BUDGETING
Profit Planning and Control

PRENTICE-HALL ACCOUNTING SERIES

H. A. Finney, Editor

PRENTICE-HALL INTERNATIONAL, INC., LONDON
PRENTICE-HALL OF AUSTRALIA, PTY., LTD., SYDNEY
PRENTICE-HALL OF CANADA, LTD., TORONTO
PRENTICE-HALL OF INDIA (PRIVATE) LTD., NEW DELHI
PRENTICE-HALL OF JAPAN, INC., TOKYO

BUDGETING
Profit Planning and Control

Second Edition

GLENN A. WELSCH, PH.D., C.P.A.

*Associate Dean of Graduate Studies
and Professor of Accounting
The University of Texas
Austin, Texas*

PRENTICE-HALL, INC. *Englewood Cliffs, New Jersey*

Preface

Profit planning and control is now recognized as one of the essentials of effective management; its usefulness extends to large, medium, and small organizations. This revised edition emphasizes the potentialities of comprehensive profit planning and control in identifying, clarifying, and strengthening the necessary relationships between the various functions and management responsibilities throughout a firm. It thereby illustrates the vital contribution profit planning and control can make to the successful life of the modern, progressive enterprise.

A full appreciation of the potential of a comprehensive program of planning and control is frequently hindered by a lack of understanding of the fundamental principles, as opposed to the mechanics, upon which it rests. In recognition of this problem, the revision stresses underlying principles and their application to underscore the significance of a comprehensive budget program as an aid to management in accomplishing its basic functions, especially those of planning, coordination, and control.

The book is written, not for the expert, but for those with a limited knowledge of the subject who seek to know more. The emphasis throughout is on a practical and understandable application of profit planning and control to the real problems of the executive. The book is designed for those interested in the practical aspects of this dynamic approach to managing as opposed to those interested in highly theoretical and complex excursions in areas of disagreement.

In this context, the book provides basic materials for a formal course at either the undergraduate or graduate level. At the graduate level, the instructor may wish to use supplementary materials in order to probe more deeply into certain aspects of the subject. To facilitate this additional study, numerous footnote references are provided throughout the text. Consideration of special and unique situations and the intricacies of cost accounting have been kept to a minimum. The text shows how a comprehensive profit planning and control program can effectively achieve the balance and co-ordination—between such diverse functions as sales, production, inventory control, cash flow, financing, capital additions, personnel, research, and cost control—which the modern business requires for its success.

Budgeting techniques that have broad business application comprise the core of the book. These techniques—in current and effective use by progressive concerns—are introduced first as general concepts, then amplified in sufficient detail to permit practical adaptation to the particular situations. Inherent in the exposition is the realization that a budget program must be tailor-made to fit the individual business; accordingly, the particular enterprise must choose those techniques best suited to its needs.

A continuous case study (simplified for instructional purposes) is outlined and illustrated throughout the book in order to provide continuity and to emphasize the interrelationships of the underlying principles and techniques of comprehensive budgeting and the functions of a business enterprise. The illustrative case runs from Chapter 3 through Chapter 14; appropriate parts are found at the end of each chapter. "Schedules" refer to the illustrative case itself, whereas other illustrative material is identified by the word "Illustration."

The case is extended for an additional fiscal year in a supplementary "Practice Case," a unique feature that provides continuity between the text materials and their practical application. The supplementary practice case is designed especially for classroom use and includes numerous "sub-cases" which correlate with assignment materials.

The new edition includes numerous short cases and additional problems related to each chapter. Discussion questions at the end of each chapter are designed to facilitate review and stimulate group discussion.

The author wishes to acknowledge the excellent suggestions received from many interested individuals with academic and active management backgrounds. Many of these suggestions have added materially to the revision. In view of the significance of their suggestions, special acknowledgement is extended to the following: Alfred P. Koch, Lehigh University; R. D. Koppenhaver, University of North Dakota; Paul W. Lindloff, Jr., University of Houston; Ray M. Powell, University of Notre Dame; H. B. Stellmacher, University of Hawaii; Roy E. Tuttle, University of Wisconsin (Madison); Robert S. Wasley, University of Colorado; Ernest H. Weinwurm, De

Paul University; Gerald Wentworth, Stanford University; and Othel D. Westfall, University of Oklahoma.

A special note of appreciation is due Mrs. Joyce Spencer for typing and checking the manuscript.

Last, but not least, my thanks and appreciation to my wife, Irma; my daughter, Mary Ann; and my two sons, Andy and Lindy. Their understanding and patience were important to me in getting this book ready for the publisher.

Comments from executives, accountants, and teachers who use this book will be sincerely appreciated by the author.

GLENN A. WELSCH

Contents

2 The Fundamental Principles of Profit Planning and Control (*Cont.*):

and limitations, 38; The fundamental of budget education, 38; Summary, 39.

Part II—BUDGET CONSTRUCTION AND APPLICATION

3 Comprehensive Budgeting for Managerial Planning and Control

Section One—Characteristics of a comprehensive budget program, 44; Outline of a comprehensive budget program, 44; The strategic or long-range plan, 46; The annual profit plan, 49; The variable expense budget, 52; Supplemental statistics, 54; Budget reports to management, 54; Length of the budget period, 55; Choosing the planning budget period, 56; Responsibility for profit planning, 57; Budget committee, 59; The budget manual, 59; *Section Two*—Comprehensive budgeting illustrated, 60. The annual profit plan (planning budget) illustrated, 60; The sales budget, 62; The production budget, 62; The direct materials budget, 64; The purchases budget, 65; The direct labor budget, 65; The building services budget, 68; The manufacturing overhead budget, 68; The inventory budgets, 68; Budgeted cost of goods sold, 69; Distribution and administrative expense budgets, 69; Budgeted income statement, 71; The budget of capital additions, 72; The cash budget, 72; The budgeted balance sheet, 73; The variable expense budget illustrated, 75; Reports to management illustrated, 76; The detailed budget program of The Superior Manufacturing Company, 78.

4 Sales Planning and Control

The concept of sales budgeting, 82; Responsibility for the sales budget, 84; Use and application of the sales budget, 85; Consideration of alternatives, 86; Pricing policy in

11 Completion and Application of the Annual Profit Plan (*Cont.*):

tion Two—Consideration of alternatives in developing the profit plan, 292. Consideration of alternatives in developing the profit plan: Sales prices to be budgeted, 293; General advertising policies, 293; Sales territory and sales-force expansion or contractions, 293; Sales mix, 294; Balance between stable production and inventory levels, 295; Expenditures for research, 295; Capital additions, 295; Testing the budget estimates, 297. *Section Three*—Application of the profit plan, 299. *Section Four*—Development of the budgeted financial statements illustrated, 302.

12 Techniques and Managerial Application of Cost-Volume-Profit Analysis (Breakeven Analysis)   325

The concept of cost-volume-profit analyses, 326; Basic assumptions underlying cost-volume-profit analyses, 330; The principle of cost variability as applied to cost-volume-profit analysis, 331; Identification of fixed and variable components of cost, 331; Straightline variability, 332; Sales price and sales mix considerations, 333; Basic managerial policies related to cost-volume-profit analysis, 336; Evaluation of the assumptions, 337; Special problems in breakeven analysis, 338; Breakeven analysis and inventory change, 340; Use and application of cost-volume-profit analysis, 345; Evaluating the effect of changing factors, 346; Cost-volume-profit analysis by organizational subdivision or product, 348; Margin of safety, 351; Cost-volume-profit analysis for The Superior Manufacturing Company illustrated, 352.

Part III—OPERATION OF THE BUDGET

13 Performance Reports for Managerial Control   359

Accounting and budget reports as a tool of communication, 361; Essential characteristics of effective performance re-

List of Illustrations

List of Schedules

(for The Superior Manufacturing Company)

CHAPTER 6

CHAPTER 7

CHAPTER 8

CHAPTER 9

CHAPTER 10

CHAPTER 11

CHAPTER 12

PART ONE

Budgeting for
Effective Management Control

O N E

Profit Planning Related to

the Basic Functions of Management

The increasing complexity of managerial problems has led to the development of certain managerial approaches, tools, techniques, and procedures generally referred to as *scientific management*. One of the more important developments in scientific management in recent years is profit planning and control (business budgeting). More and more, businessmen are coming to realize the importance of the formal planning and the dynamic control of operations.

The long-range goal of the business unit in a competitive and free economy is profit maximization. Therefore, the success or failure of a business enterprise is measured, to a large degree, in terms of profits. Keeping expenses below revenue is a never-ending problem that increases in complexity as the size of the concern increases. Efficient conduct of operations involves careful *planning*, effective *coordination*, and dynamic *control*. In order to keep pace with the competition, modern management has found that it must chart its course in advance and must use appropriate techniques to assure control and coordination of operations. Following this approach, the attainment of managerial goals is more likely. This being so, scientific management has come to recognize profit planning and control as one of the more effective managerial tools or techniques. In a recent study of well-managed companies, researchers found that 96 per cent of the companies had detailed profit plans.[1]

Plan of the book

Because this book is written for those who are not trained or experienced in profit planning and control, Part 1 (Chapters 1

[1] Burnard H. Sord and Glenn A. Welsch, *Business Budgeting, A Survey of Management Planning and Control Practices* (New York: Controllership Foundation Inc., 1958), pp. 24, 72.

and 2) starts with a brief discussion of the primary functions of management and relates them to profit planning and control. Next, the fundamental concepts underlying a profit planning and control program are outlined.

Part II (Chapters 3 through 12) considers the details of a comprehensive budget program. Primary consideration is given to the application of the fundamental concepts of profit planning and control although attention is given, when necessary, to technique. Given this general introduction to the interrelationships and mechanics of a budgeting program, even the student who lacks previous experience in the subject should be able to evaluate the applications, advantages, limitations, and strengths of the various aspects of a profit planning and control program.

Chapter 3 provides an over-all view of the primary components of a comprehensive budgeting program as preliminary to a consideration of the details in the subsequent chapters of Part II.

Part III considers performance reports that compare actual results with the profit plan. Variations are analyzed from both the technical and applied points of view.

Part IV considers important techniques related to the budget program such as standard costs and direct costing. In addition profit planning and control for nonmanufacturing and nonprofit organizations are discussed.

In order to provide a vehicle for discussing fundamentals and demonstrating mechanics, a continuous illustration (The Superior Manufacturing Company) is carried at the end of Chapters 4 through 14 inclusive. This illustration is based on an actual case. It has been simplified in order to make it manageable for instructional purposes. In line with actual procedures, budget amounts are in even hundred dollars.

Terminology

The general area of profit planning and control has no standard terminology. Numerous terms are used with considerable variation in meaning. The definitions given below indicate the context in which the various terms are used in this book.

Budgeting. This term refers to the entire process of budget planning, preparation, control, reporting, utilization, and related procedures. Budgeting is viewed essentially as a managerial process.

The word *budget* is used in two ways. First, it is used to describe the over-all plan of operations expressed in quantitative terms. The terms *planning budget, profit plan*, and *plan of operations* are used in the same context as the word budget. A business budget (profit plan) is a management plan covering all phases of operations for a definite period in the future. It is a formal expression of the policies, plans, objectives, and goals established by top management for the concern as a whole and for each subdivision thereof. Thus there will be an over-all budget, or profit plan, composed of numerous sub-budgets in the form of department and division budgets, which are in turn broken down to smaller subdivisions consistent with organizational subdivisions. Revenue goals are expressed in the sales budget; expense goals are expressed in the expense budgets. These goals must be attained in order to realize the planned net income and return on investment. In addition, the budget expresses plans relative to such items as inventory levels, capital additions, cash requirements, financing, production plans, purchasing plans, labor requirements, and so forth. Thus the budget or profit plan is a formal, quantitative statement of management plans and policies for a given period and is used as a guide or blueprint in that period.

The second connotation of the word budget refers to segments or subdivisions of the over-all plan. For example, the sales budget or the capital additions budget are subdivisions of the over-all budget.

Profit Planning and Control. This term is used in the same context as the word budgeting—see definition above. It is preferred to budgeting and will generally be used in the discussions to follow.

Budget Control. This term involves the use of budgets and performance reports throughout the period to coordinate, evaluate, and control day-to-day operations in accordance with the goals specified in the profit plan. The mere preparation of a budget may prove to be of considerable value to the average concern; but its maximum value lies in its planning aspects and in its utilization for coordination and control during the period. Budget control involves constant check and evaluation of actual results against budget goals, resulting in *corrective action* where indicated.

Comprehensive Budgeting. This term implies the application of budget principles and procedures to all phases of the operation of an individual concern and the consolidation of subdivision budgets into an over-all profit plan. It encompasses both long-range and short-range planning. This all-inclusive concept represents a complete extension of *partial budgeting* as practiced by some concerns. For example, some concerns prepare only a sales budget which is used primarily by the sales department in setting sales quotas and by the production-planning department in planning production. Other concerns maintain only a detailed capital additions budget, or use planning budget procedures but not control budget procedures. Partial budgeting may have value in some organizations, but the full potential of budgeting can best be realized through a comprehensive budget program embracing all phases of operations and used for planning, coordinating, and controlling purposes.

Profit planning and control is closely related to accounting because, like accounting, it involves financial representations of planned events. In addition, the two are closely related through historical data and certain internal management reports which compare actual results with budget objectives. Although budget procedures should be conditioned by the accounting system used —job order, process cost, standard cost, direct costing, and so forth—budgeting is a distinct process. This book presents aspects of a comprehensive budget program that are generally applicable regardless of the type of accounting system used.

In certain situations the use of profit planning and control techniques in conjunction with standard cost and/or variable (direct) costing procedures provides a particularly effective financial planning and control program.

Budgeting and the functions of management

The justification for budgeting is its potential service to management. Whereas accounting can be justified for reasons of public information, stockholders' rights, government reports and requirements, creditors' demands, and so on, budgeting is justifiable primarily for internal use. Therefore, a budget program should result in definite and tangible benefits directly related to the basic functions of management. How, then, is business budgeting related to the functions of management? Before attempting to answer this question, it is advisable to consider briefly the basic functions and needs of management.[2]

[2] For a constructive appraisal of management theory see: Harold Koontz, "Making Sense of Management Theory," *Harvard Business Review* (July-Aug. 1962.), p. 24.

With the exception of mass production methods and other technological advances, the evolution of scientific management is perhaps the most significant factor in the economic development of the United States. Scientific management does not involve a formalistic, highly complex system but is based rather upon the idea that a scientific approach—investigation, analysis, and decision making—should be used to resolve managerial problems. Along with the development of scientific management there has been serious consideration of the basic functions of management. Numerous classifications of these functions have been proposed. One that is useful in considering profit planning and control is presented in Illustration 1 (page 8). The basic functions indicated are:

(1) Conceiving business opportunities
(2) Planning
(3) Executing
(4) Controlling
(5) Appraising the planning, executing, and controlling processes to improve future action.

It is useful to view the functions of management as a cycle as indicated in Illustration 1; the cycle is continuously operative in the day-to-day, month-to-month, and year-to-year management of the business entity. The illustration further suggests the continuous and significant effects of motivation and communication. These two factors are of fundamental importance with respect to each of the basic functions. Although coordination is not listed as a basic function, the illustration suggests its importance in the effective accomplishment of the basic functions including motivation and communication. Because of the particular application of business budgeting to the planning and control functions of management, these two functions have been detailed to some extent in Illustration 1.

Scientific management recognizes a number of tools or techniques that may be used to assist management in accomplishing its basic functions. Some techniques are of more value than others. Some are adaptable only in specific situations, whereas others have a broad application. One of the latter techniques is business budgeting. A properly conceived and operated budget program goes a long way toward accomplishing the basic functions of planning and control.

Although the five functions overlap (to such a degree that they are almost indistinguishable), to facilitate discussion, each function is treated separately and related to a somewhat typical budget program. Obviously this approach necessitates some repetitions.

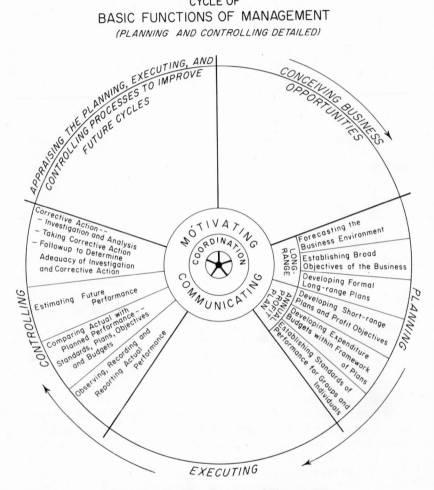

CYCLE OF
BASIC FUNCTIONS OF MANAGEMENT
(PLANNING AND CONTROLLING DETAILED)

Illustration 1. *Basic Functions of Management*

Conceiving business opportunities

Businessmen and management specialists recognize the necessity to continuously and aggressively seek out opportunities to maximize profits. Effective management requires the development of new products, new lines of endeavor, new or improved technology, and new ways of employing capital to increase the return on investment. This management function requires aggressive research and the initiative and originality to develop profitable ideas. A systematic profit planning program tends to encourage activity in developing new proprietary ideas.

The planning function related to budgeting

The managerial planning function is very broad and may be more appropriately described as strategic planning.[3] It encompasses such diverse activities as the development of the basic objectives of the firm, organizational planning, operational planning, and planning for change itself. This book is concerned primarily with profit planning, as expressed formally in quantitative terms. Thus, in Illustration 1, planning has been segmented to distinguish *long-range* profit planning and *short-range* planning.

For purposes of discussion the planning function may be outlined as follows:

(I) *Long-range planning*—Generally, planning that extends beyond one year; it may extend up to twenty years in some respects.[4]
   (a) Forecasting the business environment for the geographical and industrial areas in which the firm plans to operate.
   (b) Establishing the broad objectives of the business—Involves such objectives as types of products, marketing areas, profit objectives, return on investment objectives, and growth patterns.
   (c) Developing formal long-range plans—More and more firms are realizing the importance of reducing certain long-range plans to writing, that is, to provide a quantification of such plans as illustrated in a subsequent section.
(II) *Short-range planning*—The annual profit plan (or planning budget) is generally viewed as the first-year segment of the

---

[3] For a comprehensive treatment of planning see: Preston P. Le Breton and Dale A. Henning, *Planning Theory* (Englewood Cliffs, N. J.: Prentice-Hall, 1961); Harold Koontz and Cyril O'Donnell, *Principles of Management, An Analysis of Managerial Functions* (New York: McGraw, 1955), Chs. 20-24; Ralph C. Davis, *The Fundamentals of Top Management* (New York: Harper, 1951), Chs. 3-4.

[4] For basic treatment of this aspect of planning see: David W. Ewing (editor), *Long-Range Planning for Management* (New York: Harper, 1958); and Edward C. Bursk and Dan H. Fenn, *Planning the Future Strategy of Your Business* (New York: McGraw, 1956).

long-range plan. The annual profit plan is developed in considerable detail so as to provide a precise blueprint of management plans and policies as reflected in quantitative terms.

(a) Developing detailed plans and profit objectives.
(b) Developing expenditure (cash and expense) budgets within
the framework of the plans and policies established.
(c) Establishing definite standards of performance for individuals having supervisory responsibilities.

Planning involves the establishment of objectives and the
organization and work program (performance) required to attain
them. Objectives involve both long- and short-range plans for
the entire concern and for each of its subdivisions. After basic
planning is completed, it is necessary to organize the factors of
production available to the concern in such a way that the planned results can be attained. As applied to budgeting, planning
involves drawing up detailed plans (sub-budgets) relative to
such items as sales goals, advertising programs, production
schedules, inventory levels, raw material costs and requirements,
labor costs and requirements, personnel requirements, expense
limitations, research programs, capital additions, financing plans,
profits, and return on investment.

A pertinent question might be asked: Does management need
to plan, and, if so, to what extent? Experience has shown that
the most successful concerns are those that have definite objectives and well-drawn plans for their accomplishment. A meandering management is sure to be an inefficient management; as
one writer observed:

> In the face of such changes, the management of a company can
> if it wishes simply sit back and allow whatever is happening to
> continue to happen, whether it is good or bad, and then seek to
> adjust to the impact. When orders and sales have fallen off and
> the flow of funds into the firm has dwindled, materials and direct
> labor can be reduced proportionately. When orders and sales ex-
> pand, new workers can be hired and material purchases increased.
> But management can, if they will, seek to control the impact of
> the change rather than merely react to it. This requires an analy-
> sis of what is happening, a projection or forecast of the future, and
> actions taken anticipatory of the changes which one sees coming.
> The impact itself is thus changed.[5]

Initially management should concern itself with the develop-

[5] Neil W. Chamberlain, *The Firm: Micro-Economic Planning and Action*
(New York: McGraw, 1962), p. 9.

ment of long-range objectives, such as the desired return on investment and the desired position in the industry three, five, and ten years hence. Long-range objectives are time-segmented in detail in the short-range objectives (usually covering one year in the annual profit plan or plan of operations). The annual objectives are broken down further by period and department.

The establishment of objectives and the development of plans and work programs to accomplish those objectives are just as essential in business as they are in military operations or any other complex endeavor. It is true that many concerns plan without formal budgets. However, it is a recognized human weakness to defer activities involving precise planning. The budget program becomes important then as a technique to force management at all levels to give serious and timely attention to the planning function. The fact that plans and objectives are to be set down in black and white for all to see evokes a more careful consideration and preparation of those plans and objectives. The resulting plans and objectives are certain to be more definite and dependable and thus respected as a guide to day-to-day activity and accomplishment. One of the most frequently cited advantages of a budget program is the fact that all levels of management are brought into the planning function and are forced to give it serious consideration. The thinking of many executives in middle management is for the first time raised from a narrow concern with day-to-day departmental problems to a consideration of the company's over-all plans and objectives and those of other functional areas as well.

The importance of bringing all members of management into the planning function cannot be overemphasized. There are at least three very basic principles involved. First, active participation of all managerial levels in shaping the desired goals and the plans for achieving them has a decidedly healthful effect on interest, enthusiasm, and morale. Such personnel factors enhance esprit de corps and productivity benefits. Second, active participation by all members of management makes them aware of how their particular functional spheres fit in the total operation and of the necessity for interdepartmental cooperation. Members of middle management can see how arbitrary decisions based on the narrow considerations of single departments may create critical problems in other departments. Such decisions may, within this narrow scope, appear to be the most logical, but their over-all effect may actually be detrimental. Third, junior members of management, having participated in the planning function are adequately informed as to the future with respect to objectives, problems, and other considerations. Nothing is more discouraging and damaging to the morale of a lower-level supervisor than to be "in the dark" about what is expected in the future. Under such circumstances (which are not uncommon), lower supervisory personnel, too, find it almost impossible to make effective and adequate plans for departmental operations or to make day-to-day decisions. These conditions can best be corrected by bringing all management levels into budget planning, preparation, and operation.

The planning function varies with the level of management —top management has a much broader planning responsibility than lower management, yet each level should have definite planning responsibilities. One author has suggested the pattern of responsibility shown in Illustration 2.

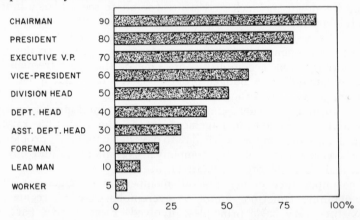

Illustration 2. *Per Cent of Time Spent on Future Planning.* (SOURCE: Ralph F. Lewis, "Management Uses of Accounting," Harper & Row, Publishers, 1961, p. 3.)

There are certain planning fundamentals that have applicability in practically all profit planning endeavors. These fundamentals may be summarized as follows:

(1) Plans must be based upon a careful evaluation of external and internal factors affecting the future.
(2) Alternative courses of action should be developed and evaluated to the fullest extent possible.
(3) Alternatives selected should be carefully drawn to express definite plans and objectives.

(4) Plans should differentiate between long-term and immediate objectives and between general and specific objectives.

(5) Short-range or immediate plans should constitute one segment of long-range plans.

(6) Plans should be formalized to the fullest extent practicable; they should be clear and comprehensive, yet as simple as possible under the circumstances. Plans should be expressed in financial and other appropriate terms.

(7) Plans and objectives should be drawn in terms of responsibilities and time; they should specify how, when, and who is responsible for carrying them out.

(8) Plans and objectives should be realistic; they should be attainable, yet should represent efficient activity.

(9) Plans and objectives should be developed through participation by those responsible for their attainment.

(10) Plans and objectives should be clearly ·understood and acceptable to those responsible for their attainment.

(11) Plans should have the basic objective of being constructive rather than restrictive.

(12) Plans should be developed so as to facilitate control.

The executing function

The executing function of management may be thought of as the action or activating phase. This function relates to all the actions taken to "start the wheels turning" in the enterprise; it is inextricably related to the broad and significant areas of communication and motivation. The executing function is most effectively carried out when based upon definite and realistic plans.

The control function related to budgeting

Control may be defined simply as the action necessary to assure that objectives, plans, policies, and standards are being achieved. Control presupposes that objectives, plans, policies, and standards have been developed and communicated to those individuals having assigned responsibilities. Thus, effective control must rest upon a firm foundation of managerial planning. The control function, in the broad sense, involves the processes of (a) evaluating performance, (b) comparing actual performance with objectives, plans, policies, and standards, (c) analyzing the deviations from such objectives, plans, policies, and standards, (d) taking corrective action as a result of the analysis, (e) following up to appraise the effectiveness of the corrective action, and (f) feeding information back to the planning process to improve future cycles.

There is a fundamental relationship between planning and control. Without effective planning there can be no effective control, and conversely, without effective control, planning is ineffective. "The better this planning is performed, the better are management's chances to get effective control. This seems to be self-evident and is why management control cannot very easily be disassociated from planning."[6]

An important aspect of effective control that is frequently overlooked is its relationship to the point of action. Control cannot be *ex post facto*, that is, an expenditure already made or an inefficiency already committed can hardly be undone. Effective control must be exercised *prior* to the commitment. This concept implies that the individual responsible for certain actions must exercise *prior* control; to do this, predetermined objectives, plans, policies, and standards must have been developed and communicated. With such information at hand the executive or supervisor is in a position to exercise control at the point of action (decision). The comparison of actual results with predetermined objectives, plans, policies, and standards constitutes *measurement* of the *effectiveness* of control during a specified *past* period; however, it may lead to improved effectiveness of control in the future. The significant concept involved here is that objectives, plans, policies, and standards fulfill two basic requirements in the over-all control process, namely: (a) to provide a basis for control at the point of action (decision) and (b) to provide a basis for measurement of the effectiveness of control historically. Control, as applied to budgeting, may be thought of as a systematized method for providing definite plans and standards for *prior* control action and a procedure for keeping management informed of conformity or lack of conformity to such predetermined plans, objectives, and policies. Control implies measurement, and this requires a yardstick for the entire organization; as we have seen, the comprehensive budget program offers such a yardstick. Bear in mind that budgeting does not in itself control, however; it is an effective approach for accomplishing the basic line reponsibilities of planning and control.

A comprehensive budget program makes control possible in

[6] William Travers Jerome III, *Executive Control—The Catalyst* (New York: Wiley, 1961), p. 25.

many ways; underlying these, however, is the comparison or measurement of actual performance against predetermined plans and objectives. This comparison extends to all areas of operation and to all subdivisions of the concern. From the point of view of methodology, it involves showing (a) actual results, (b) budget amounts, and (c) the differences (budget variations) between (a) and (b). This type of reporting is a sound application of the well-recognized management principle referred to as the *exception principle*. As applied to this situation, the exception principle holds that top management should devote detailed attention chiefly to the unusual or exceptional items that appear in daily, weekly, and monthly events, thereby leaving sufficient time for over-all policy and planning considerations. It is the out-of-line items that need executive attention; the items that are not out of line need not be referred to management. In order to implement the exception principle, techniques and procedures must be adopted to call to the attention of top management the unusual or exceptional items only. The conventional accounting report presents a mass of figures with no provision for calling the attention to the unusual or exceptional items. On the other hand, reports including a column in which meaningful *deviations* or *variations* are specifically set out immediately draw the attention of the reader to items that are significantly "out of line." It is with these items that the busy executive should be presently concerned.

A basic problem confronting executives involves the evaluation of data presented to them. Evaluation must be based upon some standard to which performance may be compared. For example, a report may show January sales of $100,000 in Sales District A, and another report may show January indirect labor costs in Producing Department X of $18,000. The pertinent problem facing the executive is whether or not these amounts represent good, poor, or indifferent performance. The *absolute amounts* certainly shed no light on the matter; some standard or yardstick is necessary by which to gauge peformance.

The traditional accounting approach has been that of comparing current results with those of some past period. For example, the sales in District A for the preceding January may have been $90,000; indirect labor in Department X may have been $20,000. Do these facts indicate satisfactory current performance in District A and Department X? The answer must be that there is still no adequate basis by which to evaluate performance. It may be that because of a change in conditions since last January, neither performance is satisfactory. For example, because of increased advertising, more salesmen, or an increase in size of territory, changes in product prices, or product lines, satisfactory sales in District A should be at least $110,000. Or in the case of indirect labor, changes in Department X operations should result in a labor cost of only $16,000. Presumably these latter amounts represent realistic budget goals. The example may be summarized:

(a) Actual compared with prior year actual (Inadequate):

	Actual This January	Actual Last January	Variations Favorable- Unfavorable*
Sales	$ 100,000	$ 90,000	$ 10,000
Indirect labor	18,000	20,000	2,000

(b) Actual compared with budget:

	Actual	Budget	Variations
Sales	$ 100,000	$ 110,000	$ 10,000*
Indirect labor	18,000	16,000	2,000*

A comparison of current results with those of some past period has value in that trends are revealed; however, the comparison is generally completely inadequate for control purposes. Such a comparison is defective for the following reasons:

(1) Conditions may have changed—reorganization, new products, new methods, price changes, volume differentials, technological improvements, and increased labor efficiency.
(2) Accounting classifications may be different.
(3) Last year's performance may have been unsatisfactory.

On the other hand, assuming the budget goals are attainable and represent efficient performance, a valid and meaningful comparison or measure of actual performance is possible. Budget control thus makes it possible for top management to feel the pulse of the enterprise throughout the year—to know specifically where there is satisfactory or unsatisfactory progress toward the over-all company objective. Progress or lack of progress must be recognized and evaluated throughout the period rather than after the end of the year, because it is then too late to take corrective action.[7]

[7] For two very practical discussions of control see: E.F. Fitzmaurice, "The Essence of Control," *The Controller* (Nov. 1950); A.M. Hartogensis, "The Accountant's Place in the Control Function," *NAA Bulletin* (Dec. 1955), pp. 473–480. Also see: Ralph C. Davis, *The Fundamentals of Top Management* (New York: Harper, 1951), Chs. 17–19. Harold Koontz and Cyril O'Donnell, *Principles of Management, An Analysis of Management Functions* (New York: McGraw, 1955), Chs. 25–30.

The primary aspects of managerial control as related to profit planning and control may be outlined as follows:

(1) There must be clearly defined lines of authority and responsibility.
(2) There must be definite policies, objectives, plans, and standards of performance.
(3) There must be definite and precise communication of authority, responsibility, policies, objectives, plans, and standards of performance.
(4) There must be enlightened and aggressive effort to attain or better the plans, objectives, and standards.
(5) There must be adequate reporting of actual performance consistent with the authority and responsibilities of those designated to carry out the plans and standards.
(6) There must be a comparison of actual results with the plans, objectives, and standards—that is, a measurement of the effectiveness of control.
(7) There must be a careful analysis of deviations from plans and objectives and a determination of the causes.
(8) There must be corrective action by persons having designated responsibilities to correct unsatisfactory performance.
(9) There must be follow-up procedures to determine the effectiveness of the corrective action.
(10) There must be a feedback of basic information to provide a basis for improving future planning and control processes.

Appraisal of functional performance to improve future action

The planning, executing, and controlling processes are rather complex and constitute a sort of cycle of managerial activities. Serious attention must be devoted to improving the cycle—that is, new approaches, ideas, techniques, and viewpoints must be evaluated, tested, and where advisable, adopted so that the management process may be continuously improved. Fundamental to improvement of the cycle of management functions is (a) the feedback of data as regards the cycle and (b) serious attention to improvement. Certainly development of effective management can never be static. Continuous change is typical; both the external environment and the internal characteristics of the firm are in a constant state of flux, necessitating constructive adaptation of the ways in which management may most effectively accomplish its basic functions.

Motivation

Motivation involves the stimulation of one or more individuals to contribute their separate or joint efforts and skills effectively in accomplishing the tasks and over-all objectives of the firm. This view of motivation is positive and implies realistic, known, and understandable objectives.[8]

Effective management is directly related to motivation of individuals and groups working together. Motivation of persons having supervisory responsibilities is accomplished through some identification of their personal interests with those of the enterprise. Financial incentives have been found to be one, but not the most important, element in motivation. Recognition of accomplishment, status, definite assignment of responsibilities, fairness in evaluation, and responsible participation in the decision-making process have been found to be especially important in motivating executives and supervisors. Undue pressure, loose organizational patterns, uncoordinated operations, lack of information, and poor communication are particularly detrimental to positive motivation. There are many avenues in developing positive motivation and a reasonable identity of personal self-interests with the the objectives of the firm. A sound profit planning and control system, if understood and wisely used, can be a significant aspect of motivation. Participation in the planning process, confidence in the measurement and evaluation process, improved communciation and coordination, are among the more important motivational aspects of a budget program.[9]

Communication

Communication involves a common understanding between two or more individuals or groups on a particular point. Obtaining a common understanding of all the policies, plans, objectives, directives, control actions, procedures, and related data is a central task of all managements. Communication is such an important facet of effective management that it should be given direct and continuous attention. Analysts have traced many of the most fundamental problems in the business unit to inadequate communication. The methods of communication useful in a firm are generally classified as oral, mechanical, and written. The problem of *precise* communication so as to avoid misunderstandings calls for extreme care in the selection of communication media. Written policies, and formal organizational, authority, and responsibility directives are generally essential.

[8] Sord and Welsch, *Business Budgeting*, pp. 37, 38, and 61.
[9] *Ibid.*

A properly designed budget program significantly enhances two-way communication by creating both formal and informal communication channels. These channels are designed primarily to transmit ideas, plans, suggestions, and constructive comments during the process of building the profit plan, as well as to transmit information about the approved plans and reports on progress and action taken. The communication media normally used in the budget process are formal conferences, informal discussions, the formal profit plan itself (or parts thereof), and control reports. The significant aspect is that formal two-way communication channels are established as a basic part of the system.[10]

Coordination related to budgeting

Coordination is the process whereby each subdivision of a concern works toward the common objective, with due regard for all other subdivisions, and with unity of effort. It means developing and maintaining the various activities within the concern in proper relationship to each other. Frequently one observes a lack of coordination when an aggressive department head expands his department out of proportion to others or bases decisions on the needs of his department only, although the decisions may implicate other departments and alter their effectiveness. For example, there must be very close coordination between the sales and production departments—sales should not plan to sell more than production can make, and vice versa. There must be coordination at all organizational levels, an objective difficult for mangement to achieve in a large enterprise.

How is coordination attained? Effective planning and organization does much to bring coordination. Control procedures are designed to check the effectiveness of coordination. A properly designed and operated budget program will contribute greatly to coordination throughout the firm. In the first place, performance of the planning function lays the proper foundation. Plans that are made sufficiently in advance, and with the care and detail necessary to meet budget requirements, are certain to be coordinated plans that take into account the objectives, problems, possibilities, and other considerations of each subdivision and of the concern as a whole. By laying down plans, and

[10] Sord and Welsch, *Business Budgeting*, pp. 26–27 and 109–120.

determining policies necessary for their accomplishment well in advance of operations, management has set up the basic foundation for effective coordination.

Second, coordination depends to a large degree upon good communication. It is important that each member of management, from the top to the lowest level, knows well in advance what is planned, and how, when, and by whom it is to be accomplished. A comprehensive budget program requires that these plans be laid down formally in the budget and, further, that copies be distributed to all management personnel. In addition, management personnel should be given timely information relative to revision of original plans and objectives, as well as current results. In this way coordination is assured because each responsible executive is fully informed as to current results and expectations with respect to his own area of responsibility, related departments, and over-all operations.

Finally, having laid the basis for effective coordination, techniques must be employed which will indicate to top management whether or not coordination is being achieved throughout the year in day-to-day operations. Management must know whether or not policies and plans are being followed throughout the organization. Management must have some indicator of defects in the plans as originally established. Control techniques are necessary if coordination is to be continuous. The control techniques discussed above are designed to achieve this end.

Managerial evaluation of alternatives

A significant phase of effective management involves careful consideration of alternative courses of action and finally a choice based on an adequate analysis of the effects, direct and indirect, of each alternative. Essentially, managerial planning consists of basic decisions to pursue particular courses of action selected from several possibilities.

Comprehensive budgeting is especially appropriate for managerial use in the evaluation and selection of alternatives because an evaluation of the probable financial effects of each alternative is generally possible during the process of budget construction, using such procedures as budget summaries, breakeven analyses, differential cost analyses, and return-on-investment analyses. The process of building a budget covering a definite period in the future involves a whole series of management policy decisions, all of which must be consistent with the desired over-all return-on-investment objective. Throughout the process of developing a coordinated plan of operations using budget procedures, management must tentatively approve definite courses of action relative to pricing, advertising, capital additions, financing, research, new products, and so on. Tentative, step-by-step approvals of budget objectives throughout the budget building process are indicated in subsequent chapters. The build-up of a budgeted plan of operations involves building, re-evaluating, tearing down, and rebuilding until the best possible plan of operations is developed. Development of certain aspects of the plan of operations may indicate that previously selected alternatives should be discarded and other courses of action reconsidered. Final approval of the budget (as opposed to tentative approvals) represents the last step in budget construction, because at this point decisions have been made on all alternatives, and their probable financial effects incorporated in the budget.

The advantages of budgeting

The preceding paragraphs indicate that the fundamental purpose of budgeting is that of assisting management in effectively accomplishing its basic functions, those of planning and control. These are rather broad aspects of profit planning. The more specific advantages of profit planning, in addition to those already discussed, may be enumerated as follows:

(1) It forces early consideration of basic policies.

(2) It requires adequate and proper organization—that is, there is a definite assignment of responsibility for each function of the business.

(3) It compels all members of management from the top down to participate in the establishment of goals.

(4) It compels all members of departmental management to make plans in harmony with plans of other departments.

(5) It forces management to put down in cold figures what is necessary for satisfactory results.

(6) It requires adequate and appropriate historical accounting data.

(7) It compels management to plan for the most economical use of labor, material, facilities, and capital.

(8) It instills in all levels of management the habit of timely, careful, and adequate consideration of all factors before reaching important decisions.

(9) It reduces cost by increasing the *span of control*,[11] hence less supervisors are needed.

(10) It frees executives from many day-to-day internal problems through the media of predetermined policies and clear-cut authority relationships thereby providing more executive time for planning and creative thinking.

(11) It tends to remove the cloud of uncertainty that exists in many firms, among lower levels of management, relative to basic policies and objectives.

(12) It pinpoints efficiency or its lack.

(13) It promotes understanding, among members of management, of their co-workers' problems.

(14) It forces management to give timely and adequate attention to the effect of the expected trend of general business conditions.

(15) It forces a periodic self-analysis of the company.

(16) It aids in obtaining bank credit.

(17) It checks progress or lack of progress toward the objectives.

The problems of budget utilization

The potentials of profit planning and control are impressive; however, it should not be assumed that budgeting is foolproof or free of problems. Its problems and limitations are significant and it is imperative that those who consider using budget planning and control be aware of them.

The principal problems in profit planning are (a) gaining top management support, (b) developing the sales budget, (c) budget education in the firm, (d) the development of realistic standards, (e) achieving flexibility in budget application, and (f) maintaining effective follow-up procedures.

In developing and using a budget planning and control system, the following four limitations should be kept in mind:

(1) *The budget plan is based on estimates.* The strength or weakness of a budget program depends to a large degree on the accuracy with which the basic estimates are made. The estimates must be based on all available facts and good judgment. The estimating of sales and expenses cannot be an exact science; however, there are numerous statistical and other techniques that may be effectively applied to the problems which, when tempered with sound reasoning and judgment, produce satisfactory results. If there is conviction that such estimates can be made, a serious effort generally gives adequate results.

[11] James H. Healey, *Executive Coordination and Control* (Columbus, Ohio: Ohio State University, Bureau of Business Research, 1956).

Because the budget plan is based entirely on estimates, judgment is necessary in interpreting and using the results.

(2) *A budget program must be continually adapted to fit changing circumstances.* A budget program cannot be installed and perfected in a short time. Budget techniques must be continually adapted, not only for each particular concern, but for changing conditions within the concern. Various techniques must be tried, improved, or discarded and replaced with others. In other words, a budget program must be dynamic. Normally it will take more than one year to attain a reasonably good budget program, and management must not expect too much during this period. Continuous budget education is necessary, especially during the formative period.

(3) *Execution of a budget plan will not occur automatically.* Once the budget is completed, the plan will be effective only if all responsible executives get behind it and exert continuous effort toward its accomplishment. Department heads must feel the responsibility for achieving or bettering department goals laid down in the budget. A continuous budget consciousness throughout the firm is implied. All levels of management must be "sold" on budgeting and must participate in the program.

(4) *The budget will not take the place of management and administration.* Budgeting does not take the place of management; it is a tool. The budget manual of one prominent concern reads as follows on this point: "The budget should be regarded, not as a master, but as a servant. It is one of the best tools yet devised for advancing the affairs of a company and of the individuals in their various spheres of activity. It is not assumed that any budget is perfect. The most important consideration is to make sure, by intelligent use of the budget, that all possible attainable benefits are derived from the budget as rendered."

Application of budgeting to various types of firms

It is sometimes said that profit planning is applicable only in very large organizations. A not unusual comment is that "budgeting is a fine idea for most concerns, but ours is different," and so on. On the contrary, profit planning in some form has application in any organization, except perhaps the smallest, irrespective of special circumstances or conditions. The fact that a company has peculiar circumstances or problems frequently is, upon proper analysis, good reason for the adoption of certain budget procedures. Budgeting has application in both manufacturing and retail situations. With respect to size, when operations are extensive enough to require more than one or two supervisory personnel, there may be a need for budgeting in some phases. A small concern certainly has different needs in this respect than a large one. As with accounting, no one system of budgeting can be designed for all alike; a system must be tailor-made to fit the particular concern.

The benefits that modern management has realized from budgeting are of such consequence that no management can afford to disregard profit planning and control.[12]

Discussion Questions

1. On what basis has scientific management come to recognize budgeting as an important tool?
2. Explain the two connotations given the word "budget" in this book.
3. What is your concept of "profit planning and control?"
4. What is your concept of "comprehensive budgeting?"
5. What reasons can you give for the fact that interest in budgeting has tended to vary with business conditions? Do you agree that management should be interested in budgeting, irrespective of business conditions? Why?
6. Why is it important that the relationship of budgeting to the basic functions of management be understood?
7. Relate the "cycle of the basic functions of management" to profit planning and control.
8. Why is it essential that top management make definite plans with regard to the future?
9. Elaborate on the statement, "A meandering management is sure to be an inefficient management."
10. Someone has said with respect to business management that "if you don't know where you are going, any old road will get you there." What are the implications of this statement?
11. Explain the statement that "control is related to the point of action."
12. Explain the exception principle and relate it to a budget control program.
13. Why is communication a serious problem in all companies? In what ways may a profit planning and control program contribute to communication?
14. It has been said that a properly designed and operated budget program *systematizes* the planning and control functions of management. Explain the reasons why a reasonable degree of systemization of these two functions is desirable. How does a budget program systematize these functions?

---

[12] Elizabeth Marting (editor), *Management for the Small Company* (New York: American Management Association, 1959).

T W O

The Fundamental Principles of

Profit Planning and Control

In the preceding chapter we looked very broadly at the basic functions of management with particular attention to planning and control. In a general way the performance of these functions was related to a comprehensive budget or profit planning program.

In Chapter 2 we identify and briefly discuss the *fundamental principles* of profit planning and control and make some distinctions that may be useful in our considerations in subsequent chapters. Because budgeting is directly concerned with planning and control, there is some duplication of the concepts discussed in the preceding chapter; however, the reader is reminded that the preceding discussions related to the broad functions whereas in this chapter we relate certain concepts directly to the budget process.

A study of successful budget programs indicates that there are certain common ingredients and basic distinctions that are essential. Failure to observe and appreciate these ingredients and distinctions may result in ineffective profit planning and control. The central idea in these considerations is that budget planning and control provides the only systematic and tangible approach so far developed for bringing, in a coordinated and practical manner, a degree of certainty and cohesiveness to management planning and control. Budget planning and control, properly operated, is a comprehensive system whereby all aspects of the management process may be brought into a coordinated whole, where the loose ends of management action and operations may be carefully tied together. This all-inclusive concept of the budget process is frequently overlooked.

Fundamental distinctions

In order to study, understand, and apply profit planning and control we must make careful distinctions between the several aspects of such a program. Failure to keep these distinctions in mind has led to much misunderstanding with respect to the budget process. Careful distinction in the study and application of budget planning and control should be made between:

(1) The mechanics of budgeting—Mechanics have to do with such matters as design of budget schedules, clerical methods of completing such schedules, and routine computations. Throughout this book some attention (primarily by illustration) is given to mechanics.

(2) The techniques of budgeting—Techniques of budgeting have to do with special approaches and methods of developing data for managerial use in the decision-making process. The techniques of budgeting are many, varying from the simple to the sophisticated. For example, we may note some of the more commonly used techniques: methods of budgeting sales volume, approaches in resolving the sales-production-inventory problem (a frequent application of operations research), breakeven analyses, capital additions determinations (such as the discounted-cash-flow approach), cash flow analyses, and variable budget procedures. The more important techniques of budgeting are discussed and illustrated in subsequent chapters.

(3) The fundamentals of the budget process—The fundamentals are concerned directly with the basic functions of management, particularly the planning and control functions. The following list includes the important fundamentals relating to the budget process. These are the fundamentals of:

(a) *Support*	(j) *Effective communication*
(b) *Organization*	(k) *Timeliness*
(c) *Confidence*	(l) *Realism*
(d) *Performance*	(m) *Flexibility*
(e) *Participation*	(n) *The significant*
(f) *Individual recognition*	(o) *Cost consciousness*
(g) *Responsibility reporting*	(p) *Follow-up*
(h) *Management by exception*	(q) *Uses and limitations*
(i) *A standard*	(r) *Continuous education*

Each of these important fundamentals is discussed briefly in the following paragraphs and its application is demonstrated in subsequent chapters.

The Fundamental of Support. In order to effectively engage in profit planning and control all levels of management, especially top management, must (a) comprehend the nature and fundamentals of budgeting, (b) be convinced that it will be useful to them, (c) be willing to devote the required effort to it, and (d) be willing to support the program in all its ramifications.

If a budget program is to be successful, it must of necessity have the full support of every member of management, starting with the president. The impetus and direction must come from the very top. The initial development of a budget program generally involves many problems; consequently a certain amount of active and passive opposition to it must be expected initially. Opposition may be due to a lack of understanding or to a realization that an effective budget program points the finger at the inefficiency, as well as the efficiency, of individuals. Therefore, it is quite obvious that to be effective such a program must be implemented by direct line authority based on a thorough knowledge of its potentials.

Before support can be expected, top management must be "sold" on the program. This is perhaps the central (and most difficult) problem facing the controller and budget director. Top management must realize, first, the real potential of a budget program, and second, that an effective and accurate budget for the firm can be constructed. If top management sees the budget program's potential as an aid in accomplishing the planning and controlling functions, effective use should result. The nature of budgeting, properly viewed, is a part of the process of management. Management without effective planning and control is a contradiction of the term. Budgeting can provide an atmosphere for teamwork and orderly accomplishment.

The central concept of budget planning is that of developing *what is desired* rather than "what will be." These ideas suggest the nature of budgeting. Even a properly prepared budget, if used ineffectively, is just poor management and an unnecessary expense to boot.

The budget director by himself cannot make a proper budget; it must be prepared by the people responsible for its operation and fulfillment. The effort and time of many executives must be involved in budget preparation. The wholehearted support of top management will result in active support of the program all the way down the line.

The Fundamental of Organization.[1] Profit planning must rest upon a sound organizational structure coupled with clear-cut lines of authority and responsibility. Plans and budgets should be developed in terms of individual responsibilities. It is people

[1] For a comprehensive treatment of this subject see: Ralph C. Davis, *The Fundamentals of Top Management* (New York: Harper, 1951), Chs. 1–14. Harold Koontz and Cyril O'Donnell, *Principles of Management, An Analysis of Managerial Functions* (New York: McGraw, 1955), Chs. 6–14.

who get things done. Planned performance, therefore, must be directly related to organizational responsibilities. Also, because *control* is exercised through people (not through things), there must be a clear-cut delineation of responsibilities from the organizational point of view as well as in terms of goals. What do we expect of the individual supervisor? Planning is fundamental in clarifying this situation; thus, sound planning is basic in establishing effective control.

The purpose of organization is to establish a framework within which current operations may be carried on with minimum direction from above. The scope and interrelationship of the responsibilities of each individual and group are specified. Prior to successful budgeting, a definite plan of organization must be established. Budget control can be effective only if every executive and supervisor knows the scope of his responsibility and authority. Careful delineation of such responsibility is management's job and is necessary to avoid overlapping effort. A formal organization chart for the company as a whole should be constructed. This over-all chart should be supplemented with auxiliary charts for each major division, these in turn being supplemented by auxiliary charts for each subdivision where authority and responsibility repose. Formal organization should not stop at this point. The organization charts should be supplemented with written directives specifying definite areas of authority and responsibility, relationships, policies, and methods of measuring performance. The formal organization charts and written supplements should be reproduced and distributed to interested parties in the form of a company organization manual.

From the accounting and budgeting point of view, definite specification of areas of responsibility is necessary because accounting and budgeting for management attempt to report and measure accomplishment in terms of individual responsibility. In drawing up the budget for a firm, it is essential that over-all plans be broken down in terms of the responsibility of each member of the management team. The duties of each supervisor or executive must be clearly defined before responsibilities can be budgeted and performance measured.

The Fundamental of Confidence. Management must be confident that it can significantly influence the course of events and that its duty is to plan such influence. Management must be convinced that realistic policies, plans, objectives, and standards can be developed in advance and that it is desirable to do so. It must operate under the belief that individuals having management responsibilities tend to tie their own success to that of the firm, and will therefore strive seriously and aggressively to attain *realistic* and *known* objectives, particularly if allowed to participate in developing these objectives. Then, too, management must be firmly convinced that the goals, objectives, and plans thus established can, and will be, attained. This conviction will lead to logical, organized, and aggressive effort to attain the predetermined goals.

The Fundamental of Performance. In profit planning, a central concept is that of developing a program of work and performance expectations by which desired goals and objectives may be achieved. The primary emphasis is on a *performance concept* as opposed to a *fiscal concept* emphasizing dollar results. If exclusive emphasis is given to estimating the dollar effect of operations, without consideration of work programs and performance expectations, the many indirect (and important) facets of profit planning and control that cannot be quantified may well be ignored.

The fiscal concept of budgeting appears to have preceded the performance concept because early emphasis in budgeting was directed toward estimating dollar values for the various accounting classifications. Unfortunately, many people today view the budget process in this same context; hence, some firms continue this emphasis and thereby significantly limit the potentials of profit planning and control. The better managements have given attention to the performance concept. A sound budget program should emphasize *both* the performance concept and the fiscal concept because there is a significant complementary relationship between them.

Throughout the discussions and illustrations to follow, primary emphasis will be given to the performance concept and secondary emphasis to the fiscal concept. Yet it must be realized that a logical and practical blending of the two concepts is necessary for effective profit planning and control.

The Fundamental of Participation. This fundamental requires clearly defined responsibilities for the input of planned data. It is basic that those having supervisory responsibilities should be responsible to the fullest extent for developing the plans and for carrying out the related responsibilities. People naturally resent arbitrary orders; they take more interest in accomplishing objectives and plans which they have had a part in formulating. Experience has shown that operating supervisors view with extreme doubt a budget prepared without their active participation; they generally make little effort to follow the budget and often try indirectly to make it unworkable. Their support is absolutely essential. The budget director should not make the budget; rather, he should supervise its compilation. The budget director, chief accountant, statistician, economist, and line executives, working in close collaboration, should construct the budget. Letting department heads actually help set their own budget estimates has several advantages. An important one is that their feeling of cooperation and responsibility is greatly enhanced. Thus they will have no occasion for making excuses that budget estimates are not fair. In addition communication is improved.

Achieving meaningful involvement in the planning process is not easy. Lower levels of management react favorably to participation, yet certain checks and restraints are necessary. No plan or estimate suggested by subordinates should be accepted without careful analysis and study. The top executives must make the final decisions; however, subordinates should be heard. Also there will always be some individual who will deliberately set budget allowances at a level that presents no challenge. This natural tendency to protect one's self can be controlled by making it clear that favorable as well as unfavorable variations between actual performance and the budget will be carefully scrutinized, and further, that this matter of budgeting is a part of their over-all rating as supervisors or executives. Differences with respect to budget estimates should be carefully discussed and analyzed, and a definite decision reached. In this way a realistic budget can be developed and, in addition, the by-products of budgeting enhanced.

Token participation is likely to create negative reactions. Participation by lower levels of management imposes a prior responsibility on higher levels of management to clearly define and circumscribe policies and premises well in advance.[2]

To indicate briefly the interdependence of the various operational executives—the budget director and the budget committee—let us outline one possible approach in developing, for example, the sales budget.

The general form for the sales budget is determined by the budget director. Several months prior to the end of the current year, say by September 15, the budget director transmits to the vice president for sales certain historical data with respect to

[2] Burnard H. Sord and Glenn A. Welsch, *Business Budgeting, A Survey of Management Planning and Control Practices* (New York: Controllership Foundation, 1958), pp. 93–107.

sales for, say, the past 12 to 20 months. He includes the necessary forms for the sales projection and indicates the due date for the estimates. The vice president for sales, being properly charged with the responsibility for preparing the sales budget, proceeds with the assistance of his staff and sales district supervisors to develop the tentative projection. The historical data provide a basis for estimating future sales. In connection with the sales estimates, the advertising and distribution expense estimates begin to take shape.

The budget director, upon receipt of the sales estimate, reviews it from a technical point of view and prepares copies for presentation to the assembled budget committee by the vice president for sales. The budget committee carefully considers the estimate, district by district and item by item, in the light of past results and the recommendations of the economist and statistician regarding future prospects. At this point the committee may recommend tentative approval as is, tentative approval with certain changes, or complete restudy and revision. Finally, upon committee recommendation, the president gives tentative approval. Using the tentative sales budget as a basis, executives in charge of other major functions prepare their respective budgets, most of which will come before the budget committee for consideration in a similar manner. Finally the budget director brings together all of the separate estimates in a master planning budget (profit plan). After due consideration, the committee recommends final approval, assuming the profit results, return on investment, and related objectives are satisfactory and attainable. From this brief summary it can be seen that budget preparation, properly accomplished, involves serious effort and cooperation on the part of the entire executive force, not just the controller and budget director.

Budget and accounting experts may design and coordinate the system, but those who have to perform should provide the input data. This procedure makes possible effective implementation of the participation principle in management.

The Fundamental of Individual Recognition. This fundametal recognizes the fact that individual accomplishment, both outstanding and substandard performance, should be identified and recognized. The system of evaluation must be fair, understandable, and reasonably accurate. It should give recognition to the abilities and performances of the individual, his aspirations, his reactions, and to the group pressures that affect him. The dignity of the individual must be respected. In profit planning and control the personal element should loom large as a factor in the design of the system, the development of input data, the method of measurement and evaluation, and the application of the system itself. By and large the human element is the dominant feature of effective management.

The Fundamental of Responsibility Reporting. We have noted that plans and controls should be developed in terms of assigned responsibilities, thus it is fundamental that the internal reports for managerial purposes must likewise be in terms of organizational responsibilities. In order to effectuate responsibility reporting, there must be an effective responsibility accounting system—that is, one tailored to the organizational structure and to assigned responsibilities so that individual performance can be evaluated. Another significant concept related to responsibility accounting is a careful distinction between controllable and noncontrollable costs (See Chapters 8 and 9). Historical cost accounting has two main objectives: (a) costing production and (b) cost control. Traditionally, cost accounting has been more concerned with costing production than with cost control; as a result, the emphasis in account classifications has been, and continues to be, on product costs rather than on the cost control aspects. In responsibility accounting, this emphasis is reversed. Cost control receives the primary emphasis. This concept does not imply that costing will be less accurate. It is a fact that costs initially accumulated for control purposes can be recast for product costing purposes just as accurately as though initial accumulation had been for product costing; however, costs initially accumulated for product costing purposes cannot generally be recast effectively for control purposes. In sum, effective budgeting requires that the traditional emphasis be reversed—the accounting system must be concerned first with control and then with product costing.

Thus a successful budget program requires close cooperation between the budgeting and accounting functions, extending to all phases of record-keeping. The budget department, and others involved in preparing estimates, depend heavily on the accounting department for the reliable historical data which necessarily form the basis for many estimates. In addition, because actual costs, revenues, and other financial amounts are periodically compared with budgeted amounts, the frameworks within which these respective amounts are classified must be identical. For these reasons the budget procedures must use precisely the same chart of accounts and employ the same classification of revenues and expenses as the accounting department. Comparisons will be meaningless if the classifications do not coincide. This in turn requires that the chart of accounts and classification of amounts recorded be consistent with the principles of budget control.

The chart of accounts must be set up in terms of areas of managerial responsibility, which is essential for managerial purposes. The chart of accounts should be supplemented with standard instructions that prescribe in detail the authorized charges and credits to each type of account. This is a requisite to successful budgeting and accounting, because the recording of an item based on an incorrect classification of accounts obviously will affect two or more accounts, resulting in erroneous budget variations in each account. As a general rule, prior to any attempt to adopt budget procedures, there should be a complete study of the chart of accounts and related classifications. Such studies frequently show the necessity of a complete revision of accounting procedures consistent with the principles of managerial accounting.

If predetermined burden (overhead) rates are used, it is necessary to budget volume and burden costs in advance in order to compute the departmental or cost-center burden rates. The author has observed cases where the cost accounting department prepared one burden (overhead) budget for costing purposes, and the budget department prepared another burden budget (at the same volume) for budget purposes. Obviously this is an unnecessary duplication of effort. The same burden budget should be used for both purposes, and it is a responsibility of the controller to see that such efforts are coordinated. The use of identical burden rates for costing and budget purposes is illustrated in a later chapter.

Standard costs provide a logical basis for budget preparation. Where standard costs are being used, they should be completely integrated with the budget program, in both budget preparation and variation analysis. (See Chapter 15).

An accounting system tailored to external needs and to "generally accepted accounting principles" is essential but is, by itself, inadequate for internal management planning and control needs.

The Fundamental of Management by Exception. This fundamental holds that the busy executive should devote his time to the unusual or exceptional items, rather than worry about those matters that are not out of line. Dealing with out-of-line items is enough of an accomplishment, without having to pinpoint them. To make this principle effective, the profit planning and control system must be designed so that the exceptions stand out. By emphasizing variations, budget planning and control provides a method whereby the attention of successively higher levels of management is called to the exception. This principle obviously requires comparison of a realistic standard with an actual result. The usual comparison with last year's results is unsatisfactory because these results frequently constitute an unreliable standard. Budgeting stands far out in front as the basic and practical approach to effective management by exception.

The Fundamental of a Standard. A system of goals, objectives, and standards is vital to control. There must be benchmarks to which performance may be related. Basically, standards are essential:

(a) to provide a target at which to shoot, and
(b) to provide a benchmark against which actual results may be compared in order to measure control—that is, to determine the degree of efficiency or inefficiency with respect to attainment of the objectives.

The Fundamental of Effective Communication. Communication implies a common understanding between two or more individuals on a given point. Communication for effective control should be such that both superior and subordinate have the same understanding of responsibilities and goals. The planning budget, built through participation and in terms of responsibilities, assures a degree of understanding not otherwise possible.

The Fundamental of Timeliness. This fundamental holds that there must be a definite time schedule for planning, performance reports, control action, and follow-up.

The schedule for planning activities should be written preferably as a *planning calendar*. Once a management firmly commits itself in this manner, procrastination in planning largely ends. Successful managers today report this result to be one of the most important indirect benefits accruing from a budget program. Whereas it was practically impossible to assemble management groups intact for planning sessions, following adoption of such a program, the planning session often assumes a priority equal to that of a meeting of the board of directors. In many companies, executives absolutely refuse to make outside commitments during the critical phases of profit planning. Many companies that budget effectively report that for the first time both strategic and detailed planning are on a rational and timely basis. Nothing is more devastating to effective planning than for the management to issue a profit plan some time after the beginning of the period involved.

Performance reports, in terms of responsibilities, should be issued for interim periods; that is, on a monthly, weekly, or in some cases, even on a daily basis. To be effective such reports must be in the hands of the responsible individual shortly after the end of the interim period. Reports, weeks after the end of such periods, are of little value; by that time the supervisor is involved in too many new problems to be much concerned about a set of historical events about which nothing can be done.

This fundamental also holds that control action to be effective must be taken immediately upon identification of a problem; the longer the control action is deferred, the greater the unfavorable financial effect becomes. In relation to this concept follow-up procedures are generally desirable to determine the effectiveness of the control action and to establish a basis for further improvement in efficiency. As with control action itself, follow-up action must be timely and decisions relative to the findings should be made forthwith. A budget program established on a firm foundation will make systematic provision for implementation of the fundamental of timeliness.

The Fundamental of Realism. In profit planning the management must avoid undue conservatism and irrational optimism. The care with which budget goals and objectives are set for such items as sales, production, costs, expenses, and productivity determines to a large degree the success of the budget planning and control program. Objectives should represent goals which are reasonably attainable and yet present a real challenge. Goals set so high as to be, for all practical purposes, impossible of attainment, tend to discourage any serious efforts to attain them. On the other hand, goals set so low that they call forth no special effort will have no meaning or incentive for supervisors.

For budget purposes, then, objectives should represent "expected actual," assuming efficient operations and satisfactory performance under the conditions that are expected to prevail during the budget period.

A problem that frequently arises is commonly referred to as *padding the budget.* This problem may be indicated by example as follows:

(1) Sales budget estimates are understated "to protect ourselves; exceeding the sales budget certainly can't be criticized."

(2) Overestimating expenses "so we will have plenty; spending less than the budget looks good to the management."

(3) Requesting more cash than needed "so that we won't have to ask for more, or if we turn some back it will look good."

Enlightened managements have developed effective ways to minimize these somewhat natural tendencies. The key lies in budget education to develop a positive attitude toward the planning and control program. An important attitude to foster is that *both* favorable and unfavorable variations will be carefully considered. Variations (whether favorable or unfavorable) due to improper planning should be identified and discussed with the responsible party by pointing up the problems created thereby. For example, a deliberately understated sales budget may have serious consequences in planning other functional activities; production and inventories may be inadequate; the advertising program and distribution expense budgets adversely affected; the cash flow plans inadequate, and so on. Each responsible executive and supervisor must understand the interrelationship of his plans to other functions of the business. Overstated expense and cash estimates likewise may seriously affect other aspects of managerial policies and planning. An important facet in preventing overestimates of expense and cash is a clear-cut policy relative to approvals. Starting with the lower levels and moving up in the management heirarchy, requests for cash and expense allowances should stand the test of logical and realistic programs and identification of specific needs. Then, too, the management must convince the lower echelons that *additional allowances* will be approved at any time, notwithstanding the budget, should sufficient reasons be presented. Lack of definite policies and failure to take sufficient time to evaluate such requests usually are prevalent where such "protection" practices exist.

A related problem has to do with the tendency to spend money unwisely near the end of the budget period when there is an excess since "our budget allowance for the next period will be cut if we turn some back." Again, the solution to this type of thinking rests upon the policies of the top management as reflected through their actions. Organizational units should be strongly encouraged to save and turn back funds not needed, and assured that such actions will have no influence upon subsequent budget allowances. Subsequent budget requests should be evaluated on the basis of proposed programs and demonstrated needs rather than upon prior expenditures.

All of these problems can be overcome through an effective and continuous budget education program having as its objective (a) effective communication of the policies of the management relative to the profit planning and control program and (b) the development of positive attitudes wherein the individual identifies

the success of the firm with his own personal success. The author
is firmly convinced that these problems exist because of inat-
tention to policy making, communication, the approval process,
and the motivational aspects of management. These problems are
commonly identified with government budgeting; but there is no
reason to assume they do not exist in the profit-making segment
of our economy.

The Fundamental of Flexibility. This fundamental holds that
there must be recognition from all levels of management that a
budget will not and should not manage the business, that flexibility in applying the budget must be the rule so that straight
jackets are not imposed and no opportunities passed up merely
because "they are not covered by the budget."

With respect to cost control this principle is especially important. Expense and cost budgets must not be used and interpreted inflexibly. The budget must not prevent the making
of rational decisions merely because an expenditure was not
anticipated.

Variable or flexible expense budgets (Chapter 9) are frequently
employed to meet the problems of cost control arising from the
volume differential. To illustrate the point, assume that the
budget for Department X carries an allowance of $2,000 for
indirect labor; 10,000 units of production are planned. Now assume that unforeseen circumstances make it necessary to actually
produce 12,000 units. Obviously, a comparison of actual costs
incurred at 12,000 units with a budget allowance based on 10,000
units would show an unfavorable, and more significantly, a meaningless variation. The variable budget procedure proves a means
of adjusting the budget allowance to the actual volume (12,000
units) prior to the comparison with actual. This does not mean
that because variable budget procedures are being used that they
should be allowed to influence the effort to develop realistic
volume forecasts.[3]

The Fundamental of the Significant. This fundamental holds
that in profit planning and control we should be concerned with
the significant rather than the irrelevant. Planning does not result
in "facts" as does historical accounting. The input data (budget
estimates) should be only as precise as is necessary to assure
sound management decisions and control. There is not enough
executive time (aside from the cost) to be concerned with insignificant and unnecessary precision. Items having no significant

---

[3] An extended discussion of flexibilty in budgeting is included in Chapter 17.

impact on the over-all profit plan should be by-passed or re-solved summarily. Budget estimates should never be expressed in cents; rounding to even $10, $100, or even $1,000 is more appropriate. The rounding should be such as to suggest the range of accuracy in the estimates. The inclusion of cents in a budget estimate obviously implies an accuracy that is not there. In the same manner, in budgeting we should not be particularly concerned with the precision that is necessary in accounting as exemplified by the system of balances, minute detail, and so on. Some accountants and executives with long experience in dealing with "precise facts" experience some difficulty in accepting the viewpoint of *the significant* that is essential to practical profit planning and control.

The Fundamental of Cost Consciousness. Both experience and investigation have demonstrated that *attitudes* of cost consciousness are fundamental to effective cost control. To illustrate, investigations have shown that if an executive is cost conscious, his subordinates tend to be more cost conscious (by a margin of approximately three to one) than the subordinates of the executive who is not cost conscious. Here we are dealing with attitudes, with the psychology of the individual and of the work group. Our planning and control system must be designed to take advantage of these psychological phenomena.

The Fundamental of Follow-up. This fundamental holds that both good and bad performance should be investigated, the purpose being threefold:

(1) In the case of poor performance, to lead in a constructive manner to immediate corrective action;
(2) In the case of outstanding performance, to recognize it and perhaps provide for a transfer of knowledge to similar operations;
(3) To provide a basis for improved planning and control in the future.

The Fundamental of Uses and Limitations. The uses and limitations of budgeting should be thoroughly understood and appreciated by each executive. Uses must be understood in terms of possible contributions to the planning, coordinating, and controlling functions. On the other hand, it is especially important that executives do not expect too much, too quickly, from a newly adopted budget program. There must be a clear realization that the budget does not manage, but rather serves as a tool to be used by management. (The uses and limitations of budgeting were discussed in Chapter 1.)

The Fundamental of Budget Education. If a budget program

is to be effective and constantly improved, supervisory personnel must be actively interested in it. The best way to assure this interest is continuous budget education. Budget education involves a sort of *public relations* job so as to educate supervisory personnel in the objectives, potentials, fundamentals, and techniques of budgeting. This result is best obtained by making the supervisory personnel an integral part of the group preparing the budget, and by requiring adequate staff assistance on the part of the budget staff. Most successful budget directors make it a policy to spend at least as much time in the plant as in the office. The budget director should, after each budget report (and during budget preparation), discuss and assist the various management personnel with any and all budget problems. Budget directors have found that direct contact with supervisors in the plant relative to budget problems contributes considerably to understanding and frequently results in constructive suggestions for improvement in budget procedures.

Summary

There are three broad aspects of profit planning and control: the mechanics, the techniques, and the underlying fundamentals. Mechanics are relatively simple, yet undue concern with them may cloud our thinking with respect to the budget process. The techniques vary from the simple to complex; they must be known and understood. The underlying fundamentals are of primary significance; they have much more in common with the process of management and enlightened human relations than with historical accounting. Profit planning and control go directly to the heart of (a) management policies, (b) organizational structure, (c) delegation of authority and responsibility, (d) accounting keyed to lines of authority and responsibility, (e) effective communication, and (f) enlightened human relations.

A budget program has great potential if designed and operated on a logical basis. The program must be sound mechanically and technically, but more important, it must rest on a firm foundation of underlying fundamentals.

Discussion Questions

1. Explain the primary distinctions between (a) the mechanics of budgeting, (b) the techniques of budgeting, and (c) the fundamentals of budgeting.

2. Why is the support of top management essential to successful budgeting? What does support imply?
3. What is meant by organization structure in a firm? How is it related to budgeting? From the budgeting point of view why is it essential that there be definite specification of areas of authority and responsibility?
4. Distinguish between the performance concept of budgeting and the fiscal concept of budgeting.
5. Why should those who are responsible for achieving budget goals participate in setting those goals?
6. Explain the significance and relationship of (a) responsibility accounting, (b) responsibility budgeting, and (c) responsibility reporting.
7. Explain the various aspects of the *Fundamental of Realism*.
8. What is meant by budget education? Is budget education important? Explain.
9. Discuss the following: "Objectives should represent goals which are reasonably attainable and yet present a real challenge."
10. In classifying costs and expenses, should the primary emphasis be on (a) costing production or (b) cost control? Explain.

PART TWO

Budget Construction
and Application

T H R E E

Comprehensive Budgeting

for Managerial Planning and Control

In Chapter 1 the budget concept was related in a general way to the basic functions of management. In Chapter 2 the fundamentals underlying a comprehensive budget or profit planning and control program were discussed. A comprehensive budget program appropriate for one firm may vary in many respects from the budget program appropriate for another firm. A budget program should be carefully tailored to the characteristics, needs, and general environment of the firm for which it is prepared.

The purpose of this chapter is to indicate, and briefly discuss, the *technical aspects* of a comprehensive budget program that appear to have general applicability. Many of the procedures outlined in this chapter will be treated in detail in subsequent chapters. The procedures reflect the latest profit planning and control techniques in use throughout industry. The techniques must be used with discrimination. Obviously, not all of them will fit every situation. Only those that are adaptable and useful in a particular circumstance should be used. Special emphasis is given in this book to integration of the numerous techniques, mechanics, and underlying fundamentals into a comprehensive budget system having significant potentials for management planning and control.

This chapter is divided into two sections. The first section is devoted to a consideration of the basic characteristics of a budget program. The second section illustrates the broad outlines of a budget program. This illustration is continued in some detail at the end of subsequent chapters.

SECTION ONE: CHARACTERISTICS OF A COMPREHENSIVE BUDGET PROGRAM

Outline of a comprehensive budget program

A comprehensive budget program encompasses much more than the traditional idea of an annual planning budget. Rather, it encompasses a variety of techniques and implies application of the profit planning and control process to all of the operational and functional areas of the business. With respect to the planning aspects, comprehensive budgeting includes both the short and long run. It also involves both *period planning* and *project planning* in their broadest senses.[1] Project planning represents an analysis of several alternatives related to specific projects or proposals, a projection of the results of each alternative, and a final selection of one of these alternatives. Project planning involves proposals that extend over varying lengths of time; the primary considerations are not in terms of time segments, but rather in terms of a specific project from its inception to completion. An example of project planning might involve: (a) deciding to construct a new plant, (b) setting the plant capacity, and (c) locating the plant in a particular region. Managerial consideration of the many related factors (after examining numerous alternatives such as one location versus other locations) may extend over a period of several years. Having made the final decisions, construction itself may extend over several years. Thus we see an example of project planning that may cover five or six years from inception to completion.

Period planning serves to explain the time segmentation that is essential in developing both long- and short-term budgets. The annual profit plan and the five-year plan (budget) are illustrative of the period planning concept. With respect to project planning, the results must, of necessity, be integrated into the periodic plans. As a matter of fact the annual profit plan and the long-range plan represent essentially an integration of many, varied project plans. To return to the project plan illustration concerning the location and construction of a new plant: the policies, costs, cash requirements, project completion, and so on, would be integrated in the periodic budgets from year to year.

In order to provide a broad view of a comprehensive budget program the principal components of such a program are outlined on pages 45 and 46.

[1] Robert N. Anthony, *Management Accounting* (Homewood, Ill.: Irwin, 1960), Chs. 16–18.

Components of a Comprehensive Budget Program

I. The Strategic or Long-range Plan (extending 3, 5, or 10 or more years into the future)
   1. Basic premises upon which the long-range plans are made
   2. Sales (or gross revenue) projections
   3. Cost projections (in broad categories)
   4. Profit and return-on-investment projections
   5. Capital additions and research plans
   6. Cash flow projections
   7. Projection of manpower requirements (particularly managerial and highly skilled)
   8. Projection of special projects and major shifts in effort
II. The Annual Profit Plan (the first chronological segment of the long-range plan)
   1. The operating budget
      (a) Budgeted income statement
         (1) Master income statement
         (2) Income statement by responsibilities
         (3) Income statement by products
      (b) Income statement supporting schedules
         (1) Sales budget
            (a) By sales district by interim periods
            (b) By product by interim periods
         (2) Production budget
            (a) Schedule of quantities to be produced
            (b) Schedule of inventories
            (c) Materials budget
            (d) Purchases budget
            (e) Direct labor budget
            (f) Manufacturing expense (overhead) budgets
               i. Service departments
               ii. Producing departments
         (3) Administrative expense budgets
            (a) Expense budgets for each administrative department.
            (b) The Personnel department budget
            (c) Manpower budget
         (4) Distribution expense budget
         (5) Appropriation-type budgets
            (a) Advertising budget
            (b) Research budget
            (c) Others
   2. The financial budget
      (a) Budgeted balance sheet
      (b) Balance sheet supporting schedules
         (1) Cash flow and funds flow budgets
         (2) Budget of receivables
         (3) Capital additions budget
         (4) Depreciation budget

III. Variable Expense Budget
   1. Provides cost formulae for budgeting:
     (a) Manufacturing expenses
     (b) Distribution expenses
     (c) Administrative expenses
   2. Provides data for dynamic cost control
IV. Supplementary Statistics
   1. Breakeven analyses
     (a) By department
     (b) By product
     (c) For over-all operations
   2. Historical growth and cost-volume-profit tables and charts
V. Budget Reports for Management
   1. Comparison of actual and budgeted costs, revenues, assets, liabilities, and equities to determine the extent to which the profit plan was met or exceeded.
   2. Analysis of variations between actual and budget to determine causes and to provide a 'basis for corrective action.

The outline indicates that there are five basic components of a comprehensive budget program: the long-range plan, the annual profit plan, variable expense budgets, supplementary statistics, and budget reports to management. Each of these components will be discussed briefly in the following paragraphs. At the end of the chapter certain aspects of each will be illustrated. As previously noted, each component will be treated in more detail in subsequent chapters.

The strategic or long-range plan

Perhaps the most significant development in scientific management within recent years has been the increasing recognition of the importance of long-range planning.[2] Long-range planning is concerned with the efforts of company executives to establish in broad terms a blueprint of what the company should attempt

----

[2] With respect to the extent of long-range planning a recent survey showed the following:

Functional Areas	Per Cent of 424 Respondents Indicating Long-Range Planning
Sales plans	63
Capital expenditure plans	63
Profit plans	54
Cash plans	50
Research plans	34

Source: Burnard H. Sord and Glenn A. Welsch, *Business Budgeting, A Survey of Management Planning and Control Practices* (New York: The Controllership Foundation, 1958), p. 122.

to do within the next three, five, or ten years, including how and when certain decisions and actions are to be taken. To quote from a well-known source:[3]

> The concept of long-term profits has far-reaching implications. It should put an end, once and for all, to the old but slow-dying idea of nineteenth-century economists that the corporation seeks only to maximize short-term profits. For the more top management thinks of its job as building a *permanent* organization—an institution for generations of managers yet to come—the more willing it will be to sacrifice short-term profits when they come into conflict with long-range objectives. Long-range planning should also add to the growing sense of responsibility to the public that is held by businessmen today. And it should give impetus to many other current trends, such as management training, product diversification, and willingness to work with the government and the military on a continuing basis. . . . It puts a premium on the *conceptual* skills of the manager, as opposed to technical and human relations skills. . . . It asks the executive to use his sixth sense. It asks that he go visionary now and then. He needs to look into the future, take calculated risks, imagine possibilities.

The very fact that the future is characterized by uncertainty indicates the importance, or even the necessity, of managerial planning. Although a distinction is made between short- and long-run planning they actually are part and parcel of the same thing. Decisions concerning short-run matters cannot be made with the degree of effectiveness possible when long-range plans for growth, development, and change have been thought out with precision. Preferably, then, the annual profit plan should be viewed as only one segment of an over-all plan.

A logical approach to long-range planning has been outlined in a series of steps as follows:[4]

(1) Establishment of the broad objectives of the enterprise for the period covered by the plan. These objectives concern such matters as: the primary purpose of the enterprise, the general goals related to operations, research, finance, personnel, public relations, management, and growth patterns.[5]

(2) Establishment of *planning premises* involving forecast data of a factual nature and basic policies expected to be applicable to the future. Premises then, are planning assumptions concerning

---

[3] David W. Ewing (editor), *Long-Range Planning for Management* (New York: Harper, 1958), pp. 4 and 5.

[4] *Ibid.*, pp. 34–39.

[5] *Ibid.*, pp. 269–274. See p. 60 for details concerning the illustrative case that is continued through Chs. 3–14.

such factors as markets, kinds of products, economic forecasts, and basic managerial decisions. Premises may be divided into three groups: (a) noncontrollable factors, such as population changes, political environment, and business cycles; (b) semi-controllable factors regarding which the firm can exercise some influence, such as share of the market, labor turnover, and pricing policy; and (c) controllable factors, such as product expansion, new plant construction, and expansion into new territories.

(3) Identification and examination of alternative courses of action.

(4) Evaluation of alternative courses of action.

(5) Selection of a course or courses of action.

(6) Formulation of necessary plans to implement the alternatives tentatively accepted.

Long-term plans (budgets) extending three, five, or ten years (five years appears to be the most common period) into the future should be considered seriously by every progressive management. Over-all, long-range planning is a function reserved to the highest levels of management. Usually such plans are known to only a very few members of the management, and are generally expressed in writing. The Controllership Foundation survey cited earlier reported that the better managed companies develop a coordinated long-range plan which includes a reasonable amount of detail in major areas such as sales, capital expenditures, product development and research, cash, and manpower.

The income-statement *component* of the long-range plan for The Superior Manufacturing Company is shown in Illustration 3. (Only sufficient data are presented to indicate the characteristics of the system.) Other aspects of the plan, involving broad objectives, planning premises, cash flow, capital expenditures, manpower requirements, and special products are not illustrated. The reader should observe how the *annual* profit plan for The Superior Manufacturing Company, as illustrated in subsequent chapters, dovetails into this long-range plan.

In larger companies long-range planning frequently is decentralized to plants or similar divisions of the company. For example an executive in one company stated:[6]

> In addition to developing the detailed one-year budget, which is broken down by months, each division prepares a four-year long-range budget which is broken down by years. Divisional managers are responsible for developing this four-year budget, which is revised

[6] Sord and Welsch, *Business Budgeting*, p. 125.

each year. Long-range plans cover all of the principal areas of activity—sales, expenses, research and development, advertising, capital expenditures, profit, and cash.

The Superior Manufacturing Company
Five-Year Plan (Profits)
(In Thousand Dollars)

	Actual			Projected				
	1960	1961	1962	1963	1964	1965	1966	1967
Sales	$5,505	$5,691	$5,963	$6,100	$7,000	$7,400	$8,000	$8,800
Variable costs	3,600	3,700	3,870	3,940	4,650	4,880	5,350	5,890
Marginal income	1,905	1,991	2,093	2,160	2,350	2,520	2,650	2,910
Fixed costs	1,220	1,100	1,160	1,310	1,400	1,430	1,470	1,580
Miscellaneous items	(30)	(15)	10	(20)	(50)	(20)	(30)	(16)
Net before taxes	715	906	923	870	1,000	1,110	1,210	1,346
Estimated taxes	290	270	325	260	490	540	590	650
Net income	$ 425	$ 636	$ 598	$ 610	$ 510	$ 570	$ 620	$ 696
Ratios								
Profit margin —pretax	13.0	15.9	15.5	14.3	14.3	15.0	15.1	15.3
Return on investment—pretax	21.0	28.0	27.6	27.4	29.6	30.0	30.0	31.0

Illustration 3. *Long-Range Plan* (*Profits*)

The annual profit plan

The annual profit plan is variously referred to as the planning budget, the plan of operations, the fixed budget, the forecast budget, the master budget, the period budget, and the static budget. The annual profit plan represents an over-all plan of operations developed by the management of the company, covering a definite period of time such as a year. It is a formal expression in quantitative terms of managerial policies and goals for a specified period, broken down in detail with respect to time, products, and *organizational responsibilities*. This component of a budget program is appropriately labeled the *planning budget* or *profit plan* since it formalizes the planning decisions of management. Illustration 4 presents diagrammatically the development and composition of the annual profit plan.

The annual profit plan consists of the operating budget, the financial budget, and certain appropriation-type budgets. The operating budget, frequently referred to as the income budget, covers revenues and expenses. The crucial elements of the

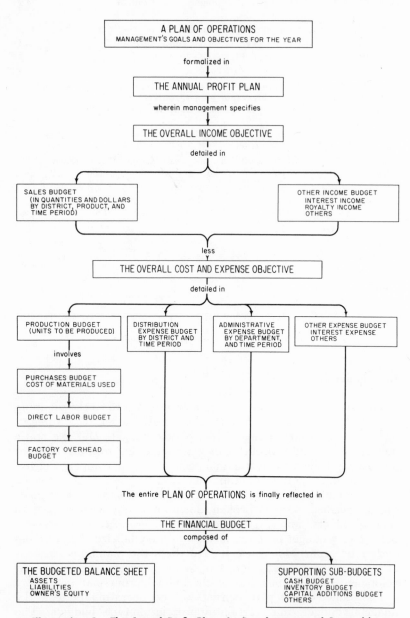

A PLAN OF OPERATIONS
MANAGEMENT'S GOALS AND OBJECTIVES FOR THE YEAR

formalized in

THE ANNUAL PROFIT PLAN

wherein management specifies

THE OVERALL INCOME OBJECTIVE

detailed in

SALES BUDGET
(IN QUANTITIES AND DOLLARS
BY DISTRICT, PRODUCT, AND
TIME PERIOD)

OTHER INCOME BUDGET
INTEREST INCOME
ROYALTY INCOME
OTHERS

less

THE OVERALL COST AND EXPENSE OBJECTIVE

detailed in

PRODUCTION BUDGET
(UNITS TO BE PRODUCED)

DISTRIBUTION
EXPENSE BUDGET
BY DISTRICT AND
TIME PERIOD

ADMINISTRATIVE
EXPENSE BUDGET
BY DEPARTMENT,
AND TIME PERIOD

OTHER EXPENSE BUDGET
INTEREST EXPENSE
OTHERS

involves

PURCHASES BUDGET
COST OF MATERIALS USED

DIRECT LABOR BUDGET

FACTORY OVERHEAD
BUDGET

The entire PLAN OF OPERATIONS is finally reflected in

THE FINANCIAL BUDGET

composed of

THE BUDGETED BALANCE SHEET
ASSETS
LIABILITIES
OWNER'S EQUITY

SUPPORTING SUB-BUDGETS
CASH BUDGET
INVENTORY BUDGET
CAPITAL ADDITIONS BUDGET
OTHERS

Illustration 4. *The Annual Profit Plan—Its Development and Composition*

50

operating budget, and hence of the profit plan, are (1) the sales budget and (2) the various expense budgets. The outline suggests the principal supporting schedules or sub-budgets which make up the operating budget.

The financial budget consists of the budget balance sheet and supporting schedules such as the cash, receivables, and capital additions sub-budgets. The financial budget is the *end result* of the operating budget.

Appropriation-type budgets are frequently found to be effective budget devices. These cover certain types of expenditures such as advertising and research. The concept involved is that management, in effect, allocates or appropriates a certain amount of funds for the budget period for a specific activity, such as advertising or research. To illustrate:

> The Ford Motor Company has guaranteed for five years the budget of its scientific laboratory, part of its Engineering and Research staff. "The budget will assure continuity of the Laboratory's operations without regard for business fluctuations," said Henry Ford II. It was also pointed out that stable long-range planning is necessary for the proper support of research, and that the five-year budget will permit the laboratory to attract the best available scientists of various specialties.[7]

The amount of an appropriation should be based on the careful planning of the activity for the period. In such cases the budget appropriation frequently constitutes managerial approval of the conduct of the specified activity. Performance reports to management during the period should indicate the progress of the planned activity and the status of the funds appropriated.

Preparation of the annual profit plan usually begins several months before the end of the current year. For example, companies whose financial year ends December 31 usually start their budget preparations around September 1. This procedure leaves time for adequate consideration of the important policies and plans involved, thus assuring completion and distribution of the approved plan on or before the first day of the period covered by the budget. Early distribution is important. Nothing detracts more from the effectiveness of budgeting than completion and, hence, distribution of the budget several months after the period has started.

Preparation of the annual profit plan begins with the development of the sales budget by the sales department. In connection

[7] "Research Notes," *The Controller* (January 1960), p. 346.

with the sales budget the advertising and distribution expense budgets are tentatively developed, because these in turn affect the sales potential. Once the sales budget is prepared, and tentatively approved, a number of other sub-budgets can be prepared simultaneously. As soon as the sales budget and the policy with respect to finished goods inventory are determined, it is possible to prepare the *production budget* which specifies the quantity and timing of production requirements. Having determined the production requirements, it is possible to develop simultaneously: (a) direct material requirements, (b) direct labor requirements, and (c) the manufacturing expense budgets. These respective budgets can be adjusted to the policies relating to work in process inventories resulting in the *budgeted cost of goods manufactured.* At the same time, budgets of such items as administrative expenses, financial expenses, research costs, capital additions, and cash budgets can be completed. These budgets are summarized in the *budgeted income statement* and *budgeted balance sheet.*

Upon completion of all aspects of the annual profit plan, the plan is reviewed by the budget committee and formally approved by the chief executive. Not infrequently it is presented to the board of directors.

The approved annual profit plan is reproduced in final form and assembled. Certain top executives are provided complete copies, others are given only that portion which relates to their particular area of responsibility.

The variable expense budget

The third principal component listed in the outline of a comprehensive budget program is the *variable expense budget*. This budget is variously referred to as the variable budget, the flexible budget, the sliding scale budget, the expense control budget, and the formula budget. The variable budget is concerned only with *expenses*. It is completely separate from the planning budget but can be used to complement it. Many firms do not employ variable budget procedures, whereas other firms integrate planning and variable budget procedures. Whether or not both techniques should be employed in a particular situation depends upon the circumstances.

Variable budgets provide data on expenses in each department that make it possible to compute budget allowances for various volumes or rates of activity in each department. In effect the variable budget provides a *formula* for each expense item in each department. The formula indicates the relationship of each expense to *output* (volume of work) in the department. Each formula includes a constant factor (fixed expense) and a variable rate (variable expense). In the case of a fixed cost, the variable rate is zero; in the case of variable cost, the constant factor is zero; and in the case of a semivariable expense, there will be a value for both the constant factor and the variable rate. To illustrate a semivariable expense assume that in Department 1 the *variable budget* formula indicates the budget allowance for supplies used is $450 per month (constant), plus $5.50 (variable rate) per 100 direct labor hours worked; the volume or rate of activity in Department 1 being measured in terms of direct labor hours. Budget allowances for this expense would be computed for various volumes in this way:

	Volume	Computation	Budget Allowance
(a)	1,000 direct labor hours	$450 plus (10 × $5.50)	$505.00
(b)	1,500 direct labor hours	$450 plus (15 × $5.50)	$532.50
(c)	2,000 direct labor hours	$450 plus (20 × $5.50)	$560.00

From this example it is obvious that if variable expense budgets are available when the planning budget (annual profit plan) is being prepared, determination of expense allowances at the *planning budget volume* involves simple computations similar to those indicated above. On the other hand, if variable expense budgets are not available, considerable analysis of expenses would be necessary to determine expense allowances for the annual profit plan.

Variable budgets are of particular importance in the control of costs. For example, assume the estimated volume in the annual profit plan for Department 1, for a given period, is 1,500 direct labor hours; therefore, the expense allowance for supplies used would be $533 (rounded) as computed above. Assume further that the actual direct labor hours during the period were 2,000 and that actual supplies used cost $550. A comparison of the actual expense of $550 with the original profit plan allowance of $533 indicates an overexpenditure or unfavorable variance of $17. Obviously the comparison is not valid because the budget allowance and the actual expense incurred were *based on different volumes*. By use of the variable budget a more meaningful control report is possible, viz.:

Budget allowance adjusted to 2,000 hours	
$450 plus (20 × $5.50)	$560.00
Actual expenditure at 2,000 hours	550.00
Budget variation (favorable)	$ 10.00

The concept just illustrated is frequently referred to as *dynamic, variable cost control.* It is significant in situations where it is impossible to budget volume or rates of activity accurately in specific departments.

The ideas presented indicate the complementary relationship or integration of annual profit planning and variable budget procedures. It is claimed occasionally that these two techniques represent a duplication; on the contary, when they are properly understood and used, they complement one another.

Variable budgets are usually constructed early in the budget preparation period because as indicated, they provide cost data for the planning budget. Variable budgets are not a part of the planning budget, and, hence, are usually bound together under separate cover; distribution to personnel is usually limited to a select few.

Supplemental statistics

The fourth component of the outlined comprehensive budget program is supplemental statistics. This component includes the application of certain managerial techniques and data that are related to planning procedures. Of particular importance is the concept of breakeven analysis, more descriptively referred to as cost-volume-profit analysis. A complete discussion of breakeven analysis is included in Chapter 12. Generally the accessory statistics, although basically not a part of the annual profit plan, are included as a supplement.

Budget reports to management

The last component in the outline of a comprehensive budget program is performance reports. This component is frequently the most critical, but is often neglected thus seriously reducing the budget's real potential to the concern. It is through performance reports to management that (a) attainment of the profit plan is assured and (b) control is achieved.

Having completed the long-range plan and the annual profit

plan, management has to a considerable degree accomplished the planning function. In addition, the basis for effective coordination has been established. Control action may be assured through a continuous reporting of *actual results* as compared with *planned results*. This continuous reporting is achieved through the medium of performance reports which indicate to management, by area of responsibility, those items which are out of line—that is, the unusual or exceptional items. It is important to note that budget reports must be timely, carefully constructed, and tailored to fit the organization's structure of responsibility. Performance reports are discussed in detail in Chapter 13.[8]

Length of the budget period

The length of the budget period varies among concerns and industries because of several factors, some internal, others largely external. Some concerns operate under conditions that make it relatively easy to plan and budget well in advance, whereas others experience considerable difficulty in estimating for the future. These variable conditions have given rise to several approaches to the problem of the length of the budget period. The two principal approaches are frequently referred to as *periodic budgeting* and *continuous budgeting*.

Periodic budgeting involves the selection of a definite planning budget period, usually a year, which generally corresponds to the accounting period. The planning budget is prepared to cover this specific period with a minimum of interim revision expected. This approach is normally used by concerns that can make reasonably accurate estimates covering the budget period.[9]

Continuous budgeting is frequently used where it is felt that definite plans and reasonably accurate estimates cannot be made except for relatively short periods, such as a quarter, or where frequent reprojection is desired. The procedure usually followed is that of preparing either a quarterly, semiannual, or even annual budget which is revised each month (or quarter) by progressively dropping the month (or quarter) just ended and adding another period in the future. For example, prior to January a budget is prepared extending, say, through June. At the end of January the semiannual budget is revised, dropping

---

[8] At this point it might be useful for the reader to turn to Chapter 17 and read pages 449 through 459 relative to budget *utilization* and *flexibility*.

[9] Sord and Welsch, *Business Budgeting*, pp. 75 and 277.

January and adding July, thereby resulting in a continuous semiannual budget for the concern. An example of an even more dynamic approach to profit planning and control is followed by a company widely recognized for its effective management. This particular company has used the continuous budget concept for many years. Each quarter an *annual* profit plan is prepared by each division of the firm; these individual plans are then combined and summarized and become the over-all profit plan. The annual profit plan is prepared *by month* for the upcoming quarter and by quarter for the remaining twelve months. Near the end of each quarter the profit plan is extended another quarter by reprojection of the upcoming quarter by month and of the following nine months by quarter. Thus under this approach the management has *monthly goals and objectives* for the immediate quarter and goals for each of the three following quarters. Continuous budgeting as practiced by this firm is perhaps the most effective approach to dynamic profit planning and control yet devised. It largely eliminates *budget revision* as a special problem.

The major distinction of the continuous approach to profit planning and control is that management has detailed and continuous plans for a fairly stable period of time in the future, whereas under periodic budgeting the short-range planning period runs out near the year's end.

Throughout this book both periodic and continuous budgeting are assumed. The illustrative case extending from Chapter 3 through Chapter 13 is developed by month for the first three months and by quarter for the remainder of the year. One can assume that either periodic or continuous budgeting is used; the timing of reprojection makes the distinction. The basic principles of budgeting are equally applicable to periodic and continuous budgeting.

Choosing the planning budget period

For planning budget purposes, where the periodic budget procedure is used, it is best in most cases to use the accounting period—usually a year—as the budget period, breaking down the annual profit plan by quarters for the last three quarters and by months for the first quarter. The last three quarters are in turn broken down by month preceding each quarter. Some firms find it feasible to prepare the entire planning budget by month at the time of original preparation. Where the continuous budget procedure is used, an annual plan, reprojected each quarter, is generally preferable.

In a recent survey it was reported that 88 per cent of the companies studied prepared a profit plan covering a twelve-month period; 8 per cent a six-month period (generally retail and finance companies), and 4 per cent used a three-month period. With respect to interim segments of the profit plan, the following practices were reported: monthly breakdown, 75 per cent; quarterly breakdown, 13 per cent; annual only, 5 per cent; and miscellaneous periods (or not reported), 7 per cent.[10]

If there is a clear understanding of the objectives, uses, and methodologies of profit planning and control, there will generally be little difficulty in determining the preferable budget period and procedure as to reprojection. In addition to the considerations noted above, such factors as the selling seasons, length of process time, merchandise turnover, seasonal cycles, natural business cycle for the industry, production periods, financial considerations, and operating conditions may influence the length of the budget period that should be used.

Responsibility for profit planning

The budget program, like any other program, must be the definite responsibility of a specified individual or group. Obviously, the chief executive has the ultimate responsibility for the profit planning and control program. However, it is necessary that a large part of the supervisory responsibility be delegated to the chief financial officer, controller, or budget director.

We have stated that a sound budget program is one of the most useful devices for achieving managerial control and efficient operation. If this is true, the position of the individual responsible for budgeting should be such that the program will command attention and respect throughout the firm. It is advisable that the individual responsible for the budget function report to the top executive. If there is a budget director, as well as a chief financial officer, it seems proper for the former to report to the latter, who should in turn report to the top executive.

---

[10] Sord and Welsch, *Business Budgeting*, pp. 75 and 277.

The organization chart for The Superior Manufacturing Company is shown in Illustration 5 (page 61). It is assumed that this chart is supplemented with detailed charts and written directives which specify definite responsibility, and commensurate authority, for each executive and supervisor. Notice the indicated position of the budget director and the composition of the budget committee.

The positions indicated for the controller and budget director do not imply that they have line authority with respect to budget enforcement. Both are strictly staff positions. Budget preparation, operation, enforcement, and control are principally line responsibilities. Staff executives generally should have no line responsibility or line authority outside their own departments. The budget director is properly charged with responsibility for *designing* the budget program and with providing technical *assistance* and *advice* to line personnel in developing and implementing it. The budget director definitely should not attempt to prepare the budget, but he should be responsible for providing technical assistance and supervision in bringing the estimates together in final form once the *input data* have been developed by the respective operating executives. The budget director should be responsible for the technical analyses needed by the various departments and for the preparation of certain budget reports. The duties of the budget director may be summarized as follows:

(1) To advise the chief executive, budget committee, and others on all budget matters.

(2) To recommend the budgeting procedures and technical requirements for each part of the budget.

(3) To assume responsibility for budget organization and the necessary time schedules.

(4) To provide over-all technical supervision of the budget program.

(5) To design and recommend essential forms, schedules, and reports necessary in the budget procedures.

(6) To supervise the preparation and revision of the budget manual for approval by the chief executive.

(7) To furnish analyses of past and future costs, revenues, and so on, to interested executives.

(8) To translate certain preliminary policy decisions into their probable or alternative financial effect on future operations.

(9) To prepare budget reports on individual and group performance.

(10) To analyze and interpret variations between actual and budget allowances.

(11) To be responsible for a certain amount of the clerical work associated with his budgeting functions.

(12) To supervise revision of both the budget and budget program

where conditions warrant.
(13) To perform statistical analyses of various types upon request.

Budget committee

It is frequently advisable for a firm to have a standing budget committee composed of the president, vice presidents, and the budget director. The chief executive officer or someone designated by him should serve as chairman. This committee should be advisory in nature. The budget manual should specify the responsibilities and duties of the budget committee, which should include the following:

(1) Receive and review budget estimates from the respective divisions or departments and make recommendations thereto.
(2) Recommend decisions on budget matters where there may be conflict between departments or divisions.
(3) Recommend changes and approval of the planning budget.
(4) Receive, study, and analyze periodic performance reports comparing the budget to actual performance. Consider policies with respect to follow-up procedures.
(5) Consider and make recommendations for revision of the budget when conditions warrant.
(6) Consider recommendations for changes in budget policies and procedures.
(7) Make recommendations for the budget manual.

There is a tendency, frequently, to establish a budget committee and then assign to it direct responsibility for the budget program. This practice represents a misuse of committees, because committees move too slowly and involve too many diverse interests to be effective in day-to-day budget work. If the committee is used, not as a directing authority, but in a consultative capacity, it will be effective from the profit planning point of view and also afford an excellent opportunity for top-level coordination. Not infrequently the top *executive committee* performs these budget functions in addition to its other functions. In such cases, a more direct authority and responsibility may rest on the committee.

The budget manual

Reference has been made to a budget manual in discussing organization and budget responsibility. A statement of budget policies in the form of a budget manual should be part of the standard operating procedure of a concern, just as there should be an organization manual. The budget manual should include the following:

(1) Statement of objectives and potentials of the program
(2) Budget preparation
    (a) Instructions and forms to be used
    (b) Responsibility for developing input data (estimates)
        (1) Operational executives
        (2) Budget committee
        (3) Budget director
(3) A budget calendar specifying definite dates for the completion of each part of the budget and submission of reports
(4) Distribution instructions specifying to whom the various budget schedules are to be sent
(5) Managerial performance reports
    (a) Responsibility for preparation
        (1) Actual data
        (2) Budget data and variations
        (3) Analysis
    (b) Form and content
    (c) Distribution
(6) Responsibility for corrective action
(7) Follow-up procedures

SECTION TWO: COMPREHENSIVE BUDGETING ILLUSTRATED

The annual profit plan (planning budget) illustrated

Details concerning the annual profit plan are developed in subsequent chapters. Right now, it is important that the reader have a general conception of a complete profit plan and its principal components. In order to provide this general conception, certain summary budget schedules for The Superior Manufacturing Company are presented in this chapter. The schedules presented deal principally with *annual results*; detailed breakdowns by months, departments, and products will be discussed and illustrated at the end of subsequent chapters. The annual summaries and discussions illustrated in this chapter include only those which are essential (a) to impart a general understanding of the annual profit plan and (b) to provide an over-all conception of a comprehensive budget program. The reader should restudy the organizational chart of The Superior Manufacturing Company, Illustration 5 (page 61) to observe how the profit plan is tailored to it, and also to note how the annual plan ties into the long-range plan.[1]

[1] See pp. 107 & 382 (footnotes) for information concerning related classroom materials for classroom use.

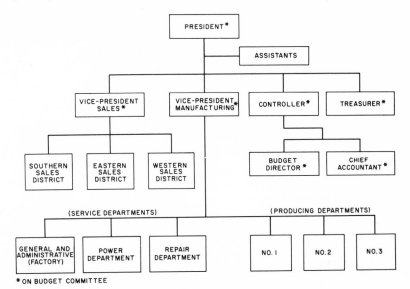

Illustration 5. *The Superior Manufacturing Company Organization Chart*

The student is urged to observe particularly the fact that the various budgets and sub-budgets illustrated below and in subsequent chapters are segmented as follows:

(a) By organizational responsibility—We have said that there should be participation in the planning process and that control can be exercised effectively only through assigned responsibilities. As a consequence, a most important fundamental of the budget process is that it be tailored, first and foremost, to the organizational structure and related responsibilities. This frame of reference is observable in practically all of the schedules including the performance reports for management.

(b) By interim periods—With respect to the annual profit plan The Superior Manufacturing Company segments the first quarter on a monthly basis; estimates for subsequent quarters are broken down by monthly periods during the year. Segmentation on a time basis is especially significant because, to be meaningful, many goals must be *immediate* goals. For example, an annual sales quota obviously would not be as effective a motivation as a series of monthly, weekly, or even daily quotas. Likewise, we have said that effective control is at the point of action; performance reports comparing actual with goals must be as soon after the point of action as is possible. The earlier problem areas are known, the sooner corrective action can be taken, thereby minimizing the cumulating effects of inefficiencies. Then too, we can hardly expect a supervisor to be much concerned about a performance report that is received months after the activity occurred—by then, he is concerned with a whole host of more current and pressing problems.

(c) By product-cost classifications—The budget program must accommodate the need for product costs, project costs, and similar cost constructions that are not necessarily based on specific responsibilities or common time periods.

It is well to point out also that many of the budget schedules illustrated in this and subsequent chapters are designed to indicate the computational aspects of developing the particular data. This approach has been adopted for instructional purposes. For inclusion in the final profit plan many of them should be redesigned to increase readability and understanding; some of them may well be omitted altogether.

The sales budget

The sales budget is the initial step in preparing the annual profit plan or planning budget. The Superior Manufacturing Company sells two products (designated X and Y) in three sales districts (designated Southern, Eastern, and Western). The sales projection provided by the executive in charge of sales, and *tentatively* approved by the president, is indicated in the annual sales budget summary, page 63. Attention is called to the heading *Ref.* which provides a line and column for indicating the source of data when taken from *prior* schedules.

The production budget

When the sales budget is completed, the next step is determination of the number of units of each product that must be manufactured to meet the sales requirements and to maintain the desired inventory levels. The determination of production requirements necessitates specification of finished goods inventory policies by management. Because production scheduling is involved in determination of the details of *when* and *where* production should take place, this budget is the primary responsibility of the factory division executives. Product X is processed through all three factory departments and Product Y through departments 1 and 3 only.

The Superior Manufacturing Company

Schedule 1

SALES BUDGET SUMMARY
By Product, By District
For the Year Ending December 31, 1963

	Ref.	Totals	Product X Units	Product X Amount	Product Y Units	Product Y Amount
Southern Sales District X—$5.00; Y—$2.00*	(Given)	$2,120,000	340,000	$1,700,000	210,000	$ 420,000
Eastern Sales District X—$5.10; Y—$2.10*	(Given)	2,907,000	500,000	2,550,000	170,000	357,000
Western Sales District X—$5.10; Y—$2.10*	(Given)	1,068,000	160,000	816,000	120,000	252,000
Totals		$6,095,000	1,000,000	$5,066,000	500,000	$1,029,000

* Average unit sales prices budgeted.

The production budget summary for The Superior Manufacturing Company is shown in Schedule 2 below.

The Superior Manufacturing Company
PRODUCTION BUDGET SUMMARY   **Schedule 2**
By Product Units
For the Year Ending December 31, 1963

		Products (Units)	
	Ref.	X	Y
Units required to meet sales budget	1	1,000,000	500,000
Add desired finished goods final inventory, Dec. 31, 1963	(Given)	200,000	120,000
Total units required		1,200,000	620,000
Less finished goods initial inventory, Jan. 1, 1963	(Given)	240,000	100,000
Planned production for 1963		960,000	520,000

The direct materials budget

The materials budget deals with the number of units of each type of *direct raw materials* that is required to produce the number of units of finished goods called for in the production budget. Preparation of this budget necessitates a careful study of raw material needs to determine material usage rates, followed by an extension of the units to be produced times the material

The Superior Manufacturing Company   **Schedule 3**
DIRECT MATERIALS BUDGET SUMMARY IN UNITS
By Raw Material, By Product, By Department
For the Year Ending December 31, 1963

		Units of Direct Raw Material Required for Production		
	Ref.	A	B	C
By product:				
X		960,000	1,920,000	1,920,000
Y		520,000	520,000	
Totals		1,480,000	2,440,000	1,920,000
By department:				
No. 1		1,480,000		
No. 2			1,920,000	
No. 3			520,000	1,920,000
Totals		1,480,000	2,440,000	1,920,000

usage rates. This budget is a responsibility of the factory division executives.

It is assumed that The Superior Manufacturing Company uses three direct raw materials designated A, B, and C. The direct materials budget summary is shown as Schedule 3. (Computations are indicated in Chapter 6, Schedules 24 and 25).

The purchases budget

The materials budget, indicating units of each type of raw material required for production, is transmitted to the purchasing department when completed. Based upon these data and management policies with respect to raw material inventories, computation of units to be purchased is possible. Once the units to be purchased are determined, it is necessary that the *timing* of purchases be budgeted in a manner consistent with the inventory policy. In addition, the purchasing department has the responsibility for estimating the planned unit purchase price for each raw material.

Computation of the units to be purchased and extension at the unit purchase prices for The Superior Manufacturing Company is indicated in the following purchases budget summary.

The Superior Manufacturing Company

PURCHASES BUDGET SUMMARY   **Schedule 4**
For the Year Ending December 31, 1963

	Ref.	Direct Raw Materials		
		A	B	C
Units required for production	3	1,480,000	2,440,000	1,920,000
Add desired final inventory, Dec. 31, 1963	(Given)	245,000	370,000	450,000
Total units required		1,725,000	2,810,000	2,370,000
Less initial inventory, Jan. 1, 1963	(Given)	220,000	360,000	460,000
Units to be purchased		1,505,000	2,450,000	1,910,000
Planned unit purchase price	(Given)	$.30	$.20	$.25
Total cost of purchases		$ 451,500	$ 490,000	$ 477,500

The direct labor budget

The factory executives prepare the direct labor budget based upon planned production, as indicated in the production budget. The labor budget is usually based upon standard labor hours and average wage rates expected. This budget should be set up in a way similar to that employed in the direct material budget; that is, by product and by organizational responsibility.

The direct labor budget summary for The Superior Manufacturing Company, using budgeted standard labor hours and average wage rates, may be constructed as follows:

The Superior Manufacturing Company

DIRECT LABOR BUDGET SUMMARY   Schedule 5
By Product, By Department
For the Year Ending December 31, 1963

	Ref.	Units to be Produced	Standard Labor Hours	Total Standard Hours	Average Wage Rate	Direct Labor Cost
		2	(Given)		(Given)	
By product:						
X		960,000	1.0	960,000	$1.50	$1,440,000
Y		520,000	.4	208,000	1.50	312,000
Totals				1,168,000		$1,752,000
By department:						
1*				488,000	$2.00	$ 976,000
2*				192,000	1.50	288,000
3*				488,000	1.00	488,000
Totals				1,168,000		$1,752,000

* Computation shown in subsequent schedules.

The Superior Manufacturing Company

BUILDING SERVICES BUDGET SUMMARY   Schedule 6
For the Year Ending December 31, 1963

	Total Year
Supervisory salaries	$ 24,000
Repairs and maintenance	18,000
Depreciation	60,000
Insurance	3,600
Taxes	2,400
Wages	27,000
Heat	13,000
Water	2,000
Total	$150,000

Occupancy cost distribution:
(based on floor space)

Selling (20%)	$ 30,000
Administrative (20%)	30,000
Factory (60%)	90,000
Total	$150,000

MANUFACTURING OVERHEAD—BUDGET SUMMARY
By Department
For the Year Ending December 31, 1963

Schedule 7

	Ref.	Producing Departments			Service Departments			Total All Depts.
		No. 1	No. 2	No. 3	General Factory Overhead	Power Dept.	Repair Dept.	
Supervisory salaries		$120,000	$22,440	$ 35,040	$ 96,000	$ 36,000	$ 3,600	$313,080
Indirect labor		145,800	3,648	44,248				193,696
Maintenance parts		10,920	624	4,240		6,800		22,584
Fuel						24,000		24,000
Supplies used		32,240	1,440	14,600			1,360	49,640
Travel & entertainment					7,040			7,040
Telephone & telegraph					7,856			7,856
Depreciation		7,320	768	4,392	1,560	5,400	120	19,560
Insurance		1,200	120	600	240	840	36	3,036
Taxes		1,800	240	720	360	960	84	4,164
Stationery & office supplies					3,744			3,744
Wages						36,000	4,800	40,800
Totals		$319,280	$29,280	$103,840	$116,800	$110,000	$10,000	$689,200
Building service allocation	6							90,000
Total factory overhead								$779,200

The building services budget

It is assumed that The Superior Manufacturing Company owns a factory building which houses the factory division and all home office installations. It is necessary to prepare a building services budget and to make allocations to the respective functional divisions served. Accordingly, the building services superintendent is requested to prepare an expense budget for the year, as shown in Schedule 6.

The manufacturing overhead budget

Once production requirements are known, the factory division executives also are in a position to prepare the manufacturing expense or overhead budget.

It will be recalled that The Superior Manufacturing Company has three producing departments and three service departments in the factory (page 61). Accordingly, factory overhead budgets for each of these six departments must be prepared. These respective cost budgets are summarized in Schedule 7.

The inventory budgets

The costs of purchases, direct material, direct labor, and overhead are now available; hence data are available to determine the budgeted value of final inventories for raw materials, work in process, and finished goods. The details of these computations are included in subsequent chapters. A summary of initial and final inventories is shown for The Superior Manufacturing Company in Schedule 8.

The Superior Manufacturing Company   **Schedule 8**

SCHEDULE OF INITIAL AND FINAL INVENTORIES

For the Year Ending December 31, 1963

		Initial Inventory			Final Inventory	
	Units	*Unit Price*	*Total Value*	*Units*	*Unit Price*	*Total Value*
Ref.	2 & 4	(Given)		2 & 4	(Given)	
Raw materials:						
Material A	220,000	$ .30	$ 66,000	245,000	$ .30	$ 73,500
Material B	360,000	.20	72,000	370,000	.20	74,000
Material C	460,000	.26	119,600	450,000	.25	112,500
Totals			$257,600			$260,000
Work in process (Prod. Y—Dept. 3)	10,000	1.38	$ 13,800	10,000	1.38	$ 13,800
Finished goods:						
Product X	240,000	3.36	$806,400	200,000	3.36	$672,000
Product Y	100,000	1.38	138,000	120,000	1.38	165,600
Totals			$944,400			$837,600

Budgeted cost of goods sold

Data are now available for preparing the cost of goods sold budget. Generally the estimates illustrated up to this point are routed to the budget director, who consolidates them into cost of goods sold and income statements. Schedule 9, cost of goods sold budget for The Superior Manufacturing Company, is self-explanatory with respect to the sources of data.

The Superior Manufacturing Company   Schedule 9

COST OF GOODS SOLD BUDGET SUMMARY
For the Year Ending December 31, 1963

	Ref.		*Annual*
Direct raw materials used:			
Inventory, Jan. 1, 1963	8	$ 257,600	
Purchases of raw materials	4	1,419,000	
Total		$1,676,600	
Less inventory, Dec. 31, 1963	8	260,000	
Cost of raw materials used			$1,416,600
Direct labor	5		1,752,000
Manufacturing expenses	7		779,200
Total charges to manufacturing			3,947,800
Add initial work in process inventory	8		13,800
			3,961,600
Less final work in process inventory	8		13,800
Total cost of goods manufactured			3,947,800
Add initial finished goods inventory	8		944,400
			4,892,200
Less final inventory of finished goods	8		837,600
Cost of goods sold			$4,054,600

Distribution and administrative expense budgets

The advertising and distribution expense budgets must necessarily be prepared, at least tentatively, in conjunction with the sales budget. The administrative expense budgets can be prepared concurrently with other parts of the profit plan. As with the factory overhead budgets, these expense budgets should be prepared under the supervision of those operating executives responsible for the respective areas being budgeted.

The distribution expense, administrative expense, and financial income and expense budgets for The Superior Manufacturing Company are summarized in Schedules 10, 11, and 12.

DISTRIBUTION EXPENSE BUDGET SUMMARY
For the Year Ending December 31, 1963

| | | *General Sales Overhead* | Sales District | | | |
| | | | *Southern* | *Eastern* | *Western* | *Total* |
	Ref.					
Supervisory salaries		$144,000	$ 72,000	$ 96,000	$ 36,000	$348,000
Travel & entertainment		38,907	25,279	30,812	11,641	106,639
Telephone & telegraph		15,861	9,379	14,828	4,915	44,983
Depreciation—office equipment		600				600
Stationery & office supplies		11,049				11,049
Auto expense		25,913				25,913
Commissions			84,800	116,280	42,720	243,800
Freight & express			19,198	19,471	7,844	46,513
Advertising		60,000	24,000	36,000	12,000	132,000
Totals		$296,330	$234,656	$313,391	$115,120	$959,497
Building service allocation	6					30,000
Total distribution expense						$989,497

ADMINISTRATIVE EXPENSE BUDGET SUMMARY
For the Year Ending December 31, 1963

| | | Departments | | | |
| | | *Administrative* | *Accounting* | *Treasurer* | *Total* |
	Ref.				
Supervisory salaries		$60,000	$48,000	$36,000	$144,000
Travel & entertaining		9,000	1,200	1,200	11,400
Telephone & telegraph		9,114	1,210	3,158	13,482
Depreciation—office equipment		600	2,400	1,200	4,200
Insurance		240	240	480	960
Taxes		240	360	120	720
Stationery & office supplies		122	610	1,829	2,561
Lawyers' retainer fee		1,800			1,800
Loss on bad debts				12,190	12,190
Audit fees		2,400			2,400
Totals		$83,516	$54,020	$56,177	$193,713
Building service allocation	6				30,000
Total Administrative Expense					$223,713

The Superior Manufacturing Company   Schedule 12

BUDGET OF OTHER INCOME AND EXPENSE
For the Year Ending December 31, 1963

	Annual	
Other incomes:		
Interest income (on building fund)	$ 500	
Other incomes	37,120	
Total		$37,620
Other expense:		
Interest expense		3,750
Net (other income)		$33,870

Budgeted income statement

Data are now available for consolidation into the budgeted income statement which is prepared in the budget department. The annual budgeted income statement and statement of retained earnings are shown below.

The Superior Manufacturing Company   Schedule 13

ANNUAL BUDGETED INCOME STATEMENT
For the Year Ending December 31, 1963

	Ref.	*Amount*	*Per cent of Sales*
Sales	1	$6,095,000	100.00
Cost of goods sold	9	4,054,600	66.52
Gross margin on sales		$2,040,400	33.48
Less:			
Distribution expenses	10	989,497	16.23
Administrative expenses	11	223,713	3.67
Totals		$1,213,210	19.90
Operating income		$ 827,190	13.57
Add net of other income & expense	12	33,870	.56
Net income before federal income taxes		$ 861,060	14.13
Federal income taxes	(Given)	258,318	4.24
Net income		$ 602,742	9.89

BUDGETED STATEMENT OF RETAINED EARNINGS
For the Year Ending December 31, 1963

	Ref.	
Balance, retained earnings, Jan. 1, 1963	(Given)	$ 522,770
Add net income budgeted	13	602,742
Total		$1,125,512
Less budgeted dividends	(Given)	12,000
Balance, retained earnings, Dec. 31, 1963		$1,113,512

The budget of capital additions

   The capital additions budget indicates such items as planned plant extensions, extraordinary repairs that are to be capitalized, building programs, machinery acquisitions, and other more or less permanent capital additions. The capital additions budget, included in the annual profit plan, represents the portion of the long-range capital additions budget that will materialize during the planning budget year. The capital additions budget for The Superior Manufacturing Company is shown below. Notice that significant 1964 items planned are also shown for information purposes.

CAPITAL ADDITIONS BUDGET SUMMARY
For the Year Ending December 31, 1963

Items	*Estimated Starting Date*	*Estimated Completion Date*	*Estimated Cost*	Year Budgeted For	
				1963	*1964*
New building	Jan. 1964	Sept. 1964	$120,000		$120,000
Machinery—Dept. 1	July 1964	Sept. 1964	10,000		10,000
Repair tools	Jan. 1963	Jan. 1, 1963	200	$ 200	
Power motor	Dec. 1963	Dec. 31, 1963	8,500	8,500	
Total			$138,700	$ 8,700	$130,000

Assets funded:	
New building	20,000
Total cash required in 1963 for capital additions	$28,700

Depreciation data:
   Repair tools—5 year life, no scrap value.
   Power motor—10 year life, no scrap value.

The cash budget

   The cash budget indicates the planned sources and disposition of cash throughout the year. The schedules prepared up to this point, with certain adjustments, provide sufficient data for development of the cash budget. Development of the cash budget is a responsibility of the treasurer. The summary cash budget for The Superior Manufacturing Company is shown below. It is obvious that cash disbursements do not always agree with expense totals, because there are certain noncash expense items such as depreciation, accrued expenses, and bad debts. Computation of the amounts shown in the cash budget summary below is illustrated in detail in a subsequent chapter.

The Superior Manufacturing Company

CASH BUDGET SUMMARY   **Schedule 16**
For the Year Ending December 31, 1963

	Ref.		
Beginning cash balance, Jan. 1, 1963	(Given)		$ 54,000
Budgeted cash receipts:			
Collections of accounts receivable*		$6,095,886	
Other income	12	37,120	
Proceeds of short-term notes payable	(Given)	100,000	
Total budgeted receipts			6,233,006
Total			$6,287,006
Budgeted cash disbursements:			
Raw material purchases—accounts payable*		$1,429,140	
Direct labor	5	1,752,000	
Factory overhead costs*		612,800	
Distribution expense*		958,897	
Administrative expenses*		173,243	
Building services*		84,000	
Capital additions	15	28,700	
Notes payable	(Given)	250,000	
Dividends	14	12,000	
Accrued and deferred items	(Given)	359,710	
Total budgeted disbursements			5,660,490
Ending cash balance, Dec. 31, 1963			$ 626,516

* Computations illustrated in subsequent chapters.

The budgeted balance sheet

The budgeted balance sheet indicates the effect of the plan of operations on the assets, liabilities, and capital of the company. The budget department compiles the budgeted balance sheet from the various schedules previously illustrated. This schedule is usually considered to be the final budget schedule prepared for the planning budget.

The budgeted balance sheet for The Superior Manufacturing Company is illustrated in Schedule 17.

BUDGETED BALANCE SHEET   **Schedule 17**
As of December 31, 1963

Assets	*Ref.*		
Current assets:			
Cash	16		$ 626,516
Accounts receivable*		$ 156,114	
Less allowance for doubtful accounts*		18,190	137,924
Raw material inventory	8		260,000
Work in process inventory	8		13,800
Finished goods inventory	8		837,600
Unexpired insurance*			17,724
Supplies inventory*			5,200
Total current assets			$1,898,764
Funds:			
Building fund*			40,500
Fixed assets:			
Land			25,000
Building		1,800,000	
Less allowance for depreciation		420,000	1,380,000
Machinery and equipment		288,700	
Less allowance for depreciation		107,740	180,960
Total fixed assets			1,585,960
Total assets			$3,525,224
Liabilities and Capital			
Current liabilities:			
Accounts payable*		$ 41,960	
Audit fee owed	(Given)	2,400	
Property taxes payable*		7,284	
Accrued interest payable*		1,750	
Federal income tax payable	(Given)	258,318	
Total current liabilities			$ 311,712
Fixed liabilities:			
Long-term notes payable	(Given)		50,000
Total liabilities			$ 361,712
Capital:			
Common stock	(Given)	2,000,000	
Premium on stock	(Given)	50,000	2,050,000
Retained earnings	14		1,113,512
Total capital			3,163,512
Total liabilities and capital			$3,525,224

* Computations explained in subsequent chapters.

The variable expense budget illustrated

The Superior Manufacturing Company uses variable expense budgets for factory overhead, distribution, and administrative costs. To derive variable budget allowances, the budget department makes an analysis of historical monthly costs, relating them to work done in each department. The results of the analysis are tempered to take into account expected conditions during the budget period and are then presented to the respective divisional executives and departmental supervisors for consideration and recommended revisions. The variable budgets are finally approved by the president.

Only the variable budget for one department of The Superior Manufacturing Company is illustrated, because the procedure for other departments is similar. The variable budget for Producing Department No. 1 is shown below.

Schedule 18
Refer to Schedule 33

The Superior Manufacturing Company

VARIABLE EXPENSE BUDGET—MANUFACTURING DIVISION
For the Year Ending December 31, 1963

PRODUCING DEPARTMENTS

	Department 1		Dept. 2	Dept. 3
	Fixed Allowance per Month Irrespective of Volume of Work	*Variable Amount per 100 Direct Labor Hours Worked*		
Supervisory salaries	$10,000	—		
Indirect labor	3,000	$22.50		
Maintenance parts	300	1.50		
Supplies used	450	5.50		
Depreciation (output basis)	—	1.50		
Insurance	100	—		
Taxes	150	—		
Totals	$14,000	$31.00		

The use of the variable budgets in preparing the expense budget schedules for the planning budget may be observed by referring to the profit plan summary for manufacturing overhead (Schedule 7, page 67). The annual allowances on Schedule 7 for Producing Department No. 1 were based on 488,000 direct labor hours (taken from direct labor budget, Schedule 5, page 66), and computed as follows:

Supervisory salaries ($10,000 × 12) plus ($0 × 4880)	$120,000
Indirect labor ($3,000 × 12) plus ($22.50 × 4880)	145,800
Maintenance parts ($300 × 12) plus ($1.50 × 4880)	10,920
Supplies used ($450 × 12) plus ($5.50 × 4880)	32,240
Depreciation ($0 × 12) plus ($1.50 × 4880)	7,320
Insurance ($100 × 12) plus ($0 × 4880)	1,200
Taxes ($150 × 12) plus ($0 × 4880)	1,800
Total ($14,000 × 12) plus ($31.00 × 4880)	$319,280

Reports to management illustrated

Preparation of the annual profit plan completes an important part of a comprehensive budget program. The next important step is putting the profit plan into operation. This procedure

The Superior Manufacturing Company   Schedule 19

SALES PERFORMANCE REPORT BY DISTRICT,
BY PRODUCT—January 1963

	Actual Sales January		Planned Sales		Variations Favorable—Unfavorable*		
Ref.	Units	Amount	Units	Amount	Units	Amount	% of Budget
Southern District:							
Product X	34,000	$170,000	30,000	$150,000	4,000	$20,000	13
Product Y	14,000	28,000	15,000	30,000	1,000*	2,000*	7*
Totals		$198,000		$180,000		$18,000	10
Eastern District:							
Product Xb	38,000	$190,000	40,000	$204,000	2,000*	$14,000*	7*
Product Y	10,000	21,000	11,000	23,100	1,000*	2,100*	9*
Totals		$211,000		$227,100		$16,100*	7*
Western District:							
Product X	16,000	$ 81,600	15,000	$ 76,500	1,000	$ 5,100	7
Product Y	9,000	18,900	8,000	16,800	1,000	2,100	13
Totals		$100,500		$ 93,300		$ 7,200	8
Grand totals		$509,500		$500,400		$ 9,100a	2
Summary by product:							
Product X	88,000	$441,600	85,000	$430,500	3,000	$11,100	3
Product Y	33,000	67,900	34,000	69,900	1,000*	2,000*	3*
Totals		$509,500		$500,400		$ 9,100a	2

a Variation due to:

(1) Variation in Units	$12,900
(2) Variation in Sales Price	$ 3,800*
Total	$ 9,100

b Authorized price reduction in this district to $5.00 per unit, in effect for entire month.

Comments:

(1) Southern District failure to meet forecast for product Y should be investigated.

(2) Eastern District needs immediate attention.

(3) Western District should be commended—investigate possibility of transfer of "know-how" to other districts.

involves conscious and continuous effort on the part of each and every executive and supervisor to meet or surpass the planned objectives in his particular functional area. The extent to which budget objectives are being attained, exceeded, or not attained is clearly and concisely indicated to all levels of management by means of performance reports.

In order to illustrate the general concept of performance reports to management, two schedules from the January 1963 Financial and Operating Report for The Superior Manufacturing Company are given (Schedules 19 and 20). On Schedule 20 the amounts in the column, Variable Budget Adjusted to Actual Volume, were derived by applying 35,000 direct labor hours (actual hours worked) to the variable budget allowances shown in the variable budget for Department No. 1 in Schedule 18 on page 75. For example, the indirect labor allowance of $10,875 was computed as follows:

$$(\$3,000) + (\$22.50 \times 350) = \$10,875.$$

In other respects the two schedules are self-explanatory.

The detailed budget program of the Superior Manufacturing Company

The budget program of The Superior Manufacturing Company has been illustrated in summary form and, up to this point, with annual data only. Because the case is continued throughout this book to illustrate the principal points developed in each chapter, it is appropriate to outline briefly some additional information concerning the budget program employed by the company.

The organization chart previously illustrated for the company is supplemented with a detailed organizational manual which specifies definite responsibility and commensurate authority for each executive and supervisor. In line with this practice, the controller has prepared an accounting manual which details the chart of accounts, and has specified precisely the type of charge or credit that will be made to each account. In addition, the manual specifies how indirect costs are to be allocated and how overhead is to be applied to production, as well as many other details relative to standardized accounting procedures.

Along these same lines the budget director has prepared a detailed *Budget Manual*. All manuals have been formally approved by the president, and hence constitute standard procedures. The following is a summary of certain pertinent information from the budget manual of The Superior Manufacturing Company.

PERFORMANCE REPORT OF FACTORY OVERHEAD
January 1963
PART I—Departmental Report of Manufacturing Expenses (Overhead)

BUDGET CONTROL REPORT

	Cost Report Month Actual	*Variable Budget Adjusted to Actual Volume*	*Variations Indicating Status of Control: Favorable— Unfavorable**	
			Amount	% of Budget
Producing Dept. No. 1:				
(Actual Volume 35,000 DLH)				
Supervisory salaries**	$10,000	$10,000		
Indirect labor	10,550	10,875	$325	3
Maintenance parts	1,500	825	675*a	82*
Supplies used	2,200	2,375	175	7
Depreciation**	525	525		
Insurance**	100	100		
Taxes**	150	150		
Total	$25,025	$24,850	$175*	1*
Producing Dept. No. 2:				
(Actual Volume 13,800 DLH)				
Supervisory salaries**	$ 1,870	$ 1,870		
Indirect labor	240	262	$ 22	8
Maintenance parts	60	48	12*	25*
Supplies used	80	109	29	27
Depreciation**	55	55		
Insurance**	10	10		
Taxes**	20	20		
Total	$ 2,335	$ 2,374	$ 39	2
Producing Dept. No. 3:				
(Actual Volume 36,200 DLH)				
Supervisory salaries**	$ 2,920	$ 2,920		
Indirect labor	3,600	3,370	$230*	7*
Maintenance parts	370	331	39*	12*
Supplies used	1,170	1,105	65*	6*
Depreciation**	326	326		
Insurance**	50	50		
Taxes**	60	60		
Total	$ 8,496	$ 8,162	$334*	4*

** These items are noncontrollable within the department.
Comments:
  a Due to breakdown of machine resulting from faulty adjustment.

(1) Budgets to be prepared
  (a) *Annual profit plan*—Annually, broken down by quarters. Each quarter to be further broken down by month during the month preceding the beginning of each quarter.
  (b) *Variable expense budgets*—For factory overhead, selling expenses, and administrative expenses
(2) Responsibility for budget preparation
  (a) *Over-all supervision*—Budget director
  (b) *Sales budget*—Vice president in charge of sales
  (c) *Expense budgets*—Statistical work done by budget department, the results being forwarded to responsible persons for recommended allowances
  (d) *Budget summaries*—Budget director
  (e) *Manufacturing budget schedules*—Vice president in charge of manufacturing; statistical work and summaries done by budget department
  (f) Other parts of the profit plan to be prepared by the supervisors responsible for the specific function involved
  (g) Controller shall furnish, upon the request of any person having budget responsibilities, historical cost and/or income data for analytical purposes
(3) Budget approval
  (a) Initially by responsible party concerned, then by next higher level
  (b) Finally by president (advised by budget committee)
(4) Budget calendar
  (a) Budget preparation
    Oct. 1—Sales budget and variable budget preparation started.
    Nov. 15—Sales budget and variable budgets completed. Decision made as to desired raw materials and finished goods inventory levels.
    Dec. 1—Production budget, materials budget, direct labor, and factory overhead budget completed. Tentative budget income statement presented to budget committee for approval or revision.
    Dec. 10—Final budgeted income statements completed.
    Dec. 22—Reproduction of the profit plan
    Dec. 30—Distribution of the profit plan
  (b) Monthly budgets
    By the end of March, June, and September respectively— submit monthly breakdown of quarterly budgets.
  (c) Expense control budgets
    By the 25th of each month submit, to the various supervisors, *Budget Expense Estimates* based on planned production for the next month.
  (d) Monthly budget reports
    By the 7th of each month distribute the *Monthly Financial*

and Budget Reports covering the preceding month. (Note—
the actual data are provided by the accounting department
and the budget allowances and variations by the budget
department. Distribution by controller's department.)

Discussion Questions

1. What are the five primary components of a comprehensive
   budget program? Briefly explain each component and indicate
   their interrelationships.
2. Explain your concept of the annual profit plan.
3. Explain the concept and use of appropriation-type budgets.
4. What is meant by long-range planning? How is it related to
   short-range planning?
5. Explain period planning and project planning. How are they
   interrelated in a comprehensive budget program?
6. Explain the concept of the variable budget. How is the variable
   budget related to the annual profit plan?
7. What is meant by variable cost control? Under what circumstances is the concept particularly useful?
8. Indicate the significant comparison or comparisons for cost
   control purposes based on the following data. Justify your
   conclusion.

	Actual Expenditure (10,000 direct labor hours worked)	Actual Last January (9,000 direct labor hours worked)	Forecast Budget Allowance (Based on 11,000 direct labor hours worked)	Variable Budget Allowance (Adjusted to 10,000 direct labor hours worked)
Indirect labor cost	$17,000	$16,200	$18,500	$17,300

9. Why are performance reports an important aspect of a profit
   planning and control program?
10. Distinguish between the periodic budget approach and the con-
    tinuous budget approach.
11. With respect to a budget program what are the responsibilities
    of (a) the budget director, (b) the line executives, (c) the
    budget committee, and (d) the top executive?
12. Why is it generally desirable to have a formal budget manual?
13. Why is the sales forecast generally considered to be the initial
    step in preparation of the planning budget?
14. What does the production budget indicate? What is the relation-
    ship between the sales budget and the production budget?
15. What is the relationship between the direct materials budget
    and the purchases budget?
16. What is the purpose of the capital additions budget? Who pre-
    pares the capital additions budget?
17. What is the purpose of the cash budget? Who should prepare it?
18. Outline the procedure for budget approval from the sales budget
    to final formal approval of the entire planning budget.

F O U R

Sales Planning and Control

The preceding chapter presented an over-all concept of a comprehensive budget program. The remaining chapters will develop the details of such a program. When attention is turned to detailed departmental and sub-budgets the sales *plan* or *sales budget* assumes primary importance.

A plan of operations for a competitive firm must necessarily be built around the amount of activity or volume of business that can reasonably be expected during the specific period covered by the profit plan. In order for a comprehensive budget program to be realistic, there must be a realistic sales or revenue budget. The seriousness with which sales and expense budgeting is viewed determines to a large degree the success or failure of a budget program. Unless a *realistic* sales budget is developed, the plans relating to other responsibilities will not be sound with a likely consequence of wrong and costly decisions. The sales budget is the foundation for periodic planning in the individual firm because practically all other company planning is based largely on it. Sales are the primary source of cash recognized in the cash budget.

Obviously there will be many technical and practical difficulties in budgeting sales quantities and sales income. Despite these difficulties, many concerns operating in extremely complex situations have been able to attain an accuracy of 98 per cent. It must be realized, however, that this accuracy is principally the result of two factors: (a) the care with which the sales budget is developed and (b) the serious effort of the sales executives to attain the sales objectives expressed in the profit plan. The second factor is particularly significant, assuming that the sales budget is not unrealistic.

If it were impossible to appraise the hazards of a business with respect to sales potentials, there would be little incentive for investment in the business initially or for the continuation of the enterprise except for highly speculative ventures.

The problem of accurately estimating market potentials in terms of quantities, prices, and timing is difficult for many concerns. In fact a recent survey found that executives reported this factor to be their primary problem in profit planning and control.[1]

In some circumstances a high degree of accuracy should not be expected. Nevertheless the problem, like most managerial problems, can be solved adequately if approached in a logical manner.[2]

The concept of sales budgeting

The sales budget represents the revenue side of the profit plan. It involves consideration of both sales quantities and sales revenue.

Sales estimates should be made for both the long and short run. Most progressive firms make serious attempts to project sales trends for the industry and the firm five to ten or more years in advance. Obviously these long-term projections are highly tentative and subject to considerable revision. Nevertheless, it is essential that the company have certain long-range objectives which emphasize the position the firm desires to occupy in each field or industry in which it intends to become an integral part. Obviously the sales projection is the key component of the long-range planning of top management. Illustration 6 suggests the nature of a long-range sales budget.

The short-term sales budget usually covers one year and brings the *current portion* of the long-range sales projection into sharp focus. The purpose in sales budgeting is not to attempt to estimate or guess what actual sales will be, but rather to develop a plan with clearly defined objectives toward which operational effort is directed.

Developing a realistic short-term sales budget involves serious and intelligent effort on the part of top management—and sales executives in particular—with the central idea of developing a

[1] Burnard H. Sord and Glenn A. Welsch, *Business Budgeting, A Survey of Management Planning and Control Practices,* (New York: The Controllership Foundation, 1958), p. 305.

[2] "Sales Forecasting: Uses, Techniques and Trends," *Special Report No. 16* (New York: American Management Association, 1956).

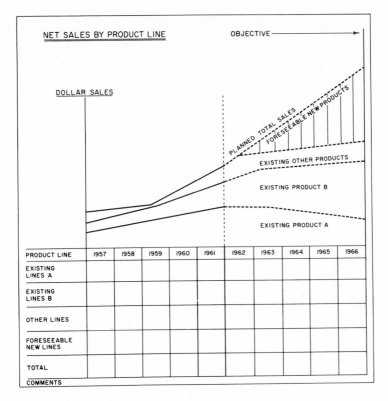

Illustration 6. A Long-Range Sales Projection. (SOURCE: Clarence A. Danielson, "How We Took Hold of Long-Range Planning," NAA Bulletin, March, 1962, Sec. 1, p. 8.)

plan which top management has reason to expect will be accomplished. Having approved such a sales plan, top management should expect the sales department to take effective steps to accomplish or exceed the goals. The development of the short-term sales budget involves detail with respect to product, time, and organizational responsibility. A complete sales budget should indicate, in addition to the *annual quantities* and *dollar revenue*, the following:

Sales by organizational subdivision (sales territories)
Sales by month and/or quarter
Sales by product

It can be seen that a complete sales budget for a medium to large concern involves numerous detailed subsidiary schedules in addition to a *summary* sales budget. The illustrative case at the end of this chapter indicates the possibilities to some extent.

In developing a sales budget a number of important policy decisions must be made by the management. For example, management must decide whether to develop the sales budget data in terms of physical units and dollars, or only in dollars. It is desirable to project both physical units and dollars wherever possible, but in some situations it may be impracticable to forecast physical units, as when numerous small products are involved. For example, a department store normally budgets much of its stock in dollars rather than physical units. Nevertheless, the sales budget data must be converted into production requirements in a manufacturing situation or into purchase commitments in a nonmanufacturing situation. This conversion is often a critical problem which taxes the ingenuity of the budget director and the executives concerned.

Responsibility for the sales budget

Responsibility for developing the input data for the sales budget should vary from concern to concern due to factors such as the concern's size, its organization, the type of industry, the complexity of the situation, the technical problems involved, and the methods of forecasting employed. Nevertheless, there are some principles that should guide the determination of responsibility.

In the first place, it is desirable that the executives and supervisors responsible for attaining the sales goals have primary responsibility for setting these goals. As a general proposition the sales budget should be a responsibility of the sales division executives. On the other hand, there are generally some technical aspects in developing the sales projection that might well be the responsibility of individuals outside the sales division. For example, a special staff section (such as an economic analysis group) may be organized to analyze and appraise the general economic picture as it relates to general managerial problems, including sales potentials.

It is essential that the various related responsibilities for sales budgeting be definitely specified by top management. These responsibilities involve the president, the sales executives, the budget committee, the accounting department, the budget director, and certain staff groups. The budget director should be responsible for furnishing technical advice and for the *mechanical design* of the sales budget procedures consistent with other portions of the profit plan. The accounting department must provide historical data needed as a basis for planning. Certain staff departments may assist in statistical analyses, economic appraisals, and financing. The budget committee and the president perform an appraisal and approval function. Notwithstanding auxiliary responsibilities, the basic responsibility for the sales budget should normally be assigned to the sales executives; the nature and extent of this responsibility must of course be determined in the light of the circumstances in each concern.

Use and application of the sales budget

The importance of the sales budget as a tool contributing to managerial planning, coordination, and control cannot be overemphasized. The active participation of numerous executives in preparation and approval of the sales budget involves participation in managerial planning in the highest degree. A completed sales budget demonstrates that management has done something tangible about its planning function.

In modern business the activities of one department have a considerable influence upon the activities of other departments. Especially important are the mutual relations and interdependence of sales department activities with other departments in the firm. Therefore coordination between the several functional areas requires a realistic sales plan. Because the planning of other departments rests so heavily upon the activities of the sales department, any failure of the sales executives to face up to their responsibilities denies other departmental executives the opportunity to develop adequate plans or define concrete objectives for their particular functions. All too frequently the various departments are forced to operate on a hit-or-miss basis because a reliable sales volume projection has not been furnished.

A sales division executive who does not give serious consideration to an accurate and meaningful sales budget is neglecting his planning and coordinating functions. There must be coordination within the sales division as well as between sales and other divisions of the firm. In a trading concern the activities of the sales division directly affect the quality, quantity, and kind of goods to be purchased, as well as the scope of activities in practically all other departments. In a manufacturing situation the sales estimate determines the requirements for raw materials, labor, plant capacity, financial measures, and many other factors. Sales, exercising such an important influence on the functioning of all other departments, should be budgeted with considerable care. Attainment of coordination between departments depends upon full knowledge of the activities of related departments; this may be accomplished through the process of building the sales budget, incorporating it in a balanced plan of operations (the planning budget), making the results available to other departments, and maintaining an adequate system of control. In addition, if the sales budget is properly used as a basis for operations in the sales division, coordination there is also assured.

The sales budget as finally approved should be converted to monthly sales quotas for each major sales division. The division sales quotas are further broken down by smaller subdivisions and then prorated to individual salesmen. Some companies go so far as to develop weekly sales quotas for each salesman.[3] Following the development and approval of sales quotas, there must be careful planning and aggressive effort toward accomplishment.

Managerial control of sales is achieved at all levels through a system of responsibility reporting that reflects performance within the sales division organization. Responsibility for attaining the sales budget rests directly upon the top executive in charge of sales. In turn, similar responsibilities are assigned to the executives having market areas under their supervision. Continuous performance reporting throughout the budget period, and in terms of this organizational responsibility, is essential. The reports should stress a comparison of results with sales budget goals, indicating by means of variations where sales results are above budget standard, below budget standard, or on budget.

Consideration of alternatives

Budgeting sales involves consideration of numerous policies and related alternatives and a clear choice from among many possible courses of action. Decisions must be made concerning

---

[3] Some firms prefer to develop sales quotas for the individual salesmen somewhat above the short-term sales budget expectations. For example one company, after having developed individual sales quotas based on the sales budget arbitrarily raised them by 15 per cent before communicating them to the salesmen. In another case, the management reported that "we have two sales budgets, one for management planning purposes and another for the sales force. The former is never made known to the lower levels of supervision."

such matters as new products, discontinuance of present products, pricing, expansion or contraction of sales areas, size of sales force, distribution cost limitations, and advertising and other promotional policies. A sound sales budget embodies a whole complex of managerial decisions. A completed sales program encompasses, in addition to the sales budget, work programs and organization for sales effort, promotion, advertising, and other activities giving rise to costs. It is desirable that these activities be given sufficient emphasis so that maximum sales potentials can be realized at minimum cost. Obviously, many possible combinations of emphasis are possible. The advertising program should be consistent with the short- and long-range sales objectives, and, conversely, the sales potential is inextricably related to the advertising program. Similarly, the volume of sales anticipated must take into account sufficient (but not excessive) expenditures for other distribution costs required to obtain that volume. There is a certain minimum cost for distribution below which the sales effort would be adversely affected.

Under any circumstances it would be necessary for the sales organization to develop the advertising and distribution expense budgets simultaneously with the sales budget. For purposes of presentation, however, the expense budgets are discussed separately in subsequent chapters.

Pricing policy in budgeting sales

Price considerations are a vital part of sales planning. Although it is desirable to develop sales potentials in terms of physical quantities, it is nevertheless essential that pricing policies be clearly stated since (a) the physical volume of goods that can be sold, and therefore budgeted, depends to a large degree upon the selling price and (b) the sales budget must of necessity be expressed in dollars as well as in physical units. The price of items offered for sale, as related to competitors' prices and the general level of prices, will definitely influence the physical volume that can be sold. Likewise the probable effect of various contemplated price changes must be given careful consideration in sales planning.

Market analysis necessarily involves a thorough analysis of the price situation. Prices must be analyzed in relation to cost, competition, the industry, and geographical areas. Generally, prices must be in line with the market. In addition to the more refined price analyses, the opinions of the salesmen should be taken into consideration. Salesmen may be in a good position to appraise the effect on physical volume of a contemplated price change.

Among other techniques that are used in determining the pricing policies is the volume-price forecast. Basically the analysis may involve setting forth in parallel columns the probable sales in physical units at varying selling prices. The varying quantities are extended at the proposed selling prices, thus giving estimated total sales dollars under different assumptions as to volume and selling price. The related estimated costs of production and distribution can then be deducted from the varying amounts of estimated sales revenue, thereby indicating the approximate profit potentials at the various assumed volume and selling-price levels. This type of analysis is significant if properly approached. Identification of all costs as either fixed or variable (Chapter 9) makes possible a useful cost-volume-profit analysis (Chapter 12), which may aid management considerably in setting its pricing policies.

Product line considerations

A basic policy area that must be resolved prior to actual development of the sales budget relates to the *number* and *variety* of products which the company will offer for sale. The long-range sales plan should include projected plans relative to new product lines to be introduced, old product lines to be dropped, innovations, and product mix. Product mix refers to the volume relationship as between two or more products. For example, assume 1,000 units of product R and 2,000 units of product S were sold, and that the budget for the coming year calls for 1,200 units of product R and 1,800 units of S. The over-all volume is still 3,000 units, but we would say that a change in *sales mix* is planned.

Assuming the long-range sales plan projects changes in the product line, with broad specification as to the timing of such changes, those changes anticipated for the coming year (the period for which the annual profit plan is being developed) must be brought into sharp focus through management policies and decisions of a short-run nature. Thus, in developing the annual profit plan top management must lay down certain very specific policies or premises concerning product line development.

Policies must be firmed relative to such matters as: What products shall be pushed? When will the new product be available for shipment? What products shall be dropped? What quality and style changes shall be made? What about "loss leaders"?

In these policy considerations concerning both long- and short-term sales plans, the effect on plans in other areas of the company, such as plant capacity, financing, territory expansion, and research, must be taken into account.

It is appropriate to point up at this time that the primary objective in sales planning should be to maximize profits in the long run rather than in the short run. For example, it is fairly obvious that certain short-run decisions may increase immediate profits but may adversely affect profits in the long run. We see then that short-run decisions may, if care is not exercised, be in conflict with long-run decisions. Obviously, careful development of long-run sales and profit plans should resolve this situation.

As an indication of the importance of product line consideration several recent surveys seeking to determine why businesses fail have revealed that one of the primary causes is the failure to keep up with competitors in product development, improvement, and design.

Lag between orders taken and shipments

In budgeting sales a careful distinction should be maintained between *sales orders taken* and *sales shipped*. Sales budgeting should be based on the latter since (a) some orders taken may be cancelled prior to shipment and (b) there may be a significant time lag between the date the order is taken and the date of shipment. Production planning, cash flow, and other aspects of the budget program must be based on shipments rather than orders. In some situations ordertaking precedes the shipment date by several months. In such cases there is likely to be a special problem in production planning; for example, this situation is typical in certain lines of wearing apparel. Production plans must proceed on the basis of orders so that stocks are sufficient at the agreed shipment date. These circumstances call for special sales budget procedures such as the development of two sales budgets—one based on expected orders and the other on shipments. Obviously, the two would be in approximate agreement except for the time lag involved.

Sales allowances and discounts

In developing the sales budget, the analyst should be concerned primarily with *net sales*. In developing net sales, all deductions from gross sales should be taken into account. Sales returns, sales allowances, discounts of all types, special allowances, and other reductions must be analyzed and carefully estimated so that net sales may be budgeted accurately. In some cases it may be desirable to develop the sales budget in terms of gross sales and to budget therein deductions for the items above. This procedure often facilitates control over the returns and allowances.

Considerations in selecting a method of forecasting sales

Numerous methods have been devised to project sales, ranging from highly refined statistical approaches to rather crude rules of thumb. Quite obviously there is no one best method for all concerns. The method used must be consistent with the peculiarities of the situation and constantly revised and improved to keep up with the growth and needs of the concern. The selection and adaptation of a particular method must take into account:

(1) *The characteristics of the concern*—Some businesses are concerned principally with local conditions, while others are concerned with regional, national, or international conditions. The size of the firm, type and variety of products, and methods of manufacturing are influencing factors. In addition, the channels and methods of distribution should be taken into account. Obviously, there are other characteristics peculiar to individual concerns that would influence the selection of a method of projecting sales, but these would be too limited in application, or detailed in analysis, to catalogue here.

(2) *The costs involved*—The cost of developing a sales budget will vary with individual concerns and with different methods. In selecting a method, the accuracy of results that might be attained must be weighed against the costs involved.

(3) *Available personnel*—The availability of personnel might be a determining factor in some cases. However, it is anticipated that, except for certain technical aspects, the sales executives will assume this responsibility as a part of their regular duties.

(4) *Status of budget education*—Upon the institution of a budget program, it may be desirable to use a rather simplified approach in projecting sales and to adopt more complicated procedures later. The method used must be consistent with the status of *budget education* in the concern. Experience has shown that

unless the executives involved in developing and using the sales budget understand the methods used and have confidence in the results, the projection is of little value.

(5) *The time covered by the projection*—Methods appropriate for developing a short-run sales projection only are, by and large, inadequate for developing long-range projections.

Steps in planning sales

A recent survey indicates the extent to which the better managed companies use sales planning. The following data are adapted from this report:[4]

	Per cent of 389 companies developing sales forecasts and plans			
	Size of Firm			
Type of sales planning	*Small*	*Medium*	*Large*	*Total*
General economic conditions	29	33	62	41
Sales estimate for industry	40	46	61	49
Share of market for company	49	49	56	51
Sales estimate for company	92	94	93	93

The same survey revealed the approaches used by these companies in developing their sales plans. The following data are adapted from the same report:[5]

	Per cent of 398 companies utilizing various procedures in developing sales estimates			
Procedures utilized in developing sales estimates	*Small*	*Medium*	*Large*	*Total*
Past sales trends of company	80	81	79	80
Salesmen's estimates	39	43	40	41
Correlation of company sales with general economic indicators	51	55	75	60
New product plans	60	54	68	60
Market surveys	47	49	67	54
Production capacity	28	51	60	47
Industry forecast and company's share of the potential	38	51	61	50
Sales department estimates	81	70	84	81
Survey of company executive opinions	44	43	48	45
Correlation of company sales with some industry economic indicator	20	33	44	33
Competitors' activities	19	17	30	22
Promotion plans	38	40	48	42
Financial capacity	16	19	31	22
Outside consultants	5	9	15	11

(Note: Per cents will exceed 100 because some companies use several methods.)

[4] Sord and Welsch, *Business Budgeting*, pp. 136, 142.
[5] *Ibid.*, pp. 136, 142.

In analyzing the several methods of developing a sales projection it appears that there are five principal steps that are common to practically all methods. These steps in broad perspective are:

(1) Analysis and appraisal of the future, general, and specific economic conditions of the nation and marketing area. In general there are three approaches used by business in forecasting general and specific business conditions. One approach used by many firms is to establish a special staff group for economic analysis. The personnel in such a group are principally economists and statisticians. Another approach revolves around the "considered judgments" of the top executives, little or no formal statistical and economic analysis being made. The judgments of the executives are based upon their own individual experiences, observations, and knowledge of the general economic outlook. A third approach involves a dependence on outside professional assistance for guidance and help in appraising the general economic picture as it affects the concern.

(2) Analysis of the market to determine its potential.

(3) Analysis of the past sales performance of the firm by interim periods (over the past 3 to 5 years) by products, sales territories, customers, size of orders, salesmen, and so forth.

(4) Consideration of the limitations of the company, such as related problems of capacity, procurement, personnel, and capital.

(5) Establishment of firm policies relating to strategies (both short and long term) that will affect sales expectations. Examples of such policies are decisions concerning advertising programs, development of the sales force, product expansion, territory expansion, research, and pricing.

(6) Translation of the results of market studies, forecasts, and other analyses into a *definite sales budget* for both the long and short run. This step fundamentally involves the acceptance on the part of the management of definite and serious sales objectives.

The difference in methods of projecting sales involves principally the relative importance attached to each of the steps above and the techniques used for the analyses.

Market analysis encompasses a very broad area of managerial problems and related policies. Although market analyses are usually not undertaken for budget purposes alone, a sound market analysis will lay the foundation for a realistic sales budget. It is not within the scope of this book to deal with the broad field of market analysis and research.[6] The objective here

---

[6] The reader is referred to books on marketing and business forecasting for details concerning market analysis. The following are representative: D. M. Phelps, *Sales Management* (Homewood, Ill: Irwin, 1951); Frederick E. Croxton and Dudley J. Cowden, *Practical Business Statistics* (Englewood Cliffs, N. J: Prentice-Hall, 1960).

is to relate market analysis to sales budgeting. It is a responsibility of the sales division executives to be familiar with and to develop market research activities for the concern. This activity is outside the scope of the budget director and controller.

In large concerns there is frequently a *market research group* which is primarily responsible for long-range sales forecasting. Both qualitative and quantitative market analyses may be performed by one department, or each may be the responsibility of separate departments. In smaller businesses it is usually not possible to have a separate market research department in which case sales and other executives are directly responsible for this function.

Sales estimates originate (a) in the field or (b) in the home office. Surveys tend to show that in large concerns the estimates generally originate in the home office, whereas in smaller concerns they generally originate in the field. In either event, both the field force and the home office should have a definite part in shaping the final sales budget.

One of the most important considerations in forecasting sales is an analysis of historical sales by years, quarters, months, and sometimes by weeks and days. The historical sales data can best be furnished by the accounting department. Therefore, it is essential that accounting records be maintained to give, where practicable, both unit and dollar sales of the following classifications:

    1. Sales by time periods
    2. Sales by products
    3. Sales by geographical sales territories
    4. Sales by salesmen

If such information is available, the basis for a meaningful sales projection is provided because past performance generally is a good indication of what can be done in the immediate future. Consideration of historical sales, however, is only one step in developing an accurate sales budget.

The forecasting method selected for a particular business should be no more complicated than is necessary to develop a sales estimate with the desired degree of accuracy. Highly refined mathematical approaches are rather rigid and unless tempered by sound judgment are likely to be misleading. In addition, complicated methods have a tendency to give a false sense of accuracy. Therefore, if the more complicated techniques are used, the results should be tempered by the sound judgment of competent individuals who have a thorough knowledge of the mathematical technique, its specialized formulas and underlying assumptions, as well as an intimate knowledge of the firm and the industry.

One survey provides some additional information concerning the practices used in industry to develop the sales budget. [7] The report covering thirty-six leading firms showed the following:

Sales forecast initiated by	*Number of Replies*
(1) Line sales organization	19
(2) Sales staff or market research staff	10
(3) Financial officer's staff	5
(4) Other headquarters staff	1
Sales forecast reviewed and/or revised by	
(1) Line sales organization	11
(2) Sales staff or market research staff	9
(3) Financial officer's staff	15
(4) Other headquarters staff (planning nature)	12
Sales forecast final approval	
(1) Committee of officers	28
(2) Chief executive officer	12
Sales forecast based on	
(1) Historical trends of own products	29
(2) Estimates of field and/or headquarters sales organizations	23
(3) Industry forecast and share of market	22
(4) Correlation of own sales with more general statistical measures	21
Sales forecasts used as a basis for financial forecasts and budgets	36

Methods of projecting sales

The methods commonly used in projecting sales in the various industries, and by large, medium, and small firms may be generally categorized as follows:

(1) Nonstatistical methods (judgment methods)
    (a) sales force composite
    (b) sales division supervisors composite
    (c) executive opinion method
(2) Statistical methods
    (a) economic rhythm method (trend analysis)
    (b) cyclical sequence method (correlation analysis)

[7] *Business Forecasting, A Survey of Business Practices and Methods* (New York: Controllership Foundation, Inc., Research Arm of Controllers Institute, 2 Park Avenue, New York, 16, N.Y.).

      (c) special historical analogy
      (d) cross-cut method
  (3) Specific purpose methods
      (a) industry analysis
      (b) product-line analysis
      (c) end-use analysis

In considering th`se various approaches it should be observed that (a) in many respects they overlap (b) certain approaches are useful only for ʳᵖecific purposes, (c) some have application for short-term sales budgeting, others for long-term planning, and (d) very rarely would a single firm use any one approach to the exclusion of all others. In the paragraphs to follow each of these methods will be discussed briefly.

Sales Force Composite—This method places a heavy responsibility on the sales force and provides for a series of screenings and approvals. A high degree of participation, from the bottom to the top, is emphasized. This approach is limited primarily to short-term sales budgeting. It may be outlined as follows:

(1) The home office provides district sales offices with (a) a record of previous sales, (b) any new or revised managerial policies relative to sales, and (c) any other data that may be of value to the sales district in making a sales estimate for the budget period. Usually the historical sales data are listed on a standard form which provides space for recording the sales forecast.

(2) The salesmen are requested to fill in their estimates based on the historical data and their knowledge of the particular territory and customers. As a usual practice, the salesmen are asked to make the estimate on the basis of current economic conditions in the area, because it is generally undesirable to have each salesman make his own appraisal of the economic future. When the salesmen provide dollar estimates, they are asked to assume current selling prices.

(3) The salesmen's estimates are reviewed by the district sales manager. The form previously mentioned may provide space for the district sales manager's estimates as well. The district sales manager may be required to provide a summarized statement of all salesmen's estimates in his district. The district estimates are transmitted to the home office by a specified date.

(4) The various district estimates are reviewed and revised by the general sales executives. Significant revisions should be discussed thoroughly with the district sales managers concerned. The home office sales executives may also convert the quantity estimates to dollar estimates by applying unit selling prices consistent

with managerial pricing policies. The general sales executives, working in cooperation with the company economist or with others who have responsibility for appraising the general economic outlook, adjust the sales estimate for this factor. Because general economic conditions can affect the sales potential to a very marked degree, it is essential that serious consideration be given to this important factor in developing the sales budget.

(5) The sales estimates are then presented to the budget committee and to the president for consideration and tentative approval. The deliberations at this level should be concerned with the soundness of the unit and dollar estimates, and may well result in (a) tentative approval, (b) tentative approval with certain changes, or (c) instructions for a complete or partial reconsideration of the sales potential. The sales estimate is judged also as to whether or not it is within the capacities of the firm.

(6) After tentative approval, copies of the tentative sales budget are distributed to the heads of other functional subdivisions so that the work of developing departmental budgets may be started. As the over-all profit plan begins to take form, it may be necessary to reconsider the sales program in some respects. This balancing of considerations, and the resulting adjustments in the profit plan as it develops, should lead to a highly satisfactory plan of operations for the firm. Final approval of the individual departmental budgets does not take place until top management approves the complete profit plan.

(7) The approved sales budget is distributed through the sales organization and becomes the basis for sales quotas and day-to-day planning in sales activities.

Obviously, the method above can have numerous variations. It is used more frequently by small concerns than by large ones, and more frequently by firms having a small number of products than those with numerous products. The principal advantages are that estimates are made by the individuals closest to the customer, and approved initially by those who have the responsibility for achieving the sales goals. On the other hand, salesmen may be too optimistic or, conversely, turn in low estimates as a matter of self-protection. They may not give sufficient attention to the problem and thus improperly evaluate the general market potential. These tendencies can be largely overcome through a program of budget education and motivation.[8]

Sales Division Supervisors Composite—This method emphasizes the responsibilities of the sales district or division supervisors rather than the individual salesmen. The method is commonly

[8] "Forecasting in Industry," *Studies in Business Policy, No. 77* (New York: National Industrial Conference Board, 1957).

used for short-term sales planning. It operates in a manner almost identical with that outlined above for the sales force composite method except that the estimates *originate* with the supervisors rather than with the salesmen. The method is widely used by firms of all sizes.

A variation of this approach is based on an informal survey of the principal customers of the firm. Under this approach the firm budgets sales on the basis of reports rendered by special company representatives who contact customers for the primary purpose of evaluating sales potentials. From the information gathered by the special representatives, and interpreted through their personal observation and judgment, an estimate for each geographical sales division is developed. These estimates should be adjusted to take into account any basic information the company has concerning such things as expected economic conditions, population trends, purchasing power, and other conditions likely to affect the market. In addition, consideration must be given to sales of the last year or two and to stock holdover on the part of customer outlets. This method might be useful in situations where there are a limited number of outlets and products.

Executive Opinion Method—Some firms find it inappropriate to send representatives into the field or to ask salesmen to make estimates. This is especially true where salesmen are not trained to perform this function, or when the market situation is somewhat complex. Therefore, it is not uncommon to see sales planning initiated, and essentially completed, in the central offices of such companies. This method, too, has numerous procedural variations.

Perhaps the simplest method, used by medium to small concerns, is known as the *jury of executive opinion method*. In its simplest form, it represents the combined judgments, or opinions, of the top executives within the firm. Although it may represent a wide range of specialized experience and knowledge, unless supplemented with facts and statistics concerning historical sales and external data, the resulting estimates must be viewed as guesses, more or less educated.

Smaller concerns are inclined to use simple procedures, starting with an analysis of historical sales data by product, territory, and salesmen, thereby developing a basis for an informed sales projection by the executives. The projection then is adjusted for such factors as expected economic conditions, management sales policies, and desired growth objectives. Next, the tentative estimates are transmitted to the respective district sales offices for consideration, review, and suggested revision. Using this procedure many concerns have been able to develop very accurate sales budgets.

The executive opinion method is used frequently because it is simple, direct, and economical.

Statistical Methods—A well-known source suggests four statistical methods of forecasting sales.[9] These methods are similar to those suggested by other authors. They are:

1. Economic rhythm method
2. Cyclical sequence method
3. Specific historical analogy method
4. Cross-cut analysis

A discussion of the technical aspects of these more refined methods is beyond the scope of this book. Consequently we will merely indicate the general characteristics of each and suggest that those who are interested in pursuing the subject further consult the selected references listed in the footnote.

Use of the statistical methods requires the services of technically trained individuals. Most companies relying on these more sophisticated approaches have organized an economic research section variously staffed by statisticians, economists, and mathematicians. In some firms the economic research section develops a detailed sales budget for the firm which is then transmitted to the sales executives and the budget or executive committee for evaluation and recommendations. In other cases the research section deals primarily with analysis of the trends in the general economy and the industry. Data concerning trends (usually expressed as indexes) are then made available to the various executives in the firm who are involved in developing the long- and short-range sales plans. To illustrate, in one well-known, highly decentralized company, each plant manager is required to develop (a) a five-year profit plan for his plant and (b) a one-year profit plan. The economic research staff (at the home office) develops projections of approximately fifteen different indexes relating to various economic indicators such as gross national product, housing starts, and regional bank deposits. These fifteen

---

[9] Frederick E. Croxton and Dudley J. Cowden, *Practical Business Statistics*, 3rd ed. (Englewood Cliffs, N.J.: Prentice-Hall, 1960); Wilson Wright, *Forecasting for Profit* (New York: Wiley, 1947); "Materials and Methods of Sales Forecasting," *Special Report 27* (New York: American Management Association, 1957); Carl A. Dauten, *Business Cycles and Forecasting*, 2nd ed. (Cincinnati, Ohio: South-Western Publishing Company, 1961), Ch 22.

or more projections (in the form of index series) are furnished to each plant manager. He may choose to use one or more of them (or none) in developing his operation plans.[10]

The *economic rhythm* method involves a projection of historical trends into the future. In projecting sales by use of this method the following steps are necessary:[11]

(a) Obtain *historical sales data* as far back as it is thought to be representative of current trends.

(b) Compute an *adjusted sales values* by dividing actual sales data (item "a" in Illustration 7) by an index (such as the wholesale price index).

(c) Use the adjusted sales values (item "b") to compute an *adjusted sales value trend* preferably by utilizing the method of least squares. If annual values are computed, the annual values are then used to develop *monthly trend values*.

(d) Develop or obtain a *cyclical forecast* (example, the index of industrial production).

(e) Develop an index of *seasonal variation* based upon the monthly historical data for the firm.

(f) The sales forecast is then developed by using each of the values indicated above in (a) through (e). These values are inserted in a work sheet similar to that shown in Illustration 7 on page 100.

From the brief outline above and the information shown in Illustration 7 it is clear that the method is rigorous and subjective. Those utilizing this method should be clearly aware of its rigidity and underlying assumptions. Basically it assumes that future data will essentially follow the patterns of historical data. All this suggests that the results should be tempered by the sound judgment, knowledge of the company, and long experience of the top executives.

The *cyclical sequence* or correlation method is widely used. It is based upon the selection of a basic series of economic or business

---

[10] Firms who have need for similar data but who do not have an economic analysis group may obtain some assistance from the following sources: National Industrial Conference Board, Economic Institute, Barron's, F.W. Dodge Corporation, Business Week, Kiplinger Washington Agency, U.S. News and World Report, Fortune "Business Roundup," and governmental aids (*Survey of Current Business, Federal Reserve Bulletin, Economic Almanac,* and *Business Statistics,* U.S. Dept. of Commerce, Bureau of the Census, Business Cycle Developments, U.S.G. Printing Office, Washington 25, D.C.). Also see: Harry W. Ketchum, "Goverment Aids in Sales Forecasting," *Methods of Sales Forecasting, Report No. 27* (New York: American Management Association, 1957).

[11] M. Whitney Greene, "Combining the Statistical Approach with Other Forecasting Methods," *Methods of Sales Forecasting, Report No. 27* (New York: American Management Association, 1957).

Build-up of monthly sales forecast based on past sales trends, cyclical movements, seasonal variations, and price changes

Year & Month	(a) Monthly Adjusted Sales Value Trend	(b) Cyclical Forecast (Index)	(c) Sales Adjusted for Cyclical	(d) Seasonal Variation (Index)	(e) Sales Adjusted for Cyclical and Seasonal	(f) Wholesale Price Index	(g) Forecasted Sales
	Source: Company records; data adjusted	Source: Based on index such as on industrial production	Source: Col. (a) times Col. (b)	Source: Based on experience of firm	Source: Col. (c) times Col. (d)	Source: Selected	Source: Col. (e) times Col. (f)
Example: 1964:							
January	$100,000	95.0	$95,000	103.0	$97,850	120.0	$117,300

Illustration 7. Worksheet—Economic Rhythm Method

data which the product sales of the company tend to follow. A statistical analysis is used to measure the correlation between the basic series and the company sales. A central problem is to locate a basic series (such as an index of bank deposits or the index of industrial production) with which company sales correlate. The basic series selected, in addition to having a high degree of correlation, should be one that is (a) available and reliable (or computable) and (b) ideally, one which is known to lead company products in movement. The aim is to discover a series that either:

(1) Changes in accord with the values to be forecast, but sufficiently in advance so that the correlated forecast data will be of value, or
(2) Changes in accord, and simultaneously, with a series of data that can be more accurately predicted than the desired series.

Once the basic economic series is selected and the correlation between it and the company sales (historically) is measured, the company must either obtain a projection of the basic series from an outside source or make one of its own. The next step is to extrapolate the company sales potential as related to the projection of the basic series.

As with the economic rhythm method a careful evaluation of the rigid results is essential, followed by the application of sound judgment on the part of the company executives.

The *special historical analogy* method is based upon the idea of selecting some previous situation and period in the past that appears to have most of the earmarks of the present situation; the implied rationale is that what happened in the past is very likely to happen again.[12] This method has found limited use and cannot be strictly considered as a statistical method. It does have some of the characteristics of the executive opinion method.

The *cross-cut-method* of forecasting sales is based on the concept that no two cycles are alike but like causes always produce like results.[13] The facts about a given situation are assembled, and relying on knowledge of economic processes, the forecaster makes some judgments as to future trends. This method has very limited use. It does not attempt to forecast the extent of sales trends. Rather it tries to determine the direction of the movement of economic activity and suggests that sales will move in the same direction and generally to the same extent. As a method

[12] Frederick E. Croxton and Dudley J. Cowden, *Practical Business Statistics,* 3rd. ed. (Englewood Cliffs, N. J.: Prentice Hall, 1960).
[13] Croxton and Cowden, *Practical Business Statistics,* 3rd ed.

of forecasting sales for a specific company, this method is not suitable; however, the concepts implied may be useful in buttressing the development of data using another method.

Industry Analysis Method—In general terms this method may be characterized in the following manner. A forecast is developed of the total volume of business for the industry in which the firm operates. Once this forecast is completed a projection is made of the share of the market that the individual company can reasonably expect. This approach is commonly used in the automotive industry. The first step in this method is to analyze industry statistics to determine historical growth rates. Next, a projection of the industry volume is developed. Next, the company's growth patterns are analyzed and compared with the industry patterns. From these analyses it can be determined whether the company's share of the market has been increasing, decreasing, or remaining about the same. The final step (and the most critical one) is to develop a projection of the share of the market the company should adopt as its objective for the period of time in the future. In this final step, a careful analysis of all identifiable factors affecting the growth of the industry should be identified and evaluated. The company itself must be prepared to take an advantage of these factors to a greater degree than the competitors. Hopeful projections of shares of the market by some firms, without adequate analysis and without sound plans to attain the projected shares have been rather common. Making such choices lightly have proved nearly disastrous for several well-known firms in the last few years. On the other hand the method is particularly sound assuming (a) industry statistics are available, (b) refined statistical approaches are used in the analyses, and (c) sound business judgments are brought to bear throughout the development of the sales projection.

The Product Line Method—This approach may be characterized as involving a detailed and separate analysis of each product sold in order to develop a sales projection, independently, for each product. The sum of the product line projections constitutes the sales projection for the company over-all. This approach is used by firms that distribute a small line of major items and use a different channel to distribute each item. In other words, the distribution system is by product rather than by geographical area or by customers. The method may vary from the more sophisticated procedures discussed above to rather simple approaches. Obviously, its effectiveness depends upon the adequacy of the analyses, evaluations, and judgments used in its application.

End-use Method—This method involves, in general, a detailed breakdown into *use* categories for the products sold and a careful analysis of the end-use of each product. Essentially this approach requires a careful analysis (and direct communication with) the major consuming industries or segments of an industry. For example, assume certain automobile manufacturers purchase, rather than manufacture, the batteries that are placed in new vehicles. Assume further that the company in question manufactures batteries and sells practically all of its output to automobile manufacturers. In projecting sales, this particular company would have to depend on one or two customers for estimates of demand. If these customers prove to be of little help, it is not unreasonable to assume that the battery manufacturer would be forced to make a projection of the market for the customer's products. Parenthetically, the battery company in this assumed example is obviously in a very untenable position in the long run. In end-use analysis, the company should take into account possible new uses and develop aggressive plans to promote such new uses. To use the battery illustration again, assume an unprecedented demand for small boats increases significantly the demand for batteries. Several battery companies, by aggressive planning, gain a considerable advantage by developing a battery that meets the peculiar use-conditions in pleasure boats. Thus, you see, the end-use method may well require use of certain nonstatistical, as well as statistical, techniques.

In a concluding note on methods of forecasting sales it is well to remember that no two companies have the same problem in budgeting sales, and therefore the approach of one company should seldom, if ever, be identical with that of another company. Then too, methods of developing a sales projection are not, by any stretch of the imagination, standardized. Differences in the characteristics of the firm, the environment in which it operates, the type of industry, size of the company, and even the state of the general economy, may significantly affect the approach that should be used. Sales budgeting cannot ever be static; the individual company must continually strive to improve the various techniques, approaches, and concepts underlying its particular method of predicting sales.

Effect on the sales budget of the concern's limitations

The preceding discussion was concerned principally with the sales potential of the market. Another important factor that must be considered before the sales budget is approved is the internal capabilities of the concern during the period covered by the sales budget. There are four principal considerations concerning internal capabilities that may influence the sales budget·

(1) Capacity of the plant for economical operation
(2) Availability of personnel
(3) Adequacy of raw materials and supplies
(4) Availability of capital

The considerations above suggest the importance of coordination with heads of other functional areas in developing a realistic sales plan.

Capacity to produce is frequently a critical factor in setting sales estimates; its evaluation involves the plant superintendent and others concerned with capital additions. There is no point in planning a greater quantity of sales than can be produced, nor is it advisable generally to operate the plant above economical capacity. The capital additions budget thus becomes involved with the sales budget because new capacity, rearrangement, extraordinary repairs, and expansion frequently need special consideration. The sales plan frequently necessitates a complete study of plant capacity.

Availability of personnel can be a very critical factor in determining the amount of goods that can be produced and, hence, sold. This factor can apply to all classes of personnel, but is more likely to be critical with respect to supervisory personnel and highly skilled workers. This situation poses a possible problem for the director of personnel with respect to recruitment and training, especially if there is to be a significant increase in sales and production. The cost of training new or replacement personnel is often a decisive consideration. Obviously, a significantly reduced sales budget can likewise create serious personnel problems.

The adequacy of funds for capital additions and working capital is also of great consequence in managerial planning. This consideration involves the company treasurer in the sales forecast, because there will be the problem of financing the production, capital additions, and sales effort implicit in the sales budget. In addition to the adequacy of capital, there is also the question of liquidity. Cash is required for capital additions, payrolls, raw materials, inventories, expenses, liabilities, and dividends, yet sales may not provide sufficient ready cash if credit sales are high and collections slow. This related problem is discussed later in connection with the cash budget.

Unless these internal limitations and the timing related to them are recognized and taken into proper account, the sales budget may not be realistic.

The sales budget illustrated

The Superior Manufacturing Company initiates its sales budget in the sales districts. During September of the current year the budget director obtains from the accounting department sales data for each district for the past twelve months. The sales data are broken down by months, by quarters, and by product. These data are set forth on *special forms* which are sent to the sales district supervisors by September 15; these forms, with the recommended sales budgets indicated on them, are returned to the vice president in charge of sales by October 15. The district estimates are then reviewed by the sales executives in the home office. The completed sales budget is presented to the budget committee by November 1.

The company follows the usual practice of preparing a detailed, budgeted income statement; therefore, the sales budget is developed by time periods, by district, and by product. The time periods for the year consist of a breakdown by month for the first quarter, and by quarters for the rest of the year. Quarters other than the first are also broken down but not until the last month of the preceding quarter.[14]

The summary sales budget for The Superior Manufacturing Company was illustrated in Chapter 3, Schedule 1. The detailed sales budget is given in Schedule 21, page 106. It may be observed that the detailed schedule includes a three-way classification of sales —by district, by product, and by time period. Because of the simplification of the illustration, one detailed budget schedule is sufficient; however, in more complex situations there would obviously be a need for several schedules in the sales budget.

The reader is reminded that it may be desirable to recast certain of the budget schedules illustrated throughout this text. It may not be desirable to incorporate budget schedules (prepared in worksheet form) into the formal budget without some recast-

[14] Throughout the illustrative problem, 1962 will be referred to as the *current year* and 1963 as the *budget year*.

The Superior Manufacturing Company

SALES BUDGET
(Detailed)
By Product, Time, and District
For the Year Ending December 31, 1963

	Ref. (Given)	Totals		Southern District		Eastern District		Western District	
		Units (Given)	Amount	Units (Given) $5.00 per Unit	Amount	Units (Given) $5.10 per Unit	Amount	Units (Given) $5.10 per Unit	Amount
Product X:									
January		85,000	$ 430,500	30,000	$ 150,000	40,000	$ 204,000	15,000	$ 76,500
February		90,000	455,500	35,000	175,000	45,000	229,500	10,000	51,000
March		95,000	481,500	30,000	150,000	50,000	255,000	15,000	76,500
Total 1st Quarter		270,000	$1,367,500	95,000	$ 475,000	135,000	$ 688,500	40,000	$ 204,000
2nd Quarter		260,000	1,317,000	90,000	450,000	135,000	688,500	35,000	178,500
3rd Quarter		190,000	962,500	65,000	325,000	90,000	459,000	35,000	178,500
4th Quarter		280,000	1,419,000	90,000	450,000	140,000	714,000	50,000	255,000
Total X		1,000,000	$5,066,000	340,000	$1,700,000	500,000	$2,550,000	160,000	$ 816,000
Product Y:	(Given)			$2.00 per Unit		$2.10 per Unit		$2.10 per Unit	
January		34,000	$ 69,900	15,000	$ 30,000	11,000	$ 23,100	8,000	$ 16,800
February		41,000	84,500	16,000	32,000	14,000	29,400	11,000	23,100
March		45,000	92,600	19,000	38,000	15,000	31,500	11,000	23,100
Total 1st Quarter		120,000	$ 247,000	50,000	$ 100,000	40,000	$ 84,000	30,000	$ 63,000
2nd Quarter		135,000	278,000	55,000	110,000	45,000	94,500	35,000	73,500
3rd Quarter		95,000	195,500	40,000	80,000	35,000	73,500	20,000	42,000
4th Quarter		150,000	308,500	65,000	130,000	50,000	105,000	35,000	73,500
Total Y		500,000	$1,029,000	210,000	$ 420,000	170,000	$ 357,000	120,000	$ 252,000
Total X and Y			$ 6,095,000		$2,120,000		$2,907,000		$1,068,000

ing. In order to conserve space, budget schedules in this book have been designed to indicate computation and build-up. Notice that the summary schedule is frequently presented after the detailed schedules. This procedure shows that it is frequently necessary to complete the detailed schedule prior to the summary. The design of budget schedules is an important responsibility of the budget director. There is no standard design suited to all purposes; the schedules must be especially designed to fit the needs and peculiarities of each concern. The schedules illustrated for the Superior Manufacturing Company are merely suggestive.[15]

Discussion Questions

1. What is the relationship of the long-range sales budget and the sales budget included in the annual profit plan?
2. Define the sales budget and relate its importance to the over-all budget program.
3. With which of the following statements do you agree? Why?
   (a) The objective in sales budgeting is to estimate what actual sales will be and then to compare actual sales with budgeted sales to determine whether or not the budget is wrong.
   (b) The objective in sales budgeting is to establish highly desirable, yet attainable sales objectives, and then to compare actual sales with budgeted sales to determine whether or not sales effort and results were adequate.
4. To whom should the responsibility for the sales budget be assigned? Discuss the related aspects of this responsibility.
5. How does the sales budget contribute to managerial (a) planning, (b) coordination, and (c) control?
6. What is the relationship between the sales budget and sales quotas for the salesmen?
7. Discuss the relationship of pricing policies to sales budgeting.
8. What is the relationship between the sales budget and the distribution expense budget?
9. What principal factors should be taken into account in developing a method of projecting sales? Should a company use one method exclusively? Why?
10. How should the sales budget be broken down with respect to detail?

[15] A continuation of this case is available for the following year from the A-Tex Publishing Company, 1005½ Guadalupe Street, Austin, Texas. The extended case is particularly useful for instructional purposes. In it the emphasis is on the overall system; pencil work has been reduced to a minimum. Included with the materials is a number of short related cases that deal with specific problems and budget application.

11. What internal limitations of the concern may affect the sales budget?
12. What factors tend to determine the number of schedules that should comprise the sales budget?

Planning Production: Finished Goods

and Work in Process

Inventory Requirements

In the preceding chapter we considered the development of the sales budget which specified the *quantity* of each product (by interim periods) that the firm plans to sell. In developing the annual profit plan the next step is to (a) establish policies relative to desirable inventory levels (*finished goods* and *work in process*) and (b) plan the quantity of each product that must be manufactured to meet the sales requirement and conform to the inventory policies. The planning of manufacturing activities is considered in the next several chapters. Illustration 8 (page 110) presents diagrammatically the areas of planning from sales through manufacturing.

With respect to production planning we are confronted with the need for planning an optimum balance between sales, inventory, and production. The problem is especially complex at this point because of the three variables only sales is known. If optimum balance is not achieved in planning this triangle of operations, many other aspects of the profit plan will be adversely affected. A well-balanced production program is necessary for economical manufacturing. Low production costs usually result from standardization of products and from stable production levels. Sales representatives are generally aggressive in requesting new products and changes in the old products. There may be pressure from both sales and manufacturing for high inventory levels. Therefore, it is essential that there be

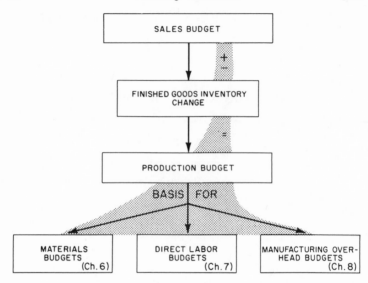

Illustration 8. *Planning Manufacturing Operations*

coordination between sales plans, production plans, and inventory policies. The production budget and the inventory policies provide the basis for obtaining this coordination.[1]

The production budget is an estimate of the *quantity* of goods that must be manufactured during the budget period. In developing the production budget, the first step is to establish policies relative to inventory levels. The next step is to determine the *total* quantity of each product that is to be manufactured during the budget period. The third step is to schedule or prorate this production to interim periods.[2]

The production budget is the initial step in budgeting manufacturing operations. In addition to the production budget, there are three other principal budgets related to manufacturing: (1) the *material budget,* which involves estimates of raw material requirements; (2) the *labor budget,* which indicates the quantity and cost of direct labor; and (3) the *manufacturing expense*

---

[1] For a particularly good discussion of these problems the reader is referred to: "Serving Sales through Planning of Production and Inventory " (a booklet), *NAA Bulletin, Accounting Practice Report No. 6* (New York: National Association of Accountants, 1959).

[2] This chapter presumes a manufacturing situation. The production budget is the manufacturing equivalent of the merchandise budget in wholesale and retail establishments. Retail budgeting is discussed in a subsequent chapter.

or *burden budget*, which includes estimates of all factory costs other than direct material and direct labor. These three budgets are discussed in subsequent chapters.

Responsibility for production budgeting

Upon completion, the sales budget should be forwarded to the chief executive in charge of manufacturing, who is responsible for translating it into a balanced production program consistent with managerial policies and certain internal limitations. Planning, scheduling, and dispatching of the actual production are functions of the production department, so it is essential that responsibility for the budget aspects of these functions be shared by production executives. These executives have first-hand knowledge of plant and personnel capacities, availability of materials, and the production situation. Although responsibility rests directly upon the production executives, top-management policies must be considered in such matters as inventory levels, stability of production, and capital additions. A balanced coordinated production program generally requires the careful attention of top management, particularly where there is multi-plant production requiring the determination of place of production as well as its timing.

To plan production properly, the manufacturing executives must have, or develop, information relative to the manufacturing operations necessary for each product. They must have information relative to the uses and capacities of each manufacturing department. The cost accounting group should provide certain historical data essential in planning production quantities and costs. The budget director should provide staff assistance when needed.

When the recommended production budget is completed by the production department, it should be submitted to the budget committee and the president for tentative approval prior to use as a basis for the materials, labor, and factory overhead budgets.

General considerations in budgeting production and inventory levels

The production budget does not attempt to establish the precise amount and timing of production that will occur during the budget period. Rather, the production budget represents the conversion of projected sales to projected production as a basis for planning (and budgeting) the various aspects of the manufacturing function—plant capacity requirements, raw material requirements, timing of purchases, labor requirements and costs, and factory overhead. These latter items can be efficiently planned only on the basis of a realistic estimate of production volume.

Generally speaking, production in manufacturing situations is: (a) for direct delivery, (b) for stock, or (c) partially for direct delivery and partially for stock. Partial production for stock is desirable from a production standpoint, because the inventory of finished goods provides a cushion for balancing sales requirements and desirable production levels.

The production budget should be developed whenever possible in terms of quantities or physical units of finished goods. Therefore, when it is possible to budget sales by units as well as by values, production budgeting is simplified.

In developing the production budget the manufacturing executives are faced with the problem of balancing sales, inventories, and production so that the lowest possible over-all cost results. To achieve an effective balance, careful consideration of a number of subsidiary, yet significant, matters is essential. The importance of this aspect of planning cannot be overemphasized because it affects so many decisions relating to cost, capital commitments, employees, and so on. Decisions required in developing the production budget are:

(1) Determination of the total production requirements (by product) for the budget period (annual).
(2) Determination of inventory policies relative to finished goods and work in process. Inventory policies should be established with some precision.
(3) Determination of plant capacity policies such as the limits of permissable departures from a stable production level throughout the year.
(4) Determination of the adequacy of manufacturing facilities (expansion or contraction of plant capacity).
(5) Determination of the availability of raw materials, purchased components, and labor.
(6) Determination of the effect of the length of the processing time.
(7) Determination of economical lots or runs.
(8) Determination of the timing of production throughout the year.

The approach used by a particular firm depends upon its size and, more importantly, the nature of its manufacturing process.

This general area is variously approached by (a) planning and controlling inventories, (b) determining economic lots or runs, and (c) planning and controlling production. It is outside the scope of this book to present or illustrate the many approaches to these problems that have been developed and described in the literature. These approaches vary from crude rule-of-thumb methods to very sophisticated approaches involving operations research, linear programming, and the use of the latest computer systems.

The remaining pages of this chapter will pose the problem from a budgeting point of view and will outline some of the principal considerations.[3]

Annual production required

The production executives must translate the quantities called for in the sales budget into unit production requirement for the *year* for each product, taking into consideration management inventory policies. For example, assume that the inventory policies have been determined and that they specify an ending inventory of finished goods of 200,000 units. The annual production requirements for The Superior Manufacturing Company for Product X may be computed as follows (see Schedule 2, page 64.):

	Units of Product X
Required for sales from sales budget	1,000,000
Add desired final inventory of finished goods (per management policy)	200,000
Total required	1,200,000
Less beginning inventory of finished goods	240,000
Budgeted production for year	960,000

Because the production budget is developed prior to the end of the current year, the beginning inventory for the budget year has to be estimated. The estimate is based on the status of the inventory at the date the budget is being prepared and is ad-

[3] The following references are recommended: P. E. Chorafas, *Operations Research for Industrial Management* (New York: Reinhold, 1958), Ch. 11; John F. Magee, *Production Planning and Inventory Control* (New York: McGraw, 1958); Thompson M. Whitin, *The Theory of Inventory Management*, 2nd ed. (Princeton, N. J.: Princeton University Press, 1957); E. H. MacNiece, *Production Forecasting, Planning and Control* (New York: Wiley, 1958); C. W. Churchman, *Introduction to Operations Research* (New York: Wiley, 1957).

justed for planned operations for the balance of the current year. Normally there will be little difficulty in estimating this inventory with reasonable accuracy.

The budgeted production (by product) having been developed for the year, the next problem is one of prorating this production by interim periods during the year (item 8 listed above). Prior to considering this basic problem we will discuss the major factors to be considered in making the proration; specifically we must consider the listed items (2) through (7) since it is the responsibility of the manufacturing executives to bring all of these considerations into optimum balance.

Inventory policies

The planning and control of inventories is one of the most neglected problems of management. The neglect frequently results in a critical shortage of goods and a consequent failure to meet sales delivery dates, or conversely, a gross overstocking of certain items. The author is reminded of one case in which a firm applied for a sizable bank loan to obtain cash for current operations. The bank's investigations revealed that the company had had no inventory-control policies on the basis that "no one in the firm would allow any appreciable overstocking." Yet an analysis of average withdrawals from inventory showed significant overstocking on many items; in fact there was about an eighteen years' supply of several slow-moving items. With respect to these items, the manufacturing department, thinking only of the trouble and cost of set-up time, had run large quantities without considering the relative turnover of the items. It was simply a case of not having definite policies and controls on inventories. The problem extends to inventories of supplies, raw materials, work in process, and finished goods. In developing production requirements, consideration must be given to the finished goods and work in process inventories. It is impossible to develop a satisfactory production program without definite inventory policies, and one of the principal advantages of production budgeting is that it forces advance consideration of the inventory problem.

Inventory policies should include (a) the establishment of inventory standards in terms of maximum and minimum limitations and (b) the application of techniques and methods that will assure conformity to inventory standards. Budgeting requires that inventory standards be established and provides for reporting variations of actual inventory levels from standard levels from month to month.

In determining inventory policies for finished goods, management should consider these important factors:

(1) Quantities needed to meet sales department requirements. This problem involves consideration of the sales budget and the related seasonality of demand. The sales department executives should be directly involved in this consideration.

(2) Perishability of items.

(3) Length of the production period.

(4) Storage facilities.

(5) Adequacy of capital to finance the cost of producing the inventory some time in advance of sales. It is not unusual to find excessive working capital tied up in inventories.

(6) Cost of carrying the inventory. There are frequently numerous and significant costs connected with stocking large quantities of goods. The principal costs involved are labor, insurance, taxes, rents, depreciation, transportation, and extra handling.

(7) Protection against raw material shortages.

(8) Protection against labor shortages.

(9) Protection against price increases.

(10) Risks involved in inventory:

　　a. Price declines

　　b. Obsolescence of stock

　　c. Casualty loss and theft

　　d. Lack of demand

Some of these factors counteract one another; the point is that a good inventory policy must express a desirable balance between these factors.

It is desirable to express the inventory policies relative to finished goods in as precise a manner as possible. To say " our policy is to keep inventory at the minimum" is obviously inadequate. In contrast, inventory standards should be expressed— *by product or by lines*—in terms such as the following:

Method	*Policy Expression*
(a) Months' supply	For Product X—Three months' supply based on moving three months average of budgeted requirements.
	For Product Y—Two months' supply based on average annual issues budgeted for the year.
(b) Maximum limit	For Product X—Inventory not to exceed 5,000 units.
(c) Maximum and minimum limits	For Product X—Maximum 5,000 units; minimum 3,000 units.
(d) Specific amount	For Product X—Double the sales of the past month.

For Product Y—Equal to the sales budgeted for the following month.

(e) Inventory turnover rates   For Product X—Turnover rate to be 6 annualized.
For Product Y—Turnover rate to be 2 on a monthly basis.

More sophisticated methods have been developed for computer application; experimentation along these lines is continuing. The method of developing and expressing a specific inventory policy must vary with the characteristics, and the nature of the inventory problems, of each company.

In order to illustrate some further inventory policy expressions, several simplified examples are presented in the next few paragraphs.

Assume the sales budget calls for 1,200,000 units of product K. Assume further that after careful consideration of the significant factors affecting inventory requirements, the management has specified a standard inventory level of two months' supply based on an annual average. The two months' supply would be 200,000 units $(1,200,000 \times 2/12)$. Although simple and direct, such a policy would be rigid; consequently, it might be quite unrealistic if sales are highly seasonal.

To illustrate a less rigid approach, assume the inventory policy to be a two months' supply of the beginning inventory based on a three months moving average of issues. This approach provides a fluctuating inventory level consistent with seasonal sales demands as is demonstrated below:

	Budgeted Units to be Sold	*Three Months' Moving Average*	*Beginning Inventory (Two Months' Supply)*
December (preceding year)	82,000		
January ⎫	85,000	85,667	171,334
February ⎬ budget year	90,000	90,000	180,000
March ⎭	95,000		
(*etc.*)			

Some firms employ a standard inventory turnover as a basis for establishing inventory levels. Inventory turnover is computed by dividing units withdrawn by units in inventory. To illustrate the procedure, assume that 150,000 units of a certain product were sold during the year and that the average inventory on hand during the year was 50,000. The inventory turnover would be computed as follows:

$$\frac{150,000}{50,000} = 3 \text{ turnovers during the year.}$$

Let us assume further that management has decided that a turnover of 4 is a desirable standard for the budget year for this particular product. Assuming the sales budget for the first three months was as indicated in column one below, a standard inventory in units related to sales trend could be readily computed as illustrated. It will be noted that the inventory level parallels the variation in sales volume.

	Budgeted Sales (Units)	Computation	Indicated Initial Inventory (Units)
January	12,000	($\times 12 \div 4$)	36,000
February	11,000	"	33,000
March	14,500		43,500

If the standard turnover figure is applied to total annual sales rather than to monthly sales, a stable inventory standard results.

Irrespective of the approach used in specifying inventory standards, it is essential that (a) definite inventory policies be established and kept current; (b) responsibility for inventory planning and control be assigned to specified individuals; (c) procedures be developed for accounting for inventories; and (d) a reporting system be designed to inform management of the status of inventory control.

Stability of production

Seasonal sales are typical in most industries; yet in most instances it is highly desirable that production levels be relatively stable. In many companies where sales are seasonal, production levels have been stabilized by developing new products that can be stored or that have opposite seasonal trends. The inventory provides a rather tempting method of leveling production; yet, as previously pointed out, there are certain pitfalls to be avoided. Stabilization of production is desirable for a number of reasons and generally results in significant reductions of costs and improvements in operations. The advantages of stable production may be outlined as follows:

    (a) Stability of employment, resulting in:
        (1) Improved morale and hence greater worker efficiency
        (2) Less labor turnover
        (3) Attraction of better workers
        (4) Reduction of expense for training new workers
    (b) Economies in purchasing raw materials as a result of:
        (1) Availability
        (2) Volume discounts

(3) Simplified storage problems
(4) Smaller capital requirements
(5) Reduced inventory risk
(c) Better utilization of plant facilities, which tends to
    (1) Reduce the capacity required to meet peak seasons
    (2) Avoid idle capacity

Undoubtedly the greatest hazard of significant ups and downs in production is the effect on personnel. Periodic layoffs, and subsequent efforts to hire employees, destroys morale, discourages the ambitious employee, and attracts unstable personalities. One of the objectives of modern management should be to offer job security. The introduction of budget control, and the consequent *planning of production and inventories*, has changed the whole pattern of operations in many companies.

Adequacy of manufacturing facilities

Planning the production program requires consideration of the adequacy of manufacturing facilities. There must be sufficient capacity to produce the planned total volume of goods and to meet the peak loads called for in the detailed production budget. The production of individual departments, processes, and machines must be carefully planned and coordinated in the production budget so as to avoid bottlenecks and idle capacity.

Plant and department capacities should be analyzed by the production executives in terms of potential or maximum plant capacity and normal or practicable capacity. Maximum capacity may be thought of as the "theoretical" engineering capacity, whereas practicable capacity is somewhat less, representing the level at which the plant or department can operate most efficiently. Practicable capacity is usually thought to be about 85 to 90 per cent of maximum capacity. Idle or excess plant capacity is the difference between the actual operating rate of activity and practicable capacity. Breakeven capacity is the rate of activity at which the sales value of the goods produced is exactly equal to the cost of producing and selling those goods. It is important that top management be informed as to the maximum capacity, practicable capacity, operating capacity, and breakeven capacity of the plant. It is usual to express capacities as percentages of maximum capacity.

Plant capacity may be expressed in one of several ways. Of course, if there is only one product or several almost identical products, capacity should be expressed in physical units of output. In other circumstances, plant capacity must be measured in terms of some common measure of output, such as direct labor hours, machine hours, dollar sales of goods produced, dollar cost of goods produced, total tonnage, or some other measure of output.

Production budgeting is directly related to the capital additions budget with respect to (a) plant additions required; (b) extraordinary repairs and rearrangements; and (c) retirement or disposal of excess plant capacity. If plant equipment appears to be inadequate, management must make plans for obtaining the additional capacity or revising the production and sales requirements. In planning capital additions, management must keep in mind the time that is required to obtain and ready the additions for production. There is also the related problem of financing. Care must be exercised lest expensive plant additions are planned to meet short-term peak demands only to remain idle for considerable periods of time thereafter. The capital additions budget is discussed in a subsequent chapter.

Availability of raw materials and labor

In some cases, the production program may be influenced by the availability of the required raw materials and labor. This situation is especially prevalent during periods of scarcity, as was the case immediately after World War II. Raw material availability may also be affected by such factors as prices, perishability, economies in purchasing, quality considerations, and quantities available. For example, canning plants obviously have to schedule production when the raw materials are in season. Even in cases where the raw materials can be stored, there is the problem of weighing the advantages of stable production against the problems and costs incident to warehousing large inventories. The availability of skilled labor and the time required to train workers are factors that may have a decided effect on the planning of production.

Length of the production period

The production budget as illustrated on page 113 indicates the *units to be completed* to meet the sales forecast and inventory requirements. A direct conversion from the sales budget to the production budget, as illustrated, assumes that the processing time is relatively short. In situations where processing requires several weeks or months, it is necessary to prepare additional schedules indicating the timing of the *units to be started*. For example, if processing requires approximately four months, the schedule of units to be started must be moved forward at least four months ahead of the dates shown in the production budget of *units to be completed*. In addition, if the product consists of many parts which are manufactured by the firm, it will be necessary to prepare a separate *parts production budget* indicating the timing of (a) parts to be completed and (b) parts to be started. The schedules indicating *starting* dates provide essential data for the purchasing department in planning raw materials purchases.

Another factor influencing the planning of production is the work in process inventory. If there is no significant fluctuation in this inventory during the year, obviously there is no material effect on production; hence, inventory fluctuation can be ignored in production planning. However, should there be a significant change in the work in process inventory, this fact must be taken into account in the planning. There are generally two possible approaches to the problem depending on the circumstances. In cases where the processing time is short, a change in work in process inventory can be incorporated into the usual production budget format along the following lines:

	Units
Units required for sales	100,000
Add final inventory of finished goods	20,000
Total	120,000
Less initial inventory of finished goods	15,000
Units to be completed for finished goods	105,000
Add *equivalent units* in final work in process inventory*	5,000
Total	110,000
Less *equivalent units* in initial work in process inventory	6,000
Equivalent units to be manufactured	104,000

* Equivalent units represent the units produced, both completed and partially completed, in a given period. For example, if a department having no beginning inventory completed 1,000 units and had on hand an ending inventory of 200 units estimated to be one-half completed, the equivalent units produced would be 1,100 [1,000+(200×1/2)].

Where the processing time is long enough to require the preparation of schedules of units to be started in addition to schedules of units to be completed, the adjustment for changes in work in process inventories can be made in these schedules rather than in the schedule of units to be completed, as illustrated above. The reasons for this procedure are obvious.

In situations where processing time is not too long, it may be more practicable to adjust production starting times to delivery times through allowed fluctuations in the work in process and finished goods inventories. The principal difficulty involved in using inventories for this purpose is that a large amount of working capital could become tied up in such inventories.

Planning production throughout the year

With the annual production requirements determined, as illustrated on page 113, the next step in the development of the production budget is the allocation of *total* (annual) production requirements to interim periods during the budget year. Interim production must also be planned so as to (a) have sufficient goods to meet interim sale requirements; (b) keep interim inventory levels within reasonable limits; and (c) manufacture the goods as economically as possible. These three objectives may not be in complete harmony. For example, assuming seasonal sales, it is possible to maintain a stable production level only if inventories are allowed to fluctuate inversely with sales. On the other hand, a stable inventory level is possible only if production is allowed to fluctuate directly with sales. From the point of view of economical operations, it is generally desirable to keep both inventories and production stable, a situation which is obviously impossible given seasonal sales. The production budget should represent the optimum balance between sales, essential inventory levels, and stable production levels.

In order to point up the problem of achieving balance between planned sales, planned inventory, and planned production, assume that planned sales for a particular product are as follows:

	Sales Budget (Units)		Sales Budget (Units)
January	1,500	July	700
February	1,600	August	600
March	1,600	September	900
April	1,400	October	1,100
May	1,200	November	1,200
June	1,000	December	1,400
		Annual Total	14,200

Assume the following additional budget data:
  (a) Inventory at beginning of year (January 1)   2,000
  (b) Inventory planned for end of budget year
       (December 30)   1,500

Query: How should production of the 13,700 units (sales 14,200 plus ending inventory 1,500 less beginning inventory 2,000) be planned or scheduled throughout the year? Note the problem of reducing inventory by 500 units.

With sales volume (highly seasonal) definitely planned, one of three basic patterns of production-inventory levels may be budgeted, viz.:

(a) *Give precedence to production stability*—Establish an inflexible production policy (such as a stable level throughout the year) and thereby cause inventory to fluctuate *inversely* with the seasonal sales pattern. This alternative is shown in Illustration 9 as Proposal (A), and graphically in Illustration 10, page 124.

(b) *Give precedence to inventory stability*—Establish an inflexible inventory policy (such as a stable level throughout the year) and thereby cause production levels to fluctuate directly with the seasonal sales pattern. This alternative is shown in Illustration 9 as Proposal (B), and graphically in Illustration 11.

(c) *Give neither inventory nor production precedence*—Establish sound inventory policies and sound production policies with due consideration to the several factors discussed in the preceding sections of this chapter so that reasonable flexibility is allowed in both inventory and production. In other words, attempt to develop the optimum balance (in terms of the effect on profits) between sales, inventory, and production. One possible alternative is shown in Illustration 9 as Proposal (C), and graphically in Illustration 12. In this case the management specified the following policies: Production should not vary more than 15 per cent (a) above or below the yearly average and (b) a maximum inventory of 1,600, and a minimum inventory of 1,400 units.

It should be noted that in this simple illustration there are two principal factors that complicate production timing: (a) highly seasonal sales and (b) a 25 per cent reduction during the year in physical inventory. Proposal (A) causes the inventory to fluctuate from a low of 500 units to a high of 1,700 units and a relatively stable production level. On the other hand, Proposal (B) causes a stable inventory level of 1,500 units. Proposal (B) calls for an immediate reduction to a standard inventory level of 1,500 units; however, this procedure causes production to fluctuate with sales from a low of 600 units to a high of 1,500 units. Taking into consideration the inventory and production policies stated, and the additional factor of vacations during July, August, and the first part of September, a workable balance is suggested in Proposal (C).

It is obvious from this rather simplified illustration that serious thought is necessary to achieve the optimum balance between sales, production, and inventory. Graphs represent one means of analyzing and presenting the related aspects of the problem. More sophisticated approaches are used in complex situations.[4]

The production budget as a planning, coordinating, and control tool

The production budget contributes to planning, coordination, and control in many ways. One prominent authority on production control stated:[5]

> The manufacturing forecast or master schedule determines in general terms (1) what will be needed, (2) when it will be needed, and (3) how much will be needed, based on estimated monthly sales for a specific period ahead.
>
> The objective of the manufacturing forecast, production forecast, or master schedule (whichever term is used), is to establish a firm production figure for an ensuing period. In continuous manufacturing the master schedule may become the manufacturing authorization and the firm goal.

The fact that a detailed production plan is developed, based on a realistic sales budget, means that a number of responsible executives have given thought and effort to the production planning function and related problems. Developing a production budget in detail requires, in addition to production plans, definite and detailed planning with respect to material requirements, labor requirements, plant capacity, capital additions, and inventory polices. The planning of production tends to divulge weaknesses and sources of potential trouble that can then be avoided by timely executive action.

Even more significant perhaps is the coordination that can result from effective production budgeting. The production program must be properly coordinated with plans related to financing, capital additions, product development, and sales. A critical

---

[4] "Computerized Production Control," *Factory Management and Maintenance*, Vol. 115, No. 7 (July 1957), p. 84. H. B. Maynard (Editor), *Industrial Engineering Handbook* (New York: McGraw, 1956).

[5] William Voris, *Production Control* (Homewood, Ill.: Irwin, 1956), p. 92.

PROPOSAL (A)

	Year	Jan.	Feb.	Mar.	Apr.	May	June	July	Aug.	Sept.	Oct.	Nov.	Dec.
Planned sales	14.200	1,500	1,600	1,600	1,400	1,200	1,000	700	600	900	1,100	1,200	1,400
Add—final inventory	1,500	1,700	1,300	900	600	500	600	1,000	1,500	1,700	1,700	1,700	1,500
Total	15,700	3,200	2,900	2,500	2,000	1,700	1,600	1,700	2,100	2,600	2,800	2,900	2,900
Less initial inventory	2,000	2,000	1,700	1,300	900	600	500	600	1,000	1,500	1,700	1,700	1,700
Planned production	13,700	1,200	1,200	1,200	1,100	1,100	1,100	1,100	1,100	1,100	1,100	1,200	1,200

PROPOSAL (B)

	Year	Jan.	Feb.	Mar.	Apr.	May	June	July	Aug.	Sept.	Oct.	Nov.	Dec.
Planned sales	14,200	1,500	1,600	1,600	1,400	1,200	1,000	700	600	900	1,100	1,200	1,400
Add—final inventory	1,500	1,900	1,800	1,700	1,600	1,500	1,500	1,500	1,500	1,500	1,500	1,500	1,500
Total	15,700	3,400	3,400	3,300	3,000	2,700	2,500	2,200	2,100	2,400	2,600	2,600	2,900
Less initial inventory	2,000	2,000	1,900	1,800	1,700	1,600	1,500	1,500	1,500	1,500	1,500	1,500	1,500
Planned production	13,700	1,400	1,500	1,500	1,300	1,100	1,000	700	600	900	1,100	1,200	1,400

PROPOSAL (C)

	Year	Jan.	Feb.	Mar.	Apr.	May	June	July	Aug.	Sept.	Oct.	Nov.	Dec.
Planned sales	14,200	1,500	1,600	1,600	1,400	1,200	1,000	700	600	900	1,100	1,200	1,400
Add—final inventory	1,500	1,700	1,300	1,100	1,100	1,300	1,500	1,500	1,600	1,600	1,700	1,700	1,500
Total	15,700	3,200	2,900	2,700	2,500	2,500	2,500	2,200	2,200	2,500	2,800	2,900	2,900
Less initial inventory	2,000	2,000	1,700	1,300	1,100	1,100	1,300	1,500	1,500	1,600	1,600	1,700	1,700
Planned production	13,700	1,200	1,200	1,400	1,400	1,400	1,200	700	700	900	1,200	1,200	1,200

Illustration 9. *Production and Finished Goods Inventory Budgets*

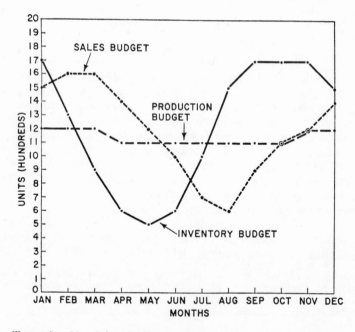

Illustration 10. *Sales, Production, and Inventory Budgets—Proposal A*

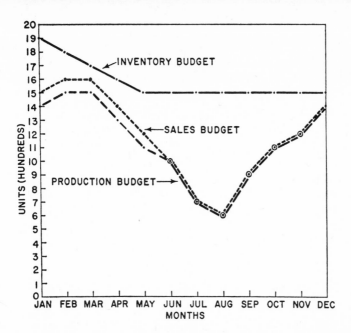

Illustration 11. *Sales, Production, and Inventory Budgets—Proposal B*

Illustration 12. *Sales, Production, and Inventory Budgets—Proposal C*

problem in all manufacturing situations revolves around the procedures established to effectively coordinate the operations of the sales and production departments. The sales executive must be as acutely aware of production problems as the production executive is aware of sales estimates. It may be desirable to revise the sales budget to emphasize those products which the factory can readily and efficiently produce. The translation of sales demands into production effort can be quite complex and, if not resolved on a sound basis, may be the cause of considerable inefficiency in the firm. Such inefficiencies can generally be attributed to a lack of timely planning and to an indefinite assignment of responsibilities. Fortunately, the production budget establishes a firm foundation for coordinated operations throughout the budget period.

The production budget as finally approved should be viewed as a master production plan to be executed by the producing department. It should not be used inflexibly, but rather as a guide to the actual, detailed, production planning and scheduling carried on by the production department on a day-to-day or week-to-week basis. It should not be viewed ordinarily as an order to proceed with production; actual production should be ordered by the production planning and scheduling department on a current basis. The production budget may be considered the framework within which current production orders are issued. Variations in actual sales and in other conditions call for departures from the original production plan.

The production budget is the primary basis for planning raw material requirements, labor needs, capital additions, cash requirements, and costs. Therefore, the production budget becomes the foundation for factory budgeting in general. It gives the factory executives something tangible upon which to base operational decisions.

An adequate production control system is essential to managerial control of costs, quality, and quantities. The principal procedures involved in production control are:

(1) Materials control
(2) Process analysis
(3) Routing production
(4) Scheduling production
(5) Dispatching production
(6) Follow-up

Production control is considered to be outside the scope of this book; the reader is referred to the several outstanding books on this subject.[6] In addition to daily and weekly controls of the production volume and the levels of the finished goods inventory, the status of these two factors should be reported on the *monthly internal management* report wherein actual results are compared with plans and standards.[7]

The production budget illustrated

It is impracticable to illustrate all the considerations affecting the production budget. It is assumed that The Superior Manufacturing Company inventory policy calls for approximately a three months' supply of finished goods and that production will be kept essentially stable. Manufacturing conditions are such that variations of approximately 15 per cent in production levels are possible without seriously affecting the permanent employees.

The vice president in charge of manufacturing, in consultation with the other manufacturing executives and, in particular, with the executive in charge of production, prepared the production schedules to meet the requirements of the sales budget. This production plan, and the resulting inventory levels, were submitted to the budget committee and tentatively approved by the president. The annual production budget for The Superior Manufacturing Company was shown in Chapter 3, (Schedule 2, page 64).

The detailed production budget, by product, for The Superior Manufacturing Company (Schedule 22) is shown on page 128. Observe that production is budgeted by month for the first quarter and by quarter for the remainder of the year as was illustrated for the sales budget.

In Schedule 22 it may be noted that the work in process inventory has been ignored. This omission is possible because it is assumed that this inventory will remain unchanged during the budget year. Assume work in process inventories to be: Product X, None; Product Y, 10,000 units throughout the year.

[6] See for example, Paul D. O'Donnell, *Production Control* (Englewood Cliffs, N. J.: Prentice-Hall, 1952).

[7] The comprehensive case that is available for use with this text presents an integrated monthly report for the management that includes these and other control points in an interrelated manner.

The Superior Manufacturing Company

PRODUCTION BUDGET DETAIL **Schedule 22**

By Product, by Time

For the Year Ending December 31, 1963

	Ref.	Required for Sales	Add Final Inventory of Finished Goods	Total Required	Less Initial Inventory of Finished Goods	Units to Be Completed
		21				
Product X						
January		85,000	225,000	310,000	240,000	70,000
February		90,000	215,000	305,000	225,000	80,000
March		95,000	200,000	295,000	215,000	80,000
Total 1st Quarter		270,000	200,000	470,000	240,000	230,000
2nd Quarter		260,000	180,000	440,000	200,000	240,000
3rd Quarter		190,000	220,000	410,000	180,000	230,000
4th Quarter		280,000	200,000	480,000	220,000	260,000
Total		1,000,000	200,000	1,200,000	240,000	960,000
Product Y						
January		34,000	100,000	134,000	100,000	34,000
February		41,000	95,000	136,000	100,000	36,000
March		45,000	88,000	133,000	95,000	38,000
Total 1st Quarter		120,000	88,000	208,000	100,000	108,000
2nd Quarter		135,000	93,000	228,000	88,000	140,000
3rd Quarter		95,000	125,000	220,000	93,000	127,000
4th Quarter		150,000	120,000	270,000	125,000	145,000
Total		500,000	120,000	620,000	100,000	520,000

In view of the fact that the finished goods inventory, *in units*, is developed concurrently with the production budget, it is appropriate at this time to prepare a budget of finished goods inventories similar to that illustrated in Schedule 23. Observe that provision is made for unit costs and total costs which can be entered later when the budgeted cost of manufacturing is determined. (See Schedule 63, Chapter 11, for the completed schedule.)

The Superior Manufacturing Company

FINISHED GOODS INVENTORY BUDGET   **Schedule 23**

For the Year Ending December 31, 1963

	Total Cost	Product X			Product Y		
	All Products	*Units*	*Unit Cost*	*Total Cost*	*Units*	*Unit Cost*	*Total Cost*
1963: Ref.							
January 1	$	240,000	$	$	100,000	$	$
January 31		225,000			100,000		
February 29		215,000			95,000		
March 31		200,000			88,000		
End of 2nd Qtr.		180,000			93,000		
End of 3rd Qtr.		220,000			125,000		
End of 4th Qtr.		200,000			120,000		

Discussion Questions

1. Define the production budget.
2. What other budgets are closely related to the production budget?
3. Who should be responsible for preparation of the production budget? Explain.
4. What are the principal considerations involved in budgeting production?
5. What is the relationship of the work in process and finished goods inventories to the production budget?
6. Discuss the apparent inconsistency between stable inventory levels and stable production in a firm having seasonal sales.
7. What is meant by "inventory policies?" List what you would consider to be some desirable inventory policies in a typical firm.
8. What are inventory standards? What purposes are served by the application of inventory standards?
9. Why is it generally desirable to maintain a stable production level?
10. In what way are manufacturing facilities related to the production budget?

11. Discuss the relationship between the production budget and the availability of (a) raw materials and (b) labor.
12. What basis should be used in determining the detailed breakdown of the production budget?
13. In what respects does the production budget contribute to managerial (a) planning, (b) coordination, and (c) control?
14. Relate the production budget to the day-to-day or week-to-week planning and scheduling of actual production throughout the year.

S I X

Planning and Controlling Materials Usage

and Purchases

A comprehensive budget program should include a system for planning and controlling the various aspects of materials used in the manufacturing process. Here we have another problem of balance similar to the one considered in the previous chapter; in this case, the *balance* to be planned and controlled is one between (1) factory requirements for raw materials, (2) raw material inventory levels, and (3) purchases of raw materials.

Once quantities of each product to be manufactured are determined in the production budget, the next step in planning the manufacturing program involves consideration of the various production costs—direct materials, direct labor, and factory overhead. This chapter is concerned with planning and controlling direct material costs.[1]

In order to assure that raw materials will be on hand in the quantities and at the time required and to plan for the costs of such materials, it is essential that the annual profit plan include (a) detailed budgets specifying quantity and cost of materials required, and (b) a related budget of raw material purchases. These considerations involve the following principal sub-budgets relating to raw materials:

> (1) *Materials budget*—This budget involves the planned *quantities* of each raw material required for planned production. It should include details by raw material, by time, and by department.

[1] "Controlling and Accounting for Supplies," *Accounting Practice Report*, a brochure (New York: National Association of Accountants, 1955), 32 pages.

(2) *Purchases budget*—Having determined in the materials budget the quantities of raw materials needed and the timing thereof, a plan for material purchases should be developed. Thus the purchases budget specifies both *quantities* and *cost* for each raw material and the required delivery dates.

(3) *Materials inventory budget*—This budget reports the planned levels of raw material inventory in terms of quantities and cost. As with production and sales, the difference between materials as specified in the *materials budget* (1 above) and the *purchases budget* (2 above) is reflected in an increase or decrease in the inventory budget.

(4) *Estimated cost of materials used budget*—This budget reports the *cost* of the materials planned for use in the materials budget (1 above). It should be observed that the materials budget cannot be *costed* until the planned cost of purchases (3 above) is developed.

The four separate sub-budgets listed above are related. Collectively,, they may be viewed as the *Materials and Purchases Budget*. In a simple situation, the four may well be combined; (1) and (4) are frequently combined. In more complex situations a separation as indicated above is almost essential—especially when the data must develop sequentially.

In designing each of these materials budgets, two basic objectives must be taken into account in the profit planning process:

(1) Raw material costs are subject to direct control; therefore, such costs are budgeted in terms of responsibility (by department), and by short, interim periods.

(2) Raw material costs are included in manufacturing costs and therefore, must be identified with the cost of finished goods (by product).

As a consequence of these basic objectives, we have a four-way classification of material costs with which to cope: by type of raw material, by usage responsibility, by interim periods, and by type of finished goods. This fact tends to complicate the mechanics of budgeting raw materials.

In paragraphs to follow we consider separately each of the four sub-budgets indicated above. Our emphasis will be on the particular problems related to budgeting raw materials. We will reemphasize the basic considerations, techniques, approaches, and decisions discussed in the preceding chapter relating to planning and controlling a balance between (a) requirements, (b) inventory levels, and (c) production or procurement. As noted above, in general, the same factors must be considered, the same approaches and techniques are applicable, and essentially the same types of decisions are involved.

The materials budget

Materials used in a factory are traditionally classified as *direct* and *indirect*. Direct or productive material is generally considered to be all material that forms an integral part of the finished product and can be directly identified with the cost of the product. Direct material cost is usually considered a *variable* cost—that is, a cost that varies in proportion to changes in output or volume. *Indirect* material is generally considered to be material used in connection with the manufacturing process, but not directly traceable to specific production. A related indirect cost, frequently referred to as factory supplies, consists of such items as grease, lubricating oils, and other maintenance supplies. *The materials budget generally deals only with direct materials; supplies and indirect materials generally are included in the manufacturing expense or overhead budget.* In some cases, however, it may be desirable to include certain indirect materials and supplies in the materials budget.

The quantities of each raw material needed for each finished product must be estimated in total for the budget period and broken down further by *interim periods* (months and quarters) in the materials budget. The product and interim period breakdown should follow the patterns used in sales and production budgets. Executives of the manufacturing division should be responsible for developing the basic input data for the raw materials budget.

The principal purposes in developing detailed raw material *quantity* requirements to meet planned production are as follows:

(1) To provide quantity data for the purchasing department so that raw material purchases can be properly planned and controlled.
(2) To provide quantity data so that the raw material costs of production by product can be budgeted.
(3) To provide data for establishing policy as to inventory levels for effective planning and control of such levels.
(4) To provide data for determination of cash requirements (cash budget) for raw material purchases.
(5) To provide data for control of raw material usage.

The basic (estimated) input data required to develop the materials budget are *standard usage rates* by type of raw material for each product. Material usage rates are applied to the production data (from the production budget) to develop the materials budget. In many manufacturing situations it is not a critical problem to determine for each unit of finished product, standard unit usage rates for unit raw materials. For example, in the manufacture of such items as furniture, clothing, mechanical equipment, appliances, and liquids such as paint, there are definite and easily determinable quantities of raw material required. Indeed, in many cases precise measurement of the quantities of raw material is essential to the desired quality of the resulting output. Such unit rates may be derived (a) during initial development of the product, (b) from engineering studies, or (c) from consumption records and bills of materials.

Where unit consumption rates cannot be derived along the lines indicated above, determination of raw material requirements may become a critical budget problem. Two principal approaches to a solution are available. One approach is to develop some reliable method of estimating total raw material *quantities* required for production through the use of adjusted historical ratios such as the ratio of material quantity usage to direct machine hours. The other approach involves the development of a relationship (usually expressed as a ratio or per cent) between material cost *in dollars* and some other series that can be projected with some degree of confidence. For example, some firms plan raw material cost as a per cent of direct labor cost. For obvious reasons the latter approach is the less desirable. In either approach the individual responsible for preparing the raw material budget must usually resort to some form of ratio. The following methods have been suggested:

(1) The ratio of the physical volume of production to the quantity of each kind of raw material. This ratio, for the past few months or year, can be calculated from historical records and adjusted for new or changed conditions;

(2) The ratio of the raw material used to some measure of production such as direct labor hours or direct machine hours;

(3) The ratio of material cost to direct labor cost;

(4) The ratio of material cost to some measure of productive output, such as direct labor or machine hours.

Irrespective of the method used, there should be considerable reliance on historical accounting data. It is frequently advisable to test the reasonableness of estimates by comparing them with historical results. If *standard costs* are being used by the cost accounting department, standard material consumption rates will have been determined and should be used for budget purposes. If the standard cost rates are considered too "tight," it may be desirable to *budget* material usage variations from standard. In determining material requirements or consumption rates, it is important that allowance be made for *normal* spoilage, waste, and scrap.

The detailed materials budget is illustrated for The Superior Manufacturing Company as Schedule 24, page 142.

The purchases and raw material inventory budgets

Careful planning of purchases may offer a significant area of cost saving in many concerns. If realistic estimates of raw material requirements (as anticipated in the material budget) have been made for the interim periods throughout the year, the purchasing officer can adequately plan his responsibilities. The purchasing officer should be assigned the direct responsibility for preparing a detailed plan of purchases for the budget year and for submitting the plan in the form of a purchases budget.

The purchases budget indicates (a) the quantities of each type of raw material to be purchased, (b) the timing of the purchases, and (c) the estimated *cost* of raw material purchases. Thus the purchases budget differs from the material budget in two principal respects. Both budgets specify quantities of each type of raw material, the difference in quantities being the *effect of planned changes in the raw material inventory levels*. The materials budget is limited to *quantities*, whereas the purchases budget specifies both quantities and *dollar costs*. The purchases budget is concerned with the timing of actual deliveries of raw materials rather than with the timing of purchase orders or commitments. It is the responsibility of the purchasing officer to order the material so that delivery will correspond to the materials budget requirements.

Planning the purchases of raw materials involves three distinct problems:

(a) Establishment of policies relating to raw material inventory levels;

(b) Determination of the number of units of each type of raw material to be purchased; and

(c) Estimating the unit cost of each type of material to be purchased.

These are the basic input data for which the purchasing officer is responsible.

Raw Material Inventory Considerations. The quantity differential between the materials budget and the purchases budget is accounted for in the change in raw material inventory levels. Thus, as with the finished goods inventory budget with respect to sales and production, the raw materials inventory budget provides a cushion between raw material requirements for production and purchases. If raw material requirements are seasonal, a stable raw material inventory level means that purchases must exactly parallel material requirements for the factory. On the other hand, in the same case, purchases could be at a uniform level only if inventory were allowed to absorb variations in factory raw material requirements. The most desirable inventory purchasing program will generally range somewhere between these two extremes. The timing of purchases will depend to a considerable degree on the *inventory policies* laid down by top management. The principal considerations in setting inventory policies are as follows:

(1) Timing and quantity of needs by the factory.
(2) Economies in purchasing through quantity discounts.
(3) Availability of raw materials.
(4) Perishability of raw materials.
(5) Storage facilities involved.
(6) Capital requirements to finance inventory.
(7) Costs of storage.
(8) Expected changes in the cost of raw materials.
(9) Protection against shortages.
(10) Risks involved in inventories.

In specifying raw material inventory policies, a standard inventory level for each type of raw material should be included. Such standards can be specified in terms of months' supplies, turnover ratios, or maximum and minimum limitations. Inventory standards are essential to adequate planning of purchases and the subsequent control of purchases and inventories. The raw material inventory problem should be approached in essentially the same manner as the finished goods inventory; therefore, the reader is referred to the discussion of inventory policies and control in Chapter 5.

Estimating raw material unit costs

The purchasing department executives have the responsibility of estimating for the purchases budget the unit cost of each raw material. Purchasing executives frequently hesitate to make such cost estimates recognizing that there can be many significant factors, external to the concern, that affect raw material prices. Nevertheless, failure to develop reasonable estimates may have far-reaching effects throughout the concern. For example, in situations where raw material is a significant part of the cost of the finished product, raw material costs are inextricably bound up with pricing policies, financing policies, and cost control, all of which must be concerned with *future* rather than historical raw material costs. Top management should insist on serious consideration of the expected trends in raw material costs, involving detailed price studies based on such factors as the general economic conditions, industry prospects, crop reports, demand for the raw materials, and current market conditions. In short, the purchasing officer has a responsibility not too different from that faced by the sales executive when he forecasts sales. A similarly comprehensive approach is required.

The cost of material includes the invoice price, less any discounts, plus freight, drayage, and handling charges incident to delivery of the goods to the warehouse or storeroom. It is frequently impracticable, however, to apply transportation costs to specific raw materials; therefore, the net purchase price is often considered to be the cost of raw materials, and transportation and handling costs are treated as factory expense or burden. From a budget point of view, unit material costs should be determined in the light of cost accounting practices in use by the firm for recording actual costs.

Contracts in existence may provide cost data. Historical costs, as indicated by the cost records, may provide a basis for estimating. If standard material costs are being used by the cost accounting department, these costs may be used for budgeting purposes. However, should such standard costs be unrealistic, a material price variance should be budgeted.

In many cases it is necessary that raw material unit prices be budgeted at *various levels* throughout the budget period. Some raw materials, such as wheat, have prices that tend to vary seasonally with production, thereby necessitating a varying budget price. Where it can be used, an *average unit price* is preferable otherwise the problem of *flow of inventory costs*, such as *fifo*, *lifo*, etc., will be encountered.

Planning, coordination and control aspects of raw materials budgeting

Formulation of detailed plans for raw material requirements, inventories, and purchases is an important part of the planning function of top management. Planning and control of raw material costs frequently are critical because the cost of production and the efficiency with which operation can be conducted on a day-to-day basis depend to a large degree on the smooth flow of raw materials (at reasonable cost) to the various subdivisions of the factory as needed. Materials planning improves coordination of effort by pinpointing responsibilities; careful thought is required to anticipate and iron out difficulties that otherwise might not become apparent until after actual operations start, resulting in delays, mix-ups, and consequent high costs. Raw materials planning prevents the accumulation of excess inventories and inventory shortages, both of which can be extremely costly. Materials budgeting forces the manufacturing and purchasing executives to face up to these significant problems and to make decisions when they *should* be made rather than when they *have* to be made. Temporizing with managerial problems and decisions is inevitably costly. With purchases planning achieved, the purchasing department has definite objectives rather than the generalized goal "to buy what is needed." Definite plans for the purchasing activities should make possible better organization and more efficiency in purchasing department operations, with consequent cost reduction.

Coordination of raw material requirements, inventory levels, and purchasing is a very significant factor in efficient operations. Material costs and inventories may have an important effect on profits, working capital, and the cash position. Buying on the spur of the moment almost always results in excess costs—if the invoiced cost is not excessive, related clerical, handling, freight, and administrative costs are certain to be. In addition, quality is frequently sacrificed when hasty purchases become necessary to prevent production stoppages. Planned purchasing results in better coordinated efforts in the purchasing and warehousing functions, with consequent reductions in these overhead costs. Perhaps the most important results are greater coordination and control of inventory levels.

In carrying out his responsibilties, the purchasing officer must continuously develop and maintain dependable sources of supply. He should be informed as to the various suppliers' potentials and limitations. Alternative sources of supply must be encouraged and developed in order to cope with such problems as (a) new sources when other suppliers fail to deliver, (b) securing improved quality, and (c) obtaining reduced prices. Needless to say, the purchasing officer has the direct responsibility of knowing the current price situation and the probable future changes. All of these responsibilities are best met when he can operate under definite policies and with a realistic projection of future needs.

Control of raw materials is facilitated in many ways by effective budgeting. Having set definitive inventory policies and standards, management has taken the first step in inventory control. Reports comparing actual inventory levels to standard inventory levels, and actual unit raw material prices with the budgeted unit prices, provide data for effective, continuous inventory control, by enabling management to exercise *management by exception.* The purchases budget, having the approval of top management, constitutes a standing order for purchasing certain qualities and quantities of raw materials at an approximate cost. Taking into account any significant variations of actual production requirements from budgeted requirements, the purchasing executive should be free to proceed with his primary responsibility of purchasing raw materials as planned. He will need to go to his superiors only when unusual circumstances arise. For example, should he get an opportunity to purchase an unusually large quantity of material at a favorable price, the proposal would be submitted to his superiors. The question, having been placed before top management, would thus be considered by others, such as the finance executive and storage personnel, who would be affected by the decision contemplated. Surely a decision based on all factors affected by the proposed action, rather than one based on the single factor of a lower unit price, would be the better. It might well be that problems in financing, warehousing, or other factors should overrule the single advantage of a lower unit price. If the raw material requirements are not known, as in cases where there is no profit plan, coordination of this type would be lacking and a large purchase at low prices might prove costly because of the expenses of warehousing, deterioration, and inventory overstocking.

Internal performance reports on at least a monthly basis should show by responsibility (a) material price variances, (b) material usage variances (including spoilage, waste, and abnormal scrap), and (c) inventory level variances from standards. To illustrate, the *two basic responsibilities* involved may be included in the monthly internal performance report along the following lines:

> (1) *Departmental supervisor's responsibility for material usage*—Actual material usage compared with standard material usage for the month and cumulative to date may be reported (a) in a separate *material usage report* segmented by using departments or (b) may be included in *departmental expense control reports* as shown in Illustration 26, Chapter 9. It may be observed that the variation

reported is due to usage because the materials are "costed" to production at standard cost. This approach is necessary for effective control since the "using" department has no control over unit material costs.

(2) *Purchasing officer's responsibility for prices, quantities purchased, and for inventory levels*—The internal report structure may vary considerably, however, Illustration 13 is suggestive.

It is important to realize that the budget responsibilities of the purchasing department chief are not ordinarily limited to direct materials budgeting. Additional budget responsibilities may involve (a) the indirect materials budget, (b) the supplies budget, and perhaps (c) the capital additions budget. The purchasing department *expense* budget is discussed in a subsequent chapter.

"X" Company

REPORT ON RAW MATERIAL PURCHASES AND INVENTORY LEVELS
For the Month of January 1963 (and cumulative to date)

	Month		Variations Above* & Below Budget	
Items	*Actual*	*Planned*	*Amt.*	*%*
Units Purchased				
Mat. A	85,000	100,000	15,000 units	15
etc.				
Unit Prices				
Mat. A	$.44	$.40	$ .04*	10*
etc.				
Dollar Outlay				
Mat. A	$37,400	$40,000	$2,600	6.5
etc.				
Inventory Levels (Turnover)				
Mat. A	2.7	2.5	0.2	8

Analysis of Variations**	Due to Price	Due to Volume	Total
Mat. A	$3,400*	$6,000	$2,600
etc.			

Comments: The unfavorable price variance of $3,400 was a result of increased market prices occasioned by shortages due to unfavorable weather in the growing areas. The favorable volume variance was due to the fact that 15,000 less units were purchased than planned because of the price increase. It is expected that the price will drop within the next 45 days.
** See Chapter 14 for computation of variances.

Illustration 13. *Performance Report on Purchases (Excerpts)*

The materials budget illustrated

The Superior Manufacturing Company uses three raw materials (A, B, and C) in producing the two products X and Y.

As indicated in Illustration 14, product X is processed through all three producing departments while product Y is processed through departments one and three only.

As shown also in Illustration 14 the standard material usage rates per unit of finished goods are:

	Units of Raw Material Required for Each Unit of Product		
	Material A	*Material B*	*Material C*
Product:			
X	1 (in Dept. 1)	2 (in Dept. 2)	2 (in Dept. 3)
Y	1 (in Dept. 1)	1 (in Dept. 3)	

The breakdown of the material budget will depend upon the particular circumstances in each concern. In turn, the breakdown will determine the number of schedules that are necessary. The Superior Manufacturing Company prepares three schedules which compose the materials budget. These schedules are as follows:

(1) *Materials budget—Unit requirements* of raw material by product, by time periods (Schedule 24).

(2) *Materials budget—Unit requirements* of raw materials by product, by time period, by departments (Schedule 25).

(3) *Materials budget summary* (Schedule 3, page 64).

The quantities shown in the three schedules were derived by multiplying the production requirements from the production budget by the raw material consumption rates given above. The unit usage rates have been included in the budget schedules for clarity of exposition. The classification of raw material by department in Schedule 25 is significant because control of raw

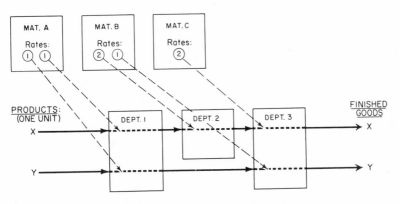

Illustration 14. *Raw Material and Product Flow*
The Superior Manufacturing Company

material usage is the responsibility of operational supervisors. Classification by product is important principally for costing purposes.

It is important to note that the materials budget shows *quantities* and *timing* of raw materials needed by the factory for specific production. Purchases must be planned in advance of these requirements. Thus the timing of raw material needs is an important factor in developing the purchases budget and in actual purchasing activities.

The Superior Manufacturing Company

MATERIALS BUDGET   **Schedule 24**
UNIT REQUIREMENTS FOR RAW MATERIALS
By Product, By Time Periods
For the Year Ending December 31, 1963

	Ref.	Product X			Product Y			Total Raw Material Required (*Units*)
		Pro-duction Planned 22	Unit Usage (Given)	Raw Material Required (*Units*)	Pro-duction Planned 22	Unit Usage (Given)	Raw Material Required (*Units*)	
Material A								
January		70,000	1	70,000	34,000	1	34,000	104,000
February		80,000	1	80,000	36,000	1	36,000	116,000
March		80,000	1	80,000	38,000	1	38,000	118,000
Total First Quarter		230,000	1	230,000	108,000	1	108,000	338,000
Second Quarter		240,000	1	240,000	140,000	1	140,000	380,000
Third Quarter		230,000	1	230,000	127,000	1	127,000	357,000
Fourth Quarter		260,000	1	260,000	145,000	1	145,000	405,000
Total		960,000	1	960,000	520,000	1	520,000	1,480,000
Material B								
January		70,000	2	140,000	34,000	1	34,000	174,000
February		80,000	2	160,000	36,000	1	36,000	196,000
March		80,000	2	160,000	38,000	1	38,000	198,000
Total First Quarter		230,000	2	460,000	108,000	1	108,000	568,000
Second Quarter		240,000	2	480,000	140,000	1	140,000	620,000
Third Querter		230,000	2	460,000	127,000	1	127,000	587,000
Fourth Quarter		260,000	2	520,000	145,000	1	145,000	665,000
Total		960,000	2	1,920,000	520,000	1	520,000	2,440,000
Material C								
January		70,000	2	140,000				140,000
February		80,000	2	160,000				160,000
March		80,000	2	160,000				160,000
Total First Quarter		230,000	2	460,000				460,000
Second Quarter		240,000	2	480,000				480,000
Third Quarter		230,000	2	460,000				460,000
Fourth Quarter		260,000	2	520,000				520,000
Total		960,000	2	1,920,000				1,920,000

The purchases and inventory budgets illustrated

It is assumed for The Superior Manufacturing Company that the average unit raw material prices for the budget period are as follows:

The Superior Manufacturing Company

UNIT RAW MATERIAL PRICE (Net of discount)
For the Year Ending December 31, 1963

Raw Material	Unit Price
A	$.30
B	.20
C	.25

It is assumed further that the initial inventories (January 1, 1963) of raw material are as follows:

Raw Material	Units	Unit Price
A	220,000	$.30
B	360,000	.20
C	460,000	.26

It will be observed that for Material C there is a different unit price as between the initial inventory and purchases; therefore, it is necessary that the *method of pricing issues* used by the cost accounting department be known. It is assumed that for raw materials The Superior Manufacturing Company uses first-in, first-out (*fifo*). Obviously, the exact initial inventory of raw materials will not be known when the budget is being prepared. The inventory units and prices given above represent, presumably, either (a) figures taken from the prior budget or (b) estimates of actual final inventory levels (for Dec. 31, 1962), based on actual levels and prices at budget preparation date, adjusted for changes expected during the remainder of the current year.

Based on the input data above, and additional quantity data from the materials budget, the purchases budget for The Superior Manufacturing Company was constructed as illustrated in Schedule 26. It will be observed that purchases are indicated in units and dollars by type of raw material by interim periods.

The illustrated purchases budget is more in the nature of a *worksheet* than an appropriate schedule for inclusion in the

The Superior Manufacturing Company

MATERIALS BUDGET—UNIT REQUIREMENTS FOR RAW MATERIALS

By Product, By Time, By Department

For the Year Ending December 31, 1963

Raw Material Unit Requirements

	Ref.	Standard Material Rates (Given)	Jan.	Feb.	March	1st Qtr.	2nd Qtr.	3rd Qtr.	4th Qtr.	Totals
Product X Scheduled Production in Units	22		70,000	80,000	80,000	230,000	240,000	230,000	260,000	960,000
Raw Material Requirements										
A used in Department 1		1	70,000	80,000	80,000	230,000	240,000	230,000	260,000	960,000
B used in Department 2		2	140,000	160,000	160,000	460,000	480,000	460,000	520,000	1,920,000
C used in Department 3		2	140,000	160,000	160,000	460,000	480,000	460,000	520,000	1,920,000
Product Y Scheduled Production in Units	22		34,000	36,000	38,000	108,000	140,000	127,000	145,000	520,000
Raw Material Requirements										
A used in Department 1		1	34,000	36,000	38,000	108,000	140,000	127,000	145,000	520,000
B used in Department 3		1	34,000	36,000	38,000	108,000	140,000	127,000	145,000	520,000
Total Material Requirements										
Department 1 Material A			104,000	116,000	118,000	338,000	380,000	357,000	405,000	1,480,000
Department 2 Material B			140,000	160,000	160,000	460,000	480,000	460,000	520,000	1,920,000
Department 3 Material B			34,000	36,000	38,000	108,000	140,000	127,000	145,000	520,000
Department 3 Material C			140,000	160,000	160,000	460,000	480,000	460,000	520,000	1,920,000

formal planning budget. It is significant to note that computation of the purchases budget *requires* that interim raw material inventory levels be determined. The purchases budget as illustrated for The Superior Manufacturing Company does not indicate inventory *valuations*. Although the schedule could be designed to show this information, it is generally desirable to set up separate inventory valuation schedules. The raw material inventory budget for The Superior Manufacturing Company, indicating inventory quantities and valuations by type of raw material by component time periods, is shown in Schedule 27.

The Superior Manufacturing Company

PURCHASES BUDGET   Schedule 26
For the Year Ending December 31, 1963

	Ref.	Units Required for Prod. 24	Add Final Inventory (Given)	Total Units Required	Less Initial Inventory (Given)	Purchases Units	Purchases Unit Cost (Given)	Purchases Total Cost
Raw Material A								
January		104,000	208,000	312,000	220,000	92,000	$0.30	$ 27,600
February		116,000	232,000	348,000	208,000	140,000		42,000
March		118,000	240,000	358,000	232,000	126,000		37,800
1st Quarter		338,000	240,000	578,000	220,000	358,000		107,400
2nd Quarter		380,000	260,000	640,000	240,000	400,000		120,000
3rd Quarter		357,000	227,000	584,000	260,000	324,000		97,200
4th Quarter		405,000	245,000	650,000	227,000	423,000		126,900
Total		1,480,000	245,000	1,725,000	220,000	1,505,000		$ 451,500
Raw Material B								
January		174,000	350,000	524,000	360,000	164,000	$0.20	$ 32,800
February		196,000	380,000	576,000	350,000	226,000		45,200
March		198,000	400,000	598,000	380,000	218,000		43,600
1st Quarter		568,000	400,000	968,000	360,000	608,000		121,600
2nd Quarter		620,000	420,000	1,040,000	400,000	640,000		128,000
3rd Quarter		587,000	400,000	987,000	420,000	567,000		113,400
4th Quarter		665,000	370,000	1,035,000	400,000	635,000		127,000
Total		2,440,000	370,000	2,810,000	360,000	2,450,000		$ 490,000
Raw Material C								
January		140,000	470,000	610,000	460,000	150,000	$0.25	$ 37,500
February		160,000	480,000	640,000	470,000	170,000		42,500
March		160,000	470,000	630,000	480,000	150,000		37,500
1st Quarter		460,000	470,000	930,000	460,000	470,000		117,500
2nd Quarter		480,000	490,000	970,000	470,000	500,000		125,000
3rd Quarter		460,000	475,000	935,000	490,000	445,000		111,250
4th Quarter		520,000	450,000	970,000	475,000	495,000		123,750
Total		1,920,000	450,000	2,370,000	460,000	1,910,000		$ 477,500
								$1,419,000

The Superior Manufacturing Company

Schedule 27

RAW MATERIAL INVENTORY BUDGET
In Units and Dollars
For the Year Ending December 31, 1963

	Ref.	MATERIAL A ($.30 per Unit)		MATERIAL B ($.20 per Unit)		MATERIAL C (See Footnotes)		Total Materials Inventory
		Units	*Amount*	*Units*	*Amount*	*Units*	*Amount*	
		26		26		26		
Beginning Inventories								
January		220,000	$66,000	360,000	$72,000	460,000	$119,600a	$257,600
February		208,000	62,400	350,000	70,000	470,000	120,700b	253,100
March		232,000	69,600	380,000	76,000	480,000	121,600c	267,200
2nd Quarter		240,000	72,000	400,000	80,000	470,000	117,500d	269,500
3rd Quarter		260,000	78,000	420,000	84,000	490,000	122,500	284,500
4th Quarter		227,000	68,100	400,000	80,000	475,000	118,750	266,850
Final Inventory		245,000	73,500	370,000	74,000	450,000	112,500	260,000

a $.26 per unit
b 320,000 units at $.26
  150,000 units at $.25
c 160,000 units at $.26
  320,000 units at $.25
d All other units at $.25

146

The Superior Manufacturing Company

ESTIMATED COST OF MATERIALS USED FOR PRODUCTION
For the Year Ending December 31, 1963

Period and Material	Ref.	Product X Units Required 25	Product X Unit Price (Given)	Product X Amount	Product Y Units Required 25	Product Y Unit Price (Given)	Product Y Amount	Totals Units 25	Totals Amount
January									
A		70,000	$.30	$ 21,000	34,000	$.30	$ 10,200	104,000	$ 31,200
B		140,000	.20	28,000	34,000	.20	6,800	174,000	34,800
C		140,000	.26	36,400				140,000	36,400
Total				$ 85,400			$ 17,000		$ 102,400
February									
A		80,000	$.30	$ 24,000	36,000	$.30	$ 10,800	116,000	$ 34,800
B		160,000	.20	32,000	36,000	.20	7,200	196,000	39,200
C		160,000	.26	41,600				160,000	$ 41,600
Total				$ 97,600			$ 18,000		$ 115,600
March									
A		80,000	$.30	$ 24,000	38,000	$.30	$ 11,400	118,000	$ 35,400
B		160,000	.20	32,000	38,000	.20	7,600	198,000	39,600
C		160,000	.26	41,600				160,000	41,600
Total				$ 97,600			$ 19,000		$ 116,600
1st Quarter									
A		230,000	$.30	$ 69,000	108,000	.30	$ 32,400	338,000	$ 101,400
B		460,000	.20	92,000	108,000	.20	21,600	568,000	113,600
C		460,000	.26	119,600				460,000	119,600
Total				$ 280,600			$ 54,000		$ 334,600
2nd Quarter									
A		240,000	$,30	$ 72,000	140,000	$.30	$ 42,000	380,000	$ 114,000
B		480,000	.20	96,000	140,000	.20	28,000	620,000	124,000
C		480,000	.25	120,000				480,000	120,000
Total				$ 288,000			$ 70,000		$ 358,000
3rd Quarter									
A		230,000	$.30	$ 69,000	127,000	$.30	$ 38,100	357,000	$ 107,100
B		460,000	.20	92,000	127,000	.20	25,400	587,000	117,400
C		460,000	.25	115,000				460,000	115,000
Total				$ 276,000			$ 63,500		$ 339,500
4th Quarter									
A		260,000	$.30	$ 78,000	145,000	$.30	$ 43,500	405,000	$ 121,500
B		520,000	.20	104,000	145,000	.20	29,000	665,000	133,000
C		520,000	.25	130,000				520,000	130,000
Total				$ 312,000			$ 72,500		$ 384,500
Total for Year				$1,156,600			$260,000		$1,416,600

The final step with respect to raw materials involves preparing a budget schedule which indicates the *cost of raw materials used for production.* This procedure is illustrated for The Superior Manufacturing Company in detail in Schedule 28. The units agree with that shown in the materials budget, with the additional factor of dollar cost. The schedule is designed primarily to show cost of raw materials used by time period for each type of *finished product*. This presentation is made so that the budgeted cost of manufacturing each product can be determined for each time period throughout the budget year. The estimated cost of materials used is summarized in Schedule 29.

The reader is reminded that, because more than one unit price is involved in Material C, some form of worksheet is necessary to derive dollar valuations for both inventory budget (Schedule 27) and the budgeted cost of materials used (Schedule 28). Because the mechanics of such a worksheet are well known it is not illustrated herein.

The Superior Manufacturing Company

ESTIMATED COST OF MATERIALS USED
FOR PRODUCTION—SUMMARY   **Schedule 29**
For the Year Ending December 31, 1963

		Totals		Product X			Product X		
	Ref.	*Units*	*Amount*	*Units*	*Price*	*Amount*	*Units*	*Price*	*Amount*
		3		3	(Given)		3	(Given)	
Materials									
A		1,480,000	$ 444,000	960,000	$.30	$ 288,000	520,000	$.30	$156,000
B		2,440,000	$ 488,000	1,920,000	.20	384,000	520,000	.20	104,000
C		1,920,000	484,600	1,920,000	a	484,600			
	28		$1,416,600			$1,156,600			$260,000

a 460,000 units @ $.26; balance @ $.25.

Discussion Questions

1. What are the principal budgets relative to raw materials? Briefly explain each.
2. Who should be responsible for preparing each of the budgets given in your answer to question 1?
3. How is material usually classified for cost accounting purposes? Relate these classifications to the materials budget.
4. What are the principal methods used in developing raw materials quantity requirements?
5. Why is it usually desirable that budget schedules as *originally* prepared be recast prior to inclusion in the final planning budget for distribution?
6. What are the principal differences between the materials budget and the purchases budget?
7. What are the principal purposes in developing the purchases budget?

8. What is the relationship between the materials budget, the purchases budget, and the raw material inventory budget?
9. What are the principal considerations in setting raw material inventory policies?
10. Generally, how should raw material unit costs be estimated?
11. Relate the materials, purchases, and cost of materials used budgets to the objectives of profit planning and control.

S E V E N

Planning and Controlling

Direct Labor Costs

In many companies labor costs (in the broad sense) are greater than all other costs combined. Even where this is not the case, careful planning and systematic control of labor costs are essential. In the broad sense planning and controlling labor costs involves the major and complex areas of (a) manpower needs, (b) recruitment, (c) training, (d) job evaluation and specification, (e) manpower evaluation, (f) union negotiations, and (g) wage and salary administration. Each of these problems may be paramount in a particular situation. A comprehensive budget program should be designed around appropriate techniques and approaches developed to apply to each of these problem areas. A budget program does not satisfy the specific needs with respect to these special personnel problems; but profit planning and control does tend to direct careful consideration to them and helps put them in proper perspective. Careful planning and realistic control of labor costs, if viewed in terms of the long as well as short run, will result in positive benefits to both the company and the employees.

Labor costs, in the broad sense, encompass all expenditures for those employed by the firm: top executives, middle management personnel, staff officers, supervisors, foremen, skilled workers, and manual laborers. To effectively plan and control labor costs, it is necessary to consider separately the several types of labor costs. This chapter is concerned with only one type of labor cost, *direct labor.*

For cost accounting purposes labor generally is classified as *direct* and *indirect*. Direct labor costs consist of the wages paid to

150

workers who are engaged directly in specific productive operations. As with direct material costs, labor costs that can be readily identified with specific production are classified as direct. Indirect labor involves all other labor costs, such as supervisory salaries, wages paid toolmakers, repairmen, storekeepers, custodians, and so forth. Direct material and labor costs are frequently referred to as *prime costs*.

The direct labor budget comprises the estimates of direct labor requirements necessary to produce the types and quantities of outputs planned in the production budget. Although some concerns prepare a labor budget that includes both direct and indirect labor, it is generally preferable to prepare a separate direct labor budget and to include indirect labor in the manufacturing expense or overhead budget. This procedure is consistent with the usual cost accounting treatment of labor costs. Overtime and premium pay related to direct labor should be budgeted as separate items. Budgeting of these latter costs should be developed along with the direct labor budget; however, such costs are generally included in the manufacturing expense category.[1]

The principal purposes of developing a detailed direct labor budget as a part of the annual profit plan are:

(1) To determine the direct labor required in terms of labor hours, and hence, the number and kind of workers needed to meet the planned production;

(2) To estimate the direct labor cost of production so that product costs can be budgeted;

(3) To provide the personnel department with manpower requirements so that it may plan recruitment activities;

(4) To provide data for determination of cash requirements (cash budget) for direct labor;

(5) To provide data for managerial control of direct labor costs.

The responsibility for preparing the direct labor budget should be assigned to the executive in charge of manufacturing. The cost accounting and personnel departments may well be called on for assistance and appropriate data. Once the direct labor budget is completed by the manufacturing division, it should be submitted to the budget director to be checked and then submitted to the budget committee at the appropriate stage in the

---

[1] Overtime and premium costs are those costs above the regular direct labor hour rate. For example, if one direct labor employee whose hourly rate was $2.00 worked one hour overtime at time and one-half, the overtime cost would be $1.00; the $2.00 is still considered as direct labor cost.

construction of the planning budget. When the direct labor budget is tentatively approved, it becomes part of the annual profit plan.

Technically, the direct labor budget may take several forms. Separate schedules are developed for (a) direct labor hours and (b) direct labor costs similar to the illustration at the end of this chapter. Assuming wage rates have been established, control of direct labor is achieved best in terms of direct labor hours rather than in dollars, hence, separate scheduling by hours is quite general.

Problems involved in planning direct labor costs

For the annual profit plan the direct labor budget should be developed in terms of both *direct labor hours* and *direct labor costs*—and by responsibilities, by interim periods, and by product. Classification by organizational responsibility and by interim periods is essential for control purposes; classification by product is essential for *costing production.*

The approach that should be used in developing these data for the direct labor budget depends principally upon (a) the method of wage payment; (b) the type of production processes involved; (c) the availability of standard labor times; and (d) the adequacy of the cost accounting records relating to direct labor costs.

Basically there are three possible approaches to the development of the direct labor budget:

(1) Estimate the standard direct labor hours required for each unit of each product, then estimate the *average wage rates* by department, cost center, or operation. Multiplication of the standard time per unit of product by the average wage rates involved gives the labor cost per unit of production for the department, cost center, or operation. Multiplication of the units of goods to be produced in the department, cost center, or operation by the unit labor cost rate gives the direct labor cost.

(2) Estimate direct ratios of labor cost to some measure of volume or output that can be projected realistically.

(3) Develop manning tables.

In recent years some companies have developed *manning tables* to aid in planning and controlling over-all labor costs.[2] Under

[2] "New Ways to Slash Labor Costs and Boost Profits," *Factory Management and Maintenance*, Vol. 115, No. 1 (Jan. 1957) p. 78.

this procedure each department is required to prepare a manning table listing individual positions classified by types of jobs. One such classification is *direct labor*. Under this classification would be listed, for specific outputs, the exact number of employees (man days) for each type of work done in the department.[3]

Estimating direct labor hours

Internal conditions will determine whether or not it is feasible to express production in terms of direct labor hours, as well as in terms of dollar cost. Similarly, internal factors will determine the most practicable approach for estimating direct labor hours.

Many firms have developed cost accounting systems that utilize direct labor hours in each department as the basis for applying manufacturing overhead to production. In such cases, generally sound methods have been developed for estimating the direct labor hours involved in production.

One of the important phases of *industrial engineering* is the development of standard labor times for various operations. In some manufacturing departments the development of reliable labor time standards is possible; in other situations, it may be impracticable except in terms of averages based on past experience. Four commonly used approaches in planning standard labor *times* may be outlined as follows:

(1) *Time and motion studies*—Such studies generally are made by industrial engineers. They involve analyzing the work on a product (or in a department) into a series of specific operations. By means of observation (and by actual timing with a stopwatch) standard time for each specific operation is determined. Obviously, the industrial engineer has to cope with the problem (and frequently the union) as to whether the fastest, slowest, or average worker shall be used for the timing. Nevertheless, time and motion studies may provide reliable information concerning the labor time necessary to perform certain operations. The result of time and motion studies can therefore provide basic input data for developing the direct labor hour requirements to meet the scheduled production; under the supervision of competent industrial engineers, time and motion studies represent the most desirable approach to the establishment of labor standards.[4]

---

[3] See Ch. 8.
[4] Ralph M. Barnes, *Motion and Time Study*, 4th ed. (New York: Wiley, 1958).

(2) *Standard costs*—If *standard costs* are being employed for labor in the cost accounting records, careful studies of direct labor hour requirements per unit of production will generally have been made. In such cases the standard labor hours per unit of product are multiplied by the quantity of production called for to derive labor hour requirements. Frequently such standards are rather exacting, so that allowances should be budgeted for variations from standard hours in order to meet the short-run goals anticipated in the annual planning budget.

(3) *Direct estimate by supervisor*—Some companies require each productive department supervisor to estimate the direct labor hours required for the budgeted output of his department. In making such estimates, the supervisor relies on (a) his judgment, (b) performance of the department as reported over the recent past, and (c) assistance from one or more staff officers.

(4) *Statistical estimates by a staff group*—Cost accounting records of past performance usually provide valuable information for converting production requirements to direct labor hours. This approach is frequently used by concerns for productive departments that process several products simultaneously. The historical ratio of direct labor hours to some measure of physical output is computed and then adjusted for any altered conditions. Obviously the accuracy of this method depends upon the reliability of the cost records and the uniformity of the production process from period to period. Even though some other method of estimating direct labor hours is used, historical ratios of direct labor hours to physical output are frequently good checks on the accuracy of the other method.

Some concerns find it desirable to use several approaches in estimating direct labor hours. A particular method applicable in one productive department or cost center may not be equally applicable in another department or cost center. There should be continuous effort to improve existing procedures and to adopt new one that are more appropriate.

Planning average wage rates

If it is possible to plan production in terms of direct labor hours and to realistically develop average wage rates for each productive department, computation of direct labor cost is merely a matter of multiplying the one by the other. Within a particular concern there may be one or more productive departments where this direct approach is feasible.

Determination of *average* direct labor wage rates in a particular productive department or cost center frequently may not present a serious problem. The usual approach is to estimate such rates on the basis of an enumeration of direct workers in the department and their expected wage rate. The union contract may be the determining factor in some cases. Another approach involves determination of the historical ratio between wages paid, and direct labor hours worked, in the department. The historical ratio is then adjusted for conditions that have changed or are expected to change.

It is important to realize that average wage rates based on historial data are useful for future planning only to the extent that there is consistency in operations and in the hours worked at different wage rates. For example, assume the following historical data;

Worker	Hours	Rate	Labor Cost
A	2,000	$1.50	$3,000
B	3,000	2.00	6,000
Totals	5,000	$1.80	$9,000

The average wage rate based on the data above is $1.80; however, should the budgeted hours for each worker be 2,500, with no changes in wage rates, the average rate would be $1.75 rather than $1.80; the difference indicates the type of adjustment that would have to be made in average rates if the ratio of hours worked to different individual wage rates changes.

In some cases the size of the department, the diversity of work done therein, and variations in hourly wages may be of such significance that the department should be subdivided into *cost centers*. Separate direct labor estimates and average wage rates would then be planned for each cost center.

If standard costs are used in the cost accounting department, the standard wage rates already developed may be used for budgeting purposes; however, it may be desirable to budget certain wage rate variances between standard allowances and planning budget allowances.

Estimating direct labor cost

The preceding discussion set forth two estimates—hours and wage rates—necessary to derive direct labor costs. This approach has definite advantages; however, practical considerations frequently make the approach inadvisable if not impossible. The other principal approach is that of estimating direct labor *cost* directly. This method involves making an estimate of direct cost (a) per unit of production or (b) in terms of some measure of production, such as direct machine hours or direct material cost.

If a straight piece-rate system of compensating labor is used, the labor cost per unit of production is known precisely. The piece-rate system bases the compensation upon the quantity produced. The various bonus systems of wage payments complicate the estimation of direct labor costs. In such cases, ratios are generally used.

The ratio approach relates direct labor cost in the past to some measure of output for the same period. The cost ratio thus derived represents the historical labor cost relationships and therefore must be adjusted for planned changes affecting such relationships. In the case of new products a rough estimate may be necessary. If accurate cost and production data are available and are carefully analyzed, accurate estimates usually are possible.

Planning and control aspects of the direct labor budget

Careful planning of direct labor requirements for the budgeted period can have beneficial results throughout the firm in a number of ways:

(1) The personnel function can be more efficiently performed because there is a basis for planning recruitment and training. The personnel department can itself be better organized as a result of knowing something of the extent of volume of work activities expected of it.

(2) The finance function can be more efficiently planned and carried out because labor may represent one of the largest demands on cash during the year. Knowing the direct labor cost enables the finance officer to estimate by interim periods the cash requirements for labor.

(3) The budgeted cost unit of manufacturing can be developed. This cost may be an important factor in several areas of decision making such as pricing policy and union negotiations.

(4) Control and reduction of direct labor costs rests upon careful planning of direct labor. The importance of stable production (which gives rise to stable employment) can be evaluated more clearly.

Control of direct labor costs may be one of the major problems facing the management of a particular company. Obviously, an important element in controlling direct labor costs is consistently competent supervision; direct observation and individual contacts with the work force by the foremen and supervisors are basic to such control. However, there is a definite need for standards by which the supervisor may gauge performance. Planning of the flow of work and arrangement of supplies, equipment, and so forth may have a definite effect on direct labor costs. From these brief observations, we see the two primary aspects of the control of direct labor costs: (1) the day-to-day concern with such costs and (2) the longer-run reporting and evaluation of results.

Considering the day-to-day concern with direct labor costs, aside from the direct supervision mentioned above, many firms have developed reasonable labor standards for many operations. Frequently these standards are compared with actual results and reported daily. For example, the author is reminded of one firm, where direct labor costs are particularly significant, that instituted a daily report on direct labor costs for the foremen. By nine o'clock each morning, each foreman has a report on direct labor performance for the preceding day. Basically the report shows (a) actual hours worked, (b) standard hours for the actual output, and (c) time variations. Such reports may be in terms of time only, or in terms of both time and dollar costs, depending upon the control elements that are vested in the foremen.[5]

Considering the longer-run reporting and evaluation of direct labor, the monthly performance report for management use should include control data, by responsibility, on direct labor as compared with the standards, however developed. These reports are essential for managerial evaluation of the status of control. They may give rise to managerial actions directed toward raising over-all operational efficiency through decisions such as adding new equipment to replace hand labor, rearrangement of operations, and redesign of products. These reports may be (a) separate schedules or (b) additions to the departmental expense control report similar to Illustration 26, Chapter 9.

Variations that are reported as a result of comparing actual direct labor costs with the standard or budget allowance, may be due to (a) labor usage (labor efficiency variation) or (b) labor wage rates (wage rate variation). Labor usage is controllable at the foreman's level by means of the approaches indicated above. On the other hand the wage rate variation is controllable at the time the wage rates are set (frequently in management-

---

[5] For another example see: Fred E. Andersen, "How We Achieve and Utilize Effective Daily Labor Reporting," *NAA Bulletin* (Jan. 1959) Sec. 1, pp. 90–95.

union negotiations) and also at the worker level. To illustrate, a foreman may create a wage rate variation by using workers with higher wage rates than the particular operation requires per the standard.[6]

The direct labor budget illustrated

In manufacturing Product X, The Superior Manufacturing Company incurs direct labor costs in each of the three producing departments. The manufacture of Product Y involves direct labor in departments one and three only. The industrial engineers in the manufacturing division, through time studies and analysis of production runs, have developed the following standard times as *budget input data* for each product:

	Direct Labor Hours per Unit of Product	
Department	*Product X*	*Product Y*
1	.4	.2
2	.2	—
3	.4	.2

An analysis of historical labor costs, together with the provisions of the union contract, provided the following expected average hourly pay rates:

Department	*Average Hourly Wage Rates*
1	$2.00
2	1.50
3	1.00

The detailed direct labor budget for The Superior Manufacturing Company is shown in Schedule 30. Units to be produced were taken from the production budget and extended, using the input data above. For clarity of understanding, computations are indicated on the schedule. It will be observed that the classification of labor cost is by product, by time period, and by organizational responsibility (department). This classification is consistent with that used for the planning budget as a whole, as indicated in all prior detailed budget schedules prepared for The Superior Manufacturing Company.

The direct labor budget *in hours only* is shown in Schedule 31. Obviously these same hours are shown in Schedule 30; however, it is generally desirable to prepare a separate schedule

[6] "Reports Which Managements Find Most Useful," Accounting Practice Report No. 9, *N.A.A. Bulletin*, Sec. 3. Also refer to Ch. 14.

DIRECT LABOR BUDGET
For the Year Ending December 31, 1963

	Ref.	Product X					Product Y					Total Labor Cost
		Units to be Produced 22	Standard Hours (Given)	Total Standard Productive Hours	Rate per Hour (Given)	Amount	Units to be Produced 22	Standard Hours (Given)	Total Standard Productive Hours	Rate per Hour (Given)	Amount	
January												
Dept. 1		70,000	.4	28,000	$2.00	$ 56,000	34,000	.2	6,800	$2.00	$ 13,600	$ 69,600
Dept. 2		70,000	.2	14,000	1.50	21,000						21,000
Dept. 3		70,000	.4	28,000	1.00	28,000	34,000	.2	6,800	1.00	6,800	34,800
Totals				70,000		$ 105,000			13,600		$ 20,400	$ 125,400
February												
Dept. 1		80,000	.4	32,000	$2.00	$ 64,000	36,000	.2	7,200	$2.00	$ 14,400	$ 78,400
Dept. 2		80,000	.2	16,000	1.50	24,000						24,000
Dept. 3		80,000	.4	32,000	1.00	32,000	36,000	.2	7,200	1.00	7,200	39,200
Totals				80,000		$ 120,000			14,400		$ 21,600	$ 141,600
March												
Dept. 1		80,000	.4	32,000	$2.00	$ 64,000	38,000	.2	7,600	$2.00	$ 15,200	$ 79,200
Dept. 2		80,000	.2	16,000	1.50	24,000						24,000
Dept. 3		80,000	.4	32,000	1.00	32,000	38,000	.2	7,600	1.00	7,600	39,600
Totals				80,000		$ 120,000			15,200		$ 22,800	$ 142,800
1st Quarter												
Dept. 1		230,000	.4	92,000	$2.00	$ 184,000	108,000	.2	21,600	$2.00	$ 43,200	$ 227,200
Dept. 2		230,000	.2	46,000	1.50	69,000						69,000
Dept. 3		230,000	.4	92,000	1.00	92,000	108,000	.2	21,600	1.00	21,600	113,600
Totals				230,000		$ 345,000			43,200		$ 64,800	$ 409,800
2nd Quarter												
Dept. 1		240,000	.4	96,000	$2.00	$ 192,000	140,000	.2	28,000	$2.00	$ 56,000	$ 248,000
Dept. 2		240,000	.2	48,000	1.50	72,000						72,000
Dept. 3		240,000	.4	96,000	1.00	96,000	140,000	.2	28,000	1.00	28,000	124,000
Totals				240,000		$ 360,000			56,000		$ 84,000	$ 444,000
3rd Quarter												
Dept. 1		230,000	.4	92,000	$2.00	$ 184,000	127,000	.2	25,400	$2.00	$ 50,800	$ 234,800
Dept. 2		230,000	.2	46,000	1.50	69,000						69,000
Dept. 3		230,000	.4	92,000	1.00	92,000	127,000	.2	25,400	1.00	25,400	117,400
Totals				230,000		$ 345,000			50,800		$ 76,200	$ 421,200
4th Quarter												
Dept. 1		260,000	.4	104,000	$2.00	$ 208,000	145,000	.2	29,000	$2.00	$ 58,000	$ 266,000
Dept. 2		260,000	.2	52,000	1.50	78,000						78,000
Dept. 3		260,000	.4	104,000	1.00	104,000	145,000	.2	29,000	1.00	29,000	133,000
Totals				260,000		$ 390,000			58,800		$ 87,000	$ 477,000
Totals for Year				960,000		$1,440,000			208,000		$312,000	$1,752,000

The Superior Manufacturing Company

DIRECT LABOR BUDGET IN HOURS

For the Year Ending December 31, 1963

	Total	Department 1			Department 2			Department 3		
		Product X	Product Y	Total	Product X	Product Y	Total	Product X	Product Y	Total
Ref.		30	30		30			30	30	
January	83,600	28,000	6,800	34,800	14,000	—	14,000	28,000	6,800	34,800
February	94,400	32,000	7,200	39,200	16,000	—	16,000	32,000	7,200	39,200
March	95,200	32,000	7,600	39,600	16,000	—	16,000	32,000	7,600	39,600
Total 1st Quarter	273,200	92,000	21,600	113,600	46,000	—	46,000	92,000	21,600	113,600
2nd Quarter	296,000	96,000	28,000	124,000	48,000	—	48,000	96,000	28,000	124,000
3rd Quarter	280,800	92,000	25,400	117,400	46,000	—	46,000	92,000	25,400	117,400
4th Quarter	318,000	104,000	29,000	133,000	52,000	—	52,000	104,000	29,000	133,000
Total Year	1,168,000	384,000	104,000	488,000	192,000	—	192,000	384,000	104,000	488,000

which specifies hours only. These data are needed in subsequent budget schedules of manufacturing overhead. The Superior Manufacturing Company uses predetermined overhead or burden rates to cost actual production in each productive department. The departmental overhead rates are based on *direct labor hours* budgeted for each department. For purposes of simplicity, payroll deductions have been disregarded.

Discussion Questions

1. Define the direct labor budget.
2. Who should be responsible for developing the direct labor budget?
3. What are the principal objectives in developing the direct labor budget?
4. What are the two principal approaches in developing the direct labor budget?
5. Generally how should direct labor hours be estimated?
6. How may the direct labor budget be related to the problem of manufacturing overhead or burden?
7. Generally, how should estimated average wage rates be developed?
8. Is direct labor normally a fixed cost, a variable cost, or a semivariable cost? Explain.
9. How should direct labor be classified in the direct labor budget? Explain.
10. How can budgeting direct labor contribute to managerial planning and control?

E I G H T

Planning and Controlling Expenses

Managerial decisions must be *forward-looking*; therefore estimates of future costs and expenses are especially significant for managerial planning and control. Cost control procedures must be tied firmly to estimates of future costs and expenses because the essence of such control is a comparison of actual costs with a *standard* of what costs *should be* under a given set of policies and conditions.

This and the following chapter are devoted to the problems of planning and controlling costs, especially as these problems relate to a comprehensive budget program. This chapter emphasizes the consideration of costs and expenses for the *annual profit plan*. The next chapter will emphasize the techniques and uses of *variable expense budgets* for cost control purposes.

Up to this point planning and control of direct material and direct labor costs have been considered from the budget point of view. It is logical next to consider other categories of cost normally incurred in business operation. Therefore, after a general consideration of certain cost concepts, this chapter will be subdivided (to facilitate discussion) as follows:

(1) Manufacturing expense (factory overhead)
(2) Distribution or selling expenses
(3) General administrative expenses
(4) Financial or other expenses

General considerations

Because we are concerned primarily with the planning and controlling of costs, it is appropriate to call attention to the discussion in Chapter 1 concerning the fundamentals of planning (pages 9–13) and control (pages 14–17). In this and the next chapter, the discussions will be directed toward specific concepts and procedures useful in applying those fundamentals. As in all discussions of costs, it is well to remember that cost constructions (classifications) are conditioned by the problem at hand; what is termed *cost* for one purpose or use may be a quite inappropriate cost construction for another purpose even though essentially the same *underlying data* may be relevant.

Classification of Costs by Responsibility. Because control is exercised through responsibilities, it is necessary that costs be planned in terms of the organizational structure. The chart of accounts used by the accounting department, and the design of the *cost side* of the budget, must be tailored to organizational responsibilities.

In considering the concept of *costs by responsibility*, it is well to call attention again (see page 32) to the fact that most of the allocations of costs that are deemed essential for *financial accounting purposes* are most inappropriate for control purposes; such allocations are generally of an arbitary nature and are seldom controllable by the organizational unit to which allocated. In principle, then, we would observe that *cost allocation generally* tends to defeat the control objectives.

Cost Reduction and Cost Control. In view of the varying discussions concerning cost control, it is useful to keep in mind a distinction that frequently is made between two related concepts, *cost reduction* and *cost control.* Cost reduction programs are directed toward specific efforts to reduce costs through improvement of such factors as methods, approaches, work arrangements, and product improvements. To illustrate, one company reported a significant reduction in costs of manufacturing a small screen designed to cover an air intake by simply reducing the number of cross wires (without reducing the utility) that needed to be "turned" as shown in Illustration 15 below. Another firm, as a result of a cost reduction program,

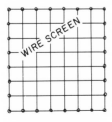
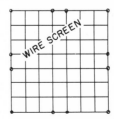

PRIOR METHOD–
ALL 28 ENDS TURNED

NEW METHOD–
ONLY 12 ENDS TURNED

Illustration 15. *Cost Reduction Example*

replaced all old-style water faucets with others that automatically turned off when released; the consequent saving was substantial.

In the broad sense, cost control includes *cost reduction*; however, in a narrower sense, cost control may be thought of as the managerial efforts to keep costs at or below a standard, i.e., to minimize costs under a given set of conditions or manner of operation. Obviously, management should attack costs from all directions—through cost reduction programs, cost planning, and continuous attention to the cost-incurring decisions. Separate attention to the two concepts of cost reduction and cost control frequently is advisable.

Classification of Costs When Related to Volume or Output. One of the most significant aspects of budgeting and managerial accounting is the analysis and classification of costs as they relate to output, volume, or activity. Knowledge of how costs relate to changes in output (however measured) has significant bearing on many managerial decisions.

Costs, when related to volume or output, may be classified as fixed, variable, or semivariable.

Fixed costs—costs or expenses that remain constant, or essentially constant, irrespective of changes in volume or activity.

Variable costs—costs or expenses that increase and decrease proportionally with increases or decreases in volume or activity.

Semivariable costs—costs or expenses that are neither fixed nor variable, but which possess some of the characteristics of both.

Determination of the relationship of costs to volume or output is fundamental to a number of important techniques such as variable budgets, breakeven analyses, direct costing, and differential cost analyses. Each of these techniques is considered in subsequent chapters; the next chapter is devoted exclusively to variable budgets.

Controllable and Noncontrollable Costs. Closely related to the classification of expenses in accordance with responsibility is the classification of expenses as controllable and noncontrollable. Controllable expenses are those which are, in the main, subject to the authority and responsibility of a specific individual. Care must be exercised in the application of this classification because the classification of an item of expense as controllable or noncontrollable must be made within a specific framework of *responsibility* and *time*. For example, the expenses of a particular department normally include some items, such as supervisory salaries, which are not ordinarily controllable within the department, but rather at higher levels of management. Thus within the framework of the department, such an expense may be classified as noncontrollable; yet when viewed in terms of larger organizational segments, or for the firm as a whole, it is controllable. Similarily, expenses such as depreciation generally are not controllable within the short run, but are definitely controllable in the long run because managerial decisions concerning capital additions in turn determine the amount of subsequent depreciation charges. In the final analysis, all costs and expenses are controllable at one level, or time, or another. Thus the concept of controllability is useful for cost control if cost classification is based upon a sound structure of authority and responsibility. The individual items of expense in each department, or other subdivision of the firm, should be clearly indentified as controllable or noncontrollable within that particular area of responsibility. This designation is especially important in cost control and in the reporting of comparisons between actual and budget which purport to measure the performance of specific individuals. Occasionally it may be advisable to establish two accounts for a particular type of expense in a department. For example, departmental salaries may be carried in two accounts, Salaries—Controllable and Salaries—Noncontrollable, and budgeted in this manner.

Some firms follow the policy of including in performance reports for a particular department only those items of cost which are controllable within the department. Other firms follow the procedure of including all departmental costs and expenses, clearly identifying the noncontrollable items. For either method, however, it is important that every cost and expense be included on some report and identified as the responsibility of some member of management. Items marked noncontrollable on departmental performance reports should be included as controllable on other reports relating to higher levels of responsibility.

Note that the classifications, controllable and fixed, and noncontrollable and variable, are not synonymous. It is generally true that in the short run, fixed costs are not subject to the same degree of control as are variable costs. Practically all variable costs, by their nature, are controllable in the short run. On the other hand it is obvious that depreciation on an output basis, for example, is a variable cost, yet noncontrollable in the short run; conversely, certain salaries are controllable in the short run, yet are fixed costs.

Planning Expenses. In developing the annual profit plan, costs and expenses for each organizational subdivision must be carefully planned. Expense planning should involve all levels of supervisory responsibilities so that an expense budget (detailed by each item of expense) is developed for each department, division, and other organizational units. In planning expenses for each organizational unit (by responsibility), it is necessary first that the volume of work, output, or activity for that unit be estimated. For example, in order to develop an expense plan for the power department, the expected demands on the power must be estimated; an expenditure plan for research and development must be related to the type and extent of research activities planned. Thus, we see that all expense planning should be directly keyed to planned or expected activities and accomplishments.

With respect to formal development of the *annual profit plan* (planning budget), we would expect to include therein separate *budget expense schedules* for each cost-incurring unit. We have already considered the development of direct material and direct labor budget schedules. As to the mechanics of developing the annual profit plan, the following sequence is suggested as typical:

(1) *Direct material and labor costs*—Budgets developed immediately after the production budget is completed and tentatively approved.

(2) *Factory overhead*—Budgets developed immediately after the production budget, as tentatively approved, is *converted* to expected output (however measured) for each producing and each service department in the factory.

(3) *Distribution costs*—Budgets developed *concurrently* with the development of the sales budget because they are mutually dependent.

(4) *Administrative costs*—Budgets developed immediately after the sales budget (and perhaps the production budget), as approved, is *converted* to expected *activity* for each administrative department involved.

Detailed expense budgets should be included in the annual profit plan for a number of reasons, principally these:

(1) So that the effects of various planned revenues and related expenses may be aggregated in a budgeted income statement.

(2) So that the cash outflow required for costs and expenses can be estimated realistically.

(3) To provide an initial expense objective (limitation) for each department.

(4) To provide a standard to be used in the period covered by

the profit plan for each item of expense in each department for comparison with actual costs and for internal management purposes.

These four reasons suggest the importance of the careful planning of expenses and the use of them for further planning, control, and evaluation.

Relationship of annual profit plan with variable expense budgets

We have already noted that variable budgets may be used to complement the planning budget (annual profit plan) procedures; therefore, it is appropriate to elaborate on their relationship to the annual profit plan and to expense control.

Many companies do not employ variable expense budget procedures. In these companies, development of the annual profit plan involves analysis of expenses, department by department, in order to develop the detailed expense budgets mentioned above for each department. The planning of expenses for the annual profit plan is further complicated by the fact that the expense budgets must be detailed for interim periods within the budget period as well as by department. A sequential problem is thus presented; the departmental expense budgets cannot be developed until the *planned* amount of *activity* for each department has been determined. Sales and productive effort in turn determine the amount of activity that must be planned for the various departments; thus we have a critical problem of converting sales expectations and production plans into departmental activity requirements. This problem was discussed in Chapter 5 and will be given further consideration subsequently. In cases where variable expense budgets are not used for cost control purposes the departmental expense budgets included in the annual profit plan are compared with actual expenses as the firm moves through the budget period. Some companies have found these original departmental expense budgets to be suitable for cost control purposes. This approach to planning and controlling expenses frequently has been referred to as *fixed budget* procedures.

In contrast, some firms employ *variable budget* procedures for planning and controlling expenses. In Chapter 3 (pages 45–46) the variable expense budget was listed as one component of a comprehensive budget program; also in that chapter, the concept of the variable budget was discussed briefly and illustrated (pages 53 and 75). It is suggested that the reader review these prior discussions. A detailed consideration of variable budgets follows in Chapter 9.

When variable expense budget procedures are employed, expression is given to the relationship of each expense to activity (department by department); thus variable budgets are based on the fixed-variable cost classification mentioned above. Because variable budgets are not related to a specific level of planned activity, but rather to the relevant range of activity, they can be developed early in the budget preparation period, perhaps concurrently with the sales and production budgets. As a matter of fact, the various formulae comprising the variable budgets should be determined prior to the timing of the development of the expense budgets for the annual profit plan. As illustrated in Chapter 3, and also at the end of this chapter (The Superior Manufacturing Company), because variable budgets are available, the expense budgets for the *annual profit plan* are developed clerically by applying the variable expense budget formulae to the planned output department by department. Thus we observe a desirable sequential change in developing the annual profit plan.

Although variable budgets may complement the development of the annual profit plan, the primary objective of variable budget procedures is the *control* of expenses. When variable budgets are available, actual expenses are compared throughout the period with *adjusted* budget allowances—that is, with budget allowances adjusted to the actual level of activity. The difference in approach to the control of costs becomes especially important when the activity of a department differs significantly from that planned in the annual profit plan.

Fixed and variable expense budget procedures for expenses are frequently viewed as if they are mutually exclusive. As has been implied, some companies use fixed budget procedures for planning and controlling expenses; others use variable budget procedures; still others use fixed budget procedures in some departments and variable budget procedures in other departments. The last situation is frequently the case and is to be preferred in the opinion of the author. The choice of approach, whether company-wide or for individual departments, should depend upon the nature of the departmental activities, the inherent control problems, and the accuracy with which activity can be planned. It is true that in some situations the classification of costs as fixed and variable is impracticable, if not impossible; however, the author is convinced that such classification can be achieved effectively in many more circumstances than is commonly supposed. Too frequently the insistence on precise theoretical distinctions obscures the more practical considerations. The test should be the needs of management and the degree of accuracy required. Management frequently does not need, nor will it pay for, an excessive degree of accuracy in these matters.

Whatever the approach, the expense budgets included in the annual profit plan must be prepared in identical form; the difference at this point is in the development of the amounts. If the variability of costs within a firm or department can be determined within practical limits of accuracy, then management may be provided with a powerful control tool. This ideal is assumed throughout this book.

Considerations in budgeting manufacturing expense or overhead

The three factory cost or expense budgets (material, labor, and overhead) are usually developed simultaneously and are consolidated in the schedule of *cost of goods manufactured*. Manufacturing expense or overhead is that part of total factory cost which is not included in direct material and direct labor cost, because it is not directly identifiable with specific products or jobs. Manufacturing expense consists of (a) indirect material, (b) indirect labor, and (c) miscellaneous factory expense items such as taxes, insurance, depreciation, power, supplies, utilities, and repairs. Each of these costs represents major problems in themselves.[1] In highly mechanized manufacturing situations, this element of cost may be of considerable significance.

The fact that manufacturing overhead includes many dissimilar types of expenses creates considerable problems for management, especially in the *allocation* of these costs to production, and in *cost control*. As there are many different types of expenses, control responsibility is often widely diffused. For example, such items as depreciation, taxes, and insurance are not generally subject to the direct control of factory management, but to that of higher level management.

There are two distinct types of departments or cost centers in practically all manufacturing situations, each involving serious

[1] To illustrate, see: "Planning, Controlling and Accounting for Maintenance," *Accounting Practice Report No. 2* (New York: National Association of Accountants, 1955), 27 pp.

---

cost accounting and budget problems: (a) direct producing departments and (b) service departments. Direct producing departments are those manufacturing departments that work directly on the products manufactured. Service departments do not work on the products directly, but rather furnish service to the direct producing departments and to other service departments. Typical service departments in a factory are: maintenance or repair department, power department, purchases department, production planning department, time and motion study department, and general factory administration. The responsibility for the operation of each department should be assigned to a single individual; the costs for each department should be classified separately in the chart of accounts used by the cost accounting department; and, finally, the costs of each department should be budgeted separately.

The Dual Problem of Manufacturing Expense or Burden. Relative to both budgeting and cost accounting, manufacturing overhead presents a unique challenge in that there is a dual problem involved:

(1) The control of manufacturing overhead.
(2) The allocation of manufacturing overhead to products manufactured (costing production)

These two phases present different problems and require different approaches for solution. All too frequently they are viewed as one problem, with a consequent limitation on the usefulness of the solution. *The difference between the two problems is critical with respect to the distribution of service department and other indirect burden costs to the producing departments.*

For control purposes it is preferable to deal with "clean" costs, that is, direct departmental costs only, exclusive of any allocated costs. For example, let us assume that Producing Department No. 1 uses a considerable amount of power produced by the Power department. In accumulating actual costs, in budgeting costs, and in cost reporting for *control purposes,* the costs of the Power department must be identified with the supervisor of the Power department only, whereas the costs of Producing Department No. 1 must be identified with the supervisor of Producing Department No. 1, exclusive of allocations of actual power cost. The supervisor of the Power department (a service department) is responsible for the costs of the services rendered; the supervisor of the using department has no control over them. What he *does* control is the *amount of the services* (power) *used*, rather than the cost of the service. Therefore the performance report of Producing Department No. 1 should reflect the quantity of power used compared with the quantity of power that should have been used in producing the volume of goods completed. In summary, it is preferable that service usage be controlled on the basis of *units of service*, when possible, rather than on the basis of dollar cost of service. If it is desirable to use dollar cost, then the using department should be charged at *standard rates* rather than at actual rates. It is obvious, then, that *cost allocation generally is inappropriate for effective cost control.*

On the other hand, in order to determine the *cost of goods manufactured* by product, it is obviously necessary that indirect costs be allocated. In the example just cited, it is necessary that the costs of power used by Producing Department No. 1 be loaded on the output of that department in order to determine realistically the total cost of producing goods in Producing Department No. 1. Thus it is obvious that *cost allocation is essential to product costing.*

These two concepts concerning the control and costing of manufacturing expense are illustrated subsequently in this chapter for The Superior Manufacturing Company.

Construction of the manufacturing expense budget

For the planning budget (annual profit plan), construction of the manufacturing expense budget involves the preparation of a budget of expense for each department of the factory. These budgets of expense should follow the expense classification used by the accounting department. Budgeted expenses generally should be indicated for the time periods within the budget period in the same manner as in the sales, production, and prime cost budgets (direct material and direct labor). At this point the problems incident to the preparation of the budget schedules of manufacturing expense will depend upon whether or not departmental *variable budgets* have been developed. At this point the firm is faced with the problem of developing manufacturing expense allowances for the specific volume called for in the production budget. The reliability with which the expense estimates can be made depends upon (a) the quality of the accounting records, and (b) the seriousness of management's attitude toward expense planning. Where there are adequate and well-kept accounting records, an important source of data upon which expense estimates can be based is available.

As is the case with most of the sub-budgets discussed up to this point, it is desirable to have estimates of manufacturing expense prepared by those individuals who have the responsibility for incurring them. Thus, each departmental supervisor should be brought into cost budget preparation. In some cases it may be impracticable for supervisors to prepare expense budgets. In such cases the budget department, or preferably some section of the factory manager's staff, may prepare the estimates. In such situations it is highly desirable that they be transmitted to the supervisors concerned for study, appraisal, and recommendations. In all cases the budget and accounting departments should provide any essential data, technical analyses, and staff assistance that may be needed.

Irrespective of the approach used in developing departmental manufacturing expense budgets for the planning budget, it is necessary that the budgeted volume of work to be done in each department be determined. The production budget expresses the budgeted quantity of *finished goods* for each component time period (see Schedules 2 and 22), yet it must be realized that this budget does not indicate the amount of work planned for such departments as the repair department, the power department, the purchases department, or even the individual producing departments. Therefore it is necessary that the volume of goods called for in the production budget be converted to expected activity for each factory department. This procedure necessitates the selection of a *base* or *factor* (frequently referred to as the factor of variability) which accurately measures the output or activity for each department. The following measures of activity for the two types of factory departments indicate some possibilities:

(1) Producing departments
   a. Units of output (if only one product)
   b. Direct labor hours
   c. Direct machine hours
   d. Direct labor dollars
   e. Raw material consumed
(2) Service departments
   a. Repair and maintenance—direct repair hours
   b. Power department—kilowatt hours delivered
   c. Purchases department—net purchase dollars
   d. General factory administration—total direct labor hours in plant or number of employees in plant

It is the responsibility of factory management to estimate, in terms of the selected base, the volume of work required in each department to produce the quantity of goods called for by the production budget. For example, the quantity of maintenance or repair work (direct repair hours) that will be needed by the several producing departments in making the budgeted quantity of finished goods is a factory management problem of considerable significance. Departmental capacity in terms of men, machines, and investment required is something that factory management should plan in advance, and then control, whether or not a budget program is in effect. A budget program enforces such planning and makes provision for effective control.

Returning again to the mechanics of the annual profit plan, once individual budgets are developed for each factory service and producing department (by responsibility and by interim periods), we are confronted with the problem of *allocating all* factory overhead on some logical basis to the products to be manufactured. Several approaches to this problem are suggested in most books on cost accounting. For purposes of discussion and illustration herein it is assumed that *annual predetermined* factory overhead rates for each producing department are used in the allocation process. This procedure necessitates the allocation of all service department costs to the several producing departments. Next, an overhead rate is computed for each producing department, the overhead rate being related to the measure of output used in that department. Thus the predetermined overhead rate for each department is computed as follows:

$$\frac{\text{Budgeted departmental overhead (annual)}}{\text{Departmental output budgeted (annual)}} = \frac{\text{Annual predetermined}}{\text{overhead rate}}$$

This is an area where cost accounting and budgeting directly overlap because departmental overhead rates computed for budget planning purposes also should be used by the cost accounting department for application of factory overhead during the year. Computation of departmental overhead rates is illustrated for The Superior Manufacturing Company in Schedule 37 (page 188).

Having developed departmental overhead rates, we must take one more step in order to identify factory overhead costs with the various types of finished goods being produced. This step, the *application of factory overhead*, involves multiplying the planned or budgeted volume of each product by the departmental overhead rates. Thus for product costing purposes we have allocated the sum of all factory overhead to cost of goods manufactured, by types of finished goods produced. Utilization of the departmental overhead rates in this manner is illustrated in Schedule 38 (page 189).

Considerations in budgeting distribution expenses

Distribution expenses include all costs related to selling, distribution, and delivery of the products to the customers. In many companies this element of cost comprises a significant percentage of total costs. Careful planning of such costs coupled with effective control vitally affects the profit potential of the firm.[2]

There are two principal aspects of distribution expense budgeting:

(1) *Planning and coordination*—In the development of the over-all plan of operations as expressed in the planning budget it is essential that the proper balance be achieved between sales effort (expense) and sales results (revenue). This balance is the result of a series of decisions as to alternatives concerning the planned sales program. The advertising program and other distribution costs must be consistent with the sales volume expected.

(2) *Control of distribution costs*—Aside from planning budget considerations, it is important that serious effort be devoted to controlling distribution costs. Control is especially important since (a) distribution costs are frequently a significant portion of total cost, and (b) both sales management and sales personnel tend to view such costs lightly, in some cases almost extravagantly. Take, for example, the not unusual extravagances with respect to entertainment costs. Distribution cost control involves the same principles of control as manufacturing overhead. Control must be built around the concepts of (a) functional responsibility and (b) cost or expense objectives.

Fundamentally the sales management is attempting to achieve through planning the *optimum balance* (as regards profit potential) between the (1) sales budget (2) advertising budget, and (3) the distribution expense budget. As a consequence,

---

[2] For comprehensive treatment of distribution costs see: Michael Schiff and Martin Mellman, *Financial Management of the Marketing Function* (New York: Financial Executives Research Foundation, Inc., 1962). Also, note the bibliography contained therein, pp. 251–256. "The Sales Department Looks at Costs" (a monogram), *Marketing Series* No. 90 (New York: American Management Association, Inc., 1953).

effective budgeting views the planning and control of *sales,
advertising,* and *distribution expenses* as one basic problem
rather than as three separate problems. The logic of this view is
obvious when we note the interrelationships between them.
The sales budget rests solidly upon the promotional program;
the amount of costs that can be expended for a given volume
of sales is limited. The practice of some companies of starting
with a sales projection, then budgeting a fixed per cent of those
sales for sales overhead, another fixed per cent for field expenses,
and still another fixed per cent for advertising, represents a
negative management approach to a serious planning problem.
In contrast, the sales executives in the better-managed companies
tentatively develop the marketing, promotional, and distribution
expense plans simultaneously. As these respective plans take
tentative shape, they become basic guideposts in developing
the final sales budget. Next the definite dollars of costs essential
to carry out the promotional, marketing, and distribution phases
are planned with some precision. These dollars of cost then
become an important part of the input data for the annual
profit plan. Although practice varies, these input data are given
expression separately in (a) the advertising budget and (b) the
budget of distribution costs.

The budget of distribution costs basically includes two major
types of costs: (1) home office expenses and (2) field expenses.
From the planning and control points of view it is essential
that these costs be planned by organizational responsibility. In
some cases this might be by sales district, in other cases by
products; in all cases the planning structure should follow the
basis upon which the sales efforts are organized. As noted in
the first part of this chapter, the concepts of controllable versus
noncontrollable costs, fixed versus variable costs, and itemization
by types of expenditure may be generally applicable to planning
and controlling such costs.

Construction of distribution expense budgets

The construction of the distribution expense budgets requires
the preparation of a budget of expense for each organizational
subdivision. The responsibility for these planning budgets, as
with other expense budgets, rests with the executives having
responsibility for the execution and for the results of the activity
being budgeted. As with all expense planning, historical data

are very useful; however, much more fundamental is that the expense budget be based upon definite plans for activity, accomplishment, and programs. Variable budgets are used by some firms to aid in control of distribution costs.

Because for accounting purposes promotional and distribution costs are not considered to be a part of the cost of goods manufactured, the critical problem of *allocating* such costs to products does not exist as it does with respect to manufacturing overhead; thus we can concentrate more directly on the problems of planning and control. In many situations, however, it is desirable to compute the profit for each product, thereby necessitating an allocation external to the accounts of some or all of the distribution costs. Such allocations when made are on a more or less arbitary basis. Such allocations and related analyses are much more meaningful if distribution costs can be classified as fixed and variable. Top management frequently needs supplementary data such as the profit contribution—by product, class of customers, market areas, and channels of distribution.

Special distribution cost problems

As in planning and controlling costs in other functional areas, there are a number of special problems in budgeting distribution expenses. It would be impractical to attempt to treat comprehensively, or even list, all of these problem areas. A good example of a problem that does not fit neatly into *general budget procedures* relates to travel expense incurred by salesmen. Many firms report that they plan and control these particular costs in relation to sales (either quantity or dollar sales); that is, they assume this particular cost should increase as sales increase and vice versa. Conversely, many sales executives say certain costs should vary inversely with sales—as sales fall off *more* effort and travel is essential to reverse the sales trend. Obviously, this particular problem, as with other special problems, must be analyzed, planned, and controlled in the particular environment in which it exists. Such problems take on an entirely different complexion when encountered in new situations. Other special problems in planning distribution costs relate to freight, entertainment, warehousing, returned goods, and advertising.

In classifying distribution costs as either fixed or variable, special problems arise. A particular problem relates to selection of the activity factor or base that measures output (work done) in the various organizational subdivisions of the sales department. To illustrate, one department store relates costs to *sales dollars* in some departments and to *number of sales* in other departments. Although variable budgets are not used in the control of distribution costs to the extent that they are in the control of factory overhead, in recent years much attention has been given to the fixed-variable classification of distribution costs. This attention is due to a growing recognition of the usefulness of the fixed-variable classification in many management decisions and the increasing utilization of such techniques as breakeven analysis, marginal cost analysis, and direct costing, each of which rests upon the concept of cost variability.

As a practical matter most firms use sales dollars as the activity base for all distribution costs, that is, for relating costs to activity in each organizational unit in the sales division. Sales dollars are often used as the measure of activity in the sales division primarily because it is felt that:

(1) to the extent that certain effort and activity does vary throughout the sales division it is "to effect changes in sales dollars or is the result of sales dollars having changed," and

(2) in a pragmatic sense certain costs "had better drop when sales drop and may increase when sales increase."

Budgeting advertising or promotional effort represents another special problem area. Although a comprehensive treatment of this subject is outside the scope of this book we might note some aspects of the problem.[3] It is recognized by most of the better managements that there are certain types of expenditures in a business that are best planned and controlled on the basis of definite *appropriations* for specific time periods. Research costs[4] and advertising costs are of such a nature that justification for unlimited expenditures might be forthcoming.[5] Therefore top management should require that such activities be programmed and planned concretely and that the attendant costs be carefully estimated. Once such plans and related expenditures are approved by top management, they constitute, in effect, managerial permission for their execution. Control is achieved through con-

---

[3] For comprehensive treatments of this subject see: James D. Scott, *Advertising Principles and Problems* (Englewood Cliffs, N.J.: Prentice-Hall, 1953). Roland B. Smith, *Advertising to Business* (Homewood, Ill.: Irwin, 1957). Franklin W. Bartle, *How to Manage Industrial Advertising* (New York: Printers' Ink Books, 1955).

[4] "Accounting for Research and Development Costs; Research Series No. 29," *NAA Bulletin*, XXXVI, No. 10 (June 1955), Sec. 3.

[5] See page 51 concerning appropriation type budgets.

tinuous reporting of progress and expenditures. In the area of distribution costs, advertising costs should be planned on an appropriation basis.

Various methods are used to determine the advertising appropriation. The more commonly used methods may be characterized as follows:

    (1) Arbitrary appropriation
    (2) All available funds
    (3) Competitive parity
    (4) Percentage of sales
    (5) Fixed sum per unit
    (6) Previous year's profits
    (7) Return on investment[6]
    (8) The task method

Under the task method, certain practical objectives to be achieved by advertising are established and then a program consistent with these objectives is set up. Recognized authorities in the advertising field generally agree that the task method is preferable.

It goes without saying that the expenditures for advertising must be within the reasonable capabilities of the firm. Accordingly, from the budgeting viewpoint, it is essential that a detailed advertising budget be prepared.

The advertising budget for the budget year should be the direct responsibility of the sales department—specifically, the advertising manager—for it is inconceivable that an accurate sales budget could be developed without at the same time developing detailed advertising plans. The detailed advertising budget should be presented to the budget committee in conjunction with the sales budget. Certainly the two budgets should be approved or disapproved as a unit. Thus the budget department receives the detailed (and approved) advertising budget for incorporation in the over-all planning budget. Control is achieved through reports of activities and actual advertising expenditures to date compared with advertising appropriations to date as indicated in the advertising budget.

From a practical standpoint costs or expenses set forth in an appropriation budget may be thought of as *fixed costs* for analytical purposes. The total amount of the cost for the period is con-

---

[6] Joel Dean "How Much to Spend for Advertising," *Harvard Business Review,* *XXIX,* No. 1 (Jan. 1951), p. 70.

stant, having been determined by management policy. Note in the illustrative case that such costs are treated as fixed costs.

In the accounting department, advertising costs, after having been budgeted for the year, may be *accrued* on a monthly basis by debiting advertising expense and crediting an advertising clearing account, actual expenditures being debited to this account. In such cases related budget procedures should be consistent.

Considerations in budgeting administrative expenses

Administrative expenses include expenses, other than manufacturing and distribution, incurred in the operation of a business. In general they are incurred in the supervision of, and service to, all major functions of the business rather than in the performance of any one function. Because a large portion of administrative expenses are fixed rather than variable, the notion persists that they cannot be controlled. Outside of certain top-management salaries which, in the case of a corporation, may be set by the board of directors, most administrative expenses are influenced significantly by managerial policies and decisions. It is not infrequent to find administrative costs top-heavy when measured by the volume of business done. In recent years a number of informed observers have expressed the opinion that a developing characteristic of industry in the United States is the high cost of administration. These costs, along with labor costs, frequently have made it difficult to price our products competitively in the international market. As general administrative costs are close to top management, there is a strong tendency to overlook their magnitude and effect on the profit potential. These facts suggest the importance of carefully planning, evaluating, and controlling this area of costs. Each administrative cost should be directly identified with some executive who then would assume responsibility for planning and controlling it. This fundamental of cost control is especially important with respect to administrative costs because there is a strong tendency not to pinpoint responsibility for costs of a general nature or those incurred in large part by top management. For these and other reasons many companies have found it useful to use the fixed-variable classification for administrative costs. In such cases the variable costs are related (correlated) with total sales dollars. This approach tends to emphasize that when volume drops, these costs should decrease also or else the profit potential is significantly affected.

Construction of the administrative expense budget

Budgeting administrative expenses involves (a) the preparation of expense budgets for the annual profit plan, and (b) expense control. Generally, the best approach for planning administrative budget allowances is to base them on specific sales plans and programs. Past experience, adjusted for anticipated changes in management policy and general economic conditions, is helpful. Because most administrative expenses are fixed, an analysis of the historical record will generally provide a sound basis for budgeting them. The preparation of administrative expense allowances should be the responsibility of the executive in charge of the specific functions being budgeted.

The principle of variable budgets has been widely accepted in the control of manufacturing expenses, but there is seldom any practical reason for not applying the concept to administrative expense for control purposes. The fact that most of the administrative expenses are fixed simplifies the application of variable budgets.

Manufacturing expense budgets illustrated

It will be recalled that the factory division of The Superior Manufacturing Company (Illustration 5, page 61) has three service departments (General and Administrative, Power department, and Repair department), and three direct producing departments (designated 1, 2, and 3). The company uses variable expense budgets. The variable budgets for the three producing and three service departments are given in Schedules 32 and 33.[7]

The Superior Manufacturing Company owns a building which houses all divisions of the company. The building is occupied by the three divisions as follows: factory division, 60 per cent of the floor space; sales division, 20 per cent; and general office 20 per cent. The occupancy costs are distributed to the three divisions on this basis. The building superintendent provided the building services budget shown in Schedule 34.

In terms of the selected measure of activity, the manufacturing division executives and departmental supervisors developed

---

[7] Derivation of the variable budgets is discussed in Ch. 9.

The Superior Manufacturing Company

VARIABLE BUDGET—MANUFACTURING DIVISION

(Service Departments)

For the Year Ending December 31, 1963

SERVICE DEPARTMENTS

	General and Administrative		Power		Repair	
	Fixed per Month	Variable per 100 Total DLH	Fixed per Month	Variable per 1000 Kilowatt Hours	Fixed per Month	Variable per Direct Repair Hour
Supervisory salaries	$8,000		$3,000		$300	
Maintenance			100	$ .28		
Fuel				1.20		
Supplies used						$.34
Travel & entertainment	100	$ .50				
Telephone & telegraph	460	.20				
Depreciation (time basis)	130		450		10	
Insurance	20		70		3	
Taxes	30		80		7	
Stationery & office supplies	20	.30				
Wages			3,000		400	
Totals	$8,760	$1.00	$6,700	$1.48	$720	$.34

The Superior Manufacturing Company

VARIABLE BUDGET—MANUFACTURING DIVISION

(Producing Departments)

For the Year Ending December 31, 1963

PRODUCING DEPARTMENTS

	Department 1		Department 2		Department 3	
	Fixed per Month	Variable per 100 Dept. DLH	Fixed per Month	Variable per 100 Dept. DLH	Fixed per Month	Variable per 100 Dept. DLH
Supervisory salaries	$10,000		$1,870		$2,920	
Indirect labor	3,000	$22.50		$1.90	800	$ 7.10
Maintenance parts	300	1.50	20	.20	150	.50
Supplies used	450	5.50	40	.50	200	2.50
Depreciation (output basis)		1.50		.40		.90
Insurance	100		10		50	
Taxes	150		20		60	
Totals	$14,000	$31.00	$1,960	$3.00	$4,180	$11.00

The Superior Manufacturing Company

EXPENSE BUDGET—BUILDING SERVICES

For the Year Ending December 31, 1963

	Ref.	Annual Total	1st Quarter			Quarters			
			January	February	March	1st	2nd	3rd	4th
		(Given)	(Given)	(Given)	(Given)	(Given)	(Given)	(Given)	(Given)
Supervisory salaries		$ 24,000	$ 2,000	$ 2,000	$ 2,000	$ 6,000	$ 6,000	$ 6,000	$ 6,000
Repairs & maintenance		18,000	1,500	1,500	1,500	4,500	4,500	4,500	4,500
Depreciation		60,000	5,000	5,000	5,000	15,000	15,000	15,000	15,000
Insurance		3,600	300	300	300	900	900	900	900
Taxes		2,400	200	200	200	600	600	600	600
Wages		26,800	2,250	2,150	2,150	6,550	6,750	6,750	6,750
Heat and light		13,200	1,800	1,000	900	3,700	2,000	2,750	4,750
Water		2,000	150	150	170	470	630	500	400
Totals		$150,000	13,200	$12,300	$12,220	$37,720	$36,380	$37,000	$38,900
Distribution of occupancy cost:									
Factory 60%		$ 90,000	$ 7,920	$ 7,380	$ 7,332	$22,632	$21,828	$22,200	$23,340
Sales 20%		30,000	2,640	2,460	2,444	7,544	7,276	7,400	7,780
Administrative 20%		30,000	2,640	2,460	2,444	7,544	7,276	7,400	7,780
Total 100%		$150,000	$13,200	$12,300	$12,220	$37,720	$36,380	$37,000	$38,900

the following budgeted quantities of work to be done by each department in the factory.

BUDGETED ACTIVITY—FACTORY DIVISION

(1) Producing departments—Budgeted direct labor hours as indicated in the direct labor budget (Schedule 31).

(2) General and Administrative Factory—Budgeted total direct labor hours for the factory as indicated in the direct labor budget (Schedule 31).

(3) Power department—Budgeted kilowatt hours planned as follows:

	Kilowatt Hours *(000's)*
January	1,450
February	1,600
March	1,600
Second Quarter	5,100
Third Quarter	4,800
Fourth Quarter	5,450
Total	20,000

(4) Repair department—Budgeted direct repair hours planned as follows:

	Direct Repair Hours
January	290
February	330
March	320
Second Quarter	1,000
Third Quarter	970
Fourth Quarter	1,090
Total	4,000

Data are now available for construction of *planning budget* schedules of manufacturing expenses for each department of the factory. These budgets are combined and summarized in Schedules 35, and 36. On each of these schedules the *annual total* is analyzed as to *fixed* and *variable* in the first two columns to facilitate (a) development of the fixed and variable components of the departmental overhead rates and (b) development of breakeven analysis as explained in Chapter 12.

By way of explaining the use of variable budgets in the computation of the planning budget expense schedules, the column héaded *January* for general and administrative factory overhead in Schedule 35 was computed as shown below. General and administrative factory overhead expense allowances are based

The Superior Manufacturing Company

FACTORY EXPENSE BUDGET

(Service Departments)

For the Year Ending December 31, 1963

GENERAL & ADMINISTRATIVE FACTORY OVERHEAD: (Based on 1,168,000 DLH)

	Annual			First Quarter			Quarters		
	Fixed	*Variable*	*Total*	*January*	*February*	*March*	*Second*	*Third*	*Fourth*
Supervisory Salaries	$ 96,000		$ 96,000	$8,000	$8,000	$8,000	$24,000	$24,000	$24,000
Travel & entertainment	1,200	$ 5,840	7,040	518	572	576	1,780	1,704	1,890
Telephone & telegraph	5,520	2,336	7,856	627	649	650	1,972	1,942	2,016
Depreciation	1,560		1,560	130	130	130	390	390	390
Insurance	240		240	20	20	20	60	60	60
Taxes	360		360	30	30	30	90	90	90
Stationery & office supplies	240	3,504	3,744	271	303	306	948	902	1,014
Totals	$105,120	$ 11,680	$116,800	$9,596	$9,704	$9,712	$29,240	$29,088	$29,460

POWER DEPARTMENT: (Based on 20 million Kilowatt Hours)

	Fixed	*Variable*	*Total*	*January*	*February*	*March*	*Second*	*Third*	*Fourth*
Supervisory salaries	$ 36,000		$ 36,000	$3,000	$3,000	$3,000	$ 9,000	$ 9,000	$ 9,000
Maintenance	1,200	$ 5,600	6,800	506	548	548	1,728	1,644	1,826
Fuel		24,000	24,000	1,740	1,920	1,920	6,120	5,760	6,540
Depreciation	5,400		5,400	450	450	450	1,350	1,350	1,350
Insurance	840		840	70	70	70	210	210	210
Taxes	960		960	80	80	80	240	240	240
Wages	36,000		36,000	3,000	3,000	3,000	9,000	9,000	9,000
Totals	$ 80,400	$ 29,600	$110,000	$8,846	$9,068	$9,068	$27,648	$27,204	$28,166

REPAIR DEPARTMENT: (Based on 4,000 direct repair hours)

	Fixed	*Variable*	*Total*	*January*	*February*	*March*	*Second*	*Third*	*Fourth*
Supervisory salaries	$ 3,600		$ 3,600	$ 300	$ 300	$ 300	$ 900	$ 900	$ 900
Supplies used		$ 1,360	1,360	99	112	109	340	330	370
Depreciation	120		120	10	10	10	30	30	30
Insurance	36		36	3	3	3	9	9	9
Taxes	84		84	7	7	7	21	21	21
Wages	4,800		4,800	400	400	400	1,200	1,200	1,200
Totals	$ 8,640	$ 1,360	$ 10,000	$ 819	$ 832	$ 829	$ 2,500	$ 2,490	$ 2,530

The Superior Manufacturing Company

FACTORY EXPENSE BUDGET
(Producing Departments)
For the Year Ending December 31, 1963

PRODUCING DEPARTMENT NO. 1 (Based on 488,000 DLH)

	Annual Fixed	Annual Variable	Annual Total	First Quarter January	First Quarter February	First Quarter March	Quarters Second	Quarters Third	Quarters Fourth
Supervisory salaries	$120,000		$120,000	$10,000	$10,000	$10,000	$30,000	$30,000	$30,000
Indirect labor	36,000	$109,800	145,800	10,830	11,820	11,910	36,900	35,415	38,925
Maintenance parts	3,600	7,320	10,920	822	888	894	2,760	2,661	2,895
Supplies used	5,400	26,840	32,240	2,364	2,606	2,628	8,170	7,807	8,665
Depreciation	—	7,320	7,320	522	588	594	1,860	1,761	1,995
Insurance	1,200	—	1,200	100	100	100	300	300	300
Taxes	1,800	—	1,800	150	150	150	450	450	450
Totals	$168,000	$151,280	$319,280	$24,788	$26,152	$26,276	$80,440	$78,394	$83,230

PRODUCING DEPARTMENT NO. 2 (Based on 192,000 DLH)

	Annual Fixed	Annual Variable	Annual Total	First Quarter January	First Quarter February	First Quarter March	Quarters Second	Quarters Third	Quarters Fourth
Supervisory salaries	$22,440		$22,440	$1,870	$1,870	$1,870	$5,610	$5,610	$5,610
Indirect labor		$3,648	3,648	266	304	304	912	874	988
Maintenance parts	240	384	624	48	52	52	156	152	164
Supplies used	480	960	1,440	110	120	120	360	350	380
Depreciation		768	768	56	64	64	192	184	208
Insurance	120		120	10	10	10	30	30	30
Taxes	240		240	20	20	20	60	60	60
Totals	$23,520	$5,760	$29,280	$2,380	$2,440	$2,440	$7,320	$7,260	$7,440

PRODUCING DEPARTMENT NO. 3 (Based on 488,000 DLH)

	Annual Fixed	Annual Variable	Annual Total	First Quarter January	First Quarter February	First Quarter March	Quarters Second	Quarters Third	Quarters Fourth
Supervisory salaries	$35,040		$35,040	$2,920	$2,920	$2,920	$8,760	$8,760	$8,760
Indirect labor	9,600	$34,648	44,248	3,271	3,583	3,612	11,204	10,735	11,843
Maintenance parts	1,800	2,440	4,240	324	346	348	1,070	1,037	1,115
Supplies used	2,400	12,200	14,600	1,070	1,180	1,190	3,700	3,535	3,925
Depreciation	—	4,392	4,392	313	353	356	1,116	1,057	1,197
Insurance	600		600	50	50	50	150	150	150
Taxes	720		720	60	60	60	180	180	180
Totals	$50,160	$53,680	$103,840	$8,008	$8,492	$8,536	$26,180	$25,454	$27,170

SUMMARY:

	Annual Fixed	Annual Variable	Annual Total	First Quarter January	First Quarter February	First Quarter March	Quarters Second	Quarters Third	Quarters Fourth
Building services	$90,000		$90,000	$7,920	$7,380	$7,332	$21,828	$22,200	$23,340
Service departments	194,160	$42,640	236,800	19,261	19,604	19,609	59,388	58,782	60,156
Producing departments	241,680	210,720	452,400	35,176	37,084	37,252	113,940	111,108	117,840
Totals	$525,840	$253,360	$779,200	$62,357	$64,068	$64,193	$195,156	$192,090	$201,336

upon total direct labor hours in the factory which were taken from the direct labor budget, Schedule 31. The total direct labor hours are applied to the variable budget allowances for general and administrative factory overhead (see Schedule 32).

Account	Fixed per Month		January DLH (00)		Variable Rate		January Budget Allowance
Salaries	$8,000	plus	836	×	$ .00	equals	$8,000
Travel & entertainment	100	"	836	×	.50	"	518
Telephone & telegraph	460	"	836	×	.20	"	627
Depreciation	130	"	836	×	.00	"	130
Insurance	20	"	836	×	.00	"	20
Taxes	30	"	836	×	.00	"	30
Stationery & office supplies	20	"	836	×	.30	"	271
Totals	$8,760	"	836	×	$1.00	"	$9,596

In order to determine the budgeted *cost of goods manufactured* for each product, the budgeted manufacturing expenses for the six factory departments must be allocated to all the products on some logical basis. It will be recalled that the direct material and direct labor costs were identified with each product in Schedules 28 and 30. Departmental factory overhead rates are used to allocate factory overhead to products manufactured.

In order to compute departmental overhead rates for each producing department, The Superior Manufacturing Company prepares a *budgeted manufacturing expense distribution sheet* as illustrated in Schedule 37. It will be observed that the *direct costs* were taken directly from Schedules 35 and 36. The next step is the distribution of service department costs to the three producing departments. The distributions of service department costs were based on the following data:

(1) *Building service*—The 60 per cent allocated to the factory is further allocated to the factory departments on the basis of relative floor space occupied (note: treated as a fixed cost):

Departments	Per cent
Power	10
Repair	5
Producing No. 1	36.890*
Producing No. 2	18.312
Producing No. 3	29.798

* Carrying per cents to decimal places in situations such as this is ordinarily impracticable. It is done here to make the burden rates come out even for illustrative purposes only.

(2) General and administrative factory overhead—The following percentages, agreed upon by factory management for accounting purposes:

Departments	Per cent
Power	10
Repair	10
Producing No. 1	50
Producing No. 2	10
Producing No. 3	20

(3) Power department—The budgeted usage of kilowatt hours by department:

Departments	Kilowatt Hours (000)
Repair	500
Producing No. 1	10,000
Producing No. 2	5,000
Producing No. 3	4,500
	20,000

(4) Repair department—The budgeted usage of direct repair hours by department:

Departments	Direct Repair Hours
Producing No. 1	1,600
Producing No. 2	800
Producing No. 3	1,600
	4,000

Building services (occupancy costs) and general factory overhead are allocated to the several producing and service departments.

Service department costs were then distributed to the three producing departments. The total costs of each department divided by the budgeted departmental direct labor hours gives the indicated departmental overhead rates. A significant aspect of this distribution worksheet is the development of the (a) fixed component and the (b) variable component of the departmental overhead rates. This development is possible because the company uses variable expense budgets.[8] This feature becomes important

---

[8] For purposes of simplicity the same basis is used for distributing fixed and variable components of service department costs. It is generally recognized that a more theoretically correct and useful distribution is possible if fixed and variable costs are treated differently. As a general proposition fixed service department costs should be distributed on the basis of *capacity to use* services, whereas variable costs should be distributed on the basis of expected actual use of service.

It will also be observed that the overhead rates are based on *expected actual volume* for the year. Generally speaking, there are three levels at which burden rates may be set. Authorities are not in agreement with respect to the preferable rate. The reader is referred to books on cost accounting for further study. The three levels are:
(1) Budgeted volume for the year.
(2) Practical plant capacity.
(3) The average volume over several years.

The Superior Manufacturing Company

MANUFACTURING EXPENSE (BURDEN) DISTRIBUTION SHEET

Schedule 37

For the Year Ending December 31, 1963

Item	Total	Power Fixed	Power Variable	Repair Fixed	Repair Variable	No. 1 Fixed	No. 1 Variable	No. 2 Fixed	No. 2 Variable	No. 3 Fixed	No. 3 Variable
		Service Departments				Producing Departments					
Direct costs	$572,400	$80,400	$29,600	$8,640	$1,360	$168,000	$151,280	$23,520	$5,760	$50,160	$53,680
Distributed costs:											
Building services—fixed	90,000	9,000		4,500		33,201		16,481		26,818	
General & administrative											
Fixed	105,120	10,512		10,512		52,560		10,512		21,024	
Variable	11,680		1,168		1,168		5,840		1,168		2,336
Power department distribution											
Fixed		$99,912		2,498		49,956		24,978		22,480	
Variable			$30,768		769		15,384		7,692		6,923
Repair department distribution											
Fixed				$26,150		10,460		5,230		10,460	
Variable					$3,297		1,319		659		1,319
Totals	$779,200					$314,177	$173,823	$80,721	$15,279	$130,942	$64,258
Direct labor hours (Schedule 31)						488,000	488,000	192,000	192,000	488,000	488,000
Burden rates (Per direct labor hour)											
Fixed						$ .6438		$ .4204		$ .2683	
Variable							$ .3562		$ .0796		$ .1317
Total						$1.00		$.50		$.40	

Standard service charges:

$$\text{Power} \left(\frac{\$99,912 \text{ plus } \$30,768}{20,000 \text{ KWH}} \right) = \$6.53 \text{ per 1,000 Kilowatt Hours}$$

$$\text{Repair} \left(\frac{\$26,150 \text{ plus } \$3,297}{4,000 \text{ Repair Hours}} \right) = \$7.36 \text{ per Direct Repair Hour}$$

MANUFACTURING EXPENSES APPLIED

For the Year Ending December 31, 1963

	Ref.	Totals	First Quarter January	February	March	Quarters First	Second	Third	Fourth
Product X									
Department No. 1									
Direct labor hours	31	384,000	28,000	32,000	32,000	92,000	96,000	92,000	104,000
Rate	37	$1.00	$1.00	$1.00	$1.00	$1.00	$1.00	$1.00	$1.00
Amount		$384,000	$28,000	$32,000	$32,000	$92,000	$96,000	$92,000	$104,000
Department No. 2									
Direct labor hours	31	192,000	14,000	16,000	16,000	46,000	48,000	46,000	52,000
Rate	37	$.50	$.50	$.50	$.50	$.50	$.50	$.50	$.50
Amount		$96,000	$7,000	$8,000	$8,000	$23,000	$24,000	$23,000	$26,000
Department No. 3									
Direct labor hours	31	384,000	28,000	32,000	32,000	92,000	96,000	92,000	104,000
Rate	37	$.40	$.40	$.40	$.40	$.40	$.40	$.40	$.40
Amount		$153,600	$11,200	$12,800	$12,800	$36,800	$38,400	$36,800	$41,600
TOTAL PRODUCT X		$633,600	$46,200	$52,800	$52,800	$151,800	$158,400	$151,800	$171,600
Product Y									
Department No. 1									
Direct labor hours	31	104,000	6,800	7,200	7,600	21,600	28,000	25,400	29,000
Rate	37	$1.00	$1.00	$1.00	$1.00	$1.00	$1.00	$1.00	$1.00
Amount		$104,000	$6,800	$7,200	$7,600	$21,600	$28,000	$25,400	$29,000
Department No. 3									
Direct labor hours	31	104,000	6,800	7,200	7,600	21,600	28,000	25,400	29,000
Rate	37	$.40	$.40	$.40	$.40	$.40	$.40	$.40	$.40
Amount		$41,600	$2,720	$2,880	$3,040	$8,640	$11,200	$10,160	$11,600
TOTAL PRODUCT Y		$145,600	$9,520	$10,080	$10,640	$30,240	$39,200	$35,560	$40,600
Total all products		$779,200	$55,720	$62,880	$63,440	$182,040	$197,600	$187,360	$212,200

with respect to variation analysis (Chapter 14) and direct costing (Chapter 15).

The departmental overhead rates are applied to the departmental direct labor hours budgeted (from Schedule 31) for each product in order to compute the budgeted amount of manufacturing expense applied to production.[9] The schedule of *manufacturing expenses applied by product* is shown in Schedule 38.

The use of predetermined overhead rates to allocate factory overhead, which includes both fixed and variable costs, results in a stable charge during the year to each unit of product for this particular element of cost. Because the departmental expense budgets show costs as they are expected to *accrue* in point of time, and the application of overhead through the rates follows the seasonal pattern of production, one can expect a *budgeted over/under-applied* factory overhead for interim periods during the year. This effect may be observed in Schedule 39 (*budgeted overhead over/under-applied*). It should be noted, however, that at year-end the total expenses planned and the total applied are equal; that is, the over/under-applied cancels out for the year as a whole (except for the possibility of a rounding error).

Schedule 39

The Superior Manufacturing Company

BUDGETED OVERHEAD OVER/UNDER-APPLIED

For the Year Ending December 31, 1963

All Departments

Time Periods:	Ref.	*Planned Accruals* 35 & 36	*Total Applied* 38	*Over*	*Under*	*Cumulative*
January		$ 62,357	$ 55,720		$ 6,637	$ 6,637
February		64,068	62,880		1,188	7,825
March		64,193	63,440		753	8,578
First Quarter		190,618	182,040		8,578	8,578
Second Quarter		195,156	197,600	$ 2,444		6,134
Third Quarter		192,090	187,360		4,730	10,864
Fourth Quarter		201,336	212,200	10,864		
Annual Totals		$779,200	$779,200	$13,308	$13,308	

[9] Although not illustrated here, it is frequently advisable to compute the application of fixed and variable burden separately, thereby maintaining such segregation in cost of goods manufactured, sold, and in inventories. This segregation may be accomplished in the accounts or as a separate analysis, and is useful as a basis for certain types of managerial decisions.

The Superior Manufacturing Company

VARIABLE BUDGET—SALES DIVISION

For the Year Ending December 31, 1963

	Southern		Eastern		Western		General Sales Overhead	
	Fixed per Month	Variable per $100 Net Dist. Sales	Fixed per Month	Variable per $100 Net Dist. Sales	Fixed per Month	Variable per $100 Net Dist. Sales	Fixed per Month	Variable per $100 Net Total Sales
Supervisory salaries	$6,000		$ 8,000		$3,000		$12,000	
Travel & entertainment	900	$ .683	1,010	$ .643	340	$ .708	916	$ .458
Telephone & telegraph	400	.216	630	.250	180	.258	824	.098
Depreciation—office equipment							50	
Stationery & office supplies							169	.148
Auto expenses		4.00		4.00		4.00	336	.359
Commissions	100	.849	140	.612	230	.476		
Freight & express	2,000		3,000		1,000			
Advertising							5,000	
Totals	$9,400	$5.748	$12,780	$5.505	$4,750	$5.442	$19,295	$1.063

All budgeted factory costs for The Superior Manufacturing Company have been identified with the various types of finished goods, *viz:*

Item of Cost	*Schedule*
Direct materials	28
Direct labor	30
Manufacturing expenses	38

The cost of goods manufactured can now be developed. This schedule is illustrated in Chapter 11.

Distribution expense budgets illustrated

It will be recalled that the sales division of The Superior Manufacturing Company (Illustration 5, page 61) has three sales districts (Southern, Eastern, and Western) and one general department (General Sales Overhead, i. e., home sales office). The company uses variable budget procedures for all distribution costs. Advertising costs are handled on the appropriation basis. The variable budgets for the three sales districts and the home office are given in Schedule 40.

The advertising budget provided by the vice president of sales is summarized in Schedule 41. Note that one twelfth of the annual allowance is shown in the variable budgets as a monthly fixed cost.

The Superior Manufacturing Company   Schedule 41
ADVERTISING BUDGET—SUMMARY
For the Year Ending December 31, 1963

Department	*Annual Appropriation*
Home Office	$ 60,000
Southern District	24,000
Eastern District	36,000
Western District	12,000
Total	$132,000

In the variable budgets (Schedule 40), the distribution expenses were related to *net sales dollars*. Therefore, in order to prepare the distribution expense budget for the planning budget, variable budget allowances were applied to net sales dollars, as indicated in the sales budget. The distribution expense budget for The Superior Manufacturing Company is illustrated in Schedule 42.

The Superior Manufacturing Company
DISTRIBUTION EXPENSE BUDGET
For the Year Ending December 31, 1963

	Annual			First Quarter			Quarters			
	Fixed	Variable	Total	January	February	March	First	Second	Third	Fourth
General Sales Overhead										
Supervisory salaries	$144,000		$144,000	$12,000	$12,000	$12,000	$36,000	$36,000	$36,000	$36,000
Travel & entertainment	10,992	$27,915	38,907	3,208	3,389	3,545	10,142	10,053	8,052	10,660
Telephone & telegraph	9,888	5,973	15,861	1,314	1,353	1,387	4,054	4,035	3,607	4,165
Depreciation—office equipment	600		600	50	50	50	150	150	150	150
Stationery & office supplies	2,028	9,021	11,049	909	968	1,019	2,896	2,868	2,221	3,064
Auto expense	4,032	21,881	25,913	2,132	2,275	2,397	6,804	6,734	5,165	7,210
Advertising	60,000		60,000	5,000	5,000	5,000	15,000	15,000	15,000	15,000
Totals	$231,540	$64,790	$296,330	$24,613	$25,035	$25,398	$75,046	$74,840	$70,195	$76,249
Southern Sales District										
Supervisory salaries	$72,000		$72,000	$6,000	$6,000	$6,000	$18,000	$18,000	$18,000	$18,000
Travel & entertainment	10,800	$14,479	25,279	2,129	2,314	2,184	6,627	6,525	5,466	6,661
Telephone & telegraph	4,800	4,579	9,379	789	847	806	2,442	2,410	2,075	2,452
Commissions		84,800	84,800	7,200	8,280	7,520	23,000	22,400	16,200	23,200
Freight & express	1,200	17,998	19,198	1,628	1,857	1,696	5,181	5,054	3,738	5,225
Advertising	24,000		24,000	2,000	2,000	2,000	6,000	6,000	6,000	6,000
Totals	$112,800	$121,856	$234,656	$19,746	$21,298	$20,206	$61,250	$60,389	$51,479	$61,538
Eastern Sales District										
Supervisory salaries	$96,000		$96,000	$8,000	$8,000	$8,000	$24,000	$24,000	$24,000	$24,000
Travel & entertainment	12,120	$18,696	30,812	2,470	2,675	2,852	7,997	8,065	6,454	8,296
Telephone & telegraph	7,560	7,268	14,828	1,198	1,277	1,346	3,821	3,848	3,221	3,938
Commissions		116,280	116,280	9,084	10,356	11,460	30,900	31,320	21,300	32,760
Freight & express	1,680	17,791	19,471	1,530	1,724	1,893	5,147	5,213	3,679	5,432
Advertising	36,000		36,000	3,000	3,000	3,000	9,000	9,000	9,000	9,000
Totals	$153,360	$160,031	$313,391	$25,282	$27,032	$28,551	$80,865	$81,446	$67,654	$83,426
Western Sales District										
Supervisory salaries	$36,000		$36,000	$3,000	$3,000	$3,000	$9,000	$9,000	$9,000	$9,000
Travel & entertainment	4,080	$7,561	11,641	1,001	865	1,045	2,911	2,804	2,580	3,346
Telephone & telegraph	2,160	2,755	4,915	421	371	437	1,229	1,190	1,109	1,387
Commissions		42,720	42,720	3,732	2,964	3,984	10,680	10,080	8,820	13,140
Freight & express	2,760	5,084	7,844	674	583	704	1,961	1,890	1,740	2,253
Advertising	12,000		12,000	1,000	1,000	1,000	3,000	3,000	3,000	3,000
Totals	$57,000	$58,120	$115,120	$9,828	$8,783	$10,170	$28,781	$27,964	$26,249	$32,126
Summary Totals										
Total all departments	$554,700	$404,797	$959,497	$79,469	$82,148	$84,325	$245,942	$244,639	$215,577	$253,339
Add building services allocated	30,000		30,000	2,640	2,460	2,444	7,544	7,276	7,400	7,780
Total company	$584,700	$404,797	$989,497	$82,109	$84,608	$86,769	$253,486	$251,915	$222,977	$261,119

The administrative expense budget illustrated

The organization chart for The Superior Manufacturing Company indicates that there are three administrative departments in the company (Administrative, Accounting, and Treasury). The company uses variable budgets in all divisions. The variable budgets for administrative departments are given in Schedule 43. The administrative expense budget schedule for inclusion in the annual planning budget is given as Schedule 44. The allowances were derived by applying the variable budget allowances to total net sales (the activity base) indicated in the sales budget.

Schedule 43

The Superior Manufacturing Company

VARIABLE BUDGET—ADMINISTRATIVE DIVISION
For the Year Ending December 31, 1963

	Administrative		Accounting		Treasurers'	
	Fixed per Month	*Variable per $100 Net Sales*	*Fixed per Month*	*Variable per $100 Net Sales*	*Fixed per Month*	*Variable per $100 Net Sales*
Supervisory salaries	$5,000		$4,000		$3,000	
Travel & entertainment	750		100		100	
Telephone & telegraph	150	$ .120	50	$ .01	60	$ .04
Depreciation	50		200		100	
Insurance	20		20		40	
Taxes	20		30		10	
Stationery & office supplies		.002		.01		.03
Lawyer retainer fee	150					
Loss on bad debts						.20
Audit fee	200					
Totals	$6,340	$ .122	$4,400	$ .02	$3,310	$ .27

Discussion Questions

1. List and define the four broad classifications of cost in manufacturing situations.
2. Discuss the importance of classifying costs in terms of *organizational responsibility*.
3. Distinguish between (a) controllable and noncontrollable costs and (b) fixed and variable costs.
4. Should the noncontrollable costs of a department be reported on the departmental cost reports? Discuss.
5. Explain the classification of costs as related to volume or activity.
6. Discuss the two basic approaches to budget treatment of expenses. Indicate the principal distinctions between them.
7. What is the principal weakness of fixed budget procedures in the control of costs?

The Superior Manufacturing Company
ADMINISTRATIVE EXPENSE BUDGET
For the year Ending December 31, 1963

	Annual			First Quarter			Quarters			
	Fixed	*Variable*	*Total*	*January*	*February*	*March*	*First*	*Second*	*Third*	*Fourth*
Administrative Department										
Supervisory salaries	$ 60,000		$ 60,000	$ 5,000	$ 5,000	$ 5,000	$15,000	$15,000	$15,000	$15,000
Travel & entertainment	9,000		9,000	750	750	750	2,250	2,250	2,250	2,250
Telephone & telegraph	1,800	$ 7,314	9,114	750	798	839	2,387	2,364	1,840	2,523
Depreciation	600		600	50	50	50	150	150	150	150
Insurance	240		240	20	20	20	60	60	60	60
Taxes	240		240	20	20	20	60	60	60	60
Stationery & office supplies		122	122	10	11	12	33	32	23	34
Lawyer retainer fee	1,800		1,800	150	150	150	450	450	450	450
Audit fee	2,400		2,400	200	200	200	600	600	600	600
Totals	$ 76,080	$ 7,436	$83,516	$ 6,950	$ 6,999	$ 7,041	$20,990	$20,966	$20,433	$21,127
Accounting Department										
Supervisory salaries	$ 48,000		$48,000	$ 4,000	$ 4,000	$ 4,000	$12,000	$12,000	$12,000	$12,000
Travel & entertainment	1,200		1,200	100	100	100	300	300	300	300
Telephone & telegraph	600	$ 610	1,210	100	104	107	311	310	266	323
Depreciation	2,400		2,400	200	200	200	600	600	600	600
Insurance	240		240	20	20	20	60	60	60	60
Taxes	360		360	30	30	30	90	90	90	90
Stationery & office supplies		610	610	50	54	57	161	160	116	173
Totals	$ 52,800	$ 1,220	$54,020	$ 4,500	$ 4,508	$ 4,514	$13,522	$13,520	$13,432	$13,546
Treasurers' Department										
Supervisory salaries	$ 36,000		$36,000	$ 3,000	$ 3,000	$ 3,000	$ 9,000	$ 9,000	$ 9,000	$ 9,000
Travel & enertainment	1,200		1,200	100	100	100	300	300	300	300
Telephone & telegraph	720	$ 2,438	3,158	260	276	290	826	818	643	871
Depreciation	1,200		1,200	100	100	100	300	300	300	300
Insurance	480		480	40	40	40	120	120	120	120
Taxes	120		120	10	10	10	30	30	30	30
Stationery & office supplies		1,829	1,829	151	162	172	485	479	347	518
Loss on bad debts		12,190	12,190	1,001	1,080	1,148	3,229	3,190	2,316	3,455
Totals	$ 39,720	$16,457	$56,177	$ 4,662	$ 4,768	$ 4,860	$14,290	$14,237	$13,056	$14,594
Summary										
Totals all departments	$168,600	$25,113	$193,713	$16,112	$16,275	$16,415	$48,802	$48,723	$46,921	$49,267
Allocated building services cost	30,000		30,000	2,640	2,460	2,444	7,544	7,276	7,400	7,780
Total company	$198,600	$25,113	$223,713	$18,752	$18,735	$18,859	$56,346	$55,999	$54,321	$57,047

8. In what way do variable budgets of expense facilitate preparation of the planning budget?
9. Are fixed and variable budget procedures for expenses inconsistent or complementary in a given situation? Explain.
10. Discuss the budget implications of (a) direct producing departments and (b) service departments.
11. What is meant by the "dual problem of burden?" What are the budget implications of the problem?
12. Discuss the problem of *cost allocation* as related to (a) product costing and (b) cost control.
13. What is meant by burden over/under-applied? Should it be budgeted? Why?
14. What are the principal problems in budgeting distribution expenses?
15. What is the relationship between the sales budget and the distribution expense budget?
16. Outline a procedure for budget control of advertising.
17. Why is it important that budget control be extended to administrative expenses?
18. Who should be responsible for preparation of expense budgets? Explain.

NINE

Controlling Costs—Variable Budgets

The preceding chapter was concerned with the development of expense budgets for inclusion in the annual profit plan (planning budget). As noted, these expense budgets may be used primarily for planning and coordination purposes. Variable budgets of expense were briefly discussed and illustrated in order to bring out their complementary relationship to the planning budget. The present chapter is concerned with (a) the theory of variable budgets, (b) the development of variable budget allowances, (c) the mechanics of variable budgets, and (d) the application of variable budgets in the control of costs.[1]

Concepts underlying the variable budget

Variable budgets are schedules of costs or expenses that indicate, for each subdivision of the firm, how each expense *should change* with changes in volume, output, or activity, i.e., what individual costs should be at various volumes rather than at one specific or fixed volume. Significantly, variable budgets express short-term cost-volume relationships within a narrow relevant range of volume. Variable budgets are said to be dynamic budgets in that expense allowances for any particular volume or rate of activity can be computed readily. This type of budget has been variously referred to as variable budget, flexible budget, sliding-scale budget, step budget, expense formula

[1] Recent surveys have indicated extensive application of the variable budget concept; see: B. H. Sord and G. A. Welsch, *Business Budgeting, A Survey of Management Planning and Control Practices* (New York: Controllership Foundation Inc., 1958), pp. 158–199; "Separating and Using Costs as Fixed and Variable," *NAA Bulletin,* Accounting Practice Report No. 10, Sec. 3 (June 1960), 39 pp.

budget, and expense control budget. General acceptance of a more descriptive title such as *planned cost-volume expense formulae* might lead to improved communication and understanding.

The principle underlying the variable budget is the *concept of cost variability*, sometimes referred to as the principle of flexibility. The concept holds that costs can be related to output or activity, and that when so related, costs are primarily the result of two factors: (a) the passage of time, and (b) activity. This means that when costs (expenses) are related to activity, two classes of costs emerge—fixed cost and variable cost.

As a practical matter, the classification of costs in accordance with the concept of cost variability requires the use of three distinct cost categories, namely:

(1) Fixed costs
(2) Variable costs
(3) Semivariable (or semifixed) costs

In order to classify costs on this basis, it is essential that each category be clearly defined. Throughout accounting and budgeting literature these classes of cost have been variously labeled and defined.[2] The above terminology has been selected for discussion purposes herein; however, each firm should select alternate terminology suitable to its own situation. The definitions and discussions that follow do not purport to be suitable for all situations. The purpose is to develop the significant aspects of each class of cost. These should be kept in mind in defining costs for application in *particular situations*.[3] Accountants and budget specialists should not let highly theoretical distinctions deter them. It must be kept in mind that the degree of accuracy management requires is the degree which permits management to reach sound conclusions and make sound decisions. Data for managerial use must be accurate, but this requirement does not forbid the inclusion of reasonable estimates. If the definition of cost variability and the subsequent classification of costs as to variability is approached from this viewpoint, useful variable budgets can be developed.

In considering the variable budget concept, the following areas are significant:

[2] For example, one company uses the following terms to apply to the concept of cost variability: product costs (variable); committed costs (fixed); managed costs (also fixed). Marshall K. Evans, "Profit Planning," *Harvard Business Review* (July-August 1959), pp. 45–54.

[3] Edwin T. Ashman, "Budgeting Direct Labor Expense in the Office," *American Business* (Aug. and Sept. 1956), p. 22.

(1) Definition of costs when related to volume or activity
(2) Selection of an activity base that appropriately measures departmental volume or activity
(3) Methods of analyzing costs to identify separately the fixed and variable components of cost
(4) Use and application of the variable budget concept

Each of these areas will be considered in this chapter.

Fixed costs defined

Fixed or constant costs are those items of cost which do not vary with volume or productive activity. They accrue with the passage of time, i.e., they are time costs. They remain constant in amount for a given short-term period irrespective of activity within a relevant range of activity. Fixed costs are occasioned by the possession of assets and the establishment of the factors of production in a state of "readiness to produce;" hence, they are frequently called capacity costs. Fixed costs are of two principal types. First, certain fixed costs are established by management decisions made in prior periods. Examples of such costs are depreciation, taxes, and insurance. Second, certain fixed costs are established by management decisions on a short-term basis such as one month or one year. Supervisory salaries, janitorial salaries, advertising expenditures, and research expenditures fall into this category. They may fluctuate by reason of changes in the basic structure of the business, methods of operations, and discretionary changes in management policy. The following list sets forth the primary factors that a company should consider in establishing and using a definition of fixed costs suitable to their particular problems and circumstances:

(1) *Controllability*—All fixed costs are controllable over the life span of a firm. Some fixed costs are subject to short-run managerial control. Numerous fixed costs are conditioned annually by the discretionary policies of management. Therefore, one of the potential areas for cost reduction frequently is the fixed-cost structure of the firm.
(2) *Relationship to activity*—Fixed costs result from the establishment of the *capacity* to produce, or to perform some activity; however, they are not a result of the performance of that activity. Fixed costs may be influenced by factors other than the passage of time, but not by the performance of activity.
(3) *Relevant range*—Fixed costs must be related to a relevant range of activity. There are few, if any, costs that would remain constant over the wide range of activity from zero to full capac-

ity. The fixed costs at one range of activity normally would be different at other ranges of activity, because increases or decreases in productive or activity capacity may cause changes in fixed costs. Therefore, in the definition and classification of costs it is essential that a well-defined range (*normal range*) of activity be anticipated. In the interpretation and application of analyses based upon this classification, it is important to realize that the relevant range of activity sets up definite limitations.

(4) *Management regulated*—The estimating of many fixed costs implies that certain managerial policy decisions have been made. Many fixed costs are dependent entirely on specific management decisions. They may vary if these decisions change. For example, in budgeting executive salaries, it is essential that managerial policies relative to salary increases or decreases be known or anticipated.

(5) *Time costs*—Because many fixed costs accrue with the passage of time, the amount of the fixed cost must be related to a specified period of time. Normally fixed costs should be related to the annual accounting period and expressed as a constant amount per month, especially for budgetary purposes.

(6) *Fixed in total but variable per unit*—This rather obvious effect is frequently the cause of much confusion. Assume, for example, fixed costs of $1,000. If 1,000 units are produced, the fixed cost *per unit* is $1.00; however, if 500 units are produced, the fixed cost per unit is $2.00. The total cost remains constant at $1,000 irrespective of the quantity produced, whereas the unit cost changes inversely with volume.

(7) *Practical application*—Practical considerations do not require a cost to be absolutely fixed to be so classified. In application, a fixed cost is one that is constant for all practical purposes.

The concept of cost variability can be presented graphically. Two types of fixed costs are portrayed in Illustration 16. Graph A illustrates a fixed cost that remains constant over the wide range of volume from zero to capacity. Graph B presents a more typical fixed cost, constant within given ranges of activity. In both cases the cost should be budgeted as a fixed cost at $3,000 if it is presumed operations will be within the indicated relevant range.

Variable costs defined

Variable or activity costs are those items of cost that vary *in proportion* to volume or activity in a department or in any other subdivision of the firm. Variable costs are activity or

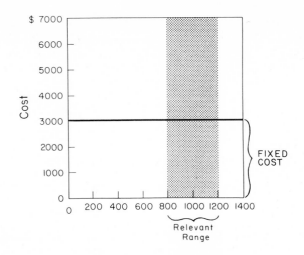

Volume – in units produced

GRAPH A- FIXED COST - CONSTANT AT ALL VOLUMES

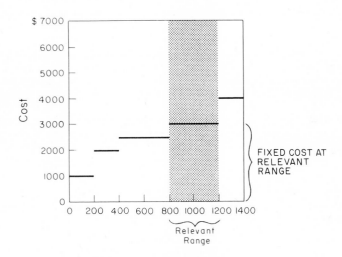

Volume – in units produced

GRAPH B - FIXED COST - RELATED TO RELEVANT RANGE

Illustration 16. *Fixed Costs Graphed*

volume costs because they accrue as a result of productive effort, activity, or work done in a department. They would not exist were it not for the performance of some activity. A variable cost is necessarily zero at zero activity. Variable costs increase or decrease directly with changes in activity; therefore, if activity is doubled, the variable cost is doubled; or if activity decreases by 10 per cent, the cost decreases by 10 per cent. The following list sets forth the primary factors a company should consider in establishing a practical definition of variable costs:

(1) *Controllability*—Variable costs generally are subject to immediate managerial control.

(2) *Proportionally related to activity*—Variable costs vary in proportion to activity or productive effort rather than to the passage of time. Because they vary in direct ratio to changes in output (however measured), they are *straightline* costs when related to some measure of activity.

(3) *Relevant range*—Variable costs must be related to activity within a normal or relevant range of operations. Outside this normal range the pattern of variable costs may well change.

(4) *Management regulated*—Most variable costs can be affected by the discretionary policy decisions of management. For example, management may decide to use a less expensive raw material than that currently used, thereby reducing the *amount* of variable cost although the cost is still variable, but at a different rate.

(5) *Activity costs*—Because variable costs fluctuate in proportion to activity in a department or other subdivision, it is important that some adequate measure of the activity of a department be selected. For example, in a producing department working on several different products simultaneously, units of output would not be additive; hence some common measure of effort, such as direct machine or man hours, must be used. The measure of output selected is generally referred to as the *activity base* or *factor of variability*.

(6) *Variable in total, but fixed per unit*—This classification recognizes the effect of activity on *total* cost. When a variable cost is related to *units*, it becomes fixed per unit. For example, assume variable cost of $1,000. If 1,000 units are produced, the variable cost per unit is $1.00. However, if 500 units (50 per cent reduction) are produced, the total variable cost would be $500 (50 per cent reduction); the variable cost per unit is still $1.00. The effect of fixed and variable costs on *unit cost* is of considerable significance in many analyses that might be made for top management as a basis for certain decisions.

(7) *Practical considerations*—A cost need not be absolutely variable to be so classified. Many so-called curved costs can be classi-

fied as variable as the curve is approximately straight within the narrow relevant range.

The concept of variable costs is portrayed graphically in Illustration 17. Graph A illustrates two different variable costs (at different rates) that vary directly with volume from zero to capacity activity. Graph B illustrates a type of variable cost that varies with production within given ranges of activity; however, the rate changes as we move to another relevant range.

Semivariable costs defined

Semivariable or semifixed costs are those items of cost that increase or decrease as volume or activity increases or decreases, but *not in proportion thereto*. This definition necessarily implies that semivariable costs possess some of the characteristics of both fixed and variable costs. In general the variability of semivariable costs may be attributed to the combined effect of (a) passage of time, (b) activity or volume, and (c) discretionary management policy decisions. Semivariable costs frequently represent a large portion of the expenses in a company.

The concept of semivariable costs is portrayed graphically in Illustrations 18 and 19. In Illustration 18, Graph A portrays the typical semivariable cost having *straightline* characteristics, showing a fixed component and a variable component. Also it may be noted that theoretically some cost is indicated at zero volume. Graph B illustrates the so-called step cost, showing both the actual cost characteristics and the application of a straightline assumption for budget purposes. Whether or not this straightline assumption can be used depends upon the significance of the steps in the relevant volume range.

In Illustration 19, curved costs are illustrated. The actual cost characteristics and the application of a straightline assumption for budget purposes are indicated. For practical purposes step and curved costs are generally classified as semivariable costs and budgeted on a straightline basis within the relevant range.

Selecting the measure of activity

Fixed costs are time costs and hence are related to a time unit such as month or year. On the other hand, a satisfactory unit to which variable costs can be related is frequently difficult to identify. In the simple case of a department producing one

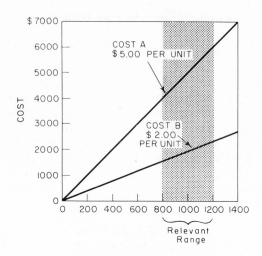

VOLUME – IN UNITS PRODUCED
GRAPH A – VARIABLE COSTS (TYPICAL)

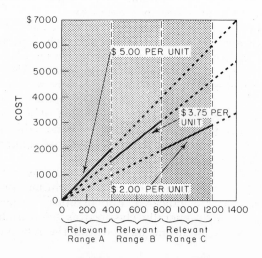

VOLUME – IN UNITS PRODUCED
GRAPH B – VARIABLE COST (REGULATED)

Illustration 17. *Variable Costs Graphed*

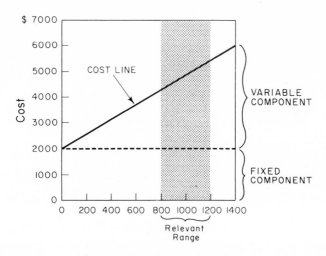

GRAPH A – SEMIVARIABLE COST (STRAIGHT LINE)

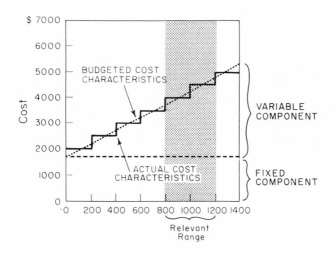

GRAPH B – SEMIVARIABLE COST – (STEP-COST)

Illustration 18. *Semivariable Costs Graphed*

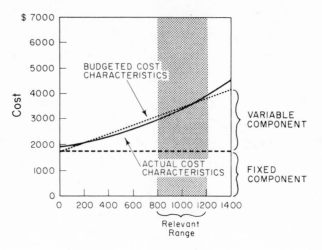

GRAPH A – SEMIVARIABLE COST (CURVED)

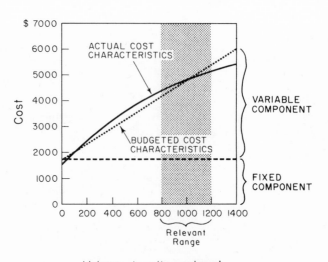

GRAPH B - SEMIVARIABLE COST (CURVED)

Illustration 19. *Semivariable Costs (Curved) Graphed*

type of output, variable costs can be related directly to the ordinary measure of that output. For example, the power department produces only kilowatt hours of electricity; hence power department costs can be related to kilowatt hours and thus accurately measure the activity of the department. In the case of departments producing more than one type of output, some common expression of activity must be established as an activity base or factor of variability. For example, one productive department may use direct labor hours, another productive department may use direct machine hours, and the repair department direct repair hours.

It can be appreciated that if costs are to be classified as to variability, and if variable budgets are to be used, there exists a serious problem of selecting an appropriate factor of variability for each department or other subdivision. The activity base must be the factor that most accurately expresses or measures the over-all activity of the organizational subdivision.

> Several considerations with respect to measuring volume should be recognized, *viz.*:
> 1. The unit must measure fluctuations in the activity which cause cost to vary.
> 2. The unit chosen should be affected as little as possible by variable factors other than volume.
> 3. The unit should be one which is easily understood.
> 4. The activity figures should be obtainable without undue clerical expenses[4]

It is generally desirable to consider seriously the measure that is used in applying overhead when the factors of variability for producing departments are being selected.

The selection of a base for control in service departments often presents a special problem. The factor of variability used in the producing departments should not be carried over into the service departments without making a thorough analysis of the service department situation. Where service departments, such as the power and repair departments, lend themselves to exact measures of activity, these measures should be used. Certain service departments, such as administrative, time and motion, and personnel do not lend themselves to single, exact units of measurement. In such cases it might be best to measure activity in terms of over-all production of the plant, or in terms of the

---

[4] "The Volume Factor in Budgeting Costs," *NAA Bulletin*, Research Series No. 18 (June 1950), p. 1306.

output of producing departments that are most frequently served.

If often happens that a base is stated in terms of over-all activity when proper analysis would show this basis to be incorrect for some service departments. For example, where direct repair hours is not an appropriate base, repair and maintenance expense may appear to be related to direct labor hours; yet 75 per cent of the repair and maintenance may be performed in a department that incurs only 25 per cent of the direct labor hours. Direct machine hours may upon analysis be found to be a better base.

Cost variability analyses frequently are meaningless because an incorrect activity base is being used, thereby showing low correlation between cost and activity. Another problem is the tendency of the activity base gradually to become inappropriate. For example, the installation of additional or new machinery in a department may necessitate a change from direct labor hours to direct machine hours as the measure of output.

Selection of an appropriate measure of departmental activity is essential in planning expenses (Chapter 8) whether or not variable budgets are utilized in the firm.

Determining the relevant range of activity

It has already been indicated that the relative range concept is important in planning and controlling costs. Although each expense item may have its own relative range (points of change) departmental considerations should prevail. As a practical matter the relevant range, on a monthly basis, should relate approximately to the monthly high (maximum limit) and monthly low (minimum limit) in activity. Obviously, the narrower the range the greater the precision in budget allowances based on variable budget formulae.

Methods of expressing variable budgets

Variable budgets may be expressed technically in several ways; however, the various methods may be grouped under three principal classifications, namely:
1. The table method
2. The formula method
3. The graphic method

The *table method*, in effect, is a multiple budget of expense showing budget allowances for several different volumes or levels of activity within the relevant range. This method of expressing variable budgets is frequently used for illustrative and instructional purposes; however, the formula method appears to be more widely used in actual practice. The table method is shown in Illustration 20. Notice that the activity base is direct machine hours and that budget allowances are given for five different volumes within the relevant range. It should also be observed that the fixed and variable components of each expense are not indicated. Therefore, this form of variable budget makes it possible to accommodate irregular step and curved costs readily without the straightline assumption.

The Bowers Corporation
VARIABLE BUDGET—DEPARTMENT X
350,000 to 500,000 direct machine hours represents
relevant range on monthly basis

Volume—Machine Hrs.	300,000	350,000	400,000	450,000	500,000
Per cent	60	70	80	90	100
Foremen salaries	$12,000	$12,000	$12,000	$12,000	$12,000
Indirect labor	12,000	14,000	16,000	18,000	20,000
Other expenses	21,000	25,000	28,000	31,000	34,000
Totals	$45,000	$51,000	$56,000	$61,000	$66,000

Illustration 20. *Variable Budget—Table Method*
(only three typical accounts shown)

It may be noted in Illustration 20 that foremen salaries is a fixed cost, indirect labor is a variable cost, and other expenses is a semivariable cost.

When the table form is used, a frequent problem arises when budget allowances are desired for some volume between two volume levels for which budget figures are provided. Two approaches to this problem have been suggested:

(1) Use the budget allowance that is nearest the desired volume. For example, if budget allowances for 460,000 direct machine hours were desired, allowances at 450,000 direct machine hours would be used.

(2) Determine the budget allowance by straightline interpolation. For example, budget allowances for 460,000 direct machine hours would be computed as follows:

	Allowance at 450,000 Hours	*Add Interpolated Increase*	*Allowance at 460,000 Hours*
Foremen salaries	$12,000	(Constant—No interpolation necessary)	$12,000
Indirect labor	18,000	$(\$20,000 - \$18,000) \times \left(\frac{460,000 - 450,000}{500,000 - 450,000} \right)$	18,400
Other expenses	31,000	$(\$34,000 - \$31,000) \times \left(\frac{460,000 - 450,000}{500,000 - 450,000} \right)$	31,600
Totals	$61,000	$(\$66,000 - \$61,000) \times \left(\frac{460,000 - 450,000}{500,000 - 450,000} \right)$	$62,000

Obviously, to determine the allowances at 460,000 hours, the allowances at 450,000 hours must be *increased* by one-fifth (10,000 hours represents one-fifth of the increase to the next column).

The *formula method* of expressing the variable budget provides a formula for each expense account in each department. The formula indicates the constant or fixed component of cost and the variable component (rate) of cost. The formula method is more compact and generally more useful, because the components of cost are indicated.

The formula method gives *straightline* expression to all costs. Steps within the relevant range may be indicated by footnote as shown in Illustration 21.

The variable budget for Department X, as expressed under the formula method, is shown in Illustration 21.

VARIABLE BUDGET—DEPARTMENT X
(Relevant Range—350,000 to 500,000 direct machine hours)

Account	Fixed Per Month	Variable Rate Per 100 Direct Machine Hours
Foremen salaries	$12,000	
Indirect labor		$ 4.00
Other expenses	4,000(a)	6.00
Total	$16,000	$10.00

(a) Decrease to $3,000 at 400,000 (or less) machine hours.

Illustration 21. *Variable Budget—Formula Method*
(only three typical accounts shown)

The *graphic method* is used primarily for significantly stepped or curved costs as was shown in Illustrations 18 and 19. Under this method budget allowances for all purposes are read directly from the graph. This method is particularly useful where it is not desired to "straighten" curved or stepped costs.

Methods of determining cost variability

When the classifications of cost relative to variability are defined and a suitable activity base for each department has been selected, the next step in the development of variable expense budgets is to determine the variability of each cost or expense in each department. It is apparent that this is the most critical problem involved in the preparation of variable budgets (and breakeven analysis), and one about which there is considerable controversy and disagreement. Numerous methods have been developed by accountants and others for resolving this difficulty. The purpose of this section is to explain and illustrate some of the techniques that have been used to some extent. Most of the methods necessarily involve an analysis of historical costs in order to form a basis for estimating the variability of future costs. It is well that the reader keep in mind that when historical costs are being analyzed, the purpose is to develop planned costs for a given period in the future.

The classification of costs as to variability should begin with a careful study of each expense account in the department under consideration, the purpose of the study being to isolate the accounts that are readily identifiable as either fixed or variable. With the fixed and variable expenses identified, the remaining accounts can be considered to be semivariable. *Each account thus determined to be semivariable must be analyzed in detail to identify the fixed and variable components of cost therein.* These procedures are based upon the assumption that semivariable costs can be analyzed in terms of fixed and variable components.

The problem of determining cost variability then narrows down to consideration of the semivariable expenses, with which the methods that are discussed and illustrated in this section are concerned. These methods may be classified under three broad categories, namely:

(1) Direct estimate methods
(2) Budgeted high and low point methods
(3) Correlation methods

Several variations of each of these methods will be discussed and illustrated.[5] In considering the several methods we should keep in mind the central objective of each—that is, to determine the fixed and variable components of individual items of cost. Further, we are interested in future costs rather than historical costs. With respect to consideration and illustration of each method, we will assume that the *activity factor* has been appropriately selected. Although the technical aspects of each method will be given primary consideration, it is well to realize that sound judgment is necessary in their development and application. In addition, it should be realized that no one parti-

---

[5] For data on reported practices see: B. H. Sord and G. A. Welsch, *Business Budgeting, A Survey of Management Planning and Control Practices* (New York: Controllership Foundation Inc., 1958), p. 174.

cular method of cost analysis is appropriate for all situations, nor for all departments or items of cost in a firm. Typically, a company will utilize several of the methods discussed below for varying internal situations.

Direct estimate methods

Direct estimate methods involve special approaches and techniques of cost analysis, not normally adaptable to routine expenses that may be analyzed and planned through less time-consuming and costly methods. Basically the direct estimate methods imply a concentrated attack upon particular cost problem areas. For our purposes we will consider two variations of the direct estimate method: (1) industrial engineering studies, and (2) direct analysis of historical data coupled with interpretation of related managerial policies.

Industrial Engineering Studies—Many companies rely heavily on industrial engineers for cost data including the variability of certain costs.[6] Because engineers are intimately involved in design of product, plant layout, production problems, and the related costs, they are in a particularly favorable position to provide certain cost data for budget purposes. Engineering studies based on analysis and direct observation of processes and operations frequently can provide the most reliable cost estimates of certain fixed and variable costs. It is important to realize that budget allowances based strictly on historical data tend to perpetuate any inefficiencies that previously existed.

Engineering studies must be relied on when historical cost data are not available, but even when they are available, engineering studies are to be preferred in many situations. In such cases analysis of historical cost data can be used as a check on the reasonableness of engineering estimates. Conversely, where cost estimates are being based principally on an analysis of historical cost data, engineering studies should be made from time to time to check against the analysis of past experience. Budget directors and others responsible for supervision of the budget program should rely heavily on the engineers for budget assistance, with particular reference to cost estimates. Duplication of cost estimating by the controller's staff and the engineers should be avoided when possible.

[6] H.B. Maynard (Ed.), *Industrial Engineering Handbook* (New York: McGraw, 1956), Sec. 6, pp. 111–207.

Industrial engineering studies provide such data as rates of material consumption (direct and indirect), labor requirements, waste and spoilage allowances. The engineering approach to cost analysis is preferable; however, the expense of applying it to all items of cost from year to year may be prohibitive.

Direct Analysis of Historical Data and Management Policies— Generally, the analyst using this approach develops and estimates the variability of a particular cost directly from information obtained through (a) an inspection of the historical activity of the cost, (b) an interpretation of managerial policies with respect thereto, or (c) a subjective decision as to its variability. Refined statistical procedures are not required.

The estimate developed is one of two types:

(1) An estimate of what the cost should be at certain specified volume levels within the relevant range. This procedure provides data for a table type of variable budget.

(2) An estimate of the fixed and variable components of the cost. This procedure provides data for a formula type of variable budget.

The steps involved in a direct estimate of cost variability of a particular cost in any one department or cost center may be summarized as follows:

(1) Selection of the factor of variability.

(2) Identification of the relevant range—the maximum and minimum limits of normal volume expectancy.

(3) Determination of the various levels within the relevant range for which allowances are to be developed if a table type of budget is being employed.

(4) Estimation of cost variability by direct analysis, inspection, and judgment.

The direct estimate approach is usually inappropriate for over-all use in the concern; however, it is of considerable use in particular departments or for individual items of cost requiring special attention.

The direct estimate methods generally are employed when:

(1) A particular expense item, by its nature, is not amenable to other methods. For example, terminal payments to employees ordinarily would have to be estimated on a direct basis after the employee turnover experience and management policies are taken into account.

(2) A new department or cost center is established for which there are no historical cost data for analysis.

(3) A new or nonrecurring activity is contemplated which gives rise to cost—for example, rearrangement of factory equipment.
(4) New machines or additional machines are installed, making historial costs inapplicable for cost estimating.
(5) Management decisions are anticipated which will significantly alter the pattern of cost variability.
(6) Changes in methods of operations are made which significantly alter the pattern of cost variability.
(7) Situations exist where direct observation of processes and operations may provide a basis for reliable cost estimates.
(8) A check on the reliability of estimates developed by other methods is desired.

Budgeted high and low point methods

These methods are based on the idea of developing for each item of cost *two expense budget allowances at two different levels of activity.* Having developed two estimates at two different levels of activity, the fixed and variable components are simply computed on an arithmetical basis assuming straightline relationships. To illustrate the approach we will consider two variations (1) the maximum and minimum method, and (2) the standby cost method.

The Maximum and Minimum Method—From point of time perhaps the first objective reported method of identifying the fixed and variable components of semivariable costs was that formulated by J. H. Williams in 1922.[7] The method involves: (1) estimating what the cost should be at two different volumes, and (2) interpolating between the two volumes to determine the fixed and variable components. The method may be outlined as follows:[8]

(1) Determine a minimum and a maximum within which the volume of business may fluctuate.
(2) Determine the total cost for the item in question at both the minimum and maximum volume of business.
(3) Subtract the minimum volume from the maximum volume of business, and the minimum cost from the maximum cost.
(4) Divide this difference in volume of business into the difference in cost to obtain the variable cost rate.

[7] J. H. Williams, "A Technique for the Chief Executive," *Taylor Society Bulletin* (April 1922), pp. 57–61.
[8] Adapted from J. H. Williams, *The Flexible Budget* (New York: McGraw, 1934).

(5) Multiply the minimum and the maximum volumes of business by the variable cost, and thus obtain the total variable cost for each.

(6) Subtract these total variable costs from the total cost. The remainder will be the fixed cost, and it will be the same in both instances.

To illustrate, assume that *indirect labor* and *activity* (direct machine hours) for Department X were analyzed with the following results: maximum volume (direct machine hours) 500,000; minimum volume 300,000; budget estimate at maximum volume $20,000, and at minimum volume, $14,000. The fixed and variable components are identified through the following computation:

INDIRECT LABOR

	Relevant Range		
	Maximum	*Minimum*	*Difference*
Volume (direct machine hours)	500,000	300,000	200,000
Budget allowance	$20,000	$14,000	$6,000

Variable cost rate: $6,000 ÷ 200,000 (DMH) = $.03 per DMH, or $3.00 per hundred Direct Machine Hours.

Fixed cost:		
Total cost (per above)	$20,000	$14,000
Variable cost:		
($.03 × 500,000 DMH)	15,000	
($.03 × 300,000 DMH)		9,000
Fixed component	$ 5,000	$ 5,000

A variable budget constructed on this basis would show the following for direct labor:

Accounts	*Fixed per Month*	*Variable Rate per Direct Machine Hour*
Indirect Labor	$5,000	$.03

Standby Cost Method—This method also involves a determination of two amounts for each cost, *viz.*, (1) a budget allowance at the budgeted level of activity and (2) the amount of the cost that would *continue* in case of a temporary shutdown or cessation of production or service department activity (the standby cost).[9] The cost that would continue in case of shutdown is considered to be the fixed component of cost because it continues despite cessation of production. The remaining portion of the cost is considered to be the variable component of the cost. Obviously the assumed shutdown does not imply a

[9] G. H. Fitch, "Distribution of Manufacturing Expenses," *NAA Bulletin* (Jan. 1, 1941), pp. 485–502.

permanent shutdown, nor is it assumed that managerial action would be taken to reduce or terminate any costs, such as supervisory salaries, that are more or less independent of minor or normal changes in output. The temporary shutdown is interpreted to be a cessation of work for one or two days, with a subsequent level of activity or volume comparable to that before the shutdown. The procedure would involve a careful study of each item of cost to determine how it would be affected by such a shutdown.

The method may be illustrated by adapting the previous illustration concerning indirect labor. Assume that a careful analysis of indirect labor has been made with the following results: budgeted cost of $20,000 at 500,000 direct machine hours; an estimated standby cost, that would continue in case of temporary shutdown, of $4,000. A variable budget constructed on the basis of the above data would include the following for indirect labor:

Accounts	*Fixed per Month*	*Variable Rate per Direct Machine Hour*
Indirect Labor	$4,000	$.032ᵃ

ᵃ Budget allowance at 500,000 DMH	$20,000
Fixed component (Standby Cost)	4,000
Variable component indicated	$16,000

Variable Rate per DMH:
$16,000 ÷ 500,000 = $.032 per DMH

The maximum and minimum method is widely used. It has the advantage of providing ample opportunity for the *participation of supervisors* in developing budget allowances. As a general rule the method is operated so that the supervisor concerned provides the two budget allowances needed, the arithmetical manipulations being done by the budget department.

Correlation methods

Correlation techniques are widely used in the analysis of costs. Such techniques provide methods for analyzing historical cost data in relation to historical volume data to determine how costs *have varied in the past* which is, in turn, the basis for estimating how costs *should vary in the future*. Because correlation techniques are based on historical data, a critical problem arises when changes in accounting classifications, methods of manufacturing, management policies, and other such changes tend to make historical data nonrepresentative.

Correlation techniques may be applied to either *monthly or annual historical data*. Monthly data are usually preferable because they provide sufficient information, yet do not go too far into the past. The correlation techniques, in general, consist of the following steps:

(1) An analysis of the relationship between cost and volume as indicated by historical data taken from the accounting records. This analysis indicates how the cost varied in the past.

(2) Following this analysis, an estimate is made of how the cost *should* vary with volume in the future, taking into account new conditions that are expected to develop during the budget year, such as changes in management policies, general economic conditions, and methods of operation.

(3) The revised estimates are presented to (a) departmental supervisors for their recommendations, and (b) the budget committee for consideration. It may be preferable in some situations to present the departmental supervisors with the resulting budget allowances for a specific volume, rather than the fixed and variable formulae components. The procedure to use should depend upon the status of budget education in the firm.

(4) The revised fixed and variable allowances are formalized in the variable budget which is approved by top management.

The techniques discussed herein assume linear relationships only; however, it may be noted that some firms have experimented with, and are using, curvilinear regression, such as the logarithmic and reciprocal regression lines. Correlation techniques discussed herein are:

(1) Graphic or visual techniques
(2) Mathematical techniques

Graphic Techniques—This method involves the use of scatter graphs in order to determine visually the fixed and variable components of cost.[10] The analysis involves the preparation of a historical graph with cost on the vertical scale (Y axis) and volume on the horizontal scale (X axis). Historical data are plotted on it and a *visual trend line* is drawn through the plotted points. The point at which the trend line intersects the

[10] See Accounting Practice Report No. 10, *NAA Bulletin*, Sec. 3 (June 1960), p. 1229.

vertical scale (*zero volume*) indicates the constant or fixed portion of the cost and the slope of the trend line as computed represents the variable cost rate.

DEPARTMENT Z
Historical Cost and Volume Data

Month	Points on Chart	Direct Machine Hours	Indirect Labor Cost
January	(1)	44,000	$ 875
February	(2)	41,000	850
March	(3)	45,000	875
April	(4)	43,000	850
May	(5)	36,000	750
June	(6)	22,000	550
July	(7)	23,000	500
August	(8)	15,000	450
September	(9)	30,000	600
October	(10)	38,000	700
November	(11)	41,000	800
December	(12)	44,000	850
Totals		422,000	$8,650

The method is illustrated below for indirect labor in Department Z using the historical data, given above, taken from the cost accounting records.

From the data presented, a scatter graph is constructed and a trend line drawn visually through the plotted points as shown in Illustration 22. The numbers on the graph identify the plotted points with the months. The fixed and variable components of cost as indicated by the trend line are determined in this manner.

Monthly fixed component (point at which the trend line intersects the *Y* axis)... $200

Variable component (interpolate between any two points on the trend line)

Cost at 40,000 DMH $800

Cost at zero DMH 200

Cost increase spread over 40,000 DMH $600

Variable rate or slope of trend line ($600 ÷ 40,000) = $.015 per DMH
The computations can be checked as follows:

Fixed cost at 50,000 DMH $200

Variable cost at 50,000 DMH (× $.015) 750

Trend line intersection at 50,000 DMH $950

The resulting variable budget would be as shown below, *assuming* an adjustment down of, say, 10 per cent in the fixed element. The adjustment down represents a *judgment* on the part

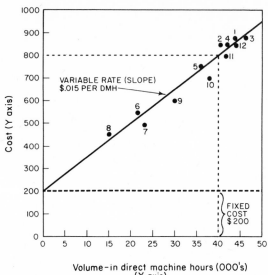

Illustration 22.   *Graphic Cost Analysis—Indirect Labor, Department Z*

of management as to what the cost *should be* as opposed to *what it was.*

Accounts	Fixed per month	Variable rate per DMH
Indirect labor	$180	$.015

Graphic analysis is one of the more important methods of analyzing a cost. The procedure is relatively simple and provides a visual and readily comprehensible picture of the interrelationships. It is difficult to grasp such relationships in a bare listing of amounts as on page 218. Graphic analysis is frequently resorted to as a preliminary study with a view to obtaining an idea of the type of additional analyses that should or should not be made. The principal weakness is the lack of objectivity in drawing the trend line; no two individuals would construct precisely the same trend line through the points. However, the margin of error is generally minor for the purposes intended. The procedure has application for individual cost items, groups of cost items, departmental cost totals, and company-wide costs.

Graphic analysis is one of the most useful, yet simple, analytical tools available to the cost analyst. Through use and experimentation, cost accountants and budget experts have found it of inestimable value. The relationship of cost to volume represents only one of the many applications of graphic analysis to cost study. It might be observed that the graphic representation of costs related to *time periods*, traditionally used by accountants, has limited significance other than to portray trends. Semilogarithmic graphs are generally preferable in this latter case. There are numerous variations of the graphic technique.

Mathematical Techniques—In the analysis of historical cost and volume data, the statistical method of least squares is a technique that may be used for computing the trend line. The method may be adapted for *curved costs;* however the *straight-line* adaptation is considered by practically all authorities to be sufficiently descriptive of the underlying cost-volume relationship for budgeting purposes.

The method of least squares is a mathematical procedure used to compute a unique line through a given series of specified points such as plotted above. In the computation of the trend line, the sum of the deviations of the points from the line will be zero, and the sum of the squares of the deviations will be less than the sum of the squares from any other straight line; thus it is a *unique* trend line. The method is purely objective in that the same trend line will be developed from the same data, whereas the graphic method trend line is subject to a judgment decision on the part of the analyst as to its position and slope.

The fitting of a unique mathematical trend line by the method of least squares involves simple linear correlation analysis of two sets of annual or monthly data—cost and volume in the present case. Simple correlation analysis is a method of defining mathematically the underlying relationship between two variables. The two variables are generally identified in this way:

(1) Independent variable (X variable)—The independent series is the one which varies or is thought to vary independently of the other (dependent) series.
(2) Dependent variable (Y variable)—The dependent series is the one which changes or is thought to change with changes in the other (independent) series.

In the mathematical definition of a trend line which expresses the relationship between two variables, the equation for a straight line may be expressed as $Y = a + bX$, where Y represents the dependent variable, a the constant factor, b the slope of the trend line, and X the independent variable. Simply, a expresses the *position of the line* and b the *slope* of the trend line. There-fore, b expresses the effect on Y (the dependent variable) of any change in X (the independent variable). The equation may be explained graphically as follows:

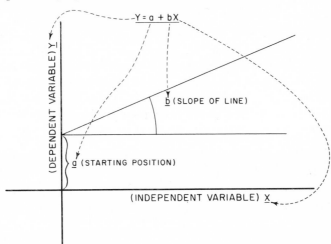

It is readily apparent from the illustration that the technique is adaptable to the analysis of costs to determine their variabil-ity or relationship to volume changes. Here, too, we are seeking an expression of the underlying relationship between two vari-ables: cost and volume. Specifically, we want to know the *effect on cost of changes in volume or activity*. In order to determine this relationship, the least squares technique is adapted to the problem at hand. The equation may be adapted:

$$Y = a + bX$$

Let the dependent variable Y
(plotted on vertical axis) represent TOTAL COST

Let a
(constant value) represent the FIXED COMPONENT OF COST

Let b (slope of trend line)
represent the VARIABLE COMPONENT (RATE) OF COST

Let the independent variable X
(plotted on horizontal axis) represent   VOLUME or ACTIVITY

It is clear from the adaptation above that the *a* value represents the *fixed per month* and the *b* value the *variable rate per direct machine hour* values in the variable budgets as illustrated for indirect labor in Department Z. Therefore, the immediate problem is to develop these respective values. It will be recalled that we are concerned with an analysis of historical cost and volume data to determine these values (*a* and *b*) which are expressive of cost variability. The *a* and *b* values may be computed by using the following equations (Note: *N* represents the number or sets of data, *i.e.*, known points on the graph; Σ, summation):

$$a = \frac{\Sigma X^2 \Sigma Y - \Sigma X \Sigma XY}{N\Sigma X^2 - (\Sigma X)^2}$$

$$b = \frac{N\Sigma XY - \Sigma X \Sigma Y}{N\Sigma X^2 - (\Sigma X)^2}$$

The equations above require computations which are best accomplished in worksheet form. To illustrate the procedure, a least squares worksheet is presented in Illustration 23. The data concerning indirect labor for Department Z given on page 218 are used for the worksheet illustration.[11]

LEAST SQUARES WORKSHEET

N	Month	Direct Machine Hours (000) X	Indirect Labor Cost Y	XY	X^2
1.	January	44	$ 875	38,500	1,936
2.	February	41	850	34,850	1,681
3.	March	45	875	39,375	2,025
4.	April	43	850	36,550	1,849
5.	May	36	750	27,000	1,296
6.	June	22	550	12,100	484
7.	July	23	500	11,500	529
8.	August	15	450	6,750	225
9.	September	30	600	18,000	900
10.	October	38	700	26,600	1,444
11.	November	41	800	32,800	1,681
12.	December	44	850	37,400	1,936
	Summations (Σ)	422	$8,650	321,425	15,986

Illustration 23.   *Indirect Labor—Department Z*

[11] The equations for computing *a* and *b* values may be rearranged in a number of different ways. As a practical matter the equations should be rearranged in such a way as to "fit" the type of calculator the analyst has at hand. The reader is referred to books on statistics for additional information.

To compute a value: $a = \dfrac{\sum X^2 \sum Y - \sum X \sum XY}{N \sum X^2 - (\sum X)^2}$

$$= \frac{(15{,}986)(8{,}650) - (422)(321{,}425)}{(12)(15{,}986) - (422)^2}$$

$$= \underline{\underline{\$191.85}}$$

To compute b value: $b = \dfrac{N \sum XY - \sum X \sum Y}{N \sum X^2 - (\sum X)^2}$

$$= \frac{(12)(321{,}425) - (422)(8{,}650)}{(12)(15{,}986) - (422)^2}$$

$= \$.01504$ per direct machine hour
($\$15.04$ per thousand DMH)

Resulting equation: $Y = a + bX$
$Y = \$191.85 + \$.01504X$

The analysis shown in Illustration 23 provides the fixed and variable components of indirect labor that existed during the period covered by the data. The next step in developing a variable budget would be to adjust the values, derived by analysis, for any conditions or changes anticipated that did not previously exist. For example, assume upon analysis it is decided that the fixed component as computed is satisfactory but that the variable component should be reduced to $\$.0145$. The variable budget for Department Z would include the following:

Accounts	Fixed per Month	Variable Rate per 100 Direct Machine Hours
Indirect labor	$192.00*	$1.45*

* Practical considerations would suggest that fixed allowances be rounded to even dollars and larger amounts to even tens or hundreds of dollars. Likewise where the number of direct hours is large in a department, the variable rate should be expressed in terms of even tens, hundreds, or perhaps thousands of hours. Rounding on variable rates must be done carefully, especially where the base is large, since the effect of a minor rounding when applied to a large number of hours might be substantial.

Although some have claimed that the least squares analysis is too involved and troublesome for pratical use, surveys show that it is frequently used. The method is not too burdensome when it is realized that the computation may be simplified, because the independent variable (volume or activity) is common to all expense accounts within a particular department or cost center, and one simplified worksheet may provide the analysis for all the accounts in a department (see Schedule 45 for The Superior Manufacturing Company). In addition, certain modern machines make significant shortcuts possible in completing the worksheet and solving the equations for the a and b values. Obviously, too, the mechanics of the computations can be readily taught to low-cost personnel.

The least squares method provides an objective method of analyzing historical data. It is important for the analyst to realize, however, that the results are rigid and often misleadingly precise, and therefore must be tempered with experience and good judgment. In addition, the underlying mathematical assumptions must be understood. If used properly, this approach to the determination of expense variation as related to activity will generally give adequate results.

Participation by supervisors in developing variable budgets

The technical aspects of variable budgets may make it difficult to achieve a meaningful participation of the departmental supervisors. Many firms have adopted the maximum-minimum method of analyses in view of the fact that the *two budget* points (allowances) for each item of expense can be (a) provided by the supervisor concerned, or (b) prepared by the budget department and then submitted to the supervisor for appraisal. On the other hand, the statistical approaches do not lend themselves to such direct participation. When statistical approaches are used, participation may be achieved by transmitting *planning budget allowances,* based on one or more specific levels of activity (within the relevant range) to the supervisors concerned. These planning budget allowances are based on the variable budget formulae developed by the budget department. Supervisors are encouraged to evaluate these allowances and to submit any recommendations with respect to them. Acceptable recommendations would lead to appropriate revision of the formulae. In view of the importance generally attached to participation, effective ways of achieving it with respect to variable budget development should be adopted.

Negative values in cost analysis

Negative fixed (or constant) computed values may result from most of the analyses described above. Likewise negative variable values (negative slope) may result from the graphic and least squares methods. Of course, these negative values can be explained mathematically. From a practical viewpoint, however, they generally should not be used. There are a number of factors that may give rise to negative values: an expense out of control, nonlinear costs, incorrect accounting, nonrepresentative data, incorrect activity base, discretionary cost decisions, and external influences.

When historical costs are being analyzed, it is important that the raw data be studied carefully prior to formal analysis. Any months showing unusual or nonrepresentative conditions should not be included in the analysis. For example, assume that during March of the past year the company participated in a trade show at considerable cost. Either the additional expenditures incurred as a result of the trade show, or data for the entire month of March, should be excluded from any analysis of the variability of the costs with volume.

Negative results persisting after adjustments of the raw data indicate the need for further analysis to determine exactly why the expense is following a random pattern. The analyst should pursue the matter to identify the causative factors so the expense can be given special treatment and attention given to the problem of variability.

Cost-volume considerations

Some authorities view the classification of cost in relation to activity or volume changes with considerable doubt and apprehension. It is generally recognized that there are some costs that are fixed and others that are variable, but there is some question as to whether or not the so-called semivariable costs can be resolved into fixed and variable components. In addition, the straightline assumption usually employed is viewed with some doubt.

In response to these arguments the proponents of the concept of cost variability have advanced the following points:

(1) Although costs in the past have varied in steps, curves, or erratically, such behavior should not be taken as normative for the future. Many costs may have been erratic because of undersirable conditions such as poor control, waste, inefficiency, faulty accounting, and discretionary management decisions.

(2) A large percentage of costs are subject to management policies.

The fact that policies have changed during the period under analysis may cause erratic cost variations. These "policy variations" should be isolated and taken into consideration in estimating future cost variability.

(3) Costs that have been erratic in the past generally will "shape up" when properly budgeted and controlled. For an excellent example see Illustration 24, page 227.

(4) Classification of actual costs in the accounts should be directed toward separate classification of unlike items. For example, certain indirect labor costs may vary in proportion to volume; however, management policy may require that any indirect laborer laid off will be paid two weeks' severance pay. This severance pay should be classified, not as a usual indirect labor charge, but as a special expense. Obviously, mixing the two in one account would tend to destroy the pattern of variability for each account. *Direct cost accounting* procedures applied in the accounts significantly simplifies the resolving of cost variability (see Chapter 15).

(5) Variable budget procedures do not necessarily require straight-line relationships, as was noted and illustrated with respect to the direct estimate method and the table-type variable budget.

(6) There will be certain costs in every firm which are influenced by special factors, some external and some internal, which will require special consideration and treatment from a budget viewpoint. The number of such items is considerably smaller than is commonly supposed.

(7) "The linearity of the total cost function in breakeven charts disturbs many economists because it conflicts with the generalized curves of theory. Net rising marginal production cost is not needed to determine the output which would theoretically maximize profits under imperfect competition. Moreover, many meticulous statistical investigations have found the total production cost function to be linear for several enterprises."[12]

(8) "In the economic research which has been done on cost, one of the important points which has been at stake is the question of whether unit variable costs fall and then rise with expanding output or are constant in their variability. Putting it another way, this is the same question as whether total variable costs would be expressed as a curve or a straight line in diagrammatic presentations. Somewhat contrary to theory, the research investigations of economists have concluded, in general, that unit variables are constant throughout the relevant ranges of volume, that is, total variable costs increase at a constant rate."[13]

[12] Joel Dean, "Cost Structures of Enterprises and Break-even Charts," *American Economic Review* (May 1948), p. 159.

[13] John H. Kempster, "Break-even Analysis—Common Ground for the Economist and the Cost Accountant," *NAA Bulletin* (Feb. 15, 1949), p. 712.

(9) Perfect linearity is not required for practical considerations. Approximate linearity is sufficiently accurate so long as sound management decisions may be based upon the analysis.

(10) Surveys of industry reveal numerous cases where cost variability with volume is identified on a practical and useful basis.

(11) The type of operations engaged in by the firm certainly determines the extent to which cost-volume relationships may be resolved.

(12) "The question of using judgment in budget allowances affects both fixed and variable expenses and affects them so much so that the better the judgment the better the budget. Strict reliance

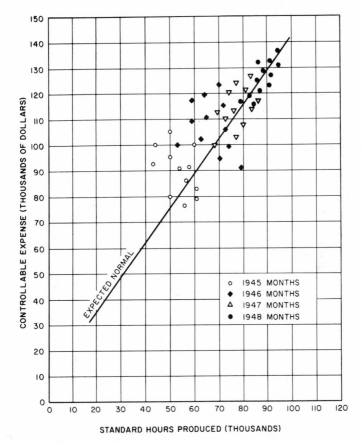

Illustration 24. *Typical Improvement in Cost Variability With Budget Control.*
(SOURCE: E. H. MacNiece, *Production, Forecasting, Planning, and Control,* 3rd ed. [New York: Wiley, 1961], p. 146).

on experience is always the *easiest* way because we can usually find out what our experience has been. But this is not budgeting—it is merely analysis. With the very real possibility of troublesome times ahead, budgeting requires judgment, good judgment, and judgment based on a realistic, economy-minded philosophy."[14]

Cost control considerations

The more complex operations become, the greater the problem of cost control. In highly complex cirumstances costs can be effectively controlled only through planning, continuous effort, and a well-designed system of control. Cost control is a line responsibility, not a staff function. A control system does not and cannot control cost; instead it places within the hands of operating management a tool of control—a tool which can be made effective only by operating management. Operating management will view cost control seriously if top management exhibits a lively interest in it. Investigations have clearly shown that lower levels of management tend to view cost control in the same light as do their superiors. If top management is lackadaisical and inconsistent with respect to cost consciousness, operating management will likewise be. Merely talking about cost control and "riding" some operating supervisor on occasion will not contribute to effective cost control. Intelligent, organized, and consistent effort is essential in order to perform effectively this vital managerial function.

The essentials of an effective cost control program may be outlined as follows:

(1) Top management must provide active and consistent support.
(2) Cost control must be clearly identified as a line responsibility.
(3) The control system must be designed to fit the peculiarities of the situation.
(4) Realistic standards (such as budget allowances) must be developed for use as a basis for gauging performance.
(5) There must be provision for adequate reporting.
(6) The control system must be simple and understandable to operating management.
(7) Cost control reponsibility must be clearly defined throughout the firm. Each cost should be definitely identified as the responsibility of some one individual.

[14] J. A. Campbell, "Common Sense Budgeting for Manufacturing Expenses," *NAA Bulletin* (July 1, 1949), p. 1260.

(8) Cost standards or allowances should be related to activity where possible.

(9) Cost control is effective *prior to cost incurrence* rather than after cost incurrence. Therefore, cost standards or allowances should be used in two ways:

    a. To control costs before incurrence. Control before incurrence is accomplished by providing operating supervisors with cost allowances (budgets), based on scheduled work, prior to the beginning of such work.

    b. To measure the effectiveness with which costs were controlled. Measurement of cost control is accomplished by comparing actual costs incurred with standards or allowances adjusted to actual work done, thereby gauging cost control performance.

(10) Cost control must be applied to costs prior to their allocation.

(11) Adequate follow-up procedures must be developed.

A properly designed and operated budget program will include an effective cost control system. Cost responsibility will have been defined, and cost standards established. The fact that operating supervisors are brought into the entire planning and control program from its inception will in itself tend to generate enthusiasm and cost consciousness.

Use of the Variable Budget Concept in Cost Control—An effective cost control system occasionally can be built around fixed budget procedures for expenses, as is explained in Chapter 8. Circumstances will determine whether or not variable budget procedures are needed. Variable budget procedures for the control of costs are desirable in circumstances in which departmental volume or activity cannot be accurately planned. As indicated previously, the application of variable budget procedures in a particular situation necessarily depends upon the feasibility of identifying the effect of activity on expense. If variable budget procedures can be adapted to the firm's operations, then a very effective and dynamic cost control system is possible.

The application of variable budgets in dynamic cost control is best explained by a simple illustration. Assume for example that we have adopted variable budget cost control procedures for Department Z. To further simplify the illustration, we shall be concerned only with Indirect Labor in Department Z. Variable budget procedures with respect to this one item of expense may be outlined as follows:

(1) *Development of variable budget allowances*—Assume the following: Fixed per month $192.00; Variable per 100 direct machine hours $1.45.

(2) *Preparation of planning budget expense schedule for Department*

Z—(Previously illustrated. Note that this phase is not a part of expense control, but is principally a planning budget function.)

CONTROL ASPECTS:

(3) *Control exerted prior to cost incurrence*—Prior to, say, January 1, the production control department furnishes the budget director with the scheduled work for the department expressed in direct machine hours. Let us assume this to be 40,000 machine hours. The budget allowance (goal) for January for Department Z is computed in this way:

Fixed	$192
Variable ($1.45 × 400)	580
Total indirect labor allowance for January	$772

Based on these computations, a *Report of Expense Allowances for Work Scheduled in January*, as shown in Illustration 25, may be prepared and delivered to the supervisor of Department Z *before* January work commences.

REPORT OF EXPENSE ALLOWANCES FOR WORK SCHEDULED
Department: *Z-Assembly*   Date: *January*
              Items   *Estimated Expense Allowance*
Controllable within department:
  Overtime wages
  Cleaners & sweepers
  Idle or delayed time
  Indirect labor $772
  Rejected production
  Maintenance—machinery & electrical
  Maintenance—general
  Miscellaneous expenses
  Rearrangement
  Shop tools
  Supplies
  Heat, light, power, & water

Noncontrollable within department:
  Supervision
  Vacation wages
  Compensation insurance
  Social Security taxes
    Total
  Direct machine hours scheduled   40,000

Note: This forecast is based on the direct labor hours scheduled for January and puts you in a position to control costs during the month in an effort to meet or better the estimated expense.

Illustration 25. *Report of Expense Allowances*

The supervisor should then utilize this report of allowances as a *guide* for cost incurrence during the month, thereby achieving control at or prior to cost incurrence. The significant point is that a cost once incurred cannot be revoked.

(4) *Measure of the effectiveness of cost control*—As soon as possible after the end of the month (January in the example) a *Departmental Cost Control Performance Report* is prepared for the supervisor of Department Z, which indicates the effectiveness of cost control during the month just ended. In case January production in Department Z actually turns out to be 40,000 direct machine hours, then a comparison of actual indirect labor cost ($825) with the original budget allowance for 40,000 hours would be a suitable measure of cost control performance on the part of the supervisor of Department Z. The comparison would look like this:

Department Z—January

Accounts	Actual Cost (At 40,000 DMH)	Budget Allowance (At 40,000 DMH)	Variation—Status of Cost Control (Unfavorable*) Amount	Per Cent
Indirect labor	$825	$772	$53*	7%*

Cost control performance is somewhat unsatisfactory on the above basis.

Now, assume instead that production plans were changed toward the end of January so that actual direct machine hours were 44,000 and actual cost still $825. The comparison would be as follows:

Accounts	Actual Cost (At 44,000 DMH)	Budget Allowance (At 44,000 DMH)	Variation—Status of Cost Control (Unfavorable*) Amount	Per Cent
Indirect labor	$825	$830ᵃ	$5	1%

ᵃ $192 plus (440 × $1.45)

Cost control in this situation is satisfactory. In the case where the department worked 44,000 hours, had we compared actual cost ($825) with the budget allowance originally computed as shown in Illustration 25 ($772), the supervisor would have had reason to complain of the unfairness of the comparison—the unfairness is due to the effect of volume differential on cost.

Cost Control Reporting. In the preceding chapters we have emphasized the importance of planning and controlling *by responsibility*. In the discussions of material, labor, overhead, distribution and administrative costs, reference has been made to this concept. Typically the better managed firms prepare four general types of reports, viz.:

(1) Those required to satisfy external requirements,
(2) Those of a statistical nature necessary to make available the mass of historical data that all firms must accumulate for various and sundry purposes,
(3) Those special nonrecurring reports related to special problems, and
(4) Those recurring internal reports needed by the management in planning and controlling operations.

At this point we are concerned with the last type of report (see Chapter 12 for a discussion of the fundamentals of reports).

The fundamental aspects of a *departmental expense perfor-mance report* are presented in Illustration 26. This report has been adapted from the procedures of a medium-size company. It is prepared monthly by department and reports year-to-date figures (not illustrated) as well as monthly data. This perfor-mance report, as illustrated, is unique in that it reports on all cost control aspects of the particular department concerned. Note that the report includes control data on (a) direct material usage and cost, (b) direct labor usage and cost, (c) factory overhead cost, and (d) service usage. Significantly, the controllable and noncontrollable costs are reported separately. As indicated in Chapter 12, the various departmental performance control reports should be combined in summaries for the higher levels of management.

Usefulness of the concept of cost variability

In this chapter we have been dealing with a concept having wide applicability in (a) profit planning, (b) managerial deci-sion making, and (c) accounting. The concept of cost variability is the foundation upon which variable budgets, breakeven anal-yses, direct costing, and variation analyses rest. These ap-plications of the variability concept are discussed in succeeding chapters. The extent to which the fixed and variable cost breakdown is useful is indicated in part in the following selected data based on surveys of some better-managed companies:

**Fixed and variable cost breakdowns are
considered useful for many purposes**

Useful for Determining	Per Cent Considering the Technique Useful
(a) The effect of volume on costs	94%
(b) Judging the efficiency of sectors of the company	89
(c) Deciding whether to drop a product	84
(d) Evaluating the effect of sales increase that may accompany a price decrease	82
(e) Determining the breakeven point for the company, its divisions and/or its products	81
(f) Choosing the best method of production	78
(g) Deciding what types of products to add	70
(h) Deciding which products to stress	66
(i) Deciding which markets to stress	50
(j) Choosing the best method of distribution and selling	49

**The majority of participants use separable fixed cost analyses
for an extensive variety of management decisions**

Useful for Determining	Per Cent Using the Technique
(a) Whether to *add to capacity* to produce an existing product	86%
(b) Whether to *close down* a plant or division	81
(c) Whether *to drop* a product or product group	72
(d) The *price and volume* at which a new product must sell to make its introduction profitable	71
(e) What types of products *to add* to a line	67
(f) Whether to open up a new *sales* office or territory	51

Source: James S. Early, *A Comparison of Practices in Costing, Pricing and Market Analysis* (a booklet), prepared by Stevenson, Jordan & Harrison, Inc., in collaboration with The American Institute of Management (adapted from the data therein).

Construction of variable budget illustrated

In the preceding chapter the 1963 variable budget for distribution expenses for The Superior Manufacturing Company was given (Schedule 40, page 192.). The worksheet that follows illustrates the method that was used in developing the variable budget allowances for *General Sales Overhead*. The company uses the least squares and graphic methods for analyzing most expenses. The least squares method was used for most of the distribution expenses.

Since the variable budgets are constructed during the first part of October, historical cost and sales-volume data cover the

DEPARTMENTAL EXPENSE CONTROL REPORT
January 1963
(Only representative figures illustrated)

Department   Z
Supervisor   A. K. Janis

Volume: Month 44,000 DMH
Year to date

Item	Actual Units	Actual Amount	Budget Adjusted to Actual Volume Units	Budget Adjusted to Actual Volume Amounts	Variations—Indicating Status of Control (Favorable-Unfavorable*) Units	Variations—Indicating Status of Control (Favorable-Unfavorable*) Amount	Variations—Indicating Status of Control (Favorable-Unfavorable*) %	YEAR TO DATE COLUMNS REPEATED
CONTROLLABLE:								
Material usage report:								
Direct material A								
Product 1	14,200	$ 7,100	14,000	$ 7,000	200*	$100*	1.4*	
" 2								
etc.								
Total direct material								
Direct labor report								
Product 1	5,300	$10,700	5,200	$10,400	100*	$300*	2.9*	
" 2								
etc.								
Total direct material								
Factory overhead report:								
Overtime								
Cleaners & sweepers								
Idle or delayed time								
Indirect labor		$ 825		$ 830		$ 5	1.0	
etc.								
Total factory overhead								
Service usage report:								
Kilowatt hours	695,000		700,000		5,000		1.0	
Direct repair hours								
Total controllable items								
NONCONTROLLABLE:								
Supervision		$15,000		$15,000				
Vacation wages								
etc.								
Total noncontrollable items								
Over-all Departmental Totals:								
Comments:								

Illustration 26.

The Superior Manufacturing Company
LEAST SQUARES WORKSHEET—GENERAL SALES OVERHEAD
(Analysis for 1963 Variable Budget)

Months	Ref.	Net Sales (000)		Travel and Entertainment		Telephone and Telegraph		Stationery and Office Supplies		Auto Expense	
		X (Given)	X²	Y (Given)	XY	Y (Given)	XY	Y (Given)	XY	Y (Given)	XY
1961											
October		$ 490	$ 240,100	$ 3,300	$ 1,617,000	$ 1,300	$ 637,000	$ 900	$ 441,000	$ 2,200	$ 1,078,000
November		520	270,400	3,400	1,768,000	1,400	728,000	910	473,200	2,250	1,170,000
December		560	313,600	3,420	1,915,200	1,350	756,000	1,020	571,200	2,300	1,288,000
1962											
January		560	313,600	3,500	1,960,000	1,380	772,800	1,000	560,000	2,300	1,288,000
February		510	260,100	3,200	1,632,000	1,290	657,900	950	484,500	2,150	1,096,500
March		440	193,600	2,950	1,298,000	1,290	567,600	830	365,200	1,950	858,000
April		390	152,100	2,700	1,053,000	1,200	468,000	750	292,500	1,650	643,500
May		350	122,500	2,400	840,000	1,170	409,500	700	245,000	1,550	542,500
June		410	168,100	2,830	1,160,300	1,190	487,900	760	311,600	1,850	758,500
July		500	250,000	3,250	1,625,000	1,350	675,000	870	435,000	2,150	1,075,000
August		520	270,400	3,300	1,716,000	1,320	686,400	900	468,000	2,200	1,144,000
September		600	360,000	3,550	2,130,000	1,400	840,000	1,070	642,000	2,450	1,470,000
Summations (Σ)		$5,850	$2,914,500	$37,800	$18,714,500	$15,640	$7,686,100	$10,660	$5,289,200	$25,000	$12,412,000

To compute a and b values:

$$a = \frac{\Sigma X^2 \Sigma Y - \Sigma X \Sigma XY}{N\Sigma X^2 - (\Sigma X)^2} \qquad b = \frac{N\Sigma XY - \Sigma X \Sigma Y}{N\Sigma X^2 - (\Sigma X)^2}$$

Travel & Entertainment

$$a = \frac{(2,914,500)(37,800) - (5,850)(18,714,500)}{(12)(2,914,500) - (5,850)^2} = \frac{688,275,000}{751,500} = \$916. \quad \text{Fixed per month}$$

$$b = \frac{(12)(18,714,500) - (5,850)(37,800)}{(12)(2,914,500) - (5,850)^2} = \frac{3,444,000}{751,500} = \$.458 \quad \text{Variable per \$100 Net Sales}$$

Telephone & Telegraph:

$$a = \frac{(2,914,500)(15,640) - (5,850)(7,686,100)}{751,500} = \frac{619,095,000}{751,500} = \$824. \quad \text{Fixed per month}$$

$$b = \frac{(12)(7,686,100) - (5,850)(15,640)}{751,500} = \frac{739,200}{751,500} = \$.098 \quad \text{Variable per \$100 Net Sales}$$

Computed in same manner: Stationery and Office Supplies

$169.   Fixed per month

$.148   Variable per $100 Net Sales

Auto Expense

$336.   Fixed per month

$.359   Variable per $100 Net Sales

12 months prior to October 1, 1962. Cost and volume data obtained from the cost department indicated:

General Sales Overhead:

(1) Supervisory salaries $12,000 per month (management anticipates no change during the coming year).

(2) Travel & entertainment—Cost data as listed on the worksheet, Schedule 45 (Y).

(3) Telephone & telegraph—Cost data as listed on the worksheet (Y).

(4) Depreciation—Office Equipment $50 per month (no change per depreciation schedule).

(5) Stationery & office supplies—Cost data as listed on the worksheet (Y).

(6) Auto expense—Cost data as listed on the worksheet (Y).

(7) Advertising—Budget per advertising schedule (Schedule 41).

Total net sales for company—As listed on the worksheet (X).

From the information given above the following budget allowances were entered on the variable budget (Schedule 40, page 192): supervisory salaries, fixed per month $12,000; depreciation, fixed per month $50; and advertising, fixed per month $5,000. The four remaining costs were analyzed as indicated in Schedule 45, page 235. It will be observed that the analysis provided fixed and variable components for each individual cost that was entered directly on the variable budget (Schedule 40, page 192). It is important to realize that, although these allowances were used directly as computed *for illustrative purposes*, they should have been tempered with judgement, taking into account new conditions such as revised operations, differing managerial policies, and changes in the general economic outlook.

Discussion Questions

1. What are the principal concepts underlying variable budgets of expense?
2. Define fixed costs. What are the two principal types of fixed cost?
3. Are fixed costs subject to managerial control? Discuss.
4. Define variable costs.
5. What is meant by *relevant range of activity*? How is it related to the classification of costs as fixed or variable?
6. What is the relationship of total fixed and total variable costs to unit costs?
7. Define semivariable costs.

8. What are "stepped" and "curved" costs? How are they usually treated for variable budget purposes?

9. What is meant by *factor of variability*? Why is it so important that the factor of variability be chosen with considerable care?

10. What are the principal considerations in selecting the factor of variability for a department?

11. Indicate the significance of the concept of the relevant range.

12. In developing variable budgets why is the analysis of semivariable costs especially critical?

13. What are the principal methods of identifying the fixed and variable components of cost in a semivariable cost?

14. Explain the three methods of technically expressing variable budgets.

15. Explain the adaptation of the equation $Y = a + bX$ to the problem of determining cost variability.

16. What should be done when negative a or b values result from a particular analysis?

17. What are the principal arguments in support of the concept that costs can be related to activity or volume with reasonable accuracy?

18. Outline the essentials of a cost control program based on budget standards.

19. What are some of the primary applications (uses) of the concept of cost variability?

Planning and Controlling

Capital Additions,

Return on Investment, and Cash

Considerations of capital additions, return on investment, and cash loom large in most, if not all, concerns. In order to control these important aspects of management, it is essential that the top executives develop, in advance, definite plans, policies, and appropriate control procedures; here again management must be forward-looking. The probable cash position for the budget year should be planned in some detail, long- and short-term plans should be developed concerning capital additions, and the trend of return on investment committed to the business should be planned and controlled.

This chapter is devoted to the budget aspects of the considerations mentioned above. For convenience in exposition, the chapter is divided into four sections:

(1) Planning and controlling capital additions
(2) Evaluation of proposed capital additions
(3) Planning and controlling return on the investment
(4) Planning and controlling cash flow

Because capital additions generally call for substantial funds, they are treated prior to discussion of the cash budget.

SECTION ONE: PLANNING AND CONTROLLING CAPITAL ADDITIONS

The importance leading firms in the United States attach to budgeting capital expenditures was clearly indicated in a recent survey of 389 companies, 97 per cent of which undertake *de-*

tailed budgeting of capital additions. Sixty-four per cent of these companies also develop such plans on a long-range basis.[1]

The capital additions budget expresses the detailed plans of top management concerning asset additions, improvements, and replacements. Capital additions represent assets purchased, the costs of which are applicable to a number of accounting periods in the future. The capital additions budget does not include ordinary repairs which should be included in the current expense budgets. Major or extraordinary repairs, the cost of which is capitalized, may be included in the capital additions budget or may be included in a separate budget of extraordinary repairs.

The capital additions budget is frequently referred to as the plant and equipment budget, construction budget, capital outlay budget, investment budget, or plant additions budget. The capital additions budget may include such items as new building, machinery, land, intangibles such as patents, and funds set aside for asset acquisition.

The capital additions budget has considerable significance from the managerial planning and control viewpoints. Top management is constantly faced with the problem of determining the amount of funds that should be invested in fixed plant. The basic problems revolve around the necessity for maintaining adequate facilities for quantity and efficiency and for meeting customer demand and competition. On the other hand, considerable planning and control are necessary to prevent (a) idle plant capacity, (b) overinvestment, and (c) investment in assets that will produce a *low return on the funds involved.*

There are a number of reasons why top management should develop a budget of capital additions. The important objectives of a budget program for capital additions are:

(1) Planning—Makes provision for sound planned capital additions.
(2) Coordination—Makes provision for adequate coordination of capital additions as related to:
    a. Financing needs—cash requirements and financing needs.
    b. Total investment committed to operations.
    c. Sales potential.
    d. Profit potential.
    e. Return on investment.
    f. Financial health of the firm.
(3) Control—Makes provision for control of (a) numerous small capital additions and (b) cost of major capital additions.

[1] Burnard H. Sord and Glenn A. Welsch, *Business Budgeting, A Survey of Management Planning and Control Practices* (New York: Controllership Foundation, Inc., 1958), p. 128.

The primary aspects of a program for planning and controlling capital expenditures may be summarized as follows:[2]

    (1) Selection of the desirable capital additions projects from the various alternative projects.
    (2) Development of the capital expenditures budgets.
    (3) Requests for authority for expenditure of funds.
    (4) Reporting actual expenditures against authorizations.
    (5) Post-completion audit or follow-up of realization from expenditures.

Managerial planning for capital additions

Because capital additions generally involve the more or less permanent commitment of large sums of money, decisions concerning them have a significant, long-term effect on the economic health of the concern. This fact suggests the need for careful analysis and planning on the part of top management. An ill-advised decision concerning capital additions frequently cannot be rectified without seriously affecting the financial health of the concern. Errors in capital additions may result in over-investment or underinvestment and a consequent deterioration of the concern's competitive position in the industry. The next section of this chapter considers several approaches that may be used by management in selecting the capital projects having the greater potential for the firm.

It is important that a distinction be made between long- and short-range capital additions budgeting. In general, budgeting of *long-range* capital additions involves the development of tentative plans for plant and equipment additions two, five, ten, and fifteen or more years into the future. On the other hand, budgeting short-term capital additions involves the development of detailed plans for the annual profit plan. Therefore, the short-term budget of capital expenditures actually represents a one-year segment of the long-term budget. In Chapter 3 a distinction was made between project planning and periodic planning. Planning capital additions primarily involves project planning, especially as regards major items extending over several budget

[2] Adapted from "The Capital Expenditure Control Program," *NAA Bulletin*, Accounting Practice Report No. 7 (March 1959), Sec. 3.

periods. These major projects are *time-segmented* for periodic planning and control purposes.

Long-term capital additions budgeting

In previous chapters the importance of long-range sales plans was emphasized. Such plans are an essential part of the development of the long-range objectives of the company—where the concern desires to be in the industry five, ten, and fifteen years hence. As a part of the development of the long-range objectives there should be tentative planning of the necessary or desired capital additions and appraisal of the long-range cash and financial position. These long-range budgets necessarily must be developed on the basis of broad and highly tentative plans and policies. Although the long-range plans must be flexible, it is desirable that they be reduced to formal expression (written) in some form, as a part of the confidential files of top management. The plans come to light primarily through the medium of the *annual planning budget*, at which point the plans become definite to the extent that there is a commitment by top management to carry them out. Long-range capital additions planning must take into account not only new additions to the plant, but probable plant and equipment replacements due to depreciation and obsolescence.

The importance of long-range top-management planning cannot be overemphasized. It is not unusual for a concern that has considerable potential to stagnate or even decline because of the failure of management to think in terms of the long-range future. One of the principal aspects of a management firmly committed to a comprehensive budget program is their related commitment to careful consideration of long-range capital additions.

Illustration 27 (page 242) presents a form used by one company to give expression to their long-term capital expenditures budget.

Capital additions in the annual profit plan

In developing the annual profit plan, top management faces the problem of reaching some definite (though still tentative) de-

The XYZ Corporation—Long-Range Plan

CAPITAL EXPENDITURE BUDGET—SUMMARY BY PROJECT AND YEARS

For the period Jan. 1, 1963 through 1967

(Expressed in Thousands of Dollars)

Description of Projects	Reference for Detail	Budgeted Date	Budgeted Amount	Amount Authorized to Jan. 1, 1963	Amount Subject to Authorization	Amount Spent to Jan. 1, 1963	Unexpended Balance of Appropriation	1963*	1964	1965	1966	1967	Subsequent Years
								Year of Expenditure—Cash Requirements					
Approved Projects													
Regular:													
Project A	A-1	1961	$1,000	$800	$200	$700	$100	$150	$75	$50	$25		
Etc.													
Special:													
Project E	E-1	1962	500	200	300	180	20	220	70	30			
Etc.													
Total Approved													
*Budgeted Projects**													
Regular:													
Project H	H-1	1963	800		800			100	150	250	200	75	25
Etc.													
Special:													
Project M													
Etc.													
Undesignated**		1963	270					50	50	50	60	60	
Total Budgeted—1963													
Total Regular													
Total Special													
Grand Total													
For Information Only													
Projects Under Study													
Project X	X-1	1964	1,700		1,700								
Etc.													
Total Special													
TOTAL—ALL PROJECTS								200	350	500	400		250

*Detailed in 1963 Profit Plan.

**To take care of minor capital additions; see annual profit plan for 1963 departmental appropriations.

Illustration 27. Long-Range Capital Expenditures Budget

cisions relative to (a) possible changes in capital additions already under way, and (b) capital expenditures that should be included in the annual profit plan. These decisions are essential so that the *annual* or short-term capital additions budget can be included in the detailed planning. To reach these decisions the various projects under consideration must be evaluated in terms of their *investment worth* to the firm (discussed in the next section of this chapter).

The capital additions budget normally will include two principal types of items. First are the *major projects*, each involving considerable funds—buildings, large items of machinery, plant sites, and so on. This type of capital expenditure frequently involves construction (and expenditures) covering more than one year. Such projects generally are considered and planned over a number of years before a final decision is reached on them. It may be observed in Illustration 27 that all projects having a specific project designation are of this type.

The second type of capital additions includes the *minor* capital additions which cannot, or need not, be planned in detail too much in advance of their incurrence. Capital additions of this type are made up of purchases of relatively low-cost machines, small additions to buildings, and other miscellaneous items that are essential to operations. This type of capital addition normally will not enter into long-range planning, except perhaps as a part of total fund requirements. Plans for capital additions for the immediate budget year should be carefully worked out and presented in as much detail as possible. It is quite obvious, however, that generally it will be impossible to project minor additions in detail; consequently, the usual procedure is to include in the capital additions budget a *blanket appropriation* for each subdivision to cover such items. The blanket appropriation should be based on past experience with adjustments for future expectancies. The blanket appropriation should be detailed by areas of responsibility. In Illustration 27, this item of capital expenditure is shown on one line as "Undesignated." The annual capital additions budget (included in the annual profit plan) is based upon the decisions of management relative to the *major projects* and the requests from the various department for appropriations to cover the *minor* capital additions. Cash requirements by interim periods during the year should be included. The annual capital additions budget for the Superior Manufacturing Company is shown on Schedule 46 (page 248).

Responsibility for budgeting capital additions

Procedures and policies should be established to encourage ideas or proposals for capital additions from any source within the company, or even from external sources. However, the primary responsibility for such proposals should rest with all members of management, including divisional and departmental supervisors. With respect to proposals for *major* capital expenditures the primary responsibility rests with top management.

For proposals involving major additions, definite procedures should be established to assure consideration. Many companies report that they must guard against a tendency to disregard a proposal that, on the surface, may not appear to have much potential but which may be quite desirable upon careful analysis. There should be established procedures (or even assistance) whereby the originator has an opportunity to express the idea in writing. If a preliminary review indicates that the idea is worthy of further consideration, steps should be taken to develop the proposal along the following lines:

(1) Description of the project.
(2) Reasons for the recommendation.
(3) Disadvantages of the project.
(4) Evaluation of *investment worth* (return on the investment)
(5) Outline of financing requirements.
(6) Probable starting and completion dates.
(7) Plans for coordinating the project with the short- and long-range objectives and potentials of the firm.

On the basis of a study along these lines, top management may decide to drop the project or to proceed with further analysis and planning. In the latter case, the data suggested above may be developed in considerable detail and re-evaluated. The plant engineering department should be assigned the responsibility of developing these data with the help of the major executives concerned. If top management eventually arrives at a favorable decision on the project, it is assigned a permanent project number to be included in the *annual planning budget* for the period in which the project will be undertaken. At this point the problem of *control* of the *major* items becomes important.

As to responsibility for the *minor* capital additions (blanket appropriation), again anyone within the firm may originate ideas or suggest the need for certain items, or day-to-day operations may indicate a particular need. However, budget requests for this type of capital addition should come chiefly from lower level (operating) management. The executives and supervisors concerned should be primarily responsible for related estimates and their subsequent control.

A definite executive, such as the chief engineer, should be primarily responsible for coordinating the development of the capital additions budget. After the approval by top management the estimates are included in the annual capital additions budget.

Capital additions plans must be consistent with the cash position and financing considerations created thereby. Both the timing of capital additions and the amount of funds that can be invested in plant involve serious policy decisions. Sales potential, related costs, and the anticipated profit potential must be carefully appraised for some time in the future. Return on investment (net profit divided by total investment) is recognized as the chief criterion of the long-run efficiency of management. Capital additions should be analyzed in terms of their probable effect on return on investment (discussed in the next section of this chapter). Prudent management ordinarily would not undertake a capital addition unless such addition would yield a return equal to, or greater than, the present return on assets or the long-range company objective for return on investment.

Control of capital additions

The importance of adequate control of capital additions cannot be emphasized too strongly. Control is not solely, nor even primarily, downward pressure on expenditures. Control must rest upon sound managerial planning that restricts expenditures to economically justifiable additions, yet guards against stagnation in the maintenance, replacement, and acquisition of capital assets.

Inclusion of major capital additions projects in the annual profit plan indicates that top management has decided to go ahead with the project at a specific time. This inclusion, however, should not constitute orders to proceed. A system of control that will indicate to management the progress, cost, and status of capital additions throughout the year is essential.

The first aspect of control involves formal authorization to undertake a project, including the appropriation of funds, even though the project was included in the planning budget. For major capital additions projects, top management should reserve to itself the responsibility for the go-ahead authorization, which may consist of formal or informal notification, depending upon the internal situation.

For *minor capital* additions, and in particular those covered by the blanket appropriation, a lower level of management is generally given the authority to issue final authorization. For example, the authority to approve such expenditures within the budget limitation may be delegated along the following lines:

Amounts	*Approval Required*
Up to $100	Department manager
$101 to $300	Plant manager
$301 to $1,000	Vice president in charge of manufacturing
Over $1,000	President

The usual practice is to seek final approval of capital additions on a *request for capital expenditure* form.

The second phase of current control of expenditures is concerned with accumulating data on costs, progress of work, and cumulative expenditures in relation to budget plans. Here again the two types of capital additions, major and minor, must be distinguished.

As soon as a major capital addition is authorized and undertaken, cost records should be set up by project number. This record should make provision for accumulation of costs by responsibility and type and for supplementary information concerning the progress of the work. *Capital addition status reports* for each project should be prepared for top management at short intervals indicating such items as:

Costs:
  Amount budgeted
  Expenditures to date
  Outstanding commitments
  Amount unexpended per budget
  Estimated cost to complete project
  Indicated over- or underexpenditure
Progress report:
  Date started
  Date originally scheduled for completion
  Estimated days needed to complete project
  Estimated date of completion
  Percentage completed to date (in terms of time)
  Percentage completed to date (in terms of cost)

Comments for top management consideration:
   Quality of work
   Unexpected circumstances

The control of minor capital additions can be achieved through the authorization procedure mentioned above and through the subsequent accumulation of actual expenditures in terms of areas of organizational responsibility. The actual expenditures are then compared with planning budget allowances in the capital additions status reports which should be rendered at frequent intervals. These reports should indicate budget variations and unexpended balances.

The final phase of control of expenditures for capital additions might be appropriately termed *follow-up*. After the project is completed, the cost records should be completed and the total cost recorded in the accounts as an asset. It is important to note that underexpenditures on one project should not be transferred to other projects without the formal approval of top management; otherwise, control may be lost. A final report on the completed project should be prepared for top management. Follow-up includes final inspections and related reports.

Another important phase of follow-up may extend several years after a major project is completed. Some concerns follow the practice of making regular studies of certain projects subsequent to completion to determine whether or not the project is producing the results anticipated in the analysis that led to the managerial decision to undertake the project. Studies of this type are important for several reasons. In the first place, they provide a good test of the adequacy of the original analysis, and secondly, they supply valuable information that may constructively influence managerial decisions in the future.[3]

Capital additions budget illustrated

The top executives of The Superior Manufacturing Company maintain a long-term capital additions budget. The 1963 segment of the long-term capital additions budget to be included in the annual profit plan is indicated in Schedule 46. It is important to note that the cash requirements for capital additions during 1963 also are indicated. Major capital additions planned for 1964 are indicated for information purposes only.

[3] "The Capital Expenditure Control Program," *NAA Bulletin*, Accounting Practice Report No. 7 (March 1959), Sec. 3.

The Superior Manufacturing Company

CAPITAL ADDITIONS BUDGET
For the Year Ending December 31, 1963

Schedule 46

Items	Ref.	Estimated Starting Date	Estimated Completion Date	Estimated Cost (Given)	1964 Budget	1963 Budget—Date of Cash Payments Annual Total	First Quarter January	February	March	Quarters First	Second	Third	Fourth
1964:													
New Building		1/64	9/64	$120,000	$120,000								
Machinery, Dept. 1		7/64	9/64	10,000	10,000								
1963:													
Repair Tools		1/63	1/63	200		$200	$200	$	$	$200	$	$	
Power Motor		12/63	12/63	8,500		8,500							$ 8,500
Totals				$138,700	$130,000	$ 8,700	$200			$200			$ 8,500
Assets Funded:													
New Building						$20,000							$20,000
Cash Required by Time Period						$28,700	$200			$200			$28,500

Depreciation Information:

	Estimated Depreciable Life	Scrap Value
New Building	Undecided	—
Machinery—Department 1	Undecided	—
Repair Tools	5 years	—
Power Motor (Power Department)	10 years	—

The Superior Manufacturing Company

SCHEDULE OF BUDGETED DEPRECIATION
For the Year Ending December 31, 1963

Item	Depreciation Rate	Asset Balance 1/1/63 (Given)	Assets Acquired 1963	Asset Balance 12/31/63	Accumulated Depreciation Balance 1/1/63 (Given)	Depreciation Charged 1963	Accumulated Depreciation Balance 12/31/63	First Quarter Jan.	First Quarter Feb.	First Quarter March	Second	Third	Fourth
Building	30 yrs.	$1,800,000	$	$1,800,000	$360,000	$60,000	$420,000	$5,000	$5,000	$5,000	$15,000	$15,000	$15,000
General Purpose Tools	5 yrs.	7,800		7,800	4,680	1,560	6,240	130	130	130	390	390	390
Power Machinery	10 yrs.	54,000	8,500	62,500	21,600	5,400	27,000	450	450	450	1,350	1,350	1,350
Repair Tools	5 yrs.	400	200	600	200	120	320	10	10	10	30	30	30
Machinery—Dept. 1	$.015*	100,000		100,000	20,000	7,320	27,320	522	588	594	1,860	1,761	1,995
Machinery—Dept. 2	.004*	20,000		20,000	12,000	768	12,768	56	64	64	192	184	208
Machinery—Dept. 3	.009*	72,000		72,000	13,500	4,392	17,892	313	353	356	1,116	1,057	1,197
Sales Office Equipment	8 yrs.	4,800		4,800	2,400	600	3,000	50	50	50	150	150	150
Accounting Office Equipment	5 yrs.	12,000		12,000	6,000	2,400	8,400	200	200	200	600	600	600
Treasurer's Office Equipment	5 yrs.	6,000		6,000	2,000	1,200	3,200	100	100	100	300	300	300
Administrative Office Equipment	5 yrs.	3,000		3,000	1,000	600	1,600	50	50	50	150	150	150
Subtotals		$ 280,000	$8,700	$ 288,700	$ 83,380	$24,360	$107,740	$1,881	$1,995	$2,004	$ 6,138	$ 5,972	$ 6,370
Grand Totals		$2,080,000	$8,700	$2,088,700	$443,380	$84,360	$527,740	$6,881	$6,995	$7,004	$21,138	$20,972	$21,370
Depreciation Expense Analysis by Function:													
Manufacturing						$19,560		$1,481	$1,595	$1,604	$ 4,938	$ 4,772	$ 5,170
Selling						600		50	50	50	150	150	150
Administration						4,200		350	350	350	1,050	1,050	1,050
Totals						$24,360		$1,881	$1,995	$2,004	$ 6,138	$ 5,972	$ 6,370

*Per Direct Labor Hour.

It is appropriate at this point to introduce the schedule of budgeted depreciation, because it is related to the capital additions budget. The schedule of budgeted depreciation for The Superior Manufacturing Company is shown in Schedule 47. This schedule may be included as a part of the planning budget. It may be observed that the depreciation estimates indicated on both the variable budgets and expense schedules included in the annual profit plan are consistent with the amounts indicated in the depreciation schedule.

SECTION TWO: MANAGERIAL EVALUATION OF PROPOSED CAPITAL ADDITIONS

In the preceding section we considered the planning and control of capital additions. There it was presumed that the basic decisions as to the allocation of funds to specific capital additions projects had been largely resolved. Within the framework of a systematized budget program for capital additions is the central problem of managerial choice between numerous alternative capital additions. When the list of "needs" for capital expenditures provided by the various divisions, executives, etc., are totaled, they may require perhaps twice the funds that can be made available. Thus, instrumental in planning and controlling capital additions is the *selection* by management of the more promising alternatives. These decisions are critical because once capital is invested in long-lived assets, management's opportunities to change the program are limited; *sunk costs* are involved and these are recoverable through use of the asset rather than through sale. In view of these considerations it is quite apparent that management must utilize systematic and reliable approaches in evaluating proposed capital additions. Basically the managerial problem is to identify and choose those projects having the highest *investment worth*—that is, the highest *rate of return* on the investment. Space precludes exhaustive treatment of the subject. The paragraphs to follow indicate briefly some of the approaches that have been used. Footnote references are included to direct the reader to comprehensive treatments of the subject.

In rationing funds among capital projects, management must, of necessity, impose an over-all budget limitation. Within this limitation specific expenditures for particular projects should be made on the basis of an objective evaluation of their *investment worth.* Minor capital additions, as explained in the preceding section, are best planned and controlled on a *blanket appropriation* basis. In some cases certain additions, replacements, and renovations are absolutely necessary. On the other hand, each major capital project proposed should stand the tests of sound judgment and investment worth.[4]

Numerous approaches are to be found in literature and in practice for managerial evaluation of alternative capital projects. The primary approaches are:

1. The pay-back method
2. The average return on investment method
3. The discounted rate of return method
4. The MAPI method[5]

We will briefly explain the first three approaches. In order to illustrate the technical aspects of each method we will utilize the following *estimates* relating to a proposed capital additions project:

(a)	Net installed cost of proposed machine—Type A	$11,000
(b)	Economic (useful) life of proposed machine	10 years
(c)	Annual earnings of machine before taxes and depreciation	$4,400
(d)	Annual depreciation (straight-line)	$1,100
(e)	Annual earnings subject to income tax	$3,300
(f)	Income tax (at assumed 50% rate)	$1,650
(g)	Annual earnings after taxes and depreciation	$1,650
(h)	Annual earnings after taxes, before depreciation ($4,400 − $1,650)	$2,750

The Pay-back Method. This method derives "The estimated period (years, months) required for the incremental cash investment in a project to be recovered from year-to-year incremental operating cash flow or throwoff.[6]

The formula for the pay-back method is:

$$\frac{\text{Net investment outlay}}{\substack{\text{Net earnings (or cost savings)} \\ \text{after taxes, before depreciation}}} = \text{Pay-back period in years}$$

[4] For an excellent treatment see: Harold Bierman, Jr., and Seymour Smidt, *The Capital Budgeting Decision* (New York: Macmillan, 1960).

[5] G. W. Terborgh, *Business Investment Policy* (Chicago: Machinery and Allied Products Institute, 1958).

[6] Herbert E. Dougall, "Payback as an Aid in Capital Budgeting," *The Controller* (Feb. 1961), p. 67.

Substituting the illustrative data:

$$\frac{\$11,000}{\$\ 2,750} = 4.0 \text{ years}$$

Thus the cash outlay for the investment will be recovered in full in four years. The pay-back method is easy to compute and understand yet it has some fundamental weaknesses. It does not measure profitability or investment worth, although the reciprocal of the pay-back figure is sometimes computed as an approximation of the rate of return ($1.00 \div 4.00 = .25$). It does not consider the *time-value* of money nor does it distinguish between alternatives having different economic lives. For example, assume we are considering an alternative machine having identical costs and income as the one above *except* that it has an estimated useful life of twenty years instead of ten. In this situation the two machines would have about the same pay-back period; however, the alternative machine would be a much better buy since it may generate income twice as long as the other machine. Despite these deficiencies the pay-back method is the most widely used. Perhaps the most effective application of the method is as a rough test to determine whether further investigation is warranted.

The Average Return on Investment Method. This method (also referred to as the financial statement method) provides a rough approximation of the rate of return on the proposed capital addition. The formula for this method is:

$$\frac{\text{Average annual earnings after taxes, before depreciation}}{\text{Average lifetime investment}} = \text{Average rate of return}$$

Substituting the illustrative data:

$$\frac{\$2,750}{\$11,000 \div 2} = \frac{\$2,750}{\$5,500} = 50 \text{ per cent return}$$

There are several variations of this particular method. For example, one variation is the average annual return on the original investment ($\$2,750 \div \$11,000 = 25\%$).

Although the average return on investment method, in contrast to the pay-back method, provides a rate of return figure, it suffers from a fundamental theoretical weakness. It does not consider the time-value of money; a dollar of income in the first year is given the same value as a dollar of income to be received in, say, the tenth year.[7]

---

[7] "Return on Capital as a Guide to Managerial Decision," Research Report No. 35 (New York: National Association of Accounts, Dec. 1953), pp. 49-56.

The Discounted Rate of Return Method. This method is variously referred to as the discounted cash flow method, and the time-adjusted rate of return method.[8] It is based on the premise that funds normally should be invested in projects that show a rate of return above a certain minimum, or alternatively, that funds should be committed to those projects indicating the highest return on the investment. The discounted rate of return method provides an interest rate that is comparable to the usual concept of an interest rate. In order to develop such a rate the present value of the various cash inflows must be determined. Fundamentally, the problem is to determine what the rate of interest return is for (a) a given investment and (b) the related series of earnings. Returning to our example, we must compute the rate of interest that the proposed investment of $11,000 will earn, assuming an annual average earnings of $2,750 (after taxes and before depreciation).

An understanding of the concept of *present value* is essential in comprehending computation of the discounted rate of return. The present value concept may be illustrated simply: What is the present value of, say, $1,000 to be received one year hence, assuming an interest rate of 10 per cent? The present value may be computed as follows:

$$PV = F\left(\frac{1}{1+i}\right)^n$$

PV = Present value
F = Future sum of money
i = Interest rate per period
n = Number of periods

Substituting:

$$PV = \$1,000\left(\frac{1}{1+.10}\right)^1$$

$$= \underline{\$909.09}$$

Proof:

Present value	$909.09
Interest ($909.09 × .10)	90.91
Value one year hence	$1,000.00

Rather than making the computation as illustrated above, we may refer to a "Present Value of $1" table (Table A, Page 254) and obtain the present value *factor* for 10 per cent, for one year. This factor (0.909) multiplied by the $1,000 gives the

[8] For a variation of this method, referred to as the present-value method, see: Harold Bierman, Jr., and Seymour Smidt, *The Capital Budgeting Decision* (New York: Macmillan, 1960).

Table A. Present Value of $1

Years Hence	1%	2%	4%	6%	8%	10%	12%	14%	15%	16%	18%	20%	22%	24%	25%
1	0.990	0.980	0.962	0.943	0.926	0.909	0.893	0.877	0.870	0.862	0.847	0.833	0.820	0.806	0.800
2	0.980	0.961	0.925	0.890	0.857	0.826	0.797	0.769	0.756	0.743	0.718	0.694	0.672	0.650	0.640
3	0.971	0.942	0.889	0.840	0.794	0.751	0.712	0.675	0.658	0.641	0.609	0.579	0.551	0.524	0.512
4	0.961	0.924	0.855	0.792	0.735	0.683	0.636	0.592	0.572	0.552	0.516	0.482	0.451	0.423	0.410
5	0.951	0.906	0.822	0.747	0.681	0.621	0.567	0.519	0.497	0.476	0.437	0.402	0.370	0.341	0.328
6	0.942	0.888	0.790	0.705	0.630	0.564	0.507	0.456	0.432	0.410	0.370	0.335	0.303	0.275	0.262
7	0.933	0.871	0.760	0.665	0.583	0.513	0.452	0.400	0.376	0.354	0.314	0.279	0.249	0.222	0.210
8	0.923	0.853	0.731	0.627	0.540	0.467	0.404	0.351	0.327	0.305	0.266	0.233	0.204	0.179	0.168
9	0.914	0.837	0.703	0.592	0.500	0.424	0.361	0.308	0.284	0.263	0.225	0.194	0.167	0.144	0.134
10	0.905	0.820	0.676	0.558	0.463	0.386	0.322	0.270	0.247	0.227	0.191	0.162	0.137	0.116	0.107
11	0.896	0.804	0.650	0.527	0.429	0.350	0.287	0.237	0.215	0.195	0.162	0.135	0.112	0.094	0.086
12	0.887	0.788	0.625	0.497	0.397	0.319	0.257	0.208	0.187	0.168	0.137	0.112	0.092	0.076	0.069
13	0.879	0.773	0.601	0.469	0.368	0.290	0.229	0.182	0.163	0.145	0.116	0.093	0.075	0.061	0.055
14	0.870	0.758	0.577	0.442	0.340	0.263	0.205	0.160	0.141	0.125	0.099	0.078	0.062	0.049	0.044
15	0.861	0.743	0.555	0.417	0.315	0.239	0.183	0.140	0.123	0.108	0.084	0.065	0.051	0.040	0.035

Table B. Present Value of $1 Received Annually for N Years

Years (N)	1%	2%	4%	6%	8%	10%	12%	14%	15%	16%	18%	20%	22%	24%	25%
1	0.990	0.980	0.962	0.943	0.926	0.909	0.893	0.877	0.870	0.862	0.847	0.833	0.820	0.806	0.800
2	1.970	1.942	1.886	1.833	1.783	1.736	1.690	1.647	1.626	1.605	1.566	1.528	1.492	1.457	1.440
3	2.941	2.884	2.775	2.673	2.577	2.487	2.402	2.322	2.283	2.246	2.174	2.106	2.042	1.981	1.952
4	3.902	3.808	3.630	3.465	3.312	3.170	3.037	2.914	2.855	2.798	2.690	2.589	2.494	2.404	2.362
5	4.853	4.713	4.452	4.212	3.993	3.791	3.605	3.433	3.352	3.274	3.127	2.991	2.864	2.745	2.689
6	5.795	5.601	5.242	4.917	4.623	4.355	4.111	3.889	3.784	3.685	3.498	3.326	3.167	3.020	2.951
7	6.728	6.472	6.002	5.582	5.206	4.868	4.564	4.288	4.160	4.039	3.812	3.605	3.416	3.242	3.161
8	7.652	7.325	6.733	6.210	5.747	5.335	4.968	4.639	4.487	4.344	4.078	3.837	3.619	3.421	3.329
9	8.566	8.162	7.435	6.802	6.247	5.759	5.328	4.946	4.772	4.607	4.303	4.031	3.786	3.566	3.463
10	9.471	8.983	8.111	7.360	6.710	6.145	5.650	5.216	5.019	4.833	4.494	4.192	3.923	3.682	3.571
11	10.368	9.787	8.760	7.887	7.139	6.495	5.988	5.453	5.234	5.029	4.656	4.327	4.035	3.776	3.656
12	11.255	10.575	9.385	8.384	7.536	6.814	6.194	5.660	5.421	5.197	4.793	4.439	4.127	3.851	3.725
13	12.134	11.343	9.986	8.853	7.904	7.103	6.424	5.842	5.583	5.342	4.910	4.533	4.203	3.912	3.780
14	13.004	12.106	10.563	9.295	8.244	7.367	6.628	6.002	5.724	5.468	5.008	4.611	4.265	3.962	3.824
15	13.865	12.849	11.118	9.712	8.559	7.606	6.811	6.142	5.847	5.575	5.092	4.675	4.315	4.001	3.859

same present value, $909.09, computed above.* Similarly, we may determine the present value of, say, $4,500 to be received three years hence, assuming an interest rate of 6 per cent. Reading from the table (the 6 per cent column, the line for three years) we find the factor 0.840. The present value is ($4,500 × 0.840) $3,780. The following table indicates the correctness of the computation:

Year	Principal Invested at Beginning of Year	Add Earnings (6% × Col. 1)	Principal Plus Earnings Invested at End of Year
1	$3,780.00	$226.80	$4,006.80
2	4,006.80	240.41	4,247.21
3	4,247.21	254.83	4,502.04*

*$2.04 due to rounding error since table is carried to only three places

A somewhat different situation involving the concept of present value is posed when the present value of a *series of equal annual payments* is involved. To illustrate, what is the present value of $1,000 to be received at the end of each of three years, assuming an interest rate of, say, 6 per cent? Stated somewhat differently, what would you have to pay (in lump sum) at the beginning of year one for an annuity contract which pays you in return $1,000 at the end of each of three years, assuming an interest rate of 6 per cent? The cost of the annuity contract (present value of the future receipts) may be computed by formula. However, if a table of "Present Value of $1 Received Annually for N Years" (Table B, Page 255) is available, the computation is quite simple. From the table we obtain the discount factor of 2.673 (6 per cent column, line for year three). The present value may be directly computed (2.673 × $1,000) as $2,673. The computation may be verified as follows:

Year	Principal Invested at Beginning of Year (a)	Year End Earnings (6% × Col.[a]) (b)	Annuity Payments to be Returned at Year End (c)	Balance Invested at Year End (a) + (b) − (c)
1	$2,673.00	$160.38	$1,000.00	$1,833.38
2	1,833.38	110.00	1,000.00	943.38
3	943.38	56.62	1,000.00	–0–

With the present value concept in mind, let's return to our

* Tables may be based on several assumptions, viz.: that the cash flow occurs (1) at year-end, (2) in uniform monthly installments, or (3) continuously during the year. For purposes of illustration herein tables under assumption (1) are utilized, although the second and third assumptions generally are more representative of actual conditions. See "Return on Capital as a Guide to Managerial Decisions," Research Report No. 35, National Association of Accountants, New York, Dec. 1959, pp. 97-104.

original problem, that of determining the rate of return for an investment of $11,000 that generates earnings (cash inflow) of $2,750 per year for ten years. *The discounted rate of return is that rate of interest that will discount the future earnings of the asset so that the sum of the discounted incomes (present value of the incomes) exactly equals the original investment in the asset (cost).*

Calculation of the discounted rate of return inherently separates that portion of each year's income that represents *return of cost* from the portion that represents income; therefore, in the computations income is not reduced by depreciation charges. Income *is* reduced by income taxes because they require cash. As a consequence of these adjustments, the computation is based on a strictly *cash flow* concept of income for the project.

The rate of return cannot be computed directly; we must utilize a method of elimination (trial runs) to estimate the rate. Note that this problem is different from that illustrated above in that (a) the rate is not known as it was above, and (b) the investment is known whereas it was not known above. The steps shown below can be used when (a) the estimated annual earnings are *equal* each period, and (b) when there is *no salvage value.* (Based on data given on page 251.)

Step 1: State the data in the following equation:
Investment = Earnings (discounted for ten years at an unknown rate of return)
$11,000   = $2,750 (discounted for ten years at an unknown rate of return)

Step 2: Divide the investment by the annual earnings to determine the "Table Factor."
$11,000 ÷ $2,750 = 4.0 (Table B Factor)

Step 3: Enter the table "Present Value of $1 Received Annually for N Years" (page 255) on the line "ten years" and find the factor closest to 4.0. In this case the 4.0 falls between 20 per cent (4.192) and 22 per cent (3.923). From this we can deduce that the approximate rate of return is 22 per cent.

Step 4: If more precision is desired we can interpolate between 20 and 22 per cent as follows:

22%—3.923 ┐ .077
? —4.000 ┘   .269
20%—4.192 ────────┘

$\frac{.077}{.269} \times 2\% = .572\%$

$22\% - .572\% = 21.428\%$ Rate of return

In order to illustrate the computation when the earnings (cash inflows) are *irregular* from period to period, consider a proposal costing $15,000 with incomes (after tax, before depreciation) over a five-year useful life as follows: 1st, $5,050; 2nd, $4,550; 3rd, $4,050. 4th, $3,550; and 5th, $3,050. Because the earnings are irregular we must consider each year separately by using Table A, "Present Value of $1," on page 254. In this case we simply estimate the rate by inspection, then test it. Let's assume we estimate that the rate will be approximately 15 per cent; our "tests" would be as follows:*

Investment cost $15,000; five-year life

Year	Earnings (Cash Inflow Estimated)	First Trial @ 15% Discount Factor From Table	Present Value	Second Trial @ 14% Discount Factor from Table	Present Value	Third Trial @ 12% Discount Factor from Table	Present Value
1	$ 5,050	.870	$ 4,394*	.877	$ 4,429	.893	$ 4,510
2	4,550	.756	3,440	.769	3,499	.797	3,626
3	4,050	.658	2,665	.675	2,734	.712	2,884
4	3,550	.572	2,031	.592	2,102	.636	2,258
5	3,050	.497	1,516	.519	1,583	.567	1,729
Totals	$20,250		$14,046		$14,347		$15,007

* $5,050 × .870 = $4,394

Our first trial demonstrated that the 15 per cent rate was too high (since the sum of the discounted values was below $15,000); the second trial demonstrated that 14 per cent also was too high. The third trial at 12 per cent equates the investment cost of $15,000 with the sum of the present values of the earnings for the five years, thus the rate of return for the proposal is 12 per cent.

The discounted rate of the return might be: (a) compared with a minimum standard rate established by the management, (b) used to rank the project against other alternative proposals, and (c) compared with the expected return on the investment for the firm over-all. The discounted rate of return meets all theoretical considerations and at the same time is a very practical approach in that the rate developed is comparable to other interest rates.[9] Complexity of computation has deterred some firms from utilizing the approach, although those who have worked with it a short time report that this disadvantage is of little consequence.[10]

* The reader should realize that the computation is more complex when such factors as salvage value, multiple investment dates, partial disinvestment, and cost savings (rather than earnings) are involved.

[9] Joel Dean, "Profitability Indexes for Capital Investment," *The Controller* (Feb. 1958), p. 64.

[10] Joel Dean, *Capital Budgeting* (New York: Columbia University Press, 1951).

The results of the three methods as applied to the continuing illustration may be summarized as follows:

ANALYSIS OF PROPOSAL—Asset cost $11,000, average
annual earnings $2,750 and estimated life ten years
1. Pay-back:
    Years   4.0 years
    Return   25%
2. Average Return on Investment:
    on average investment   45.8%
    on original investment   25%
3. Discounted rate of return   21.4%

Some firms follow the practice of developing all of the analyses listed above; most firms using the discounted rate of return analysis also compute the pay-back. In comparing and ranking various proposals, consideration may be given to a number of analyses, practical considerations, and value judgments.

In using the results of the various evaluation techniques discussed in this section, the role of *judgment* must not be overlooked. Because all of the evaluations are of necessity based upon *estimates* of future potentials, the result can be no better than the estimates. In large measure the estimates themselves are subject to judgments. In addition there may be numerous factors related to the proposal that cannot be quantified. For example, the effect of a particular proposal on employee morale, and hence output, cannot be expressed in figures; yet it may be an over-riding factor in the decision. In many cases the nonquantitative factors may be clearly controlling. A keen appreciation of the assumptions underlying the computations in each technique is essential.[11] In decision making we must guard against accepting a quantitative expression as being infallible and thus allow ourselves to be lulled into a false sense of confidence. The role of managerial judgment and experience still looms large despite the mathematical results obtained through techniques such as those discussed above.

SECTION THREE: PLANNING AND CONTROLLING RETURN ON THE INVESTMENT

Simply stated, return on investment is derived by dividing income by investment (assets). Return on investment is variously referred to as capital yield, return on assets employed, return on capital, or simply rate of return. Broadly speaking, return

[11] Robert N. Anthony, "Some Fallacies in Figuring Return on Investment," *NAA Bulletin* (Dec. 1960), pp. 5-13.

on investment has two significant applications in business situations:

> (1) Evaluating individual proposed capital additions (discussed in the preceding section).
> (2) Measuring the absolute and relative success of a company and its subdivisions.

Return on investment as a measure of managerial effectiveness

One of the central problems of top management in the development of a planning budget is an evaluation of the budgeted profit that is a *residue* when budgeted incomes and costs are "built up," as previously explained and illustrated. The profit residue may be appraised as to adequacy on the basis of judgment, past experience, and on what is known concerning competitors' profits. Another common practice is to appraise the adequacy of a profit figure as a per cent of net sales (profit margin), but this latter ratio does not take into account an important factor—the *amount of capital required* to produce the profits. Another ratio frequently used is the ratio of profit to owners' equity. This ratio indicates how effectively owner equity (original investment and undistributed profits) is being employed, but its neglects the important factor of debt financing.

The concept of return on investment provides a more meaningful approach to the evaluation of profit. Return on investment applied to a company, or its subdivisions, is derived by dividing net income by *total* assets employed. The procedure may be applied to historical data thereby constituting a realized rate of return, or it may be applied to budgeted data, constituting a planned or projected rate of return. From a budgeting point of view, it has been suggested that it is generally desirable to develop the revenue side of the budget and then to apply a standard rate of return to the assets employed, the results of which are deducted from revenue, leaving a residual for *costs*. On the other hand, it is frequently argued that the better approach is to develop the revenue and costs, leaving profits as the residual. After this process is completed, the profits are evaluated in terms of return on investment. If the return is inadequate, the entire plan of operations (budget) must be surveyed and restudied with a view to increasing sales, decreasing costs, decreasing investment, or some combination thereof, any of which accomplishments would have a favorable effect upon the return on investment figure.

The tendency in considering action to increase profits is to look to increased sales and decreased costs irrespective of the additional capital that might be involved. The entire triangle of financial management—sales, profits, and investment—must be considered. A concern can grow through profitability as well as through increased sales. Return on investment, properly computed, thus makes possible a simple and understandable over-all evaluation of the effectiveness of financial management.

The important relationship of return on investment to all phases of operations is indicated in Illustration 28. The formula for direct computation of return on investment is:

$$\frac{\text{Profit}}{\text{Investment}} = \text{Return on Investment}$$

The ratio assumes more significance when it is realized that it is the direct result of two other ratios, the *profit margin* and *investment turnover:*

(1) $\dfrac{\text{Profit}}{\text{Sales}} = \text{Profit Margin}$

(2) $\dfrac{\text{Sales}}{\text{Investment}} = \text{Investment Turnover}$

(3) Profit Margin × Investment Turnover = Return on Investment

To illustrate, assume: sales, $100,000; profit, $10,000; and investment, $50,000. The ratios are apparent:

(1) $\dfrac{\$10,000\ (\text{Profit})}{\$50,000\ (\text{Investment})} = 20\%$ (Return on Investment)

−or−

(2) $\dfrac{\$10,000\ (\text{Profit})}{\$100,000\quad (\text{Sales})} = 10\%$ (Profit Margin)

(3) $\dfrac{\$100,000\quad (\text{Sales})}{\$50,000\ (\text{Investment})} = 2$ (Investment Turnover)

(4) 10% (Profit Margin) × 2 (Investment Turnover) = 20% (Return on Investment)

From this simple example the significance of the three factors (sales, profits, and investment) on the return on investment is apparent. Illustration 28 in turn traces graphically the interrelation of all financial aspects of operations as they affect the rate of return on investment. This type of illustration is excellent for presenting the concept to management and for suggesting approaches to improving the rate in particular situations.

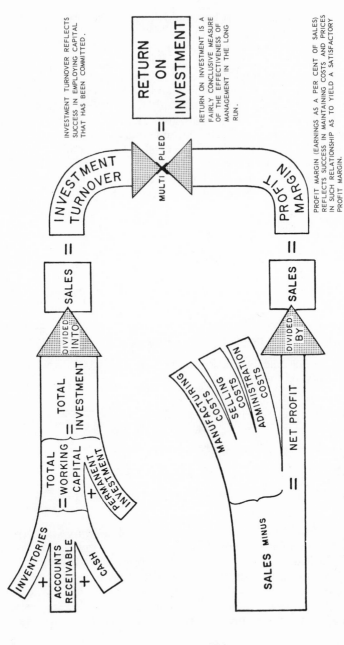

RELATIONSHIP OF FACTORS AFFECTING RETURN ON INVESTMENT

Illustration 28. Relationship of Factors Affecting Return on Investment

For example, the chart readily shows the effect of a reduction either in cost or in capital outlay on the return on investment. Similarly an increase in sales or reduction in inventories is apparent.

In computing return on investment, for a company as a whole or for each division separately, it is essential that *investment* and *income* be carefully defined. Actual practice reveals considerable variation in the way these two terms are defined and, therefore, determined in dollars. It would seem desirable that the definitions be determined by a firm in the light of its particular situation and its use of the results.

Basically investment may be defined as (a) total funds committed to the business (total assets as reported on the balance sheet), or (b) as total owners' equity. Most companies using the concept of rate of return compute and use *both* concepts because each tells a somewhat different story. However, for internal evaluations most firms define investment as total assets. In defining *investment* the following items should be given special attention:

(1) Idle assets—There is a basic question as to whether or not such items as excess cash, temporary investments, idle plant, land being held for future plant sites, and special funds should be included. As a general proposition it would seem that such items, if under the control of the management, should be included.

(2) Accumulated depreciation—In view of the facts that some assets frequently are used after being fully depreciated and depreciation rates are inconsistent with real economic use-value to the firm, some companies add accumulated depreciation balances back to total assets. For example, they note that if this is not done, an old plant may well show a higher rate of return than a new, and much more efficient, plant. For the company overall it would seem that assets net of depreciation should be used as the investment base. For internal segments of the firm, adding back depreciation may be justified when such segments are being compared on this basis. This problem suggests a note of caution about attempts to compare two *unlike* segments on a precise mathematical basis.

(3) Intangible assets—Items such as deferred charges, patents, copyrights, and goodwill pose a particular problem as to their exclusion or inclusion. Again, there is much disagreement on these items; however, it would appear that except for special purposes, such items should be included if they represent funds committed to the business.

(4) Valuation of the assets—There is the question as to whether book values or current market values should be used. In view of the subjectivity of current market valuations and application of the "going-concern" concept, book values are normally used. In the case of potential sale of the business a return based on current market values may be especially useful.

Basically, *income* may be defined as (a) operating income or (b) net income as reported on the income statement. Obviously, the definition of income should be consistent with the definition of investment. For example, if depreciation is omitted with respect to investment, it should also be omitted in the definition of income. In defining income the following items should be given special consideration.

(1) Depreciation expense.
(2) Interest on liabilities—If the total asset amount is used as the investment base, interest on debt should be added back to income (having been deducted in computing income) because it represents that part of income on the total investment that is paid to creditors.
(3) Income taxes—Many firms prefer to compute the return prior to income taxes for the very practical reason that there is much variation in income taxes that is not related to short-term profits. These companies feel that a more stable and internally useful return figure is derived thereby. Some firms compute the rate both before and after taxes.
(4) Earnings and losses on investments, funds, and nonoperating activities.

In addition to the budget application of return on investment in evaluating the adequacy of planned profits, some concerns have developed return on investment as the basic concept underlying their entire control system.[12] Concerns using this system compute rates of return for the concern as a whole and for each major subdivision. The rate of return measures the effectiveness of each particular management, because it relates the profit-making ability of the subdivision to the capital employed, thereby serving as a guide in evaluating the effectiveness of capital utilization The objectives of the company (and subdivisions) include, in addition to a dollar-profit objective, a return-on-capi-

[12] See "How the duPont Organization Appraises Its Performance," *Financial Management Series*, No. 94 (New York: American Management Association, 1950). Also "A Program of Financial Planning and Controls, The Monsanto Chemical Company," *Financial Management Series*, No. 103 (New York: American Management Association, 1953).

tal-employed objective. Some concerns have applied the concept as a control tool to different lines of products. Application of the concept to organizational subdivisions of the concern or to different lines of products involves serious allocation problems, not only for incomes and costs, but for investment as well.

The application of return on investment to major profit-producing subdivisions of a firm is suggested in Illustration 29, page 266. It may be observed in the illustration that *Investment Turnover* is on the vertical scale and *Profit Margin* on the horizontal scale. The curved line on the graph indicates the company standard or desired return on investment (20 per cent). The chart indicates that Division A is below the standard, and the reason (low profit margin) is apparent. Division C is also below the desired standard return despite a high profit margin; the investment turnover is low. Division B is above the standard as a result of a good investment turnover (same as A) and a good profit margin (same as C). The usefulness of this method of presentation is readily apparent, particularly when it is realized that a minimum of top management time and technical understanding is required for immediate comprehension of the data and their underlying implications. In addition, if the graph is read vertically and horizontally from various points on the curved line, the combinations of profit margin and investment turnover required to attain the standard return are readily apparent.

From the budgeting viewpoint it is important to keep in mind that in actual cases in which return on investment has been developed as an over-all control technique, budget planning and control continues to be a vital part of the complete control plan. In extended applications of the concept, the rate of return becomes the focal index of over-all effectiveness. Behind it lie the budget plans, cost control procedures, ratios, and performance reports and comparisons for operating management, which are equally important.

Return on investment is a tool of analysis that should be part of the over-all control plan of management. It has the distinct advantage that, through it, managerial attention is clearly and forcefully directed toward the overriding objective—to make the best profit possible with the capital available. It tends to direct attention to a combination of the three principal factors —sales, capital employed, and costs—instead of allowing an obsession with any one of them to develop. Despite problems of allocation, the application of return on investment to major sub-

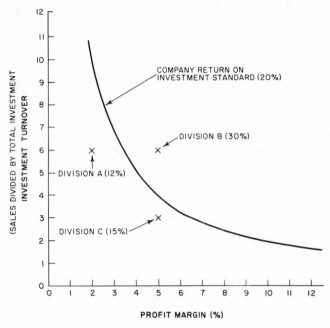

Illustration 29. *Return on Investment, Profit Margins, and Asset Turnovers.*

Managerial Analysis:

Division A—The *turnover* of six appears to be adequate; good utilization of assets indicated, approximately the same as Division B. On the other hand, the *profit margin* of 2 per cent is very unsatisfactory; there is indicated a need to attack manufacturing costs and other operating expenses. By raising this margin to approximately 3½ the standard return is achieved.

Division B—The *turnover* of six coupled with the *profit margin* of five results in a *return* of 30 per cent, well over the standard of 20 per cent.

Division C—The *profit margin* of 5 per cent appears to be adequate, approximately the same as B. On the other hand, the *turnover* of three is completely unsatisfactory, indicating poor utilization of assets relative to sales. Inventory levels and other assets, as well as sales, should be scrutinized.

divisions of the firm cannot be denied. On the other hand, it must be realized that, as with other control techniques, the technique is not a cure-all. To be effective the procedure must be integrated with other control techniques so that a sound financial planning and control system is developed.[13]

SECTION FOUR: PLANNING AND CONTROLLING CASH FLOW

One of the principal advantages of a comprehensive budget program is that it makes possible the development of an accurate cash budget. Control of the cash position is a vital phase of the financial management of a concern. There must be balance between cash and the cash-demanding activities—operations, capital additions, and so on. Too often the need for additional cash is not realized until the situation becomes quite critical. A carefully developed estimate of cash position and cash needs projected for some time into the future is a necessity to sound financial management. Many lending agencies require such estimates before granting credit.

A cash budget is a projection of the cash position by interim periods for a specific duration of time. Many concerns make both long- and short-term projections of their financial position. The short-term projection is included in the annual profit plan. The cash budget consists of two parts: (1) the projected cash receipts, and (2) the planned cash disbursements.

Determination of probable cash receipts and cash payments makes possible an evaluation of the probable cash position for the immediate budget period. Evaluation of the cash position in this manner may indicate (a) the need for some form of financing to cover indicated cash deficits, or (b) the need for management planning to put excess cash to profitable use. The facts above indicate that the cash budget is closely related to the sales plan, expense budgets, and capital additions budget. Nevertheless it must be realized that planning and control of these factors does not automatically bring about a desirable cash position. This statement suggests an essential distinction between the cash budget and other budgets. The cash budget

[13] "Experience With Return on Capital to Appraise Management Performance," *NAA Bulletin*, Accounting Practice No. 14 (Feb. 1962), Sec. 3. For an exhaustive treatment of this subject see: E. J. Blakely, "A Critical Analysis and Evaluation of the Theory and Application of Return on Investment in Measuring Managerial Performance," unpublished dissertation, The University of Texas, 1961.

is concerned with the *timing* of receipts and disbursements of cash (cash basis), whereas the other budgets are concerned with the timing or incurrence of the transactions themselves (accrual basis).

The principal purposes of the cash budget may be outlined as follows:

(1) To indicate the probable cash position as a result of planned operations.

(2) To indicate cash excess or shortages.

(3) To indicates the need for short-term borrowing, or the availability of idle cash for investment.

(4) To make provision for the coordination of cash in relation to (a) total working capital, (b) sales, (c) investment, and (d) debt.

(5) To establish a sound basis for credit.

(6) To establish a sound basis for current control of the cash position.

The preparation of the cash budget should be a responsibility of the treasurer or some other executive charged with financial responsibility in the concern. Since the cash budget is based on numerous plans and budgets originating throughout the firm, the treasurer must work very closely with other executives.

Basically there are two approaches that may be used in developing a cash budget that is sufficiently detailed and accurate for profit planning and control purposes. The method most widely used for short-term cash planning is known as the *cash receipts and disbursements method*. This method is the most simple and appropriate when a comprehensive budget program is used. The underlying plans (such as sales) that give rise to cash inflow, and the budgets of expenses and capital additions that require cash outflow, are carefully planned and estimated (as illustrated in the previous chapters for The Superior Manufacturing Company case). The second method has been referred to as the *net cash flow method*. Under this approach the starting point in the analysis is *net income,* similar to the approach commonly used in the analysis of working capital.

Cash receipts and disbursements method—Estimating cash receipts

The method of estimating cash receipts depends upon the particular situation and upon the extent of budgeting being done in other areas. Cash receipts arise in most situations from cash sales, collections of accounts and notes receivables, interest on loans and investments, sales of capital assets, and miscellaneous sources. If these amounts have been estimated along the lines discussed and illustrated up to this point, the estimating of cash receipts is considerably simplified.

Receipts from cash sales are relatively easy to plan on the basis of historical ratios of cash to credit sales, adjustment being made for expected changes in the general business trend and other indicated conditions. Cash sales give rise to immediate cash; therefore, there is no problem of lag between point of sales and realization of cash.

In the case of charge sales the lag between point of sale and realization of cash presents a problem. The principal approach to the problem must be based on the collection experience of the past—the average period between the date of sale and the date of collection. The department in charge of credit and collections should conduct continuous analyses to determine, for example, the efficiency of collections. Data such as the percentages of credit sales collected in thirty days, sixty days, and so forth, are invaluable in estimating the cash receipts from accounts receivable. It may be advisable to accumulate such information for various sales districts or for different classes of customers. Estimates derived on the basis of past experience must be tempered with careful judgment.

The treasurer will not usually have difficulty in estimating miscellaneous cash receipts from sources such as royalties, rent income, and dividend income.

Estimating cash receipts illustrated

The Superior Manufacturing Company receives cash from sales and miscellaneous sources. Based upon past experience, assume the treasurer estimates losses from bad debts will be $.20 per $100 total net sales (see *Variable Budget*, Schedule 43, page 194). Analysis of collections of net accounts receivable in prior periods as adjusted also indicates that collections on total sales should be planned as follows during 1963:

> 82% in month sold
> 10% in the first month following sale
> 5% in the second month following sale
> 3% in the third month following sale
> Quarterly basis—92% collected in quarter sold
>   8% collected in next quarter

The Superior Manufacturing Company

ESTIMATED COLLECTIONS FROM ACCOUNTS RECEIVABLE

For the Year Ending December 31, 1963

Schedule 48

	Ref.	Sales	Less Allowance for Doubtful Accounts	Balance to be Collected	First Quarter — January	First Quarter — February	First Quarter — March	Quarters — Second	Quarters — Third	Quarters — Fourth	Balance Uncollected 12/31/63
Balance in Accounts Receivable and Allowance for Doubtful Accounts 12/31/62:											
Prior Accounts	(Given)	$ 10,000	$ 6,000	$ 4,000						$ 4,000	
October, 1962	(Given)	20,000	400	19,600	$ 19,600						
November 1962	(Given)	40,000	800	39,200	24,500	$ 14,700					
December, 1962	(Given)	90,000	1,800	88,200	49,000	24,500	$ 14,700				
		160,000	9,000								
1963 Budgeted Sales:	21										
January		500,400	1,001	499,399	409,507	49,940	24,970	$ 14,982			
February		540,000	1,080	538,920		441,914	53,892	43,114			
March		574,100	1,148	572,952			469,821	103,131			
1st Quarter		1,614,500	3,229	1,591,810				1,464,465	$ 127,345		
2nd Quarter		1,595,000	3,190	1,155,684					1,063,229	92,455	
3rd Quarter		1,158,000	2,316	1,724,045						1,586,121	
4th Quarter		1,727,500	3,455								$ 137,924
Total Year		$6,095,000	$12,190	$6,233,810							
Totals		$6,255,000	$21,190		$502,607	$531,054	$563,383	$1,625,692	$1,190,574	$1,682,576	$137,924
Less Bad Debts to be Written Off		3,000	3,000								
Budgeted Balance in Allowance for Doubtful Accounts			$18,190								
Less Net Uncollected on 12/31/63				137,924							
Total Budgeted Cash Receipts for 1963		6,095,886		$6,095,886	$502,607	$531,054	$563,383	$1,625,692	$1,190,574	$1,682,576	
Balance in Accounts Receivable Dec. 31, 1963		$ 156,114									

Accounts receivable as of December 31, 1962, and the related allowance for doubtful accounts, classified by billing date, are estimated to be as follows:

Date Sold	Uncollected Accounts Receivable	Allowance for Doubtful Accounts
October, 1962	$20,000	$ 400
November, 1962	40,000	800
December, 1962	90,000	1,800
Prior accounts	10,000	6,000

The $10,000 (prior accounts) includes $3,000 to be written off as uncollectible during 1963. It is expected that $4,000 of these prior accounts will be collected in the fourth quarter.

On the basis of the *sales budget* and the data above, the treasurer prepared the *estimated collections from accounts receivable* shown in Schedule 48, page 270. It may be observed that the treasurer carried cash sales through the analysis on the same basis as credit sales.[14] This is because the statistical analysis of collections is based on total sales in the concern. Analysis of miscellaneous sources of cash provided the data for the *budget of other income* shown in Schedule 49. The results of these two schedules are summarized in Schedule 50. It is important to note that cash receipts are developed for interim periods throughout the year.

The Superior Manufacturing Company
BUDGET OF OTHER INCOME (Cash Basis)   **Schedule 49**
For the Year Ending December 31, 1963

	Budgeted Amount (Given)
January	$ 3,390
February	2,950
March	3,620
Total 1st Quarter	9,960
2nd Quarter	9,510
3rd Quarter	8,220
4th Quarter	9,430
Total for Year	$37,120

---

[14] Generally it is preferable to relate collection experience to credit sales.

The Superior Manufacturing Company
SUMMARY OF BUDGETED CASH RECEIPTS
For the Year Ending December 31, 1963

			Sources of Cash	
	Ref.	*Total*	*Accounts Receivable* 48	*Other Incomes* 49
January		$ 505,997	$ 502,607	$ 3,390
February		534,004	531,054	2,950
March		567,003	563,383	3,620
Total 1st Quarter		1,607,004	1,597,044	9,960
2nd Quarter		1,635,202	1,625,692	9,510
3rd Quarter		1,198,794	1,190,574	8,220
4th Quarter		1,692,006	1,682,576	9,430
Total for Year		$6,133,006	$6,095,886	$37,120

Estimating cash payments

Cash disbursements are made principally for purchases of raw materials, direct labor, out-of-pocket expenses, capital additions, retirement of indebtedness, and corporate disbursements such as dividends. The budgets for these items (already prepared as illustrated in prior chapters), therefore, provide the basis for estimating the cash requirements. The cash receipts and disbursements approach involves the elimination of *noncash items,* such as depreciation from the appropriate budget schedules of expense previously prepared. Experience and company policy relative to discounts must be taken into account in estimating the lag between the incurrence of accounts payable and the payment. Accruals and prepayments must be taken into account in determining the timing of related cash disbursements. Interest payments on indebtedness and property taxes can be readily estimated. Federal income taxes cannot be estimated until the budgeted net income is known. Cash requirements for such items as dividends may present a problem, but in many firms a relatively consistent dividend policy simplifies the problem. In other cases, cash requirements for dividends must be estimated by top management on the basis of whatever information is available at the time.

Estimating cash payments illustrated

The treasurer of The Superior Manufacturing Company assumes that all purchases of raw material are charged to accounts payable. The company follows the policy of taking all cash discounts; hence purchases and payables are recorded in the accounts at *net of discount*. Payments are made as a general policy on the last day of the discount period. The result is that, on the average, *one-third* of the purchases for a particular month are carried over to the next month for payment. For quarterly estimates the treasurer estimated that one-ninth of the purchases for the quarter will not be paid until the following quarter.

It is estimated that the December 31, 1962, balance in accounts payable will be $52,100. Based on these data and data from the *raw material purchases budget* (Schedule 26), a schedule of *budgeted cash required for purchases of raw materials* is prepared as indicated in Schedule 51. It should be noted that computations are carried to even $10 and that cash requirements are developed by component time periods. As with previous schedules the form illustrated below is primarily a computation schedule. It is frequently desirable to recast certain schedules such as this one for inclusion in the formal planning budget.

The Superior Manufacturing Company
BUDGETED CASH REQUIRED FOR   Schedule 51
PURCHASES OF RAW MATERIALS
For the Year Ending December 31, 1963

	Ref.	Beginning Balances Accounts Payable	Raw Material Purchases 26	Total Payable	Estimated Balance of Purchases to be Paid Next Month	Cash Required (Invoices Payable)
January		$52,100	$ 97,900	$150,000	$32,630[a]	$ 117,370
February		32,630	129,700	162,330	43,230	119,100
March		43,230	118,900	162,130	39,630	122,500
Total 1st Quarter			$ 346,500	$474,460		$ 358,970
2nd Quarter		39,630	373,000	412,630	41,440	371,190
3rd Quarter		41,440	321,850	363,290	35,760	327,530
4th Quarter		35,760	377,650	413,410	41,960	371,450
Total for Year			$1,419,000			$1,429,140

Ending balance in Accounts Payable 12/31/63 $41,960

[a] ⅓ of $97,900.

The expense budgets were illustrated in preceding chapters (Schedules 34, 35, 36, 42, and 44). These schedules indicated the total expenses for each department by time periods. The treasurer converts these schedules to cash requirements by eliminating the noncash items. The *budgeted cash required for expenses* is illustrated in Schedule 52. The noncash items are indentified as *exclusions*. Preparation of this schedule involved an assumption that the Lawyer Retainer Fee is paid monthly and that the annual Audit Fee is payable on March 1 for the past year; that is, the 1962 audit fee is payable on March 1, 1963. For illustrative purposes Supplies Used was treated as an exclusion (inventory basis), whereas Stationery and Office Supplies was treated on a cash basis. Cash expenditures for advertising were assumed to be the same as those in the expense budget.

The capital additions budget previously illustrated (Schedule 46) indicates the cash requirements for this purpose. The remaining items requiring cash are deferrals, accruals, dividends, and income taxes.

It is assumed that the data summarized below relative to deferred items, accrued items, dividends, and income taxes have been received from the accounting department and from other sources by the treasurer.

(1) Unexpired Insurance—Balance on December 31, 1962, $2,532. (4 months' premium.) Policy renewal date May 1, 1963; $22,788 cash paid for 3-year premium.

(2) Accrued Property Taxes—Unpaid taxes as of December 31, 1962, $4,982, payable during February, 1963. Estimated taxes for 1963 as indicated in the expense schedules previously prepared from the variable budgets.

(3) Federal Income Taxes—1962 income taxes payable on April 15, 1963, $279,400. (Assume for simplicity that the 1963 income tax rate is 30 per cent of net income.)

(4) Accrued Interest Expense—Balance on December 31, 1962, $7,000. (Represents $10\frac{1}{2}$ months' interest on $200,000, 4 per cent long-term notes. Interest payable each February 15.) $150,000 of these notes are due and payable on February 15, 1963.

(5) Dividends—It is anticipated that an annual dividend of $12,000 will be declared in June, 1963, payable in August, 1963.

(6) Interest Income—There will be no accrued interest income on December 31, 1962; however, on December 31, 1963, the bank will credit $2\frac{1}{2}$ per cent interest on the building fund ($20,000) to the fund.

(7) Direct Labor and Other Wages—Assume no accruals.

The Superior Manufacturing Company

BUDGETED CASH REQUIRED FOR EXPENSES
For the Year Ending December 31, 1963

Schedule 52

Cash Requirements

	Ref.	Total Expense	Less Exclusions	Total Cash Required	First Quarter January	First Quarter February	First Quarter March	Quarters First	Quarters Second	Quarters Third	Quarters Fourth
Manufacturing Division:											
General & Administrative Overhead	35	$ 116,800	$ 2,160	$ 114,640	$ 9,416	$ 9,524	$ 9,532	$ 28,472	$ 28,700	$ 28,548	$ 28,920
Power Department	35	110,000	7,200	102,800	8,246	8,468	8,468	25,182	25,848	25,404	26,366
Repair Department	35	10,000	1,600	8,400	700	700	700	2,100	2,100	2,100	2,100
Department No. 1	36	319,280	42,560	276,720	21,652	22,708	22,804	67,164	69,660	68,076	71,820
Department No. 2	36	29,280	2,568	26,712	2,184	2,226	2,226	6,636	6,678	6,636	6,762
Department No. 3	36	103,840	20,312	83,528	6,515	6,849	6,880	20,244	21,034	20,532	21,718
Totals		$ 689,200	$ 76,400	$ 612,800	$ 48,713	$ 50,475	$ 50,610	$149,798	$154,020	$151,296	$157,686
Buildings Services	34	150,000	66,000	84,000	7,700	6,800	6,720	21,220	19,880	20,500	22,400
Sales Divisions:											
Southern District	42	234,656		234,656	19,746	21,298	20,206	61,250	60,389	51,479	61,538
Eastern District	42	313,391		313,391	25,282	27,032	28,551	80,865	81,446	67,654	83,426
Western District	42	115,120		115,120	9,828	8,783	10,170	28,781	27,964	26,249	32,126
General Sales Overhead	42	296,330	600	295,730	24,563	24,985	25,348	74,896	74,690	70,045	76,099
Totals		$ 959,497	$ 600	$ 958,897	$ 79,419	$ 82,098	$ 84,275	$245,792	$244,489	$215,427	$253,189
Administrative Division:											
Accounting	44	54,020	3,000	51,020	4,250	4,258	4,264	12,772	12,770	12,682	12,796
Treasurer	44	56,177	13,990	42,187	3,511	3,538	3,562	10,611	10,597	10,290	10,689
Administrative	44	83,516	3,480	80,036	6,660	6,709	6,751*	20,120	20,096	19,563	20,257
Totals		$ 193,713	$ 20,470	$ 173,243	$ 14,421	$ 14,505	$ 14,577	$ 43,503	$ 43,463	$ 42,535	$ 43,742
Grand Totals		$1,992,410	$163,470	$1,828,940	$150,253	$153,878	$156,182	$460,313	$461,852	$429,758	$477,017

* Does not include 1962 Audit Fee; see Schedule 53.

The Superior Manufacturing Company

SCHEDULE OF ACCRUED ITEMS, DEFERRED ITEMS, DIVIDENDS, AND INCOME TAXES AND CASH REQUIREMENTS THEREFOR
For the Year Ending December 31, 1963

	Balance 12/31/62 (Given)	Renewals and Payments 1963 (Given)	Total	Expirations and Accruals 1963	Balance 12/31/63	Cash Requirements — First Quarter: January	February	March	Quarters: First	Second	Third	Fourth	Total
Unexpired Insurance	$ 2,532	$ 22,788	$25,320	$ 7,596	$ 17,724	$	$	$	$	$22,788	$	$	$ 22,788
Accrued Property Taxes	4,982*	4,982		7,284*	7,284*		4,982		4,982				4,982
Federal Income Taxes	279,400*	279,400		258,318*	258,318*			279,400	279,400				279,400
Accrued Interest Expense	7,000* (10½ Mos.)	8,000 (12 Mos.)	1,000	2,750* (12 Mos.)	1,750* (10½ Mos.)		8,000		8,000				8,000
Interest Income on Building Fund ($20,000 at 2½% credited to Building Fund on December 31)													
Supplies Inventory	13,700	41,140	54,840	49,640*	5,200	3,400	3,300	3,500	10,200	10,400	10,400	10,140	41,140
Audit Fee	2,400*	2,400		2,400*	2,400*			2,400	2,400				2,400
Dividends											12,000		12,000
Total Cash Requirements						$3,400	$16,282	$285,300	$304,982	$33,188	$22,400	$10,140	$370,710

* Credit.

Note—Notes Payable will be included in Schedule 54.

The Superior Manufacturing Company

SUMMARY OF CASH REQUIREMENTS
For the Year Ending December 31, 1963

	Ref.	Annual Total	1st Quarter			Quarters			
			January	February	March	First	Second	Third	Fourth
Material	51	$1,429,140	$117,370	$119,100	$122,500	$ 358,970	$ 371,190	$ 327,530	$ 371,450
Labor	30	1,752,000	125,400	141,600	142,800	409,800	444,000	421,200	477,000
Expense	52	1,828,940	150,253	153,878	156,182	460,313	461,852	429,758	477,017
Capital Additions	46	28,700	200			200			28,500
Accrued & Deferred Items	53	370,710	3,400	16,282	285,300	304,982	33,188	22,400	10,140
Notes Payable	(Given)	150,000		150,000		150,000			
Totals		$5,559,490	$396,623	$580,860	$706,782	$1,684,265	$1,310,230	$1,200,888	$1,364,107

(8) Stationery and Office Supplies—Assume no inventory.

(9) Supplies Used—Inventory on December 31, 1962, $13,700. Budgeted purchases during 1963: January, $3,400; February, $3,300; March, $3,500; 2nd Quarter, $10,400; 3rd Quarter, $10,400; and 4th Quarter, $10,140. Supplies Used as indicated on expense schedules previously prepared. Assume supplies paid for as purchased.

(10) Annual Audit Fee—The 1962 audit fee of $2,400 is payable on March 1, 1963, and the 1963 fee of $2,400 is payable on March 1, 1964.

(11) Contingent Liabilities—Litigation currently in progress may result in a payment of approximately $620,000 as an adjustment of prior years' federal income taxes.

The data above were used to develop a *schedule of accrued items, deferred items, dividends, and income taxes and cash requirements therefor* as illustrated in Schedule 53. It may be observed that, because of the simplified illustration, numerous items are included in the one schedule. This is not the typical situation; generally, separate schedules and computations would be necessary for each separate type of expenditure. Although the estimates and requirements for income taxes are indicated on the schedule at this point, it must be realized that the schedule, of necessity, would be constructed initially without this item. It is generally advisable to complete the schedule with a rough estimate of income taxes so that the probable cash position can be determined. As soon as net income is computed and the tax estimate prepared, the schedule can be recast as illustrated.

The cash requirements indicated in Schedules 46, 51, 52, and 53 are summarized in Schedule 54. Notes Payable, to be paid during the immediate budget year, are also included.

Determination of financing needs

Computation of estimated cash receipts and estimated cash payments, together with the estimated beginning cash balance for the budget period, make possible an evaluation of the resulting cash position. Schedule 55, *Comparison of Estimated Cash Receipts and Disbursements*, is an evaluation of the cash position of The Superior Manufacturing Company by time period for the budget year. It is assumed that the cash balance at the beginning of the budget year will be approximately $54,000. Cash receipts and cash disbursements were taken from Schedules 50 and 54 repectively.

The Superior Manufacturing Company
COMPARISON OF ESTIMATED CASH   **Schedule 55**
RECEIVED AND DISBURSEMENTS
For the Year Ending December 31, 1963

	Beginning Cash Balance	Cash Receipts	Total	Cash Disbursements	Ending Cash Balance
Ref.		50		54	
January	$ 54,000	$ 505,997	$ 559,997	$ 396,623	$163,374
February	163,374	534,004	697,378	580,860	116,518
March	116,518	567,003	683,521	706,782	23,261*
2nd Quarter	23,261*	1,635,202	1,611,941	1,310,230	301,711
3rd Quarter	301,711	1,198,794	1,500,505	1,200,888	299,617
4th Quarter	299,617	1,692,006	1,991,623	$1,364,107	627,516
Totals		$6,133,006		$5,559,490	

* Credit Balance Indicated.

The last column (Ending Cash Balance) indicates a favorable cash position for each period except one. There is a cash deficit of $23,261, for the month of March, indicating a need for some form of financing. Estimated cash balances for the following periods suggest that a short-term bank loan would be sufficient to protect the cash position. After consideration of all factors involved, the treasurer decided that the following short-term financing should be included in the cash budget:

Date Needed:	March 1, 1963
Amount Needed:	$100,000
Repayment Date:	April 30, 1963
Interest Rate:	6%
Type of Financing:	Interest bearing note

The short term financing, interest thereon, and effect on cash is presented in Schedule 56, *Budgeted Short-Term Financing Requirements.*

Determination of budgeted financing completes all aspects of the cash budget. Utilizing the data in Schedules 55 and 56, the treasurer prepared the *final cash budget* indicated in Schedule 57.

It may be re-emphasized at this point that the schedules concerning the cash budget as illustrated in this chapter are primarily

Schedule 56

The Superior Manufacturing Company
BUDGETED SHORT TERM FINANCING REQUIREMENTS [1]
For the Year Ending December 31, 1963
(a) *NOTES PAYABLE—SHORT TERM*

	Ref.	Beginning Account Balance	Cash Received (Loan Incurred)	Subtotal	Cash Payment (Loan Paid)	Ending Account Balance
January		—				—
February		—				—
March[a]		—	$100,000	$100,000		$100,000
1st Quarter			$100,000	$100,000		$100,000
2nd Quarter		$100,000		$100,000	$100,000	—
3rd Quarter		—				—
4th Quarter		—				—
Total		—	$100,000	$100,000	$100,000	—

[a] $100,000, 60 day, 6% interest bearing note, dated March 1, 1963, due April 30, 1963.

(b) *INTEREST EXPENSE ON SHORT-TERM NOTES*

	Ref.	Beginning Account Balance	Expense Incurred	Subtotal	Cash Payments	Ending Account Balance
January		—				—
February		—				—
March		—	$ 500	$ 500		$500
1st Quarter		—	$ 500	$ 500		$500
2nd Quarter		$500	$ 500	$1,000	$1,000	—
3rd Quarter		—				—
4th Quarter		—				—
Total		—	$1,000	$1,000	$1,000	—

[1] In view of the fact that only *one* loan is contemplated, this schedule is superfluous. It is included simply to indicate one possible format for situations involving numerous loans and repayments.

computation schedules. The form included in the planning budget should be adapted to the peculiarities of the particular concern and to the personalities involved. No type of presentation that would be universally applicable can be formulated.

The Superior Manufacturing Company
FINAL CASH BUDGET
For the Year Ending December 31, 1963

	Ref.	Beginning Cash Balance	Cash Receipts	Total	Cash Payments	Ending Cash Balance
		50			54	
January		$ 54,000	$ 505,997	$ 559,997	$ 396,623	$163,374
February		163,374	534,004	697,378	580,860a	116,518
March		116,518	667,003b	783,521	706,782	76,739
2nd Quarter		76,739	1,635,202	1,711,941	1,411,230c	300,711
3rd Quarter		300,711	1,198,794	1,499,505	1,200,888d	298,617
4th Quarter		298,617	1,692,006	1,990,623	1,364,107	626,516
Totals			$6,233,006		$5,660,490	

a Includes $150,000 payment on long term note payable.
b Includes $100,000 short term note payable.
c Includes payment of short term bank loan and interest $101,000.
d Includes $12,000 dividend payment.

Net cash flow method

The *net cash flow method* of planning cash is used by some firms in planning for the short run; however, it is used much more frequently in long-term cash planning. The method requires less detail and fits well the broad projections common in long-range planning.

Basically, this method involves the development of cash flows starting with *net income;* adjustments are made for noncash items affecting reported net income. Essentially net income is converted from the *accrual* basis to a cash basis. Outflows of cash are estimated for nonprofit items such as capital additions, payment of debt and dividends in a manner similar to that discussed above for the cash receipts and disbursements method. Technically the net cash flow method is similar in approach to that commonly utilized in the analysis of working capital.[15] capital.[15]

[15] For a technical treatment of the method see: G. A. Welsch, C. T. Zlatkovich, and J. A. White, *Intermediate Accounting* (Homewood, Ill.: Irwin, 1963), Chap. 29. Also see: Almand R. Coleman, "Funds Statements and Cash Flow," *The Controller* (Dec. 1961), pp. 592-595.

The AK Corporation

BUDGETED NET INCOME AND CASH FLOW FOR THE YEAR ENDING DECEMBER 31, 19—

(In thousand dollars: Only 100% column partially completed with hypothetical amounts for illustrative purposes)

Revenues and costs	At 80% capacity Amount	per cent	At 90% capacity Amount	per cent	At 100% capacity Amount	per cent	At 110% capacity Amount	per cent	At 120% capacity Amount	per cent
Sales	$8,000		$9,000		$10,000	100	$11,000		$12,000	
Variable costs:										
Direct material										
Direct labor										
Factory overhead										
Distribution cost										
General administrative cost										
Total variable costs					7,000	70				
Marginal income					3,000	30				
Fixed costs:										
Factory overhead										
Distribution										
General administrative										
Total Fixed costs					2,500	25				
Operating income					500	5				
Provision for income taxes					250	2.5				
Net income					250	2.5				

Cash flow analysis

Beginning cash balance	$ 40
Cash Sources:	
Net income	250
Add: Depreciation & amortization	100
Decrease in inventory	12
Deduct: Increase in prepaid items	5*
Increase in receivables	7*
Net cash income	350
Sale of capital stock	100
Total cash inflow	450
Total cash available	490
Cash requirements:	
Dividends	40
Decrease in long-term liabilities	30
Net increase in fixed assets	300
Total cash required	370
Ending cash balance	120

Illustration 30. *Net Income Cash Flow Method—Short Term*

The RB Company
LONG-RANGE PLANS—ANALYSIS OF CASH FLOW

Items	Current Year	Future Projections				
	1963	1964	1965	1966	1967	1968
Beginning Cash Position						
Cash Inflows						
Net Income Planned (after tax)						
Adjustments:						
Add: Depreciation & Amortization						
Increase in working capital other than cash						
Deduct: Decrease in working capital other than cash						
Net Income on cash basis						
Other sources of cash:						
Capital stock sales						
Long-term loans						
Sales of fixed assets						
Total cash inflow						
Cash Outflows						
Sinking fund requirements						
Dividend payments						
Payment on long-term debt						
Additons to fixed assets						
Total cash outflow						
Ending Cash Balance Indicated						

Illustration 31. Net Income Cash Flow Method—Long Term

In order to indicate the approach and its potential applications two illustrations are presented. Illustration 30, which was adapted from the procedures of a well-known company, is developed in connection with the annual profit plan; it emphasizes the variable budget concept *extended* to the budgeted income statement and the cash flow projection. Illustration 31 is an adaptation from the planning procedures of another company. In this case the approach is used in the long-range planning program.

Maintaining control of the cash position

The company financial officer is directly responsible for control of the cash position subject, of course, to the decisions of the chief executive. Actual cash receipts and payments will be somewhat different from those anticipated in the planning budget. This discrepancy may result from (a) variation in factors affecting cash, (b) sudden and unexpected circumstances influencing operations, or (c) lack of adequate cash control.

It is important that control procedures for cash be developed so that the effect of each of the factors listed above is evaluated and reported. A good system of control is especially important because of the consequences that may result from lack of managerial control of the financial function. Frequently it is possible for management to make decisions or to alter existing policies in such a way that the cash position is enhanced. For example, an unexpected change in the cash position giving rise to a possible serious cash shortage is not unusual, but mangement may be able to avoid, or at least to minimize, the undesirable situation through action on such matters as (a) increased effort to collect receivables, (b) reduction of out-of-pocket expenses, (c) deferment of certain expenditures (such as capital additions), (d) deferment of payment of certain liabilities, (e) reduction of purchases (inventories), and (f) better timing of operations affecting cash. Obviously, the effect of decisions such as those just enumerated on the cash position is contingent upon the timing of the decision as related to the cash position. The earlier the decision, the greater the effect on the ultimate cash position. Therefore, it is essential that management be fully informed relative to the *probable* cash position as far in advance as possible.

Assuming adequate planning, control of the cash position

generally should be based upon two policies. First, an adequate and continuous evaluation of both the present and the probable cash position should be made. This procedure involves a periodic evaluation and reporting—say monthly—of the actual cash position to date, coupled with a reprojection of the probable future cash flow, taking into account budgeted conditions as affected by unusual and unexpected developments that were not originally anticipated in developing the cash budget. Assume, for example, that at the end of February there is an actual cash balance of $11,000, whereas the original budgeted balance was $32,000. The factors giving rise to the $21,000 unfavorable variation should be carefully analyzed, with particular emphasis placed on the probable future effect. Next, the budgeted cash receipts and payments for the *remainder* of the year should be carefully evaluated *and adjusted for any new conditions* that may affect them. The final step, then, in evaluating the probable future cash position is to start with the $11,000 actual cash balance at the end of February, adding to it the reprojected budget receipts for each time period during the rest of the budget year, and deducting therefrom the reprojected budget payments for the same period. In this way a completely new evaluation of the probable future cash position is developed for top management. The procedure provides management with what might be termed a running or *continuous budget* evaluation of the cash position, making possible continuous control through policy decisions that, by the very nature of the situation, must be made some time in advance in order to have the desired effect on the cash position. This procedure is indicated in Illustration 32, which was adapted from the procedures of a medium-sized firm.

The second aspect of cash control involves procedures for maintaining data on the day-to-day (or week-to-week) cash position. In order to minimize interest costs, yet to assure adequate cash, many treasurers use a daily evaluation of the cash position along the lines indicated in Illustration 33. This approach is particularly useful in companies having (a) widely fluctuating cash demands, and (b) widely dispersed branches through which significant amounts of cash flow. Many companies have come to realize the significant reduction of interest costs that can be achieved through *daily* control of cash balances. For example, one company estimated that it saved approximately $40,000 in one year through daily control. Prior to instituting daily control it was not uncommon for one division of the com-

X Company

MONTHLY REPORT OF CASH POSITION

At March 31, 1963

Particulars	Actual Cash Position		Reprojection of Cash Position for Remainder of Year				
	Month of March	Cumulative Jan. 1-Mar. 31	April	May	June	3rd Quarter	4th Quarter
Cash Receipts:							
Accounts receivable							
Trade notes receivable							
Cash sales							
Other sources							
Total cash inflow							
Cash payments:							
Raw material							
Accounts payable							
Current expenses							
Dividends							
Other payments							
Total cash outflow							
Indicated cash position from operations							
Financing Required (net of interest): *							
Short-term							
Long-term							
Total							
Indicated cash position (after financing)							

*Indicates payment of debt.

Illustration 32. Report of Cash Position—Monthly

DAILY REPORT OF CASH POSITION
For the Month of ____

| | | | Cash Inflow | | | | Cash Outflow | | |
Date	Day	Running Cash Balance	Total Cash Inflow	Collection on Receivables	Other Sources of Cash	Total Cash Outflow	Payment Current Liabilities	Payroll Requirements	Operating Expense	Other Disbursements
1	Th									
2	Fri									
3	*									
4	*									
5	Mon									
6	Tue									
7	Wed									
8	Th									
9	Fri									
30	Fri									
31	*									

End of Month Balances:
    Actual:
        Amount $ _____
        Average daily balance** $ _____
    Budgeted:
        Amount $ _____
        Average daily balance** $ _____

*Nonworking day
**Based on number of working days in the month

Illustration 33. Report of Cash Position—Daily

287

pany to have excess cash of several million dollars while another division was borrowing substantial amounts on a short-term basis and paying 6 per cent interest.

Many companies have achieved effective control of cash through their comprehensive budget program which includes (a) systematic projection of the cash flows for both the long and short range, (b) daily evaluation of the cash position, and (c) monthly projection of the cash position along the lines discussed above.[16]

Discussion Questions

1. Define and indicate the scope of the capital additions budget.
2. Distinguish between long- and short-term budgeting of capital additions. Indicate the importance of each and relate them to a comprehensive budget program.
3. Outline the reponsibility for capital budgeting in a typical concern.
4. With respect to short-term capital budgeting why is it generally desirable to differentiate between (a) major capital additions and (b) minor capital additions?
5. Explain how capital additions may be controlled, making a distinction between minor and major capital expenditures.
6. What is the relationship between depreciation shown in the (a) planning budget expense schedules, (b) depreciation schedule, (c) variable budgets?
7. Explain the concept of the pay-back method of evaluating proposed capital additions. Indicate its principal advantages and disadvantages.
8. What is meant by (a) present value of $1 and (b) present value of $1 received annually for N Years?
9. What is the basic concept of the discounted cash flow method of evaluating proposed capital additions. Indicate its principal advantages and disadvantages.
10. Define return on investment. What are the two principal applications of return on investment?
11. In what way does return on investment measure the effectiveness of managerial effort?
12. Assuming return on investment for the concern as a whole is too low, what lines of action may be open to management to improve the return?
13. Explain how return on investment may be affected by accounts receivable.

[16] "Cash Flow for Managerial Control," *NAA Bulletin*, Research Report No. 36 (Oct. 1961).

14. If a particular concern makes rather complete return on investment analyses, are there any reasons for also using budget procedures?

15. Outline the possible relationships between a budget program and return on investment procedures.

16. What are the two basic approaches that may be used in projecting cash flow?

17. Who should be responsible for developing the cash budget? How is it related to the annual profit plan?

18. Elaborate on the following statement: "Many companies effectively control cash by (a) projection of cash flows, (b) daily evaluation of the cash position, and (c) monthly reprojection of the cash position.

E L E V E N

Completion and Application of

the Annual Profit Plan

Throughout the preceding chapters a sequential approach to building an annual profit plan was discussed and illustrated. In those chapters approaches to planning and control were considered for each functional area. At this point we can consider completion of the profit plan and its application throughout the period it covers. From this point, completion of the annual profit plan involves compilation of summary schedules (budgeted financial statements) that report the over-all financial results as planned. Further, we can now consider several other problems related to the budget program.

Consequently, this chapter discusses four essential aspects of budgeting that were deferred for practical reasons. These considerations are presented in the following order:

(1) Completion of the annual profit plan
(2) Consideration of alternatives in developing the profit plan
(3) Application of the profit plan
(4) Development of the budgeted financial statements, illustrated

SECTION ONE: COMPLETION OF THE ANNUAL PROFIT PLAN

The build-up of the annual profit plan terminates with the budgeted income statement and the balance sheet. These two statements summarize and bring together the details of the plans developed by management for the period involved. The details of the build-up follow.

Responsibility for completion of the profit plan

At this point in the program of profit planning, the budget director has a particularly heavy responsibility. Up to this point, aside from designing and improving the over-all system, the budget director has been viewed as an advisor to the various executives and supervisors in the development of the plans for their particular areas of responsibility. Now the parts must be put together as one complete profit plan, and this is the responsibility of the budget director. The principal sub-budgets essential to complete the annual profit plan are these:

(1) Budgeted cost of goods manufactured
(2) Budgeted cost of goods sold
(3) Budgeted income statements
(4) Budgeted statement of application of funds
(5) Supplementary statistics (such as breakeven analysis, discussed in the next chapter)

In combining the sub-budgets, each of which has been only *tentatively* approved, the budget director is bringing all the plans to the focal point of *net income* and *return on investment;* these are the final tests of the adequacy and realism of the detailed plans. Bringing together the various detailed plans is a technical problem that can be best presented by illustration. Accordingly, the last section of this chapter demonstrates this process for the illustrative case, The Superior Manufacturing Company. Careful study of the sequential development of the summary statements in the illustration is suggested for better understanding of the profit planning process generally.

Prior to distribution, it is generally desirable to recast certain budget schedules (previously illustrated as worksheets) so that technical accounting mechanics and terminology are avoided as much as possible. The presumption must be that most of the users are not accountants, and are not particularly impressed by rows of figures. On some of the sub-budgets it may be desirable to report results for the *past year* for comparative purposes. This procedure is especially applicable to the budgeted annual income statement, and the balance sheet.

The redesigned schedules should be assembled in a logical order of presentation, reproduced, assembled as one complete package, and distributed on or before the first day of the upcoming budget period. When assembled and bound, the completed profit plan is variously referred to as *the planning budget, the plan, the master budget, the forecast budget, the financial budget, the operating plan,* or *the plan of operations.* Throughout this text the author has chosen to use the terms *annual profit plan* or *annual planning budget.* The current trend is to drop the word "budget" entirely, and to use instead such terms as *the profit plan* or simply *the plan.* There are good psychological reasons for this recent trend. Over the years the word "budget" has come to connote restrictions, pressure devices, or other limitations. This unfavorable attitude can be traced directly to misunderstanding and misuse of budget techniques and procedures. But aside from these considerations, terms such as *profit plan* are more descriptive of the characteristics and objectives of the annual budget.

In arranging the schedules to be included in the final profit plan, the budget director should take into consideration management preferences, as well as the principles of good presentation. No one arrangement is perfect. As a general rule, however, it is desirable to place the *estimated financial statements* ahead of the supporting schedules such as the sales, expense, cash, and capital additions budgets.

The budget director should have a limited number of copies of the profit plan appropriately bound with a simple but well designed cover. It may be desirable to use some loose-leaf arrangement for binding, because the budget should be viewed as a flexible document to be revised as circumstances warrant. Revision may involve one or more schedules, depending upon the nature of the revision. (Revision is considered in Chapter 17.)

The date of completion of the profit plan is of considerable importance. The issuance of a planning budget some time after the beginning of the budget period is one sure way of destroying a good part of the budget potential. Obviously the psychological importance of issuing the planning budget prior to the beginning of the budget period is considerable. Timely completion of the planning budget suggests the need for a *budget calendar* as previously noted in Chapter 3 (pages 59 and 79).

SECTION TWO: CONSIDERATION OF ALTERNATIVES IN DEVELOPING THE PROFIT PLAN

If one were to concentrate on the *mechanical aspects* of the development of the annual profit plan, the impression might be that the sales executives develop a sales projection and that this is followed by a somewhat clerical approach to the development of the production, inventory, purchases, labor, materials, and other components of the planning budget. However, throughout the preceding discussions we have attempted to emphasize the fundamental importance of managerial decision making, policy formulation, and consideration of alternative courses of action in the planning process. We have also emphasized the importance of participation by all members of the management.

Top management's choice of policies from numerous alternative courses of action is essential to the building of a realistic plan of operations. References were made throughout the preceding chapters to *tentative approval* of particular parts of the planning budget by the budget committee and the president. To make these tentative choices and decisions requires serious step-by-step consideration of alternatives during the build-up. Only tentative approvals are indicated in most cases because the full impact of a selected alternative may not be fully realized until the profit plan has progressed to the stage of budgeted financial statements.

The build-up of a plan of operations normally will not, and probably should not, involve a smooth flow of planning and decision making from one phase of the plan to another. Subsequent development of the plan may indicate that a previously selected alternative should be discarded and other alternatives considered. Through this process of building, tearing down, and rebuilding, a desirable plan of operations can be developed. It not infrequently happens that a plan practically completed, has to be torn down, restudied, and rebuilt. This may be the result, for example, of an unsatisfactory profit margin or return on investment ratio. Management is then faced with the problem of attacking one or more of the factors that might produce undesirable results. Of course, to be realistic, there may be circumstances where a *loss* will have to be planned—though every possible effort should be directed toward minimizing it. The use of procedures such as breakeven analysis, differential cost analysis, and return on investment analysis should be used during the planning process to *test* and *evaluate* proposed courses of action. These techniques are especially important in pinpointing and evaluating the effect of applying alternative proposals.

Numerous situations can be cited to show how management, in the process of developing the planning budget, is faced with alternative decisions. The following are representative of the more important areas where alternatives must be considered and choices made:

(1) *Sales prices to be budgeted*—Management is faced with the serious problem of establishing pricing policy and estimating the quantities that can be sold at given prices. Evaluation of such factors as cost, the market, economic trends, and competitor prices is essential in selecting the desirable alternative.

(2) *General advertising policies*—The financial limitation on advertising expenditures, local versus national, and specific versus institutional advertising, represent areas where alternative choices must be made early in the planning process.

(3) *Sales territory and sales force expansion or contraction*—Decisions

as to the preferable alternatives should be based on careful studies of market areas and market potentials either by company personnel or outside professional help.

(4) *Sales mix*—Sales mix refers to the relative sales emphasis to be given the various products sold by the concern. Decisions concern, principally, the relative profitability of products, the more profitable products being given special emphasis. These decisions must be based necessarily upon cost analysis by product. In this connection, it is important that the costs be accurate. Identification of fixed and variable costs, as in the variable budgets, provides a valuable tool for differential cost analysis by product, and in addition makes possible a more accurate allocation of indirect costs. Cost allocation is generally more accurate, because fixed costs should be allocated ordinarily on a different basis than for variable costs. The concept of differential cost analysis may be illustrated as follows:

Assume that under ordinary procedures the following data concerning products A and B are available:

	Product A		Product B	
	Units	*Total*	*Units*	*Total*
Estimated sales potential	10,000 @ $4.00	$40,000	10,000 @ $4.00	$40,000
Estimated costs	10,000 2.60	26,000	10,000 2.60	26,000
Estimated profit potential	10,000 1.40	14,000	10,000 1.40	14,000

Indicated Conclusion: Since there appear to be no differentials involved, no alternatives are available; therefore push both products equally.

Now assume the following differential cost analysis is made:

	Product A		Product B	
	Units	*Amount*	*Units*	*Amount*
Estimated sales potential	10,000 @ $4.00	$40,000	10,000 @ $4.00	$40,000
Variable costs (differential costs)[a] from variable budgets	10,000 1.20	12,000	10,000 1.40	14,000
Contribution to cover fixed costs and profit (Marginal income)	10,000 2.80	28,000	10,000 2.60	26,000
Fixed costs from variable budgets	10,000 1.40	14,000	10,000 1.20	12,000
Potential profit	10,000 1.40	14,000	10,000 1.40	14,000

[a] The example above assumes that variable cost is also differential cost. This is true in this specific illustration. Broadly speaking, differential cost is the cost difference between two or more possible alternatives. In estimating differential costs of each of a given set of alternatives, one of the alternatives must be selected as the standard. Frequently the standard alternative is a continuation of the current plan.

Indicated Conclusion: The line "Contribution to Cover Fixed Costs and Profit" indicates a unit differential between the two products. Product A contributes $2.80 per unit, whereas Product B contributes $2.60, a difference of $.20 per unit. The two products are equated at 10,000 units only. Above this volume product A makes superior profits by the differential of $.20 per unit. In view of this differential the indicated alternative is to push Product A over Product B, other things being equal. Similar analyses can be made with respect to differentials by sales territory and by other subdivisions of the concern.

(5) *Balance between stable production and inventory levels*—Techniques to aid in the selection of the most desirable alternative in this respect were discussed in Chapter 5 under "Stability of Production."

(6) *Expenditures for research*—This is one of the alternative decision areas that must be based upon long-range objectives, executive judgment, competitive activities, and the ability of the concern to finance research.

(7) *Capital additions*—Alternatives in the area of capital additions must be given attention in most concerns. Analytical cost and income studies, evaluation of cost and income differentials, and return on investment computations, represent the principal considerations for sound capital additions decisions. The application of return on investment computations to specific contemplated capital additions was suggested in Chapter 10.

(8) Perhaps the principal aspect of alternative decisions has to do with evaluating the probable profit result *while the planning budget is being built*, rather than waiting until the budgeted financial statements are finally determined. Breakeven analysis represents a technique that is especially valuable for this purpose. It makes possible evaluation of the effect of varying combinations of (a) sales prices, (b) sales volumes, (c) sales mix, (d) fixed costs, and (e) variable costs. The effect on profits, breakeven points, and margins of safety can be evaluated in general terms concurrent with planning budget development. The application of breakeven analysis to this and other problems is discussed in the next chapter. At this point it is appropriate to illustrate the usefulness of variable budgets in evaluating profit potentials *concurrently* with budget development. For this reason variable budgets should be completed early in the budget development period.

To illustrate this last point, assume that the sales plan, materials, and direct labor budgets have been tentatively approved. From the data for The Superior Manufacturing Company, the resulting *profit from operations* is readily determinable, as shown in Illustration 34. Note in particular the use of variable budget *totals* to derive summary expense allowances. This procedure illustrates the important use of variable budgets as a tool to assist management in the selection of desirable alternatives. In the absence of variable budgets, estimating expense allowances at *various volumes* would present an almost impracticable task at that particular point in planning budget development. In Illustration 34 additional columns might be added to develop *operating profit* for a whole series of assumed sales volumes (for other examples see Illustration 30, page 282 and Illustration 62, page 452).

Source Sch. No.				
1	Sales			$6,095,000
	Costs for year:			
29	Direct material	$1,416,600		
30	Direct labor	1,752,000		
	Manufacturing overhead:			
33 and 31	Dept. 1 ($14,000 × 12) + ($31. × 4,880)	319,280		
33 and 31	Dept. 2 ($1,960 × 12) + ($3. × 1,920)	29,280		
32 and 31	Dept. 3 ($4,180 × 12) + ($11. × 4,880)	103,840		
33 and 31	General and administrative ($8,760 × 12) + ($1.00 × 11,680)	116,800		
33 and Estimate	Power ($6,700 × 12) + ($1.48 × 20,000)	110,000		
33 and Estimate	Repair ($720 × 12) + ($.34 × 4,000)	10,000		
Estimated	Building services	90,000		
	Total	$ 779,200		
Estimated	Add inventory decrease	106,800	4,054,600	
	Indicated gross margin		2,040,400	
	Distribution costs:			
21 and 40	Southern district ($9,400 × 12) + ($5.748 × 21,200)	234,656		
21 and 40	Eastern district ($12,780 × 12) + ($5.505 × 29,070)	313,391		
21 and 40	Western district ($4,750 × 12) + ($5.442 × 10,680)	115,120		
21 and 40	General sales overhead ($19,295 × 12) + ($1.063 × 60,950)	296,330		
Estimated	Building services	30,000		
	Total	$ 989,497		
	Administrative costs:			
21 and 43	Administrative department ($6,340 × 12) + ($.122 × 60,950)	83,516		
21 and 43	Accounting department ($4,400 × 12) + ($.02 × 60,950)	54,020		
21 and 43	Treasurer's department ($3,310 × 12) + ($.27 × 60,950)	56,177		
Estimated	Building services	30,000		
	Total	$ 223,713	1,213,210	
	Indicated operating profit		$ 827,190	

Illustration 34. *Worksheet to Estimate Operating Profit.*

These data may also be presented graphically as a breakeven chart (Chapter 12). As a matter of fact, many budget directors maintain an informal *worksheet* and *breakeven graph* throughout the profit planning process. These are continually revised as the numerous sub-budgets are received from the various executives and supervisors—each being worked into the informal figures to test their effect on the final income figure. The importance of this informal step-by-step pretesting cannot be overemphasized—it may save considerable revision later.

Returning to our illustration, at this point the indicated operating profit of $827,190 should be evaluated to determine whether or not it is satisfactory in terms of:

(a) Historical profits
(b) Long-range profit objectives
(c) Industry high and average profits
(d) Return on investment (see Chapter 10)
(e) Breakeven point (see Chapter 12)

If the profit is deemed satisfactory, preparation of the planning budget can be continued. If the profit is deemed unsatisfactory, management should reconsider the alternatives selected up to this point as well as other alternatives.

By testing alternative choices at the time they are made, a plan that otherwise might turn out to be unfavorable may possibly be revised so that more favorable results are planned. Many alternatives have to be considered before the most favorable plan of operations can be developed.

Testing the Budget Estimates. Throughout the development of the annual profit plan sound practice suggests that the *ratio test* be applied to key estimates and finally to the resulting income. The ratio test is simply the comparison of certain ratios based on budget data with the same historical ratios (a) for the firm, and (b) for the industry (when available). Any significant difference between the budgeted ratio and the historical trend of the ratio should be carefully investigated to determine the cause. If the cause can be related to specific decisions, policies, or assumptions that have been changed or revised (and that should influence projected results), the ratio has survived the ratio test. On the other hand, should there be no identifiable factors that would affect the planned results, the assumption should be that some facet of the plan is deficient or in error.

The ratio test should be applied by the budget director step-by-step during the process of developing the profit plan. When the test shows a particular ratio to be out of line, the executive

WORKSHEET FOR RATIO TESTS ON 1963 BUDGET

Items Tested Ratio		Historical				Annual Profit Plan 1963	Long-Range Projection			
		1959	1960	1961	1962		1964	1966	1968	1970
Sales										
Operating Profit										
Profit/Sales	%	6.33	6.51	6.08	5.92	7.21*	6.20	6.20	6.40	6.40
Sales/Investment		2.12	2.23	1.97	1.96	2.14	2.26	2.25	2.30	2.30
Return on investment		13.42	14.52	11.98	11.60	15.43*	14.01	13.95	14.72	14.72

* Ratio appears to be out of line; potentially indicates (a) an error or (b) a deficiency in planning. Projected profit primarily is suspect.

Illustration 35. Worksheet for Ratio Tests

responsible for the particular projection should be informed to make appropriate investigation. Should there be a mistake, action should be taken to prevent the effect from being carried into other aspects of the plan. The ratio tests are generally represented by a worksheet maintained by the budget director. One type of worksheet adapted from the procedures of a well-managed company is shown in Illustration 35. Although in this company the budget director applies the tests using a total of 63 ratios, only three representative ratios related to operating profit are illustrated. We might note at this point that the ratio test has even more significance in evaluating the reasonableness of the quantified results of long-range planning (see Illustration 3, page 49).

SECTION THREE: APPLICATION OF THE PROFIT PLAN

In preceding chapters, considerable attention was given to the use of the various segments of the annual profit plan, particularly for control purposes. It is appropriate at this point to generalize in some respects relative to use. Obviously the final test of whether the efforts and cost expended in developing the profit plan are worthwhile depends upon its usefulness to the management; thus some fundamental questions are posed. How should this tool be utilized? How should the plans and policies expressed in the profit plan be made effective? Should it be viewed as a rigid plan to be followed under any and all circumstances? Should it be used as a pressure device? How should it be used by the lower levels of management?

In the early chapters it was emphasized that the planning budget should represent attainable goals and objectives, yet goals and objectives set high enough to present a challenge to the firm. The plan should be developed with the firm conviction that it is going to meet or exceed all major objectives. Through the principle of participation, communication (both downward and upward) is enhanced. If this principle is made effective, the various executives and supervisors will have a clearer understanding of their responsibilities and what accomplishments are expected of them.

The next step is the distribution of the profit plan, as finally approved, to various segments of the firm. In Chapter 3 (page 60) *distribution instructions* were included as an important part of the *budget manual*. The policy relative to distribution of the profit plan is significant. We have said that a limited number of copies of the *complete* profit plan should be prepared. The copies of the complete plan should be distributed to the members of top management specifically designated, and perhaps to each member of the board of directors. Normally the distribution of the complete plan should be limited to vice presidents and to the heads of certain staff groups. The guiding principle in establishing the policy on distribution might be expressed as follows: provide one copy to each member of the management team consistent with the problem of *security*. Some companies have had the experience of having a copy of their annual profit plan finding its way into the hands of unauthorized parties, say, a competitor. The reader can well appreciate the seriousness of this possibility. Most firms number each copy of the complete profit plan and keep a record of the distribution of each copy. At year end the copies are returned to the budget director for destruction.

The distribution policy should make provision for distribution of *parts* or segments of the profit plan to middle and lower management personnel. For example, a sales district supervisor would not be given a copy of the entire budget but should receive those parts that apply to his particular responsibility, such as the sales budget, expense budget, and advertising budget for his district. In preceding discussions concerning the design of the budget form, we suggested that it should articulate internally (each segment should tie in with other related segments), but at the same time the various sub-budgets should be complete and stand alone.

After distribution of the annual profit plan, a series of *profit plan conferences* should be held. Usually the chief executive calls meetings of the top executives for the specific purpose of discussing the plans, expectations, and steps in implementation. At this meeting the importance of *action, flexibility* (see Ch. 17), and *continuous control* may well be emphasized. In particular, it must be realized by all executives and supervisors that the budget is merely a *tool* for their use. The profit plan, no matter how well designed and how carefully drawn, cannot *manage;* in the final analysis men, not budgets (or other similar tools), perform the management functions. Use of the profit plan as a guide to action and performance, directed toward attaining or bettering the goals quantified in the annual profit plan require continuous managerial effort and attention.

Similar conferences should be conducted until all levels of management are reached. It is vitally important that each executive and supervisor clearly comprehend his particular responsibilities as specified. These conferences will induce the necessary profit consciousness throughout management and, if followed properly, will insure active support to attain the objectives. Basically this is a problem of communication from the top down—a generally neglected problem in industrial management.

The profit plan provides the supervisor of each major subdivision of the firm with a basis for the detailed operating plan for his subdivision. For example, the advertising director has an approved over-all plan of advertising adequately related to company objectives. Within this plan he can make detailed plans from day to day and month to month to execute the advertising function. Similarly, the treasurer, having definite information concerning such things as expected cash receipts, cash disbursements, and capital additions, can proceed with effective and detailed financial planning. Thus the planning budget becomes the basis for current operations, and exerts considerable coordinating and controlling effects.

Performance must be measured and reported to top management. It is through control that execution of the plan is assured. Procedures must be established so that accomplishment, or its lack, is immediately known, and effective action taken to correct or minimize any undesirable effects. Short-term performance reporting is absolutely essential. For example, control of sales is achieved in some respects by comparing actual sales with budgeted sales by areas of responsibility. Such a comparison at the end of the year would be of little or no value, because it is then too late to take effective action. On the other hand, daily, weekly, or even monthly sales reports may serve as a basis for effective managerial action. If January sales are below the quota in the sales budget, investigation is in order to determine the reasons. It may be that the condition is due to circumstances over which the firm has no control and little can be done to compensate for it. On the other hand, it may be that managerial action can be taken to correct the condition, or action may be taken to increase the possibility of volume in excess of budget figures for subsequent months of the year. It is important that management know about the trouble spots as they occur so that immediate attention can be given to them. Actual figures standing alone do not indicate weak spots; they must be compared with a good standard (budget) in order to be properly evaluated. Chapter 13 is devoted to the problem of performance reporting to management.

One of the most important aspects of budget operations is the principle of *flexibility*. To view the annual profit plan as an inflexible blueprint of operations is to invite trouble. Obviously, it is impossible at the outset to anticipate all contingencies. Each day may present contingencies not anticipated in the planning budget. Therefore, it is necessary that current adjustments be made in operating plans despite the original budget program. This is as it should be; the budget should not be viewed as a restrictive influence, but rather as a specification of the general objectives of the firm. Certainly every advantage should be taken of favorable circumstances as they arise despite their not having been anticipated in the planning budget. Taking advantage of favorable opportunities as they arise means that the budget objective as a whole will be exceeded and, after all, budget goals can be viewed as *minimum objectives*. The aim is to exceed them whenever possible.

A budget program properly viewed and administered does not hamper or restrict management; instead, it provides definite and concrete objectives around which day-to-day and month-to-month decisions are made. It makes possible effective implementation of the exception principle discussed in Chapter 1 (page 15). Use and application of both the annual planning budget and the variable budgets are considered in detail in Chapters 9, 13, 14, and 17. Flexibility in budget application is absolutely essential and increases the probabilities of achieving or bettering the objectives as laid down.

SECTION FOUR: DEVELOPMENT OF THE BUDGETED FINANCIAL STATEMENTS, ILLUSTRATED

The budget schedules for The Superior Manufacturing Company case illustrated in preceding chapters provide the essential data for completion of the estimated financial statements. Preparation of a schedule of *estimated cost of goods manufactured* is the next logical step to illustrate in building the annual profit plan. The budgets of raw materials used (Schedule 28), direct labor (Schedule 30), factory overhead applied (Schedule 38), and production (Schedule 22), together with work in process inventory information, provide data which may be assembled in a schedule of cost of goods manufactured. This procedure is illustrated in Schedule 58. Beginning work in process inventories (January 1, 1963) are as follows:

Product X—No work in process inventory throughout the year.
Product Y—10,000 units valued at $13,800. (This inventory is in Department 3 and remains relatively constant throughout the year.)

The breakdown by product and by time periods should be particularly observed. The reader is urged to trace the source of data as indicated in the "Ref." column.

The cost of goods manufactured is summarized in Schedule 59. As with certain other summary schedules, this is an optional one that may or may not be needed, depending upon the complexities of the situation.

The Schedule of *budgeted cost of goods sold* may be developed next from data concerning cost of goods manufactured and finished goods inventories. The Superior Manufacturing Company uses first-in, first-out in pricing issues of finished goods. In order to compute cost of sales by sales district, it is assumed that withdrawals from initial inventories are in the ratio of district *unit* sales for the period involved. Initial inventories (January 1, 1963) of finished goods are estimated to be:

	Product X	Product Y
Units	240,000	100,000
Valuation	$806,400	$138,000

Cost of goods sold is developed by product, by time period, and by sales district. A worksheet (Schedule 60) is used for this purpose. The results are shown in detail in Schedule 61 (budgeted cost of goods sold), and in summary in Schedule 62.

In Chapter 5 the *finished goods inventory budget* (Schedule 23) was illustrated. At that point *units only* were known. Data developed in Schedule 60 (*budget worksheet—cost of goods sold and finished goods inventory*) make possible the completion of

The Superior Manufacturing Company

ESTIMATED COST OF GOODS MANUFACTURED

For the Year Ending December 31, 1963

	Ref.	Annual Total	First Quarter January	First Quarter February	First Quarter March	Quarters First	Quarters Second	Quarters Third	Quarters Fourth
Product X:									
Materials used	28	$1,156,600	$ 85,400	$ 97,600	$ 97,600	$280,600	$288,000	$276,000	$ 312,000
Direct labor	30	1,440,000	105,000	120,000	120,000	345,000	360,000	345,000	390,000
Prime cost		2,596,600	190,400	217,600	217,600	625,600	648,000	621,000	702,000
Burden applied	38	633,600	46,200	52,800	52,800	151,800	158,400	151,800	171,600
Cost of goods manufactured		3,230,200	236,600	270,400	270,400	777,400	806,400	772,800	873,600
Units produced	22	960,000	70,000	80,000	80,000	230,000	240,000	230,000	260,000
Unit cost			$3.38	$3.38	$3.38	$3.38	$3.36	$3.36	$3.36
Product Y:									
Materials used	28	$ 260,000	$ 17,000	$ 18,000	$ 19,000	$ 54,000	$ 70,000	$ 63,500	$ 72,500
Direct labor	30	312,000	20,400	21,600	22,800	64,800	84,000	76,200	87,000
Prime cost		572,000	37,400	39,600	41,800	118,800	154,000	139,700	159,500
Burden applied	38	145,600	9,520	10,080	10,640	30,240	39,200	35,560	40,600
Cost of goods manufactured		717,600	46,920	49,680	52,440	149,040	193,200	175,260	200,100
Units produced	22	520,000	34,000	36,000	38,000	108,000	140,000	127,000	145,000
Unit cost			$1.38	$1.38	$1.38	$1.38	$1.38	$1.38	$1.38
All Products:									
Materials used	28	$1,416,600	$102,400	$115,600	$116,600	$334,600	$358,000	$339,500	$ 384,500
Direct labor	30	1,752,000	125,400	141,600	142,800	409,800	444,000	421,200	477,000
Prime cost		3,168,600	227,800	257,200	259,400	744,400	802,000	760,700	861,500
Burden applied	38	779,200	55,720	62,880	63,440	182,040	197,600	187,360	212,200
Total manufacturing cost		$3,947,800	$283,520	$320,080	$322,840	$926,440	$999,600	$948,060	$1,073,700
Add initial work in process inventory		13,800	13,800	13,800	13,800	13,800	13,800	13,800	13,800
Deduct ending work in process inventory		(13,800)	(13,800)	(13,800)	(13,800)	(13,800)	(13,800)	(13,800)	(13,800)
Cost of goods manufactured		$3,947,800	$283,520	$320,080	$322,840	$926,440	$999,600	$948,060	$1,073,700

The Superior Manufacturing Company

ESTIMATED COST OF GOODS MANUFACTURED—SUMMARY

For the Year Ending December 31, 1963

	Ref.	Annual Total	1st Quarter			Quarters			
			January	February	March	First	Second	Third	Fourth
Product X:									
Cost of goods manufactured	58	$3,230,200	$236,600	$270,400	$270,400	$777,400	$806,400	$772,800	$ 873,600
Units produced	22	960,000	70,000	80,000	80,000	230,000	240,000	230,000	260,000
Unit cost	58		$3.38	$3.38	$3.38	$3.38	$3.36	$3.36	$3.36
Product Y:									
Cost of goods manufactured	58	$ 717,600	$ 46,920	$ 49,680	$ 52,440	$149,040	$193,200	$175,260	$ 200,100
Units produced	22	520,000	34,000	36,000	38,000	108,000	140,000	127,000	145,000
Unit cost	58		$1.38	$1.38	$1.38	$1.38	$1.38	$1.38	$1.38
All Products:									
Cost of goods manufactured	58	$3,947,800	$283,520	$320,080	$322,840	$926,440	$999,600	$948,060	$1,073,700

The Superior Manufacturing Company

BUDGET WORKSHEET—COST OF GOODS SOLD AND FINISHED GOODS INVENTORY

(First-In, First-Out)

For the Year Ending December 31, 1963

Schedule 60

	Total			Sales Districts					
				Southern		Eastern		Western	
	Units	Unit Cost	Cost	Units	Cost	Units	Cost	Units	Cost
Product X:									
January									
Initial Inventory	240,000	$3.36	$ 806,400						
Production	70,000	3.38	236,600						
Total	310,000		$1,043,000						
Sales at cost	85,000	3.36	285,600	30,000	$ 100,800	40,000	$ 134,400	15,000	$ 50,400
Inventory	155,000	3.36	757,400						
	70,000	3.38	270,400						
February Production	80,000	3.38							
Total	155,000	3.36	$1,027,800						
	150,000	3.38	302,400						
Sales at cost	90,000	3.36		35,000	117,600	45,000	151,200	10,000	33,600
Inventory	65,000	3.36	725,400						
	150,000	3.38	270,400						
March Production	80,000	3.38							
Total	65,000	3.36	$ 995,800						
	230,000	3.38	218,400						
Sales at cost	65,000	3.36	101,400	20,526[a]	68,967	34,211	114,949	10,263	34,484
	30,000	3.38	676,000	9,474	32,022	15,789	53,367	4,737	16,011
Inventory	200,000	3.38	806,400						
2nd Quarter Production	240,000	3.36							
Total	200,000	3.38	$1,482,400						
	240,000	3.36	676,000						
Sales at cost	200,000	3.38	201,600	69,231[b]	234,000	103,846	351,000	26,923	91,000
	60,000	3.36	604,800	20,769	69,784	31,154	104,677	8,077	27,139
Inventory	180,000	3.36	772,800						
3rd Quarter Production	230,000	3.36							
Total	410,000	3.36	$1,377,600						
Sales at cost	190,000	3.36	638,400	65,000	218,400	90,000	302,400	35,000	117,600
Inventory	220,000	3.36	739,200						
4th Quarter Production	260,000	3.36	873,600						
Total	480,000	3.36	$1,612,800						
Sales at cost	280,000	3.36	940,800	90,000	302,400	140,000	470,400	50,000	168,000
Inventory	200,000	3.36	672,000						
Total Sales at Cost	1,000,000		$3,364,600	340,000	$1,143,973	500,000	$1,682,393	160,000	$ 538,234

Computations:

[a] March Sales in Dist. = Sch 5 × $\dfrac{\text{March Sales costing } \$ 3.36}{\text{March Total Sales — Sch 5}}$ = $\dfrac{30,000 \times 65,000}{95,000} = 20,526$ = Allocation to District

[b] $\dfrac{90,000 \times 200,000}{260,000} = 69,231$

Product Y:	Totals Units	Unit Cost	Cost	Southern Units	Cost	Eastern Units	Cost	Western Units	Cost
January									
Initial inventory	100,000	$1.38	$ 138,000						
Production	34,000	1.38	46,920						
Total	134,000	1.38	$ 184,920						
Sales at cost	34,000	1.38	46,920	15,000	$ 20,700	11,000	$ 15,180	8,000	$ 11,040
February Production	100,000	1.38	138,000						
Inventory	36,000	1.38	49,680						
Total	136,000	1.38	$ 187,680						
Sales at cost	41,000	1.38	56,580	16,000	22,080	14,000	19,320	11,000	15,180
March Inventory	95,000	1.38	131,100						
Production	38,000	1.38	52,440						
Total	133,000	1.38	$ 183,540						
Sales at cost	45,000	1.38	62,100	19,000	26,220	15,000	20,700	11,000	15,180
2nd Quarter Inventory	88,000	1.38	121,440						
Production	140,000	1.38	193,200						
Total	228,000	1.38	$ 314,640						
Sales at cost	135,000	1.38	186,300	55,000	75,900	45,000	62,100	35,000	48,300
3rd Quarter Inventory	93,000	1.38	128,340						
Production	127,000	1.38	175,260						
Total	220,000	1.38	$ 303,600						
Sales at cost	95,000	1.38	131,100	40,000	55,200	35,000	48,300	20,000	27,600
4th Quarter Inventory	125,000	1.38	172,500						
Production	145,000	1.38	200,100						
Total	270,000	1.38	$ 372,600						
Sales at cost	150,000	1.38	207,000	65,000	89,700	50,000	69,000	35,000	48,300
Inventory	120,000	1.38	165,600						
Total Sales at Cost	500,000	1.38	$ 690,000	210,000	$ 289,800	170,000	$ 234,600	120,000	$ 165,600

The Superior Manufacturing Company
BUDGETED COST OF GOODS SOLD
For the Year Ending December 31, 1963

	Ref.	Total All Districts		Southern District		Eastern District		Western District	
		Units 21	Cost 60	Units 21	Cost 60	Units 21	Cost 60	Units 21	Cost 60
Product X:									
January		85,000	$ 285,600	30,000	$ 100,800	40,000	$ 134,400	15,000	$ 50,400
February		90,000	302,400	35,000	117,600	45,000	151,200	10,000	33,600
March		95,000	319,800	30,000	100,989	50,000	168,316	15,000	50,495
Total 1st Quarter		270,000	907,800	95,000	319,389	135,000	453,916	40,000	134,495
2nd Quarter		260,000	877,600	90,000	303,785	135,000	455,677	35,000	118,138
3rd Quarter		190,000	638,400	65,000	218,400	90,000	302,400	35,000	117,600
4th Quarter		280,000	940,800	90,000	302,400	140,000	470,400	50,000	168,000
Total Product X		1,000,000	$3,364,600	340,000	$1,143,974	500,000	$1,682,393	160,000	$ 538,233
Product Y:									
January		34,000	$ 46,920	15,000	$ 20,700	11,000	$ 15,180	8,000	$ 11,040
February		41,000	56,580	16,000	22,080	14,000	19,320	11,000	15,180
March		45,000	62,100	19,000	26,220	15,000	20,700	11,000	15,180
Total 1st Quarter		120,000	165,600	50,000	69,000	40,000	55,200	30,000	41,400
2nd Quarter		135,000	186,300	55,000	75,900	45,000	62,100	35,000	48,300
3rd Quarter		95,000	131,100	40,000	55,200	35,000	48,300	20,000	27,600
4th Quarter		150,000	207,000	65,000	89,700	50,000	69,000	35,000	48,300
Total Product Y		500,000	$ 690,000	210,000	$ 289,800	170,000	$ 234,600	120,000	$ 165,600
All Products:									
January			$ 332,520		$ 121,500		$ 149,580		$ 61,440
February			358,980		139,680		170,520		48,780
March			381,900		127,209		189,016		65,675
Total 1st Quarter			1,073,400		388,389		509,116		175,895
2nd Quarter			1,063,900		379,685		517,777		166,438
3rd Quarter			769,500		273,600		350,700		145,200
4th Quarter			1,147,800		392,100		539,400		216,300
Total for Year			$4,054,600		$1,433,774		$1,916,993		$ 703,833

The Superior Manufacturing Company
BUDGETED COST OF GOODS SOLD—SUMMARY
For the Year Ending December 31, 1963

Schedule 62

SALES DISTRICTS

	Ref.	Total All Districts		Southern		Eastern		Western	
		Units	Cost	Units	Cost	Units	Cost	Units	Cost
Products:									
X	60	1,000,000	$3,364,600	340,000	$1,143,974	500,000	$1,682,393	160,000	$ 538,233
Y	60	500,000	690,000	210,000	289,800	170,000	234,600	120,000	165,600
Total Cost			$4,054,600		$1,433,774		$1,916,993		$ 703,833

The Superior Manufacturing Company
FINISHED GOODS INVENTORY BUDGET
For the Year Ending December 31, 1963

		Product X			Product Y		
Ref.	Total Cost	Units	Unit Cost	Total Cost	Units	Unit Cost	Total Cost
		23	60		23	60	
January 1, 1963	$944,400	240,000	$3.36	$806,400	100,000	$1.38	$138,000
January 31, 1963	895,400	225,000	a	757,400	100,000	1.38	138,000
February 28, 1963	856,400	215,000	b	725,400	95,000	1.38	131,100
March 31, 1963	797,440	200,000	3.38	676,000	88,000	1.38	121,440
End of 2nd Quarter	733,140	180,000	3.36	604,800	93,000	1.38	128,340
End of 3rd Quarter	911,700	220,000	3.36	739,200	125,000	1.38	172,500
End of 4th Quarter	837,600	200,000	3.36	672,000	120,000	1.38	165,600

a 70,000 units at $3.38, and 155,000 units at $3.36.
b 150,000 units at $3.38, and 65,000 units at $3.36.

The Superior Manufacturing Company
BUDGETED INCOME STATEMENT, BY TIME PERIODS
For the Year Ending December 31, 1963

	Ref.	Annual	First Quarter			Quarters			
			January	February	March	First	Second	Third	Fourth
Sales	21	$6,095,000	$500,400	$540,000	$574,100	$1,614,500	$1,595,000	$1,158,000	$1,727,500
Less cost of goods sold	61	4,054,600	332,520	358,980	381,900	1,073,400	1,063,900	769,500	1,147,800
Gross margin		2,040,400	167,880	181,020	192,200	541,100	531,100	388,500	579,700
Less:									
Selling expenses	42	989,497	82,109	84,608	86,769	253,486	251,915	222,977	261,119
Administrative expenses	44	223,713	18,752	18,735	18,859	56,346	55,999	54,321	57,047
Totals		1,213,210	100,861	103,343	105,628	309,832	307,914	277,298	318,166
Operating profit		827,190	67,019	77,677	86,572	231,268	223,186	111,202	261,534
Add:									
Interest income	53	500	42	41	42	125	125	125	125
Other income	49	37,120	3,390	2,950	3,620	9,960	9,510	8,220	9,430
		864,810	70,451	80,668	90,234	241,353	232,821	119,547	271,089
Less interest expense	53	3,750	667	416	667	1,750	1,000	500	500
Profit before income tax		861,060	$ 69,784	$ 80,252	$ 89,567	$ 239,603	$ 231,821	$ 119,047	$ 270,589
Per cent of sales		14.13	13.9	14.8	15.6	14.8	14.5	10.3	15.7
Federal income taxes	53	258,318							
Net income		$ 602,742							

the *finished goods inventory budget,* which is illustrated in Schedule 63.

At this point the compilation of the budgeted income statements involves merely the assembling of the appropriate estimates from schedules already developed. The Superior Manufacturing Company prepares the following budgeted income statements:

(1) Annual (Schedule 13)
(2) By time periods (Schedule 64)
(3) By sales districts (Schedule 65)
(4) By product (Schedule 66)

Schedule 65

The Superior Manufacturing Company

BUDGETED INCOME STATEMENT, BY SALES DISTRICTS
For the Year Ending December 31, 1963

				Sales District	
	Ref.	*Total*	*Southern*	*Eastern*	*Western*
Sales	21	$6,095,000	$2,120,000	$2,907,000	$1,068,000
Cost of goods sold	61	4,054,600	1,433,773	1,916,993	703,834
Gross margin		2,040,400	686,227	990,007	364,166
District sales expenses	42	663,167	234,656	313,391	115,120
District direct operating profit		1,377,233	451,571	676,616	249,046
Per cent of net sales		22.6	21.3	23.3	23.3
Allocations:					
General sales overhead	42	296,330			
Administrative expenses	44	193,713			
Building services	34	60,000			
To be allocated		550,043	191,305	262,370	96,368
Allocation basis*			(34.78%)	(47.70%)	(17.52%)
District operating profit		827,190	$ 260,266	$ 414,246	$ 152,678
Per cent of net sales		13.57	12.3	14.2	14.3
Add net of other incomes and expenses	49 & 53	33,870			
Profit before income tax		861,060			
Federal income tax	53	258,318			
Net income		$ 602,742			

* On basis of net sales.

The Superior Manufacturing Company
BUDGETED INCOME STATEMENT, BY PRODUCT
For the Year Ending December 31, 1963

			Product	
		Total	*X*	*Y*
	Ref.			
Sales	21	$6,095,000	$5,066,000	$1,029,000
Cost of goods sold	61	4,054,600	3,364,600	690,000
Gross margin		2,040,400	1,701,400	339,000
Allocations:				
District sales expenses	42	663,167		
General sales overhead	42	296,330		
Administrative expenses	44	193,713		
Building services	34	60,000		
Total to be allocated		1,213,210	1,008,420	204,790
Allocation basis*			(83.12)	(16.88)
Operating profit		827,190	$ 692,980	$ 134,210
Per cent of sales		13.57	13.68	12.07
Add net of other incomes and expenses	49 & 53	33,870		
Profit before income tax		861,060		
Federal income tax	53	258,318		
Net income		$ 602,742		

* On basis of net sales

The budgeted balance sheet may be developed directly from prior schedules along the same lines as the income statement. The budgeted balance sheet requires the application of the *operating budget* schedules, cash budget, capital additions budget, and other miscellaneous budgets to the estimated balances in the real accounts at the beginning of the budget year. Thus the process is more involved than is the development of the income statements. Although it is possible to develop the balance sheet directly, it is usually desirable to set up a special worksheet for this purpose. Such a worksheet for The Superior Manufacturing Company is illustrated in Schedule 67. The worksheet is developed from the estimated trial balance as of December 31, 1962, as follows:

The Superior Manufacturing Company
Estimated Trial Balance as of December 31, 1962

	Debits	Credits
Cash	$ 54,000	
Accounts receivable	160,000	
Allowance for doubtful accounts		$ 9,000
Raw material inventory	257,600	
Work in process inventory	13,800	
Finished goods inventory	944,400	
Unexpired insurance	2,532	
Supplies inventory	13,700	
Building	1,800,000	
Land	25,000	
Machinery and equipment	280,000	
Allowance for depreciation (Building, machinery and equipment)		443,380
Building fund	20,000	
Accounts payable		52,100
Audit fee payable		2,400
Notes payable—short term		
Property taxes payable		4,982
Accrued interest expense		7,000
Federal income taxes payable		279,400
Notes payable—Long term (4% interest payable February 15; $150,000 principal due February 15, 1963)		200,000
Common stock (20,000 shares)		2,000,000
Retained earnings		522,770
Premium on common stock		50,000
	$3,571,032	$3,571,032

The following entires were taken from the various budget schedules indicated and entered on the budget worksheet (Schedule 67) under the column "Entries 1963 Budget."

	Debits	Credits
1—Sales Budget Schedule 21		
Accounts receivable	$6,095,000	
Sales		$6,095,000
2—Purchases Budget Schedule 26		
Raw material inventory	1,419,000	
Accounts payable		1,419,000
3—Cost of Materials Used Schedule 28		
Raw material used	1,416,600	
Raw material inventory		1,416,600

	Debits	*Credits*

4—Direct Labor Budget Schedule 30

Direct labor	1,752,000	
Cash clearance		1,752,000

5—Building Services Budget Schedule 34

Building services	150,000	
Cash clearance		84,000
Allowance for depreciation		60,000
Prepaid insurance		3,600
Property taxes payable		2,400

6—Factory Expense Budgeted Schedule 36

Factory overhead	689,200	
Supplies inventory		49,640
Allowance for depreciation		19,560
Prepaid insurance		3,036
Property taxes payable		4,164
Cash clearance		612,800

7—Building Services Allocated Schedule 34

Selling expenses	30,000	
Administrative expenses	30,000	
Factory overhead	90,000	
Building services		150,000

8—Distribution Expense Budget Schedule 42

Selling expenses	959,497	
Allowance for depreciation		600
Cash clearance		958,897

9—Administrative Expense Budget Schedule 44

Administrative expense	193,713	
Allowance for depreciation		4,200
Property taxes payable		720
Audit fee payable		2,400
Prepaid insurance		960
Allowance for doubtful accounts		12,190
Cash clearance		173,243

10—Collection of Accounts Receivable Schedule 48

Cash clearance	6,095,886	
Accounts receivable		6,095,886

11—Bad Debts Written Off Schedule 48

Allowance for doubtful accounts	3,000	
Accounts receivable		3,000

	Debits	*Credits*

12—Other Income Budgeted Schedule 49

Cash clearance	37,120	
Other income		37,120

13—Payment of Accounts Payable Schedule 51

Accounts payable	1,429,140	
Cash clearance		1,429,140

14—Capital Additions Budgeted Schedule 46

Machinery and equipment	8,700	
Building fund	20,000	
Cash clearance		28,700

15—Accrued and Deferred Items Schedule 53

Prepaid insurance	22,788	
Accrued property taxes	4,982	
Income taxes payable	279,400	
Accrued interest expense	8,000	
Supplies inventory	41,140	
Audit fee payable	2,400	
Retained earnings	12,000	
Notes payable—long term	150,000	
Cash clearance		520,710

16—Interest Expense Schedule 56

Interest expense	1,000	
Cash clearance		1,000

17—To clear out Cash Clearance

Cash clearance	5,560,490	
Cash		5,560,490
Cash	6,133,006	
Cash clearance		6,133,006

18—Building Fund Interest Credit Schedule 53

Building fund	500	
Interest income		500

19—Accrued Interest on Notes Schedule 53

Interest expense	2,750	
Accrued interest expense		2,750

20—Income Taxes Payable

Income tax expense	258,318	
Income taxes payable		258,318

The Superior Manufacturing Company
BUDGET WORKSHEET
For the Year Ending December 31, 1963

	Trial Balance Dec. 31, 1962 Dr	Cr	Entries 1963 Budget Dr	Cr	Work in Process Dr	Cr	Profit and Loss Dr	Cr	Balance Sheet Dec. 31, 1963 Dr	Cr
Cash	$ 54,000		17-$6,133,006	17-$5,560,490					$ 626,516	
Accounts receivable	160,000		1-6,095,000	10-6,095,886 11-3,000					156,114	
Allowance for doubtful accounts		$ 9,000	11-3,000	9-12,190						$ 18,190
Raw material inventory	257,600		2-1,419,000	3-1,416,600					260,000	
Work in process inventory	13,800				$ 13,800	$ 13,800			13,800	
Finished goods inventory	944,400						$ 944,400	$ 837,600	837,600	
Prepaid insurance	2,532		15-22,788	5-3,600 6-3,036 9-960					17,724	
Supplies inventory	13,700		15-41,140	6-49,640					5,200	
Land	25,000								25,000	
Building, machinery & equipment	2,080,000		14-8,700						2,088,700	
Allowance for depreciation		443,380		5-60,000 6-19,560 8-600 9-4,200						527,740
Building fund	20,000		14-20,000 18-500						40,500	
Accounts payable		52,100	13-1,429,140	2-1,419,000						41,960
Audit fee payable		2,400	15-2,400	9-2,400						2,400
Accrued interest expense		7,000	15-8,000	19-2,750						1,750
Property taxes payable		4,982	15-4,982	5-2,400 6-4,164 9-720						7,284
Income taxes payable		279,400	15-279,400	20-258,318						258,318
Notes payable—Long term		200,000	15-150,000							50,000
Common stock		2,000,000								2,000,000
Retained earnings		522,770	15-12,000							510,770
Premium on stock		50,000								50,000
	$3,571,032	$3,571,032								

	Trial Balance Dec. 31, 1962 Dr	Cr	Entries 1963 Budget Dr	Cr	Work in Process Dr	Cr	Profit and Loss Dr	Cr	Balance Sheet Dec. 31, 1953 Dr	Cr
Sales				1-$6,095,000				$6,095,000		
Raw material used			3-$1,416,600		$1,416,600					
Building services			5-150,000	7-150,000						
Factory overhead			6-689,200 7-90,000		779,200					
Direct labor			4-1,752,000		4-1,752,000					
Selling expenses			7-30,000							
Administrative expenses			8-959,497 7-30,000				$ 989,497			
Interest expense			9-193,713				223,713			
Interest income			16-1,000	18-500			3,750	500		
Other income			19-2,750	12-37,120				37,120		
Income tax expense			20-258,318				258,318			
Cost of goods manufactured						$3,947,800	3,947,800			
						$3,961,600				
					$3,961,600					
Net income							602,742			$ 602,742
							$6,970,220	$6,970,220	$4,071,154	$4,071,154

Schedule 68
Note*

The Superior Manufacturing Company
BUDGETED BALANCE SHEET—JANUARY
For the Month Ending January 31, 1963

ASSETS

Current Assets:			
Cash	$		$ 163,374
Accounts receivable	157,793		
Less allowance for doubtful accounts	10,001		147,792
Raw material inventory		253,100	
Work in process inventory		13,800	
Finished goods inventory		895,400	
Prepaid insurance		1,899	
Supplies inventory		13,457	1,488,822
Funds:			
Building fund			20,042
Fixed Assets:			
Land		25,000	
Building	1,800,000		
Less allowance for depreciation	365,000	1,435,000	
Machinery and equipment	280,200		
Less allowance for depreciation	85,261	194,939	1,654,939
Deferred Charges:			
Factory overhead under applied			6,637
Total Assets			$3,170,440

LIABILITIES AND CAPITAL

Current Liabilities:			
Accounts payable	$	$ 32,630	$
Audit fee payable		2,600	
Property taxes payable		5,589	
Accrued interest expense		7,667	
Federal income taxes payable[a]		300,335	348,821
Fixed Liabilities:			
Long term notes payable			200,000
Capital:			
Common stock		2,000,000	
Premium on common stock		50,000	
Retained earnings	522,770		
Add January net income	48,849	571,619	2,621,619
Total Liabilities and Capital			$3,170,440

* See Schedule 17, Chapter 3, page 74, for Annual Balance Sheet.

a Litigation currently in progress may result in payment of approximately $620,000 as an adjustment of prior years' Federal Income Taxes.

The reader is reminded that the trial balance just presented (December 31, 1962) is needed before the end of the current operating period if the budget is to be completed and distributed before the beginning of the budget year. This requirement should be no deterrent to completion of the planning budget. The trial

BUDGETED CHANGES IN WORKING CAPITAL
For the Year Ending December 31, 1963

	Ref.	Balances 1/1/63 67	Balances 12/31/63 67	Working Capital Increase or Decrease*
Current Assets:				
Cash		$ 54,000	$ 626,516	$ 572,516
Accounts receivable (net)		151,000	137,924	13,076*
Raw material inventory		257,600	260,000	2,400
Work in process inventory		13,800	13,800	—
Finished goods inventory		944,400	837,600	106,800*
Unexpired insurance		2,532	17,724	15,192
Supplies inventory		13,700	5,200	8,500*
Total current assets		$1,437,032	$1,898,764	$ 461,732
Current Liabilities:				
Accounts payable		$ 52,100	$ 41,960	$ 10,140
Audit fee payable		2,400	2,400	—
Accrued interest expense		7,000	1,750	5,250
Property taxes payable		4,982	7,284	2,302*
Income taxes payable		279,400	258,318	21,082
Total current liabilities		$ 345,882	$ 311,712	$ 34,170
Working Capital		$1,091,150	$1,587,052	$ 495,902

balance generally can be estimated with reasonable accuracy by the budget and accounting departments, using the November actual balance and the current December forecast. This fact suggests the need for a worksheet similar to Schedule 67 that includes these data. In some cases it becomes necessary to revise parts of the planning budget after initial distribution. This revision should be made if the estimated end-of-the-year trial balance is materially incorrect. Immaterial differences should cause no concern.

The resulting annual balance sheet for The Superior Manufacturing Company is shown in Schedule 17 (Chapter 3). Monthly budgeted balance sheets may or may not be prepared. Since they require little time to prepare, they may be justified. The January balance sheet is illustrated in Schedule 68. The reader should particularly note the contingent liability indicated in the footnote and the treatment of *manufacturing overhead over under applied* on the monthly balance sheet. The latter item does not appear on the annual balance sheet. Preparation of the monthly balance sheets may be facilitated through the use of a worksheet similar to Schedule 67.

The Superior Manufacturing Company prepares an analysis of working capital which includes (a) a statement of changes in working capital and (b) a funds flow statement. The *budgeted*

(1) Net income for the year (Schedule 13)		
Funds provided	$602,742	
Retained earnings		$602,742
(2) Cash dividends paid (Schedule 53)		
Retained earnings	12,000	
Funds applied		12,000
(3) Purchase of capital additions (Schedule 46)		
Building, machinery & equipment	8,700	
Funds applied		8,700
(4) Depreciation for the year (Schedule 47)		
Funds provided (adjustment)	84,360	
Allowance for depreciation		84,360
(5) Cash contribution to building fund (Schedule 46)		
Building fund	20,000	
Funds applied		20,000
(6) Interest credited to building fund		
Building fund	500	
Funds applied		500
(7) Notes paid (Schedule 54)		
Notes payable—long term	150,000	
Funds applied		150,000
(8) Funds applied to increase working capital (Schedule 69)		
Working capital	495,902	
Funds applied		495,902

changes in working capital are shown in Schedule 69. The beginning and ending balances were taken directly from Schedule 67.

Preparation of the funds flow statement is facilitated through the use of a worksheet similar to that illustrated in Schedule 70[1]. The two trial balances were taken from the worksheet shown as Schedule 67. The component entries, for changes in the noncurrent accounts, were developed from numerous schedules. The entries on the worksheet are listed above with explanatory notes and source information.

[1] G. A. Welsch, C. T. Zlatkovich, and J. A. White, *Intermediate Accounting* (Homewood, Ill.: Irwin, 1963), Ch. 29.

The Superior Manufacturing Company
WORKSHEET—FUNDS FLOW STATEMENT
For the Year Ending December 31, 1963

	Ref.	Trial Balance 1/1/63 67	Interim Entries 1963 Debit	Interim Entries 1963 Credit	Trial Balance 12/31/63 67
Non-Fund Accounts:					
Land		$ 25,000			$ 25,000
Building, machinery, and equipment		2,080,000	(3) $ 8,700		2,088,700
Allowance for depreciation		443,380*		(4) $ 84,360	527,740*
Building fund		20,000	(5) 20,000		40,500
			(6) 500		
Notes payable—long term		200,000*	(7) 150,000		50,000*
Common stock		2,000,000*			2,000,000*
Retained earnings		522,770*	(2) 12,000	(1) 602,742	1,113,512*
Premium on stock		50,000*			50,000*
Working capital (Schedule 69)		1,091,150	(8) 495,902		1,587,052
		———			——
Funds Provided:					
From operations:					
Net income			(1) 602,742		
Adjustment for non-fund items:					
Depreciation			(4) 84,360		
Funds Applied:					
Cash dividends paid				(2) 12,000	
Purchases of equipment and tools				(3) 8,700	
Contribution to building fund—cash				(5) 20,000	
Contribution to building fund—interest credit				(6) 500	
Notes payable—long term				(7) 150,000	
Funds applied to increase working capital				(8) 495,902	
			$1,374,204	$1,374,204	

* Credit Balance

The budgeted funds flow statement taken directly from the worksheet (Schedule 70) is illustrated in Schedule 71.

The Superior Manufacturing Company
BUDGETED FUND FLOW STATEMENT   Schedule 71
For the Year Ending December 31, 1963

Funds Provided:			
From operations:			
Net income		$602,742	
Add Nonfund charges:			
Depreciation		84,360	
Total funds provided			$687,102
Funds Applied:			
Cash dividends paid		$ 12,000	
Cash transferred to building fund	$20,000		
Add interest credit	500	20,500	
Notes Paid—long term		150,000	
Purchases of equipments and tools		8,700	
Total Funds Applied			$191,200
Budgeted Increase in Working Capital			$495,902

After completion of these summary schedules, the annual profit plan is presented to the budget committee and then to the chief executive for approval. Upon final approval the budget director reproduces it for distribution to specified executives.

Discussion Questions

1. Why is it desirable that estimated financial statements be developed as a part of the planning budget?
2. What should the budget calendar indicate? Why is it frequently important to have a budget calendar?
3. Outline the responsibilities of the budget director (and others) in putting together the components of the annual profit plan.
4. During the process of planning budget development why should the various sub-budgets be given only tentative approval?
5. Discuss the statement, "Planning-budget construction is essentially a matter of managerial policies and decisions concerning *alternatives.*"
6. Why is it sometimes necessary to rebuild the planning budget several times before final approval?
7. Explain the use of the variable budgets in "testing" the appropriateness of the profit plan during the process of its development rather than at the time the budgeted income statement and balance sheets are completed.

8. What is meant by the ratio tests? Explain their applicability (a) with respect to development of the annual profit plan and (b) with respect to long-range planning.

9. The planning budget should be completed prior to the beginning of the period for which the budget is made. In order to complete the planning budget, the trial balance as of the end of the current year is needed. What can be done to resolve the apparent inconsistency?

10. Outline the distribution of the planning budget in a typical situation.

11. Why should the planning budget and variable budget be assembled under separate covers?

12. Discuss the advantages of two alternatives concerning distribution of the annual profit plan—alternative 1, distribute by company mail (or messenger); alternative 2, distribute through line channels coupled with *planning conferences.*

13. Discuss the following criticism of planning budget procedures: "The planning budget exerts a restrictive influence on management."

14. Why is it essential that management apply the planning budget in a flexible way?

15. Discuss the statement: "Budgeting cannot take the place of management."

T W E L V E

Techniques and Managerial Application

of Cost-Volume-Profit Analysis

(Breakeven Analysis)

Although a complete and perhaps adequate budget program may be developed without using cost-volume-profit (breakeven) techniques, the use of such techniques may significantly add to the understanding and usefulness of budget procedures and estimates. In addition, cost-volume-profit analyses provide valuable information bearing on many types of managerial decisions.

There is a very close relationship between budgeting and cost-volume-profit analyses. Although such analyses may be applied to historical data, the significant application is to *future estimates.* The latter application, using budget data, indicates its importance in comprehensive budgeting. If variable budgets are used, as illustrated in The Superior Manufacturing Company case, the basic data for cost-volume-profit analyses are available. If variable budgets are not used, then costs and expenses are not expressed in terms of variability (identification of the fixed and variable components), consequently, cost-volume-profit analysis involves a critical problem in expense analysis. Current literature is replete with discussions of breakeven analysis. Most of these discussions are concerned with arithmetical aspects of the analysis which *assume that the variability of costs has been determined;* yet the latter is the critical problem. It is important to realize that breakeven analyses rest upon a valid identification of cost variability with volume, i.e., an identification of the fixed and variable components of cost.

A title more descriptive of the underlying concepts is *cost-volume-profit* analysis. The breakeven point, defined as that volume level at which revenue exactly equals total cost, is somewhat incidental to the comprehensive scope of cost-volume-profit analysis. Cost-volume-profit analysis is directly concerned with the effect on profits of (a) changes in fixed costs, (b) changes in variable costs, (c) changes in sales quantities, (d) changes in sales prices, and (e) changes in sales mix. An analysis that may provide management with an insight into these effects and interrelationships obviously has considerable significance in many areas of managerial decisions. If such an analysis can be made with reasonable accuracy, its importance cannot be overlooked by the controller, budget director, nor by management in general.

The purposes of this chapter are (a) to explain the basic concepts underlying cost-volume-profit analysis, (b) to indicate some of its applications, and (c) to consider its interrelationship with budgeting.

The concept of cost-volume-profit analyses

Understanding cost-volume-profit analysis requires an appreciation of the underlying concepts. The underlying concepts are best indicated in the familiar breakeven chart shown in Illustration 36 which, together with Illustrations 37 and 38, are based on the following budget data.

Annual Profit Plan—XYZ Company

	Fixed	Variable	
Budgeted sales (200,000 units @ $25)			$5,000,000
Budgeted costs:			
Direct material		$ 900,000	
Direct labor		1,000,000	
Factory overhead	$ 700,000	300,000	
Administrative expenses	600,000	100,000	
Distribution expenses	500,000	300,000	
Totals	$1,800,000	$2,600,000	4,400,000
Budgeted profit			$ 600,000

(Capacity production 240,000 units)

The vertical scale on the chart (Illustration 36) represents dollars of revenue and cost. The horizontal scale reflects volume or activity—in this case, *units of output*. The three lines representing total fixed costs, total costs, and sales may be located readily

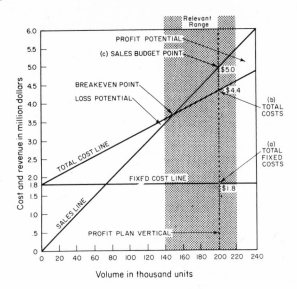

Illustration 36. *Breakeven Chart of XYZ Company*

by placing the *profit-plan vertical* at the budgeted volume of 200,000 units and marking thereon the budget level of (a) fixed costs ($1.8 million), (b) total costs ($4.4 million), and (c) sales dollars ($5.0 million). The fixed cost line is drawn *horizontally* through the fixed cost point of $1.8 million. The total cost line is drawn through (1) the total cost point of $4.4 million and (2) the intersection of the fixed cost line with the left vertical scale. The sales line is drawn through the budget sales point ($5.0 million) to the zero-zero point at the left. If the same distance is used on the horizontal scale for volume of sales as on the vertical scale for the revenue realizable from that volume, the sales line will connect opposite corners of the graph at 45°.

The point at which the *sales* and *total cost* lines intersect is the breakeven point ($3.75 million). The spread to the right of this point (between the two lines) represents the profit potential, and the spread to the left represents the loss potential.

From point of view of graphing technique, there are two additional and important variations of the breakeven chart. In Illustration 36 fixed costs were charted *below* variable costs. Another variation frequently used shows fixed costs charted *above* variable costs, as may be seen in Illustration 37. The latter method has the advantage of indicating the recovery of fixed costs at various volume levels before profits are realized. It may be observed also

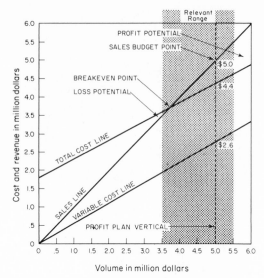

Illustration 37. *Breakeven Chart of XYZ Company*

from Illustration 37 that output or volume is expressed in *budget-ed sales dollars* rather than in units, the units being converted to sales dollars at the budgeted unit sales price of $25.

A third plan is that of showing the various fixed and variable costs in a particular sequence: for example, in income statement order for major classifications such as separate graphing of manufacturing, distribution, and administrative expenses, as shown in Illustration 38.

Obviously the breakeven point is the same in each of the three methods of graphing. Illustration 36 indicates the breakeven volume in both units (150,000) and dollars ($3.75 million), whereas Illustrations 37 and 38 show the breakeven volume in dollars only.

The breakeven point, as well as other significant data, may be determined through the use of simple mathematical procedures. There are a number of formulas that may be used for such computations; the two usually employed are as follows:

(1) BREAKEVEN COMPUTATION BASED ON BUDGET TOTALS:

$$BES = \frac{Fixed\ Costs}{1 - \dfrac{Variable\ Costs}{Corresponding\ Sales}}$$

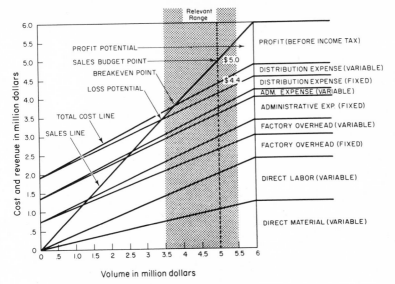

Illustration 38. *Detailed Breakeven Chart of XYZ Company*

Substituting the illustrative data we have

$$BES = \frac{\$1.8 \text{ million}}{1 - \dfrac{\$2.6 \text{ million}}{\$5.0 \text{ million}}} = \frac{\$1.8 \text{ million}}{1 - .52} = \frac{\$1.8 \text{ million}}{.48}$$

$$= \$3.75 \text{ million} \quad (\$3.75 \text{ million divided by } \$25)$$
$$= 150,000 \text{ units}$$

Analysis of the formula provides an insight into the mechanics of the breakeven point. Dividing variable costs by sales results in the *variable cost ratio*. For example, the .52 ($2.6 ÷ $5.0) derived in the illustration above indicates that variable costs are 52 per cent of sales, or, to express it differently, $.52 of every sales dollar is necessary to recover, exactly, the variable costs. Subtracting the variable cost ratio from one gives the *marginal profit ratio*. For example, the .48 (1 − .52) derived in the illustration above, indicates that 48 per cent of sales are available to cover fixed costs (and generate profits) or, to express it differently, $.48 of each sales dollar is available to cover fixed costs and make a profit. Since profit at breakeven is zero, dividing fixed costs by the profit margin ratio (.48) (also referred to as the P/V ratio) gives the number of dollars of sales revenue that is necessary to exactly recover fixed costs ($1.8 million ÷ .48 = $3.75 million).

The computations can be verified readily as follows:

Breakeven sales		$3,750,000
Deduct:		
Fixed costs	$1,800,000	
Variable costs ($3,750,000 × .52)	1,950,000	
Total		3,750,000
Net Profit		Nil

(2) BREAKEVEN COMPUTATION BASED ON BUDGETED UNIT PRICE AND COSTS:

Unit sales price ($5.0 million ÷ 200,000 units)	$25
Unit variable cost ($2.6 million ÷ 200,000 units)	13
Contribution of *each unit* sold to cover fixed costs and profits	$12

Fixed costs to be recovered of $1.8 million divided by unit recovery of $12 gives a breakeven volume of 150,000 units (150,000 × $25 = $3.75 million breakeven.)[1]

Obviously computations based on unit prices and costs can be used only in the case of a single product or in the application of breakeven analysis to each product separately.

Basic assumptions underlying cost-volume-profit analyses

The simplified breakeven charts and the illustrative computations above indicate the basic assumptions underlying cost-volume-profit analyses. These underlying assumptions are:

(1) That the *principle of cost variability* is valid.
(2) That costs can be resolved into their fixed and variable components.
(3) That fixed costs remain constant.
(4) That variable costs vary proportionally with volume changes expressed in terms of a common measure of activity.
(5) That the revenue and cost estimates, and hence the results of the analysis, are valid only within a definite relevant range of activity.
(6) That selling price is not to change as volume changes.

---

[1] Note that computations based on *total cost* give the breakeven point in dollars of sales whereas the unit cost approach gives the breakeven point in units.

(7) That there is only one product or, in the case of multiple products, that sales mix remains constant.

(8) That basic managerial policies relative to operations will not change materially.

(9) That there will be no change in the general price level.

(10) That there is synchronization between production and sales— that is, that there will be no change in inventory.

(11) That efficiency and productivity per worker will remain essentially unchanged.

The principle of cost variability as applied to cost-volume-profit analysis

In the illustrations in this chapter all costs are identified by their fixed and variable components. Obviously the accuracy and hence the reliability of cost-volume-profit analysis depend upon the precision with which cost variability is determined. The principle of cost variability was defined and discussed in Chapter 9 with respect to variable budgets. Also at that point the concepts of fixed and variable costs were defined and illustrated. The concepts of cost variablility, fixed costs, and variable costs discussed at that point are precisely the same concepts that are involved in cost analysis for cost-volume-profit.

Cost-volume-profit analyses are developed under the assumption that the concept of cost variability is valid and, further, that it is possible to identify fixed and variable components of cost. Many leading firms have demonstrated that such determination is not only possible, but that it can be done with reasonable accuracy.

Identification of fixed and variable components of cost

A rough estimate of cost variability and the breakeven point may be derived by plotting historical revenue and cost data for several successive periods. Such an estimate may give a general idea of the economic characteristics of a firm. However, it is an unsophisticated approach and must be viewed with considerable caution because, in most cases, each set of historical data represents varying conditions such as changes in the general price level, managerial policies, accounting classification, productivity, methods of manufacturing, and products. Because this approach estimates the *historical* relationship, there is the implicit assumption that the historical trends will continue in the future as in the past. Some firms use this approach to approximate competitor breakeven points for comparison with their own.

Since the accuracy of cost-volume-profit analysis depends upon the accuracy with which cost variability is determined, a more scientific approach is required. Thus a careful study and analysis of each cost or group of costs must be made. Preliminary analysis will readily indicate certain costs to be fixed for all practical purposes and certain other costs to be approximately variable in nature. In addition there will be a group of costs possessing the characteristics of both fixed and variable costs, i.e., semivariable costs. These are the costs that require special analysis, the objective being to separate the fixed and variable components. Generally the most logical starting point to resolve this problem is an analysis of historical data. Numerous methods have been suggested for determining cost variability. The principal approaches are discussed in detail in Chapter 9 in connection with variable budget construction. These same approaches may be applied to the analysis of costs for breakeven purposes.

The fact bears reiteration that, if variable budgets have been constructed, cost variability is already determined and may be readily used for breakeven analysis. This interrelationship of variable budgets and breakeven analysis suggests that, once reliable variable budgets are constructed, numerous cost-volume-profit analyses can be developed with little effort and cost. This application is illustrated at the end of the chapter based on the Superior Manufacturing Company data previously developed.

Straightline variability

The fixed and total cost lines on the breakeven chart normally are shown as *straight* or linear from zero to capacity. The assumptions that fixed costs remain constant at all volume levels, and that variable costs vary *proportionally* at all volume levels, is seldom, if ever, literally true. A casual glance at the breakeven chart may convey this impression; however, a practical analyst will readily note that such is not the case. In Illustrations 36-38 a portion of the breakeven chart was shaded to indicate the *relevant range*. The concept of relevant volume range was discussed in Chapter 9 in connection with variable budgets. The relevant range may be thought of as the area of significance.

Although the lines may be extended to the left and right of the relevant range, the analysis has meaning only in this range. What the analysis purports to show is what fixed costs *should be* and how variable costs *should vary* within the relevant volume range *as determined by existing managerial policies.* Within this relevant volume range operational conditions and managerial policies can be assumed to be relatively stable and consistent, and hence the results predictable on a straightline basis. Outside this range, different operational conditions and managerial policies will (and should) prevail, resulting in a completely new pattern of cost valiability and, consequently, new cost-volume-profit relationships. To apply the analysis outside the relevant range, without adjustment for a different set of conditions, is poor judgment and will surely lead to erroneous conclusions. The analysis purports to show what would happen at the various volume levels, assuming that conditions and policies remain stable.

Sales price and sales mix considerations

The breakeven chart assumes a constant unit sales price; hence, the revenue line is straight. This simplifying assumption is necessary for two reasons. First, it is desirable to show the effect of the expected or budgeted sales price. The effect of other contemplated selling prices can be shown (page 347). Secondly, since the sales line expresses the combined results of *volume* and *sales price*, any attempt to show the effect on the physical volume of sales of changes in unit selling prices would involve price (demand) theory. It may be noted that if it is possible to make a reliable estimate of the net effect of a price increase or decrease on total sales revenue, the breakeven analyst would have no difficulty in including such estimate in his analysis. There is no reason why the sales line cannot be expressed as a curve, or in steps, provided a realistic determination can be made of what the line (curve) should be.

A cost-volume-profit analysis may be developed for each product separately or for multiple products. If only one product or very similar products are involved, the complication of *sales mix* is avoided. Sales mix refers to the relative quantities of the various products making up the "sales line." The analysis of sales mix may be simply illustrated. Assume that the following budget data are available concerning two products.

| | Product A | | | Product B | | |
	Units		*Amount*	*Units*		*Amount*	*Totals*
Sales	10,000	$1.00	$10,000	7,500	$1.33⅓	$10,000	$20,000
Costs:							
Fixed			2,000			5,500	7,500
Variable		.60	6,000		.40	3,000	9,000
Total			8,000			8,500	16,500
Net profit		.20	$ 2,000		.20	$ 1,500	$ 3,000

The breakeven chart and computation of the breakeven point are shown in Illustration 39, Graph A. The *sales line* and *total cost line* assume a 10 to 7.5 quantity ratio between the two products at all points up and down the volume scale. It may be observed that, although the profit per unit is indicated to be $.20 for each product, this figure would be different for each product at all other sales volumes due to the effect of fixed costs.

Now assume top management is considering the effect of a change in sales mix, the objective being to determine which product should be pushed. Casual observation of the budget data provides no direct clue as to which product is potentially the more profitable; in fact, it may appear that they are equal in profit potential ($.20 profit per unit for each product); hence the budgeted sales mix is appropriate. In order to demonstrate the effect of a change in sales mix, assume the controller prepared the following analyses:

1st Assumption: 20% quantity increase in product A, no change in product B.

| | Product A | | | Product B | | |
	Units		*Amount*	*Units*		*Amount*	*Totals*
Sales	12,000	$1.00	$12,000	7,500	$1.33⅓	$10,000	$22,000
Costs:							
Fixed			2,000			5,500	7,500
Variable		.60	7,200		.40	3,000	10,200
Total			9,200			8,500	17,700
Net profit			$ 2,800			$ 1,500	$ 4,300

2nd Assumption: 20% quantity increase in product B, no change in product A.

| | Product A | | | Product B | | |
	Units		*Amount*	*Units*		*Amount*	*Total*
Sales	10,000	$1.00	$10,000	9,000	$1.33⅓	$12,000	$22,000
Costs:							
Fixed			2,000			5,500	7,500
Variable		.60	6,000		.40	3,600	9,600
Total			8,000			9,100	17,100
Net profit			$ 2,000			$ 2,900	$ 4,900

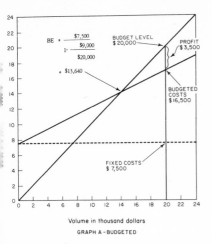

GRAPH A - BUDGETED

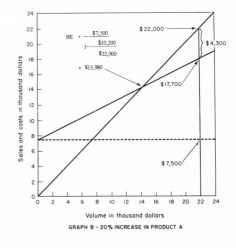

GRAPH B - 20% INCREASE IN PRODUCT A

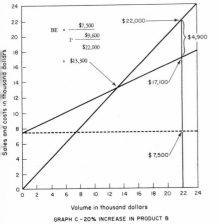

GRAPH C - 20% INCREASE IN PRODUCT B

Illustration 39. Breakeven Charts—Sales Mix: (a) Budgeted;
(b) 20 Per Cent Increase in Product A; (c) 20 Per Cent Increase
in Product B.

The analysis may be summarized as follows:

	Results at Present Budget	Results of 20% Increase in Product A	Results of 20% Increase in Products B
Net profit	$ 3,500	$ 4,300	$ 4,900
Percentage profit change (increase-decrease*)		23%	40%
Breakeven point	$13,640	$13,980	$13,300

The analysis above indicates that it would be desirable to push product B, because in the second assumption (a) greater profits result, and (b) the breakeven point is lowered. The analysis is graphically illustrated and the effects demonstrated in Illustration 39, Charts B and C. It is important to observe that a new cost-volume-profit analysis is developed for each new sales mix ratio, wherein both the sales and cost lines are based upon the new sales mix or quantity ratio between the two products at all points up and down the volume scale. Obviously, this application provides a significant tool for management in that it clearly indicates the dramatic effect on the profit and loss picture (and the breakeven point) of pushing or failing to push the more profitable lines. Therefore, the sales mix assumption inherent in breakeven analysis, if viewed properly, is an advantage rather than a disadvantage. It may be observed that the breakeven points for the two products computed separately (which assumes independence) will not sum to the breakeven point based on combined data, which assumes a dependence imposed by the prescribed sales mix limitation.

Basic managerial policies related to cost-volume-profit

Cost-volume-profit analysis carries implicit assumptions relative to the basic managerial policies. The revenue data introduced into the computations implies definite policies that have been set relative to such items as sales prices, sales mix, and products. The fixed cost data implies specific policies such as salary scales, number of indirect employees on fixed salaries, specific depreciation methods, insurance coverage, research effort, advertising, and plant capacity—that is, those policies that determine the fixed cost structure of the company. The variable cost data imply specific policies that determine the variable cost structure of the firm, such as quality of raw materials, technology in the manufacturing process, wage rates for direct labor employees, and sales commissions.

Because cost-volume-profit analysis implies a definite set of policies affecting the revenue and cost characteristics of the firm —and this is one of its most significant applications—it tells management in effect, "Here are the approximate results to be expected at varying volume levels of operations presuming a *specific set* of policies and decisions. If one or more of these policies or decisions are not changed, this is the approximate result." For example, if the firm is approaching the breakeven point in operations, or profits are dropping, managerial action aimed at lowering the breakeven point *before it is reached* should be forthcoming. This distinction is important, for management must know what the effect of present policies is in order to know when and why they should be changed, how they should be changed, and what the probable effect would be. Not one, but a series of breakeven analyses under varying assumptions as to costs, operational conditions, and policies, may constitute a valuable guide for managerial decisions.

Evaluation of the assumptions

The last three assumptions listed on page 331 are generally of little consequence in cost-volume-profit analysis because it is a short-term analysis. The analysis as generally developed assumes a stable price level. This assumption, of course, is not completely valid, but for periods of one year or less (and the analysis must be kept current) the change is generally negligible. Should there be a significant price level change affecting revenue or costs, the entire analysis should be developed anew.

The assumption of efficiency and productivity per worker is particularly important in the long run; however, these seldom change materially in the short run. If they do, the existing relationships between volume and costs will change and, hence, a new analysis is required.

Should there be a material change in the inventory upon which the analysis is based, appropriate adjustment must be made in the computations for the increase or decrease in inventory along the lines suggested in a later section of this chapter.

Various aspects of the eleven assumptions discussed above are the basis for most criticisms leveled at cost-volume-profit analyses. Although some of them are difficult to resolve in specific situations, none is beyond the realm of reasonable solution under most circumstances. Whether or not they can be validated in a particular situation will depend to a large degree upon the persistence, perspective, ability, and practical judgment of the analyst.

Special problems in breakeven analysis

In the previous examples in this chapter, volume was expressed in units of product or net sales dollars. The *base or factor of variability* usually employed is net sales dollar, as the best measure of over-all activity or volume in a concern. Units of product are preferable if the analysis is applied to one product. In cases of multiple products, the factor used to measure total volume must be in units that are additive—that compose a common denominator of volume. For the concern as a whole, net sales dollars are generally the only satisfactory common denominator because manufacturing, selling, and administrative activities are expressed in combination.

If variable budgets are available, they may be summed for cost-volume-profit purposes. This process may give rise to some complications because the several departmental variable budgets are related to different activity bases. For example, selling expenses may be related to sales dollars, factory overhead related to direct labor or machine hours, and power department costs related to kilowatt hours. In adding such variable budget allowances, it is assumed that the departmental activity factors correlate to a reasonable degree with the over-all base selected for breakeven purposes. The usual procedure in constructing breakeven analysis based on variable budgets is simply to add the *fixed* component of costs shown in the several variable budgets and to treat the remaining costs (determined by subtraction from total costs) as variable. This procedure is illustrated subsequently for The Superior Manufacturing Company case. Selection of an appropriate activity base for departments was discussed in Chapter 9.

Other incomes and other expenses, if significant in amount, present another special problem in cost-volume-profit analyses.

Preferably nonoperating items such as these should be omitted from the analysis; however, if they are included, it is preferable to include the *net* of other income and other expenses. If the excess is expense, it should be added to fixed expense, whereas if the excess is income, it should be deducted from the fixed expense. When graphed the effect of these amounts should be indicated with additional lines; thus the economic characteristics of the firm before and after such nonoperating items are indicated. The computational procedure may be illustrated simply. Assume the following budget data are available:

Budgeted sales (10,000 units @ $3.)		$30,000
Less:		
Fixed costs	$18,000	
Variable costs	9,000	27,000
Operating profit		3,000
Add:		
Other incomes	$ 3,000	
Less other expenses	1,000	2,000
Budgeted net income		$ 5,000

To compute the breakeven points:

Case A—Omitting other incomes and expenses;

$$\text{BES} = \frac{\$18,000}{1 - \dfrac{\$9,000}{\$30,000}} = \underline{\$25,714}$$

Case B—Including other incomes and expenses:

$$\text{BES} = \frac{\$18,000 - \$2,000}{1 - \dfrac{\$ 9,000}{\$30,000}} = \underline{\$22,857}$$

The computations may be verified for Case B as follows:

Sales		$22,857
Less:		
Fixed costs	$18,000	
Variable costs (.30 × $22,857)	6,857	24,857
Operating loss		($2,000)
Add:		
Other incomes	$ 3,000	
Less other expenses	1,000	2,000
Net income		NIL

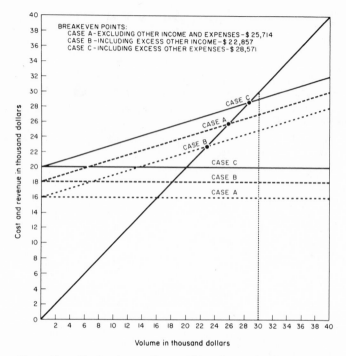

Illustration 40. Breakeven Chart—With Other Income and Expenses

Case C—Assuming other incomes of $1,000 and other expenses of $3,000; that is excess expense of $2,000:

$$BES = \frac{\$18,000 + \$2,000}{1 - \dfrac{\$9,000}{\$30,000}} = \underline{\underline{\$28,571}}$$

The graphic analyses for each of the three cases are shown in Illustration 40.

Breakeven analysis and inventory change

In most cases budgeted inventory changes (finished goods and work in process) will be immaterial in amount and thus may be disregarded in cost-volume-profit analyses. On the other hand, when the budgeted inventory changes are significant, the analyst should seriously consider introducing this factor into the computations. In this connection it is appropriate to note that when *direct costing* (only variable costs are considered as production and inventory costs), as opposed to *full costing*, procedures are used, inventory changes have no effect on the breakeven computations. This fact is often cited as a significant advantage by the proponents of direct costing. (See Chapter 15.)

Introduction of the effect of inventory changes in cost-volume-profit analyses involves (a) subjective judgement as to what management might do (relative to inventory changes) at levels of operation above or below the budgeted level, and (b) the degree of theoretical precision that the analyst desires. In the discussions to follow one practical approach that is used with some frequency is illustrated, although it does overlook some theoretical distinctions in the interest of simplicity and practicality.[2]

In order to pinpoint the problem and to illustrate one practical approach, the following simplified data are used:

Budgeted sales (90,000 units @ $2)		$180,000
Budgeted production (100,000 units):		
Fixed costs	$ 80,000	
Variable costs ($.60 per unit)	60,000	
Total costs	140,000	
Less inventory increase (10,000 units @ $1.40)	14,000	126,000
Gross margin		54,000
Less administrative & distribution costs:		
Fixed costs	10,000	
Variable costs ($.10 per unit)	9,000	19,000
Budgeted income		$ 35,000

Note that (a) only one product is involved (so that the effects may be seen clearly), and (b) there is a budgeted *increase* in inventory amounting to 10 per cent of production. It is also assumed that the increase in inventory is at the same unit cost as budgeted production ($1.40 per unit).

If it is desired to *disregard* the inventory change in computing the breakeven point (which is a common practice), the breakeven point may be computed as follows:

[2] For excellent discussions of this problem see: R. Lee Brummet, *Overhead Costing*, Bureau of Business Research, School of Business Administration, University of Michigan, 1957. Roy E. Tuttle, "The Effect of Inventory Change on Breakeven Analysis," *NAA Bulletin* (January 1959), pp. 77–87.

Based on budget totals:

$$\text{BES} = \frac{\$80,000 + \$10,000}{1 - \dfrac{\$60,000 + \$9,000 - \$6,000}{\$180,000}} \quad {}^3$$

$$= \frac{\$90,000}{1 - .35}$$

$$= \frac{\$9,000}{.65}$$

$$= \$138,462 \text{ or } 69,231 \text{ units } (\$138,462 \div \$2)$$

Because there is only one product, computations giving the same results may be

Based on budgeted unit prices and costs:

Unit sales price		$2.00
Less unit variable costs:		
Factory	$.60	
Administrative & selling	.10	.70
Contribution to cover fixed costs & profit		$1.30

Fixed cost to be recovered $90,000 divided by unit recovery of $1.30 gives 69,231 units at breakeven or $138,462.

The computations may be verified by omitting the inventory change, viz.

Breakeven sales (69,231 units at $2)		$138,462
Less production costs:		
Fixed	$80,000	
Variable (69,231 × $.60)	41,539	121,539
Gross margin		16,923
Less administrative & selling:		
Fixed	10,000	
Variable (69,231 × $.10)	6,923	16,923
Profit or loss		Nil

If we regard the inventory change as *significant* and therefore introduce it in the analysis, we must assume either: (a) that the management will tend to maintain a constant *ratio* of inventory change to production—that is, in the above example the inventory increase will tend to be 10 per cent of production at various levels of operations, or (b) that the inventory change

---

[3] In all cases the *variable costs* and the *sales figure* must relate to the same level of activity. The subtraction of $6,000 (10,000 units at $.60) reduces the variable costs to a 90,000 unit basis which is necessary in this case since the $180,000 sales figure is based on 90,000 units, whereas the production costs are based on 100,000 units. The production level could be "run up (or down)" to agree with sales, thereby changing only variable production cost.

will be constant as to unit change—that is, in the above example management will maintain the 10,000 unit increase in inventory irrespective of the level of operations. In addition, we may assume (a) that a beginning inventory is, in effect, a fixed cost or (b) that it is in part a fixed cost and in part a variable cost. The theoretical aspects are complicated by these assumptions and the additional factor of factory *overhead over- or under-applied.*

In order to avoid complexity, yet to derive a reasonable approximation, many firms simply assume (1) that the inventory increase or decrease will tend to be proportional to changes in production, and (2) that the inventory change carries the same ratio of fixed and variable costs to total cost as is budgeted for current production.

Returning to the illustrative data, the inventory change (increase of 10,000 units or 10 per cent of production) may be analyzed as follows:

Costs in inventory change:

Fixed component: $\dfrac{10,000 \text{ units}}{100,000 \text{ units}} \times \$80,000 = \$8,000$

Variable component: $\dfrac{10,000 \text{ units}}{100,000 \text{ units}} \times \$60,000 = 6,000$

Total (10,000 units) $\underline{\$14,000}$

Accepting the two simplifying assumptions listed immediately above, the breakeven point may be computed as follows:

Based on budget totals:

$$\text{BES} = \cfrac{\$80,000 + \$10,000 - \$8,000}{1 - \cfrac{\$60,000 + \$9,000 - \$6,000}{\$180,000}}$$

$$= \frac{\$82,000}{.65}$$

$$= \$126,154 \text{ or } 63,077 \text{ units } (\$126,154 \div \$2)$$

Because there is only one product, computations giving the same results may be:

Based on budgeted unit prices and costs:

Unit sales price		$2.00
Less unit variable cost:		
Factory	$.60	
Administrative & selling	.10	.70
Contribution to cover fixed costs and profit		$1.30

$$BES = \frac{\$80,000 + \$10,000 - \$8,000}{\$1.30}$$

$$= 63,077 \text{ units or } \$126,154 \ (63,077 \times \$2)$$

Note that the $8,000 (computed above) subtracted from fixed costs in both computations represents the *fixed cost* component of the inventory change. It is subtracted because this amount of fixed cost is "going to inventory" rather than to cost of sales because inventory is *increased*.

The computations may be verified in terms of the two simplifying assumptions as follows:

Breakeven sales (63,077 units @ $2)		$126,154
Less costs:		
Production (63,077 ÷ .90 = 70,085 units)		
Fixed costs	$ 80,000	
Variable costs (70,085 × $.60)	42,051	
Total production costs	122,051	
Less inventory (10% of production)	12,205	
Cost of goods sold		109,846
Gross margin		16,308
Less selling & administrative costs		
Fixed	$ 10,000	
Variable (63,077 × $.10)	6,308	16,308
Net income		Nil

If we assume the budget presented above with the exceptions that (a) budgeted sales are 110,000 units and (b) production is 100,000 units, a 10,000 *decrease* in inventory results. The breakeven point under the two simplifying assumptions would require that the $8,000 fixed costs *withdrawn* from inventory be added to fixed costs as follows:

$$BES = \frac{\$90,000 + \$8,000}{\$1.30}$$

$$= 75,385 \text{ units (or } \$150,769)$$

The application of this *practical* method is illustrated in The Superior Manufacturing Company case at the end of the chapter. When dealing with the somewhat heterogeneous and detailed data common to an actual situation, some practical approach is generally preferable to a complicated, theoretical approach, assuming the practical approach provides a reasonable approximation of the results.

Use and application of cost-volume-profit analysis

In situations where cost-volume-profit analyses can be developed with a reasonable degree of accuracy, they can be of considerable value as a managerial tool. Essentially cost-volume-profit analysis is a technique that provides greater insight into the *economic characteristics* of a firm and may be used to determine the approximate effect of various alternatives. It should be realized that cost-volume-profit analysis is based on *estimates,* and the arithmetical manipulations generally involve *averages,* hence the results should never be viewed as precise. Rather, the analysis may be characterized appropriately as a "slide-rule" approach that may be used to develop and test, with a minimum of effort, the approximate effect on costs and profits of several types of managerial decisions.

Illustration 41 is shown below to indicate a few of the *economic characteristics* of the firm, viz:

(1) Fixed costs, variable costs, and total costs at varying volumes.
(2) The profit and loss potential, before and after income taxes, at varying volumes.
(3) The margin of safety—the relationship of budget volume to breakeven volume.
(4) The breakeven point.
(5) The preferred dividend or danger point—the point below which preferred dividends are not earned.
(6) The dead point—the point where management earns only the "going" rate on the investment.
(7) The common dividend or unhealthy point—the point below which earnings are insufficient to pay the preferred dividends and the expected dividend on the common stock.

It may be observed that all these points as well as others can be computed readily if data are developed for cost-volume-profit purposes. The remaining paragraphs of this chapter are intended to indicate some of the more significant applications of breakeven analysis.

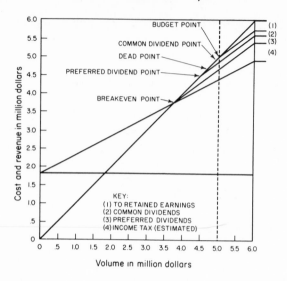

Illustration 41. *Breakeven Chart—Economic Characteristics*

Evaluating the effect of changing factors

An important aspect of cost-volume-profit analysis is the flexibility with which the effect of a contemplated change in one or more factors influencing the analysis can be evaluated. This aspect of cost-volume-profit analyses is of considerable importance to management during the process of developing the annual profit plan because it makes possible early and continuous *testing* to determine the probable over-all effect of any number of alternatives under consideration.

The methods and techniques of identifying the effect of a change in sales mix were illustrated earlier in this chapter (pages 333–335). This section considers the evaluation of changes in (a) fixed costs, (b) variable costs, and (c) sales price.

Returning to the original illustration in this chapter (page 326) concerning the XYZ Company, assume it is desired to evaluate the effect of a contemplated 10 per cent increase in *fixed costs*. The computation simply would be:

(a) Effect on BES:

$$\text{BES} = \frac{\$1.8 \text{ million} \times 110\%}{1 - \dfrac{\$2.6 \text{ million}}{\$5.0 \text{ million}}} = \$4.125 \text{ million}$$

(b) Sales necessary to earn the originally budgeted profit of $600,000:

$$\text{BES} + \text{``Profit'' sales} = \frac{(\$1.8 \text{ million} \times 110\%) + \$.6 \text{ million}^4}{1 - \dfrac{\$2.6 \text{ million}}{\$5.0 \text{ million}}}$$

$$= \$5.375 \text{ million}$$

The computations may be verified:

	At Breakeven		To Earn $.6 million profit
Sales (millions)		$4.125	$5.375
Fixed costs	$1.8		$1.8
10 per cent increase	.18		.18
	1.98		1.98
Variable costs (52% rate)			
$4.125 × 52%	2.145	4.125	
5.375 × 52%			2.795 · · · · 4.775
Net income		Nil	$ .600

Now assume instead that it is desired to evaluate the effect of a contemplated 10 per cent increase in *variable costs*. The computation could be made as follows:

(a) Effect on BES

$$\text{BES} = \frac{\$1.8 \text{ million}}{1 - \dfrac{\$2.6 \text{ million} \times 110\%}{\$5.0 \text{ million}}} = \$4.2 \text{ plus million}$$

(b) Sales necessary to earn the originally budgeted profit of $600,000:

$$\text{BES} + \text{``Profit'' sales} = \frac{\$1.8 \text{ million} + \$.6}{1 - \dfrac{\$2.6 \text{ million} \times 110\%}{\$5.0 \text{ million}}}$$

$$= \$5.6 + \text{ million}$$

These two changes are shown graphically in Illustration 42.

Finally, assume it is desired to evaluate the effect of a contemplated 10 per cent increase in sales price. The computations are:

(a) Effect on BES:

$$\text{BES} = \frac{\$1.8 \text{ million}}{1 - \dfrac{\$2.6 \text{ million}}{\$5.0 \text{ million} \times 110\%}} = \$3,413,795 \text{ or } 124,138 \text{ units}$$

---

[4] Note that the desired profit figure is merely added to the fixed costs because the contribution of sales above variable costs "cover fixed costs and profits."

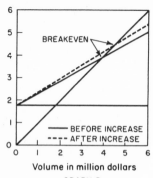

GRAPH B
EFFECT OF 10% INCREASE IN VARIABLE COSTS

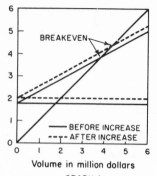

GRAPH A
EFFECT OF 10% INCREASE IN FIXED COSTS

Illustration 42. *Change in Cost Structure*

(b) Sales necessary to earn the originally budgeted profit of $600,000; assume further that the price increase will reduce units sold by approximately 5%:

$$\text{BES} + \text{“Profit” sales} = \frac{\$1.8 \text{ million} + \$.6 \text{ million}}{1 - \dfrac{\$2.6 \text{ million} \times 95\%}{\$5.0 \text{ million} \times 95\% \times 110\%}}$$

$$= \$4{,}551{,}720 \text{ or } 165{,}517 \text{ units}$$

Significantly the effect of contemplated decisions such as those illustrated above may be plotted on the graph easily as shown in Illustration 43. In plotting a *price change*, care must be exercised as indicated in Illustration 43. Note that when volume is expressed in *units*, a price change may be indicated by merely raising or lowering the *sales line*. In contrast, when volume is expressed in *sales dollars* the *total cost* line rather than the sales line must be changed.

These illustrations should be sufficient to indicate the wide application of cost-volume-profit analyses for *testing* the effect of proposed action and for consideration of numerous alternative proposals. For example, the technique lends itself to ready determination of the effect on the profit potential of replacing old machinery with new machinery, which change may result in a shift of fixed and variable costs.

Cost-volume-profit analysis by organizational subdivision or product

In many instances it is useful to develop cost-volume-profit analyses by product, plant, or other subdivision of the concern. An actual incident may be noted to dramatize the application of such analyses. A particular sales division executive, whose

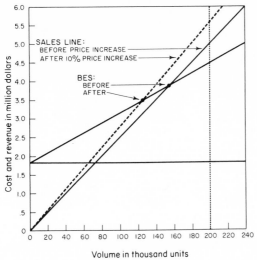

PLOTTING 10% PRICE INCREASE

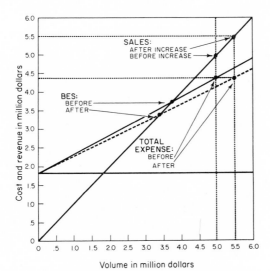

PLOTTING 10% PRICE INCREASE
WHEN VOLUME SCALE IS IN SALES DOLLARS

Illustration 43. *Change In Unit Sales Price*

349

BUDGET DATA

	Eastern District			Western District			Company		
	Fixed	*Variable*	*Total*	*Fixed*	*Variable*	*Total*	*Fixed*	*Variable*	*Total*
Sales			$300,000			$200,000			$500,000
Cost of goods sold	$ 36,000	$ 84,000	120,000	$ 24,000	$ 56,000	$ 80,000	$60,000	$140,000	200,000
Gross margin			180,000			120,000			300,000
Direct district sales expenses	30,000	99,000	129,000	20,000	64,000	84,000	50,000	163,000	213,000
Direct district operating profit			51,000			36,000			87,000
Cost sub-totals	66,000	183,000		44,000	120,000		110,000	303,000	
Allocated general sales and administrative costs a	21,600	14,000	36,000	14,400	9,600	24,000	36,000	24,000	60,000
Total costs	87,600	197,400		58,400	129,600		146,000	327,000	
Net income			$ 15,000			$ 12,000			$ 27,000

a Allocated on same basis for simplicity.

Breakeven computation:

Before allocations:

Eastern District

$$BE = \frac{\$66,000}{1 - \frac{\$183,000}{\$300,000}}$$
$$= \$169,231$$

Western District

$$BE = \frac{\$44,000}{1 - \frac{\$120,000}{\$200,000}}$$
$$= \$110,000$$

After allocations:

Eastern District

$$BE = \frac{\$87,600}{1 - \frac{\$197,400}{\$300,000}}$$
$$= \$256,140$$

Western District

$$BE = \frac{\$58,400}{1 - \frac{\$129,600}{\$200,000}}$$
$$= \$165,909$$

Company

$$BE = \frac{\$146,000}{1 - \frac{\$327,000}{\$500,000}}$$
$$= \$421,965$$

Illustration 44. Breakeven Analysis By Sales Districts.

variable costs to sales ratio was 75 per cent, was contemplating an increase in divisional fixed costs. The president inquired as to the amount of sales necessary to maintain the present profit position after the increase in fixed costs. The sales executive replied that for each dollar increase in fixed cost, sales volume would have to be increased one dollar to maintain the same profit position. Needless to ﹍ay, the sales executive was not nearly so enthusiastic about increasing fixed costs when told by the controller (based on the cost volume-profit analysis) that for each \$1 increase in fixed costs, sales volume must be increased by no less than \$4, in order to maintain exactly the present profit position (\$1 ÷ 25% = \$4).

Breakeven analysis by organizational subdivisions or products presents a special problem to the analyst—that of indirect costs. It is generally best to develop an analysis (a) before and (b) after allocation of indirect costs. In this connection allocations frequently can be made on a more logical basis if the allocation basis used for fixed costs differs from the one used for variable costs. One application of breakeven analysis by sales districts is shown in Illustration 44.

For preparation of breakeven charts based on the analysis above, it may be desirable to plot the data both before and after cost allocations on the same chart.[5]

Margin of safety

The margin of safety is the relationship of budgeted volume (or actual volume) to the breakeven volume. It is useful for management to realize how close to the breakeven point the concern is operating. For example, assume the following data concerning two concerns:

	Company A	Company B
Budgeted sales	\$100,000	\$100,000
Budgeted costs:		
Fixed	70,000	20,000
Variable	20,000	70,000
Budgeted income	\$ 10,000	\$ 10,000
Indicated breakeven points	\$ 87,500	\$ 66,667

[5] For an excellent treatment of the problem see R.J. Barber, "When Does Part of a Business Break Even?" *NAA Bulletin* (May 1951), p. 1040. For a comprehensive treatment of breakeven analysis see Fred V. Gardner, *Profit Management and Control* (New York: McGraw-Hill, 1955) and John Y.D. Tse, *Profit Planning Through Volume-Cost Analyses* (New York: Macmillan, 1960).

Although the two concerns budget the same profit figure, there is a basic difference in their economic characteristics. Company A is much closer to the breakeven point than Company B. Whereas Company A will operate at a loss if volume drops more than $12\frac{1}{2}$ per cent, Company B will not operate at a loss until volume drops more than $33\frac{1}{3}$ per cent; in other words, they have different margins of safety. The margin of safety may be expressed (a) as a ratio of budget of breakeven, or (b) as the ratio or per cent of the difference between sales and breakeven to budgeted sales. The following figures are illustrative for the two concerns mentioned above:

	Company A	Company B
(a) Margin of Safety expressed as a per cent of budget to breakeven:		
(100,000 ÷ 87,500)	114.3%	
(100,000 ÷ 66,667)		150.0%
(b) Margin of Safety expressed as the per cent of the difference to budgeted sales:		
($12,500 ÷ $100,000)	$12\frac{1}{2}$%	
($33,333 ÷ $100,000)		$33\frac{1}{3}$%

Cost-volume-profit analysis for The Superior Manufacturing Company illustrated

The annual income statement for The Superior Manufacturing Company is recast for cost-volume-profit purposes in Schedule 72. It is assumed that the inventory contains the same ratio of fixed to variable cost as in current production.

Derivation of the fixed and variable components of the inventory change was as follows on Schedule 72:

(1) Determine per cents on line "Per cent of fixed and variable to total" from the data on the preceding line ($525,840 ÷ $3,947,800 = 13%).

(2) Determine *total* change in inventory (last column) as a squeeze figure between "Total manufacturing costs" and "Cost of goods sold" ($4,054,600 − $3,947,800 = $106,800).

(3) Determine fixed and variable components of inventory change on the line "Add decrease in finished goods inventory" using the per cents developed on the preceding line ($106,800 × 13% = $13,884).

Data now are available on Schedule 72 for computing the breakeven point under several assumptions:

(1) Omit inventory change, but include other incomes and expenses.
(2) Omit both inventory change and other incomes and expenses.
(3) Include inventory change, but omit other incomes and expenses.
(4) Include both inventory change and other incomes and expenses.

The Superior Manufacturing Company

INCOME AND COST DATA FOR COST-VOLUME-PROFIT ANALYSIS
For the year ending December 31, 1963

		Company		
	Ref.	*Fixed*	*Variable*	*Total*
Budgeted sales	1			$6,095,000
Manufacturing costs:				
Material	29		$1,416,600	1,416,600
Labor	30		1,752,000	1,752,000
Prime cost			3,168,600	3,168,600
Factory Overhead:				
General factory	35	$105,120	11,680	116,800
Power	35	80,400	29,600	110,000
Repair	35	8,640	1,360	10,000
Producing Department 1	36	168,000	151,280	319,280
2	36	23,520	5,760	29,280
3	36	50,160	53,680	103,840
Buiding services	36	90,000		90,000
Total factory overhead costs		525,840	253,360	779,200
Total manufacturing costs		525,840	3,421,960	3,947,800
Per cent of fixed and variable to total		13%	87%	100%
Add decrease in finished goods inventory		13,884	92,916	106,800
Cost of goods sold	60	539,724	3,514,876	4,054,600
Gross margin				2,040,400
Distribution:				
General sales overhead	42	231,540	64,790	296,330
District	42	323,160	340,007	663,167
Building service	42	30,000		30,000
Total distribution		584,700	404,797	989,497
Administrative:				
Administrative Department	44	76,080	7,436	83,516
Treasurer's Department	44	39,720	16,457	56,177
Accounting Department	44	52,800	1,220	54,020
Building services	44	30,000		30,000
Total administrative		198,600	25,113	223,713
Total selling & administrative expense		783,300	429,910	1,213,210
Operating profit				827,190
Add net of other income and expense	13			33,870
Net profit before income taxes	13			861,060
Less Federal income taxes	13			258,318
Net income	13			$ 602,742
Total fixed costs *excluding* inventory decrease		$1,309,140		
Total variable costs *excluding* inventory decrease			$3,851,870	

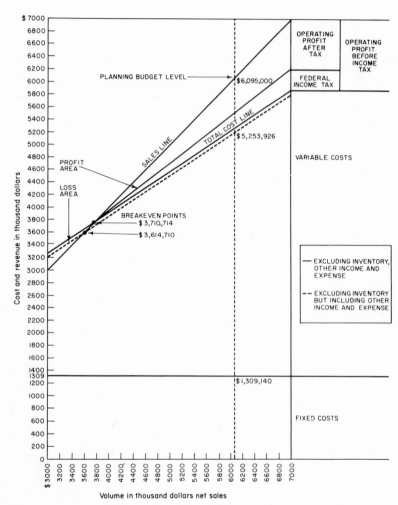

BREAKEVEN CHART OF THE SUPERIOR MANUFACTURING COMPANY

Representative computations are shown below for the first and second assumptions. The related breakeven chart is shown in Schedule 73. Note that for practical reasons the volume scale at the left does not extend to zero.

Computation of breakeven point:

Assumption 1—Omit inventory change but include other incomes and expenses.

$$\text{BES} = \frac{\$1,309,140 - \$33,870}{1 - \dfrac{3,851,870 + 92,916}{\$6,095,000}}$$

$$= \frac{\$1,275,270}{1 - .6472}$$

$$= \$3,614,710$$

Assumption 2—Omit both inventory change and other incomes and expenses.

$$\text{BES} = \frac{\$1,309,140}{1 - .6472}$$

$$= \$3,710,714$$

Discussion Questions

1. Outline the relationship between budgeting and cost-volume-profit analysis.
2. List the principal assumptions underlying cost-volume-profit analysis.
3. Discuss the advantages and disadvantages of the three principal methods of graphic presentation of breakeven analysis.
4. Why is it important to define clearly the "relevant range" in breakeven analysis?
5. Why is the assumption of straightline variability of costs usually considered sufficiently valid for cost-volume-profit analyses?
6. What is the relationship between management policies and cost-volume-profit analyses?
7. What is meant by the "economic characteristics" of a firm? Why is a knowledge of them of significance to management?
8. What is meant by "margin of safety." In what way is it of significance to management?
9. How would a change in the productivity per worker in a firm influence the breakeven point? Explain.
10. In what way would a change in the general price level affect the breakeven point? Explain.
11. List and explain several uses of cost-volume-profit analysis.

PART THREE

Operation of the Budget

THIRTEEN

Performance Reports for Managerial Control

In the preceding chapters we have considered development of both long- and short-range profit plans. In those discussions problems and approaches relating to managerial control were also considered. Performance reports for internal managerial use constitute an important part of a comprehensive budget system. The purpose of this chapter is to consider (a) some of the fundamentals that should be observed in establishing a system of performance reports, and (b) the characteristics and mechanics of an integrated performance reporting system that ties in directly with the annual profit plan and the actual results of operations as reported by the accounting department. The performance reporting phase of a comprehensive budget program is very critical and the manner in which it is handled will in turn have a significant effect upon the extent to which the planned goals and objectives are achieved.

To indicate the extensive reporting requirements the business firm must satisfy and to pinpoint the specific aspect of reporting that we are considering in this chapter, the following broad classification of reports is presented and briefly explained:

(1) *External reports*—Under this classification are reports to government agencies, regulatory commissions, creditors, investigative agencies, and other such groups external to the active management. Frequently, these reports are quite extensive and comprise a significant aspect of the over-all reporting activities of the business enterprise. In sum total these reports are very costly and considerable management attention is devoted to them.

(2) *Report to owners*—Under this classification are the traditional annual report to the owner (to stockholders in case of a corporation) and other special reports prepared for the owners relative to special problems or items of interest. These reports, by and large, are based upon "generally accepted accounting principles"

and generally report data that have been subject to audit by an independent C.P.A. This phase of reporting is frequently referred to as *financial accounting*.

(3) *Internal reports*—These are reports prepared within the firm and for internal use only; in this respect they may be considered *confidential* reports. They do not have to meet the rules of external groups, nor the test of "generally accepted accounting," but rather the test of *internal management needs*. For purposes of discussion this category of reports is subdivided into three distinctly different subclassifications.

(a) *The statistical reports*—These are accounting reports that carry the vital historical statistics concerning all phases of operations. The data included in these reports constitute the detailed financial and operating history of the firm. The accumulation of these data is essential on a continuing basis for both contemplated and unknown uses in the future. These statistics include the basic data for the two categories of reports outlined above; they also provide the basic data for special-purpose studies that are made from time to time. Separate reports of this type are common in the better-managed companies and are made on a repetitive basis (usually monthly).

(b) *Special reports*—These are internal reports that are prepared irregularly, each one being related to a specific problem. Their design, scope, and comprehensiveness depend upon the particular problem involved.

(c) *Repetitive control or performance reports*—These reports are generally prepared on a monthly basis and follow a fairly standardized format from period to period (but not standardized as between companies or industries). These reports are specifically designed to facilitate internal managerial control. They should comprise carefully selected series of data related to specific responsibilities. Fundamentally, they report actual results compared with objectives, or budgeted plans. Frequently they give rise to special reports since they are designed to pinpoint both efficient and inefficient performance.

All firms irrespective of size have reporting requirements involving all of the categories listed above. In the smaller firm most of the basic reporting needs may be accomplished with a *single* general purpose report. However, as the size and complexity of the firm increases, there is increasing need for segmentation of the reporting as suggested above. Many firms make the mistake of mixing these several categories despite the increasing size and complexity of operations. As a firm changes and grows, the system of financial reporting must be adapted to meet the changing needs. It is not unusual to find an antiquated accounting and financial reporting system in an otherwise dynamic company; in such cases, it is safe to say that the full potentials of the management (and the company) are jeopardized. It is important to realize that the usual accounting report prepared for external use has limited application for internal managerial purposes. Accountants who attempt to meet the problems of modern management with the types of reports designed for external purposes are failing in their responsibilities. Obviously, accounting reports containing budget data are rarely prepared for external use.

In this chapter we are concerned only with internal reports, (3) above, and more specifically with *repetitive performance reports*, (3, c) above. In considering this particular aspect of reporting, which we have considered an integral part of a comprehensive budget program, we will first consider some of the essential characteristics and mechanical aspects. In the latter part of the chapter we will discuss a somewhat typical monthly performance report related to the annual profit plan.

Accounting and budget reports as a tool of communication

In most business situations, management must rely to a great extent upon information contained in reports developed within the concern—the more so as operations become more complex because management cannot easily observe, analyze, and assemble all facts relative to operations. Accounting and budget reports comprise a large proportion of the reports needed by the various levels of management. Reports concerning the financial situation are essential to most, if not all, managerial policy decisions. As stated in a recent study:

In order to be useful to management, accounting information must be communicated to management personnel. Communication implies that a person receiving the information understands the nature and significance of material contained in the reports he receives. When communication is genuinely effective, management's actions and decisions are likely to be based on the facts which they receive rather than on untested impressions and guesses. However, there is reason to believe that accounting reports to management have not always achieved their intended purpose because the reports were not understood, recipients lacked time required to grasp the meaning, or the content of reports was not relevant to problems facing the persons who received them.[1]

Reports that communicate effectively to all levels of management stimulate action and influence decisions. Those charged with the design and preparation of reports for managerial use must know and understand the problems and methods of management.

Essential characteristics of effective performance reports for managerial use

Performance reports should be adapted to the particular company, yet we may generalize with respect to certain criteria. These criteria are as follows:

(1) Reports should be tailored to organizational structure (responsibilities).
(2) Reports should be designed to implement the management exception principle, therefore, should include a basis for evaluation of performance.
(3) Reports should be simple and understandable.
(4) Reports should contain only essential information.
(5) Reports should be adapted to the needs and personal preferences of the primary user.
(6) Reports should be designed with particular consideration of their primary use.
(7) Reports should be accurate.
(8) Reports should be prepared and presented promptly.
(9) Reports, when possible, should convey a constructive tone rather than implied criticism.
(10) Reports should be standardized where feasible.

Reporting by areas of organizational responsibility

Mention has been made in the preceding chapters of the importance of accounting and budgeting in terms of the organizational responsibilities. This procedure is essential in that organizational responsibilities are identified and reported on. It follows that an effective control system of performance reporting must be likewise developed along organizational lines. Performance reports should be *integrated* in such way that it is possible to trace favorable or unfavorable performance to the original source.

---

[1] "Reports Which Management Find Most Useful," *NAA Bulletin,* Accounting Practice Report, No. 9 (Feb. 1960), Sec. 3.

The performance report system also must be designed so that management can readily observe the salient facts in each report. Condensed summaries should be provided for the successively higher levels of management, and all performance reports should be designed to implement the exception principle—that is, so that the *exception* or the *unusual* stands out.

In order to illustrate the manner in which reports may be (a) related to the organizational structure, and (b) designed to identify the exceptional items, a hypothetical manufacturing company is assumed. The organization chart for The SP Manufacturing Company is shown in Illustration 45, page 364. Note the four levels of management indicated and the line organization from president down to the foreman of the No. 2 Machining Department as an example. The blocked out segment of the chart is used for the illustrative cost reports to follow. Illustration 46 shows the related February *cost report* for each level of management and the integration between them. It will be observed that the lower cost report (for Machining No. 2) indicates the *status of cost, control* for the month and year to date for each controllable cost in the department. This report is designed especially for the foreman of Machining No. 2. Similar reports would be prepared for the other producing departments (Machining No. 1, Drill Press, Assembly, and Others). Obviously the foreman of each department would normally receive only the report pertaining to his department.

Moving one step up the organizational ladder (to the production manager), a *productive department summary cost* report is prepared. This report is simply a summary of the five producing department reports. The report is designed especially for the production manager and clearly pinpoints, *by department,* any weakness in cost control. Should the production manager desire to trace the source of either favorable or unfavorable cost control performance to *accounts* within the department involved, he can refer to the appropriate departmental reports, each of which should be attached to his summary. For example, the *productive department summary* (last column) calls attention to two departments (Machining No. 2 and Assembly) having unfavorable cost variances. Tracing the $130 unfavorable variance in Machining No. 2, one immediately identifies the specific item of cost (direct labor) as the primary problem that needs attention.

It may be observed that noncontrollable costs (see Chapter 8) are not reported in the simplified example. A policy problem exists in this respect—that is, whether or not to show all costs

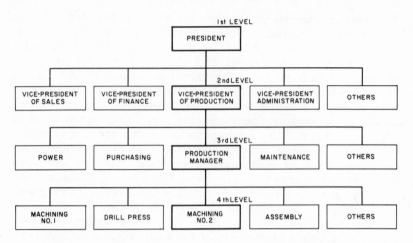

Illustration 45. Organization Chart—The SP Manufacturing Company

chargeable to the particular organizational subdivision or to show just the controllable costs. Although many firms report only controllable costs on departmental cost reports, others prefer to show all costs chargeable to the department on the theory that the supervisor should be aware of the full cost of operating his department. The former procedure generally is preferable.

This simplified illustration for The SP Manufacturing Company also shows the application of the exception principle in performance reports. For example, the production manager does not have to delve into numerous figures to identify the source of trouble (the exception); he merely checks the last column of the summary for *significant variations*. In connection with the application of the exception principle it may be observed that it cannot be applied to actual (historical) figures standing alone; there must be some standard (budget in this case) against which actual figures may be compared in order to identify the exceptions.

Moving to level 2, the build-up of the *factory cost summary* for the vice-president of production is accomplished by listing the summary data for each of the five organizational subdivisions (Power, Purchasing, Production, Maintenance, and Others). In a like manner, the summary for the president is developed. The result of these procedures is an integrated cost report system built around (a) the organization structure, (b) the budget objectives, and (c) the exception principle. The system is simple,

The SP Manufacturing Company
COST REPORT   Feb. 1963

LEVEL No. 1

Division Cost Summary

Controllable Costs:	Actual		(Over) or Under Budget	
	This Month	Year to Date	This Month	Year to Date
Sales	$32,900	$ 65,200	($1,720)	($3,280)
Finance	3,150	5,990	420	760
Production	21,800	44,740	(200)	(510)
Administration	17,700	35,300	760	980
Others	8,500	15,900	(200)	100
Totals	84,050	167,130	(940)	(1,950)

$510 etc.

The SP Manufacturing Company
COST REPORT   Feb. 1963

LEVEL No. 2

Factory Cost Summary   Executive   M. R. Bryan

Controllable Costs:	Actual		(Over) or Under Budget	
	This Month	Year to Date	This Month	Year to Date
Power	$. 3,200	$ 6,650	$ 210	$ 350
Purchasing	1,120	2,590	120	170
Production	13,600	27,760	(90)	(310)
Maintenance	2,950	5,850	(360)	(750)
Others	930	1,890	(80)	30
Totals	21,800	44,740	(200)	(510)

$310 etc.

The SP Manufacturing Company
COST REPORT   Feb. 1963

LEVEL No. 3

Dept.   Productive Department Summary   Supervisor   P. M. Cain

Controllable Costs:	Actual		(Over) or Under Budget	
	This Month	Year to Date	This Month	Year to Date
Machining No. 1	$ 3,400	$ 7,000	$ 120	$ 80
Drill Press	1,850	3,600	80	150
Machining No. 2	4,200	8,600	(90)	(130)
Assembly	2,950	6,100	(250)	(450)
Others	1,200	2,460	50	40
Totals	13,600	27,760	(90)	(310)

$130 etc.

The SP Manufacturing Company
COST REPORT   Feb. 1963

LEVEL No. 4

Dept.   Machining No. 2   Foreman   A. B. Smith

Controllable Costs:	Actual		(Over) or Under Budget	
	This Month	Year to Date	This Month	Year to Date
Direct Labor	$2,150	$4,400	($70)	($150)
Direct Material	1,200	2,500	10	30
Supervision	400	800	-	-
Set Up	150	310	(10)	(30)
Repair	140	260	(20)	10
Supplies	60	140	-	(10)
Others	100	190	-	20
Totals	4,200	8,600	(90)	(130)

Illustration 46. Cost Control Reports—The SP Manufacturing Company

easily understood, and enables the executives to keep their fingers on the performance pulse of the concern with a minimum of time and study.[2] Obviously, this same system should be applied to sales performance reporting and other operational areas as well.

Keep reports simple and understandable

In the design and preparation of control reports, it is important to keep in mind that the reader will generally not be an accountant and that the report is to serve a user other than the report-maker. Careful attention to form is important. Titles and headings should be descriptive, column headings and side captions should clearly identify the data presented, and technical terminology should be avoided.

Reports should not be too long or involved; extensive and complex tabulations of figures should be avoided. Reports should be carefully screened to eliminate all nonessential information. Many reports include too much data rather than too little. An example of report simplification may be observed in Illustration 46, where actual costs and budget variations are indicated, budget allowances having been omitted. Obviously the inclusion of a column "Budget Allowance" adds little to understanding or usefulness and, in addition, tends to make the report too bulky. Another possibility for report simplification is the rounding of amounts to the nearest significant figures.

Standardization of recurring reports is a desirable objective. Executives become accustomed to certain forms and methods of presentation, and know where to look to find the specific information they desire. Thus, changing report forms indiscriminately can become a considerable source of annoyance. Despite the desirability of standardizing certain reports, constant attention must be given to improving the system of reports. Improvement necessarily involves changes; but desirable changes, if made at an opportune time and adequately presented, can be accomplished usually with a minimum of confusion.

Reports must be kept current. It is not uncommon to find data in some reports (or even entire reports) which serve no useful purpose. Such data are there, frequently, because someone in upper management, months or even years before, requested it for a

---

[2] For a comprehensive discussion of these concepts see John A. Higgins, "Responsibility Accounting," *The Arthur Andersen Chronicle*, Vol. XII, No. 2.

special purpose. Although there is no further use for the information, no one has taken the initiative to discontinue it. It is not surprising that busy executives, in requesting special information, may not think of giving a date beyond which such data will no longer be needed; nor do they necessarily think to tell someone to discontinue presenting certain information.

It is well known that surveys reveal that a considerable percentage of the data on internal financial reports are not used. Effort directed toward simplification of reports should be continuous and should be supplemented by periodic surveys to divulge the extent of extraneous information being presented to the various levels of management.

Control reports must be suited to user

The extent to which the several levels of management will use performance reports is a basic communications question. Communication is enhanced if the reports are adapted to (a) the different needs and requirements of the several management levels and (b) the personalities and requirements of the *principal* users.

In developing an effective system of managerial reports, careful consideration must be given to the organization structure, particularly with respect to the three basic levels of management—top, middle, and lower. The three levels of management have different responsibilities, and these frequently call for different kinds of information. The uses to be made of the information by the several levels of management should be the principal guide as to the content and design of the respective reports.[3]

Top management must have reports that give a complete and readily comprehensible summary of the over-all aspects of operations. Therefore accounting and budgeting reports to top management must pinpoint both high and low efficiency throughout the firm.

In reviewing figures presenting current operating results, management concentrates on deviations from predetermined objectives or changes from past experience. Where operations are progressing according to plans expressed in the budget, little time is spent in studying the figures. Moreover, reliance is placed upon the controller for screening out the important items and for bringing out the significance of the figures. However, ex-

---

[3] For an excellent discussion of reporting to the several levels of management, see "Presenting Accounting Information to Management," *NAA Bulletin*, Research Series No. 28 (Dec. 1954), pp. 596–626.

perience has shown that the executive who receives too much detail is not necessarily well informed. He may become confused by details and be unable to visualize the trends and the broader aspects which are after all more important than the individual items.[4]

Because *top management* spends considerable time in planning for the future, *historical data* are of value primarily to the extent that they provide an insight into the future. The planning budget as discussed in previous chapters is one of the most significant reports for top management. Performance reports covering current operations, the principal consideration in this chapter, constitute an important aspect of top management's planning and control procedures.

Middle management is usually defined to include those members of management in charge of the major subdivisions of the concern, such as sales, production, and finance. Middle management is responsible for carrying out the responsibilities assigned to the subdivisions within the broad policies and objectives established by top management. Middle management is closer and more concerned with operations than top management, although it also has important planning functions. Accounting and budget reports for middle management, although summary in nature, must be more concerned with day-to-day operations.

Lower level management (supervisiors and foremen) is principally concerned with coordination and control of day-to-day operations; therefore, control reports must be designed to facilitate the control of current operations. These reports are principally concerned with the control of production and costs. Reports to foremen and supervisors must be simple, understandable, and limited to items having a direct bearing on the supervisors' operational responsibilities.[5]

In the design of reports suited to the *principal user,* consideration must be given to the method of presentation. Those executives who are going to use the reports have different backgrounds, working methods, personalities, and personal preferences. Executives having controllership backgrounds may prefer tabulated and detailed data whereas those having engineering backgrounds may prefer graphic presentations and highly summarized data. Because executives who have sales backgrounds tend to minimize financial reports, the ingenuity of those responsible for designing and preparing financial reports for them is heavily taxed.

Media of presentation of financial data may be broadly classified as follows:

[4] Ibid., pp. 605 and 606.
[5] "Use of Graphs in Internal Reporting," *NAA Bulletin,* Accounting Practice Report, No. 13 (Oct. 1961), Sec. 3.

(1) Written
   (a) Formal financial statements
   (b) Tabulated statistics
   (c) Narration and exposition using words
(2) Graphic
   (a) Charts
   (b) Diagrams and pictures
(3) Oral
   (a) Group meetings
   (b) Conferences with individuals[6]

A concern should not limit itself to use of specific media for presentation of reports to top management. In most concerns all of the media listed above should be employed from time to time. Selection of the appropriate method should depend upon such factors as type of report, data involved, level of management using the report, purpose of the report, peculiarities and background of the principal user, and the nature of the concern's operations. Some executives are chart-minded, others are figure-minded. Because accountants by training and tradition are figure-minded, financial reports likewise have been predominantly tabulations of financial statistics. Those preparing accounting and budget reports must remember that financial reports are generally used by nonaccountants with varied backgrounds. In view of these considerations some concerns have adopted combination forms that are very effective. A very useful combination of media for recurring reports employs both charts and figures. To illustrate, assume the following data taken from a somewhat conventional report (employing the traditional form):

REPORT OF OPERATING PROFITS AND SALES
1953 TO DATE

Year	Operating Profits	Sales
1953	$14,000	$150,000
1954	14,000	147,000
1955	14,500	154,000
1956	14,700	160,000
1957	14,400	158,000
1958	14,800	161,000
1959	14,600	164,000
1960	14,500	165,000
1961	14,500	165,000
1962	18,000*	166,000
1963	14,600**	168,000**

* Includes fixed assets sold at a gain of $4,000.
**Budgeted.

[6] Adapted from "Presenting Accounting Information to Management," *NAA Bulletin Research Series No. 28.* (December 1954), p. 637.

REPORT OF ACTUAL AND BUDGETED SALES
MARCH 31, 1963

Month	Actual Sales	Budgeted Sales	Variations from Budget (Under*)
January	$11,800	$ 12,000	$200*
February	12,100	12,000	100
March	14,300	14,000	300
April		15,000	
May		16,000	
June		15,000	
July		14,000	
August		12,000	
September		13,000	
October		14,000	
November		15,000	
December		16,000	
Total		$168,000	

Although the first report accurately presents historical profits and sales over a period of years, comparisons and trends are not

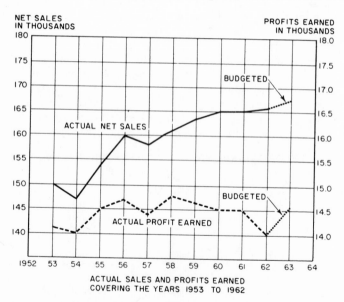

ACTUAL SALES AND PROFITS EARNED
COVERING THE YEARS 1953 TO 1962

Illustration 47a. *Graphic Presentation—Sales and Profits*

readily comprehended. The same data are represented in Illustrations 47a and 47b. Similarly, the performance report shown above is presented somewhat differently in Illustrations 48a and 48b. The procedure suggested by this simple example indicates the advantages of presenting certain types of information both graphically and in figures. The charts effectively communicate the overall aspects of the data; the figures provide exact data when needed. Some concerns follow the practice of maintaining a "financial report book" for individual executives. The book is generally a loose-leaf binder containing the financial reports of importance to the particular executive. If the combined and graphic procedures are used, the graphs might be printed on the back of the page and the corresponding figures on the front of the next page so that, when the report is opened at any particular page, the graphs are always on the left and figures on the right. It will be observed that Illustrations 47 and 48 are presented in this manner.[7]

Many top executives have a strong preference for narrative summaries of internal reports. Words frequently tell the story much more effectively than bare figures. Analyses of the causative factors that are involved, for example, in a financial report show-

SUMMARY OF ACTUAL SALES AND PROFITS
EARNED FROM OPERATIONS COVERING
THE YEARS 1953 TO 1963

Year	Actual Net Sales	Profits Earned (excluding unusual or nonoperating items)	Profit as Per Cent of Sales
1953	$150,000	$14,000	9.3
1954	147,000	14,000	9.5
1955	154,000	14,500	9.4
1956	160,000	14,700	9.1
1957	158,000	14,400	9.1
1958	161,000	14,800	9.2
1959	164,000	14,600	8.9
1960	165,000	14,500	8.8
1961	165,000	14,500	8.8
1962	166,000	14,000	8.4
1963 (Budgeted)	168,000	14,600	8.7

Illustration 47b

[7] Robert A. Blake, "The Management Data Book," *NAA Bulletin* (May 1962), pp. 43–50.

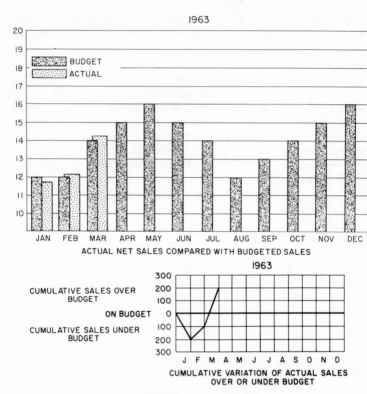

Illustration 48a. *Graphic Presentation—Sales and Profits*

ing significant exceptions, generally should be presented in narrative form.

Oral presentation of financial reports should occupy a significant part of the reporting system in all concerns. Controllers and budget directors should encourage conferences of executives where the financial report is presented, explained orally, and discussed. Oral presentation is very important, because interpretation and emphasis that are lacking in other forms are possible. In addition, executives have the opportunity of asking questions and bringing up points that are not clear, thus assuring good understanding and communication. Oral presentation and explanation of financial results to the several executives simultaneously saves considerable executive time and effort.

SUMMARY OF ACTUAL NET SALES COMPARED WITH
BUDGETED SALES FOR THREE MONTHS
ENDING MARCH 31, 1963

Month 1963	Actual Net Sales	Budgeted Net Sales	*Variation of Actual Sales from Budget (*Amounts below budget)*	
			Monthly Variation	*Cumulative Variation*
January	$11,800	$12,000	$200*	$200*
February	12,100	12,000	100	100*
March	14,300	14,000	300	200
April		15,000		
May		16,000		
June		15,000		
July		14,000		
August		12,000		
September		13,000		
October		14,000		
November		15,000		
December		16,000		
Total		$168,000		

Illustration 48b

Minimize the time gap between the decision and the reporting

As a rule, executives, supervisors, and foremen are very busy tending to their respective responsibilities. Also they are continually (daily) involved in the decision-making process, varying from major decisions to relatively insignificant ones. It is the sum total of these decisions that determines the success or failure both of the firm as a whole and the segments thereof. In view of the significance of the decision-making process and its immediate and continuous effect on efficiency, the gap between the point of decision and the reporting of the results of such decisions must be minimized. In any situation both good and bad decisions must be expected; the degree of over-all efficiency depends then upon the *ratio* of the good decisions to the total. Advance planning minimizes the risk of an excessive number of bad decisions; likewise a sound system of performance reporting minimizes this risk. The time gap between the decision point and performance reporting must be minimized because (a) unfavorable situations and problems are most significant to the supervisor at the time they occur; as time passes the supervisor becomes more concerned with new events and less concerned with past events; (b) the longer an unfavorable situation continues before correction the greater the financial loss to the company; and (c) with the passage of time there is a tendency to regard inefficiency as "normal" or "the best we can do under the circumstances." Here we may observe a parallel with Gresham's law that "bad money drives out the good money"; similarly inefficiency tends to drive out efficiency.

Consistent with the cost of detailed record-keeping and reporting, control reports should be available on a timely basis. In order to achieve a realistic balance between immediate reporting and the costs of detailed reporting, monthly performance statements are widely used by industry. When special problem areas are involved, weekly and even daily reporting may be necessary, if not continuously, at least for a time.[8]

The tendency of some accountants to hold up the issuance of performance reports until all the "facts are in" frequently detracts from the usefulness of the reports. Because accounting data can seldom be exact (there will always be some element of estimation, such as depreciation), those preparing such reports should not hesitate to make reasonable estimates of "actual" items, so that an early report is possible. It is not unusual, even in simple situations, to find monthly performance reports being issued after the twentieth of the following month. Objective analysis will usually show no valid reason for the reports being issued later than the fifth to seventh day in the following month. Some accuracy may have to be sacrificed, but not enough to impair the effectiveness of the resulting data for *managerial purposes*. It bears repeating that external reporting presents communication problems which are entirely different from internal reporting.

Managerial follow-up procedures

The better-managed concerns issue monthly performance reports covering all aspects of operations. These reports indicate favorable and unfavorable variations between actual performance and planned performance for the month just ended and, cumulatively, for the year to date. Executives should examine the monthly control report carefully to become familiar with both *high* and

---

[8] D. L. Wilson, "Daily Profit Estimates Are Practicable," *NAA Bulletin*, Sec. 1 (July 1958), pp. 73-78.

low performance in the various organizational subdivisions for which they are responsible. Analyses of the reasons for the high and low performance should be given immediate priority. However, the process should not stop at this point. *Follow-up procedures* constitute a very important aspect of effective control. Some concerns require written explanations of significant variances. The follow-up procedures preferred by other firms involve constructive conferences where the causes are discussed and corrective action is decided upon. Follow-up procedures should begin at the top management level—in the executive committee meeting, for example, where both unsatisfactory and satisfactory conditions are discussed and analyzed. Decisions should be made concerning ways and means of correcting unsatisfactory conditions. Favorable variances should be given equal consideration (a) to determine whether or not the objectives were realistic, and (b) to give recognition to those responsible for high performance, and (c) to possibly transfer some "know-how" to other subdivisions of the firm.

Technical aspects of control reports

Some few concerns purport to issue separate internal "accounting" and "budget" reports; however, because separation of these two reports for internal managerial purposes seems illogical, it is assumed in this book that they are combined into a single performance report.

Control reports are variously called performance reports, financial and operating reports, accounting reports, budget reports, or simply financial reports. The significance of a combined accounting and budget report lies principally in the comparison of actual results with budget objectives and in the study of the resulting variations. There are numerous methods of expressing the differences. Variations expressed only as absolute amounts are not always satisfactory because the absolute amount is frequently not indicative of the significance of the variation. Although *statistical control limits* can be developed, most concerns find it entirely satisfactory to establish a general "rule-of-thumb" policy relative to variations. For example, a medium-sized business might establish a policy that variations up to $25 or 5 per cent of budget are to be considered insignificant. Certainly a realistic policy along this line should be established because neither actual figures nor budget objectives will be absolutely accurate.

In Illustration 46 the reports contained columns for actual and budget variations only; budget objectives were not included. Many concerns prefer to show actual, budget, dollar variations, and percentage variations. The mechanics of several methods of expressing variations may be simply illustrated as follows:

	(1)	(2)	(3)	(4)	(5)	(6)
				Per Cent of	*Per Cent*	*Per Cent*
			Variation	*Variation*	*of Budget*	*of Actual*
	Actual	*Budget*	*in Dollars*	*to Budget*	*Realization*	*to Budget*
			(1−2)	(3÷2)	(2÷1)	(1÷2)
Expense	$ 110	$ 100	$ 10*	10%*	90.9%	110%
Sales	$11,000	$10,000	$1,000	10%	110%ᵃ	110%

*Unfavorable
ᵃFor incomes the dividend and divisor must be reversed.

Reports should normally carry *actual* (column 1); however, there is a serious question as to which of the remaining columns illustrated immediately above should be used in a particular situation. In most cases it would seem desirable to report data shown in columns 1, 3, and either 4, 5, or 6. Column 4 is more generally used than 5 or 6, because it relates the variation directly to the objective. In the illustration column 4 indicates that expense was 10 per cent over budget (*Unfavorable). Sales were also 10 per cent over budget, which is favorable. In computing this column, the mathematical process is the same for incomes or expenses, that is, column 3 divided by column 2. If the budget variation is negative (unfavorable), the resulting percentage will be negative (unfavorable). Column 5, "Per Cent of Budget Realization," is used by many concerns, because it is easily understood. In the above case the budget realization of 90.9 ($100÷$110) indicates that the efficiency of cost control was only 90.9 per cent; had actual expense been $100, budget realization would have been 100 per cent; that is, exactly "par." On the other hand had actual expense been $90, budget realization would have been 111 per cent. When dealing with incomes, the mathematical process must be reversed, that is, actual is divided by budget. Thus budget realization for sales in the illustration is 110 per cent because actual sales were 10 per cent above budgeted sales. The latter method is simple to understand, because a percentage figure above 100 per cent always indicates a favorable condition, whereas a percentage figure below 100 per cent indicates an unfavorable condition. The method illustrated in column 6 is seldom used.

Monthly performance reports covering operations should generally show (a) variations for the month being reported and (b) cumulative variations to date. Those preparing performance reports covering operations should make judicious use of footnote comments where the reasons for specific variations are known. In addition, footnotes should be used to direct the attention of management to specific conditions that may require managerial consideration. It is frequently desirable to include recommendations in footnotes.

The examples on pages 378 and 379 illustrate methods used by some leading concerns in presenting data in budget reports.[9]

Group and individual conferences should be held at the various levels of management aimed toward effective corrective action. Follow-up procedures should embody constructive action to correct unfavorable conditions rather than punitive action for failures the results of which obviously cannot be erased. Another important aspect of follow-up procedure is that the resulting *action* is strictly a *line function* rather than a staff function. The budget director, controller, or other staff officer definitely should not undertake, nor should he be assigned, the responsibility for enforcing the budget.

The integrated control report

At the beginning of this chapter it was indicated that the primary type of report under consideration was the *repetitive control* or *performance report*. To be of maximum usefulness the monthly control or performance report should be carefully designed to indicate the performance of each individual having supervisory responsibility. The periodic performance report should be designed as *one package* comprised of a number of summaries, subsummaries, and detailed statements along the lines suggested in Illustration 46.

⸱ [9] See also "Reporting Data to Top Management," American Management Association, Special Report 25 (1957).

Square D Company[1]

MONTHLY STATEMENT OF EXPENSE

Department No. _24_   Department Name _Machine Shop_   Supervisor _Joe Doaks_   Plant _Detroit_

Month of October   Year to Date Through—October 31

	Controllable Expense				Controllable Expense	
Month Actual $	Managerial Policy $	Actual $	Policy $	Total Actual $	Managerial Policy $	Actual $	Policy $

Description of Expense Account

Division B

SUMMARY OF DEPARTMENTAL BUDGET REALIZATION
BY LINES OF RESPONSIBILITY

Month of October

(these columns repeated for year to date)

	Variable Expense			Per Cent of Budget Realized %
Dept.	Actual $	Budget $	Variation $	

Dept. Head

Description

[1] Adapted from A.A. Kasper, "Budgetary Control Works at Square D Company," *NAA Bulletin* (December 1951), Sec. 1, pp. 456 and 458.

A Manufacturing Company[1]

MANUFACTURING EXPENSES BY DEPARTMENTS—
AUGUST, 19—

		This Month			Saving or (Loss)	
Department	Operating Activity	Should Spend †	Actually Spent	This Month	Year to Date
1 Receiving	110%	$35,680	$36,750	$(1,070)	$(6,125)
2 Sorting and Storing	95	24,215	24,800	(585)	1,210
4 Grinding	115	8,615	7,800	815	5,700
5 Cracking	110	9,450	10,960	(1,510)	(8,615)
6 Mixing	80	12,870	13,970	(1,100)	2,850

Explanation of Saving or Loss—Principal Items
Dept. 1—Repairs to lift truck, not budgeted, $1,200.
Dept. 5—Overtime high due to breakdown of Cracker #1, $450; Repairs of
    Cracker #1, $1,450.
Dept. 6—Indirect labor high in relation to volume, $850.

† Based upon budget for month adjusted for percentage of activity in each
department.
[1] Adapted from Ernest A. Carlson, "Techniques for Effective Reporting to
Management," *NAA Bulletin* (February 1952), Sec. 1, p. 693.

A particularly distinguishing feature of a well-designed control
report is that it should be completely *integrated*—that is, each
of the segments should link, on a responsibility basis, schedule
to schedule. Integration in the system is particularly important
(a) so that significant variations may be traced down to the
source of the problem and (b) so that the various segments
comprise within themselves a complete report. The latter aspect
is essential for proper distribution of the performance report and
segments thereof.

Distribution of the various segments of the annual profit plan
was discussed in Chapter 11. Distribution of the monthly performance report (and segments thereof) should follow essentially
the same pattern. The financial officer or budget director should
develop (as a part of the accounting or budget manual) a *performance report distribution schedule.* Certain executives have
need for, and should get, the complete monthly performance report. Other members of management need get only those schedules related to their particular area of responsibility. The tendency to provide everyone with a complete copy of the monthly
report should be discouraged. The receipt of a bulky financial
report by a department supervisor tends to discourage concern
with even the part that directly concerns his department. Lower

levels of management may receive only one or two of the *detailed segments*. On the other hand, the higher the levels of management, the greater the need for *summaries*, yet these summaries must be supported by adequate detail so that it is possible to identify the details of any particular aspect of operations. The distribution of reports to the various levels of management may be indicated in a simple way by referring to Illustrations 45 and 46. The distribution schedule could well be as follows:

Position and Name	*Report to be Received*
Foreman, A.B. Smith	Cost Report, Machining No. 2
Supervisor, P.M. Cain	Cost Report, Productive Department Summary
	Cost Reports, All Productive Departments
Executive, M.R. Bryan	Factory Cost Summary
	Productive Department Summary
	Cost Reports, All Productive Departments
	Service Department Summary
	Cost Reports, All Service Departments
President	Complete Report

January performance report for The Superior Manufacturing Company

Space limitations preclude inclusion of the monthly performance report employed by this company. The report is completely integrated and includes two types of comparisons, viz., (1) actual compared with the annual profit plan and (2) actual compared with adjusted budget allowances for costs (variable budget allowances). The report carries actual, budget, and variations for the month and cumulative for the year to date. Schedules 19 (page 76), and 20 (page 78) and Illustration 26 (page 234) are representative of the general format and composition of the various segments of the integrated report.

Illustration 49 is a listing of the various segments of the complete performance report. Note that the schedule indentification (first column) indicates the interrelationship of the detailed and summary schedules. For example, Schedule G2 is a *summary* performance report of distribution expenses which is supported by Schedules G2.1, G2.2, G2.3, and G2.4 which are the individual expense performance reports for the four sales districts. The column to the right, "Order of Preparation," is included to suggest the sequence that is used by this company in developing

The Superior Manufacturing Company

PERFORMANCE REPORT—LIST OF SCHEDULES
January Report—Schedules

Sch. No.	Title	Department	Supervisor	Order of Preparation
A	Balance Sheet with Budget Comparisons (with Original Plan)			26
B	Income Statement (compared to Original Plan and Adjusted Budget)			23
C	Cost of Goods Sold			—
D	District Income Statements (compared with Adjusted Budget)	By district		25
E	Sales Control Report	By district		22
F	Summary of Manufacturing Costs (by Product)	Mfg.	A.B. Works	24
G	Departmental Expense Control Report (Summary)	Company	Gen. Management	20
G1	Departmental Expense Control Report (Summary)	Gen. Adm.	B.R. Taylor (Ex. VP)	7
G1.1	" (Dept. only)	Adm.	P.A. Johnson	4
G1.2	" "	Accounting	H.H. Harrison	5
G1.3	" "	Treasurer	I.M. Cash	6
G2	" (Summary)	Sales	G.A. Beloit	12
G2.1	" (Dept. only)	Southern	Ray C. Nixon	8
G2.2	" "	Eastern	C.C. Campbell	9
G2.3	" "	Western	W.W. Anderson	10
G2.4	" "	Gen. Sales	T.K. Rielly	11
G3	" (Summary)	Factory	A.B. Works	19
G3.1	" (Dept. only)	No. 1	K.R. Mason	13
G3.2	" "	No. 2	A.B. Ross	14
G3.3	" "	No. 3	W.E. Cox	15
G3.4	" "	Repair	C.R. Medford	16
G3.5	" "	Power	K.W. Haus	17
G3.6	" "	Gen. Fac.	A.R. Carson	18
G4	" "	Bldg. Serv.	Sam Adams	3
G5	Report of Noncontrollable Expenses at Dept. Level (Summary)	Company	Gen. Man.	21
H	Report of Material Purchases	Pur.	T.E. Merton	2
I	Report of Other Income and Expenses (compared with Orig. Plan)	Treasurer	I.M. Cash	1
J	Analysis of Mfg. O.H. Over/Under Applied	Factory	Gen. Man.	27

Illustration 49

the various detailed reports, the summaries, and finally the complete report. Special note should be taken of the structure of the complete report in terms of organization responsibilities.[10]

Discussion Questions

1. Outline and briefly explain the broad classification of the reporting structure of a medium to large firm.
2. Why should financial reports for internal purposes be different from those for external purposes?
3. What are the principal purposes of financial reports to the management of the firm?
4. What are the essential characteristics of effective reports for internal managerial use?
5. Why should certain internal financial reports be prepared in terms of organizational responsibilities?
6. Relate the *exception principle* to accounting and budget reports.
7. Draw a distinction between internal reports for (a) top management, (b) middle management, and (c) lower management.
8. Why is it essential that several media of presenting financial data be used in a company?
9. Discuss the advantages and disadvantages of requiring written explanations of unfavorable variations.
10. What criteria might be used to determine whether or not a variation is significant?
11. Why is it generally undesirable to distribute complete copies of the monthly financial and budget report to all supervisory personnel?
12. Assume that a particular report shows for item A a $500 unfavorable variation and for item B a $500 favorable variation. Should equal consideration be given to the two variations? Discuss.
13. Explain the *time gap* in performance reporting. Why is it critical?
14. What is meant by "integration in the monthly performance report"? Is it significant? Why?

[10] As noted earlier a continuation of the illustrative case (The Superior Manufacturing Company) is available separately as a continuing case study wherein the annual profit plan, variable budgets, and the January performance report are developed for the following year (1964). This continuing case is especially useful for supplementing the text discussions for classroom instructional purposes.

F O U R T E E N

Analysis of Budget Variations

Throughout the preceding chapters a comparison of actual results with budgeted objectives has been stressed as an important aspect of control. In the last chapter the monthly performance report was considered. A distinguishing feature of this monthly report was the development of *variations* between actual and budget. It was further indicated that the important aspect of a variation is that if significant, it should result in careful investigation to determine the *underlying causes*, for the causes rather than the results provide the basis for appropriate corrective action.

In evaluating and investigating significant variations to determine the underlying causes the following possibilities should be considered:

(1) That the variation is not significant—both favorable and unfavorable variations should be investigated to determine significance.

(2) That the variation is due to reporting errors—both the budget objective and the actual data supplied by the accounting department should be appraised to be sure there are no clerical errors. For example, a single accounting entry charged to the wrong department may cause an unfavorable variance in one department and a favorable variance in another department.

(3) That the variation is due to a specific managerial decision—from time to time the management, in the interests of improved efficiencies or to meet certain exigencies, will make decisions that may create variations. For example, it may be decided to raise a given salary (say, to meet competitive efforts by another firm to attract a key employee), or to undertake a special advertising project not previously planned. Such discretionary decisions of management will result in reported variations. Such variations must be identified because they need no further in-

vestigation. When the decision was made it was recognized what the result would be.

(4) That many variations are explainable in terms of the effect of uncontrollable factors which are apparent.

(5) That those variations for which the precise underlying causes are not apparent should be of primary concern and should be carefully investigated. In other words, we are concerned with the variations that "need explaining"; these are the exceptions that generally require corrective action.

There are numerous ways to investigate significant variations to determine the underlying causes. Some of the primary approaches are as follows:

(1) Conferences with supervisors, foremen, and sometimes other employees of the particular operational area involved;

(2) Analysis of the work situation including the flow of work, coordination of activities, effectiveness of supervision, and other prevailing circumstances;

(3) Direct observation;

(4) On-the-spot investigations by *line* officials;

(5) Investigations by *staff* groups (specifically designated as to responsibilities);

(6) Audits by the internal audit staff;

(7) Special reports (See Chapter 11); and

(8) Variance analysis.

This chapter is concerned with *variance analysis,* which is only one of the possible approaches that may be used in investigating significant variations. The discussions are simplified because our objectives are (1) to present the concept of variation analysis and (2) to relate the analysis to the monthly (budget) performance report. Variance analysis involves a mathematical manipulation of two sets of data in order to shed some light on the underlying causes of variation between the two sets of data. One of the amounts is treated as the base, standard, or reference point. Variance analysis has wide application in financial reporting; it frequently is applied in the following situations:

(1) Investigation of variations between actual results of the current period with the actual results of a prior period; the prior period being considered as the base.[1]

---

[1] G. A. Welsch, C. T. Zlatkovich, and J. A. White, *Intermediate Accounting* (Homewood, Ill.: Irwin, 1963), Ch. 28.

(2) Investigation of variations between actual results and standard costs, the latter being treated as the base. (Discussed in Chapter 15.)

(3) Investigation of the variations between actual results and budget objectives, the latter being treated as the base.

In each of these three uses of variation analysis, the same analytical approach is used—the arithmetic is essentially the same—the only difference is in the data that are being analyzed. This chapter is concerned with the latter application only—that is, the analysis of budget variations. We will consider variance analysis related to (a) sales, (b) raw material, (c) direct labor, and (d) manufacturing overhead.

Analysis of sales variances

An appreciation of both the significance and limitations of the results of variance analysis is enhanced if the mathematical manipulations involved are understood. The following simplified example is used to present the mathematics underlying variance analysis and to suggest how the analysis of certain *budget* variations may provide management with a better insight into the causes underlying the unfavorable situation. First we will consider sales variances. Assume the top management of a particular company receives the following report:

SALES PERFORMANCE REPORT—SUMMARY
For the month of January

Sales Districts:	Actual Results	Objectives (from Profit Plan)	Variation Unfavorable*
No. 1	$ 481,500	$ 500,000	$18,500*
No. 2	198,800	200,000	1,200*
No. 3	402,100	400,000	2,100
Total	$1,082,400	$1,100,000	$17,600*

The attention of top management is drawn immediately to the *exceptional* items, that is, the $17,600 and $18,500 unfavorable variations in sales for the month. As each variation is identified with a specific sales district, responsibility is pinpointed. However, the *cause* of the unfavorable situation is not apparent. Assume management is interested in pursuing the matter further and turns to another schedule in the report as follows:

SALES PERFORMANCE REPORT—DISTRICT NO. 1
For the month of January

Products	Actual Results		Profit plan		Variation Unfavorable*	
	Units	Amount	Units	Amount	Units	Amount
M	35,000	$182,000	40,000	$200,000	5,000*	$18,000*
N	49,900	299,500	50,000	300,000	100*	500*
Total		$481,500		$500,000		$18,500*

Again the exceptional item stands out—Product M in District No. 1. The alert executive would inquire as to what caused the $18,000 unfavorable variance in Product M. It is obvious that *quantity* sold was substantially less than the profit plan objective. At this point a mathematical (variance) analysis of the $18,000 may provide some useful data for the management. The first step is to determine both the actual and budgeted average sales prices, viz.:

$182,000 ÷ 35,000 units = $5.20 actual average sales price
$200,000 ÷ 40,000 units = $5.00 budgeted average sales price

At this point it is obvious that the $18,000 unfavorable variation was due principally to the fact that the actual quantity sold was 5,000 units below budget, although this is offset to some extent by a $.20 increase in average selling price. The effect of these two factors—quantity and price—might be computed as in the table that follows.

Quantity factor (sales volume variation)
  Sales price held constant:

Actual sales at budget sales price (35,000 × $5)	$175,000	
Budget sales at budget sales price (40,000 × $5)	200,000	$25,000*

  [The computation may be simplified:
    (40,000 − 35,000) × $5 = $25,000*]

Price factor (sales price variation)
  Sales quantity held constant:

Actual sales at actual sales price (35,000 × $5.20)	$182,000	
Actual sales at budgeted sales price (35,000 × $5.00)	175,000	7,000

  [The computation may be simplified:
    35,000 × ($5.20 − $5.00) = $7,000]
Sales variation $18,000*

Interpretation of the results of the above analysis may be briefly narrated as follows:

    There was an $18,000 unfavorable variance for Product M, in District No. 1 when actual sales are compared with the profit plan.

Analysis of this variance indicates that the number of units sold was 5,000 below plan; when valued at the budgeted sales price, an unfavorable *quantity variance* of $25,000 resulted. This unfavorable quantity variance was offset in part by a favorable sales *price variance* of $.20 per unit on the 35,000 units actually sold, the offset totaling $7,000. The factors causing the substantial quantity variance should be investigated further.

With respect to the mathematical operations involved in the analysis, note that (a) in computing the quantity variance the *price* factor is held constant and the quantity is variable; (b) in computing the price variance the *quantity* factor is held constant and the price is variable.[2]

Analysis of raw material variances

Raw material variances shown on the monthly performance report are frequently analyzed mathematically to determine (1) the material price variation, and (2) the material usage variation. Assume the following data are available for the month from the performance report of a particular producing department.

	Actual	Planning Budget	Variations (Unfavorable*)
Units of finished goods produced	87,500	100,000	
Raw materials:			
Units (2 units of raw material per unit of finished goods)	176,000	200,000	
Average unit cost	$.224	$.20	
Total raw material	$39,424	$40,000	$576

A favorable raw material variation of $576 is reported. Sufficient data are available to analyze this variation. It should be obvious that this variation standing alone has limited meaning because the number of units actually produced was 12,500 *less* than the planned production of 100,000 units. In this case we

---

[2] Some analysts prefer a three-way analysis rather than the two-way analysis illustrated above. The three-way analysis is computed as follows:

Quantity variance (40,000 − 35,000) × $5	$25,000*
Price variance ($5.20 − $5.00) × 40,000	8,000
Combined quantity-price variance (40,000 − 35,000) × ($5.20 − $5.00)	1,000*
Total variance	$18,000*

See: G. A. Welsch, C. T. Zlatkovich, and J. A. White, *Intermediate Accounting* (Homewood, Ill.: Irwin, 1963), Ch. 28.

expect a favorable variance because material costs actually incurred in processing 87,500 units are compared with a budget material cost based on 100,000 units. This fact suggests an additional factor in analyzing this particular variance—that is, the effect of *volume* as well as usage and price. Using *fixed budget procedures*, three separate variations may be computed as follows:

Fixed Budget Analysis:

Volume Variation (the variation in raw material usage due to the fact that actual production was less than planned production):

Budgeted raw material usage (200,000 units × $.20)	$40,000	
Raw material that should have been used in making 87,500 units (87,500 × 2 × $.20)	35,000	$5,000

Material Usage Variation (the variation due to inefficient use of raw materials):

Raw material that should have been used in making 87,500 units (87,500 × 2 × $.20)	$35,000	
Raw material actually used at budgeted price (176,000 × $.20)	35,200	200*

Material Price Variation:

Budget price minus actual price times actual units of raw material used ($.20 − $.224) × 176,000		4,224*
Total Material Variation		$ 576

The results of the analysis may be explained, for example, as follows:

> When comparing actual material costs with the budgeted material costs included in the *original* profit plan a $576 favorable variance is reported. However, there was a significant difference between actual production and planned production (12,500 units). The effect of this *volume* differential is $5,000 (favorable); it does not represent efficiency or inefficiency in raw material costs because it was occasioned solely by the units produced. Analysis of the data shows a $200 unfavorable *usage* variance. This variance is significant and reflects the fact that the producing department involved used more than the standard units of raw material in processing 87,500 units. The reasons for this over usage should be discussed with Mr. X, the departmental supervisor, because it may indicate inefficiency, an adverse effect on product quality, or an inappropriate standard. Further analysis shows that there was an unfavorable material *price* variance of $4,224. This particularly significant variation was due to the fact that the purchasing department paid

more than the budgeted price for raw material. This variation should be discussed further with Mr. Y, the purchasing officer.

It should be obvious that the performance report comparison might have been made more effective for control purposes by comparing *actual* (based on 87,500 units of output) with an *adjusted budget* allowance (also based on 87,500 units of output) as follows:

Raw Materials:	Actual (at 87,500 units output)	Budget (at 87,500 units output)	Variations (Unfavorable*)
Units	176,000	175,000	
Amount	$39,424	$35,000	$4,424*

In this report the total variation of $4,424 (unfavorable) may be analyzed using *variable budget procedures* to compute the usage and price factors as follows:

Variable Budget Analysis:
  Material Usage Variation:
    Raw material that should have been used in making
      87,500 units (87,500 × 2 × $.20) $35,000
    Raw material actually used at budgeted price
      (176,000 × $.20)   35,200 $200*

  [The computation may be simplified:
    (176,000 − 175,000) × $.20 = $200*]

  Material Price Variation:
    Budgeted price minus actual price times actual units of
      raw material used ($.20 − $.224) × 176,000 $4,224*

  Total Material Variation[3] $4,424*

The results of this analysis may be explained, for example, in exactly the same way as the preceding analysis except for the *first three* sentences. These sentences are not appropriate because the *volume effect* was not allowed to affect the performance report (Variation $4,224*).

The reader should note that the two different analyses of raw material cost variance were due to the fact that (1) in the first instance actual was compared with the original budget, and (2) in the second instance actual was compared with an adjusted

---

[3] Some analysts prefer a three-way analysis where a usage-price factor is identified similar to that noted on page 387.

budget allowance. Both analyses are common with respect to the usage and price variances. Normally only the second analysis is used because most firms compare actual with adjusted budget for raw materials in the performance report.

Analysis of direct labor variances

In approach, mechanics, and interpretation the analysis of direct labor variances as reported on the monthly performance ٬eport parallels that discussed and illustrated above for materials. Assume the following data for the month are available from the performance report of a particular department:

	Actual	Planning Budget	Variations (Unfavorable*)
Units of finished goods produced	87,500	100,000	
Direct labor:			
Direct labor hours (.4 DLH per unit of finished goods)	35,357	40,000	
Average wage rate	$1.96	$2.00	
Total direct labor cost	$69,300	$80,000	$10,700

The report shows a favorable direct labor variance of $10,700. Because actual production was 12,500 less than planned volume, there should be a favorable variance. Thus, as in the situation with raw materials, the effect of the volume of output differential must be identified. Actually, the effect of *three* factors must be identified in order to explain the $10,700 variation. The analysis may be developed as follows:

Fixed Budget Analysis:
   Volume Variation (the variation in labor usage due to the fact that actual production was less than planned production):

Budgeted labor usage (40,000 DLH × $2)	$80,000	
Labor that should have been employed in making 87,500 units (87,500 × .4 × $2)	70,000	$10,000

   Labor Usage Variation (variation due to inefficient usage of labor):

Labor that should have been employed in making 87,500 units (87,500 × .4 × $2)	$70,000	
Labor actually used at budgeted wage rate (35,357 × $2)	70,714	714*

   Wage Rate Variation:

Budgeted wage rate minus actual wage rate times actual direct labor hours ($2.00 − $1.96) × 35,357		$ 1,414
Total Direct Labor Variation		$10,700

Again, as with direct material, it should be obvious that the performance report comparison would be more effective (for control purposes) if actual labor costs incurred (in producing 87,500 units of output) were compared with an adjusted budget allowance (also based on 87,500 units of output) as follows:

	Actual (at 87,500 units output)	Budget (at 87,500 units output)	Variations (Unfavorable*)
Direct labor:			
Direct labor hours	35,357	35,000	
Amount	$69,300	$70,000	$700

In this report the $700 favorable variation may be analyzed directly as to labor usage (efficiency) and wage rate factors as follows:

Variable Budget Analysis:
Labor Usage Variation:
Computed as above or more directly (35,357 − 35,000) × $2 $ 714*

Labor Wage Rate Variation:
Computed as above ($2.00 − $1.96) × 35,357   1,414
Total Labor Variation[4] $ 700

The results of the latter analysis may be explained, for example, as follows:

> The monthly performance report showed a favorable direct labor variance for Department XX of $700. This variation resulted from comparing labor costs actually incurred in producing 87,500 units of output with a budget allowance adjusted to this same volume of output. Although the over-all variance is favorable, further analysis indicates an *unfavorable* labor usage or efficiency variation of $714. This unfavorable condition was due to the fact the department incurred 357 more direct labor hours than standard for the actual output. This unfavorable condition should be discussed with the supervisor concerned. On the other hand, there was a significant *favorable* wage rate variation of $1,414 since the average wage rate per hour in the department was $.04 below the standard. This favorable variance should be further investigated to determine the fundamental cause. It is possible that the supervisor of the department was able to maintain a higher proportion of lower paid employees which is desirable assuming quality of product and employee relations are not adversely affected. This latter factor may have been the cause of the excess hours used.

---

[4] Some analysts prefer a three-way analysis where a usage-wage rate factor is identified similar to that noted on page 387.

With respect to the two different analyses of direct labor illustrated above, it bears repeating that (1) in the first illustration actual was compared with the original budget and that (2) in the second illustration actual was compared with an adjusted budget allowance. Normally the second approach is used for control purposes.

Analysis of manufacturing overhead (burden) variances

The analysis of manufacturing overhead or burden variances is considerably more complex than for sales, raw materials, and direct labor. This subject has been a primary concern of cost accountants for many years; as a result, practically every book dealing with the subject of cost accounting, or even managerial accounting, has discussions and illustrations of this analysis. Although the mathematical analyses of manufacturing overhead variances are fairly simple, the analysis itself is not too precise because of the numerous opportunities for theoretical and practical distinctions in manipulating the data. The problem is further complicated by a lack of standardization in terminology; practically every writer on the subject has his own "pet" terms. The student pursuing this subject may be understandably confused by the maze of terminology, theoretical distinctions, practical distinctions, and the resulting volume of alternative procedures. There is another factor that adds to the complexity of the problem and that is the type of data available for the analysis—specifically, the type of *budget data* that are available. If actual manufacturing overhead is being compared with planning budget data only, the analysis (and the results) are significantly different than when *variable budget* data (where overhead expenses are identified as to their fixed and variable components) as well as planning budget data, are available.

In this discussion we do not dwell on theoretical distinctions, but stress rather the relationship of the analysis of manufacturing overhead (burden) variations to the monthly performance reports as applied to a comprehensive budget program.[5]

To illustrate (a) the mathematical aspects, (b) the interpreta-

---

[5] Readers interested in a study in depth of the analysis of manufacturing overhead are referred to one or more of the several excellent textbooks on cost accounting and managerial accounting.

tion of the results, and (c) the relationship of variance analysis to a budget program, assume the following data for Department XX.

(1) Computation of the departmental overhead rate (See Chapter 8 for discussion of this problem):

From the annual profit plan:	Factory Overhead Budgeted	Volume in DLH's Budgeted[6]	Factory Overhead Rate Budgeted (per DLH)
Fixed Costs	$192,000	480,000	$.40
Variable Costs	120,000	480,000	.25
Total	$312,000	480,000	$.65

(2) Data for the month of January:

(a) Units produced during January	87,500
(b) Actual direct labor hours incurred in January	35,357
(c) Output in units planned (planning budget) for January	100,000
(d) Standard direct labor hours for January actual output (87,500 × .4 DLH's per unit)	35,000
(e) Planning budget allowance for manufacturing overhead for January: DLH's	40,000
Amount	$26,000
(f) Actual departmental overhead incurred (debited to the manufacturing overhead control account)	$24,550
(g) Departmental overhead applied for the month (credited to the manufacturing overhead control account and debited to the manufacturing account) (35,000 DLH's × $.65)	$22,750
(h) Manufacturing overhead under-applied (debit balance in the manufacturing overhead control account—to be analyzed)	$ 1,800

(i) The variable budget for the department summarized (on a monthly basis) is:

	Fixed Cost per month	Variable Rate per DLH
Manufacturing overhead (total)	$16,000	$.25

6 Throughout this discussion of variation analysis of manufacturing overhead, it is assumed that productive volume (output) is measured in terms of direct labor hours. Other measures of productive volume might be more appropriate depending on the circumstances. It is assumed also that annual predetermined overhead rates are used for accounting purposes and that overhead is applied by multiplying the standard rate by the *standard hours* for the output of the period. This latter point suggests the standard cost approach. In absorption costing the standard rate is frequently multiplied by the actual hours for the output. In either case a useful variation analysis of the overhead over/under-applied is possible. The reader is referred to leading cost accounting books for further considerations of this product costing problem.

To restate the problem at hand, let's assume the monthly performance report for January showed the following:

	Actual Incurred	Overhead Applied	Variation (Over—Under*)
Manufacturing overhead (Dept. XX)	$24,550	$22,750	$1,800*

We will discuss and illustrate the analysis of the overhead variance (under-applied, hence unfavorable) of $1,800 under two assumptions, viz.:

    (1) That *both* planning budget and variable budget data for manufacturing overhead are available.

    (2) That *only* planning budget data are available—that is, the fixed and variable components of overhead costs are not known.

Assumption No. 1—Planning and variable budget data are available, hence the fixed and variable components of both the (a) overhead costs and (b) the annual departmental overhead rate are known (given above). In this case a particularly meaningful analysis of the $1,800 under-applied overhead may be developed as follows (amounts rounded to even dollars; * means unfavorable):

Variable Budget Analysis:

  Budget or Spending Variation:

Variable budget allowance adjusted for *actual* hours worked [$16,000 + ($.25 × 35,357)]	$24,839	
Actual burden incurred (at 35,357 DLH's)	24,550	$ 289

  Idle Capacity Variation (Volume or Idle Time Variation):

Burden applied (35,000 DLH's × $.65)	$22,750	
Variable budget allowance adjusted for *standard* hours in production [$16,000 + ($.25 × 35,000)]	24,750	$2,000*

  Manufacturing Overhead Efficiency Variation:

Variable budget allowance adjusted for standard hours in production [$16,000 + ($.25 × 35,000)]	$24,750	
Variable budget allowance adjusted for actual hours worked [16,000 + ($.25 × 35,357)]	24,839	89*
Total Variation		$1,800*

In order to facilitate computation of variations, the data may be arranged as follows:

Data :

   (1) Manufacturing overhead applied (35,000 DLH's × $.65) $22,750

   (2) Variable budget allowance adjusted for actual hours worked
       [$16,000 + ($.25 × 35,357)]   24,839

   (3) Variable budget allowance adjusted for standard hours in pro-
       duction [$16,000 + ($.25 × 35,000)]   24,750

   (4) Actual manufacturing overhead incurred (given)   24,550

Variation Analysis:[7]

Budget or spending variation	(Item 2 minus Item 4)	$ 289
Idle capacity variation	(Item 1 minus Item 3)	2,000*
Manufacturing overhead efficiency variation	(Item 3 minus Item 2)	89*
Total Variation	(Item 1 minus Item 4)	$1,800*

The variations may be evaluated and interpreted as follows:

Budget or spending variation—The variation as computed is a valid measure of the effectiveness of overhead *cost control* because actual costs are compared with budget allowances *adjusted to actual work done*. The variation can be reconciled with departmental variations as reported on the departmental performance report. For example, if there were ten expense items listed on the performance report for the department, the variations between these actual costs and the variable budget allowances would sum to the total budget variation as computed ($289).[8]

Idle capacity variation—The variation as computed correctly measures the *cost of idle plant capacity*. In the illustration the planning budget anticipated that the average monthly capacity was 40,000 standard DLH's (480,000 ÷ 12). Actual production volume was equivalent to only 35,000 standard direct labor hours. The variation as computed shows the portion of monthly *fixed costs* related to the idle plant capacity. The 5,000 direct labor hours of idle plant capacity multiplied by the *fixed* component of the overhead rate ($.40) gives the variation ($2,000). This point may be further clarified by computing the variation as follows on page 396.

---

[7] A two-way analysis, combining the idle time and efficiency variations, frequently is used, viz.:

Controllable variation	(Item 2 minus Item 4)	$ 289
Uncontrollable variation	(Item 1 minus Item 2)	2,089*
		$1,800*

[8] In some cases adjustments may have to be made for service department volume differentials.

$$\frac{5{,}000 \text{ DLH}}{40{,}000 \text{ DLH}} \times \$16{,}000 \text{ (monthly fixed costs)} = \underline{\$2{,}000}$$

Overhead efficiency variation—This variation as computed measures the *excess burden costs* that were incurred as a result of the fact that more direct labor hours were required than should have been (357 DLH's). Since variable costs (but not fixed costs) increase and decrease as direct labor hours increase and decrease, the burden efficiency variation should be expressed as variable costs only. That the variation as computed precisely fits these specifications may be demonstrated as follows:[9]

Standard hours in production	35,000
Actual hours incurred	35,357
Difference—Inefficient hours	357*
Multiply by variable portion of overhead rate	$.25
Overhead efficiency variation (wholly variable)	$ 89

Assumption No. 2—It is assumed that only planning budget data are known and that fixed and variable components of cost and the overhead rate are *not known*. In this case analysis is possible as illustrated below; however, it has some serious theoretical flaws:

Fixed Budget Analysis:
Overhead Budget or Spending Variation:

Planning budget allowance minus actual overhead incurred	
($26,000 − $24,550)	$1,450
Idle Capacity Variation (Volume Variation):	
Actual direct labor hours minus planning budget direct labor hours times the overhead rate	
(35,357 − 40,000 = 4,643* DLH × $.65)	3,018*
Overhead Efficiency Variation:	
Standard hours allowed for work done minus actual hours multiplied by burden rate	
(35,000 − 35,357 = 357* DLH × $.65)	232*
Total Variation	$1,800*

[9] It may be convincingly argued that overhead efficiency variation should include some fixed costs since workers who waste time also waste the cost of space, machinery, supervisory effort, and so forth, which they occupy, use, and require. If this position is accepted the computations in the example could be made so that the portion of fixed costs related to the 357 hours of inefficiency also are included in the efficiency variation and excluded from idle capacity or volume variation. The amount of fixed costs in question may be readily computed:

$$\$16{,}000 \times \frac{357}{40{,}000} = \underline{\$143}.$$

In order to facilitate computations, the data are frequently recorded on a worksheet as follows:

Data:

(1) Planning budget allowance	$26,000
(2) Burden applied (standard hours times overhead rate— 35,000 DLH's × $.65)	22,750
(3) Actual hours times overhead rate (35,357 DLH's × $.65)	22,982
(4) Actual burden incurred	24,550

Variation Analysis:

Overhead budget variation	(Item 1 minus Item 4)	$1,450
Idle capacity variation	(Item 3 minus Item 1)	3,018*
Overhead efficiency variation	(Item 2 minus Item 3)	232*
Total Variation	(Item 2 minus Item 4)	$1,800*

Mathematical analysis of a variation, such as illustrated above, can be useful for managerial purposes only to the extent that the variations are *understandable* and correctly measure the effect of each factor. This being the case, the analysis immediately above must be viewed with considerable caution.

The latter analysis of the manufacturing overhead variation may be appraised as follows:

> *Overhead budget variation*—This variation represents the difference between actual overhead incurred in producing 87,500 units and the overhead budgeted for 100,000 units. The variation as computed is not significant as an indicator of the efficiency with which manufacturing overhead costs were controlled during the period because the effect on costs of the *volume of work done* is not taken into account—that is, the effect on costs producing 12,500 units is completely overlooked. The variation as computed is meaningful only in those instances where actual output and budgeted volume are approximately the same.
>
> *Idle capacity variation*—This variation is a measure of the cost of *idle plant capacity.* Assuming that the volume of work in the planning budget represented approximately the practical capacity of the plant, there existed during the year idle plant capacity to the extent of 4,643 DLH's (40,000 − 35,357). The idle capacity variation places a dollar tag on this idle capacity. The idle capacity variation as computed above ($3,018*) is deficient in two respects. First, idle capacity in hours is considered to be the difference between average plant capacity on a monthly basis (40,000 DLH's) and actual hours worked (35,357), rather than the difference between average plant capacity and standard hours in production. Secondly, the idle capacity is valued at the standard overhead rate [40,000 − 35,357) × $.65

= \$3,018*]. This latter assumption is incorrect, because only *fixed* costs should be identifiable with idle capacity.

Overhead efficiency variation—This variation is termed "efficiency" because it is a dollar evaluation of the difference between actual hours worked and standard hours in production. The dollar valuation is in terms of the standard overhead rate [$(35,000 - 35,357) \times \$.65 = \$232*$]. The variation represents excess burden costs because of the fact that more hours were required than should have been required for the resulting production. The dollar evaluation in terms of the full overhead rate is not theoretically sound, because fixed costs do not vary with either standard or actual direct labor hours.

The above illustrations and related comments indicate that a particularly useful analysis of manufacturing overhead variance is possible if the fixed and variable components of such costs are known. Consequently, the analysis under Assumption 1 (above) is clearly preferable.

Use of variance analysis

In developing analyses along the lines discussed in this chapter, the analyst should constantly keep in mind the overriding fact that the results must (a) be understandable by those expected to use them, (b) measure with reasonable accuracy that which they are supposed to measure, and (c) be subject to concise presentation and explanation. It is unrealistic to expect top executives to devote undue time to a consideration of highly technical accounting and budget analyses.

Whether or not the additional analyses considered in this chapter should be used depends upon their potential use in the particular situation. These analyses can be significant when carefully developed, properly interpreted, and wisely used. However, the analyst must realize that these analyses involve concepts that are difficult to express in a simple manner and, therefore, should be used with caution.

With respect to presenting the results of variance analyses, two approaches are observed in practice. First, the analyses are frequently developed as one aspect of a *special report* concerning specific (but not recurring) problems with which the management is concerned. Second, the analyses are frequently included as a part of the *monthly performance report* discussed in Chapter 11. In this situation the results generally are reported in the "comment" section of the related report schedule. For example, the sales quantity and sales price variations may be reported at the bottom of the sales performance report as shown in Schedule 19. (page 76). It is generally desirable to include *narrative* comments concerning variation analysis.[10]

Discussion Questions

1. What important factors should be considered in evaluating a significant variation between actual and budget?
2. Explain the primary approaches to be used in determining the cause, rather than the effect, of significant variations.
3. Define (a) sales volume variation and (b) sales price variation.
4. Assume that a report showed the following data for product T:

		Actual	*Budget*	*Variation*
Sales		$9,690	$10,000	$310*
Average sales price		$.95	$1.00	
Volume variation	$200			
Price variation	510*			
	$310*			

   Explain how the volume and price variations were computed and give the interpretation of each.
5. With respect to the analysis of variations in raw material costs, explain (a) material usage variation and (b) material price variation.
6. Explain (a) wage rate variation and (b) labor quantity variation.
7. Explain volume variation related to (a) raw material and (b) direct labor. Explain why the analyst frequently does not compute it for control purposes.
8. Explain "manufacturing overhead over/under-applied." What are the primary factors that may cause it for a particular period?
9. Define the following: (a) budget or spending variation, (b) idle capacity variation, and (c) efficiency variation.
10. Explain why variable budgets make possible a more meaningful analysis of manufacturing overhead.
11. Why should technical analyses along the lines discussed in this chapter be used with caution?

[10] "Development and Reporting of Variances," *NAA Bulletin*, Accounting Practice Report, No. 15 (July 1962), Sec. 3.

PART FOUR

Miscellaneous

Budget Considerations

FIFTEEN

Budgeting Related to Standard Costs

and Direct Costing

Up to this point the discussions and illustrations have been concerned with the principal techniques and applications of a comprehensive budget program. With respect to the relationship of accounting to budgeting, historical accounting (full costing) procedures were assumed. This chapter considers two situations, viz., (1) where a *standard cost* system is used, and (2) where a *direct costing* system is used.

The objective in this chapter is to outline the principal interrelationships between a comprehensive budget program, a standard cost system, and a direct costing system. In order to accomplish this aim, some of the basic concepts underlying each accounting system will be briefly discussed. There are a number of variations both in standard cost procedures and in direct costing procedures. In order to simplify the discussion, a typical standard cost procedure and a typical direct costing procedure are explained. Alternative procedures are adequately covered in several books on cost accounting.[1]

Standard costs

Historical costs are actual costs reported after operational activities take place—that is, after the cost is incurred. Historical costs comprise a significant part of the financial history of a

[1] Clinton W. Bennett, *Standard Costs* (Englewood Cliffs, N.J.: Prentice-Hall, 1957).

firm. Standard costs, on the other hand, are costs determined before there is production or activity which gives rise to costs. Standard costs are predetermined costs which, presumably, represent what costs *should be*, as opposed to historical costs, which represent what costs *were*. Proponents of standard cost systems view the standard cost as the *true* cost of activity or production, whereas historical or actual costs generally represent the true cost *plus* losses due to inefficiency, faulty operations, and inadequate control.

Cost systems may also be broadly classified either as job order or process. In this context the type of system used generally depends upon the type of operation being carried on. For example, a machine shop would normally use a job order cost system, whereas a flour mill would use a process cost system. In this context, standard costs do not represent "another system"; they may be used with either a job order or a process cost system or some combination thereof. The standard cost concept is usually applied to manufacturing costs; however, within recent years the concept has been applied to a limited extent to administrative and distribution costs.

Standard cost systems also differ from "actual (historical) cost" systems in that in the former *both* actual and standard cost figures are recorded in the accounts and subsequently reported. In a standard cost system, the standard costs are recorded directly in the accounts, separate accounts being established for recording the *variations* between actual costs and standard costs. Thus, both the standard costs and the standard cost variations are an integral part of the formal accounting procedures. It will be recalled from previous chapters that budget figures are *not* incorporated in the accounts.

Standard costs and budget costs compared

The concept of budget costs, as developed in the preceding chapters, suggests that budget costs should represent reasonably attainable goals under expected operating conditions. Budget costs should be fairly "tight," because efficient operations should be assumed in establishing budget allowances. Budget costs then represent *expected actual costs* under normal operating conditions, assuming a high, yet attainable, efficiency level.

There are numerous theories (and opinions) as to what level of efficiency standard costs should represent. It is generally conceded that standard costs should be based upon analytical studies and precise specifications representing highly efficient operations. The diversity of opinion concerning the efficiency level of standard costs has resulted in differentiation of the following types of standard costs:

(1) Basic or Bogey Standards—Basic standards represent standard cost allowances set for the first or base year and are seldom if ever changed. They represent a yardstick or benchmark from which actual costs are measured in order to determine trends.[2] Thus, basic standard costs may be used in a manner similar to the method used by the statistician in determining trends in terms of the base year. Actually, basic standard costs are seldom used.

(2) Ideal Standards—Ideal standards represent what the minimum cost should be under ideal operating conditions. They assume the highest possible level of efficiency and maximum output from a plant in peak operating condition. Ideal standards represent strict engineering standards and are generally unattainable in the short run; hence, they, too, are seldom used.[3]

(3) Normal Standards—Normal standards represent what costs should be over a complete cycle of operations for the particular firm. Normal standards are goals generally attainable by the firm over its operating cycle. Many concerns find it difficult to define and precisely identify their particular operating cycle. Cycles may vary from a few months in some industries to several years in others. Obviously cyclical effects within the period covered frequently cause variations from standard.

(4) Expected Actual or Current Standards—Expected actual standards represent what short-run costs should be under the company's normal expected operating conditions. The period usually agrees with the accounting and budgeting fiscal year. These standards represent attainable goals in the light of current conditions and expectations. Generally, firms have found this type of standard the most useful, principally because the variations shown can be considered as adequate measures of immediate or short-term efficiency or lack of efficiency.

Standard costs relate closely to the budgeting of costs. The discussions to follow will attempt to explain and illustrate the direct relationship between standard costs and budget planning and control of costs. The definitions above provide the principal

---

[2] See Eric A. Camman, *Basic Standard Costs* (New York: American Institute Publishing Company, 1947).

[3] See John J.W. Neuner, *Cost Accounting* (Homewood, Ill.: Irwin, 1957), Ch. 20.

clue to this relationship. *If expected actual standards are developed for use in the standard cost system, these same standards should be used for cost estimates in the annual profit plan and also for cost control purposes.* Obviously, then, expected actual standards and budget costs are *identical*, thus the budget variations and standard cost variations should be identical. This point will be illustrated subsequently.

On the other hand, if standards other than expected actual are used in the standard cost system, there will be differences between standard costs and budget costs. As a general rule standards other than expected actual will be "tighter" than is desirable for budget purposes. Even so, standard costs calculations may still be used for budget construction but, in that event, the budget should include amounts for *budgeted variations between expected actual and standard costs.*

The importance of a clear-cut understanding of the interrelationship of budgets and standard costs cannot be overemphasized. To quote one author:

> Standards have been ably discussed from both a managerial and an accounting point of view in current books and periodicals, but one important consideration has not been given adequate attention. The part that budgets and systems of budgetary control play in the development and operation of standards is important enough to deserve careful consideration. In fact, the statement can safely be made that budgeting must precede the accurate and effective determination of price standards for material, labor, and overhead and that, conversely, a plan of budgetary control is more successfully installed in concerns having standardized production processes and operating under standard cost accounting systems. Budgetary control and standard costs are inseparable, and each is an important adjunct to managerial planning.[4]

The standard cost specification

Standard cost specification (standard cost card) represents one of the basic components of a standard cost system. Basically it specifies the standard costs of material, labor, and overhead for each product or job. The standard cost specification generally is the culmination of a series of cost analyses and engineering studies to develop reliable standards. In the case of standardized products there would be a standard cost card (specification)

[4] John G. Blocker and W. Keith Weltmer, *Cost Accounting* (New York: McGraw-Hill, 1954), p. 562.

for each product. In job order situations the standard cost card is developed for each job on the basis of specifications for the job. The procedure for each job involves predetermination of the raw material requirements, labor requirements, and overhead, in view of the various departments or cost centers through which the work must pass. Whether production is for stock or on a job order basis, many firms find it more practicable to develop a separate standard cost card for each major component, operation, or assembly so that the total standard cost may be determined by adding the various standard costs for the components. Obviously the standard cost specification card should be designed to fit each particular situation.

Standard Cost Specification (Card)

Product: _____ *P* _____ Date _____ *1/1/—* _____

Specifications _____ *Attached* _____

Department #1:			
Material R	2 Units @ $1.50	$3.00	
Direct labor	3 Hours @ 2.00	6.00	
Overhead	3 Hours @ 1.00[5]	3.00	$12.00
Department #2:			
Material M	4 Units @ $ .50	2.00	
Direct labor	2 Hours @ 3.00	6.00	
Overhead	2 Hours @ 2.50[5]	5.00	13.00
Total standard cost			$25.00

Illustration 50

A simplified standard cost card for a standardized product is shown in Illustration 50. It will be observed that the product passes through two departments (#1 and #2). Raw material R is used in Department 1 and raw material M is used in Department 2. Direct labor is required in both departments. Standard overhead rates based on departmental direct labor hours are used to charge manufacturing overhead or burden to the product in each department.

Standard costs for material—accounting and budgeting procedures

The development of standard costs for material involves the determination of standard quantities of material required for each unit of product and standard raw material unit cost. Multiplication of the standard quantity of raw material by the

[5] See page 418 for computation of these overhead rates.

standard material price gives the standard raw material cost per unit of product.

The development of standard quantities of raw material required for each unit of product involves an analysis, in terms of product specifications, drawings, and blueprints, of each type of raw material used. This is essentially an engineering problem that might involve procedures such as chemical analyses, mechanical analyses, and test runs. Such procedures are desirable also for developing budget costs, even though standard costs are not employed.

The development of standard material prices is a responsibility of the purchasing department, subject to top management approval. Standard material prices should represent expected actual conditions and should be developed in the same manner as budgeted material costs (see Chapter 6). Because material prices are frequently affected by the quantities of raw material to be purchased, production and raw materials budgeting are generally essential to the establishment of meaningful standard material prices.

In most situations standard material costs should be suitable for budget purposes. Therefore, in situations where standard material quantities and prices have been established, development of the materials and purchases budgets merely involves the application of these standards to the budgeted quantities of goods to be manufactured, as indicated in the production budget.

In order to illustrate the accounting procedure for raw materials when standard costs are used, assume that during January the company purchased 2,100 units of material R at $1.55 per unit and 4,200 units of material M at $.49 (refer to Illustration 50). These purchases would be recorded in the accounts of the standard cost system as follows:

For material R purchase

Raw materials control (2,100 units @ $1.50)	$3,150	
Material price variance (2,100 units @ $.05)	105	
Cash (2,100 units @ $1.55)		$3,255

For material M purchase

Raw materials control (4,200 units @ $.50)	$2,100	
Material price variance (4,200 @ $.01)		$ 42
Cash (4,200 @ $.49)		2,058

The Raw Materials Control account is debited with the *standard cost of material purchased* during the period, the difference between standard cost and actual cost being debited or credited to a Material Price Variance account. Referring to the above entries, the Material Price Variance Control account shows a debit balance for the month of $63, which represents an unfavorable standard cost variation. Detailed records supporting the control account would indicate the amount of variance for *each item or class of raw material* and specifically which purchases gave rise to the variation. It is significant to note that it is not necessary to wait until the end of the period in order to determine the price variance. Variations on weekly or even on individual purchases may be determined and reported to management so that corrective action may be taken whenever possible. The responsibility for controlling material price variances rests with the purchasing department. The Material Price Variance account is usually closed at the end of the period to the Income Summary account because it represents a *loss* due to inefficiency rather than a cost of production.[6]

Materials used in production may be charged to the Materials in Process account for standard quantities valued at standard prices. For example, assume that 1,000 units of product P (Illustration 50) were produced in January and that raw material issues were: 2,050 units of raw material R; 4,020 units of raw material M. Entries in the accounts would be:

For raw material R

Material in process—Dept. 1 (2,000 units @ $1.50)	$3,000	
Material quantity variance (50 units @ $1.50)	75	
Raw materials control (2,050 units @ $1.50)		$3,075

For raw material M

Material in process—Dept. 2 (4,000 units @ $.50)	$2,000	
Material quantity variance (20 units @ $.50)	10	
Raw materials control (4,020 units @ $.50)		2,010

In the above entries, the Work in Process account is charged with standard quantities of raw material required for 1,000 units of product produced, whereas the Material Control account is

---

[6] Another method of entering standard material costs in the accounts debits the Raw Material Control account at actual for purchases and, for issues, credits the Material Control account at actual, the Materials in Process account being debited at standard. The effect of this procedure is to record both price and quantity variations at the time the material is issued. The result of this procedure is that the material price variance is based on issues (which is inconsistent with with the control responsibility for unit cost) rather than on purchases and the Raw Material Control account is carried at actual unit material prices rather than at standard.

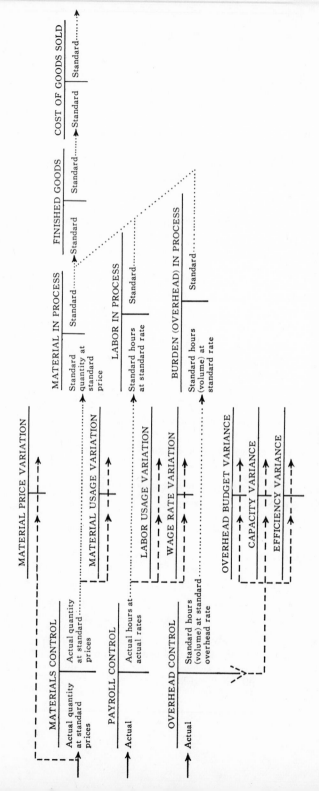

Illustration 51. Simplified Standard Cost Flow Chart.

credited with actual quantities used, both quantities being valued at the standard material prices given.[7] The material *quantity* variance account has a debit balance of $85, which represents the standard cost of excess material used. This variance measures the effectiveness with which raw materials were used. It is significant that the variance is expressed in terms of the standard material unit cost rather than of the actual material unit cost, since the departmental supervisors (factory Departments 1 and 2) have no control over material prices, but do have control over material *usage*. It should be noted at this point that the Raw Materials Control account carries the final inventory of raw materials valued at standard prices. The Material Quantity Variance account is closed at the end of the period to the Income Summary account on the assumption that the balance represents a *loss* due to inefficiency, therefore it is not a proper cost of production.

The flow of costs in a standard cost system is shown graphically in Illustration 51.

If standard costs for material were used for budget purposes also, then obviously standard cost variations and budget variations for material would be the same.

A distinct advantage resulting from standard costs for material is that the accounting is simplified for inventories of raw material and work in process. If raw material purchases are recorded in the Materials Control account at standard unit prices, the troublesome problem of pricing individual issues on the stores card (using some method such as first-in, first-out) is avoided. Stores cards can be kept in terms of units only, because both issues and inventories are valued at the standard unit material price. The use of standards for material reduces the cost of the accounting function and at the same time increases the possibilities of control through accounting.

Standard costs for direct labor—accounting and budgeting procedures

The establishment of standard costs for direct labor generally is more complex than for material. Standard costs for labor are developed along the lines previously discussed in Chapter 7. Just as it is generally necessary to develop separately standard quantities and standard unit prices for material, it is likewise

---

[7] Another method debits the in-process accounts at actual, crediting them at standard, thereby drawing off the variances at the point of completion. The reader is referred to cost accounting books.

generally desirable to develop hourly labor requirements and standard wage rates per hour by department or cost center for each unit of product. The development of labor standards, as with budget labor cost, necessitates subdivision of the factory into departments which frequently must be further subdivided into cost centers so that each kind or type of direct labor is segregated. For example, cost centers are usually established for such activities as drilling, grinding, polishing, assembly, and painting. Direct labor standards are then developed for each cost center. Standard labor hour requirements in a cost center are usually developed by the engineering department, utilizing time and motion studies. With standard times for the various operations developed, the standard time for any item to be processed through the cost center can be determined by adding the standard time required for each operation involved in the cost center. The wage rates of the direct labor workmen in each department are analyzed, taking into account both hourly pay and relative time for each rate, to develop a standard wage rate for the cost center. The standard wage rate is applied to the standard hours to compute the standard direct labor cost per unit of product. As with budget standards for direct labor, standard cost must be fair and equitable to both employee and employer. The standard should be attainable yet present a challenge which represents a high degree of efficiency.

The procedures mentioned above are equally applicable for setting budget standards, aside from standard cost considerations. Occasionally budget standards for direct labor are not determined as carefully as they should be, nor as carefully as they presumably would be for standard cost purposes. Obviously, if standard direct labor costs have been developed, they should be used directly for budgetary purposes.

A typical standard cost accounting procedure for direct labor may be illustrated; refer to Illustration 50. Continuing the assumption that 1,000 units of product P are produced in January, assume further that actual direct labor data were: Department 1, 3,100 actual direct labor hours at an average hourly actual rate of $2.05; Department 2, 1,960 direct labor hours at an average hourly actual rate of $3.10. Entries in the accounts would be:

For Department 1

Labor in process—Dept. 1 (3,000 DLH @ $2.00)	$6,000	
Labor usage variance (100 DLH @ $2.00)	200	
Wage rate variance (3,100 DLH @ $.05)	155	
Accrued payroll (3,100 DLH @ $2.05)		$6,355

For Department 2

Labor in process—Dept. 2 (2,000 DLH @ $3.00)	$6,000	
Wage rate variance (1,960 DLH @ $.10)	196	
Labor usage variance (40 DLH @ $3.00)		$ 120
Accrued payroll (1,960 DLH @ $3.10)		6,076

The in-process accounts are charged (debited) with the standard cost of direct labor, the difference between actual and standard being debited or credited to appropriately titled *variance accounts* in a manner similar to that used for raw material. The labor variance accounts are closed at the end of the period and are generally accorded the same treatment as that previously outlined for material variance accounts. Again it may be observed that the standard cost variations for labor generally should be identical with the related budget variations. The inclusion in the ledger accounts of standard costs for labor and the resulting variances tends to increase their significance to management. The responsibility for direct labor *usage* variances rests directly on production foremen and supervisors. Wage rate variances may be due primarily to economic conditions beyond the control of management; yet they are not infrequently affected by personnel and administrative policies. Labor time or usage variances should be analyzed by cost center (areas of responsibility), shifts, or groups of workers. It is fairly obvious that labor usage variances can be determined and reported on a monthly, weekly, or even daily basis. It is not unusual to find daily and cumulative reports of labor variances posted on bulletin boards or charts in the factory.

The analysis of standard cost variations for either material or labor should not stop with the identification of time and responsibility. Significant variations should be carefully investigated to determine precisely *what caused the variation*, so that appropriate managerial action may be forthcoming.

Standard costs for overhead—accounting and budgeting procedures

The development of standard costs for manufacturing overhead (burden) must be based on an adequate budget system for the manufacturing division. Adequate budgeting is essential because standard overhead or burden rates must be developed in advance for each department or cost center. The problem is analogous to that encountered in actual cost systems when overhead is costed into production through the use of predetermined burden rates. It will be recalled that predetermined overhead rates are computed as follows (see Chapter 8):

$$\frac{\text{Budgeted overhead for year}}{\text{Budgeted volume for year}} = \text{Standard overhead rate per unit of volume}$$

The formula requires that (a) annual volume (work) be budgeted for each department or cost center, and (b) annual overhead costs be estimated for each department or cost center for the budgeted volume. It is generally thought that these estimates should be subjected to more careful analysis when standard costs are being developed than when they are to be used in historical cost systems. There is no real logic for the distinction. When a complete budget program is in effect, the volume forecasts and overhead cost budgets should be used as the basis for computation of the standard overhead rate as was illustrated in Chapter 8 for The Superior Manufacturing Company.

The standard cost accounting procedure for factory overhead may be illustrated by referring to Illustration 50. Continuing the assumption that 1,000 units of product P are produced in January, assume further the following data for overhead: Actual overhead for January in Department 1, $3,500; in Department 2, $5,373. Direct labor hours as given on pages 412 and 413. Entries in the accounts under a standard cost system would be:

For Actual Overhead Incurred

Overhead control—Department 1	$3,500	
Overhead control—Department 2	5,373	
Various accounts		$8,873

For Overhead Applied—Department 1

Overhead in process (3,000 DLH @ $1.00)	$3,000	
Overhead control—Department 1		$3,000

For Overhead Applied—Department 2

Overhead in process (2,000 DLH @ $2.50)	$5,000	
Overhead control—Department 2		$5,000

For Overhead Variances—Department 1
(see page 416 for computation)

Overhead budget variance	$ 160	
Overhead idle capacity variance	300	
Overhead efficiency variance	40	
Overhead control—Department 1		$ 500

For Overhead Variances—Department 2
(see page 416 for computation)

Overhead budget variance	$ 100	
Overhead idle capacity variance	333	
Overhead efficiency variance		$ 60
Overhead control—Department 2		$ 373

In the above entries it will be observed that, as with material and labor, the Overhead in Process account is charged (debited) at standard. The three Work in Process accounts (Material, Direct Labor, and Overhead) are *credited* at standard for goods completed, leaving the work in process inventory valued at standard. In the above example the overhead (burden) *under-applied* for January was $500 for Department 1 and $373 for Department 2. In historical cost accounting procedures it will be recalled that the usual procedure is to close such items to a special account entitled *Overhead Over/Under-Applied*. In standard cost systems overhead over/under-applied is analyzed and recorded in separate variance accounts as illustrated.

The overhead budget or spending variance is the net of all variations between *actual costs* and *budget allowances* adjusted to actual volume attained in each department.[8] Therefore, it measures the efficiency with which overhead costs were controlled. The overhead budget demonstrates a direct relationship between standard costs and budgeted costs. Because budget variance represents loss due to inefficient cost control, it should be closed directly to the Income Summary account.

Overhead idle capacity variance represents the amount of overhead over/under-applied as a result of the fact that actual volume for the period was more or less than the productive capacity for the period. For example, in the illustration, Department 1 output for January represented 3,000 standard direct labor hours. Department 1 capacity (in direct labor hours) for the year was budgeted at 42,000, a monthly average of 3,500.[9] Therefore, the department worked 500 hours below capacity; this deficit, when multiplied by the *fixed component* of the overhead rate ($.60), gives the unfavorable capacity variance of $300. This variance is frequently due to seasonal conditions which will be offset in later

[8] This statement assumes variable budget standards are available. See next section.

[9] This statement assumes capacity variance is measured from expected actual rather than plant capacity, practical capacity, or normal capacity.

periods; therefore it should be treated as a deferred item rather than as a profit-and-loss item.

Overhead efficiency variance is due to the fact that actual hours in work done was different from standard hours in work done. For example, in the illustration, Department 1 actual hours were 3,100, standard hours, 3,000—a difference of 100 (excess) hours, which, when multiplied by the *variable component* of the overhead rate ($.40), gives the unfavorable efficiency variation of $40. Since this variance is generally indicative of plant inefficiency, it is closed to the Income Summary account for the period.

The overhead variances recorded in the last two entries on pages 414 and 415 were computed as follows:[10]

	Dept. 1	*Dept. 2*
(1) Overhead applied	$3,000	$5,000
(2) Variable budget adjusted to actual hours		
$2,100 + (3,100 × $.40)ª	3,340	
$2,333 + (1,960 × $1.50)		5,273
(3) Variable budget adjusted to standard hours		
$2,100 + (3,000 × $.40)	3,300	
$2,333 + (2,000 × $1.50)		5,333
(4) Actual overhead incurred	3,500	5,373
Variations (unfavorable*):		
Overhead budget variance (2−4)	$ 160*	$ 100*
Overhead idle capacity variance (1−3)	300*	333*
Overhead efficiency variance (3−2)	40*	60
Total variance (1−4)	$ 500*	$ 373*

ª See Variable Budgets on page 418.

We may reemphasize that if *expected actual standards* for overhead are used, the resulting standard cost variations are identical with those obtained with budget variation analysis procedures, as illustrated in Chapter 14. Computational procedures are identical in both situations.

Several methods of analyzing overhead variances are to be found in current literature and practice.

The standard cost income statement

In order to complete the illustration developed thus far in this chapter a simplified income statement based on the standard cost concept is presented in Illustration 52.

---

[10] This analysis is identical conceptually and mathematically with the analysis discussed and illustrated in Chapter 14 (pages 394 through 396). The interpretation given on pages 395 and 396 are appropriate for the standard cost variations illustrated above.

INCOME STATEMENT—STANDARD COST APPROACH
(Based on standard cost data)
For the month of January 19—

Sales—product P (1,000 units @ $40)		$40,000
Less: Standard cost of goods sold (1,000 units @ $25)		25,000
Standard gross margin		15,000
Deduct standard cost variances (unfavorable*):		
Material price variance—Material R	$105*	
Material price variance—Material M	42	
Material quantity variance—Material R	75*	
Material quantity variance—Material M	10*	
Labor usage variance—Department 1	200*	
Wage rate variance—Department 1	155*	
Labor usage variance—Department 2	120	
Wage rate variance—Department 2	196*	
Overhead budget variance—Department 1	160*	
Overhead efficiency variance—Department 1	40*	
Overhead budget variance—Department 2	100*	
Overhead efficiency variance—Department 2	60	819*
Actual gross margin		$14,181
Selling and administrative costs		9,261
Net income		$ 4,920

(Note: On monthly statements idle capacity variance is usually shown
as a deferred item on the balance sheet.)

Illustration 52

Observe that the variances, except for idle capacity, are written off as a loss in the period in which they were incurred;
thus the losses due to inefficiency do not affect cost of goods
sold nor are they carried forward in inventory as an asset. In
developing the monthly performance report, the standard cost
variances may be reported on the income statement as shown
and need not be repeated as *budget variations*. Obviously, subsidiary schedules (related to responsibilities) would normally be
needed to supplement the summary variances reported on the
income statement.

Variable expense budgets related to standard costs

Variable expense budgets as discussed and illustrated in Chapter
9 complement standard cost procedures in that they provide
data (1) for computation of departmental or cost center overhead rates, and (2) for overhead variance analyses.
The development of budgeted (standard) overhead rates was

discussed and illustrated in Chapter 8. The same procedures apply with respect to standard costs. For example, the standard overhead rates shown on the cost card on page 407 and used in the illustrations on pages 414 and 415 were computed as follows:

Budgeted data:

	Dept. 1	Dept. 2
Direct labor hours budgeted for the year	42,000	28,000
Variable budgets:		
Fixed cost per month	$ 2,100.00	$ 2,333.33
Variable rate per DLH	.40	1.50

Computation of standard overhead rates for the year:
Dept. 1
$$\frac{(12)\ (\$2,100) + (42,000 \times \$.40)}{42,000} = \$1.00 \text{ per DLH}$$
Dept. 2
$$\frac{(12)\ (\$2,333.33) + (28,000 \times \$1.50)}{28,000} = \$2.50 \text{ per DLH}$$

In the analysis of standard cost overhead variances, data from the variable budget were utilized in the illustration on page 416. The procedures used there are identical with those discussed and illustrated in Chapter 14. In those discussions the significance of variable budget data in developing meaningful variance analyses was demonstrated.[11]

Integration of standard costs and budgeting

An appraisal of standard costs and budgeting reveals that there is a considerable amount of overlapping with respect to objectives, advantages, and internal applications. It must be recognized, nevertheless, that there are distinct and significant aspects of each procedure that are not common to the other.

---

[11] In Chapter 14 the discussions and illustrations indicated that variance analysis (whether budget data or standard cost data) depends upon the data available, viz.: (1) variable budget procedures where the fixed and variable components of cost are known, and (2) fixed budget procedures where the fixed and variable components of cost are not known. Another classification of variance analyses is based on the number of resulting variances: (1) two-way analyses and (2) three-way analyses. The reader is referred to leading cost accounting books for consideration in depth of these aspects of variance analyses.

There are many situations in which it may be desirable to have a standard cost system in addition to a complete budget program. Whereas a comprehensive budget program is concerned primarily with the development of a coordinated plan of operations covering a given period of time as well as control of all aspects of operation, the primary objectives of a standard cost system are (a) to control manufacturing costs, and (b) to simplify certain cost accounting procedures.

It is not unusual to observe situations in which cost estimating is done somewhat haphazardly for budget purposes. The development of standard costs for material, labor, and even administrative and distribution costs may greatly improve the accuracy with which the budget is developed. Certainly the two procedures complement one another in many ways.

In addition to the budget aspects of standard costs, there are numerous accounting aspects involved. Standard costs can simplify the cost accounting procedures in several ways, of which the principal ones have already been indicated—accounting for raw materials, work in process, and finished goods inventories at standard costs.

In systems integrating standard costs and budgeting it is not uncommon to find standard cost procedures used for manufacturing costs and budget procedures used for distribution and administrative costs.

The integration of standard costs, as a part of the accounting system with a comprehensive budget program, represents a progressive advance in the cost control function of a concern. Such integration provides an effective basis for systematic planning, coordinating, and controlling of operations.

DIRECT COSTING

Within recent years considerable attention has been given to an accounting procedure variously referred to as *direct costing*, variable costing, or marginal costing. As with any new concept that affects traditional procedures, there has been much discussion, disagreement, and misunderstanding concerning direct costing. The purpose of including a brief discussion of the concept of direct costing is to indicate potential relationships between it and a comprehensive budget program. At the outset it may be helpful to note that in better-managed companies using the direct costing approach, the companies also follow standard cost procedures and employ comprehensive budget procedures including the variable budget concept. Thus, one may say that a combined *planning budget, standard cost, direct costing,* and *variable budget* system has been evolved by a number of companies. The obvious implication of this development is that these four tools or techniques in combination complement each other in significant manners.

The nature of direct costing

Although there are numerous aspects of direct costing, the concept involves four significant and distinct features, viz.:[12]

    (1) The fixed and variable components of all costs (manufacturing, administrative, and distribution) are formally segregated in the accounts at initial recording. This segregation of fixed and variable components of cost requires special provision in the chart of accounts. For example, manufacturing expense control accounts might appear as follows:
        14191 Variable manufacturing expense control
        14192 Fixed manufacturing expense control
    (2) Only variable costs (direct material, direct labor, and variable manufacturing overhead) are treated as costs of production; therefore, cost of goods sold and inventories of work in process and finished goods are accounted for, and reported, at the related variable cost only. Fixed costs are considered to be *period* costs rather than product costs. As a consequence, all fixed costs are written off and reported as a direct deduction on the income statement for the period in which incurred. No fixed costs are carried to cost of goods sold or capitalized in inventory.
    (3) The income statement is rearranged to emphasize the *contribution margin* or *marginal income*—that is, the excess of sales revenue over variable production, distribution, and administrative costs. The fixed costs are deducted in full as period costs.
    (4) The reported net income fluctuates directly with increases and decreases in sales revenue from period to period. This effect is in contrast to full costing (absorption costing) where reported net income is significantly affected by the amount of increase or decrease in inventories. For example, one company reported

---

[12] For a comprehensive treatment of the subject of direct costing see: Wilmer Wright, *Direct Standard Costs* (New York: McGraw-Hill, 1962).

the following comparative results (amounts simplified for illustrative purposes) where inventory of finished goods changed significantly from month to month:

	Net Sales	Reported net income under Full Costing	Reported net income under Direct Costing
January	$30,000	$5,000	$5,000
February	27,000	5,600	3,200
March	27,000	800	3,200
Total for Quarter		$11,400	$11,400

The nature of direct costing is further indicated through a proforma income statement and related breakeven analysis using simplified amounts as shown in Illustration 53.

INCOME STATEMENT—DIRECT COST APPROACH

Net sales			$200,000	100 %
Less variable cost of sales:				
Beginning inventory (variable costs)		$ 10,000		
Variable costs:				
Direct material	$50,000			
Direct labor	40,000			
Variable factory overhead	20,000			
Variable administrative costs	5,000			
Variable distribution costs	6,000	121,000		
Total		131,000		
Less ending inventory (variable costs)		11,000		
Variable cost of sales			120,000	60 %
Marginal income (and P/V ratio)			80,000	40 %[13]
Less period (fixed) costs:				
Fixed factory overhead		$ 10,000		
Fixed administrative cost		25,000		
Fixed distribution costs		35,000		
Total period (fixed) costs			70,000	35 %
Operating income (pre-tax)			$ 10,000	5 %

Breakeven point computation:

$$BES = \frac{\text{Fixed Costs}}{\text{P/V Ratio}}$$
$$= \frac{\$70,000}{40\%}$$
$$= \$175,000$$

Illustration 53

[13] The P/V ratio is computed by dividing *marginal income* by *sales revenue* (*volume*); it is the complement of the variable cost ratio (variable costs/sales revenue).

Direct costing related to budgeting

The above discussion of the nature of direct costing should be sufficient to indicate the potential relationships between it and a comprehensive budget program. We may summarize the primary aspects of these relationships as follows:

(1) If variable expense budgets are used as a part of the budget program, the problem of resolving the variability of costs (Chapter 9) is simplified because the historical cost data will be segregated as to the fixed and variable components.

(2) Development of the budgeted cost of goods sold is simplified because the problem of allocating fixed costs is avoided.

(3) The historical data as recorded and reported by the accounting department emphasizes the cost-volume-profit relationships, hence the extension of this particular analysis to data relating to the future (in the budget) is facilitated.

(4) The comparison of actual costs with budgeted costs (or standard costs) in terms of responsibility has more meaning because there is less allocation of costs (see Chapter 8, pages 170 and 171 relative to the effect of allocations in cost control).

Despite the preceding discussions, the reader should realize that there are a number of disadvantages to direct costing and that many accountants do not favor the approach. On the other hand it does appear that there is a trend toward greater use of the direct costing approach.[14]

As noted earlier, a number of companies are integrating budgeting, standard costs, direct costing, and variable budget procedures. The objective is to build a completely integrated planning and control system. One writer outlined four tools to control costs as follows:[15]

(1) A good cost system
(2) A direct-cost income statement
(3) A sound budget program
(4) An appropriation system (for certain types of expenditures)

The author also stressed the importance of flexibility in adapting them to a particular situation. Much of the work that is being done in this direction is experimental; certainly some prevalent ideas will be discarded and new concepts developed that will improve the over-all system. It appears clear that direct

[14] Wilmer Wright, "Why Direct Costing Is Rapidly Gaining Acceptance," *The Controller* (July 1962), pp. 40–46.

[15] Adapted from: Cecil L. Clark, "Control Costs—With Sharp Tools," *NAA Bulletin* (August 1955), pp. 1634–1642.

costing and the integration of this approach with budgeting and standard costs has not reached a state of maturity. We can expect changes in this area of financial management in the next few years. At the present time, it seems safe to say that the integration of budgeting, standard costs, and direct costing as currently conceived does not have universal application; however, there are many situations where such integration may prove particularly effective.[16]

Discussion Questions

1. What are standard costs? Compare them with historical costs.
2. Distinguish between (a) basic standards, (b) ideal standards, (c) normal standards, and (d) expected actual standards.
3. What is the purpose of the standard cost card?
4. How are standard material costs usually determined?
5. Assuming the standard cost of raw material per unit is $1.00, give the standard cost entry for the purchase of 1,000 units of raw material at $1.05.
6. Assume from question 5 that 210 units of the raw material purchased is issued to the factory for the production of 100 cans of finished goods. The standard raw material requirement is 2 for 1. Give the standard cost entry indicated.
7. Explain what is recorded in each of the following accounts and their disposition: (a) Raw material price variance account and (b) Raw material usage variance account.
8. How are standard labor costs usually developed?
9. Give the standard cost entry indicated assuming that: 100 cans of finished goods are being produced, the standard labor hours per can are 3, the standard wage rate is $2.00, and actual labor incurred is 290 hours at $2.10.
10. Explain what is recorded in each of the following accounts and their disposition: (a) Labor usage variance account and (b) Wage rate variance account.
11. Review the procedure and purpose of computing standard overhead or burden rates.
12. What is meant by idle plant or idle capacity variation?
13. Relate standard cost variations to budget variations.
14. When is it necessary to budget *standard cost variations?*
15. Relate standard costs to (a) the annual profit plan, and (b) variable expense budgets.
16. What are the primary characteristics of direct costing procedures?
17. Relate direct costing to (a) the annual profit plan, and (b) variable expense budgets.

[16] "Current Applications of Direct Costing," *NAA Research Report No. 37,* (January 1961).

SIXTEEN

Budget Planning and Control

for Nonmanufacturing Concerns

and Nonprofit Organizations

NONMANUFACTURING CONCERNS

The preceding chapters have emphasized budget procedures for manufacturing concerns. The purpose of this chapter is to discuss some of the particular problems and procedures involved in budgeting for wholesale and retail concerns, and for nonprofit organizations.

Instead of converting raw materials into finished products, a merchandising concern purchases goods and resells them in essentially the same form. Obviously, a nonmanufacturing concern would not develop budgets convering production, raw materials, purchases, direct labor, or manufacturing overhead. Instead, the principal aspect of budgeting for nonmanufacturing concerns revolves around the *merchandise budget.*

Although industrial budgeting has received much more attention in general business literature, it is a fact that comprehensive budget control has been employed to a greater extent in retailing than in manufacturing situations. The reason is that the operating margin in merchandising concerns is typically very low. In addition the purchasing function is particularly critical. While it is not unusual for a manufacturing business to make 10 per cent profit on net sales, a 2 to 3 per cent profit on net sales is considered good in many merchandising concerns. Another factor is that, historically, more importance appears to have been attached to the financial control function in retail concerns (particularly in department stores) than in manufacturing concerns.

Wholesale and retail concerns are smaller on the average than manufacturing concerns; however, it does not follow that there is less need for formal budgeting. On this point one authority states:

> It is sometimes argued that the smaller firms need not follow the practice of formal budgeting. Unquestionably there are thousands of small retailers who hold this view. Moreover, some of these firms consistently show a substantial profit. Such examples, however, do not discredit budgetary practice. In some of these cases, success can be traced to the retailer's superior managerial ability along other than planning lines. In other instances the merchant does devote a substantial amount of time and thought to the problem of anticipating demand trends, and he does plan his purchases and stocks in the light of these appraisals. But because most of the calculations are carried on informally in his mind or on a piece of scratch paper, he is not aware that he is performing the budget function. For every business that succeeds without the aid of careful planning, there are many more that fail because of this weakness.[1]

Effective budgeting for wholesale and retail concerns encompasses the same basic procedures as profit planning and control for manufacturing concerns; viz.:

(1) The development of a realistic plan of operations (profit plan) covering a definite period of time.
(2) Intelligent and continuous effort to assure attainment of the objectives formally expressed in the plan of operations.
(3) The development of a control system based upon performance reports in terms of organizational responsibilities.

General considerations

The essentials to successful budgeting discussed in Chapter 2 have equal application to wholesale and retail situations. As in manufacturing concerns, the controller or budget director should be assigned the responsibility for supervising and designing the budget program, but the basic plans and estimates comprising

[1] Paul L. Brown and William R. Davidson, *Retailing Principles and Practices* (New York: Ronald, 1960) p. 289.

the profit plan should be provided by those responsible executives whose functions are being budgeted. Departmental managers, buyers, divisional merchandise managers, and other executives should be brought into budget planning individually as well as through the budget committee.

Definite and clear-cut organizational structure is as essential to effective budgeting and control in nonmanufacturing concerns as in those previously discussed, and for the same reasons. A simplified organization chart is presented (Illustration 54) so that the reader may visualize the way in which department stores typically are organized. As with manufacturing concerns, budgeting for nonmanufacturing concerns should be expressed in terms of organizational responsibilities.

Budget planning activities should start about three months prior to the beginning of the period being budgeted. In non-manufacturing concerns it is desirable that the budget period correspond to the seasonal cycle; most retail concerns set up their budget on a six months' basis with a breakdown by months within the period. The periods frequently are February through July and August through January because they represent the two major merchandising seasons: spring-summer and fall-winter. Where practicable it is desirable that the budget cover a twelve-month period, with a breakdown by months.

For purposes of discussion, profit planning and control for nonmanufacturing concerns may be outlined as follows:

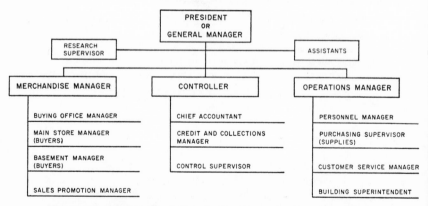

Illustration 54. *Simplified Organization Chart of a Department Store (buying and selling functions integrated)*

I. Budget planning
    a. Sales planning
    b. Stock and purchase planning
    c. Budgeting expenses
    d. Budgeting professional services
    e. Budgeting capital additions
    f. Budgeting cash
    g. Budget summaries—income statement and balance sheet
II. Budgetary control

The term *merchandise budget* is frequently used with reference to budgeting in nonmanufacturing situations. The term merchandise budget is usually considered to encompass planning of sales, stocks (inventory), reductions, markdowns, employee discounts, stock shortages, purchases, and gross margins.

Sales planning

The first basic item to be budgeted in retail as well as manufacturing concerns is expected sales volume. Two general approaches are used in nonmanufacturing situations. One approach is to estimate *unit* sales by price lines. This approach is practicable only in situations where there are a limited number of relatively high-value items. Another approach, extensively employed, is that of estimating sales by appropriate classifications in *sales dollars*.

Frequently two sales projections are developed independently, viz.:

    (1) On a departmental (or merchandise line) basis
    (2) On a total sales basis

If the two projections are approximately equal, the departmental sales estimates are generally used. In case of considerable differences, both estimates should be carefully studied to reconcile the discrepancy. It is generally desirable to break the sales into cash, charge, and C.O.D.[2]

In budgeting sales a number of factors should be given consideration, the principal factors being these:

, [2] See *Manual of Budgetary Procedure and Control for Departmentized Stores*, Rev. ed., Controllers' Congress New York, National Retail Dry Goods Association, pp. 11 and 12.

1. Outside Conditions[3]
   a. The general business conditions expected to prevail during the coming period.
   b. Local business conditions expected to prevail.
   c. The trend of population in the trading area.
   d. Probable changes in purchasing power.
   e. Expected changes in the competitive situation.
   f. Fashion movements expected.
2. Inside Conditions[4]
   a. Changes in promotional policies.
   b. Changes in location and space.
   c. Changes in personnel policies.
   d. Changes in physical arrangement and merchandise layout.
   e. Changes in price policy.
   f. Changes in credit policy.

In order to illustrate sales budgeting, assume the over-all sales estimate for the six-months period beginning February 1 is $590,000 net sales (after discounts and other reductions). When the *total sales approach* is used, the total amount is usually broken down by time periods and by departments on the basis of *experience percentages*. For example, the total may be broken down by months as shown in Illustration 55.

Month	Projected Experience Percentages by Month	Planned Net Sales by Month (rounded)
February	15.25	$ 90,000
March	16.10	95,000
April	17.29	102,000
May	18.98	112,000
June	18.65	110,000
July	13.73	81,000
Total	100.00	$590,000

Illustration 55. Distribution of Planned Net Sales by Month.

Similarly, the estimated sales may be further distributed by department for each month. The projected experience percentages should be carefully developed on the basis of local conditions, past experience, and then adjusted for future expectations. Distribution of net sales by department for each month is shown in Illustration 56. Note that the only *input* data are (1) the

[3] Adapted from D.J. Duncan, and C.F. Phillips, *Retailing Principles and Methods* (Homewood, Ill.: Irwin, Inc., 1955), Ch. 12.

[4] Adapted from F.M. Jones, *Retail Merchandising* (New York: Pitman, 1957), Ch. 27.

Department	February %	February Amount	March %	March Amount	April %	April Amount	May %	May Amount	June %	June Amount	July %	July Amount	Total Amount
Women's Coats & Suits	9	$ 8,100	7	$ 6,650	5	$ 5,100	5	$ 5,600	4	$ 4,400	4	$ 3,240	$ 33,090
Women's Dresses	33	29,700	35	33,250	40	40,800	38	42,560	39	42,900	40	32,400	221,610
Men's Furnishings	18	16,200	20	19,000	21	21,420	19	21,280	20	22,000	18	14,580	114,480
Draperies, Curtains, Etc.	12	10,800	15	14,250	15	15,300	12	13,440	13	14,300	10	8,100	76,190
Others	28	25,200	23	21,850	19	19,380	26	29,120	24	26,400	28	22,680	144,630
Totals — Amount	100	$ 90,000	100	$ 95,000	100	$102,000	100	$112,000	100	$110,000	100	$ 81,000	$590,000
" — %		15.25		16.10		17.29		18.98		18.65		13.73	100.00

Illustration 56. Distribution of Planned Net Sales by Month, by Department.

over-all sales estimate ($590,000) and (2) the projected experience percentages by time periods, by department.

Stock and purchase planning

After planning net sales, three things are required, viz.: (a) decisions as to the amount of stock (inventory) that should be on hand at the beginning of the month (BOM), (b) determination of the goods to be purchased during the period, and (c) estimates of desired inventories of stock at the end of the month (EOM). Since the end of the month inventory for one month is also the beginning of the month inventory for the next month, consideration narrows to the BOM monthly stock levels and purchase requirements.

Because stock inventory is one of the most critical problems facing the retailer or wholesaler, primary consideration is given to this factor. With sales accurately estimated and stock requirements determined, purchase requirements can be computed as a residual quantity.

Principal factors to be considered in setting beginning of the month (BOM) stock figures have been stated as follows:

(1) Basic stock requirements, i.e., the investment necessary to maintain adequate assortments of those items for which the demand is relatively stable.

(2) Promotional merchandise needed to get planned volume for the month.

(3) Policy in regard to the department: Is it to be a dominant policy so far as competition is concerned?

(4) What is the relation of stock to sales? Does this relation insure maximum turnover and at the same time afford complete stocks?

(5) Outlook for prices.[5]

Planning Inventory Levels—The retailer and wholesaler must determine the amount of stock that should be on hand at the beginning of the month as related to the planned sales. Stocks plus the planned inflow of goods during the month must be adequate to support planned sales. On the other hand stocks must be kept at reasonable levels to minimize potential losses through style changes, obsolescence, and excess capital tied up in inventory. The delicate balance of stocks requires the exercise of considered judgement in addition to the use of the usual

---

[5] *The Buyer's Manual*, Rev. ed. (New York: National Retail Dry Goods Association, Merchandising Division, undated), p. 178.

analytical approaches. Nonmanufacturing concerns rely to a considerable degree on *stock-sales ratios* in determining suitable stock levels. Two methods of computing the stock-sales ratio are:

(a) $\dfrac{\text{Average inventory at retail}}{\text{Net sales}} = $ Stock-sales ratio (at retail)

(b) $\dfrac{\text{Average inventory at cost}}{\text{Cost of sales}} = $ Stock-sales ratio (at cost)

The two methods will give the same figure only if the markups on sales and inventories are the same. The usual practice in retail concerns is to base the computation on retail rather than on cost figures. Trade publications provide information concerning stock-sales ratio experiences that may be of considerable value in budgeting stock levels.

To illustrate application of the BOM stock-sales ratio, assume that a stock-sales ratio of 2 for February is projected in the Women's Coats and Suits department (Illustration 56). Because planned sales for February are $8,100, the planned stock at the beginning of February would be $16,200 at retail. The planned February stock levels (BOM) for each department may be computed as follows:[6]

Department	Projected BOM Stock Sales Ratio Desired	Planned Net Sales (Feb.)	Planned BOM Stock (at retail)
Women's Coats & Suits	2	$ 8,100	$ 16,200
Women's Dresses	3	29,700	89,100
Men's Furnishings	2.5	16,200	40,500
Draperies, Curtains, Etc.	1.5	10,800	16,200
Others	3.5	25,200	88,200
Totals	2.78 (average)	$90,000	$250,200

Illustration 57. Computation of BOM Stock Levels.

It is important that stock levels and stock-sales ratios be related to each particular department or kind of merchandise. For example, turnover of 5 may be required for the store as a whole, yet a turnover of 2 may be satisfactory for an individual line.

Planning Purchases—The following formula is usually employed to compute the required purchases at *retail value:*

$$\begin{array}{l}\text{PLANNED} \\ \text{PURCHASES} \\ \text{(Retail Value)}\end{array} = \begin{array}{l}\text{Planned} \\ \text{Net Sales}\end{array} + \begin{array}{l}\text{Planned} \\ \text{Reductions}\end{array} + \begin{array}{l}\text{Planned} \\ \text{EOM Stock}\end{array} - \begin{array}{l}\text{Planned} \\ \text{BOM Stock}\end{array}$$

[6] Paul L. Brown and William R. Davidson, *Retailing Principles and Practices* (New York: Ronald, 1960), p. 300.

Department	(1) Planned Net Sales (Illustration 56)	(2) Planned Reductions (Assumed)	(3) Planned EOM Stock (BOM for following month)	(4) Planned BOM Stock (Illustration 57)	(5) Planned Purchases (1 + 2 + 3 − 4)
Women's Coats & Suits	$ 8,100	$ 500	$ 16,200	$ 16,200	$ 8,600
Women's Dresses	29,700	2,000	87,100	89,100	29,700
Men's Furnishings	16,200	1,000	41,500	40,500	18,200
Draperies, Curtains, Etc.	10,800	800	17,000	16,200	12,400
Others	25,200	1,200	86,000	88,200	24,200
Totals	$90,000	$5,500	$247,800	$250,200	$93,100

Illustration 58. Computation of Purchases at Retail.

The formula is logical in that purchases must be equivalent to sales, plus or minus changes in the inventory of goods on hand, assuming all are valued at retail. In addition, enough goods must be purchased (at retail) to cover all reductions in goods at retail value.

Reductions include (a) markdowns, (b) discounts given to employees, (c) discounts given to certain types of customers such as clergymen, and (d) inventory shortages due to theft and other causes. The formula may be further clarified by illustrations:

	Case A	Case B	Case C
Planned sales	$10,000	$10,000	$10,000
Add planned reductions	—	1,000	1,000
Total	10,000	11,000	11,000
Add planned final inventory (EOM, Stock)	—	—	5,000
Total	10,000	11,000	16,000
Less planned beginning inventory (BOM)	—	—	4,000
Purchases required at retail value	$10,000	$11,000	$12,000

The formula may be applied to a stock classification, department, time period, or to an entire store. The purchases (at retail value) for February for the planned net sales shown in Illustration 56 may be computed as shown in Illustrations 57 and 58.

In Illustration 58 *planned purchases* are indicated at *retail;* consequently the amount that should be budgeted for purchases *at cost* is not indicated. The conversion of purchases at retail to purchases at cost is made by multiplying the retail value by the "cost multiplier" which is the complement of the planned *initial* markup percentage (on sales price). Computation of purchases at cost is shown in Illustration 59.

Department	Planned Purchases (*Illus. 58*— at retail)	Planned Initial Markup on Sales price	Cost Multiplier	Purchases (at cost)
Women's Coats & Suits	$ 8,600	60%	40%	$ 3,440
Women's Dresses	29,700	70%	30%	8,910
Men's Furnishings	18,200	50%	50%	9,100
Draperies, Curtains, Etc.	12,400	40%	60%	7,440
Others	24,200	50%	50%	12,100
Totals	$93,100			$40,990

Illustration 59. *Computation of Purchases at Cost.*

The last column in Illustration 59 represents the *purchases budget at cost*. These amounts are used as the basis for buying merchandise for the several departments. It should be observed that the illustrative data were developed for only one month (February); the procedure would be identical for each month.

The planned purchases computed along the lines just illustrated are incorporated in the budgets of cash, and profit and loss, in a manner similar to that previously illustrated for manufacturing costs in manufacturing situations.

Markup considerations

In the preceding discussions (Illustration 59), the *planned* initial markup was based on retail value (sales price). The term *markup* refers to the difference between cost and the selling price of an article. Markup is variously expressed as a dollar amount or as a percentage of either (a) cost or (b) retail price. For example, if 100 items costing $60 were marked to sell for $100, the markup would be $40, or $.40 each. The markup as a percentage could be expressed either:

(a) On cost $\dfrac{\$40}{\$60} = 66\tfrac{2}{3}\%$

(b) On retail price $\dfrac{\$40}{\$100} = 40\%$

In nonmanufacturing situations, it is particularly important that a distinction be drawn between *initial markup* and *maintained markup* (gross margin). This distinction is especially vital for pricing, budgeting, and accounting purposes. Initial markup represents the difference between the cost and the original, or first, retail price placed on goods. Using the figures given in the preceding paragraph, the initial markup was $40, or $.40 each. Maintained markup, or gross margin, is the difference between cost of goods sold and actual sales. For example, if, in the case above, the 100 articles were marked down from $100 to $90 and then sold, the maintained markup or gross margin would be $30, or $.30 each. The examples may be summarized in this way:

	Initial Markup	*Maintained Markup (Gross Margin)*
Sales (100 units)	$100	$90
Cost of sales	60	60
Initial markup	$ 40 (40% on sales)	
Maintained markup		$30 (33⅓% on sales)

It is obvious that the difference between initial markup and maintained markup is due to the effect of reductions (see page 433), whether they be markdowns, discounts, or stock shortages. In budget planning it is necessary that very careful consideration be given to developing (a) planned initial markup and (b) planned gross margin (maintained markup). The procedure may be illustrated by the following example: Assume planned net sales in a department for February to be $8,100 after planned *reductions* of $500. Assume further that, after careful consideration of past trends and future expectations, the store management decided that this department should realize a *gross margin* (maintained markup) of 57.53 per cent of net sales. The question is what should be the *initial markup:* (a) on retail, and (b) on cost, in order to realize a *maintained markup* of 57.53. The gross margin and cost of sales in dollars should be:

Planned net sales	$8,100
Planned gross margin ($8,100 × 57.53)	4,660
Difference—Planned cost of sales	$3,440

The *initial markup* on retail value that should be planned for the department may be computed as follows:

$$\frac{57.53\% + 6.17\%**}{100\% + 6.17\%} = 60\%$$
$$** \ (\$500 \div \$8,100 = 6.17\%)$$

Thus an initial markup of 60 per cent on retail, that is, 150 per cent on cost,[7] would be necessary under the conditions anticipated to realize a maintained markup of 57.53 per cent on retail. The computations may be verified as follows:

Planned net sales		$8,100
Less: Cost of goods sold		
Net sales	8,100	
Add reductions	500	
Total merchandise required (at retail)	8,600	
Initial markup ($8,600 × 60%)	5,160	
Cost of goods sold		3,440
Maintained gross margin		4,660
Maintained markup percentage ($4,660 ÷ $8,100)		57.53%

Markup Conversion—Although in retail circles markups are usually expressed on retail price, when the goods arrive a markup on cost must be applied to give the desired markup on retail.

---

[7] See next section for method of converting from a markup on retail to a markup on cost.

For example, an item costing $.60 must be marked up $66\frac{2}{3}$ per cent *on cost* to sell at a price which will give 40 per cent *on retail* price, viz.:

Markup based on cost price:

1. Cost	$.60		
2. Sales price ($.60 × 166⅔%)		$1.00	
3. Markup on cost ($.60 × 66⅔%)			$.40

Markup based on sales price:

1. Sales price		$1.00	
2. Markup on retail price ($1.00 × 40%)			$.40
3. Cost ($1.00 × 60%)		$.60	

Tables for ready reading of equated markup figures may be available; however, a simple procedure may be used to convert from markup on retail to markup on cost, or *vice versa*. Observe the relationship between the two columns below:

EQUATED MARKUPS

	Markup Based on Retail (retail fraction always smaller)	Markup Based on Cost (cost fraction always larger)
⅓ on retail	$\frac{1}{3}$ (33⅓%)	$\frac{1}{2}$ (50%)
40% on retail	$\frac{40}{100}$ (40%)	$\frac{40}{60}$ (66⅔%)
30% on retail	$\frac{30}{100}$ (30%)	$\frac{30}{70}$ (42.8%)
50% on retail	$\frac{50}{100}$ (50%)	$\frac{50}{50}$ (100%)

Conversion from the retail fraction to the cost fraction merely involves carrying over the numerator and taking the *difference* between the retail numerator and denominator for the cost denominator. Converting from the cost fraction to the retail fraction may be accomplished through using the reverse procedure: the retail denominator is the sum of the cost numerator and denominator. The method is easily remembered when it is realized that the cost fraction must always be a larger fraction than the retail fraction.

Open-to-buy planning

Open-to-buy is a term that is generally used in nonmanufacturing concerns to refer to that amount which a buyer may spend for a specified period of time. For example, if the cost of planned purchases for a particular department for the month is $2,000, open-to-buy is $2,000 before any purchases are made. If by the 15th the buyer has spent $1,200, he is then open-to-buy $800.

Control of purchases is frequently exercised through open-to-buy reports. Computation of open-to-buy throughout a specific period may involve consideration of several factors. For example, assume the following data for Women's Coats & Suits (Illustration 58):

	At Retail
Planned sales for February	$ 8,100
BOM inventory	16,200
Planned EOM inventory	16,200
Planned reductions for the month	500
Actual sales to date (February 20)	5,000
Actual reductions to date	300
Merchandise received to date (at retail)	6,000
On order for February delivery	2,000
Planned initial markup 40% on retail (i.e., 66⅔% on cost)	

The open-to-buy may be computed as follows:

Needed Stock

Planned EOM inventory			$16,200
Planned sales for remainder of month			
Planned sales		$ 8,100	
Less actual sales		5,000	3,100
Planned reductions for remainder of month			
Planned reductions		500	
Less actual reductions		300	200
Total			$19,500

Available Stock

Stock on hand at present			
BOM inventory	$16,200		
Goods received to date	6,000	22,200	
Less:			
Actual reductions to date	300		
Actual sales to date	5,000	5,300	16,900
Stock on order for February delivery		2,000	
Total			18,900
Open-to-Buy at Retail			600
Cost multiplier (100% − 40%)			60%
Open-to-Buy at Cost (on February 20)			$ 360

If available stock was in excess of needed stock the department would be "overbought."

Budgeting expenses

In nonmanufacturing situations, expenses typically are broken down into natural classifications, such as salaries, taxes, repairs, and insurance. In addition, and certainly more significantly for control, they should be further classified in terms of operating responsibilities as determined by the organizational structure of the firm. In a manner similar to that described for manufacturing concerns, each individual having cost-incurrence responsibilities should actively participate in setting expense allowances for his particular department or function. It is not unusual to find expenses being classified as either fixed or variable, and variable expense budgets similar to those previously discussed being used. Again, the critical problem concerning variable budgets is the selection of suitable factors or measures of activity with which to correlate variable costs. Net-sales dollars are appropriate for some expenses, while the number of transactions may be more appropriate for others.

For evaluation and adjustment of expense budgets prepared by the various supervisory and executive personnel, a computation similar to the following is usually employed:

Planned February sales (Illustration 56)	$90,000
Planned cost of sales, at cost (Illustration 59)	40,990
Planned gross margin (maintained markup)	49,010
Necessary *net profit margin* (3% of net sales)	2,700
Expense Limitation	$46,310

If the expense budgets when added together amount to more than $46,310, they must be carefully restudied for the express purpose of reducing them to the expense limitation. Since the profit margin is generally small in nonmanufacturing situations, expense control through budget planning becomes very significant.

When the expense budgets are finally pared down to the expense limitation, they are incorporated into the profit plan and provide essential data for budgeting cash and profit and loss in the manners previously discussed and illustrated.

Budgeting professional services

Budgeting professional services such as legal and accounting should be based upon the going rates and should be incorporated in the expense budgets as illustrated in Chapter 8.

Budgeting capital additions

Budgeting capital additions in nonmanufacturing situations presents essentially the same problems as those encounted in a manufacturing situation. The procedures discussed in Chapter 10 relating to budgeting capital additions are equally appropriate for retail and wholesale concerns. The capital additions budget as finally approved is incorporated into the profit plan and provides essential data for planning cash requirements and the budgeted financial statements.

Budgeting cash

In concerns of all types, budgeting the cash position throughout the budget period, and the related control of cash, are two of the more significant aspects of management planning and control. In retail and wholesale concerns particularly, these factors can be most critical because inventories of considerable value must frequently be maintained. In addition, it is not unusual to find extensive credit being granted. The development of a complete plan of operations covering a definite future period of time is essential in developing a reliable cash budget. The establishment of a line of credit with banks and other lending agencies is frequently dependent upon an adequate cash forecast supported with a well-conceived plan of operations. The cash budget in retail and wholesale concerns may be developed in a manner similar to that previously discussed and illustrated for manufacturing concerns. Control of the cash position may be exercised in a similar manner.

Budget summaries

Although some retail firms budget only sales, stock levels, and purchases, the usual procedure is to use a comprehensive budget program extending to all phases of operations. In such cases the several sub-budgets (sales, stock, purchase, expense, capital additions, cash, and so on) are summarized in budgeted income statements and balance sheets.

Budgetary control

The establishment of a realistic plan of operations constitutes one of the primary functions of management in retail and wholesale concerns. The creation of such a plan covering a definite period of time in the future is one of the best ways of assuring reasonable success for the concern. Nevertheless, it is equally true that the planning activities must be complemented with an adequate system of control, geared to the planned objectives.

A control system in all but very small operations must necessarily be based upon an efficient reporting system that provides a running account of whether or not actual operations are satisfactory. The evaluation of actual operations as the business moves through the planned period is accomplished through a comparison with budget objectives. The control reports must (a) cover all significant aspects of operations, (b) be consistent with the assigned responsibilities (organizational structure), and (c) use the management exception principle. The principles of budget control reports previously discussed are equally applicable to nonmanufacturing concerns.

NONPROFIT ORGANIZATIONS

Within recent years it has become the rule rather than the exception for *nonprofit* organizations to develop *planning budgets* for their operations and special events. Professional organizations, clubs, churches, welfare organizations, special conference groups, athletic organizations, parent-teacher groups, fraternal organizations, and other similar nonprofit groups should carefully develop a detailed budget to establish the expected (or authorized) expenditures required to carry out their programmed objectives and as a basis for planning amounts and sources of revenues necessary to support these objectives.

Planning budgets for nonprofit organizations should be developed on a program basis. Also they should be developed on a *participation* basis, that is, the chosen officers of the organization, through a series of meetings, should agree upon the general objectives and the specific programs to be undertaken. Once these basic decisions are reached, this same group should then consider the expenditure and revenue problems. The next step involves, therefore, decisions as to the amount of funds that *should* be committed to each aspect of the program. Having determined on a tentative basis the funds that should be committed, the next step for this group involves consideration of the *sources* of funds and the amount that might realistically be derived from such sources. The final, and generally most critical, step for the governing group is to balance (or reconcile) programs, expenditures, and revenues so that there is a coordinated and financially sound plan of operations (planning budget) for the organization or endeavor.

Having developed a definite program of activities and the related financial plans, the governing group may present them to the membership for approval. Developing plans in this manner, and making adequate presentation of the plans to the membership, is perhaps the most effective way of getting the enthusiasm and support of the membership in accomplishing both the broad objectives and the specific programs. Similarly, such presentations are frequently fundamental to success because they help in obtaining the required *revenues.* Obviously such groups tend to provide financial support to sound programs that they understand, rather than to vague programs about which they know little.

In order to illustrate in a general way the application of budgets to nonprofit organizations, two examples from small but representative situations are presented, viz.:

Illustration 60 shows the budget and actual results for the season for a junior league baseball program. Several aspects may be noted that indicate special adaptations to fit the particular situation. First, it was decided to budget and account on a cash basis. Second, note that each item is numbered to the left and that there are detailed schedules to support this summary report. Finally, note the *explanations* that supplement the basic data on the budget. This particular report was at the end of the season; similar reports were prepared at the end of each month and presented to the elected officers.

Illustration 61 shows the budget summary for the annual convention of a professional organization covering a three-day period. Two distinctive aspects of this budget may be noted. First, the variable budget concept is used. Note the incomes and costs are identified as to fixed and variable (rate) components. Second, by introducing this concept it was possible to develop budget estimates for various assumed registration levels. This particular feature is quite significant in planning conventions since the attendance is difficult to project. In this particular case, after observing the strong possibility of a loss if there were less than 500 registrations, the executive committee undertook an intensive effort to encourage attendance. As a result, in this particular instance the registrations were 512. Again we may note the left column suggesting the necessity for detailed supporting schedules.

		Cash Basis	
Receipts:		*Budget*	*Actual*
Acc't No.			
R-1	Concessions	$ 2,500.00	$ 2,114.42
R-2	Game collections	700.00	420.49
R-3	Special events	2,200.00	2,063.25
R-4	Sponsors	1,300.00	1,350.00
R-5	Sponsor club	2,000.00	1,750.00
R-6	Sale of signs (Total sold $2,450.00)	2,400.00	2,200.00
R-7	Funds borrowed	4,000.00	4,000.00
R-8	Pictures (net) baseball	170.00	55.85
R-9	Miscellaneous & donations	50.00	15.81
R-10	Coin purse project ($1,195.33 − $580.68)		614.65
	Total receipts	$15,320.00	$14,584.47
	Add: Beginning cash balance	140.93	140.93
	Total cash available	$15,460.93	$14,725.40

Expenditures:			
E-1	Franchise & conference	$ 55.00	$ 45.00
E-2	Insurance	700.00	433.21
E-3	Playing equipment	2,300.00	1,913.71
E-4	Field upkeep—Contract	1,000.00	1,045.00
E-5	Umpires	700.00	500.00
E-6	Concession purchases	600.00	519.03
E-7	Sign upkeep	600.00	576.00
E-8	Payment on liabilities	1,600.00	1,095.75
E-9	Field equipment purchases	1,000.00	661.00
E-10	Field improvements	5,000.00	6,817.87
E-11	Printing and mailing	250.00	164.00
E-12	Interest expense (Does not include accrued)	400.00	350.00
E-13	Miscellaneous	225.00	160.58
E-14	General field maintenance & equipment repair	950.00	398.91
	Total expenditures	$15,380.00	$14,680.06
	Ending cash balance	$ 80.93	$ 45.34

Explanations:

(a) Additional cash to be collected per attached schedule $1,260.00

(b) Unpaid liabilities per attached schedule $3,710.00

(c) See attached schedules designated by Account Number for detailed analysis of receipts and expenditures.

(d) Expenditure per boy ($14,680.06 ÷ 240 boys) $61.17 each

(e) Expenditure per boy excluding equipment purchases and field improvements ($7,201.19 ÷ 240 boys) $30.00 each

Illustration 60. *Budget Report, Nonprofit Organization.*

The Society of "XXXX"
BUDGET OF INCOME AND EXPENSE—SUMMARY
Annual Meeting of Members—June 15-17, 19XX
(Location)
(Hypothetical Figures)

Detail Schedule No.		Average Unit Rate	At Registrations Levels (expected)		
			450	500	550
	Incomes:				
I-1	Registration Fees	$ 7.50	$ 3,375	$ 3,750	$ 4,125
I-2	Social events and luncheons	36.00	16,200	18,000	19,800
I-3	Exhibitor booth rental—net	Fixed	1,500	1,500	1,500
I-4	Miscellaneous	Fixed	200	200	200
	Total incomes		$21,275	$23,450	$25,625
	Expenditures:				
E-1	Social events and luncheons	$31.00	$13,950	$15,500	$17,050
E-5	Printing, postage, art work, etc.	Fixed	2,000	2,000	2,000
E-6	Speaker expense (travel, hotel, flowers, complementary tickets, etc.)	Fixed	2,700	2,700	2,700
E-7	Public relations	Fixed	1,000	1,000	1,000
E-8	Hospitality rooms	Fixed	150	150	150
E-9	Reception committee	Fixed	100	100	100
E-10	Headquarters	Fixed	500	500	500
E-11	Pre-convention costs	Fixed	300	300	300
E-12F	Miscellaneous	Fixed	600	600	600
E-12V	Miscellaneous	$ 1.00	450	500	550
	Total expenditures		$21,750	$23,350	$24,950
	Gain (or loss)		($475)	$100	$675

Illustration 61. *Budget for Nonprofit Organization—Annual Meeting.*

As a concluding note, the preparation of a budget for nonprofit organizations, as with other types of organizations, is only the first step. The *managing* is yet to be done. The budget should be viewed as a guide and should not be used inflexibly. If unforeseen changes or events occur, appropriate action should be taken, notwithstanding the budget. Finally, subsequent to the development of the budget there must be periodic reporting, in terms of responsibility, wherein actual results are compared with budget objectives. Resulting variances should be seriously evaluated and corrective action taken when needed.

Discussion Questions

1. Outline the needs for budgeting in retail and wholesale concerns.
2. Discuss responsibility for budgeting in nonmanufacturing concerns.
3. What should be the length of the budget period in retail concerns? Discuss.
4. Define the term *merchandise budget*.
5. Outline the general procedure in developing the sales budget for a typical department store.
6. In developing the merchandise budget, why is primary consideration frequently given to stock levels, rather than to purchases?
7. What is meant by rate of stock turnover? How is the rate computed?
8. Assume the following budget data are available: Sales, $70,000; EOM stock, $120,000; Planned reductions, $3,000; BOM stock, $140,000. Compute the amount of goods that should be purchased at retail value. Explain the formula you used.
9. Define reductions. Why must they be considered in computing purchases?
10. What is meant by *open-to-buy?* How is it used?
11. Distinguish between (a) initial markup and (b) maintained markup.
12. Assuming an item costing $5.20 is to be marked up 27.5 per cent on retail, compute the selling price. Explain your computations.
13. Why is the problem of expense control specially critical in nonmanufacturing concerns?
14. Discuss the basic considerations concerning the development of an adequate system of control reports in retail and wholesale concerns.
15. Outline the principal steps in establishing a budget planning and control program for a nonprofit operation.

SEVENTEEN

Adaptation and Use of Budget

Procedures

In the preceding chapters we have emphasized the concept of comprehensive budgeting. This concept encompasses two main ideas: first is the idea that profit planning and control, to be of maximum potential, should extend to all phases of operations; second is the idea that profit planning and control should involve both the long and short run. The annual profit plan is the current year's segment of management plans. Many observers of managerial decision making have noted that short-run decisions made within a context of realistic long-run plans generally are sound decisions. On the other hand, these same observers have noted that very frequently short-run decisions made without adequate consideration of long-run consequences prove deficient in the long run. Thus some decisions that seem entirely logical when made may be most deficient when put under the scrutiny of long-run considerations. Unfortunately, short- rather than long-range considerations predominate in the decisions of many firms. One of the essential ingredients of managerial success is that the decision-making process must rest firmly on long-range considerations. A second ingredient is that decision making must operate in the context of the over-all effect on the firm, rather than on the individual segments thereof. The purpose of this final chapter is to point up some of the principal problems in applying the comprehensive budget concept to particular situations and to reemphasize some of the primary aspects of effective budget use.

Budget adaptation

One of the central problems in initiating and developing an effective budget program is that of selecting appropriate techniques and adapting them to the peculiarities of the situation. Further, as the concern grows, changes its characteristics, and becomes more complex, there is the continuing problem of discarding techniques that have lost their usefulness and replacing them with more appropriate procedures. Both the accounting and the budgeting systems must be revised as the concern changes.

It is not uncommon to find a situation in which an installed budget system does not fit the environment within the concern. This result usually occurs when a "system" that has been developed in another concern is literally transplanted without change. It is doubtful whether any two budget programs should be identical for the obvious reason that no two concerns are identical.[1]

Appropriate methods of planning sales and other revenue vary between concerns depending upon (a) certain external factors that affect the firm, (b) the internal characteristics of the firm, and (c) the status of budget education or sophistication. Likewise the approach to the determination of expense allowances necessarily should vary. Variable budget procedures for expenses do not have universal application, to be sure, but the idea of adjusting budget expense allowances to output (volume of work) should be given serious consideration by every concern. The variable budget idea may not have application with respect to all costs of operation in a concern, yet it may be particularly useful in certain areas of responsibility. Breakeven analysis may have considerable application in one firm but not in another. The design of internal accounting and budget performance reports certainly should be based upon the characteristics of the firm and the particular needs of the principal users. A profit planning and control system should not be static; for example,

[1] Marshall K. Evans, "Profit Planning," *Harvard Business Review* (July-Aug. 1959), pp. 45–54.

variable budgets and breakeven analysis may not be useful currently in a particular concern, yet five years from now they may be highly desirable. The system of budgeting sales that is appropriate today may be entirely inadequate a few years hence.

Budget installation

Budget installation can be very troublesome for a number of reasons. In the first place, there is a natural tendency on the part of many individuals, irrespective of their position in the organization, to resist change of any type. This tendency may be due to several factors such as conservatism, insecurity, lack of understanding, and fear of the unknown. Second, as a result of unfortunate misuse, budgeting has come to have bad connotations in the minds of some people. Some supervisors may think of budgeting initially as another "infernal device" through which management seeks to increase undesirable pressure. In the third place, budgeting, properly viewed, requires time and effort on the part of executives, supervisors, and foremen. These reasons make it imperative that a profit planning and control program be carefully thought out and intelligently instituted.

It has been said that a concern should not hope to develop an adequate budget program in less than two years; generally, by the end of the third year, the program should be in good shape. Although the size and characteristics of the concern are the determining factors, it may be undesirable to attempt to budget all phases of operations the first year. Sales is often one of the best areas in which to initiate budget procedures. Manufacturing firms frequently find it advisable to start with expense budgeting of factory operations. Many concerns, through necessity, have initiated budget procedures in the area of capital additions, subsequently extending budget procedures to other phases of operations. Where practicable, however, it is advisable to start on company-wide budgeting for the first year.

Once the program is started, its development must be aggressively supported by top management. Initial resistance may be overcome only through active and continuous *budget education* carried down to the lowest supervisory level. The objectives of the profit planning and control program should be made clear to executives and supervisors alike. Adequate understanding and appreciation of the program can best be accomplished through conferences and discussions aimed toward getting across the ways in which the program may not only benefit the firm but also the individual executives and supervisors themselves. Management personnel must be shown how the program may make their particular jobs easier; how they may participate in management planning; and, consequently, how they may directly contribute to the over-all success of the firm. It has been stated —and certainly it is not an overstatement—that budget installation involves approximately 25 per cent technique and 75 per cent education. A somewhat common top-management mistake is that of hiring a budget director to "come in and set up a budget program in the shortest possible time." The error is then compounded when top management fails to follow through to assure (a) a positive internal climate (b) proper line-management participation, and (c) effective budget education. In budget education the idea of some executives that "everyone but me" needs to be educated frequently must be overcome. Budget education, in most cases, should start at the very top and be carried down through the lowest level of supervision. Line executives should actively participate in conducting budget education within their particular areas of responsibility.

The way in which a budget control system is installed can have a marked effect upon its acceptance throughout the concern. Psychological factors are important. Careful planning on the part of top management prior to budget installation is most essential. It is generally desirable that a committee of top-management officials be appointed to analyze the budgetary needs of the concern, to develop specific objectives of a budget program for the concern, and to recommend an approach to budget installation. Mr. M. K. Evans, Budget Director of Westinghouse Electric Corporation, in an excellent article listed nine basic steps in budget design and installation:

1. Define the objective(s) of the installation.
2. Decide on a basic approach.
3. Analyze the situation, i.e., get the facts.
4. Design appropriate techniques and procedures.
5. Clarify line and staff responsibilities under the budget.
6. Plan the installation program.
7. Recruit and train personnel.

8. Measure and maintain the system.
9. Use the information produced.[2]

Budget use

Effective budget use depends upon (a) an appreciation of the human factor in each situation and (b) an understanding of the ways in which the budget system may be used as a tool of management. The psychology of motivation is an important aspect of managerial accounting. A budget system may partially fulfill the basic psychological necessity for group planning and also include effective control devices which may provide an incentive for individuals. Budgeting may help satisfy the fundamental psychological demand of individuals for a strong sense of purpose.[3]

Because budgets tend to point the finger at individual inefficiency, the psychological impact is considerable. If budgeting as a tool of management is used with a proper consideration for the human factors, it can be a positive factor. The point has already been made that for some individuals budgeting has a connotation of rigidity and a police type of restrictiveness; consequently, many firms do not use the term budgeting at all. On the other hand, it is generally recognized that a certain amount of discipline is good. One writer made this point as follows:

> The preparation of a formal forecast is a discipline which is good for management. The re-examination of plans and estimates required periodically forces attention to the over-all situation. Managers are constantly dealing with specific situations—"putting out brush fires" as some call it. People and crises clamor for their attention. On the other hand, next quarter's sales, or next year's capital expenditures or profits, may never come up insistently for the manager's attention unless he imposes upon himself the self-discipline of a periodic forecast. A manager never has enough time to do everything he wants to do. The periodic forecast insures

---

[2] M. K. Evans, "A Stairway to Budgetary Control," *NAA Bulletin* (Dec. 1955), p. 481.

[3] For an excellent discussion of the psychology of motivation, see Franklin A., Callaby, "Accounting for Human Nature: Management Accounting in Action," *The Accountants Journal*, England (Dec. 1955), p. 353.

appropriate priority for planning and helps to keep it from being crowded out by execution. . . any forecast should be the product of management planning as a whole and not confined to any group of management. A forecast made by the general manager alone, without participation or acceptance by the lower management levels, is of little value. It must be put together by management as a whole; it must be known to management as a whole, it must have the support of management as a whole.[4]

The above quotation provides the basis for proper use of the budget. Upon final approval of the planning budget, immediate steps should be taken to insure that all levels of management understand the operating plan as expressed in the budget. It is especially important that each member of management understand fully his responsibilities as expressed in *the profit plan*. The best way to assure adequate communication in these respects is to arrange a series of budget meetings, starting at the top-management level and continuing throughout the firm. At these meetings the *approved profit plan* is explained in detail and "sold." The controller and budget director should participate in these conferences; however, it is especially important that line management actively participate in this phase of budget education. It is through such procedures that the foundation is laid for effective use of performance reports for control purposes by those in charge of organizational units throughout the period.[5]

It is not unusual to find individuals who view budget control and cost control as one and the same thing. Although cost control is an important aspect of budgeting, budget control should involve all aspects of operations. In the preceding chapters, budgeting has been related to control of revenue, capital additions, production, costs, financing, cash, and all other aspects of operations.

Budget use should be based upon the idea that the *planning budget* represents highly desirable goals and objectives. Managerial effort should be organized and directed so that attainment of the planned objectives will be assured if at all possible. A fine, but important, distinction can be drawn between two different objectives of profit planning. These objectives are not the same,

---

[4] Joel Hunter, "Accounting in Management," *The Journal of Accountancy* (Nov. 1955), p. 64.

[5] For an excellent treatment of this idea, see M. K. Evans, "Accounting Problems in Measuring Performance by Organizational Units," *NAA Bulletin* (Aug. 1955), p. 1739.

yet they are complementary. The two objectives may be expressed as follows:

1. The planning budget represents desirable objectives which management believes can be attained—objectives to which management is willing to commit itself; and objectives toward which intelligent effort will be directed to assure reasonable attainment thereof.

2. The planning budget is significant from the management point of view in that it enables management *"to know where we are going,"* if present policies are continued.

Procedures should be developed to accommodate both of these objectives. The second objective frequently is overlooked or at least inadequately met. This objective may be largely met through the concept of *reprojection* discussed below.

Flexibility and Budget Revision. Consideration of the two objectives in the preceding paragraph leads to another important aspect of budget use, that of *flexibility.* The concept of flexibility in budgeting is rather broad. To indicate the various connotations of this term we might note the following:

(1) Variable budgets—flexibility may be introduced in cost control through use of the concept of variable or flexible budgets as discussed in Chapter 9.

(2) Continuous budgeting—this approach to budgeting, discussed in Chapter 3, is particularly conducive to flexibility.

(3) Step profit planning—Under this approach the profit plan is developed simultaneously for several levels of sales expectations.

(4) Reprojections—Flexibility may be introduced effectively by means of reprojections of plans.

(5) Revision of the profit plan—Flexibility may be introduced by a systematic reconsideration and revision of the annual profit plan.

(6) Profit plan as a guide to action—Flexibility may be introduced if management views the profit plan as a *guide to action* rather than as an inflexible limiting device.

Each of these approaches (except the variable budget concept which was treated in detail in Chapter 9) will be discussed briefly in the following paragraphs.

The continuous budgeting approach (defined on page 55) is particularly effective in introducing flexibility in the profit planning and control program. Under this approach as each period ends it is dropped from the budget and another comparable

1958 BUDGET—PRODUCT E AT VARIOUS SALES LEVELS—ANNUAL BASIS

	$11,500,000	$12,000,000	$12,500,000	$13,000,000	$13,500,000	$14,000,000	$14,500,000	$15,000,000	$15,500,000	$16,000,000
Gross sales										
Less discounts	55,200	57,600	60,000	62,400	64,700	67,100	69,500	71,900	74,400	76,800
Less royalties	131,500	137,300	142,900	148,700	154,400	160,200	165,900	171,600	177,300	183,000
Less allowances	66,300	69,100	72,100	74,900	77,900	80,700	82,600	86,500	89,300	92,200
Net sales	11,247,000	11,736,000	12,225,000	12,714,000	13,203,000	13,692,000	14,182,000	14,670,000	15,159,000	15,648,000
Cost of sales	8,775,650	9,157,200	9,536,750	9,920,300	10,301,850	10,683,400	11,064,950	11,446,400	11,827,950	12,209,500
Gross operating profit	2,471,350	2,578,808	2,686,250	2,793,700	2,901,150	3,008,600	3,117,050	3,223,600	3,331,050	3,438,500
Selling expense	980,000	980,000	980,000	980,000	980,000	980,000	980,000	980,000	980,000	980,000
Service expense	164,500	171,600	178,700	185,900	193,000	200,200	207,350	214,500	221,650	228,800
Warehouse expense	144,000	144,000	144,000	144,000	144,000	144,000	144,000	144,000	144,000	144,000
Advertising	784,076	796,576*	809,076	821,576	834,076	846,576	859,076	871,576	884,076	896,576
Commissions	38,870	40,560	42,250	43,940	45,630	47,320	49,010	50,700	52,390	54,080
Freight out (net applicable)										
Bad debts	55,200	57,600	60,000	62,400	64,800	67,200	69,600	72,000	74,400	76,300
Engineering and product design	212,000	212,000	212,000	212,000	212,000	212,000	212,000	212,000	212,000	212,000
Total expense	2,378,646	2,402,336	2,426,025	2,449,816	2,473,506	2,497,296	2,521,036	2,544,776	2,568,516	2,592,256
Division profit or loss	92,704	176,464	260,224	343,884	427,644	511,304	596,014	678,824	762,534	846,244
Interest on investment	264,000	264,000	264,000	264,000	264,000	264,000	264,000	264,000	264,000	264,000
Company profit or loss	$ (171,294)	$ (87,536)	$ (3,776)	$ 79,884	$ 163,644	$ 247,304	$ 332,014	$ 414,824	$ 498,534	$ 582,244

*Calculation Per Formula in Exhibit 5
$12,000,000 × 2.50% (Variable) Plus $496,576 (Fixed) = $796,576

Illustration 62. *Step Profit Planning.*

1958 BUDGET—PRODUCT E AT VARIOUS GROSS SALES LEVELS—FOUR-WEEK PERIOD

	$600,000	$800,000	$1,000,000	$1,200,000	$1,400,000	$1,600,000	$1,800,000	$2,000,000	$2,200,000	$2,400,000
Gross sales										
Less discounts	2,880	3,840	4,800	5,760	6,720	7,680	8,640	9,600	10,560	11,520
Less royalties	6,840	9,120	11,400	13,680	15,960	18,240	20,520	22,800	25,080	27,360
Less allowances	3,480	4,640	5,800	6,960	8,120	9,200	10,440	11,600	12,760	13,920
Net sales	586,800	782,400	978,000	1,173,600	1,369,200	1,564,000	1,760,400	1,956,000	2,151,000	2,347,200
Cost of sales	457,860	610,480	763,100	915,720	1,068,340	1,220,960	1,373,580	1,526,200	1,678,820	1,831,440
Gross operating profit	128,940	171,920	214,900	257,880	300,860	343,840	386,820	429,800	472,780	515,760
Selling expense	78,600	78,600	78,600	78,600	78,600	78,600	78,600	78,600	78,600	78,600
Service expense	6,840	9,120	11,400	13,680	15,960	18,240	20,520	22,800	25,080	27,360
Warehouse expense	11,520	11,520	11,520	11,520	11,520	11,520	11,520	11,520	11,520	11,520
Advertising	54,724	59,724*	64,724	69,724	74,724	79,724	84,724	89,724	94,724	99,724
Commissions	2,028	2,704	3,380	4,056	4,732	5,408	6,084	6,760	7,436	8,112
Freight-out (net applicable)										
Bad debts	2,886	3,848	4,810	5,772	6,734	7,696	8,658	9,620	10,582	11,544
Engineering and product design	16,980	16,980	16,980	16,980	16,980	16,980	16,980	16,980	16,980	16,980
Total expense	173,578	182,496	191,414	200,332	209,250	218,168	227,086	236,004	244,922	253,840
Division profit or loss	(44,638)	(10,576)	23,486	57,548	91,610	125,672	159,734	193,796	227,856	261,920
Interest on investment	21,120	21,120	21,120	21,120	21,120	21,120	21,120	21,120	21,120	21,120
Company profit or loss	$(65,758)	$(31,696)	$ 2,366	$ 36,428	$ 70,490	$ 104,562	$ 138,614	$ 172,676	$ 206,738	$ 240,800

*Calculation Per Formula in Exhibit 5
$800,000 × 2.50% (Variable) Plus 4/50 of $495,576 = $59,724

Source: "Responsibility Reporting," a mimeographed booklet, edited by Kenneth S. Axelson, Partner (New York: Peat, Marwick, Mitchell & Co., Jan. 1961), p. 133.

Illustration 62. Step Profit Planning (continued).

period added. For example, one outstanding company operates under a twelve-month profit plan detailed by month for the up-coming quarter, and detailed by quarter for the remaining nine months of the twelve-month period. As a quarter passes, it is dropped; then the next quarter is replanned by month and another quarter in the future is added. Through this approach the company is *always* looking forward for three months in detail and nine more months by quarter. The need for budget revision is eliminated and the opportunity for replanning is routine on a quarterly basis. This is a particularly effective approach to profit planning and control.

Step profit planning is used by only a small number of firms because of the amount of detail required. Under this approach flexibility is introduced by developing the planning budget for several levels of sales activity rather than for the projected level.[6] The central problem in this approach is whether to develop a *complete* profit plan for several levels of activity or to develop only certain parts of the complete profit plan. For example, one company develops a complete profit plan at the *budgeted level of sales*, but develops income statements (only) for several levels of sales above and below that expected. Illustration 62 (page 452) indicates one adaptation of step profit planning.

A system of *reprojections* is used by some companies within the framework of the annual profit plan (periodic budget approach). Under this approach, as practiced by one company, the annual profit plan is not revised (except under extreme circumstances); however, each division manager (having profit responsibility) is required to submit by the end of the *current month* a reprojection of his expectations for the following month. Should this reprojection be materially different in any respect from the original profit plan a complete explanation of the reasons is required. In addition to flexibility it should be noted that this procedure is used by the management for a very specific and important purpose. The purpose is to provide top management with data concerning all developments expected in the immediate future that may have a significant financial effect. It puts management in a position to take effective *advance* action relative to a dynamic situation. Significantly, it emphasizes

[6] F. E. Baridon, "Profit and Loss Budget by Volume," *NAA Bulletin* (Nov. 1960), pp. 83–89.

that control must be exercised *prior to, or at the point of,*
action rather than after the fact. This concept thus meets a need
that the annual profit plan and the end-of-the-month performance
reports do not fully satisfy.

A second approach to reprojection is similar to that outlined
immediately above. The difference is that the reprojection is
made at the end of each month (or quarter) for the *remaining*
months covered by the annual profit plan. For example, at the
end of August a reprojection is made for the remaining four
months of the year and added to the *actual* for the first eight
months in order to provide management with an estimate of
"how we will probably come out by year end." A recent study
noted the significance of this procedure which was referred to
as *Estimation of Future Performance;* to quote:[7]

> Since the budget is an instrument of both planning and control,
> provision should be made for periodic examination of *performance*
> against budget goals. The interviews revealed two types of analyses
> of performance. One type of analysis is concerned with an evaluation
> of *past* performance compared with the original budget or plan of
> operations. The other analysis relates to actual results to date
> coupled with an estimation of *future* performance to determine the
> probable outcome for the period in view of new developments
> originally unforeseen. Both analyses usually are made on a periodic
> (monthly or quarterly) basis. The latter, in effect, constitutes a
> reexamination of the primary economic factors in the light of known
> conditions to date and reestimates of the future, to recast probable
> results for the original planning period.

The concept was indicated with respect to sales taken from
the same source is shown in Illustrations 63 and 64. The report
further noted that "the procedure of estimating future performance may be applied to all aspects of the plan of operations;
however, particular application noted relates to sales, cash,
capital additions, and profits."

It appears that the concept of reprojection has been neglected
in the literature despite the fact that this is a very significant
and sophisticated aspect of effective profit planning and control.

---

[7] B. H. Sord and G. A. Welsch, *Business Budgeting; A Survey of Management*
Planning and Control Practices (New York: Controllership Foundation, Inc.,
1958), pp. 253–257.

ILLUSTRATIVE DATA FOR ESTIMATION OF FUTURE
PERFORMANCE

(Illustrative Data simplified)

	Plan of Operations (Sales Budget)		Actual		Re-evaluation	
	Monthly	*Cumulative*	*Monthly*	*Cumulative*	*Monthly*	*Cumulative*
Jan.	10	10	14	14		
Feb.	14	24	16	30		
March	16	40	12	42		
April	10	50	7	49		
May	20	70	19	68		
June	40	110	32	100		
July	30	140	28	128		
Aug.	10	150	7	135		
Sept.	10	160			13	148
Oct.	20	180			20	168
Nov.	40	220			34	202
Dec.	20	240			23	225
Totals	240	240				225

**Illustration 63. *Illustrative Data for Estimation
of Future Performance.***

In case the operating picture of the company is changed
materially during the year, and periodic budgeting is being
followed (see page 55), complete *revision* of the profit plan
may be in order. Such circumstances may be due, for example,
to the rearrangement of internal organizational structure, changes
in manufacturing methods, strikes, fire or storm damages, unexpected wage increases, and fluctuation of general economic
conditions. Revision may involve minor changes in the budget
for the remainder of the year, or significant revision. If significant changes occur, the profit plan should be revised unless the
end of the year is near. Complete revision would involve considerable work and would follow normal planning budget procedures.

It may develop, during the year, that the original plan of
operations was either too optimistic or too pessimistic. To allow
for this, many companies review the profit plan at the beginning
of each quarter to determine whether or not it should be revised.
In addition, division heads generally may initiate budget revisions
if they know of future changes in the operating situation relative
to their divisions. Requests for revision should follow the normal
line channels, finally coming before the appropriate management
level for consideration and final decision. *As a general policy,
budget revisions should be held to a minimum.* It is frequently

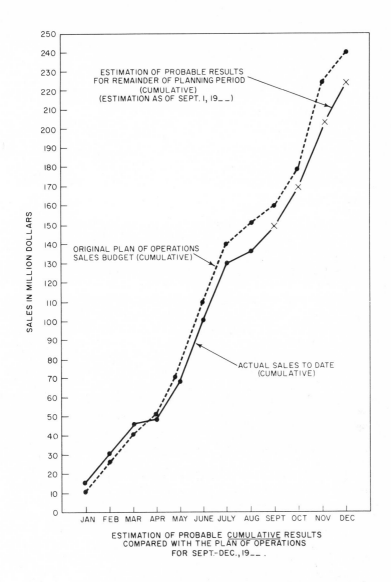

ESTIMATION OF PROBABLE RESULTS
FOR REMAINDER OF PLANNING PERIOD
(CUMULATIVE)
(ESTIMATION AS OF SEPT. I, 19_ _)

ORIGINAL PLAN OF OPERATIONS
SALES BUDGET (CUMULATIVE)

ACTUAL SALES TO DATE
(CUMULATIVE)

ESTIMATION OF PROBABLE CUMULATIVE RESULTS
COMPARED WITH THE PLAN OF OPERATIONS
FOR SEPT.-DEC., 19_ _ .

Illustration 64. *Estimation of Future Performance*

457

desirable, in the case of minor changes, to let the effect show up on the budget reports as *explainable* variations rather than to go to the trouble of revising the budget.

If *variable budgets* are being used, they should be kept in line with current conditions and operating policies, because they are used throughout the year to determine adjusted budget allowances for cost-control purposes.

Although the profit plan should be viewed as a *guide to action*, it should not be viewed as an inflexible plan. Obviously, when the profit plan is constructed, some significant events cannot be anticipated, nor can those that may be anticipated always be accurately evaluated far in advance. Current managerial decisions and efforts must be conditioned by current events and conditions, as well as by the original plans expressed in the profit plan.

When conditions have materially changed, the plan of operations should be adjusted accordingly. If favorable opportunities arise which were not anticipated in the original plan of operations, this fact should be no deterrent to immediate managerial action to take advantage of the situation. Likewise, should conditions change so that it appears undesirable to carry out certain planned projects such as a costly capital addition, there should be no hesitancy to make the indicated decision, irrespective of the budget program. All of these suggestions imply that the budget should not be viewed as a rigid, inflexible plan, but rather as a *flexible plan* that should be adjusted as circumstances warrant. On the other hand, it is essential that the budget not be changed with every whim, nor that it be viewed lightly as expressive of desirable goals to be attained. When viewed as a desirable goal of operations, to be adjusted when circumstances warrant, the budget becomes an important tool in the management kit that makes possible effective management by exception.

In the preceding paragraphs six approaches to achieving flexibility in the application of profit planning and control have been suggested and discussed briefly. Although each approach was considered separately we do not mean to imply that one should be used to the exclusion of the others. In order to introduce flexibility into the budget process, and to help attain the budget's full potential, not one but several of these approaches should normally be adapted and used by a particular firm. We cannot overemphasize the fact that budgets do not manage; only people manage.

Human relations aspects of budgeting

We have continually emphasized that the successful use of budgets rests heavily upon the application of good human relationships. The problem of good human relations is certainly a critical one in modern industry.[8] Many of the shortcomings attributed to budgets are due to poor human relations and improper attitudes on the part of management. In the case of weak management, techniques such as budgeting frequently are used as the "whipping boy." Obviously a technique by itself can do nothing—the individuals using it determine its good or bad administration. Sound budgeting must be based upon "such fundamentals as recognition of accomplishment, consideration for the rights of individuals, fair play—in other words, enlightened relationships among people."[9]

The way in which top management views budgeting is of utmost importance. As one prominent writer has expressed it:

> In exploring budgeting principles as they relate to people, the first consideration should be the motivation for the budget system. Why have one at all? Is the budget a part of a system of over-all planning, in order that all concerned may have a measure of the amounts to be spent, and in order that action may be by design rather than by expediency? Or is the budget a pressure device designed to goad people into greater efforts? It takes a little soul-searching to determine honestly which of these concepts represents the position of a particular management.[10]

In Chapter 2, the essentials to successful budgeting were discussed. Budget use depends upon the degree to which these essentials are observed.

[8] Harold Leavitt, *Managerial Psychology* (Chicago: The University of Chicago Press, 1958).

[9] James L. Peirce, "The Budget Comes of Age," *Harvard Business Review* (May-June 1954), p. 58. Note: This is one of the outstanding statements concerning the fundamentals of budgeting that has been written in recent years. The reader is urged to obtain a copy of it for careful study.

[10] Peirce, *op. cit.*, p. 59.

Another important aspect of successful budget practice and use is a careful distinction between staff and line responsibilities. The controller and budget director are staff personnel, and as such they are concerned principally with service. Staff personnel should not attempt, nor give the impression of attempting, to usurp line authority. A misconception of the function of the controller and budget director in their accounting and budgeting activities frequently creates friction. Staff personnel should not be asked, nor should they take it upon themselves, to exercise authority over operating (line) personnel. The controller and budget director should not develop the profit plan because this is strictly a line function. Neither should the controller or budget director take operating personnel to task for unfavorable results related to the budget. The duties of the budget director have been previously outlined; basically they involve responsibility for design and direction of the budget program, but certainly include no responsibility for enforcing the budget. In this connection it is important that we make a clearcut distinction between (a) enforcing the budget and (b) reporting actual results compared with budget objectives. The controller and budget director are responsible for reporting to all levels of operating management the results of operations related to budget plans. Corrective action resulting from either favorable or unfavorable results are strictly line functions. The controller or budget director should not allow himself to be put in the position of (a) approving budgets or (b) taking line action concerning efficient or inefficient operating results outside his particular department. The controller and budget director should not be responsible for cost control and reduction; rather they may be properly charged with the responsibility for designing an effective system of cost control. In the final analysis line executives and supervisors should be charged with the direct responsibility for cost control and reduction. A careful distinction between line and staff is essential to good management; the distinction must not only be drawn by top management, but there must also be assurance that the distinction is being *practiced* throughout the firm. The wise controller and budget director will insist that responsibilities for budget planning and control be carefully specified and formalized in written instructions to be distributed to all supervisory personnel. A company budget manual is an important vehicle for disseminating general budget responsibilities and policies.

The following principal points have been listed as especially important in establishing a sound budget program based on enlightened human relations:

1. Establish your budget system on the highest possible level of motivation.
2. Anchor your budgeting firmly in a foundation of company planning.
3. Establish the meaning of control, and then put it into practice.
4. Insist on clear-cut organizational structure.
5. Arrange for good, common sense accounting and complete, simple, and prompt explanations of the content of the items.
6. In the field of cost control, use your budget as a tool to be placed in your foremen's hands—not as a club to be held over their heads.
7. Insure the active participation of top management.
8. See that the controller and his staff express the correct attitude for the responsibility they undertake with respect to budgets. It is the controller's job to establish, maintain, and coordinate a budgetary system—in fact a complete system of planning and control. But this work must be accomplished through authorized management. He must not enforce his instructions nor issue orders.[11]

Machine and computer applications in budgeting

The development of machine accounting methods and the application of computers in the development and processing of data has led a number of concerns to adaptation of these techniques to certain aspects of the budget process. The replacement of manual procedures and computations by these new methods is significant. It is not unusual to find companies that have "computerized" their budgeting; a few are experimenting with the adaptation of these methods to long-range planning problems.

In viewing the budget process, as in accounting, one quickly observes the necessity for (a) testing the financial effect of numerous alternatives, and (b) processing large quantities of data. The modern computers and tabulating equipment are especially useful for these two purposes. The computer may be thought of as a machine that can perform arithmetical calculations in tremendous quantities at fantastic speeds. It can retain

11 Peirce, *op. cit.*, pp. 64-66.

or remember vast quantities of data. On the other hand, the computer can only do what it is told to do—that is, there must be a programmed input which tells the machine what data to select and what operations to perform on the selected data. Thus we have two basic sets of input data: (a) programming input (instructions) and (b) basic data to be used by the computer in connection with the programmed instructions. The latter data are enhanced by the machine only to the extent that mathematics can improve it. Fundamentally, the output data can be no better than the basic input data and the programmed instructions. Tabulating equipment is particularly useful for processing budget data because complete budget schedules can be printed directly. For example, one company reported one of their procedures as follows:[12]

The following information is entered on the tabulating card:

Detail	Source of Data
Sales quantity	Sales forecast
Bulk standard cost	Production cost standard
Bulk cost at plant budget unit	Plant estimate of cost
Plant budget packing unit	Plant estimate of cost
Plant budget shipping unit	Plant estimate of cost
Interdivision profit paid	Analysis of interdivision products consumed

After the above information has been entered, the cards are forwarded to the tabulating department for key-punching and the preparation of the cost of sales tabulation. The cost of sales tabulation, prepared on an I.B.M. 604 computer, provides the following ten-column information on each product for which a quantity was forecast:

1. Month	6. Packing expense amount
2. Quantity	7. Shipping expense amount
3. Net sales amount	8. Interdivision profit paid
4. Standard bulk cost amount	9. Totals of Columns 4 to 7
5. Budget bulk cost amount	10. Gross profit—Columns 3 minus 9

Electronic data processing (EDP) may be particularly useful in budgeting by (a) handling the burden of mass calculations, (b) reducing the time span required for such calculations, (c) computing the probable effects of numerous alternatives and (d) providing more time for executive consideration of the basic decisions underlying the budget. On the other hand, several

---

[12] Joseph M. Palecek, "Machine Accounting Tabulations for Budgetary Planning," *NAA Bulletin* (November 1960), pp. 80–81.

disadvantages may be cited, viz.: (a) equipment cost that is prohibitive for the smaller firms, (b) tendency of the mathematical exactness of the results to restrict the imagination of the planners, (c) the necessity to follow "exact rules of the game," (d) the cost of programming, and (e) the shortage of qualified computer experts. Despite these disadvantages, computer applications in the area of managerial profit planning and control are particularly significant and, consequently, will receive increasing attention and use.

Prior to efforts to adapt machine data processing techniques, the budget program should be well organized and established. In order to indicate in a simple way the application of machine data processing, we may consider the continuing illustrative case (The Superior Manufacturing Company). An initial step would be to divide the process of developing the *annual profit plan* into sequential phases along the following lines:

Phase 1—Sales budgeting and manufacturing planning
Phase 2—Expense budget development (including the input of variable budget formulae)
Phase 3—Cash planning, capital additions, and depreciation
Phase 4—Preparation of budgeted financial statements
Phase 5—Preparation of monthly performance reports

Phase 1 is sufficiently detailed in Illustration 65 to indicate the general procedures. In connection with this illustration it should be clear that fundamentally the *basic input budget data* that represent the plans, objectives, and policies of the management must be developed as discussed in the preceding chapters. In other words the basic decisions, judgments, and alternative choices must be made by the management irrespective of the machines. The illustration also indicates the time-saving potentials in manipulating the mass of details involved.

Budgets related to accounting

Accounting and budgeting are significant managerial tools of communication. Communication is achieved only if the one receiving the information understands it. Adequate understanding of accounting and budget reports is essential to effective management in modern industry. This fact places a heavy responsibility upon those who are responsible for the accounting and budget functions. To develop accounting and budgeting systems that

SCHEDULE NO.	INPUT DATA	SCHEDULE NO.	OUTPUT DATA
	Sales quantities budgeted (by product & district)	1	Sales budget summary
	Budgeted unit sales price	21	Sales by product, by district, by time period
	Initial inventory Inventory levels (or days supply or turnover) and Production limits	2	Production budget summary
		22	Production budget, by product, by time period
	Units of raw material required, by product	3	Materials budget summary
		24	Materials required by product (unit only)
	Price per unit of raw material	25	Materials required by department
	Initial raw material inventory	4	Purchases budgeted summary
		26	Purchases budgeted detailed
	Inventory levels	28	Cost of materials required for production
		29	Cost of materials required for production summary
	Standard labor time (hours)	30 & 31	Direct labor budget
	Average rate per hour	5	Direct labor budget—summary
32 & 33	Variable expense budgets (manufacturing)	35	Expense budgets, service departments
	Budgeted direct repair hours	36	Expense budgets, producing departments
34	Budgeted kilowatt hours Budget of occupancy costs	7	Factory expense budget summary
		37	Budgeted overhead distribution sheet
		38	Manufacturing overhead applied to production
	Overhead percentage allocation	39	Manufacturing overhead — under- or over-applied
			Statement of gross margins

Illustration 65. Phase 1—Mechanized Sales and Manufacturing Cost Planning

will effectively serve management, there must be a clear conception of the methods and problems of management. This additional requirement places a responsibility upon the accountant to inform himself of managerial techniques, and especially of the many tools of scientific management.

An effective financial control system should be built around certain well-known techniques appropriately adapted for the particular situation. Among the principal techniques of financial control are the following:

1. Planning budget procedures
2. Variable expense budget procedures
3. Historical cost systems
   a. Job-order
   b. Process
   c. Others
4. Standard cost systems
5. Direct cost systems
6. Breakeven analysis
7. Return on investment and other ratio analyses
8. Special cost and financial analyses

Reports to management are one of the more critical problems involved in developing an effective system of financial control. A perfect system of control is ineffective unless there is timely and effective communication through the medium of reports—written, graphic, and oral. Information supplied to management must be accurate; however, this requirement should not preclude the inclusion of reasonable estimates. It has been appropriately stated that "the accuracy which management requires is only that which permits it to reach sound conclusions and make sound decisions." Adherence to this idea by accountants will generally make possible timely and effective internal managerial reports. Internal reports must be completely divorced from reports for external purposes, because the objectives involved are totally different.

Discussion Questions

1. Company X hired John Doe as budget supervisor to "install a budget system." John had been assistant budget director for Company Y and planned to install a system identical to that of Company Y. Discuss.

2. Discuss the necessity for continuous development and change in a budget program for a particular firm.

3. What are the principal problems connected with budget installation in a firm?

4. Why is it essential that once a budget program is initiated, the program be aggressively pushed by top management?

5. Discuss the importance of budget education in situations in which a budget program is being initiated.

6. Who should participate in the budget education program? As discussion leaders? As participants?

7. What are the principal factors in effective budget use?

8. Discuss the problem of budget flexibility as related to budget use.

9. From the budgeting point of view, what is the importance of a careful distinction between line and staff responsibilities?

10. Discuss the implications of the statement: "The accuracy which management requires is only that which permits it to reach sound conclusions and make sound decisions."

Problems and Cases

Chapter 1

1-1. THE TEXMO SERVICE COMPANY performs services for the oil industry. Texmo is classified as a medium-sized firm and has been in operation since 1948. The firm operates in the United States and Canada.

Operations at the field level are under the supervision of division managers who usually are engineers. The typical division covers a wide territory, the extent of the territory depending upon the amount of oil exploration and production activities within it. For example, one state is divided into three divisions whereas another division encompasses two states. Similarly, the amount and type of equipment used in a division depends upon the amount of activity in the area and the characteristics of that activity. For example, a district involved in production requires somewhat different services than a district involved in exploration.

Each month's activities are reported on the basis of the (a) number of jobs by type, (b) total revenue by type of job, and (c) average revenue per job. Expenses are reported by division and by type of job.

Prior to each six-months' period, each division manager is required to prepare a budget (see Exhibit 1). At the end of each month a report is prepared for each division comparing budget (as revised by higher management) with actual (see Exhibit 2).

In discussing the procedure, one division manager commented: "The operating report is not fair as far as I am concerned. For example, if my jobs are above budget, which is a good thing, my expenses show unfavorable variations against my original estimates. On the other hand, if my jobs are down by say 10 per cent, my expense allowances are cut 10 per cent. Can't we do something about this?"

Required:

Discuss the problems posed. Give your recommendations and the basis for them.

The Texmo Service Company

Six-Month Budget for the Period _____ to _____

Division _____

Manager _____

Approved _____

Date _____

Particulars	Jan.	Feb.	Mar.	Apr.	May	June	Total
Revenues:							
Type X jobs — No.							
$ Amount							
Type Y jobs — No.							
$ Amount							
Total jobs — No.							
$ Amount							
Av. per job							
Expenses:							
Type X jobs (Itemized)							
Type Y jobs (Itemized)							
Division overhead (Itemized)							
Total expenses							
Division net revenue							
Per cent on total revenue							

468

Exhibit 1.

The Texmo Service Company

Operating Report, dated _____

Division _____

Manager _____

Particulars	Month of _____			Cumulative _____ months to date _____		
	Actual	Budget	Variations	Actual	Budget	Variations
Revenues:						
Type X jobs — No.						
$ Amount						
Type Y jobs — No.						
$ Amount						
Total jobs — No.						
$ Amount						
Av. per job						
Expenses:						
Type X jobs (Itemized)						
Type Y jobs (Itemized)						
Division overhead (Itemized)						
Total expenses						
Division net revenue						
Per cent on total revenue						

Exhibit 2.

1-2. KRANDALL-KNOX COMPANY. Samuel Krandall, who had been for a number of years selling a line of supplies used by hotels, motels, and similar establishments, had managed to save a tidy amount which he invested in common stocks. At the age of forty-four, Sam, with his brother-in-law Harry Knox, decided to open a small wholesale distribution firm in another state (where Knox resided). In 1952 the Krandall-Knox partnership was formed to distribute a line of supplies similar to that sold by Krandall over the years. Sam invested $25,000 and Harry invested $10,000. Two salesmen were employed initially. Sam was to sell and to work directly with the salesmen in developing statewide distribution. Harry was to do the purchasing, shipping, and other administrative duties.

The firm was rather successful, as a result principally of Sam's work with the sales force, as well as the fact that the chief competitor was an old "family" corporation operated by two men who had married the daughters of the founder. Harry believed the competitor still operated "in the horse and buggy days," and he was about right.

Within ten years Krandall-Knox had grown substantially. The following is indicative of the growth at the end of the first, fifth, and tenth years:

	First Year	Fifth Year	Tenth Year
Home office employees	2	4	14
Sales force	3	8	18
General employees	0	1	2
Total assets	$27,500	$ 60,000	$240,000
Sales dollars	34,000	110,000	480,000
Partners' salaries	12,000	20,000	36,000
Income (after salaries)	($7,500)	4,200	14,500

In accordance with the partnership agreement, an annual audit was prepared by an independent C.P.A. After submission of the last audit report the C.P.A. handed Mr. Knox a separate memorandum. In it the C.P.A. noted the profit trend and other data relating to internal efficiencies. The memorandum suggested that, in view of the size of the firm, serious consideration be given to establishing a profit planning and control program. The memorandum stated that such a program could be particularly effective in (a) setting prices, (b) increasing sales volume, (c) controlling expenses, and (d) managing inventory. The memorandum noted that inventory control appeared to be a serious problem in the firm.

Mr. Knox was impressed with the suggestions: "Sam, I believe the C.P.A. has something; why don't we get a program started right away. Our profit margin certainly is shrinking." "Well, I don't know, Harry; I'd have to oppose a budget if that is what they mean. The company I used to sell for had a budget and they were always hounding me on the expense budget and sales quota budget. I didn't need a budget. If I could have saved the time and worry, I could have sold even more," was Sam's reply.

Required:

(a) Analyze the situation.
(b) Identify the central problem or problems.
(c) Provide recommendations with the basis therefor.

1-3. THE SIMPLEX CORPORATION sells two similar products—
Super and Super D. The company estimated that, aside from over-all
volume increases, an increase in sales of one product would, on a unit
basis, proportionately decrease the sales of the other product. Management is considering two possible alternatives for profit planning purposes,
viz.: (1) push Super sales or (2) push Super D sales. The following
budget estimates have been prepared:

	Super	*Super D*
Unit sales price	$10.00	$13.00
Fixed overhead ($120,000 allocated on a 1:3 ratio)	1.00	3.00
Unit variable cost of sales	6.00	7.00
Sales commissions (20% of sales)	2.00	2.60
Net profit per unit	$ 1.00	$ .40

Required:

(a) How many units of Super and Super D were used in computing
the above budget estimates?
(b) Compute the budgeted gain or loss in this case.
(c) Based on the data given, what alternative should management
select? Support your decision with figures and appropriate comments.

1-4. THE LAMAR AIR CONDITIONING SALES COMPANY sells
residential and industrial air conditioning units in a twenty-county area
in one of the midwest states. The units are purchased from three different manufacturers and are sold direct to contractors and users. Company
salesmen call on potential buyers, the territory being divided into five
sales districts. The following data were developed at the end of May,
19B.

SALES REPORT

	ACTUAL SALES		Year to Date	
District	*May 19A*	*May 19B*	*19A*	*19B*
1	$43,000	$47,000	$130,000	$135,000
2	56,000	57,000	165,000	164,000
3	37,000	35,000	113,000	110,000
4	76,000	79,000	220,000	227,000
5	62,000	60,000	190,000	191,000

DISTRICT SALES EXPENSE REPORT

ACTUAL EXPENSES

District	May 19A	May 19B	Year to Date 19A	Year to Date 19B
1	$ 4,500	$ 4,800	$ 15,000	$ 18,000
2	5,400	5,600	16,000	17,000
3	3,800	3,500	14,000	11,000
4	7,200	7,400	19,000	20,000
5	6,100	5,800	21,000	22,000

BUDGET REPORT

District	Budgeted Sales May 19B	Budgeted Sales Year to Date	Budgeted Expenses May 19B	Budgeted Expenses Year to Date
1	$46,000	$133,000	$ 4,900	$ 17,000
2	60,000	170,000	5,700	18,000
3	32,000	105,000	3,200	10,000
4	82,000	230,000	7,000	18,000
5	60,000	190,000	5,700	23,000

During the past year the above data were reported essentially in the form shown above. As a member of the newly established controller's staff you have been asked to design an appropriate report form for top management, summarizing the sales volume and related expenses by district, and emphasizing the exception principle. Recast the above data in your recommended format. Also provide narrative comments pointing up strong and weak performances for each district. Be prepared to defend your format and narrative comments

Chapter 2

2-1. THE SNYDER SERVICE COMPANY was organized as a corporation by eight contributors, one of whom had acted as promoter and who subsequently served as general manager. The company was organized to render a particular service. This service involved local business enterprises and varied somewhat from client to client. The price charged for the service varied accordingly. Each separate job was priced as a unit. One client might use the service a number of times during the year with varying requirements and charges.

The Snyder Company operated in an area having a population of approximately 200,000. There were two competitors in the area who had been in business for over ten years. Although there was a limit to the total demand for the service, it was felt by the organizers that (a) demand above that currently being met by the competitors could be generated, and (b) that some business could be taken away from the competitors who were moderately successful. The organizers were firmly convinced that quality of service would be the key to success.

The company obtained a charter authorizing 10,000 shares of $5 par value stock. Each shareholder invested $3,000 in cash, receiving in return 600 shares of stock. The remaining shares were held as unissued. The by-laws carried a provision that in case any shareholder desired to sell shares, the shares would have to be offered first to the corporation and second to existing shareholders.

The manager proceeded to rent especially desirable space somewhat in excess of immediate needs. He also purchased top quality furniture and equipment. All of this represented a substantial investment. Initially, five individuals were employed in addition to the general manager. Several of the shareholders (all of whom were on the board of directors) were concerned about the overhead and other costs that would have to be met every month.

During the first year of operations the board met about every sixty days. Being rather busy with their own firms they gave relatively little attention to this "side" investment. The manager gave an oral report at each meeting concerning operations and business done; generally, he painted an optimistic picture. A local C.P.A. firm was engaged to prepare the tax returns.

At the end of the first year the C.P.A. was directed, in accordance with the by-laws, to prepare an audited financial report for the board. The audit report came as a considerable shock to the board because it showed a net loss approximating 20 per cent of the original investment. In addition, the firm was in debt up to approximately 40 per cent of the original investment. Accounts receivable were relatively high. The board immediately considered two alternatives: (a) close the business and take their loss (assets on hand including receivables could be liquidated for approximately 30 per cent of the original investment), or (b) borrow or invest another $6,000 and continue the business. There was considerable opposition to the latter alternative. After a rather lengthy discussion it was decided that outside advice should be sought concerning the alternatives. A consultant was engaged and within two weeks he made the following recommendations:

a. That the business be continued
b. That a strict system of profit planning and contol be adopted and an appropriate accounting system be used
c. That the general manager and his assistant (advised by the consultant) draw up a detailed monthly budget for the next twelve months
d. That the manager and his assistant be paid a monthly base salary of one-half that paid during the past year
e. That the manager and his assistant be given a monthly bonus computed by deducting expenses for the month from the cash collections for the month; negative bonuses were to be deducted from the following month's bonus.

The board approved this proposal and directed that the profit plan be developed. The next day the three designated individuals completed the plan which included a budgeted income statement (Exhibit 1) and a budget of cash flow (Exhibit 2).

In developing the budget the first question asked the consultant was, "How do we proceed?" The consultant suggested that the first step should be to budget income, forgetting about expenses and cash for the moment. The next question was, "Should we be optimistic or pessimistic in estimating jobs and income?" The reply: "Neither, we should budget realistically because...."

Upon completion of the revenue estimates, expenses were estimated, again "realistically." "Now," the consultant said, "let's see what the difference is month by month." The results (profits) were quite disappointing and would not be acceptable to the board.

The next step suggested by the consultant was, "Let's see what we can do 'realistically' about both revenues and expenses." After considerable discussion it was decided that little could be done about the revenue estimates, but approximately $450 per month could be taken out of expenses without significantly affecting operations.

Two telephone extensions could be removed, one employee dropped, advertising cut, free meals and drinks to various individuals stopped, travel reduced, and one room of office space subleased. For the first time the general manager analyzed the expense structure in terms of how revenues would be affected.

Next, the cash flow budget was developed, anticipating a $6,000 loan. With reasonable restraint, progress in the year ahead appeared to be possible.

The board adopted the profit plan including a monthly performance reporting system (Exhibits 3 and 4).

At the end of the second year the company reported the following:

a.	Revenue—Jobs	1% below budget
	—$ Amount	9% above budget
b.	Expenses	12% below budget
c.	Cash	2% above budget
d.	Reduction of debt	$1,500
e.	Accounts receivable	40% reduction from beginning of year

Required:

(a) Be prepared to discuss all aspects of this case with particular attention to:
  1. The recommendations of the consultant,
  2. The size of the firm, and
  3. Evaluation of the format of the various exhibits.
(b) What additional recommendations would you have made? Why?

The Snyder Service Company, Incorporated

BUDGETED INCOME STATEMENT

For the period September 1, 19A to August 31, 19B

	September	October	November	December	January	July	August	Year
REVENUE:								
Service jobs—Number								
—Dollar amount								
Miscellaneous								
Total								
EXPENSES:								
1. Accounting								
2. Advertising								
3. Bank charges								
4. Depreciation and amortization								
5. Dues and subscriptions								
6. Public relations								
7. Interest								
8. Machine rent								
9. Operating supplies								
10. Rent								
11. Repairs								
12. Payroll taxes								
13. Telephone								
14. Travel								
15. Part-time help								
16. Postage								
17. Licenses, fees, and franchise tax								
18. Fidelity bond expense								
19. Taxes								
20. Miscellaneous expense								
Total expenses								
Balance to cover salaries, debt, and dividends								
Base salaries								
Balance								
Bonus								
To retained earnings								

Exhibit 2.

The Snyder Service Company, Incorporated
BUDGETED CASH FLOW

	September	October	November	December	January	July	August	Year
Cash position—beginning								
Cash provided:								
Net income*								
Add: Depreciation and amortization								
Increase in accruals								
Increase in payables								
Miscellaneous								
Total cash provided								
Cash applied:								
Capital additions								
Increase in receivables								
Increase in prepayments								
Payments on long-term debt								
Tax payments								
Dividends								
Bonus payments								
Miscellaneous								
Total cash payments								
Cash position—ending								
Increase (decrease) in cash position								

* "To retained earnings" from Exhibit 1.

Exhibit 3.

The Snyder Service Company, Incorporated

FINANCIAL REPORT
April 30, 19B

	Month of April		Cumulative September 1, 19A to April 30, 19B	
	Profit plan	*Actual*	*Profit plan*	*Actual*
REVENUE:				
Service jobs—Number				
—Dollar amount				
LESS: Adjustments—Number				
—Dollar amount				
Estimated additional adjustments—Number				
—Dollar amount				
Net revenues—Jobs				
—Number				
—Dollar amount				
Miscellaneous				
TOTAL REVENUES				
EXPENSES:				
1. Accounting				
2. Advertising				
3. Bank charges				
4. Depreciation and amortization				
5. Dues and subscriptions				
6. Public relations				
7. Interest				
8. Machine rent				

Exhibit 3. (Continued)

9. Operating supplies
10. Rent
11. Repairs
12. Payroll taxes
13. Telephone
14. Travel
15. Part-time help
16. Postage
17. License, fees, and franchise tax
18. Fidelity bond expense
19. Taxes
20. Miscellaneous expense
TOTAL EXPENSES
Gross income
Less: Salaries
      Bonus
Net income (loss)

CASH POSITION
Projected through May 19B

April 30 cash balance (from balance sheet attached) .... $
Add: Estimated collections in May ....
     Total cash available .... $
Deduct: Estimated cash needed for May bills............................ $
        Bonus .... $
        Payment on liabilities... $
Estimated cash balance at end of May.................................... $

Exhibit 4.

The Snyder Service Company, Incorporated
BALANCE SHEET
April 30, 19B

Assets
Petty cash
Cash
Accounts receivable
  Less: Allowance for doubtful accounts
Payroll advances
Equipment
  Accumulated depreciation
Furniture and Fixtures
  Accumulated depreciation
Leasehold improvements
  Accumulated depreciation
Organization expense
  Accumulated amortization
    Total assets

Liabilities
Accounts payable
Notes payable
F.I.C.A. payable
WH taxes payable
Accrued interest payable   -
  Total liabilities

Capital
Capital stock
Retained earnings
Adjustments
Accumulated income (per income statement attached)
  Total capital
Total liabilities and capital

Computation of February Bonus

Cash collections on February jobs:
  In February . . . . $_____
  In March . . . . $_____
  In April . . . . $_____
Cash collections on prior jobs . . . . $_____ $_____

Less: February expenses
  (from February report) . . . . $_____
  February salaries . . . . $_____ $_____
Net subject to bonus . . . . $_____

Division: Company . . . . $_____
         Manager . . . . $_____
         Assistant manager . . . . $_____
             Total . . . . $_____

479

2-2. THE SUPREME CORPORATION is a small firm manufacturing three different models of a simple household item. The product is sold through independent wholesale outlets in a three-state area. Recently, a competing device appears to have been removed from the market. The management of Supreme is concerned with the effect on operations because they feel that an increase in volume may be anticipated.

The management of the company has never been involved in profit planning and control. Planning has been on an informal and nonsystematic basis. In discussing the new development with the board of directors (who meet quarterly) the general manager raised both the volume and price aspects of the new situation. At his suggestion the board approved a resolution to have the company's C.P.A. help with some analyses and decisions.

Subsequently, in analyzing the situation (following certain procedures recommended by the C.P.A. firm), the management made the following estimates for the coming year:

(1) Physical volume of sales will increase by 20 per cent
(2) Material prices will rise by 15 per cent
(3) Administrative expenses will increase *in total* by 10 per cent
(4) Direct labor wage rates will increase by 20 per cent
(5) Selling expenses will increase *in total* by 30 per cent if sales prices are increased. If sales prices are not increased these expenses will increase in total by 10 per cent
(6) There will be a 10 per cent reduction in the material content of each unit of finished goods
(7) Fixed manufacturing expenses of $20,000 will not change.

The audited report for the past year showed the following (simplified and rounded):

Sales		$500,000
Cost and expenses:		
Direct materials	$110,000	
Direct labor	80,000	
Manufacturing expenses—Fixed	20,000	
Manufacturing expenses—Variable	40,000	
Administrative expenses	30,000	
Selling expenses	120,000	
Total		400,000
Net income		$100,000

Among other considerations it is desired to determine (1) the per cent that selling prices (on the average) should be increased to bring a 20 per cent return on $655,000, the amount of the total assets, and (2) the net income that might be expected for the coming year assuming no change in selling price.

Required:

(a) Present computations showing the development of the desired information.

(b) Provide comments relative to evaluation (usefulness and limitations) of the results.

(c) What additional approaches and analyses would you suggest?

2-3. TECHNICAL EQUIPMENT CORPORATION was organized in 1935 to conduct geophysical services for oil producing companies in the Southwest. Its expansion since that time, both as to areas of operations and revenues, has been phenomenal. It now also manufacturers equipment in related fields and sells to the U.S. Government as well as to private operators. Sales for the calendar year 1962 are expected to reach $65 million. The company has manufacturing plants located in two large Southwestern cities and has subsidiaries in nine foreign countries.

The firm is alert to the latest management developments. Likewise, it is alert for new fields which it may enter profitably and for methods of improving present products and operations.

The attached chart (Exhibit 1) shows the organizational relationships within the firm.

The activities included in the Control and Finance Division (a staff group) are centered in the five following departments: a Central Plant and Office Services department; the secretary-treasurer, who has responsibility for matters concerning corporate affairs and financial policy; the Planning department, which coordinates preparation of the annual budget; the Central Accounting department, where consolidation accounting is handled and where internal auditing is done only to a limited extent; and the Management Services department, which prepares special reports and studies.

The product divisions are decentralized as to profit responsibility, each division head being solely answerable to top management for the operations of his division. Staff department managers in the product divisions report to the division head and have only a functional relationship with their staff counterparts at the central level. TEC believes that the experience gained in specific product areas enables these individuals to develop their abilities to the fullest extent possible and thus justifies the possible extra cost resulting from some duplication of effort in performing staff functions.

There is no line of authority from the vice president of Control and Finance, Mr. Watson, to the six product division controllers. Informal communication results from regular monthly meetings held by the vice president of Control and Finance and attended by the seven controllers. At these meetings problems of concern to the majority are discussed.

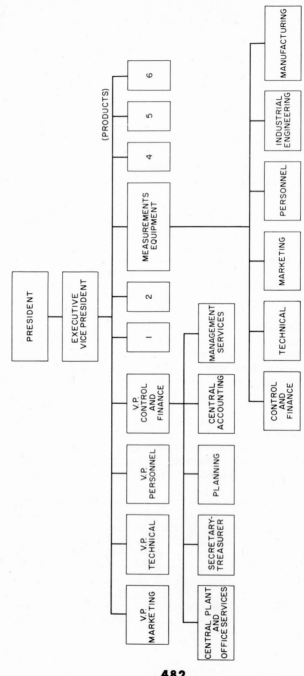

Exhibit 1. Organization Chart

482

Each division controller can thus learn how the others are handling problems similar to his own, or can receive suggestions from them.

In addition, each product division controller prepares a monthly report for the division manager, a copy of which goes directly to the vice president of Control and Finance. The latter officer reviews these reports and submits pertinent comments to the executive vice president, the Product Division head, or the Product Division controller, depending on the nature of the matter. The vice president of Control and Finance has been assigned over-all responsibility for the reporting function (accounting and budget control reports).

A typical situation illustrates the relationships:

In examining the monthly reports from the Measurements Equipment Division, Mr. Watson observed that the inventory of manufactured parts had increased from $50,000 to $200,000 in a period of three months. Mr. Watson had missed the last two group meetings; apparently the increasing inventory had not been noticed by his assistant who conducted the meetings when Mr. Watson was absent. He questioned Mr. Nolan, the Measurements Equipment Division controller, who had no specific information relative to the increase, stating that "it was nothing to be alarmed about." In view of the large amount of funds involved, Mr. Watson pursued the subject rather forcefully suggesting to Mr. Nolan that he should have investigated the reasons and propriety of the increase. The following day Mr. Watson received a telephone call from Mr. Sumner, head of the Measurements Equipment Division. Mr. Sumner appeared to be annoyed, stating that "Nolan felt that you were too hard on him. Incidentally, he reports to me and the inventory is my responsibility." Nevertheless, Mr. Watson inquired about the unusual increase in inventory. Mr. Sumner gave the distinct impression that he had not been aware of the increase and flatly stated that he did not know why it had increased. The telephone conversation ended with neither party indicating any further action.

Mr. Watson was deeply concerned about the matter and felt strongly that some action should be taken. Consequently, he discussed the situation in detail with Mr. Porter, the executive vice president, who requested complete details (in writing) from Mr. Sumner.

Required:

Be prepared to discuss the significant problems and policies suggested by this situation.

2-4. THE COLIN STEEL WORKS, INCORPORATED was organized during World War II and for a period of about five years produced almost exclusively for firms having defense contracts. The company was organized by fourteen local businessmen to process ore and scrap. Due to the continuing strong demand immediately following the war and during the Korean conflict, the company had experienced a reasonably strong demand for the semi-finished products produced. By the end of the Korean conflict the company had moved into manufacturing some products for general distribution. Because the firm was located in the southwest a substantial freight advantage existed, particularly on the heavier items manufactured.

As a result of increased competition and fall-off in the profit margin during the last two years, the management had found it necessary to tighten up on operations. The management had devoted considerable efforts to improving supervisory skills and to up-grading hourly paid workers. During the period, there had been some lay-offs; in such cases the management attempted to carefully evaluate employees so that the less efficient were laid off. The management felt that they had been fairly successful in keeping the better workers.

During the last several years, considerable efforts had been devoted to reducing costs. The accounting system had been revised in accordance with the concept of responsibility accounting. Standards has been developed in some operations and there had been some adaptation of the accounting system toward a standard cost system. These adaptations related to direct labor and direct material standards only. Among the procedures recommended had been a budget planning and control program.

Although competition remained strong and pressure on prices heavy, the company had experienced a slight annual increase in gross business except for the last year. The company had approximately 225 employees on a regular basis. From time to time ten to fifty temporary employees were employed.

During the past year the management had made strong efforts to develop a profit planning program for the company. The president of the firm had become convinced that such a program would be worthwhile. He was strongly influenced by the discussion at a conference he had attended conducted by the American Management Association.

The president felt that the budget program would be of value in management planning and control. In addition, he felt that some effective approach was needed to control factory overhead and general overhead costs.

The budget program during the past year had involved numerous problems; however, the president felt that this was to be expected during the first year. The budget supervisor was a long-time employee and not having had previous experience with a budget program, he too was learning. Meetings were scheduled at the end of the year to review the procedures, progress, and related problems.

The factory manager and the budget supervisor recently had a meeting of the second-line supervisors, excluding the foremen. The purpose of the meeting as described in the announcement was "to critically examine our budget experience during the past year with a view to improving procedures."

During the discussions, Sam Grant, one of the factory supervisors, commented: "I don't like this participation idea that we keep talking about. Last year I followed the instructions and let the foremen participate all over the place and it has given me nothing but trouble. I used to have firm control over these men, but after this year I'm about ready to throw in the sponge." "What's the problem?" replied Bill Winter, the budget supervisor. "Well, it's like this. First, I spend a lot of time telling these guys that they are to draw up their own expense budgets; they were not too happy about it and I had a heck of a time getting them in on time. Then they were all wrong and I had to change them. Now I had to spend a lot of time in cozy little chats trying to explain to them why they had to be changed. Finally, we got them in; then comes the reports. Of course, they had all kinds of unfavorable variations and you should hear the excuses. After I get through with all the conferences, I don't have much time left to supervise. But more important, I feel that I have lost control over the foremen. They are giving me too much static and excuses now. I feel we should tell them what to do, how much to spend, and not encourage them to question everything. You need discipline and respect at this level and the only way to get it is to be firm and rule with an iron hand, otherwise we supervisors will lose our authority. Too much talk with the foremen is not good." "But Sam," replied Fred Matson, the factory manager, "we let you participate; don't you think that is working?" "Well, the management will have to decide on that; I think supervisors have enough sense to know how to get along with their superiors. They realize you can't run an operation by mob rule." After a few more comments the meeting was adjourned for lunch.

Required:

Analyze the situation and present recommendations.

2-5. RECTOR IMPLEMENT COMPANY. In 1946, C.Q. Davis, Lee Watson, and Paul Rector purchased a retail implement franchise from the old, established seed and implement company, Whitaker Brothers. Whitaker Brothers was engaged primarily in the retailing of a well-established line of farm machinery in a seven-county area having 250,000 acres in cultivation. The remaining acreage was in large ranches.

The name Rector Implement Company was given to the new firm because Rector was to manage the firm and it was anticipated that he would eventually buy the other interests. Rector had been manager of the implement department of Whitaker Brothers for about ten years. In 1952, he purchased the interests of Watson and Davis. Sales and profits in the postwar era were good but a drought from 1953 through 1958 caused a rapid fall in sales and profits. The revenue and profit history are shown in Table 1.

Year (ended 8-31)	Total Assets*	Revenue	Profits and (Losses)
1946	$ 92,000	$ 250,000	$ 12,000
1947	115,000	275,000	16,000
1948	256,000	400,000	30,000
1949	372,000	450,000	42,000
1950	375,000	550,000	50,000
1951	400,000	600,000	75,000
1952	410,000	700,000	80,000
1953	515,000	650,000	49,000
1954	420,000	300,000	(30,000)
1955	380,000	270,000	(17,000)
1956	351,000	270,000	(6,000)
1957	350,000	250,000	2,000
1958	328,000	290,000	(8,000)
1959	340,000	400,000	5,000
1960	566,000	675,000	60,000
1961	601,000	800,000	65,000
1962	526,000	1,000,000	70,000

* Major fluctuations were in inventory (equipment) and receivables

Table 1. Revenue and Profit History

The principal source of revenue was new equipment sales which generally amounted to about 75 per cent of the total. Parts and miscellaneous hardware accounted for about 12 per cent of the revenues with shop work providing the remainder. In dry years the new equipment sales fell rapidly while the repair parts and shop revenues remained stable.

In June, 1959, Joe Rector, the son of Paul Rector, joined the firm as general manager, a position which had not previously existed. Joe, at the age of 22, had just graduated from college with a major in retailing. Joe was already married and had planned for two years to join his father in the business. Joe's background, academically, was good, but his primary interest, like that of his father, was in sales work. Joe had a knack for getting along with the customers who were older men who had farmed in the area since childhood. Paul Rector laid a good "ground" for his son in the firm and the employees were aware of the fact that Joe would be their "boss" someday. Joe had worked in various departments of the store during vacations and after school. By August, 1962, his place in the organization was the key position. (See Table 2.)

Paul Rector, president, started in the implement business in early 1930 after "going broke long before it became fashionable" in the hardware business. He traveled for an implement manufacturer and then

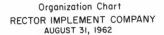

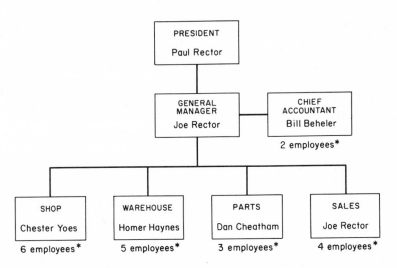

Organization Chart
RECTOR IMPLEMENT COMPANY
AUGUST 31, 1962

PRESIDENT

Paul Rector

GENERAL MANAGER

Joe Rector

CHIEF ACCOUNTANT

Bill Beheler

2 employees*

SHOP	WAREHOUSE	PARTS	SALES
Chester Yoes	Homer Haynes	Dan Cheatham	Joe Rector
6 employees*	5 employees*	3 employees*	4 employees*

*Number of employees in addition to department head

Table 2.

joined a subsidiary of this firm. After two years with the subsidiary, he transferred to a branch of the parent company as a sales representative. In 1936, he joined Whitaker Brothers as manager of their implement department. By 1946, Mr. Rector was well-known in agricultural circles in the area and had little trouble making the infant Rector Implement Company a success. By 1962, Mr. Rector was sixty years of age and under the care of a physician because of a stroke in 1960. He welcomed the coming of his son to the business because it gave him an opportunity "to slow down and hunt and fish a little." His long-range dream of having at least one son join him in business was fulfilled. As President of Rector Implement in 1962, he worked Joe into the business to take over his duties and "just went down to the store for a while later in the day." "Later in the day" meant 8:30 a.m. instead of 7:00 a.m.

The chief accountant, Mr. Bill Beheler, joined Rector Implement Company in 1960 after retiring from another job. Mr. Beheler, age fifty-five, was instrumental in installing the present accounting system based on the four operating departments of the firm. Costs and revenues were accounted for on the basis of the department in which they were incurred. Accounting reports were not sent to operating personnel at the departmental level.

Chester Yoes, age fifty-five, head of the Shop, joined Whitaker Brothers before World War II as a mechanic. He rejoined Rector Implement Company as a tractor mechanic after the war. As head of the Shop, his duties were the same as the other mechanics except for the fact that he allotted the work among the men. He received a commission on the work he did and a slightly higher weekly base wage to compensate for his administrative tasks.

Homer Haynes, age fifty-eight, joined Rector Implement Company in 1948 as a truck driver. As head of the Warehouse department his duties included supervision of assembly of new implements and the servicing of new tractors prior to delivery. Also he supervised deliveries to customers and the receipt and storage of car loads of merchandise. His orders came from the general manager or president.

Dan Cheatham, age forty-four, joined Whitaker Brothers in 1941 in the Parts department. He had been head of the Parts department since the formation of Rector Implement Company. He had been "the man in charge" when Mr. Rector was away until Joe Rector joined the firm. Mr. Cheatham was in charge of the purchasing and selling of parts, hardware, and other miscellaneous items peculiar to farm equipment stores.

Joe Rector headed the Sales department in addition to being general manager because it was felt that none of the regular salesmen should be burdened with the over-all responsibility for sales. Joe also sold merchandise when he was at the store or had the opportunity.

After Joe Rector entered the firm, he was swamped with the detailed day-to-day operating decisions of all departments. He spent the majority of his time talking with and supervising various employees of the several departments. The employees were very cooperative and tried to please him in every way. However, Joe Rector and his father often made different decisions on the same problem. For example, when walking around the Warehouse, Shop, or Parts department Mr. Rector would suggest that certain things be done, not knowing that Joe had requested that the men do differently. In loyalty to Mr. Rector the employees would stop what they were doing and carry out his suggestion even though a bottleneck might be created.

Competition was particularly strong in 1962, consequently Joe Rector spent a great deal of time in sales supervision and actual selling. Late in 1962 while in the office of the chief accountant Joe commented that he needed someone to "take my orders on a departmental level and carry out the detail work without having to ask me whether or not to tighten the nut one more round." Bill Beheler had been awaiting such an opportunity to talk about the operation of the business. During the course of the conversation Joe indicated that "the organization looks good on paper but doesn't work like the one in the textbook." In order to get all the details taken care of Joe had been arriving for work at 6:00 a.m. and leaving about 6:30 p.m.

Bill asked, "What do you think is wrong with the organization?" Joe replied, "Well, I am not sure, but perhaps this incident will give you an idea of what is happening. The other day Chester wanted to buy some new hand cleaner for the shop boys to use. The cost was about the same as the soap we had been using but he had to come ask me if he could change. He said that all the boys in the shop liked it and had voted on it. Of course I said yes. But it took at least thirty minutes of his time and mine." Bill said, "It looks like that is a rather minor thing for you to worry about. Just be glad you are making a profit." Joe answered, "Yes, a profit, but I have no time for my family. I have to make every decision around here, except in your department. How can I make every decision and run this place the way it should be run?" "Well, have you ever considered establishing more authority and controlling through a system of budget control?" asked Bill. "No, my brother is always talking about budgets and how they can help in operating a firm, but I never did understand accounting so I don't know. And it is probably like that organization chart from a textbook—fine on paper but not in practice." "I have seen a few systems in operation and they work if properly installed and the people understand what is happening," said Bill.

Joe continued, "How could I ever get Dad to see the picture? He is just like Dan in the Parts department—never willing to change or experiment." Bill replied, "Dan is rather consistent in what he does and so is Paul. However, why don't we talk to him about it?" Joe answered, "If you really think it will do any good at all I want to try it. We need something new around here!"

About two weeks later Mr. Rector, Joe, and Bill Beheler went on a two-day quail hunt. On the return drive Joe brought up the subject of budget control by saying. "Dad, do you think a budget program would help me—and you—in running the business? A budget program would make possible more delegation of responsibilities to the departments. I don't know how you have done it all these years—but the details are driving me crazy." Paul answered, "It might work, Joe, but there is one big problem and that is getting the boys—Dan, Chester, and Homer —to do things on their own." "That is a problem, all right," admitted Joe. "Now, how do we correct it?" Bill spoke up, "Mr. Rector, perhaps an outsider could help us on this since we will all need assistance in a budget program." After some further discussion, Mr. Rector said, "It is all right with me. I'll do everything I can to help even though I am not at the store much anymore and I have some doubts."

Joe contacted a local C.P.A. firm. The managing partner outlined a budget program for Mr. Rector, Bill Beheler, and Joe. Subsequently the department heads were called in for a group discussion. As the C.P.A. explained the program Joe noted Dan shaking his head and Chester looking as though struck by a wrench. A question and answer period followed which involved only a few minor questions.

After the C.P.A. left, Paul asked, "What do you think of it, boys?" Homer said, "It sounds all right to me even through I don't understand all the details. I believe it means I am going to be fully responsible for operating the warehouse and will run it to the best of my ability, cooperating with Joe, Dan, and Chester." Bill said, "That's right, and I will send you the results of your operations so that you can compare them with the budget for your department." Dan interjected, "What is the matter with the way it is? I am happy now and I thought everybody was happy—especially since the drought is over." Mr. Rector said, "Thank goodness the drought is over, Dan. But the company has grown a lot since those days and everyone needs to be responsible for his own department." Chester said, "I had rather work on those old G and A model tractors all day than keep up with all the customers and newfangled hydraulic systems they have now—much less any paper work." Mr. Rector replied, "Ches, you are a good mechanic and the customers like you. You will have a chance to make yourself more money and help Joe out, too." Dan shook his head again and said, "Why don't we just keep on going. It looks like we are doing fine. Besides, it probably won't work." On this note the meeting was adjourned with Mr. Rector asking the fellows to sleep on it. The next week Mr. Rector called a meeting for the purpose of discussing the budget program further. No agreement was obtained from Chester and Dan. The C.P.A., who had been asked to attend the meeting, recommended that "the best thing to do for the time being is to take no action, but hold it for further consideration."

After the C.P.A. left, Mr. Rector, Joe, and Bill had the following discussion: Bill said, "I am sorry that it didn't pan out the way we had talked. I wonder what we should do next." Mr. Rector observed, "All the boys in the Shop apparently feel the same way Chester does and the rest of the men in the Parts department are not capable of handling the job of supervision." Joe stated, "There must be some way to get to the heart of our problem. Dad, will it be all right with you if I ask Bill and the C.P.A. to study the problem we have for a couple of months with a view to making definite recommendations?" Mr. Rector answered, "Sure, Joe, do what you think is best."

Required:

(a) Analyze the pertinent aspects of the situation.

(b) Evaluate the respective roles of Mr. Rector, Joe, Bill, and the C.P.A. both in the light of what was done and what should have been done.

(c) Suggest appropriate recommendations by Bill and the C.P.A.

Chapter 3

3-1. CONSOLIDATED CORPORATION had been operating for a period of eight years. During this period profits fluctuated considerably and were never particularly good. Within the last two years two wholly owned subsidiary corporations had been formed. There was no program of planning by the management and control was a definite problem.

The members of the board of directors were particulary disturbed by the evidence of inadequate coordination and control. Accordingly they engaged a consultant to make a study of the management procedures currently employed. The consultant submitted a comprehensive report to the board including specific recommendations. Included in the recommendations were concrete proposals relating to organization structure and policy formulation. In addition, a revision of the accounting system was recommended so that accounting and reporting by responsibility would be possible.

Excerpts from the consultant's recommendations relative to a budget control program follow:

PROFIT PLANNING AND CONTROL

General

Management planning and control are essential to the success of business operations. The more complex and decentralized operations become, the greater the need for sound budget control.

Profit planning and control involve the development of a definite *plan of operations* (budget) by those directly responsible for administration of the functions involved; the formal expression of the plan in financial terms; formal approval of the plans by the policy-making body: and finally, conformance with the approved plans, except to the extent that the original plans are revised by the approving authority. Control and conformance are assured by means of periodic performance reports to the approving authority, showing (a) plans (budget), (b) actual, and (c) differences or variations.

Application to Consolidated and Subsidiaries:

The concept of profit planning and control should be applied to the operations of Consolidated Corporation and the two subsidiary corporations:

    (1) Consolidated Corporation
        (a) The board of directors initially should establish broad policies and lay down broad operational decisions relative to the functions of the company within which operations and activities should be planned and conducted.
        (b) The president of Consolidated should establshed detailed operational policies for the company within the framework referred to in (a) above.
        (c) The president should communicate appropriate aspects of the plans and policies referred to in (b) above to those employees of the

firm having direct administrative responsibilities for specific functions., viz.:

  (1) Administrative—B. K. Adams
  (2) Operations—John Cason
  (3) Subsidiary management—P. M. Bowers & R. T. Brown
  (4) Others

(d) Each executive having direct administrative responsibilities (c above) should develop a budget or plan of operations relating to their specific function. Each plan should specify:

  (1) Time covered (1 year)
  (2) Planned revenues
  (3) Planned expenses
  (4) Planned expenditures for capital assets
  (5) Cash requirements
  (6) Other items partinent to operation.

Items 2 through 6 should be *dated*, preferably scheduled by month.

The plans thus developed should be presented to the president of Consolidated whose responsibilitiy it is to assure they are in conformance with his policies, and those of the board of directors. The president is responsible for the soundness of the final plans.

(e) The president should work these several plans into an over-all coordinated plan for presentation to the board of directors. This should be accomplished prior to the beginning of the budget year.

(f) The Board of Directors should carefully study the plan and give final approval after making any changes deemed advisable.

(g) The president should be allowed to assume full responsibility within the framework of the approved plan of operations. He should be assigned direct responsibility to see that operations (including all expenditures) conform to the plan to the fullest extent possible. Desirable revisions in the plan should be brought before the board for prior approval.

(h) Records should be maintained so that monthly performance reports can be presented to the board of directors. These reports should be as follows:

	Month			Year to Date		
Item	*Plan*	*Actual*	*Variation*	*Plan*	*Actual*	*Variation*
Wages etc.	$2,000	$2,100	($100)	$6,000	$5,800	$200

The board should evaluate performance and keep in touch with operations through the president and by means of the performance reports.

(2) Subsidiaries

(a) The board of directors of Consolidated should prescribe broad policies and operational decisions for the subsidiaries.

(b) The subsidiaries should follow budget contʳol in a manner similar to that outlined above. Authority (and hence budget control) should be as follows: functional supervisors to general managers to Consolidated president to Consolidated board of directors.

At the next meeting of the board of directors the consultant's report was discussed. During this discussion the president made the following comments: "I'm afraid this budget will put me in a straight jacket. Conditions around this area are just too dynamic for such precision—

every day new problems arise that could not possibly have been in the budget. We just can't plan ahead like this—there would be so many changes necessary that it would be a waste of time. We've got to meet these problems as they arise. Further, if I took all the time needed to develop a budget, I wouldn't have time to do much else. I know Bowers and Brown pretty well and I don't think either of them would take to it at all; they like action. Their operations are just starting; we have to feel our way along there too."

Required:

(a) Be prepared to discuss and evaluate the recommendations relating to profit planning and control.
(b) Consider the points raised by the president. What would you suggest relative to them?
(c) Would you suggest the company proceed with the budget program? Why?

3-2. THE SUMMARY MANUFACTURING COMPANY produces seat covers for automobiles. Two models are produced, designated as Custom and Standard. The covers are sold in two states, Texas and Arizona. Three materials are used, designated as A, B, and C. There are two producing departments—Cutting and Finishing. The following profit plan estimates have been made for the coming year.

(1) Sales budget—Custom 10,000 in Texas, 4,000 in Arizona; Standard 30,000 in Texas, 10,000 in Arizona. Sales prices to retailers—Custom $15; Standard $12.
(2) Inventories (*fifo*)

	Beginning		Ending	
	Units	*Unit Cost*	*Units*	*Unit Cost*
Raw material:				
A	500	$1.25	1,000	$1.25
B	2,000	.50	2,000	.50
C	3,000	.40	2,000	.40
Work in process	—		—	
Finished goods:				
Custom	200	$11.00	200	12.00
Standard	400	7.00	300	8.00

(3) Raw material requirements—Each unit of Custom produced requires 1 unit of material A and 2 units of B. Standard requires 2 units of B and 2 units of C.
(4) Estimated cost of material—Material A $1.25; B $.50; C $.40.
(5) Estimated unit direct labor cost—Custom $3.00 in Cutting and $4.50 in Finishing. Standard $2.50 in each department.
(6) Overhead budgets have been prepared which show the following unit overhead rates:

	Custom	*Standard*
Cutting	$1.00	$.50
Finishing	1.25	.70

(7) Expenses: Distribution $70,000 (including non-cash items $10,000)

Administrative 50,000 (including non-cash items $5,000)

Net of other expenses over other incomes 2,825

Federal income tax average rate 30%

Other Data:

(8) Beginning balance in retained earnings $125,000.

(9) Planned dividends to be paid during year: $30,000.

(10) Planned cash receipts:

Cash sales	$475,000
Accounts receivable collections	225,000
Other incomes	175
Proceeds of bank loan	10,000
Sale of treasury stock	15,000

(11) Planned cash disbursements (in addition to those previously indicated):

Accounts payable (assume all raw materials are purchased on account)	$105,000
Capital additions	40,000
Accrued and deferred items (assume no unpaid wages)	15,000
Other expenses	3,000
Estimated income taxes to be paid during the year	20,000
Payment on long term note	50,000

(12) Beginning cash balance $60,000.

(13) Non-cash items in the overhead budget amounted to $10,380.

Required:

Prepare the following schedules utilizing the profit-plan estimates provided above. Design the schedules so they provide the essential data in easily understood form. Use the schedule numbers and titles listed below.

Schedule
Number   *Title*

1   Sales plan summary—By product, by district
2   Production plan summary—By product units
3   Direct materials plan summary (In units)—By material, by product
4   Purchases budget summary—By material
5   Cost of raw materials required for production—By material, by product
6   Schedule of initial and final inventories
7   Direct labor plan summary—By product, by department
8   Overhead plan summary (Overhead Applied)—By product, by department
9   Cost of goods manufactured and sold summary
10   Profit and loss summary
11   Planned statement of retained earnings
12   Cash plan summary

3-3. THE COMPTE SALES COMPANY uses a continuous profit plan covering a six-month period. The plan is revised monthly. Summary profit plan data for one six-month period are shown below.

	March	April	May	June	July	August	Total
Sales	$210,000	$216,000	$224,000	$208,000	$190,000	$180,000	$1,228,000
Cost of goods sold	84,000	86,000	90,000	83,000	76,000	72,000	491,000
Gross margin	126,000	130,000	134,000	125,000	114,000	108,000	737,000
Distribution expenses	52,000	53,000	55,000	51,000	49,000	47,000	307,000
Administrative expenses	26,000	27,000	27,000	25,000	24,000	24,000	153,000
Operating margin	48,000	50,000	52,000	49,000	41,000	37,000	277,000
Financial expenses	1,000	1,000	1,200	1,200	900	900	6,200
Income (before income tax)	47,000	49,000	50,800	47,800	40,100	36,100	270,800
Income taxes (40%)	18,800	19,600	20,320	19,120	16,040	14,440	108,320
Net income	$ 28,200	$ 29,400	$ 30,480	$ 28,680	$ 24,060	$ 21,660	$ 162,480

In accordance with company budget procedures the following data were provided the budget director:

(a) Sales department revised estimates: Sales—April $220,000; May $225,000; June $210,000; July $192,000; August $182,000; September $195,000. Distribution expense—a straight 2 per cent increase; September $50,100.

(b) The executive vice-president estimates—administrative expenses for September $25,000.

(c) The treasurer estimates—financial expenses for July through September $1,100 per month.

(d) Accounting department estimates—cost of goods sold will increase in proportion to the increase in sales for each month, September $78,000.

Required:

(a) Prepare a revised profit plan following the concept of continuous budgeting, including appropriate comments concerning the estimates and an evaluation of the changes.

(b) Prepare a separate narrative appraising the budget approach and procedures utilized by the company.

3-4. X COMPANY. Assume you have been engaged to make an independent evaluation of the operations of the X Company, which is experiencing certain difficulties. You have concluded that a comprehensive budget program is advisable. In an executive meeting the company controller, an elderly man, comments in your presence, "Oh, I realize that budgeting is perhaps OK in a few extremely large firms, but not ours. We have special problems, such as sales forecasting, because we have five different products distributed all over the U. S. In addition, you just can't tell what our expenses for the year are going to be. Besides, I don't have the time or help to prepare a budget. I probably couldn't make those sales people follow it anyway." The rest of the executives look at him with what you interpret to be possible agreement. Narrate your reply exactly as you would give it to the executive group in the presence of the controller.

3-5. MICRO CORPORATION uses variable budget procedures to aid in the control of costs. The variable budget for Cost Center 23 is shown below:

The Micro Corporation
VARIABLE EXPENSE BUDGET
For the year 19—
COST CENTER NO. 23

Accounts	*Fixed Allowance per Month*	*Variable Rate per 100 Direct Machine Hours*
Supervisory salaries	$ 900.	$ —
Indirect labor	200.	.90
Maintenance parts	50.	.05
Supplies used	—	.60
Power used	30.	.10
Miscellaneous expenses	40.	.12
Depreciation on machinery	100.	—
Totals	$1,320.	$1.77

Required:

(a) The annual profit plan is being developed. It includes an estimate of the planned volume of work for Cost Center 23. What amounts should be included in the planned *schedule of costs* for Cost Center 23, (1) for the January estimate of 20,000 direct machine hours? (2) for the annual estimate of 260,000 direct machine hours? Show your computations.

(b) Assume the profit plan is completed and that January of the new year has passed. Actual machine hours in January were 24,000. Actual expenses were: Supervisory salaries $900, Indirect labor $415, Maintenance parts $65, Supplies used $140, Power used $50, Miscellaneous expenses $70, and Depreciation $100. Using these data and the planned allowances developed in requirement (a), prepare a performance report comparing actual expenses with planning budget allowances. Set up four amount columns: (1) Actual expenses, (2) Original profit plan allowances, (3) Variations—amount, (4) Variations—per cent of budget.

(c) Prepare another performance report comparing actual with variable budget allowances *adjusted to actual work done;* 24,000 DMH.

(d) Which report would the supervisor of Cost Center 23 prefer? Why?

3-6. THE MAXWELL COMPANY. The home office of The Maxwell Company was located in a large metropolitan area; the main plant was located in another state approximately 200 miles from the home office. At the end of 1955, the company employed approximately 175 full-time people and had average annual sales of 5.5 million dollars for the five-year period ending 1955.

Although the company had been in operation over twenty-five years, it had experienced considerable difficulty during the period 1950-1955. The management had been unable to reverse a slight downward trend in over-all sales volume and a serious decline in profits. The company annual report showed a net loss for 1953 and 1955.

During the early part of 1956, the president (and founder) retired, and a new president was hired from the outside. This change resulted in several other changes in the management personnel including the employment of a controller. Prior to this time, there had been no controller as such; the chief accountant carried out the controllership function which consisted primarily of supervision of the cost accounting system and the tax section.

The new president was forty-seven years of age and had been quite successful in a prior management position with a somewhat smaller company. He immediately instituted a number of changes in the organizational structure of the company. The home office was relocated in the same city as the plant. During the two-year period 1956-1957, the new management team was able to increase sales slightly and to increase net income by a greater percentage. The favorable increase in net income was primarily due to cost reductions resulting from moving the home office and from a forceful cost control program throughout the company. The changes instituted by the new president were not accepted without considerable "stresses and strains" throughout the company.

The new controller reorganized the cost accounting system during 1956. The president directed that a complete budget planning and control program be instituted at the beginning of 1957. The controller strongly favored the budgetary planning and control program; in fact, he had suggested from the beginning that such a program was needed. The controller forcefully pushed the budget program and felt generally satisfied with the results at the end of 1957, although there were numerous incidents and remarks which indicated that the lower levels of management (particularly the longtime supervisors) were resisting the program.

During 1958 the budget program seemed to operate more smoothly, and by bringing the several levels of management into the planning function, acceptance seemed to improve. Although he had no prior experience with a long-range planning program, the controller was particularly interested in experimenting with such a program (on a formal basis) as soon as possible. Both the president and the controller were careful to *instruct* the executives and supervisors not to use the budget as a *pressure device*, but as a constructive tool to improve internal planning, coordination, and control.

Encouraged by the latest response to the budget program, as evidenced by the actions of the top executives, the president and the controller decided to push ahead with a long-range planning program. Because both had limited experience with long-range planning on a formalized basis, a long-range planning committee was established to study (a) the feasibility of formalized long-range planning procedures for the company, and (b) to make recommendations relative to such a program. An outside consultant was employed to provide technical advice and assistance. The committee spent considerable time on the assignment. The controller served as chairman of the committee. Pertinent aspects of the report of the committee dated June, 1959, are shown in Exhibit 1.

During the process of developing the annual planning budget, the controller developed a tentative long-range plan that attempted to express the tentative plans that evolved in the meetings of the executive committee, following the committee report (Exhibit 1). The general approach visualized by the controller is indicated in the representative schedules. (Exhibits 2–5—only representative data are shown.)

Required:

Be prepared to discuss the significant aspects of Exhibits 1 through 5. (Note: Sufficient data are not given to appraise the reasonableness of the figures.)

Exhibit 1.

THE MAXWELL COMPANY
Long-Range Planning for Management
(Tentative Report, June 1, 1959)

Long-range planning is that activity in a company which sets long-term goals for the firm and then proceeds to formulate specific plans for attaining these goals.[1]

Long-Range Planning vs. Business Forecasting

One of the many new tools for dynamic management which has come into existence since World War II is formalized long-range planning. A distinction should be made between business forecasting and long-range planning. Business forecasting is only a part of future planning, as it primarily involves the measurement of future economic fluctuations. Long-range planning, on the other hand, involves the determination of definite and realistic goals to be met in the light of the future economic conditions and the formulation of specific, though flexible, plans for meeting the goals set. In addition, it is important to distinguish between informal discussions of future plans and formalized long-range planning. In the latter case, plans are formalized in writing.

Long-Range Planning Must Consider the Company as a Whole

Successful long-range planning involves more than mere projection of the results of past experience. On the other hand, past experience is

[1] Note: Many of the ideas included in Exhibit 1 were taken from *Long-Range Planning for Management* (a collection of outstanding articles), edited by David W. Ewing (New York: Harper, 1958).

important in setting budget objectives for the future. If long-range planning follows the same procedures as used in setting short-range budget goals, some important aspects of long-range planning may be overlooked. Long-range planning is more than adding on so much more men, facilities, and capital. Planning future objectives involves consideration of the company as a whole. If, for example, the company were to set a goal of a 75 per cent increase over present sales by the end of seven years with a 5 per cent improvement over present return on investment, the problem of achieving these objectives involves much more than additional salesmen, plant expansion, etc. The problem involves a multitude of other factors such as: How can we achieve a better system of control? How can we improve customer service? How can we improve the morale and motivation of our employees?

The committee believes that it would be advantageous to the company to institute formalized long-range planning at an early date.

Length of the Long-Term Planning Period

How far into the future should long-range planning extend? A great deal of variance appears to exist from company to company in this respect. Some long-range plans involve only two to three years, whereas others are for 20 to 30 years. This difference is understandable considering the differences between companies, firms, and managements. One authority[2] believes the long-range plan should cover the *shorter* of the two periods listed below:

1. The plan should not extend so far into the future that it can have no influence on near-term decisions.
2. The plan should extend into the future only as far as correct assumptions can be made with a sufficient degree of certainty.

    In this way the establishment of goals and methods of achieving them is substantially more likely to lead to the desired results than to mislead into undesired results.

The committee believes that the company should develop, in addition to the annual budget, a long-range plan extending five years in advance in major detail and ten years in advance indicating broad objectives only.

Long-Range Planning Must Be a Responsibility of Top Management

Long-range planning is a responsibility of top management. Due to the confidential nature of long-range planning and to the fact that long-range planning can only be achieved by those not bogged down in specific day-to-day operating decisions, future planning must be a responsibility of the top echelon of management. This type of activity responds to group or committee effort so that the particular abilities of of several people are utilized in determining and deciding the specific plans and goals set for the future.

[2] *Ibid.*, pp. 157–158.

The committee recommends that the operative committee assume the responsibility for long-range planning. The controller (a member of the committee) should be charged with design and coordination of long-range planning procedures.

Steps Involved in Planning[3]

The first step in the long-range planning process is the establishment of basic planning objectives. Basic decisions included in this step are: Are we going to stay in business? Are we going to buy or sell? The second step in the planning process is the establishment of planning premises or assumptions. This step involves the forecasting part of long-range planning mentioned earlier. At this point, the planners must decide on such matters as: What kind of markets should the company enter? What volume of sales should be our objective? What should be the price policy? What products ,should be sold? What cost objectives are realistic? What are the financial aspects of the plan?

The third step is the search for alternative courses of action. Few cases exist where alternatives to a business plan cannot be found. Even if all the alternatives prove unfeasible, they serve the purpose of securing confidence in the original plan.

The fourth step in long-range planning is the evaluation of available alternatives. This evaluation involves the determination of the strong and weak points of each plan and the weighing of the various factors involved.

The fifth planning step is that of selecting the course or courses of action to be undertaken. The sixth step is taken after the plan is once adopted. This step involves the drawing up of derivative plans which support the basic plan. Plans do not accomplish objectives by themselves. Plans require a breakdown into further plans for each segment of the company, and each manager concerned is charged with executing the subsidiary plans necessary for making the basic plan a reality.

Criteria for Effective Long-Range Plans[4]

Once a feasible long-range plan has been developed, how can the management have confidence that the plan is the best one for their company? One authority has suggested the following six items as earmarks of a good plan:

1. Has the planning team determined the key influences in the growth of the industry and evaluated the influence of each?
2. Have the strengths and weaknesses of the company been accurately evaluated?

[3] *Ibid.*, pp. 11–43.
[4] *Ibid.*, pp. 113–134.

3. Have the capacities of different company functions to support the plan been projected far enough ahead?
4. Is there a practical timetable?
5. Have alternatives been considered?
6. What provisions have been made for future reverses?

Forecasting Techniques

The relative success or failure of long-range planning depends to a large extent on the planners' ability to make accurate forecasts of the future economic activity. Three basic strategies, useful in economic forecasting, have been suggested.[5]

The first strategy is the ability of the planners to get economic information fast and accurately. To do this, internal as well as external information must be made available to the planners on a continuous and timely basis. To employ this strategy, the planners must have the ability to separate superfluous information from material facts. The planners must be able to quickly pinpoint the trends, if any, which the information contains, and then determine the effect the trends may have on future economic activity.

The second strategy is based on the premise that the future is not identical with the present but is an outgrowth of it. This strategy involves the use of various mathematical computations—some relatively simple, others more complicated. Such devices as trend extrapolation, leading series, and diffusion indexes are sometimes used. The whole theory of this strategy ". . . is the notion that change through time is rhythmic or cyclic—and that, like the life and death cycles of plants and animals, business activity also has its expansions and contractions. . . ."

The third strategy is that forecasting stems from the concept of certain underlying theories or principles of economics. This strategy makes use of classic economic analysis. The technique is to discover relationships among economic factors and apply them to situations in the past, present, or future. This strategy has met with failures in the past (e.g., the Great Depression), but has made tremendous improvements in the past few years. The primary reasons for this improvement have been the "Keynesian revolution" and the creation of the valuable system of national income accounts developed by the National Bureau of Economic Research. Other developments in this area have been the construction of economic models, where some success in forecasting has been found by the results of certain relationships between the dependent and independent variables subjected to the models.

In order to meet these needs, the committee feels that outside sources must be depended upon for general economic analysis. The present size of the company precludes extensive internal economic analysis efforts.

[5] *Ibid.*, pp. 378–394.

Long-Range Planning Must Be Flexible

A good practice is to review the long-range plans at least every year
and more often when conditions warrant. Long-range plans cannot possibly be developed to preclude revision—flexibility is particularly important. The human element alone is enough to make long-range planning
something less than precise. But the very fact that management has
thought seriously about the future and determined the basic strategy to
use makes it easier to cope with unexpected situations.

Just as in short-range budgeting, the value of long-range planning may
not lie so much in the tangible results, but in the very fact that it
forces management to set realistic goals and policies, to consider the
most effective use of available resources, and to give serious attention
to the trend of business conditions—all of these on a timely basis.

Exhibit 2.

THE MAXWELL COMPANY
Long-Range Plan

Planning Premises (Hypothetical for illustrative purposes):

1. Aggressive, dynamic, and efficient management
2. Effective research essential to maintaining an aggressively competitive
   position
3. No major war or other national catastrophe
4. Moderate inflation through 1969
5. Adequate capital and financing will be available
6. Growth in general economy 3 per cent per year—growth in industry
   slightly greater than the general economy
7. Major moves planned by management:
   a. Product R to be introduced in 1961—large distribution and tooling
      expenses anticipated
   b. Price increase of one dollar planned for Product X—to go into
      effect in 1963
   c. Renovation of plant to be completed in 1964—factory overhead
      expenses should show improvement in 1965
   d. Product A dropped once Product R becomes established; estimated
      date, 1965
   e. When production of 450,000 units of Product A is reached, a price
      decrease of 10 per cent will take effect for Product R; estimated
      date, 1964
   f. Western plant to be completed near end of 1969
8. Major expense increases
   a. Labor contract to be renegotiated at end of 1961. Wages, on the
      average, will increase 5 per cent. Non-union personnel will also
      benefit with roughly the same increase.
   b. Introduction of state income taxes in 1965—roughly 5 per cent of
      net income

Exhibit 3.

THE MAXWELL COMPANY
Annual Budget and Long-Range Plan—Summary of Sales, Costs, and Income
(in thousands of dollars)

	Ref.	Actual Results					Annual Planning Budget 1960	Long-range Projection				
		1955	1956	1957	1958	1959		5 year				10th year
								1961	1962	1963	1964	1969
Sales		$5,604					$6,870				$8,963	$9,712
Variable costs:												
Materials		1,410					1,731				2,241	2,541
Direct labor		2,300					2,117				2,844	3,012
Factory overhead		273					280				359	470
Distribution costs		441					455				490	511
Administrative costs		27					29				38	43
Total		4,415					4,612				5,972	6,577
Plus (or minus) variable costs associated with decrease (or increase) in inventories		(36)					(77)				40	51
Total variable costs		4,451					4,535				6,012	6,628
Marginal income		1,189					2,335				2,951	3,084
Fixed costs:												
Factory overhead		448					535				563	525
Distribution costs		562					603				590	601
Administrative costs		205					202				220	223
Plus (or minus) fixed costs associated with decrease (or increase) in inventory		(5)					(10)				6	7
Total fixed costs		1,210					1,330				1,379	1,356
Operating income		(21)					1,005				1,572	1,728
Other (expenses) and income—net		(2)					37				45	38
Net income before income tax		(23)					1,042				1,617	1,766
Less income taxes		—					484				889	971
Net income after taxes		($23)					$ 558				$ 728	$ 795
Analysis:												
Profit margin		—					8.12%				8.12%	8.19%
P/V ratio		.21					.34				.33	.32
Breakeven point (millions)		$5.76					$3.91				$4.18	$4.14
Margin of safety (% above B. E.)		—					76%				114%	135%
Variable cost ratio		.79					.66				.67	.68
Fixed cost ratio		.22					.19				.15	.14

Exhibit 4.

THE MAXWELL COMPANY
Annual Budget and Long-Range Plan—Summary of Balance Sheet Projection
(in thousands of dollars)

	Ref.	Actual Results					Annual Planning Budget	Long-range Projection					
								5 year				10th year	
		1955	1956	1957	1958	1959	1960	1961	1962	1963	1964	1969	
Current assets		$1,610					$1,833				$1,170	$1,112	
Funds		—					20				10	50	
Fixed assets (net)		1,560					1,633				2,824	3,455	
Other assets		2					1				1	1	
Total assets		$3,172					$3,487				$4,005	$4,618	
Current liabilities		$ 397					$ 429				$ 309	$ 359	
Long-term liabilities		20									100		
Total liabilities		417					429				409	359	
Capital stock (par $100)		2,240					2,240				2,240	2,670	
Paid-in surplus		10					10				10	20	
Retained earnings		505					808				1,346	1,569	
Total capital		2,755					3,058				3,596	4,259	
Total liabilities and capital		$3,172					$3,487				$4,005	$4,618	
Analysis:													
Current ratio		4.1-1					4.3-1				3.8-1	3.1-1	
Fixed assets to totals assets		49%					47%				71%	75%	
Capital to total assets		87%					88%				90%	92%	
Long-term liabilities to total assets		.6%					—				2.5%	—	
Book value per share of stock		$123					$137				$161	$160	
Earnings per share of stock		—					$24.91				$32.50	$29.78	
Return on investment		—					16.01%				18.18%	17.22%	

Exhibit 5.

THE MAXWELL COMPANY
Annual Budget and Long-Range Plan—Summary of Cash Flow
(in thousands of dollars)

	Ref.	Actual Results					Annual Planning Budget 1960	Long-range Projection		5 year 1963	1964	10th year 1969
		1955	1956	1957	1958	1959		1961	1962			
Sources of Cash												
Net income		($23)					$ 558				$ 728	$ 795
Add back non-cash expenses												
Depreciation and amortization		83					88				147	182
Sale of fixed assets		8									14	15
Sale of capital stock		—										440
Capital additions fund							41					100
Decrease in current assets (other than cash)											45	
Increase in current liabilities		32					67					
Financing (long-term)												100
Other sources		3										
Total Cash Inflow		103					754				934	1,632
Beginning cash balance		127					627				218	488
Total cash available		230					1,381				1,152	2,120
Cash Requirements												
Dividends		15					60				132	264
Capital additions		20					135				422	1,300
Increase in building fund		—					20				40	
Payment of long-term liabilities											50	
Payment of prior year's tax liability							613					
Increase in current assets (other than cash)		54					112					
Decrease in current liabilities											120	150
Other requirements		2									10	10
Total Cash Outflow		91					940				774	1,724
Ending cash balance		$ 139					$ 441				$ 378	$ 396
Analysis:												
Cash to current assets		8.6%					24.1%				32.3%	35.6%
Cash to total assets		4.4%					12.6%				9.4%	8.6%
Cash to current liabilities		35.0%					102.8%				122.3%	110.3%
Cash to sales		2.5%					6.4%				4.2%	4.1%

Chapter 4

4-1. THE STRAND-WALKER CORPORATION. One of its members presented the following proposal to the executive committee during a discussion of policies for the upcoming budget preparation period.

> I propose that top management adopt a *policy* that the current concept of a *realistic* sales budget be changed. Under my proposal, the policy would require a *highly conservative* sales budget. The Sales department should be free to establish whatever sales *quotas* they deem suitable for their sales efforts, but these should not tie in with the sales budget since such quotas normally should be very optimistic whereas the sales budget should be very conservative.
>
> The sales budget should be very conservative so that expense budgets will likewise be conservative. This is the best means of achieving cost control. In addition, should actual sales significantly exceed budgeted sales it is easy to raise expense allowances as needed. On the other hand, if sales should be significantly under budget it is hard to cut expenses adequately. A high sales budget carries with it high expenses and can be disastrous if sales do not materialize.
>
> I have been talking with a friend of mine in another company and they really got caught last year on expenses when actual sales came out far below budget. They sure regret having budgeted sales too high.
>
> I think we should adopt this policy now and prevent such trouble in the future.

Required:

Present your reply exactly as you would give it before the group, assuming you are another member of this executive committee.

4-2. THE MITE MANUFACTURING COMPANY makes two products, S and T, which are distributed in two sales districts. The sales plan for the coming year showed the following (gross sales):

	Product S (Units)		Product T (Units)	
	Comal District	*Dibol District*	*Comal District*	*Dibol District*
January	2,000	3,000	3,000	4,000
February	2,200	3,400	3,300	4,500
March	2,300	3,400	3,500	4,600
2nd Quarter	6,600	9,000	8,000	10,000
3rd Quarter	7,000	9,900	8,500	10,300
4th Quarter	5,000	7,000	6,000	8,000

Additional Data:

    (1) Sales prices to be budgeted:
        Product S—Comal District $3.30, Dibol District $3.40
        Product T—Comal District $4.30, Dibol District $4.40
    (2) It is estimated that sales returns and allowances will be as follows:
        Product S—One per cent of gross sales
        Product T—One and one-half per cent of gross sales

Required:

    Prepare schedules in good form for
    (a) Planned sales—Detailed
    (b) Planned sales—Summary.
The company follows the practice of budgeting sales returns and allowances.

4-3. THE OK MANUFACTURING COMPANY has for many years manufactured a line of stoves. The line is fairly broad, varying from simple heating stoves to large combination heating and air conditioning units up to seven-ton capacity. The firm also distributes an external condensing unit to complete the heating-air conditioning package. The condensing units are purchased from another manufacturer and the OK trade name is placed upon them prior to sale. In addition to selling the line to various trade outlets in a three-state area, the company manufactures the combination unit for another company that operates on a national basis. These units are sold under the trade name used by the other company. The combination unit manufactured by the company is recognized as one of the better units produced anywhere. On units sold in the three-state area OK has a definite freight advantage.

    The OK company has been moderately successful—that is, the sales have been steady with a gradual and consistent increase in the three-state area. Orders from the national firm have increased from year to year during the past ten years at a rate approximately twice that of the distribution through trade outlets under the OK trademark. The OK company realizes about 30 per cent more profit per unit, after allocation of all overhead, on the trade business than on the business from the national outlet. Profits for the OK Company over-all have been good when related to investment.

    The OK company executives have decided to expand into three additional states. The company has an effective budget planning and control program. The sales budget has been quite accurate for the past six years except for 1962 when sales were approximately 15 per cent below budget.

    A preliminary study by the controller of the OK company provided the following sales potentials for the new territory: 1963, $150,000; 1964,

$200,000; and 1967, $500,000. A representative of the sales department worked with the controller in developing these preliminary estimates.

You have been engaged as an outside consultant to advise with respect to preparing a realistic sales budget for the new territory convering the period indicated above. The company has been using the *field approach* in developing the annual sales budget. It is expected that the 1963 estimate in the new territory will be considered with particular care because purchases of component parts, materials, employment of additional personnel, etc., will be based upon this projection.

You are expected to advise with respect to (a) factors that should be considered in deriving a realistic projection and (b) an approach in budgeting sales in the new territory. Feel free to comment on any related matters.

4-4. THE WALLIS SALES COMPANY sells a line of paint and related supplies through sales outlets covering a three-state area. Six salesmen are employed and contact each outlet about every three weeks. A salesman will write up orders (four copies) at the time of the call. One copy is left with the customer, one is retained by the salesman, and two are sent to the home office. The Sales department reported that goods are shipped, on the average, about 3 weeks after the order is written; orders average $350 each. From time to time customers alter (up or down) or cancel an order. The Wallis company has a rather liberal policy relative to such changes or cancellations. In addition, goods may be returned by the customer because Wallis accepts returns within 30 days of shipment if the goods are undamaged. From time to time discounts are allowed customers to induce them to keep, rather than return, items. The liberal policies with respect to orders, returns, and discounts "are forced upon us by the competition." Certain actual data for the past 12 months are as follows:

	Orders Taken	Shipments	Returns	Allowances
Jan.	$150,000	$118,000	$1,400	$ 200
Feb.	165,000	130,000	1,100	900
Mar.	180,000	144,000	600	1,100
Apr.	200,000	156,000	1,200	300
May	175,000	175,000	400	800
June	150,000	191,000	1,400	100
July	90,000	169,000	900	900
Aug.	75,000	140,000	800	600
Sept.	90,000	88,000	200	500
Oct.	100,000	72,000	1,900	100
Nov.	125,000	84,000	800	1,100
Dec.	140,000	93,000	300	600

The executive committee has decided to start a budget program; hence, it is in the process of developing the sales budget covering the ensuing year. Certain budget policy decisions are under consideration. You have been asked to make recommendations with respect to them.

The Sales department executives have taken the position that separate projections must be made with respect to each of the four items listed in the table above. Certain members of the planning committee feel equally strong that a budget of *net sales* is not only desirable, but sufficient. What would you recommend? Why? Indicate your recommendations relative to any particular budgeting problems involved in the basic approach you select.

4-5. RICHARDS SALES COMPANY. The executives of the Richards Sales Company are considering pricing policies in connection with the sales budget currently being developed. One particular problem concerns the price of the principal product. The current selling price is $10.50 per unit. The Sales department generally feels that the price should be reduced to $10; the other executives feel that this decrease in price would not be offset by increased volume as is claimed. As a result of the discussions concerning the various alternatives that exist, a rather complete study has been made. The following data were developed:

(1) Sales price-volume data:

Assumed Selling Price	Estimated Market at Given Price (Units)
$10.00	12,000
10.20	11,500
10.40	11,300
10.50	11,000
10.60	10,600
10.80	9,500
11.00	9,000

(2) Total fixed costs, $35,000. (It is assumed this cost will be constant at all the volumes listed above.)

(3) Estimated variable cost per unit of product, $6.00.

Required:

(a) Assume you are the staff representative that developed the above data. You are to present it to the executive committee. Prepare a volume-price forecast which suggests the alternative that should be selected. Prepare the forecast in a form suitable for submission to the executive committee, supplementing it with comments or graphs if these would add to the effectiveness of the presentation.

(b) Indicate some approaches you may have used in developing the sales price-volume data.

4-6. THE ECONOMY MANUFACTURING COMPANY executives are in the process of developing the sales budget (and planning budget as well) for the coming year 19B. A meeting of the budget committee is scheduled for next Monday at 9:00 A.M. This is the third meeting concerned with the sales plan. Data developed to date are as follows:

(a) The Sales division has prepared the following sales plan: Product X, $200,000; Product Y, $315,000. The long-range plan calls for a 12 per cent increase in sales in 19C and a 7 per cent increase in 19D.

(b) The treasurer has prepared a tentative cash budget at the budgeted sales volume (excluding capital additions requirements) which indicates a cash deficit during the 3rd and 4th quarters. The deficit is approximately $60,000 in September.

(c) The Manufacturing division has estimated the present plant capacity for economical operation to be 450,000 direct machine hours (DMH).

(d) The personnel supervisor is concerned about the estimate of the vice-president in charge of manufacturing that 10 additional highly skilled workers would be required to meet the production requirements of the sales forecast. It is believed that the workers can be hired, but that the wage demands likely will be above what is currently paid the 137 skilled workers in the same category.

(e) The purchasing agent anticipated no difficulty in obtaining the required quantity and quality of raw materials and supplies. In fact there may be a slight cost saving due to increased volume.

(f) The Sales division recommended the following budgeted sales prices: Product X, $2.00; Product Y, $2.25.

(g) The company had established a line of credit for $100,000. The treasurer felt it would be difficult to increase this amount materially. The company has 10,000 shares of unissued common stock; the current market price is $9.50 per share. Two years ago the board of directors voted not to sell the shares.

(h) The industrial engineers have developed the following standard direct machine hours per unit of product: Product X, $1\frac{1}{4}$; Product Y, $2\frac{1}{2}$.

(i) A survey of plant capacity indicated additions to plant and machinery could be made as follows at the cost indicated:

Increase in Capacity DMH	Estimated Cost
25,000	$ 40,000
50,000	70,000
100,000	110,000
150,000	150,000

Required:

After considering all the facts as given, what would you recommend to the budget committee relative to the sales plan and related problems? Narrate your recommendations, supplementing them with appropriate analyses.

4-7. HEALEY DEPARTMENT STORE. Healey's is the largest department store in a metropolitan area with a population of approximately 150,000. Healey's is a family-owned store having been organized by the senior Healey 42 years ago. The success of the store has been due in large part to two factors: (a) service to the customers and (b) a wide line of quality goods. Customers liked to deal with Healey's because of a liberal credit policy and the knowledge that the store would stand behind anything sold. Both competitively priced and quality lines were carried in most departments. There was a bargain basement.

In recent years competition became progressively stronger, forcing lower margins and lower profits. Approximately five years ago a system of departmental sales quotas was adopted. Under the quota plan weekly sales quotas were developed by the management for each of the 23 departments of the store. The quotas were set approximately 15 per cent higher than the management realistically thought would be sold. Over the five-year period departments met their sales quotas for the week about 10 per cent of the time. The management felt that the system of sales quotas had been generally effective in increasing sales volume. The management recognized that the department managers felt that they could "meet the quota only if we are lucky." Nevertheless, the management felt that the high quotas were an incentive to most of the managers.

Cash and inventory problems in particular had practically forced the management to consider the adoption of a budget program. The new controller had worked very hard during the past year to set up an appropriate budget program. He had attempted to complete a budget on a semi-annual basis, including budgets of sales, advertising, costs, purchases, cash, etc.

The primary problem encountered by the controller was one of *educating the management*—many of the executives had practically grown up with the company. This problem involved, according to the controller, "the concepts and objectives of budget planning and control. They simply did not get the idea, although I can truthfully say that most of them wanted to see the idea succeed. It is just foreign to their traditional way of thinking and doing things." Apparently the top management was not aware of their own reluctance, because they appeared to be satisfied with the new controller and clearly stated that they wanted to push the program.

One point of direct disagreement concerned the quota system and the sales budget. The controller proposed that realistic sales quotas be developed for each department and that these quotas be used both as departmental goals and as a basis for building the rest of the budget, including the over-all sales budget. He took the position that the accuracy of the cash budget, purchases budget, and all other budgets for that matter, depended upon an accurate sales budget. In addition, he felt that realistic sales quotas for each department would offer more incentive than the present quota system.

The three top officers strongly disagreed. They felt that the present quota system should be retained on the basis that "we know how these sales people operate; you've got to give them a high quota, otherwise they will lay down on the job. They understand the present quota system; they know they have to work like the dickens to even come close; it has been proven, and it gets results. Believe me, you must know the psychology of the situation." They felt that a "second" sales budget could be developed to satisfy the needs pointed out by the controller. Either the controller "could develop such a sales budget or simply take the quotas as presently being set and multiply them by 85 per cent." They realized the effect on departmental supervisors should they learn about the two sales budgets. It was proposed that the second sales budget be kept confidential. The controller felt that this secrecy would be impossible because "the budget otherwise would divulge indirectly the lower sales budget figures."

Over the past 10 years you have performed services for the management of Healey's as an independent professional man. The management has contacted you and requested that you study this matter and make definite recommendations, including the basis for your conclusions. Feel free to comment upon any related matters.

Chapter 5

5-1. THE THOMAS MANUFACTURING COMPANY produces soil pipe, sewer pipe, fittings, joints, and numerous related items in many sizes and of several different materials. Most of the finished goods are stored outside between date of completion and date of shipment to customers.

Production problems are critical particularly in view of high set-up costs. In order to produce soil pipe, for example, considerable rearrangement is necessary and the special forms must be taken out of storage and prepared for use. As a result of the high set-up costs large runs are usually made in order to keep unit costs within reason.

Inventory storage costs are low (roughly estimated by the management to be about $.10 per unit per year) and deterioration is not a problem. Obsolescence is considered to be a relatively minor factor in terms of two or three years. The company finances the inventory locally, paying an average of 7 per cent interest.

Other than the fixed factory overhead (approximating $125,000 per year), production costs for material and labor tend to vary directly with the number of units produced.

The company has just started a budget program. A tentative sales budget has just been developed as shown on Exhibit 1. Other pertinent data available are:

	Inventory On Hand	Average Unit Cost*	Average (lot) Production	Average Set-up Cost
Soil pipe	21,000	8.50	30,000	$15,000
Sewer pipe	34,000	6.00	40,000	20,000
Fittings	22,000	1.50	25,000	10,000
Joints	4,000	4.50	10,000	8,000
Etc.				

* Includes set-up costs based on average (lot) production.

You have been requested to advise with respect to developing a realistic production budget. What basic problems would you consider in advising on the production budget? What would you recommend relative to these problems? What production schedule would you recommend for soil pipe for the coming year?

Exhibit 1.

THE THOMAS MANUFACTURING COMPANY
Sales data and budget

	19A	19B	19C	Jan.	Feb.	Mar.	2nd	3rd	4th
				1st			Current Year		
SOIL PIPE									
Actual	11,000	12,000	15,000	1,500	1,200	1,000	3,000	4,000	4,500
Budget, next year				1,500	1,500	1,200	3,500	4,000	4,500
SEWER PIPE									
Actual	8,000	8,000	9,000	1,000	1,100	1,100	4,000	2,500	1,500
Budget, next year				1,200	1,200	1,200	4,800	3,000	1,500
FITTINGS									
Actual	15,000	16,000	23,000	2,400	2,200	2,000	6,500	6,500	6,000
Budget, next year				2,600	2,600	2,200	7,500	7,000	5,500
JOINTS									
Actual	4,000	4,500	4,800	700	700	800	2,200	2,300	1,900
Budget, next year				800	800	800	2,300	2,400	2,000
ETC.									

5-2. THE PRODUCTO COMPANY manufactures five principal products. The planning budget is being developed for the coming year. The tentative annual sales budget prepared by the Sales division showed the following:

Product	Units Budgeted
1	100,000
2	150,000
3	80,000
4	200,000
5	250,000

Sales are highly seasonal—for example, the sales budget showed the following for Product 1:

Jan.	10,500	July	5,200
Feb.	10,300	Aug.	5,000
Mar.	9,400	Sept.	7,500
Apr.	8,500	Oct.	8,800
May	8,000	Nov.	9,500
June	7,000	Dec.	10,300

The following inventory levels have been tentatively decided upon:

| | FINISHED GOODS | | WORK IN PROCESS | | | |
| | Initial | Final | Initial | | Final | |
Product			*Units*	*% Complete*	*Units*	*% Complete*
1	10,000	12,000	0	—	0	—
2	10,000	8,000	2,000	100	2,000	100
3	5,000	5,000	2,000	50	6,000	50
4	20,000	20,000	5,000	100	4,000	100
5	25,000	28,000	7,000	80	8,000	80

Required:

(a) Prepare the annual production budget summary for the company.

(b) What policies would you suggest relative to monthly inventory and production levels for the company? Give support for your recommendations.

(c) Prepare a production budget for Product 1 in conformance with your recommendations.

5-3. LAX METAL WORKS. For some time the Lax Metal Works has been experiencing a critical shortage of cash to meet payrolls and to pay for raw materials. During July of the current year (19D) the situation became extremely critical. A request was made to the bank for a $200,000 loan. The company was unable to furnish the bank with an audited financial statement. The bank refused to consider the loan further until a C.P.A. was called in to conduct an examination of the present financial condition of the firm and to report to them. The company agreed to these conditions. The C.P.A. developed the following data (as well as other pertinent data) concerning the finished goods inventory:

| | | *Current* | Number of Units Sold | | |
| | *Units on* | *Average* | | | |
Item	*Hand*	*Unit Cost*	*19A*	*19B*	*19C*
A	12	$18	15	12	8
B	100	9	150	170	180
C	21,000	4	2,000	1,900	1,600
D	6,000	7	8,000	8,000	8,000
E	79,000	5	4,000	4,200	4,500
F	48,000	6	8,000	7,800	7,500
G	34,000	8	2,000	1,800	1,500
H	—	32	100	150	175
I	900	21	1,500	1,700	2,000
J	10,000	10	14,000	16,000	18,000

There are unusually high *set-up costs* on items E and G. Item C has a relatively long processing period (23 days). The inventory condition is due to the fact that the *production man* consistently overproduced on each order received from sales *to save set-up costs*, and had no knowledge of inventory policies or levels; also, the Sales division maintained no formal record of inventory levels. Most of the items were stored outside in the yard.

Required:

(a) Estimate the overinvestment in inventory.
(b) Set forth your recommendations, in narrative form, relative to inventory and production, supplementing them with adequate supporting analyses. In the process of examination of the company assume the C. P. A. came to the conclusion that there is no good reason why any item should be stocked in excess of a 2 years' supply.

5-4. THE STALEY MANUFACTURING COMPANY executives are presently concerned with the establishment of inventory policies as a part of the development of a budget program. Several alternatives have been discussed concerning inventory levels, among them the moving average method and the average withdrawal method. The sales budget shows the following data for the main product:

Date	Units
December (preceding year)	800,000
January	780,000
February	780,000
March	810,000
April	830,000
May	820,000
June	800,000
July	700,000
August	600,000
September	650,000
October	700,000
November	780,000
December	820,000
January (following year)	810,000

Required:

You are requested to prepare a table for presentation to the company executives, assuming a three-month moving average is used, showing inventory levels by month for (a) a half month's supply and (b) a one and one-half months' supply. Explain by way of comment the principal characteristic of this method and compare it with an inventory level based on monthly average withdrawals budgeted during the year. You

515 correction:

may feel it advisable to compare the three inventory levels on a graph; plot units on the vertical scale and months on the horizontal scale. What conclusions would you draw relative to inventory and production policies as a result of comparing the three inventory levels?

5-5. THE XY MANUFACTURING COMPANY has been budgeting operations for several years. The president stated (with justification) that inventory control and production planning through the budget had not been satisfactory. This had been due primarily to poorly planned production and inventory budgets.

Accordingly, you are directed to make a detailed analysis and recommendation on the matter for the 19B planning budget currently in preparation. Your analysis and recommendations are to be presented to the budget committee.

Despite a seasonality problem, the Sales department has been quite successful in accurately planning sales on a monthly basis for the year. The following data are available:

(1) Sales plan for 19B:

	Units		Units		Units
January	36,000	May	32,000	September	26,000
February	38,000	June	26,000	October	30,000
March	38,000	July	22,000	November	36,000
April	36,000	August	20,000	December	40,000

(2) The January 1, 19B finished goods inventory is estimated at 96,000 units.

(3) Work in process inventory to remain constant.

(4) Annual sales for 19A, including the December estimate, were 350,000 units.

(5) Average finished goods inventory for 19A was 70,000 units.

Required:

(a) Prepare the *annual* production budget, assuming the policy of management is to budget the finished goods final inventory at a standard amount based on the 19A historical inventory to sales turnover ratio.

(b) Prepare a table showing monthly sales, production and inventory levels assuming (1) a stable inventory (2) stable production, and (3) *your* recommended inventory-production levels. In developing your recommendations assume the following policies have been established:

    (1) The president feels that a maximum inventory of 85,000 units must be observed and agrees with the vice president of Sales that the minimum should be 75,000.

(2) A stable level of production is highly desirable, except that during vacation season (July and August) production can be reduced by 25 per cent; also, a 7.5 per cent variation in production will not result in undesirable conditions.

(c) Narrate your reasons and/or arguments in support of your recommendations as you would present them to the budget committee. You may need one or more graphs to supplement your narrative and table. Note and defend any recommendations at variance with policies (1) and (2) above. Comment on the reasons why the first two production budgets developed in requirements (a) and (b) are not desirable.

Chapter 6

6-1. THE MODEL MANUFACTURING COMPANY uses two major raw materials in manufacturing one primary product. The company is in the process of developing the purchases and materials budgets. For the past three years the company had developed a sales budget and had recently decided to extend budgeting to all phases of operations. The sales budget showed the following (units): Jan., 1,500; Feb., 2,500; March, 4,000; 2nd quarter, 9,000; 3rd quarter, 5,000; and 4th quarter, 2,000. In working on the problem the following data relating to raw materials had been assembled.

	Material T*			Material U		
	Units Required (Budgeted)	Days Required For Delivery (Average)	Unit Price Last Year	Units Required (Budgeted)	Days Required For Delivery (Average)	Unit Price Last Year
January	3,500	14	$8.50	12,250	8	$3.00
February	4,000	14	8.50	14,000	7	3.10
March	4,500	18	9.20	15,750	6	3.10
Second Quarter	14,000	18	9.30	49,000	6	3.20
Third Quarter	11,000	10	8.60	38,500	5	3.30
Fourth Quarter	8,000	7	8.10	28,000	5	3.50

* Standard usage 2 units of material T for each unit of finished product.

The management is confronted with three problems about which they have requested your assistance. In view of the increasing price of material U, it has been proposed that a lower quality of material be used. This step, it is estimated, would reduce the unit cost for such material by 15 per cent. Another problem relates to the unit price to be used for budget purposes. The purchasing agent feels that an average price for the year should be used because, "It is only a guess anyway;

I have no control over the price." The chief accountant feels that the price for each interim period should be budgeted since, "We use *fifo* in accounting for raw materials, and an average price would produce meaningless variations particularly in view of the typical fluctuating price of our raw materials." The third problem has to do with freight charges—that is, should the unit price be budgeted *before or after freight charges?* Experience has shown that freight charges on T average about 5 per cent of the cost, whereas freight charges on U average about 10 per cent. The problem is complicated by the fact that the freight charges are paid upon delivery of the materials, whereas the materials are paid for at the end of the discount period.

What are your recommendations regarding each of these problems and any related items? Indicate the basis for your recommendations.

6-2. THE SIMPLE PRODUCTS COMPANY manufactures two products, S and P, processing them through two departments. Product P is processed through both departments, whereas product S is processed through Department 1 only. Raw material A is used in Department 1 for both products and raw material B is used in Department 2 only. A profit plan is prepared on a semi-annual basis. Budget estimates developed to date include the following:

(1) Production budget (Units)

Product	January	February	March	2nd Quarter
S	5,000	6,000	7,000	20,000
P	8,000	9,000	10,000	30,000

(2) Estimated beginning inventories

    Material A— 70,000 units @ $3.00
    Material B—120,000 units @ $2.20

(3) Budgeted material prices (for purchases)

    Material A—$3.00
    Material B— 2.00

(4) Raw material requirements for finished goods

Product	Material A	Material B
S	5	0
P	6	7

(5) Ending raw material inventories planned

    Material A—January and February 70,000, March 80,000, 2nd Quarter 90,000
    Material B—To remain constant at 120,000

Required:

Prepare appropriate profit plan schedules relative to:
(a) Materials

(b) Purchases

(c) Raw materials inventory (use *fifo*)

(d) Cost of raw materials used (by department, product, material, and time period)

Be prepared to justify your particular approach.

6-3. THE CONWAY MANUFACTURING COMPANY prepares an annual profit plan which is broken down by months for the first quarter and by quarters for the remainder of the year. The fiscal year begins July 1. The following data have been developed to date:

(1) Production plan (Units)

	1st Quarter			Quarter		
Product	*July*	*August*	*September*	*2nd*	*3rd*	*4th*
C	5,000	4,500	5,200	15,000	18,000	12,000
O	9,000	8,000	9,500	30,000	20,000	18,000
N	12,000	14,000	16,000	50,000	45,000	55,000

(2) Raw material requirements

Unit Raw Material Usage Rates

Product	#1	#2	#3
C	2	5	3
O	3	0	2
N	1	4	2

(3) Raw material prices budgeted

Raw Material	*Unit Purchase Price*
#1	$1.50
2	2.00
3	3.00

(4) Raw material final inventories budgeted (The company uses *fifo*.)

	#1	#2	#3
July	60,000	100,000	122,000
August	60,000	100,000	125,000
September	62,000	103,000	135,000
2nd Quarter	65,000	108,000	140,000
3rd Quarter	68,000	104,000	130,000
4th Quarter	70,000	100,000	125,000

(5) Raw material inventories at end of current year estimated to be: Material #1, 60,000 @ $1.50; Material #2, 100,000 @ $2.00; and Material #3, 120,000 @ $3.10.

Required:

Prepare the following sub-budgets (detail and summary) in good form. Identify each schedule and cross reference them.

(a) Materials budget

(b) Purchases budget
(c) Raw materials inventory budget
(d) Estimated cost of raw materials used

6-4. HOWE SERVICE COMPANY was started in 1921 by Mr. Howe and one helper. The company has had phenomenal growth in servicing one particular industry. At the present time there are approximately 3,000 employees. In addition to services the company sells manufactured products, principally in connection with service jobs; however, some items are sold to retail outlets. The company manufactures some of these products and purchases others. The company operates on a nation-wide basis, having 10 operating divisions, each under a division manager. Division personnel are responsible for sales efforts as well as performance of services. There is a central manufacturing plant that produces some of the items sold and a shop division that designs and manufactures service equipment used in the field.

The six top executives (president, and five vice presidents, of manufacturing, engineering, research, operations, and finance, respectively) constitute an executive committee that passes on all major decisions. The vice president of finance, after several years of effort, convinced the executive committee of the desirability of formal profit planning and was authorized to employ a budget supervisor to install a complete budget program. The budget supervisor reports directly to the vice president of finance. Although the vice president of finance strongly favors budgeting, he admittedly knows little about the technical aspects. The other executives are not at all familiar with budget techniques or applications.

The budget supervisor has been asked to appear before the executive committee to outline a budget program appropriate for the situation. Near the close of the last meeting the following comments were made by the vice president of operations (in charge of field operations):

> This budget program is OK with me; it won't bother us in operations; our gross sales and service revenues are good. We are 15 per cent above the same period last year, and this is the best indicator of how well my divisions are doing. Our expenses are up some in most of the divisions, I'll admit, but we have done all that is humanly possible to reduce them—we watch the monthly accounting statements carefully. I do think the budget might help Jim (vice president of manufacturing) with some of those high overhead costs. By the way, I will be very interested in the budget director's forecasts of divisional gross revenues and expenses for next year.

Required:

Narrate an appropriate reply to the vice president of operations to be given at the next meeting of the executive committee (by the budget supervisor).

Chapter 7

7-1. THE STINSON MACHINE WORKS is a small company with approximately 145 employees. The corporation operates a machine-shop type of manufacture. Two regular products are manufactured that are sold to distributors. In addition, the company accepts *jobs* to manufacture items according to specifications furnished by the customer. These items vary from small, simply constructed bearings to complex subassemblies. Orders may vary from ten units to several thousand, with frequent repeat orders.

The company has been budgeting for the past two years. Although direct labor is controlled primarily through labor standards and by close supervision at all times, a direct labor budget is prepared so that *income, cash, and certain other budgets* may be realistically developed.

The direct labor budget is developed rather simply by relating labor costs to sales dollars. Because small inventories of finished goods are involved, the management feels that this is the best approach. It is also felt that this is the simplest procedure and about the only approach available because specific jobs (other than regular production) cannot be projected. A revenue or sales budget is developed, then the labor cost is determined by means of a ratio based on historical experience.

In connection with the development of the direct labor budget, the management has encountered two troublesome problems. The budget is being prepared for the coming year and it is hoped to have it completed by December 15.

The first problem has to do with overtime. Some producing departments are forced to work overtime during certain periods. Although there is some seasonality in the overtime, unusually large orders with tight delivery dates may come in at any time. The union contract requires that time and one-half be paid for overtime up to 10 hours per week; above this the pay is double-time. During the past two years considerable discussions have taken place in the budget meetings as to how the overtime should be treated in the budget. The practice so far has been to "sorta average it in." The executive in charge of operations feels that the "inaccuracy of the direct labor budget has been due primarily to this approach, if we didn't have this problem we could budget direct labor with some assurance."

The second problem relates to upcoming union contract negotiations. Because the company has not had to consider this problem since the adoption of the budget program, no procedures have been established. The union contract expires at the end of February of the coming year. Preliminary discussions have been held with the union representatives. The union has presented a proposal that calls for a 15 per cent increase in average hourly pay. The management has taken the position that the outlook does not justify a wage increase. It is felt that competition is stronger than ever; price resistance is very stiff; and any attempt to raise prices, as would be necessary in the face of a wage increase, would cause serious loss of business. The company would have to lay off workers. In a closed meeting of top management it was tentatively decided that they would be willing to sign a new contract with a wage rate increase of 5 per cent.

There is disagreement in the executive committee as to whether or not a wage increase should be included in the budget for the year currently being constructed. Several feel that "we don't want to develop another budget at the end of February."

These two problems have been referred to you for your recommendations, with specific reasons for your recommendations. Feel free to comment on any related matters.

7-2. THE BOSTRAND COMPANY produces two products, AX and BX. The products are processed through two departments, #1 and #2. Planning budget data developed to date are:

(1) Production (Units)

	AX	BX
January	5,000	14,000
February	4,000	12,000
March	6,000	15,000
2nd Quarter	18,000	50,000
3rd Quarter	22,000	60,000
4th Quarter	16,000	45,000

(2) Standard times developed by the industrial engineers are (hours per unit of finished product):

Product	Department #1	Department #2
AX	4	3
BX	2	5

(3) Average wage rates to be budgeted:

Dept. #1	$2.10
Dept. #2	1.90

Required:

(a) Prepare the following direct labor budget schedules: (By time, department, and product)
(1) Direct labor hours
(2) Direct labor cost
(3) Summary of labor hours and cost
(b) Be prepared to outline the uses of each of the three budget

schedules. Relate them to (1) the annual profit plan and (2) the monthly performance report.

7-3. THE DRYDEN CORPORATION produces products X, Y, and Z. All three products are processed through process #1; Y and Z through process #2; and Z through process #3. The company prepares a semi-annual profit plan and follows the practice of including both direct and indirect labor in the labor budget. Profit plan data developed to date are:

(1) Production budget (Units)

	X	Y	Z
July	5,000	3,000	21,000
August	7,000	6,000	26,000
September	10,000	8,000	30,000
4th Quarter	25,000	18,000	75,000

(2) Indirect labor cost estimates

	Process #1	Process #2	Process #3
July	$35,000	$20,000	$15,000
August	37,000	21,000	16,000
September	38,000	24,000	18,000
4th Quarter	98,000	62,000	48,000

(3) Direct labor standard hours per unit of product

	Process #1	Process #2	Process #3
X	$1\frac{1}{2}$	—	—
Y	$1\frac{1}{2}$	3	—
Z	$1\frac{1}{2}$	2	5

(4) Average wage rates budgeted

Process #1	$2.00
Process #2	2.20
Process #3	1.80

Required:

Prepare labor budget schedules showing:
(a) Direct labor hours only
(b) Direct and indirect labor cost
(c) Labor budget summary

7-4. THE DORAN COMPANY prepares an annual profit plan which is broken down by months. At the end of each month control reports are prepared for management which compare actual costs with budget allowances. At the end of March the following data are available:

(1) Actual direct labor costs

	Dept. A	Dept. B	Dept. C
January	$53,000	$53,000	$67,000
February	44,000	47,000	62,200
March	40,000	44,000	48,800

(2) Direct labor allowances in the profit plan:

	Dept. A		Dept. B		Dept. C	
	Hours	Amount	Hours	Amount	Hours	Amount
January	30,000	$60,000	27,000	$56,700	28,000	$61,600
February	24,000	48,000	23,000	48,300	27,000	59,400
March	23,000	46,000	23,000	48,300	20,000	44,000

(3) Actual units produced

	Dept. A	Dept. B	Dept. C
January	13,000	8,500	30,000
February	11,000	7,500	28,000
March	10,000	7,000	22,000

(4) Standard labor hours per unit of product

Dept. A	2
Dept. B	3
Dept. C	1

(5) Average wage rates budgeted

Dept. A	$2.00
Dept. B	2.10
Dept. C	2.20

Required:

Prepare a direct labor control report showing the status of direct labor control for March and year to date. Be prepared to justify your approach.

Chapter 8

8-1. THE WALKER FOOD PROCESSING COMPANY employs approximately 375 people and distributes the products in a three-state area. The company had never prepared a budget. In support of an increased line of credit the bank has requested the management to furnish a budgeted income statement, a cash flow projection, and a balance sheet covering the next six months. The sales and related production budgets have been tentatively approved by the management. No substantial change in inventories is planned.

The sales manager has developed the following budget of distribution costs:

	Actual last six months	Per cent of Total	Proposed Budget
Sales volume	$6,800,000		$7,956,000
Expenses:			
Salaries	181,600	15.0	212,400
Commissions	340,000	28.1	397,800
Promotion	160,600	13.3	188,300
Travel	275,400	22.8	322,800
Entertainment	40,300	3.3	46,700
Freight	179,200	14.8	209,500
Depreciation, taxes, & insurance			
on autos	17,500	1.4	19,800
Miscellaneous	15,400	1.3	18,400
Totals	$1,210,000		$1,415,700

The production manager has developed the following budget of factory costs:

	Actual last six months	Proposed Budget
Direct material	$2,924,000	$3,500,000
Direct labor	1,571,000	1,880,472
Factory overhead:		
Salaries	253,800	253,800
Wages	204,200	224,620
Supplies	87,500	102,375
Utilities	135,100	135,100
Depreciation, taxes & insurance		
on autos	165,200	165,200
Services	58,400	64,240
Miscellaneous	68,200	79,794
	972,400	1,015,129
Total	$5,467,400	$6,395,601

Required:

You have been asked to analyze the budget procedures and the resulting projections. What are your recommendations?

8-2. FOWLER MANUFACTURING COMPANY, a casting manufacturer, employed John T. Simmons to install a budget control program in the company. A new system of production control had been installed recently, product lines were new, and operations had been completely changed.

John's first step in introducing budget control of factory costs was to obtain planned production for the year from the Production Planning department. Using the planned production volume for the year and historical cost figures, expense projections for the year for each department were developed. The estimates were broken down as to material, labor, and factory overhead, and detailed by account. Monthly budget allowances were then derived by dividing the annual expense estimates by twelve.

The next step involved a meeting of all foremen by the works manager, Fred Wagner, who explained the production budget; then John briefly discussed the budget cost estimates he had developed. Fred observed that "we should get behind John on these cost budgets and help him control costs." Next Fred asked John to explain the budget control program to the foremen. Because this was the start of the budget program, John, as expected, sensed some feelings of doubt and suspicion on the part of the foremen. Accordingly, he tried to "sell" the program by pointing out to the foremen that he would carry the ball, and that they could benefit, if costs were reduced, because a successful firm profit-wise would be more apt to pay good salaries and provide steady employment. Fred stressed the point that "we must not lose sight of the cost per pound. For example, if a forge shop foreman can reduce labor cost, while increasing overhead cost at the same time, we should always recognize the total savings and not be concerned about the lesser increase in fixed overhead." The foremen appeared to be impressed with this viewpoint. The foremen were told by John that they would be called, by telephone, for individual meetings in his office to discuss their expense budgets in detail. John felt that the foremen would prefer individual meetings and would rather meet in his office to save time and prevent interruptions.

At the individual conferences John showed each foreman the detailed cost estimates for his department, discussed them; then told him to take the figures, look them over in view of the budgeted production, and write down any revisions thought necessary. The estimates had been entered on budget forms developed by John; extra columns were provided for the suggested revisions by the foremen. Each foreman took the forms for review, to be returned by internal courier in five days.

During the review period John was careful to remain in his office so that the foremen could contact him personally or by phone at any time. After receiving the forms from the foremen, John had his secretary call each foremen and arrange for another series of individual conferences for a final discussion of the cost budgets. John was surprised by the small number of revisions suggested by the foremen. Several of the foremen informed the secretary that the budget estimates were "OK"; therefore, there was no use wasting more time in another conference. As a final step, John sent the foremen a memo stating that the cost budgets would be restudied by him, then recommended to operating management, and that final approval would be given by top management.

After final approval by top management each foreman was sent a copy of the cost budget for their particular area of responsibility. The budget estimates showed all costs normally charged against them by the accounting department, including allocations of indirect costs. Attached to each cost budget was a memo to the foremen, signed by John, to the effect that next year the budget procedure would be reversed—

that each foreman would be required to originate his own expense budget.

During the first few months of the new year actual production was approximately 15 per cent above that originally called for in the production budget. This was due to the fact that sales volume was considerably above that originally estimated by the budget staff. The foremen were annoyed by the "red herrings" on the new monthly cost report which, for the first time, showed *actual, budget,* and *variations* (unfavorable in red). John received numerous indications of these annoyances, but discounted them as a normal reaction; however, he had received no complaints or comments from Fred.

Required:

(1) In what respects did John and Fred use good or bad cost control procedures the first year.

(2) How do you think John and Fred should proceed next year?

8-3. THE XY MANUFACTURING COMPANY produces two products, X and Y. The manufacturing division consists of two producing (#1 and #2) and two service (#3 and #4) departments. The company uses a historical cost system, except that predetermined (budgeted) overhead rates are used in the producing departments to allocate factory overhead to the products. Department #1 rate is based on direct machine hours (DMH) and Department #2 rate on direct labor hours (DLH). In applying overhead the standard rates are multiplied by actual hours. The following budget and actual data are available:

(1) Annual planning budget data:

    a. Overhead budgeted for the year: Dept. 1, $85,000; Dept. 2, $72,500; Dept. 3, $20,000; Dept. 4, $15,000. Machine operators salaries are treated as an overhead cost.

    b. Budgeted units to be produced: Product X, 50,000; Product Y, 30,000.

    c. Budgeted raw material cost per unit of product (all used in Dept. #1): Product X, $4.00; Product Y, $5.00. No material is added in Dept. 2.

    d. Budgeted time required for production: Direct machine hours in Department #1 for each unit of finished goods—Product X, $1\frac{1}{2}$; Product Y, 1. Direct labor hours in Department #2 for each unit of finished goods —Product X, 2; Product Y, $2\frac{1}{2}$.

    e. Average wage rates budgeted in Department #2: Product X, $2.40; Product Y, $2.50.

    f. Allocation of service department cost:
Dept. #3—Allocate $\frac{1}{2}$ to #1 and $\frac{1}{2}$ to #2.
Dept. #4—Allocate $\frac{2}{3}$ to #1 and $\frac{1}{3}$ to #2.

(2) January actual data:

    a. Units actually produced in January—Product X, 4,000; Product Y, 3,000.

    b. Actual direct machine hours in Dept. #1—Product X, 6,100; Product Y, 4,150.

c. Actual costs incurred:

Dept.	Overhead	Raw Material	Direct Labor Hours	Amount
1	$7,700	X—$16,300		
		Y— 15,200		
2	6,800		X—8,200	$19,730
			Y—7,400	18,400
3	2,000			
4	1,600			

Required:

(a) Compute the annual budgeted overhead rate for each department.
(b) Using the rates developed in (a), prepare a schedule of actual cost of manufacturing for January (assume no work in process inventory).
(c) Prepare a performance report showing the status of cost control by department. Use one-twelfth of the planning budget allowances for overhead as the monthly budget allowance. Indicate by way of comment the reasons why this procedure may not be suitable for control purposes.

8-4. Prepare a detailed schedule of expenses for Department X to be used for planning budget purposes. Indicate fixed and variable costs thereon. Budget data available are as follows.

(a) Planned production in direct labor hours:

January	15,000
February	16,000
March	18,000
2nd Quarter	55,000
3rd Quarter	40,000
4th Quarter	60,000

(b) Variable expense budget for Department X:

Accounts	Fixed per Month	Variable per Direct Labor Hour
Salaries	$1,000	
Wages	400	$.050
Supplies used	50	.006
Rearrangement costs	150	
Maintenance—labor		.017
Maintenance—parts		.008
Utilities		.020
Power		.010
Depreciation	80	
Taxes and insurance	40	
Miscellaneous	60	.015
Totals	$1,780	$.126

8-5. THE DANDY CORPORATION manufactures three products, A, B, and C, processing them through two separate processes referred to as Process #1 and Process #2. There are two service departments; Factory Administrative, and Maintenance. The company utilizes variable budgets for factory costs but not for distribution and general administrative costs. There are six sales districts and three general administrative departments. A planning budget is developed on a semi-annual basis, being broken down by month at time of preparation. The following planning data have been developed to date.

(a) Variable expense budgets:

SERVICE DEPARTMENTS

	Factory Administrative		Maintenance	
	Fixed per Month	Variable per 100 DMH	Fixed per Month	Variable per Direct Repair Hour
Supervisory salaries	$ 7,000		$3,000	
Indirect labor	3,000	$1.20	2,000	$.50
Supplies used	100	.20	400	.10
Depreciation	300		200	
Insurance & taxes	80		200	
Miscellaneous	200	.10	200	.20
Totals	$10,680	$1.50	$6,000	$.80

PRODUCTION PROCESSES
(Fixed per month; variable per 100 DMH)

	Process #1		Process #2	
	Fixed	Variable	Fixed	Variable
Supervisory salaries	$ 9,000		$ 6,000	
Indirect labor	6,000	$15.00	4,000	$12.00
Maintenance parts	500	1.00	200	1.00
Depreciation	1,000		800	
Insurance & taxes	200		100	
Miscellaneous	300	2.00	200	2.00
Totals	$17,000	$18.00	$11,300	$15.00

(b) Production budget data:

	Units of Finished Goods		
	A	B	C
January	7,000	4,000	10,000
February	7,000	4,000	10,000
March	8,000	5,000	9,000
April	8,000	5,000	9,000
May	10,000	8,000	9,000
June	10,000	7,000	8,000

(c) Direct machine hours required for each unit of finished product:

Product A—3 hours in Process #1 and 1 hour in Process #2
Product B—2 hours in Process #1 and 1 hour in Process #2
Product C—1 hour in Process #1 and 1 hour in Process #2

(d) Direct repair hours budgeted:

January	600
February	600
March	650
April	650
May	650
June	600

(e) Building service budget summary:

January	$10,200
February	10,500
March	11,000
April	11,500
May	12,000
June	11,400

(f) Building service allocation:

Factory	70%
Selling	18%
Administrative	12%

Required:

(a) Prepare a budget of direct machine hours by department, product, and month.

(b) Prepare detailed planning budget expense schedules for the four factory departments, indicating fixed and variable costs, and including building service allocations.

Chapter 9

9-1. THE BOWLES MANUFACTURING COMPANY produces parts for certain manufacturers. These parts are made of various kinds of metals; consequently the production of a particular part usually involves such activities as heat treating, machining, drilling, and finishing.

The parts are made in various quantities according to specifications furnished by the customer. Orders vary from as few as 10 to 1,000 or more. There are many repeat orders frequently involving both minor and major changes in design. Production activities are such that work is scheduled in lots or jobs; consequently, a job order cost accounting system is employed. The company also prepares an annual planning budget to aid in determining capital additions requirements and in planning and controlling such items as cash, expenses, and other expenditures.

When a job is started through the plant the cost accounting department sets up a job cost sheet on which all costs for each job are accumulated as work progresses. A typical job cost sheet is reproduced below.

JOB COST SHEET

Job No._____

Customer_____

Item_____

Specifications_____

Quantity to be completed_____

Date ordered_____ Date started_____ Inspections_____

Date of delivery_____ Date completed_____

MATERIAL COSTS			LABOR COSTS			MFG. COSTS		
Date	Ref.	Amount	Date	Ref.	Amount	Date	Ref.	Amount
Totals								

Summary

Selling price $_____

Costs to manufacture:

    Materials $_____

    Labor   _____

    Overhead   _____

        Total cost to manufacture $_____

Less: Estimated selling

        costs $_____

      Estimated admini-

        strative costs   _____   _____

    Total cost to make and sell

Profit (estimated) $_____

For purposes of simplicity, it is assumed that the company has two service departments (Repair department and General Factory Overhead department) and two producing departments (Metal Working department and Finishing department). All jobs go through the two producing departments; the service departments do not work on *jobs* but render *services* to the producing departments.

During December of the past year a contract was signed with the Jackson Corporation that called for 100 units of "Components Part XY-138" at a contract price of $14 per unit, to be delivered not later than

February 10 (of the current year). At the time the contract was signed the Jackson representative indicated that there probably would be numerous repeat orders for increasing quantities over the next few years. The prospect of repeat orders was an important factor in the $14 bid price. The factory manager and cost accountant worked together very closely in developing the bid price; they later received information that led them to believe that the next lowest bid (by a local competitor) was $16.19.

Job No. 101 was assigned to the Jackson order and work was started on it on January 3. The factory manager kept a careful check on the progress of the job, realizing the importance of quality workmanship and the necessity of meeting or even beating the deadline. Similarly, the chief cost accountant carefully checked the accumulation of cost data because the experience on the initial order would provide a basis for pricing subsequent orders from Jackson.

The cost department received a report on February 4 showing Job 101 complete. The 100 units were delivered to the Jackson Corporation on February 5. The Jackson representatives were quite pleased with the workmanship and early delivery. Subsequent negotiations resulted in a contract with the Jackson company for the delivery of additional "Components Parts XY-138" as follows at a unit price of $12.50:

	Units
March	200
May	250
June	290
Sept.	350
Nov.	350
Dec.	360

The cost accounting department accumulated the following direct costs with respect to Job 101:

Metal working department
Direct material (from material requisitions) $180
Direct labor (from labor time tickets—50 hours)   120
Finishing department
Direct material (from material requisitions) $250
Direct labor (from labor time tickets—75 hours)   150

The cost accounting department recently completed a study of the two service departments which resulted in a decision to allocate the indirect overhead cost as follows:

Repair department: Allocate 2/3 to metal working and 1/3 to finishing.
General factory overhead department: Allocate 1/2 to metal working and 1/2 to finishing.

The following data were available at the dates indicated:

	Last year actual (Dec. 31 last year)	Current year budget (Prepared Dec. 20 last year)*
Sales	$397,000	$418,000
Prime costs		
(mat. & labor)	187,000	196,200
Repair dept.		
costs (F)**	14,000	15,000
Gen. factory		
overhead (F)	22,000	24,000
Metal working		
dept. (F)	45,000	45,000
Metal working		
dept. (V)	12,000	13,000
Finishing dept. (F)	23,000	24,000
Finishing dept. (V)	18,100	19,000
Selling costs (F)	28,000	29,260
Admin. costs (F)	12,400·	12,540
Net income	35,500	40,000
Direct labor hours:		
Metal working dept.	41,200 (hrs.)	40,000 (hrs.)
Finishing dept.	19,900 (hrs.)	20,000 (hrs.)

*Includes Job 101 and excludes other business with Jackson
**F—fixed; V—variable

Required:

(a) Complete the job cost sheet for Job 101 as it would have been completed for accounting purposes.

(b) For accounting purposes how should the costs of Job 101 have been recorded.?

(c) Analyze cost experience on Job 101 in a manner suitable for determining the bid price on the new contract. Evaluate the new contract price of $12.50. At what unit price would Bowles break even on XY-138? What pertinent factors should have been considered in establishing the contract price?

(d) What reservations would you have on the overhead costs allocated to both Job 101 and the new contract?

(e) Evaluate the over-all profit potential of the firm.

9-2. THE McKAY TOOL COMPANY. The stock of The McKay Tool Company, a manufacturer of small, specialized tools, was closely held by three members of the McKay family—one brother, Samuel, and two married sisters. Samuel had been president of the company since the death of the senior McKay in 1947. The recent death of Samuel, resulting from a heart attack, came as a shock to the other officers of the company, all of whom had been hired by the senior McKay before World War II. Samuel McKay's stock passed to his wife and three daughters, none of whom were affiliated with the company. These events resulted in the employment of a new president from the outside. The new president, Richard E. Johnson, brought in two of his former associates who were given the positions (newly created) of executive vice president (Robert Conklin) and controller (Henry Mohle).

During the first year the new officers succeeded in completing a rather extensive internal reorganization. Simultaneously, the controller revised the accounting system to emphasize the control aspects by adapting it to the new organization structure. The other officers appeared to accept the new officers and the changes instituted. This acceptance was due to three principal factors: (a) the competence of the new officers, (b) company loyalties existing among the old employees, and (c) recognition that the company gradually had become less competitive in the industry.

Subsequent to the revision of the accounting plan, immediate steps were taken to institute a system of sales budgeting which tied in with the newly adopted quota system whereby monthly quotas would be developed for each salesman.

With historical cost data for approximately two years, classified in accordance with the new system of accounts now available, Mr. Mohle felt that the next major step was to develop a complete budget program including effective cost control procedures.

During a conference of supervisors called by Mr. Mohle and the plant supervisor to discuss problems of cost control, Mr. Ralph Mellon, supervisor of Producing Department 5, commented: "I have had no experience with expense budgets, but a friend of mine who works for another plant in the city has warned me about how they work in his company. He is asked to prepare a detailed annual expense budget for his department. When the monthly reports come out, his actual expenses are compared with one-twelfth of the annual budget. Frankly, he says it causes a lot of trouble and is of no use as far as he is concerned. He is trying to get rid of it."

After some discussion it was suggested that monthly expense budgets for each department might be prepared during the preceding month. Mr. Mohle pointed out that although this procedure might be useful, planning expenses only one month in advance would not meet the planning needs of the management. Another suggestion was to have each supervisor develop an annual expense budget detailed by month. Another supervisor commented that "we cannot guess expenses for December twelve months in advance for a number of reasons. Perhaps the most important one is that we have no idea as to how much work we will be doing in future months. We get production orders about ten days in advance now. I cannot see how guessing expenses will help control them." Another supervisor interjected, "In my department expenses are determined by the work we do more than anything else. I would hate to see my June expenses (when production is at the top) set up against the same budget as my August expenses (when production is at the bottom)."

Mr. Mellon, who had evidenced an appreciation of the need for some new cost control procedures in the company, suggested that "we might establish percentages or rates for each expense in each department so that the budget allowance would be doubled in a month where output was doubled compared with another month."

Mr. Mohle, who had been participating in the discussions on an advisory basis, had indirectly guided the discussions. At this point, he suggested that the company experiment with *variable budget cost control.* He explained that this procedure would require:

(a) Identification of controllable and noncontrollable costs related to individual supervisory responsibilities
(b) Identification of the *fixed costs*
(c) Identification of the *variable costs*
(d) Agreement on variable budget allowances relating the department costs to some measure of department output such as indirect labor hours
(e) Monthly reports for each supervisor comparing actual costs with *adjusted budget* allowances.

After some discussion of these ideas, the meeting closed with this comment by Mr. Mellon: "But many of my costs, such as indirect labor, are neither fixed nor variable." Sam Spears, another supervisor, stated: "It appears to me that tying budget allowances to direct labor hours would encourage supervisors to incur more direct labor hours, which itself adds to cost, so that budget allowances would be higher.

Another meeting was scheduled for the following day. In preparation for the next meeting Mr. Mohle decided to use Department 5 costs and production as a basis for discussion of the variable budget idea.

Producing Department 5 was one of the departments that had a high ratio of machines to manpower. Practically all of the different types of tools manufactured passed through Department 5; therefore, it appeared that over-all productive activity in the department was best measured in direct machine hours (DMH) rather than units of output. The Accounting department used DMH as a basis for applying departmental overhead costs to production.

Inspection of the actual controllable expenses incurred in the department during the past year indicated that a few expenses, such as depreciation and salaries, were fairly constant from month to month in spite of the fact that the DMH varied considerably from month to month during the same period. A few expenses such as direct material used and direct labor, appeared to vary directly with output. On the other hand, most of the expenses appeared to vary in some degree, although not directly, with the related productive activity. Indirect labor appeared to be typical of the latter type of expense as indicated by the following historical data provided by the Accounting department (simplified for illustrative purposes):

Month (Numbered for Convenience)	Department 5	
	DMH's (000)	Indirect Labor Cost
1	170	1650
2	160	1470
3	160	1480
4	150	1450
5	150	1460
6	140	1450
7	130	1420
8	120	1200
9	130	1440
10	150	1490
11	160	1490
12	170	1500

In preparation for the meeting Mr. Mohle prepared a graph plotting thereon indirect labor (vertical scale) against productive activity (horizontal scale). He intended to lead the discussion to two questions: (1) What indirect labor (in Department 5) did last year in relation to productive activity, and (2) What indirect labor should do next year in relation to planned production activity.

Required:

(a) Be prepared to discuss the procedures listed by Mr. Mohle related to *variable budget cost control*.

(b) Construct the graph of indirect labor. Be prepared to present an explanation of the analysis and its application to the situation.

(c) What would you recommend as the *variable budget allowance* for indirect labor?

(d) What budget variance would be reported for January of the coming year, assuming actual expense of $1570 and production output of 180,000 DMH's?

(e) How should the following individuals be involved in setting the variable budget allowances for Department 5: Mr. Mohle, Mr. Mellon, Mr. Mellon's next superior, the budget committee, the president?

(f) How would you answer the comment by Mr. Spears?

9-3. Producing Department A factory overhead costs have been analyzed with the following results (costs are related to direct machine hours; normal range of activity is 7 to 9 thousand DMH):

(a) Depreciation $Y = \$600 + 0X$
(b) Indirect labor $Y = \$400 + .08X$
(c) Power costs $Y = - + .02X$

In Producing Department B supplies used have been analyzed as follows (monthly basis):

Activity (Directly Labor Hours)	Budget Allowance
7,000	$406
9,000	472

Required:

For Department A:

(a) Prepare a formula type variable budget for the department (increments of 1,000 starting with 7,000).
(b) Identify and define the type of cost represented by each item.
(c) Graph each cost.
(d) Compute the budget allowance for each cost for January, assuming budgeted activity to be 7,500 DMH.

For Department B:

(e) What is the fixed component of supplies used? The variable rate?
(f) Assume annual budget activity of 100,000 DLH, compute the annual budget allowance.
(g) Graph the account.

9-4. THE CARLSON COMPANY. Based on the data given below for the Carlson Company indicate for each account what you would recommend as the variable budget allowance, and also indicate factor of variability. Justify the decisions you make.

(a) Sales supervisory salaries budgeted for the year $236,400.
(b) Office supplies used ¼ of 1 per cent of net sales (budgeted net sales $400,000).
(c) Maintenance (monthly basis)
    Budget allowance at volume of 100,000 direct machine hours $20,000
    Budget allowance at volume of 80,000 direct machine hours $17,000
(d) Indirect labor is estimated to be $15,000 at 80,000 DMH; at standby $3,800 per month.
(e) Direct labor is estimated to be $42,000 at 100,000 DMH.
(f) Miscellaneous expenses are estimated to be $1,000 at a monthly volume of 100,000 DMH; the cost is estimated to be 60 per cent variable and 40 per cent fixed.
(g) Property taxes last year were $880; it is estimated that there will be a 12½ per cent increase in taxes.

(h) The *method of least squares* analysis on a monthly basis indicates the following for indirect materials when related to DMH: Fixed $1,500, Variable $1.50. The economist estimates a general price level increase of 8 per cent, however, the budget committee feels that the variable portion is at least 10 per cent too high now (at present prices).

9-5. (a) Using the data given below, prepare a variable budget for distribution costs, District #1.

(1) The method of least squares analysis of monthly data for the past 12 months (using dollar sales as the base) provided the following results, adjustment already having been made for "anticipated future conditions."
Promotion costs (other than advertising) $Y = \$1,000 + .05X$
Traveling expenses $Y = \ \ \ \ 100 + .08X$

(2) A graphic analysis of sales commissions, and miscellaneous expenses, showed the following:

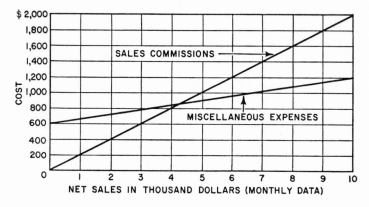

(3) Advertising is handled on an appropriation basis, the annual appropriation being $1,800. (The firm follows the practice of crediting a reserve for advertising each month for one-twelfth of the annual allowance.)

(b) The sales budget included an estimated sales volume for February of $8,200. Using the variable budget developed in (a), compute the distribution cost allowances that should be included in the planning budget for February and used as a guide for cost control during the month.

(c) Assume *actual* sales volume attained in February were $8,500, and actual expenses incurred were: sales commissions $1,700, promotion costs $1,437, traveling expenses $775, miscellaneous expenses $1,130, and advertising $200. Prepare a performance report for management indicating the status of cost control in District #1 during February.

9-6. THE XY COMPANY. The data given below were taken from the cost records of the XY Company:

Department X

Month	Direct Labor Hours (thousands)	Indirect Labor	Mainte- nance	Supplies Used	Salaries	Miscel- laneous Expenses
1	8.0	$750	$620	$690	$300	$170
2	9.0	820	680	790	300	180
3	9.5	850	685	820	300	195
4	8.1	760	625	700	300	175
5	7.0	690	600	600	300	140
6	6.8	675	590	580	300	125
7	6.0	610	520	490	300	110
8	6.1	600	512	475	300	100
9	6.7	660	585	565	300	120
10	7.2	700	610	625	300	150
11	8.0	740	690	685	300	165
12	9.8	880	685	880	300	200

Department Y

Month	Direct Machine Hours	Maintenance	Supplies Used
1	19,000	$250	$475
2	18,000	230	450
3	18,000	240	440
4	17,000	225	430
5	17,000	210	420
6	16,000	200	410
7	14,000	190	360
8	14,000	200	350
9	17,000	230	425
10	19,000	240	480
11	20,000	260	510
12	21,000	280	515

Required:

Department X:

(a) Prepare a graphic analysis of the above data, relating each cost to volume.

(b) Using the graphs developed in (1), construct a formula type variable budget for Department X.

(c) Prepare a table showing the budget allowances at 7,000 and 9,000 direct labor hours. (Note the relevant range is 6 to 10 thousand DLH.)

(d) Comment on supplies used.

Department Y:

(e) Analyze each cost, using the method of least squares.

(f) Prepare a graph showing the least squares results plotted thereon.

(g) Indicate the variable budget allowances.

Chapter 10

10-1. NATIONAL MANUFACTURING COMPANY. "Gentlemen, I have invited the two plant managers to meet with the executive committee today to discuss plant problems. Concerning the plants, I have listed a number of items for discussion as you will note from the agenda and other papers before you. This union problem is getting serious." These were the opening remarks of Melvin C. Robb, president of National Manufacturing Company.

"The first item I would like to discuss is this statement. (see Exhibit 1.) My chief clerk says these statements about plant 2 have been all wrong. Now, I don't have much time to devote to bookkeeping problems, but I don't like this report all the time showing plant 2—with all due respect to Jim Carnes—doing worse than plant 1. I think Jim does a terrific job with that old plant, but these figures on profit margin and return on investment don't make sense to me. Before the company decided to construct plant 2, all these things were settled; otherwise we would not have built it," was the somewhat defensive comment of Ralph Wilson, manager of plant 2.

Exhibit 1

NATIONAL MANUFACTURING COMPANY
Summary of Plant Results
Year ended December 31, 19—

	Plant No. 1	Plant No. 2
Incomes	$14,000,000	$30,000,000
Costs:		
Materials	6,450,000	13,850,000
Direct labor	4,970,000	9,800,000
Depreciation on plant	425,000	1,900,000
Other manufacturing costs	527,000	1,260,000
Administrative costs	338,000	590,000
Home office allocation	800,000	1,700,000
Total costs	$13,510,000	$29,100,000
Income (before income taxes)	$ 490,000	$ 900,000
Profit margin	3.5%	3.0%
Investment:		
Cash	$ 53,000	$ 86,000
Other current assets	272,000	219,000
Land	25,000	47,000
Plant	8,500,000*	21,000,000**
Accumulated depreciation	(6,375,000)	(3,900,000)
Other assets	532,000	478,000
Home office allocation	500,000	1,070,000
Total	$ 3,507,000	$19,000,000
Return on investment	14%	4.7%

*St. line—20 years
**SYD—20 years

"Now Ralph, we don't want to get excited about these figures, although I did want to discuss them with you. Since you mentioned them we might analyze the situation a bit. Two years ago, when plant 2 was completed, we all thought it would be a very efficient operation. We have ceased purchasing from outsiders and are now manufacturing everything we sell. I believe we now have plant 2 close to normal operating capacity. Yet, these figures might indicate that plant 1, and all of you know how old it is, is operating more efficiently, that is, at lower cost, higher profit margin, and higher return on capital. Jim appears to be doing a terrific job with that old plant. Ralph, what do you think is wrong at plant 2?" came the reply of Mr. Robb.

"All of you will recall that I argued very forcefully for the construction of plant 2. It is the latest in machinization—cuts labor costs, produces better quality, and will help us on this union problem. I know it is an efficient plant and should be able to produce much more cheaply, taking quality into consideration, than plant 1. The sales department is certainly conscious of quality in our products. I'm glad that we were able to get the plant up to normal capacity in about 18 months. Ralph has certainly worked hard and efficiently on this. I doubt that we should plan on keeping plant 1 in operation more than 5 more years; quality and costs will be critical. Yet, I don't understand how these figures were developed," interjected the vice president of sales.

"I certainly envy Ralph with that new plant. I think he has performed miracles in getting it going full tilt. I don't think there is a problem —no use quarreling with these figures, they look O. K. to me—you can't compare one plant with the other," commented Jim Carnes, manager of plant 1.

"Looks as if we should do some investigating at plant 2 to see what is the matter. Maybe plant layout is to blame. If the plant is at normal capacity, the figures should be better than plant 1. Perhaps some pressure to reduce costs would help," commented Mr. Robb.

"Before we go too far, let me get in a word or two. I think plant 2 is efficient—we're doing a good job. These figures just are not right. I want to talk to the accounting people. What does this SYD—20 years mean? Who shall I contact down there?" was the immediate reply by Ralph Wilson.

"It appears to me that we ought to have someone on this committee representing accounting and finance. If we don't have someone capable, we should hire somebody," interjected the newest member of the executive committee, Johnny Crow, son-in-law of Mr. Robb.

Feeling that the discussion was getting nowhere, Mr. Robb said: "Let's forget about the figures at this time and get on this union problem. Here we have a serious problem."

Required:

(a) Was the position taken by the manager of plant 2 sound? Explain.
(b) What are your recommendations?

10-2. WALTON CORPORATION. The capital budget committee of the Walton Corporation was established to appraise and screen departmental requests for plant expansions and improvements at a time when these requests totaled ten million dollars. The committee is establishing minimum performance standards which it would demand of these projects in the way of anticipated rates of return before interest and taxes.

The Walton Corporation is a closely held family corporation in which the stockholders exert an active and unified influence on the management. At this date, the company has no long-term debt and has 1,000,000 shares of common capital stock outstanding. It is currently earning $5 millon (net income before interest and taxes) per year. The applicable tax rate is 50 per cent.

Should the projects under consideration be approved, management is confident the $10 million of required funds can be obtained either:

(1) By borrowing—via the medium of an issue of $10 million, 4 per cent, 20-year bonds.

(2) By equity financing—via the medium of an issue of 500,000 shares of common stock to the general public. It is expected and anticipated that the ownership of these 500,000 shares would be widely dispersed.

The company has been earning 12 1/2 per cent return on owners' equity after taxes. The management and the dominant stockholders consider this after-tax rate of earnings to be a minimum capitalization rate (8 times earnings) as long as the company remains free of long-term debt. An increase to 15 per cent after tax rate on owners' equity (6 2/3 times earnings) would constitute a minimum adjustment to compensate for the risk of carrying $10 million of long-term debt. They believe that this reflects, and is consistent with, current market appraisals.

The committee requested:

(1) A columnar schedule comparing the minimum returns on owners' equity for each proposal, considering interest, taxes, and earnings ratios, which should maintain the present capitalized value per share (on owners' equity), and

(2) A columnar schedule showing the effect of each proposal on earnings per share, the capitalized value per share, and the *capitalized-earnings* ratio.

Required:

(a) Prepare the two schedules requested by the committee.

(b) Evaluate the approach used by the committee.

(AICPA Adapted)

10-3 In developing the cash budget for the year 19B you were asked to analyze the accrued and deferred items. Among the items considered were the three given below.

(a) Accrued property taxes—Property taxes are payable in February. The balance in the tax liability account at the end of 19A is $204.00. The 19B variable expense budget shows property taxes to be $19.00 per month (fixed) and no variable. Prepare a schedule to show cash requirements and tax liability account balances by time periods. (Note—the company prepares an an⌐ual budget detailed by quarters; the first quarter is detailed by month.)

(b) Unexpired insurance—The present policy expires and will be renewed on February 1, 19B; thε new 5-year premium is $1,740. The balance in the prepaid insurance account on December 31, 19A is $35. Prepare a schedule similar to that required in (a) above.

(c) Accrued interest expense—The accrued interest expense account has a balance of $450.00 as of December 31, 19A (after closing). There are two notes payable outstanding as follows:

Date	Time	Interest Rate	Face	Type of Note
4/1/19A	1 yr.	4%	$15,000	Bank Loan—interest bearing
1/1/19B	1½ yrs.	5%	26,000	Bank Loan—interest bearing

Required;

Prepare a profit plan schedule showing cash requirements, interest expense, and accrued interest.

10-4. Based on the budget data given below determine the estimated cash receipts from collections of accounts receivable by time period.

(a) Balance in Accounts Receivable account as of December 31, 19A $1,000.

(b) Balance in Allowance for Doubtful Accounts as of December 31, 19A $600.

(c) Budgeted Sales for 19B:

January	$10,100
February	12,120
March	11,110
2nd Quarter	30,300
3rd Quarter	33,330
4th Quarter	32,320

(d) Estimated losses on accounts receivable due to bad debts—1 per cent of sales, rounded to even $10.

(e) Experience indicates collections, after provision for bad debts, should be: 80 per cent in month sold; 10 per cent in first month following sale, and 10 per cent in second month following sale. On quarterly basis assume 90 per cent will be collected in quarter sold and balance in next quarter. One-fourth of the net in accounts receivable as of December 31, 19A will probably be collected in June, balance uncertain.

10-5. THE FEDER COMPANY prepares an annual profit plan covering all phases of operations. The plan is broken down by quarters, the first quarter being detailed by months. The following planning data have been developed to date:

(1) Capital additions budget—Cash requirements as follows: Machinery to be purchased: March $2,500, 3rd Quarter $6,000. Contribution to building fund: $30,000 on December 15. Blanket appropriations for minor capital additions: 1st Quarter $600, 2nd Quarter $500, 3rd Quarter $500, 4th Quarter $700.

(2) Sales budget (averages 70 per cent cash sales)—January $90,000, February $85,000, March $85,000, 2nd Quarter $250,000, 3rd Quarter $230,000, 4th Quarter $300,000.

(3) Collections on credit sales, after allowance for bad debts, are expected to be as follows: 80 per cent in month sold, 10 per cent in first month following sale, 7 per cent in second month following sale, and 3 per cent in third month. On a quarterly basis 94 per cent collected in quarter sold and 6 per cent in the next quarter.

(4) Estimated balances at beginning of the budget year:

Accounts receivable	$20,000	(Estimated collections: 2nd
Allowance for doubtful accounts	7,000	Quarter $5,000, 4th Quarter
Cash	15,000	$7,000)

(5) Estimates of Other Incomes and Other Expenses (Cash basis)

	Other Incomes	Other Expenses
January	$1,500	$2,000
February	1,000	2,000
March	1,000	1,500
2nd Quarter	3,000	5,000
3rd Quarter	3,000	5,000
4th Quarter	4,000	6,000

(6) Allowance for bad debts is one-half of 1 per cent of credit sales. (Round to even $10.)

(7) Cash required for purchases is estimated to be as follows: January, $14,408; February, $16,272; March, $15,230; 2nd Quarter, $46,380; 3rd Quarter, $39,370; and 4th Quarter, $48,496.

(8) Expense budget totals are as follows (assume exclusions for noncash items such as depreciation total $4,500 per month): January, $70,900; February, $67,710; March, $70,120; 2nd Quarter, $200,620; 3rd Quarter, $174,630; and 4th Quarter, $212,010.

(9) Estimated miscellaneous cash requirements:
   (a) Insurance policy to be renewed on June 1, cost $750.
   (b) Property taxes to be paid in February $1,400.
   (c) March 15, annual payment of interest (4 per cent) on long-term Notes Payable, principal $50,000. $20,000 is also paid on the principal at this time.
   (d) Dividends $20,000 (June).
   (e) Legal retainer fees $150.00 per month. *
   (f) Audit fee payable $2,500 (February).

*Not included in (8).

(g) Federal income taxes: April, $21,000; November, $3,000; and December, $3,000.

Required:

Prepare the following schedules for the profit plan:
(a) Estimated cash collections from receivables.
(b) Summary of cash receipts detailed by source and time periods.
(c) Summary of cash payments—detailed by reason and time periods.
(d) Tentative cash budget.
(e) Schedule of short-term financing recommended. (Assume 5 per cent interest rate.)
(f) Final cash budget—set out financing and repayment separately.

10-6. THE CONWAY COMPANY utilizes a comprehensive budget program. The profit plan is developed on a semi-annual basis, being detailed by months. The company has had considerable difficulty with working capital, especially cash. A serial bond issue is being paid which constitutes a heavy drain on cash; the last payment is to be made in 19A. Certain data as of March 31, 19A, are given below.

(a) Cash budget for the 6 months ending June 30, 19A (page 546).
(b) Actual results of operations relative to cash for 3 months ending March 31, 19A:

  Cash receipts—Cash sales: Jan.-Feb., $173,000; March, $81,000. Receivable collections: Jan.-Feb., $61,000; March, $34,000. Notes collected: Jan.-Feb., $8,000; March, $3,000. Other incomes: Jan.-Feb., $6,200; March, $3,400.

  Cash payments—Raw mat. purchases: Jan.-Feb., $36,000; March, $18,000. Accounts paid: Jan.-Feb., $51,000; March, $28,000. Notes paid: Jan.-Feb., $10,000; March, $10,000. Expenses paid: Jan.-Feb., $115,700; March, $68,200. Other expenses: Jan.-Feb., $13,000; March, $5,500. Capital additions: Jan.-Feb., $10,500; March $900.

Required:

(a) Prepare a performance report of cash receipts and disbursements as of March 31, 19A, to be presented to top management. Provide comments where appropriate.
(b) Prepare an analysis of the probable cash position for the remainder of the year, including your recommendations for additional financing. The present line of credit is $50,000. Provide comments where appropriate.

The Conway Company Cash Budget

	January	February	March	April	May	June	Total
Beginning cash balance	$ 20,000	$ 33,500	$ 40,800	$ 47,500	($ 21,300)	($ 15,300)	$ 20,000
Cash receipts:							
Cash sales	80,000	90,000	90,000	75,000	70,000	65,000	470,000
Receivable collections	30,000	35,000	36,000	25,000	20,000	20,000	166,000
Notes collected	5,000	2,000	3,000	8,000	3,000	6,000	27,000
Other incomes	3,000	3,000	3,500	3,000	2,500	2,500	17,500
Sale treasury stock				18,000			18,000
Total receipts	$118,000	$130,000	$132,500	$129,000	$ 95,500	$ 93,500	$698,500
Total cash available	$138,000	$163,500	$173,300	$176,500	$ 74,200	$ 78,200	$718,500
Cash payments:							
Raw material purchases	$ 15,000	$ 17,000	$ 16,000	$ 8,000	$ 14,000	$ 13,000	$ 83,000
Accounts paid	25,000	28,000	26,000	12,000	17,300	25,000	133,300
Notes paid	10,000		10,000				20,000
Expenses paid	48,500	61,700	66,600	54,800	52,700	49,500	333,800
Dividends						15,000	15,000
Bonds				40,000			40,000
Other expenses	5,000	6,000	6,000	4,500	4,500	4,000	30,000
Income taxes				78,000			78,000
Capital additions	1,000	10,000	1,200	500	1,000	500	14,200
Total payments	$104,500	$122,700	$125,800	$197,800	$ 89,500	$107,000	$747,300
Ending cash balances (before financing)	$ 33,500	$ 40,800	$ 47,500	($ 21,300)	($ 15,300)	($ 28,800)	($ 28,800)
Budgeted financing				35,000[a]			35,000
Ending cash balances (after financing)	$ 33,500	$ 40,800	$ 47,500	$ 13,700	$ 19,700	$ 6,200	$ 6,200

[a] Six months bank loan $35,000 @ 5%.

10-7. THE BASE MANUFACTURING COMPANY. The management of the Base Manufacturing Company is purchasing a machine required for a special operation. They are considering two machines. The following data have been developed to provide a basis for selecting one alternative over the other.

	Machine A	Machine B
Cost of machine	$120,000	$120,000
Estimated life-years (straightline)	8	15
Estimated average annual income (before deducting income taxes)	$ 24,000	$ 16,800
Residual value	—0—	—0—
Income tax rate	40%	40%

You are requested to develop the following analyses.
(a) Payback—years and return.
(b) Average return on investment—on average investment and on original investment.
(c) Discounted rate of return
(d) Evaluate the results

10-8. THE XYZ COMPANY is considering two machines. As a basis for selection of one of them the following data were developed:

	Machine A	Machine B
Investment (original cost)	$26,563	$26,563
Annual estimated income after depreciation and income taxes		
Year 1	$ 687	$ 4,687
Year 2	1,687	3,687
Year 3	2,687	2,687
Year 4	3,687	1,687
Year 5	4,689	689
Total	$13,437	$13,437
Estimated life—straightline (years)	5	5
Estimated residual value	—0—	—0—
Estimated average income tax rate	40%	40%

Required:

(a) Compute the cash inflow on each machine.
(b) Compute payback and average return on each machine.
(c) Compute the discounted rates of return.
(d) Evaluate the results.

Chapter 11

11-1. THE MONROE COMPANY manufactures a medium-priced line of furniture which is sold in a four-state area. Twenty-one different items are manufactured and there are several variations in about one-half of the items. For example, there are four different styles of "TV-Lounger" chairs although they are all built around the same chassis. The variations are principally in the type and design of the covering used on the chairs, although one type utilizes a more expensive material for the padding.

The company has been in operation for over twenty years and is owned by thirty-one stockholders. The board of directors, consisting of four members of the active management and three other stockholders, meets monthly to review operations and to formulate basic policy. Since World War II the company has experienced a steady growth in sales volume, having increased approximately 180 per cent to an annual volume of about 18 million dollars.

For several years the company has budgeted sales and to a limited extent the cash position. During the past year a complete planning budget was used for the first time. The management was generally pleased with the results despite the fact that some aspects of the plan appeared to have been unrealistic. During the year there had been numerous suggestions that some part of the budget be revised. The president had taken the position that no changes should be made in the plan of operations under any circumstances. This policy caused some concern especially when the monthly performance reports were distributed.

The budget for the coming year had just been completed and was being considered by the executive committee (composed of the four top operating executives who were also on the board of directors) prior to submission to the board of directors at the next meeting. The company had followed what they considered good budget procedure in bringing intermediate members of the management into the budget building activities. It appeared that these supervisors were quite interested in the program although they were frank to admit that they needed to know more about the whole picture.

The executive committee first considered the sales budget, which had been discussed previously by them and tentatively approved. In view of the experience during the past several years it was generally agreed that the sales budget was realistic. The inventory policy seemed sound, consequently there was little questioning about the production budget. The expense budgets were considered next. At this stage of the discussions Ray Crandall, the executive in charge of manufacturing, remarked that "the production budget looks OK; however, these expense budgets still bother me as they did last year. My supervisors who worked on them have recommended that our revision policy be relaxed. Once we set the budget there appears to be an inflexible policy that it cannot be revised. It seems to me that we should establish a more flexible policy on this matter. Now as to production, we can plan it on a week-to-week basis; the budget of production is merely a guide. But on expenses the budget is the master." "Well, Ray, we have held the line on all revisions (and not only expense) in the past year because requests for budget changes can very quickly become a habit; every time someone falls down on the job we get a request for a change in the budget. Before long the budget means nothing, particularly since some supervisors can anticipate an unfavorable report of their operations and, for self-protection, request a budget change before the report is prepared. We have operated under the concept that we will build a good sound plan and that we should know where and when we fall down. As top management, we need a firm plan with some force behind it; we need to know where we are heading. If we continually change the budget, our plan becomes so vague and changeable that it will be of little use to us. If we keep changing our goals, we will lose sight of where we should be going; in fact we will be wandering in the dark just as if we had no plan of operations. Besides we can't be revising the budget at every whipstitch; we have other things to do," replied the president, Harry Rapides. "What do you think, Rich?" "I'm not sure just what we should set as policy on this matter, Harry," replied Glen Richards, the executive in charge of sales. "We spend a lot of time developing our plan of operations; obviously we can't foresee all events and conditions; yet we can't be changing our plans all the time. If conditions get too far from that anticipated in our budget, comparisons won't mean much. If we are willing to look carefully at the variations to determine those causes beyond our control and those due to inefficiency, we might get along without too much revision." Benny Hughes, the executive in charge of finance and accounting, had responsibility for coordinating the budget activities; consequently, he had very definite ideas about the matter. He observed that "we should be very reluctant to change the budget; only when major events that were unforeseen occur should we consider revision." Mr. Rapides noting that it was about lunch time stated: "Let's knock off until tomorrow at 2:00. At that time let's get together here and agree on a basic policy relative to budget revision for the coming year. Remember we are experimenting; we can always change the policy for the next year. In the meantime, I would like for each of you to do some serious thinking on the matter."

Required:

What policy would you recommend relative to budget revision? Provide the basis for your recommendations.

11-2. THE NAPKO COMPANY is currently developing a planning budget for 19A. Certain data developed to date are given below.

(a) Budgeted cost of goods manufactured

	Product A		Product B	
	Units	*Unit Cost*	*Units*	*Unit Cost*
January	20,000	$1.00	14,000	$2.00
February	20,000	1.00	15,000	2.00
March	21,000	1.00	16,000	2.10
April	23,000	1.00	15,000	2.10
May	23,000	1.00	14,000	2.10
June	23,000	1.00	13,000	2.10

(b) Sales budget (Units)

	Product A		Product B	
	District 1	*District 2*	*District 1*	*District 2*
January	10,000	7,000	6,000	6,000
February	12,000	8,000	7,000	6,000
March	13,000	11,000	9,000	8,000
April	15,000	12,000	9,000	7,000
May	14,000	11,000	8,000	7,000
June	9,000	8,000	5,000	5,000

(c) Beginning inventories: Product A, 20,000 units @ $.90; Product B, 30,000 units @ $1.90. The company uses *fifo*.

Required:

(a) Prepare a worksheet to compute cost of goods sold by product, by sales district. Assume shipments to districts from stock to be in the ratio of budgeted sales on a unit basis.

(b) Prepare a budgeted cost of goods sold by product, district, and time.

(c) Prepare a budget of finished goods inventories by product and time period.

(d) Indicate the sources of the input budget data utilized in requirements (a), (b), and (c). Is the assumption in (a) sound? Why?

11-3. THE ADOLPH COMPANY is in the process of developing a profit plan covering the year 19B. Certain budget data developed to date are:

(1) Net income budgeted $54,500
(2) Addition to building $10,000
(3) Machinery purchased $21,000
(4) Sale of machinery $5,000 (cash), costing $20,000 (80 per cent depreciated)

(5) Depreciation on machinery $8,000
(6) Payment on bonds payable $20,000
(7) Sale of stock at par $20,000
(8) Dividends $7,500
(9) Trial balances:

	Actual Balances 12/31/19A	Budgeted Balances 12/31/19B
Cash	$ 33,000	$ 61,000
Accounts receivable	78,000	73,000
Allowance for doubtful accounts	(8,000)	(7,000)
Notes receivable	15,000	16,000
Inventories	40,000	47,000
Prepaid expenses	5,000	6,000
Supplies on hand	7,000	5,000
Buildings	100,000	110,000
Accumulated depreciation	(40,000)	(45,000)
Machinery	60,000	61,000
Accumulated depreciation	(20,000)	(12,000)
Land	50,000	50,000
	$320,000	$365,000
Accounts payable	$ 44,000	$ 47,000
Notes payable	30,000	25,000
Accrued taxes payable	6,000	6,000
Bonds payable	50,000	30,000
Capital stock	150,000	170,000
Retained earnings	40,000	87,000
	$320,000	$365,000

Required:

Prepare the following schedules:
   (a) Budgeted changes in working capital
   (b) Worksheet—budgeted application of funds
   (c) Budgeted application of funds statement

11-4. THE R. T. ZECK COMPANY executives are considering alternatives concerning company autos. The profit plan for the coming year is being developed and a definite policy is need. The company now owns one company car which is over 3 years old and is to be disposed of. Extra cars are being rented from the Jett Rent-A-Car Agency as needed. Some executives feel that the company should purchase additional autos; others feel that it is more economical to rent cars when needed. Maintenance on the car presently owned is performed by the local dealer at regular rates. The following data have been developed to date under your supervision:

(1) Estimated requirements for the next year:
    (a) Four cars per day—Monday through Friday each week
    (b) Two additional cars each week on Monday and Friday
(2) Rental costs per auto quoted by the Jett Company:
    (a) Weekly rate (5 days)—$22.50 plus 8 cents per mile
    (b) Daily rate (8:00 A.M. to 6:00 P.M.)—$6.00 plus 8 cents per mile
(3) Estimated mileage per car for the year:
    (a) On the four cars used daily—20,000 miles
    (b) On the two extra cars—6,000 miles
(4) Estimated variable costs for company owned cars:
    (a) Gas and oil—$3\frac{1}{2}$ cents per mile
    (b) Repairs and service—1 cent per mile
(5) Estimated fixed costs for company owned cars:
    (a) License and taxes per car $40.00
    (b) Insurance per car   90.00
    (c) Garage rental per year   1,500.00 (based on space required)
    (d) Outside maintenance per car:
        On the four cars used daily   30.00 (per month)
        On two extra cars   16.50 (per month)
    (e) Dispatcher for six cars   250.00 (per month)
(6) Cost of new cars $1,950 (The company uses straight-line depreciation.)
(7) Estimated trade-in value at end af 3 years $450 per car.

Required:

(a) You have been asked to analyze the situation and to present a report to the executive committee with recommendations. Use the above data as you deem appropriate.

(b) What additional data would you need to support your analysis and recommendations? Why?

11-5. THE CENTRAL MANUFACTURING COMPANY. The budget committee of The Central Manufacturing Company has had one meeting concerning the sales budget proposed by the sales division. During the meeting there was considerable discussion concerning profits and the effect of sales volume on cost and profits. Profits for the past several years have been rather low, averaging 2 per cent of sales, whereas the industry average is 4.5 per cent (before income taxes). Tentative planning data already developed are as follows:

(1) Annual sales forecast:

District	Amount
1	$5,000,000
2	4,000,000
3	4,000,000
4	7,000,000

(2) Raw material cost averages 6 per cent of sales.
(3) Direct labor cost averages 10.6 per cent of sales.
(4) Variable budget totals:

		Fixed per Month	Variable
Producing Dept. #	1	$ 81,667	$ 3.47 per hundred direct machine hours
Producing Dept.	2	80,000	2.50 per hundred direct machine hours
Producing Dept.	3	68,333	35.00 per hundred direct labor hours
Producing Dept.	4	80,833	12.60 per hundred direct labor hours
Producing Dept.	5	92,500	33.70 per hundred direct labor hours
Service Dept.	21	34,167	.44 per hundred total direct machine hours
	22	22,500	2.10 per hundred total direct labor hours
	23	26,667	.20 per hundred total sales dollars total
Administrative			
Dept.	30	70,000	.003 per total sales dollar
	31	85,000	.007 per total sales dollar
	32	70,000	.005 per total sales dollar
Sales:			
Home Office		130,000	.004 per total sales dollar
District	1	33,000	.06 per district sales dollar
	2	35,000	.085 per district sales dollar
	3	36,000	.085 per district sales dollar
	4	34,000	.046 per district sales dollar

(5) Inventory changes—none.
(6) Assume federal income tax average rate of 40 per cent.
(7) Volume data:

	At Sales Forecast	At 105% of Sales Forecast
Sales volume	$20,000,000	$21,000,000
Direct machine hours (hundreds)		
Department 1	150,000	157,500
Department 2	120,000	126,000
Direct labor hours (hundreds)		
Department 3	16,000	16,800
Department 4	38,000	39,900
Department 5	22,000	23,100

Required:

Prepare tentative income statements at (a) the forecast volume, and (b) assuming a 5 per cent increase in the sales forecast of each district. Detail the expenses by department. (c) What would you recommend relative to increasing the profit margin?

Chapter 12

12-1. THE DUNCAN COMPANY. The Duncan Company profit plan for the year is summarized below.

Sales (400,000 units)		$20,000,000
Manufacturing costs:		
Material	$1,700,000	
Labor	1,600,000	
Fixed overhead	2,500,000	
Variable overhead	3,800,000	
Distribution costs:		
Fixed	3,400,000	
Variable	1,900,000	
Administrative costs:		
Fixed	1,750,000	
Variable	350,000	
Total costs		17,000,000
Net Profit (before income taxes)		$ 3,000,000

Required:

(a) Compute the breakeven point using total costs.
(b) Compute the breakeven point using unit costs.
(c) Using the results of (a) and (b) prepare a breakeven chart showing the several components of cost.
(d) Explain and evaluate the results.

12-2. THE METAL PRODUCTS COMPANY manufactures three models of a single product. From the following data you are to prepare a schedule, supported by computations, showing sales quantity and sales dollars for each model necessary to enable the company to cover its variable and nonvariable costs (AICPA adapted).

Model No.	Annual Sales Budget (Units)	Budgeted Unit Sales Price	Budgeted Sales Allowance for Year	Quantity Budgeted for Production
100	30,000	$15	$1,260	30,500
200	16,000	18	480	15,000
300	10,000	25	410	10,000

Model No.	Over-all Total Cost (Per Unit)	Estimated Cost per Unit	
		Variable	*Non-variable*
100	$15.072	$ 9.871	$5.201
200	17.335	10.250	7.085
300	23.756	15.436	8.320

12-3. THE K CORPORATION. Certain planning budget data for the year for the K Corporation are summarized below:

Sales		$15,000,000
Costs:		
Fixed	$4,150,000	
Variable	9,450,000	13,600,000
Net Profit		$ 1,400,000

Required:

(a) Compute the breakeven point.

(b) Compute the breakeven point assuming fixed costs are increased 10 per cent.

(c) Compute the breakeven point assuming variable costs only are increased 10 per cent.

(d) Compute the breakeven point assuming sales prices are increased 10 per cent. Disregard requirements (b) and (c).

(e) Compute the breakeven point assuming sales volume is increased 10 per cent. Disregard requirements (b), (c), and (d).

(f) Prepare a breakeven chart for requirements (a) and (d).

12-4. Certain annual budget data for two similar companies are as follows:

	Company A		Company B	
Sales	$200,000		$200,000	
Costs:				
Fixed	$120,000		$ 60,000	
Variable	60,000	180,000	120,000	180,000
Net income		$ 20,000		$ 20,000

Required:

Evaluate and compare the economic characteristics of the two companies. Support your computations with appropriate comments.

12-5. THE EGON CORPORATION, in evaluating profit potentials, considers the effect of sales mix. Budgeted fixed costs are $3,312; variable cost ratios: Product A, 70 per cent; Product B, 80 per cent; and Product C, 90 per cent. The following sales mix alternatives are being considered:

	Sales—Alternative No. 1		Sales—Alternative No. 2	
Product	Amount	Mix Ratio	Amount	Mix Ratio
A	$12,000	50%	$16,800	70%
B	7,200	30	4,800	20
C	4,800	20	2,400	10

Required:

Based on the data given, evaluate the two alternatives. Select the preferable one, explaining the basis for your choice.

12-6. THE CORDING MANUFACTURING COMPANY prepares a cost-volume-profit analysis for each plant. For Plant No. 1 annual budgeted fixed costs are $120,000; variable costs, $84,000; and sales value of production, $220,000. Allocated home office costs are $32,000.

(a) You are asked to prepare the analysis (and chart) indicating the breakeven points before and after cost allocations.

(b) Plant No. 2 produces a product which costs $3.00 per unit when produced in quantities of 10,000 and $2.50 per unit when produced in quantities of 20,000. What are the total fixed costs?

(c) Plant No. 3 income and cost estimates are as follows:

Sales (annual)		$100,000
Costs:		
Fixed	$40,000	
Variable	30,000	
Home office allocated	35,000	105,000
Net loss		$ 5,000

Sale of Plant No. 3 is under consideration; what is your recommendation based on the data given? Justify your recommendation.

(d) Plant No. 4 income and cost estimates are as follows:

Sales (annual)		$200,000
Costs:		
Fixed	$ 75,000	
Variable	135,000	
Home office allocated	50,000	260,000
Net loss		$ 60,000

Sale of Plant No. 4 is under consideration; what is your recommendation based on the data given? Justify your recommendation.

12-7. COMPANY X. The annual planning budget for Company X shows sales of $18,000,000 and total costs of $13,600,000, of which $10,000,000 are fixed costs. Published financial data of competitor Y for the past 10 years are as follows:

Year	Sales	Total Costs
(1)	$ 8,000,000	$ 8,100,000
(2)	8,000,000	8,200,000
(3)	8,400,000	8,300,000
(4)	8,800,000	8,500,000
(5)	9,500,000	8,700,000
(6)	10,200,000	9,000,000
(7)	10,700,000	9,300,000
(8)	11,600,000	9,700,000
(9)	12,100,000	9,800,000
(10)	13,000,000	10,100,000

Required:

On the basis of the data given, evaluate and compare the two companies.

12-8. THE EASTERN COMPANY. The proposed annual profit plan for the Eastern Company showed the following simplified data:

	Product X			Product Y			*Total*
	Units	*Price*	*Amount*	*Units*	*Price*	*Amount*	*Amount*
Sales	1,000	$1.00	$1,000	2,000	$3.00	$6,000	$7,000
Costs:							
Fixed			200			2,700	2,900
Variable			600			2,400	3,000
Total			800			5,100	5,900
Net income			$ 200			$ 900	$1,100

Required:

(a) Compute separate breakeven points in sales dollars and units for each product assuming complete independence.

(b) Compute the company breakeven point in sales dollars assuming a constant sales mix quantity ratio of 1:2.

(c) Using the answer derived in (b) and the data above, compute the number of units of each product at breakeven (quantities ratio 1:2). Present proof of computations.

(d) Compute the company breakeven point in sales dollars assuming a constant sales mix as follows:

Case A—Product X, 2,000 units; Product Y, 2,000 units
Case B—Product X, 1,000 units; Product Y, 3,000 units

(e) What basic evaluations and conclusions can you draw from the preceding computations?

(f) Based on the data given, what product should be push·d? Why?

12-9. THE SHORT MANUFACTURING COMPANY manufactures two products, A and B. The company is having difficulty making sufficient sales to employ present plant capacity. A new customer offers a large repeating contract for Product A at $10 each and for Product B at $18 each. The following data are available (assume the old market will not be affected):

	Product A	Product B
Direct labor	$ 6,000	$15,000
Direct material	3,000	5,000
Variable factory overhead	3,000	4,000
Fixed factory overhead	12,000	20,000
Packing, shipping, and other variable costs	4,800	1,000
Administrative and sales overhead	9,000	15,000
Current sales: Average quantity	4,000 units	2,500 units
Unit sales price	$ 14	20

Assume the new contract will not increase fixed costs and administrative and selling overhead.

Required:

(a) Compute the breakeven point for each product separately.

(b) Based on the data given, should the contract be accepted? Support your conclusion with computations.

(c) What is the minimum price and volume for each product that could be accepted under the new offer?

12-10. A small-job printing firm is preparing a bid for 10 to 15 thousand advertising pamphlets, to which the following figures relate:

Estimated cost of setting up and fixed overhead	$390
Estimated cost of material and variable overhead	$5.00 per hundred
Estimated cost of labor	$3.00 per hundred
Estimated selling price	.11 each

Required:

(a) How many pamphlets must be sold to break even?

(b) What is the profit per pamphlet above breakeven?

(c) What should be the bid price for 10,000 pamphlets if a 10 per cent profit on sales is to be made? On 14,000 pamphlets?

12-11. Cost analysis of a typical service station, *type A*, indicated the following: Average annual investment (including building), $30,000; fixed costs per month, $2,500; and for each $1 sale of gasoline (4 gallons) variable costs of $.75.

Required:

(Each requirement is independent of the others unless otherwise indicated.)

(a) How much volume per month (average) must the operator attain to break even?

(b) How much profit can the operator expect (1) in January, if sales are 48,000 gallons, and (2) in February, if sales are 32,000 gallons?

(c) What average monthly volume must the operator attain in order to earn 10 per cent return on the investment?

(d) The operator is considering an increase in fixed costs of $500 per month; what volume must he attain to (1) break even, (2) earn 10 per cent on the average investment?

(e) Variable costs are increased 10 per cent. What volume is necessary to break even? What volume is necessary to earn 10 per cent return on the investment? Disregard requirement (d).

(f) The operator considers increasing investment by stocking certain miscellaneous items for sale. He contemplates an average stock costing $1,000, having a markup on cost of 20 per cent. Anticipated sales per month are $240 (at selling price). What is the breakeven point assuming no change in fixed costs? What is the volume necessary to earn 10 per cent on the investment?

(g) A retail price reduction of one cent per gallon is contemplated. What is the new breakeven point and volume necessary to earn 10 per cent on the investment, (1) assuming the operator absorbs the price reduction, and (2) assuming the operator and supplier absorb the price reduction equally? Disregard requirements (d) to (f) above.

12-12. THE FASTWEAVE COMPANY. Early in 1953, after numerous experiments, Mr. James R. Smith, a textile engineer, perfected a satisfactory working model of a loom that was far superior to anything on the market.

After discussing the new invention with friends and relatives, Mr. Smith decided to organize a corporation to manufacture the new loom. He applied for a patent and began looking for manufacturing equipment and a suitable factory building.

The Fastweave Company was incorporated in North Carolina in 1953. Mr. Smith purchased 1,500 shares of the common stock at par ($20 per share). Friends and relatives purchased an additional 2,650 shares of the stock at par. The company planned to make available to selected individuals the remainder of the 15,000 shares authorized.

Mr. Smith was able to obtain some surplus government machine shop equipment at very reasonable prices. A small, but suitable warehouse was rented for the factory building.

Early in 1954, a small work force was hired and the company began manufacturing and selling the new looms. Net sales during 1954 approximated $30,000, total costs amounted to $42,000 including approximately $30,000 fixed costs, and book value of the assets at end of the year amounted to $116,000. However, more textile companies became interested in the new loom; consequently, net sales increased to around $60,000 for 1955, resulting in a profit of approximately $5,000 for the year (liabilities at the end of the year amounted to $30,000).

In anticipation of a continued increase in demand, the board of directors recognized that additional heavy equipment would have to be purchased before sales could be increased much beyond $70,000. The board authorized the purchase of sufficient equipment (costing $160,000) to increase capacity to approximately $250,000 sales volume. The company arranged for immediate delivery during January 1956. To raise capital, an additional 7,850 shares of common stock were sold during 1956 at $20 per share. In considering the purchase of the new equipment, the directors noted that the new equipment would increase present fixed costs by approximately 100 per cent, including a 125 per cent increase in the annual depreciation charge to approximately $27,000.[1]

Many textile mills were interested in purchasing the Fastweave loom, but were extremely cautious about installing the new machine before the completion of extensive and lengthy field tests. However, purchasers of the new machine supported Mr. Smith's claim that it wove with more speed, efficiency, and quietness. Smith felt that field tests also confirmed the fact that the new loom outproduced the old standard models and was much easier to operate and maintain. The major resistance offered by prospective purchasers was that the new loom had not been tested with all types of fabrics.

Although net sales increased in 1956 to approximately $90,000, a net loss of $18,000 was sustained (book value of assets $234,000). Net sales increased again in 1957 to around $100,000 with a loss of $10,000 (liabilities at the end of the year amounted to $27,000). In view of a $4,000 profit in 1958 (net sales $120,000; book value of assets $221,000) and a shortage of cash, Mr. Smith recognized that additional funds again would be necessary to see the company through the next several years. The directors had never declared a dividend.

Mr. Smith felt that sales volume was the key to success; consequently, he felt that the company should spend at least $10,000 per year on an extensive advertising campaign, and also add four salaried salesmen (average salary $8,000 per year) to contact distributors. The company had found it difficult to get distributors because of the established position of older manufacturers. These plans would also require substantial cash outlays.

The directors desired to maintain control over the company, and were

---

[1] The fixed assets are being depreciated on the basis of an average life of ten years (straightline).

reluctant to make public offerings of the common stock. Consequently, they instructed Mr. Smith to contact a local financing institution with the view of arranging an $80,000, 6 per cent loan, payable at the end of three years.

Mr. Smith contacted the loan officer of a local financing institution for an appointment. Mr. Smith was requested to bring "figures" relating to operations for the past five years; accordingly, he had the bookkeeper prepare the following summary of sales, incomes, assets, and liabilities:

The Fastweave Company

SUMMARY OF SALES, INCOME, ASSETS, AND LIABILITIES

	1955	1958
Sales	$ 60,000	$120,000
Net profit	5,000	4,000
Assets—Book value	106,000	221,000
Assets—Market value	130,000	300,000
Liabilities	30,000	12,000

After a discussion of the business with Mr. Smith and a study of the summary, the loan officer made the following statement:

"These historical figures reflect what has happened in your company— and frankly, it doesn't look too good. We need to examine the future. What are the profit potentials? What is your breakeven point? What can be done to increase the company profit margin? These questions are vital in evaluating the possibility of repayment because cash is generated by profits. We need a projection for the next three years before your request for a loan can be considered properly."

Mr. Smith indicated that he would have "some figures" ready the next morning. The figures summarized below were developed by Mr. Smith assuming the loan would go through:

			Cash	
Year	Sales	Profits	Payment on Loan	Excess
1959	$180,000	$ 20,000		$10,000
1960	225,000	25,000	$20,000	5,000
1961	250,000	40,000	30,000	10,000
1962	250,000	40,000	30,000	10,000
	$905,000	$125,000	$80,000	$35,000

Required:

(a) Evaluate the profit and cash potentials of the company assuming you have made a study of the sales projections and believe they are realistic.

(b) Evaluate the balance sheet potentials (past and future.)

(c) Suggest reasonable answers to the questions posed by the loan officer.

(d) Do you think the loan should be made? Why?

Chapter 13

13-1. THE DISHON-WRIGHT COMPANY. For several years The Dishon-Wright Company had used a planning budget. Several revisions in the over-all budget program had been adopted on an experimental basis during the past year. One of the changes involved the adoption of variable budget procedures in several of the departments in the factory. An evaluation of the results had convinced the management that these procedures would improve cost control if understood and used properly. One problem related to controllable and noncontrollable costs. There had been no distinction made along these lines as far as departmental costs were concerned; all costs related to the department were listed on the departmental cost report. There had been considerable discussion at the lower-supervisory levels during the past few months concerning this practice. Many of the lower-level supervisors felt that they should not be held responsible for items over which they had little or no control. In thinking about this problem the management had come to the conclusion that every cost should be the responsibility of some individual with supervisory or executive status. In attempting to implement this concept, problems were encountered with respect to certain costs, particularly those over which little control could be exercised and those that tended to overlap more than one department. Consequently, the top management was considering a policy to the effect that "whatever department exerts the *most* influence over a particular item of cost, irrespective of the degree of influence, shall be held responsible for that cost."

During the discussions one executive remarked that "we should not be concerned about insignificant variations." "What do you consider to be insignificant?" another asked.

Another problem being considered by the management had to do with the type of departmental cost report that would best fit the situation, particularly in view of the recent concern about controllable costs. The form of report used during the past year is shown in Exhibit 1 on page 563.

The president had requested the budget committee to make recommendations relative to (a) the policies mentioned above and (b) the format of the budget report. A short meeting had been held subsequently at which time these matters were discussed. Two proposals concerning the cost report were submitted by the controller, who had supervisory responsibilities with respect to the budget. The two proposals are shown in Exhibits 2 and 3 (page 564). The committee did not make a definite decision with respect to either of them. Some members of the committee felt that all expenses should be shown on the departmental cost report so that, as one member stated, "supervisors will know the total costs involved in their departments; this will make them more cost conscious." There was no objection to showing controllable and noncontrollable costs separately "assuming we can agree on a policy that makes sense and can be made practical." Other members of the committee felt strongly that only the controllable costs should show on the departmental cost reports. "Why clutter up the reports with noncontrollable items? Besides, the foremen and supervisors strongly resent their being shown even though they are separately listed. They feel that they will get blamed for unfavorable variations even though they are listed as noncontrollable.

"I have checked with many of them and they just don't want them listed," reported one member of the committee. "But we don't want these expenses going unreported and hence uncontrolled," reported another.

Required:

(a) What would you recommend relative to the policy decisions facing the management?

(b) Indicate your choice as between Exhibits 1, 2 and 3, or draft a more suitable format for the company. Give support for your choice.

The Dishon-Wright Company   Exhibit 1.

DEPARTMENTAL COST REPORT, ___March 31, 19—___
                                                          (date)

___(Department)___   ___(Supervisor)___

	Month of March			3 Months through March		
	Actual	Adjusted Budget	Variation	Actual	Adjusted Budget	Variation
Raw materials used	$	$	$	$	$	$
Direct labor						
Vacation wages						
Maintenance						
Supplies used						
Indirect labor						
Insurance						
Taxes						
Utilities						
Miscellaneous						
Total	$	$	$	$	$	$

Exhibit 2.

(Heading)

	Month of _____		_____ months through __	
	Actual	Variation	Actual	Variation
Materials used (lbs.)				
Labor (hrs.)				
*Vacation wages Maintenance	$	$	$	$
Supplies used Indirect labor *Insurance *Taxes Utilities Miscellaneous Total *Noncontrollable				

Exhibit 3.

(Heading)

	Month of _____			_____ months through __		
CONTROLLABLE:	Actual	Budget	Variation	Actual	Budget	Variation
Materials used Labor Maintenance	$	$	$	$	$	$
Supplies Indirect labor Utilities Miscellaneous Total						

13-2. THE "X" SERVICE COMPANY, situated in the Southwest, has rendered services to the oil industry for approximately 35 years. Services rendered are technical and cover a fairly broad range of jobs.

Two years ago the sales organization, which is a part of operations, came up with a new idea regarding a service that they thought involved a vast new market. The idea was discussed with field operations and with higher levels of management. As a result, the research and engineering department was directed to study the idea and to come up with plans for a prototype of the equipment required. Based upon these plans, research and engineering was directed to build and test a prototype. The general policy laid down with respect to this idea was that speed in development was important and that cost was not a critical factor. A target date for completion of the equipment and related testing was set. The time involved approximated twenty months. During this period of time, research and engineering spent some $300,000 in development and testing. Testing involved numerous field tests by engineers working closely with the field personnel. The tests indicated that the equipment was quite effective and performed as anticipated. In addition to the $300,000 spent for research and development, approximately $75,000 was spent in constructing the prototype and in adapting it for field use.

The prototype unit was assigned to field operations and used in a particular area for a period of six months. Although the equipment worked satisfactorily and the resulting services were of considerable value to the customers, field operations recommended that the whole project be discontinued because it was uneconomical. Field operations felt that the service was too costly in that the customers, although they liked the service, would not pay the necessary price. After careful study of the entire project, top management decided not to continue the service.

With respect to the expenditures, the $300,000 was charged off as a research expense, and the $75,000 was capitalized as operating equipment.

As a result of this sequence of events, two problems arose: (a) what accounting treatment should be accorded the $75,000, and (b) allocation of the $75,000 against budget appropriations.

With respect to accounting treatment, it has been proposed that the item be (a) expensed or (b) capitalized and depreciated over a period of five years as an engineering prototype.

With respect to budget allocations, the executive in charge of engineering and research felt that his budget should be charged with the $300,000 only, on the basis that "we did what operations and sales asked us to do. They took it; now they should have to bear the cost of turning it down. Our budget appropriation does not include the cost of capital additions or expenses of operating the field organization." The executive in charge of field operations stated, "Sure, you built it for us, but it is not economical to operate; consequently, it does not meet our needs. If you can bring it up to our standard on economics, we will take it. Further, there was no provision in our budget for this item."

What are your recommendations relative to the budget problems and why?

13-3. THE ENNIS MANUFACTURING COMPANY was organized to manufacture aluminum windows and doors for homes. Over the past 10 years the firm has grown rapidly although at a somewhat lower relative rate than that experienced by the industry generally. Profitwise the company has been moderately successful, particularly in view of a definite freight advantage in the territory served. The company has experienced some trouble with quality of product due in some cases to design and in others to inadequate supervision of assembly operations.

The company recently purchased a suitable building for manufacturing operations and moved to it from rented quarters. As a part of the move the company installed some new equipment, rearranged plant layout, and made considerable efforts to improve quality control. It was felt that all the "bugs" had been taken out of the products manufactured. The company also started a training program for the workers on the assembly line.

All of these activities required considerable cash which had been obtained through a loan from a local bank. There were 11 shareholders; however, three men owned 72 per cent of the outstanding shares. Prior to the changes a new manager was employed who had had experience with a larger manufacturer of aluminum products. The new manager was given an option to purchase up to 20 per cent of stock outstanding at a favorable option price. Most of the changes were made at the insistence of the new manager who has been on the job for about two years. During this period seven of the 16 supervisors employed were replaced.

Six months after assuming management responsibilities, the new manager, with the assistance of several of the supervisors, drew up a plan of operations covering the following six-month period. The board of directors was pleased with the results. As one director expressed it, "These figures make sense to me. For the first time I have some feeling about what the future prospects are. I don't mind assuming some responsibilty for this loan if there is evidence of what we can do." Each month a financial report was presented to the board by the new manager. A copy was also transmitted to the bank. The report compared actual results with the original budget figures. At the end of the first four months the comparisons showed generally favorable results.

More recently, the manager appointed a special committee of supervisors to work on cost control. The committee quickly came to a consideration of standards in the manufacturing operations and in control reporting procedures.

The engineer on the committee developed material standards for each type of window and door manufactured. He prepared a "Standard Materials List" for each item and recommended that materials be drawn from storage based upon the items scheduled for production and the standard material list. He further recommended that variations in materials usage should be reported by production order, by department, upon completion of the order. In a similar manner standard direct labor times were tentatively estimated for each type of item manufactured. The data was developed on a form captioned "Standard Labor Time, By Operation." It was realized that the labor time standards were not too accurate; however, it was contemplated that with experience they could be improved. It was recommended that average material and labor rates be used in connection with the unit standards.

The overhead had been budgeted originally by the general manager on the basis of a specific, expected work load. The committee proposed to relate overhead costs to volume of products manufactured. Initially, it was decided that direct labor hours should be used as the measure of output for this purpose.

At the last meeting of the committee considerable time was spent discussing the problems of standards and measuring, evaluating, and reporting operations at the end of each month. The committee appeared to be in agreement that current month and year-to-date results should be reported. There appeared to be considerable confusion and disagreement relative to reporting procedures. At the conclusion of the meeting a subcommittee of two was appointed to "prepare a presentation to clear the air on these points so we can consider them intelligently and reach some conclusions." Accordingly, the subcommittee prepared the exhibits following (Nos. 1-3), using simplified figures, to bring out the central problems pertinent to the discussions in the last committee meeting. The subcommittee felt that separate illustrations would be useful to "educate" the committee as to the issues and to bring out the advantages and disadvantages of the alternatives that might be considered. The subcommittee assumed no responsibility for making recommendations—only for "clearing the air."

Required:

(a) Do you agree that the three problems posed by the subcommittee are pertinent to the situation?

(b) What other pertinent problems, if any, are posed?

(c) Analyze each of the exhibits and present your recommendations relative to each of the problems posed by the subcommittee. Substantiate your recommendations.

(d) What recommendations do you have relative to your response to requirement (b) above?

Exhibit 1

Problem: What variations and analyses should be reported?

Sales:	Actual		Budget		Variations
	Units	*Amount*	*Units*	*Amount*	
Product *X*	4,500	$94,000	5,000	$100,000	
" Y					
" Etc.					

Expenses	*Actual*	*Original Budget*	*Adjusted Budget*	*Variations*
Dept. 1				
Units	5,500	5,000	5,500	
DLH's	11,500	10,000	11,500	
Amounts(by accounts)	$17,000	$15,000	$17,250	

Exhibit 2

Problem: What is output for control purposes?

Expenses	Actual	Original Budget	Adjusted Budget	Adjusted Budget	Variations
Dept. 1					
Units	5,500	5,000	5,500	5,500	
DLH's	11,500	10,000	11,500	11,000	
Amounts (by					
accounts)	$17,000	$15,000	$17,250	$16,500	
Dept. 2					
Etc.					

Exhibit 3

Problem: How should the variations be reported?

Sales:	Actual	Budget	Variations Amount	Per cent	Realization
Product X					
Y	$48,000	$52,000	$4,000*	7.7*	92.3
Z	77,000	70,000	7,000	10.0	110.0
Expenses;					
Dept. 1					
Dept. 2					
(by accounts)	$26,400	$24,000	$2,400*	10.0*	90.9
Dept. 3					
(by accounts)	36,800	40,000	3,200	8.0	108.7
Etc.					

13-4. THE LELON MANUFACTURING COMPANY. Certain cost and budget data as of June 30 are given below for The Lelon Manufacturing Company. You are requested to prepare detailed and summary reports suitable for control purposes.

	June		January-May Inclusive	
Costs	*Actual*	*Budget*	*Actual*	*Budget*
Divisions:				
Sales	$65,000	$60,000	$333,000	$322,000
Financial	7,000	7,100	36,000	36,500
General administrative	16,000	15,700	82,000	81,000
Research	21,000	22,000	120,000	110,000
Factory				
Departments (factory only):				
Purchasing	6,000	5,600	30,000	28,800
Maintenance	4,000	3,500	24,000	21,000
Factory administrative	9,000	8,800	44,000	45,000
Production (five cost centers)				
Production Cost Centers:				
No. 1	18,000	17,700	95,000	93,800
2	27,000	26,000	130,000	132,000
3	32,000	30,500	168,000	168,500
4 (see below)				
5	11,000	10,000	67,000	66,000
Cost Detail for Production Cost Center No. 4:				
Salaries	2,500	2,500	12,500	12,500
Wages	8,000	7,800	43,000	42,500
Material used	4,500	4,500	24,000	24,000
Supplies	420	380	2,000	1,500
Maintenance	200	160	1,100	950
Depreciation*	100	100	500	500
Taxes*	20	20	100	100
Insurance*	50	50	250	250
Power	120	115	720	700
Miscellaneous	80	90	440	400

* Non-controllable in this cost center.

13-5. It is important that a clear-cut distinction be made between line and staff authority. When acting in a staff relationship, one must realize that one's job is to advise, not command, to sell, not tell; and that it is the line supervisor who must assume responsibility for making decisions and issuing instructions through the scalar chain below him.

A case at point is the one concerning a competent young auditor, who had unusual industrial experience as controller and internal auditor of several large business enterprises, and who was hired by the executive vice president of an expanding company as his assistant. The assistant's charge was clear—to bring to the attention of the executive vice president means and places for reducing costs of operations, expending scarce capital wisely and in an orderly fashion. But some uncertainty existed in his mind, or in that of his superior, as to whether he was limited to a staff position, or whether he had line authority from the executive vice president to see that these things were done. In any event, he gathered a large organization of statisticians, production efficiency experts, planners, economists, budget control personnel, and organization specialists. With their help the assistant readily discovered numerous places where costs could be reduced, production and service improved, management bettered, and money most efficiently expended.

The accuracy of the findings was extraordinarily high; yet the entire program[1] failed, and the executive vice president was forced to abandon it. The reason was simple.

Discuss.

Chapter 14

14-1. Actual and budget sales data for the month of June for the three products sold are summarized below.

	Gulf District			Inland District		
	X	Y	Z	X	Y	Z
Budget Data:						
Units	25,000	30,000	40,000	15,000	30,000	50,000
Average unit price	$2.00	$.75	$1.00	$2.00	$.70	$1.10
Actual Data:						
Units	26,000	30,500	39,000	14,000	25,000	62,000
Amount	$52,260	$23,027	$38,610	$28,560	$18,750	$62,620

Required:

Prepare summary and detailed sales performance reports indicating thereon the sales quantity and price variations.

14-2. THE SUPREME COMPANY manufactures two products, HO

---

[1] Taken directly from: Harold Koonz and Cyril O'Donnell, *Principles of Management* (New York: McGraw-Hill Book Company, 1955), p. 141.

and MO. Certain planning budget data for the month of March are as follows:

	HO	MO
Units to be manufactured	150,000	280,000
Units of raw material #1 required (based on standard rates)	495,000	
Units of raw material #2 required (based on standard rates)		224,000
Average unit cost of raw material—#1 $.80; #2 $1.20		
Direct labor hours per unit of finished goods	$\frac{3}{4}$	$1\frac{1}{4}$
Direct labor cost (total)	$299,250	$689,500

Actual date for the month of March:

	HO	MO
Units actually manufactured	160,000	260,000
Raw material cost #1 (Total)	$434,190	
#2		$246,285
Average unit cost of raw material—#1 $.82; #2 $1.17		
Total direct labor hours	125,000	323,000
Total direct labor cost	$337,500	$629,850

Required:

Prepare summary and detailed reports of direct material and direct labor, emphasizing usage and price variations.

14-3. THE CLYTON PROCESSING COMPANY processes three products through two separate processes designated Process No. 1 and Process No. 2. Manufacturing overhead is applied by means of predetermined overhead rates. Process No. 1 rate is based on direct labor hours whereas Process No. 2 rate is based on direct machine hours. The overhead rates are computed on the basis of planning budget overhead allowances and the related volume of work. Certain budget and actual data for the year are summarized below.

(a) Planning budget annual data:

	Process No. 1	Process No. 2
Overhead budgeted: Fixed	$40,000	$90,000
Variable	$48,000	$60,000
Direct labor hours budgeted	40,000	12,000
Direct machine hours budgeted	10,000	200,000

(b) Actual annual data:

	Process No. 1	Process No. 2
Overhead incurred: Fixed	$39,500	$90,500
Variable	$48,000	$64,500
Direct labor hours: Actual	36,000	13,000
Allowed at standard	35,000	12,500
Direct machine hours: Actual	8,900	207,000
Allowed at standard	8,800	205,000

Required:

(a) Prepare a statement showing manufacturing overhead incurred, applied, and over/under-applied for each process. Assume overhead is applied on the basis of allowed hours.

(b) Prepare an analysis of manufacturing overhead over/under-applied for each process. Show computations.

(c) Write a narrative explaining the interpretation of Process No. 2 variations.

14-4. THE CORD COMPANY. The following data were taken from the performance report of the Cord Company for January (the first month of the fiscal year).

(a) Sales Performance Report—Central Sales Division:

	Actual		Profit Plan		
					Variations
	Units	*Amount*	*Units*	*Amount*	*(Unfavorable*)*
Product AK	109,000	$182,030	100,000	$180,000	$2,030
Product BK	57,000	136,230	60,000	138,000	1,770*
		$318,260		$318,000	$ 260

(b) Departmental Performance Report—Producing Department 1

	Actual		*Budget Adjusted to Actual Output*	*Variations (Unfavorable*)*
Raw material	5,300 units	$8,639	$8,500	$139*
Direct labor	2,900 DLH	$5,529	$5,000	529*

Additional data:

Units of output—Department 1:
     Budgeted   2,200
     Actual   2,000
Budget rates per unit of output:
     Material usage   2 1/2 units
     DLH rates $2.00

(c) Departmental Performance Report—Summary

	Manufacturing Overhead		
	Actual	*Budget Adjusted to Actual Output*	*Variations (Unfavorable*)*
Dept.			
1	$14,360	$14,860	$ 500
2	19,660	18,830	830*
3	35,350	34,280	1,070*
Totals	$69,370	$67,970	$1,400*

Department variable budget totals:	Dept 1	Dept 2	Dept 3
Fixed per month	$5,000	$8,000	$17,000
Variable rate per DLH	$3.40	$1.90	$2.70
Annual output (DLH's)	60,000	70,000	80,000
January output (DLH's)			
Actual	2,900	5,700	6,400
Standard	2,500	5,500	6,500

Required:

(a) Prepare an analysis of the sales variations by product.

(b) Prepare brief comments on the results of requirement (a), suitable for the sales performance report.

(c) Prepare an analysis of the raw material and labor variances.

(d) Prepare brief comments on the results of (c).

(e) Prepare an analysis of manufacturing overhead by department. The following computations should be made:

(1) Compute annual departmental overhead rates.

(2) Manufacturing overhead over- or under-applied by department—overhead is applied on the basis of standard DLH.

(3) Compute variances.

(f) Explain the variances developed in requirement (e) above.

Chapter 15

15-1. THE STANDARD PRODUCTS CORPORATION records expected actual standard costs in the accounts. Variances between actual costs and standard costs are recorded in separate variance accounts. The standard-cost card for Packer No. X-1 showed the following:

	Departments		
	X	Y	Z
Materials—#1 ($1.00 per unit)	2 units		
#2 ($1.20 per unit)		3 units	
#3 ($1.50 per unit)		1 unit	4 units
Direct labor: Hours	3	2	4
Average wage rate	$2.00	$2.20	$3.00
Burden rate per direct labor hour	$ .50	$1.00	$1.40

During January the company manufactured 2,000 No. X-1 Packers, of which 1,900 were sold at $75 each. Other transactions during the month are summarized below.

(1) Raw material purchases:

> Material #1—4,200 units @ $1.05
> #2—5,800 units @ $1.20
> #3—10,000 units @ $1.45

(2) Material issues:

> Dept. X—4,100 units of material #1
> Dept. Y—6,150 units of material #2
> 1,900 units of material #3
> Dept. Z—8,200 units of material #3

(3) Direct labor:

> Dept. X—6,250 hours @ $2.10
> Dept. Y—3,900 hours @ $2.10
> Dept. Z—8,000 hours @ $3.05

(4) Burden:

> Burden is applied on the basis of standard hours. Actual burden incurred: Dept. X—$3,500; Dept. Y—$4,600; Dept. Z—$11,000.

(5) Burden variances are determined on the basis of variable budget allowances. Variable budget summaries are as follows:

Department	Fixed per Month	Variable per Direct Labor Hour
X	$2,100	$.20
Y	3,100	.40
Z	4,100	.90

(6) Selling and Administrative costs $30,000.

Required:

(a) Prepare a standard-cost card for Packer No. X-1.
(b) Record the transactions. (Assume cash payments.)
(c) Prepare a simplified profit and loss summary.

15-2. Prepare journal entries for the following transactions, assuming standard costs are recorded in the accounts.

(1) Purchased 15,000 units of Material K at $2.73 per unit. The standard price is $2.70.

(2) Purchased 9,000 units of Material L at $4.17 per unit. The standard price is $4.20.

(3) Issued 14,300 units of Material K to the factory to manufacture 10,000 units of finished goods. The standard material usage rate is 1.4.

(4) Issued 8,950 units of Material L to the factory to manufacture 10,000 units of finished goods. The standard material usage rate is .9.

(5) Direct labor incurred in manufacturing 10,000 units of finished goods; Dept. 1—31,500 hours @ $2.05; Dept. 2—17,450 hours @ $2.47. Standard wage rates are: Dept. 1—$2.00; Dept. 2—$2.50. Standard labor hours per unit of finished goods are: Dept. 1—3 hours; Dept. 2— $1\frac{3}{4}$ hours.

(6) Burden incurred: Dept. 1—$50,000; Dept. 2—$37,500.

(7) Burden is applied on the basis of standard direct labor hours. Burden application rates (per direct labor hour): Dept. 1—$1.60; Dept. 2—$2.10.

(8) Variable budget summary:

Department	Fixed per Month	Variable per Direct Labor Hour
1	$30,000	$ .62
2	17,500	1.05

15-3. THE ANONYMOUS COMPANY. The following comments and illustrative data were taken from the notes and discussions of The Anonymous Company:

COMMENTS—Proponents of direct costing call attention to the fact that the controller using *ordinary* or *absorption* costing procedures would be hard put to explain to management why profits do not rise and fall as sales volume rises and falls even though prices were not changed. Under *direct costing* procedures, reported profits rise and fall as sales rise and fall.

The unrealistic profit figures reported under *ordinary* costing procedures are due to the effect of fixed manufacturing costs capitalized in, or withdrawn from, inventory. These fixed costs affect reported profits illogically when sales volume and productive volume are different.

In order to demonstrate the effect, the actual data for one quarter have been selected. The illustration is simplified by assuming that (a) budgeted and actual sales prices are identical and (b) budgeted and actual costs are identical. The latter simplification also is assumed so that the "manufacturing overhead over/under-applied is composed of only one variation, the idle capacity variation."

ILLUSTRATIVE DATA

Standard Costs

(a) Direct material and direct labor—$.40 per unit of finished goods.

(b) Manufacturing overhead:

	Amount	Units Fin. Gds.	Overhead Rate per unit Fin. Gds.
Annual fixed costs budgeted	$ 96,000	240,000	$.40
Annual variable costs budgeted	48,000	240,000	.20
	$144,000	240,000	$.60

(c) Actual results (1st Quarter):

Schedule of finished goods (in units)

	January	February	March
Beginning inventory	—0—	—0—	6,000
Units manufactured	20,000	24,000	12,000
Units available for sale	20,000	24,000	18,000
Units sold	20,000	18,000	18,000
Final inventory	—0—	6,000	—0—

Actual manufacturing overhead incurred:

Fixed	$ 8,000	$ 8,000	$ 8,000
Variable	4,000	4,800	2,400
Total	$12,000	$12,800	$10,400

Actual distribution and administrative costs incurred:

Fixed	$ 5,000	$ 5,000	5,000

Sales at $1.50 per unit: January 20,000; February 18,000; March 18,000 (units).

Required:

(a) Prepare income statements by month (especially arranged) under (1) ordinary costing procedures (include over- or under-applied overhead on a separate line immediately preceding cost of goods sold figure) and (2) direct costing procedures so as to bring out the distinctions between them as clearly as possible.

(b) Prepare a statement relative to the distinctions indicated in requirement (a).

15-4. *The Fable of the President and the Accountant*[1]

Once upon a time a company was losing money; although its plant had a normal capacity of 30,000 widgets it was selling only 10,000 a year, and its operating figures looked like this:

Price per unit	$ 1.00
Total fixed cost	$ 6,000.00
Fixed cost per unit	.60
Variable cost per unit	.65
Total unit cost	1.25
Total manufacturing cost	$12,500.00
Value of closing inventory	—0—
Cost of goods sold	$12,500.00
Sales income	10,000.00
Operating loss	(2,500.00)

[1] Adapted from *Business Week*, Jan. 15, 1955.

Then one day a bearded stranger came to the board of directors and said: "Make me president, pay me half of any operating profit I produce, and I'll put you on easy street."

"Done," they said.

So the bearded stranger set the factory running full tilt, making 30,000 widgets a year. So his figures looked like this:

Total fixed cost	$ 6,000.00
Fixed cost per unit	.20
Variable unit cost	.65
Total unit cost	.85
Total manufacturing cost	$25,500.00
Value closing inventory	17,000.00
Cost of goods sold	8,500.00
Sales income	10,000.00
Operating profit	1,500.00

"Pay me," said the bearded stranger.

"But we're going broke," said a director.

"So what?" said the stranger. "You can read the figures, can't you?"

WHAT IS YOUR REPLY?

Chapter 16

16-1. THE MIET DEPARTMENT STORE. Assume you are working on the sales budget for the fall season for the Miet Department Store. The following data are available:

Actual sales for the same period last year	$400,000
Expected decrease in consumer prices	2%
Expected decrease in number of transactions	1%

Expected distribution of Sales:

By department:

Dept. X	40%
Dept. Y	50%
Dept. Z	10%

By department, by months:

	Dept. X	Dept. Y	Dept. Z
August	15%	13%	10%
September	17	18	12
October	18	12	12
November	16	14	18
December	24	30	27
January	10	13	21

Required:

(a) Prepare appropriate sales budget schedules.
(b) Evaluate the approach used by the company.

16-2. Budget objectives for Department A (Men's Furnishings) during a particular period are as follows (assume no inventory change):

Planned sales	$10,000
Planned markdowns	100
Planned discounts	400
Planned stock shortage	200

Required:

(a) Compute the initial markup per cent that should be budgeted to attain a planned gross margin of 55 per cent on sales.
(b) Compute the resulting gross margin per cent assuming a planned initial markup of 60 per cent.

16-3. THE TEX DEPARTMENT STORE. The following data are for Departments X and Y of the Tex Department Store as of March 15.

	Department X	Department Y
Planned sales for the month	$25,000	$ 7,000
Actual sales to date	11,000	3,700
BOM inventory	55,000	18,000
EOM inventory	58,000	17,000
Merchandise received to date	16,000	4,500
Merchandise ordered for March delivery	6,000	2,500
Planned reductions	2,000	400
Actual reductions to date	800	300
Planned initial markup	30%	35%

Required:

Compute the open-to-buy as of March 15 for each department.

16-4. THE DUNCAN DEPARTMENT STORE is currently developing the budget for the period August to January. The budget is detailed by months. Planned net sales for the six months' total $900,000, distributed 13 per cent to Jewelry, 43 per cent to Men's Furnishings, 41 per cent to Women's and Misses' Coats and Dresses, and Miscellaneous 3 per cent. Distribution of sales by months are as follows:

	Jewelry	Men's Furnishings	Women's and Misses' Coats and Dresses	Micellaneous
August	8.0%	8.2%	14.4%	12.1%
September	9.8	8.3	20.8	16.3
October	11.3	9.1	18.9	15.7
November	18.5	20.7	16.7	18.2
December	45.3	47.4	13.7	27.3
January	7.1	6.3	15.5	10.4

Planned BOM stock sales ratios for August are: Jewelry, 3.9; Men's Furnishings, 4.8; Women's and Misses' Coats and Dresses, 2.0; and Miscellaneous, 3.1.

Planned reductions for August are: Jewelry, $700; Men's Furnishings, $2,500; Women's and Misses' Dresses, $3,600; and Miscellaneous, $100.

Planned BOM stocks for September are: Jewelry, 3.6; Men's Furnishings, 4.6; Women's and Misses' Coats and Dresses, 2.0; and Miscellaneous, 3.0.

Planned initial markups are: Jewelry, 45 per cent; Men's Furnishings, 40 per cent; Women's and Misses' Coats and Suits, 40 per cent; and Miscellaneous, 50 per cent.

Required:

(a) Prepare a summary sales budget by department.
(b) Prepare a sales budget by department, by months.
(c) Compute the August stock levels (BOM) for each department.
(d) Schedule of August purchases at retail and cost.
(e) Compute the maintained markup by department (per budget).

16-5. TRACY'S DEPARTMENT STORE operates in a large metropolitan area having a population of over one million in the immediate area. There are approximately 100 separate sales departments in the store, each supervised by a department manager.

Department managers, who have sales and general departmental responsibilities, are responsible for purchasing also. Although the merchandise is purchased through a central purchasing group, the department managers select the merchandise specifying specific brands, quality, and quantities within the departmental budget. Thus the departmental managers clearly understand that top management holds them directly responsible for purchasing.

Department managers are allowed to raise the selling price (additional markups) within their own discretion subject to the general policy of Tracy's to be "competitive in all lines." In addition, department managers have authority to mark down merchandise subject to an over-all limitation of "10 per cent of total sales for the month."

After a recent extended conference with the controller, the general manager of the store was particularly concerned about "the theft of merchandise by customers and employees" and "inventory manipulations by department managers to cover poor buying."

Tracy's employs a small force of store detectives, approximately 10, having responsibility for "continuous surveillance to catch customers and employees in the act of stealing store merchandise." Store detectives do not work "in cooperation" with floor personnel. The supervisor of the store detectives feels that there is a need for at least 20 detectives. Cost has been the determining factor in limiting the number of detectives.

Tracy's follows the retail industry tradition in using the retail inventory method with an adjustment to LIFO at the end of the calendar year. The retail inventory results are' used for monthly statements and for control in some respects. An annual end-of-the-year physical inventory is taken, and in addition, physical counts by department are made on a "spot" basis throughout the year. Physical inventory results (valued at retail) are always checked against the book inventory (retail inventory results).

The store budgets a merchandise shortage (for theft) of 1 per cent of sales. All department stores recognize that theft is inevitable, but that continuous action is necessary to minimize the loss. When a department shortage is over 1 per cent of sales, top management wants to know why and expects definite action to correct the condition. The controller has the direct responsibility to see that "proper control procedures are maintained." The store detectives are under his supervision.

In the recent conference with the general manager the controller made it very clear that the "amount of shortages due to theft are not known principally because department managers manipulate the retail inventory results to cover up poor buying." Retail inventory calculations when compared with physical counts, frequently indicate a shortage several times greater than would be probable through theft. On the other hand, it is not unusual for the comparison to show overages. The controller felt that "one can safely conclude that inventory manipulation is the cause. More specifically the inventory manipulation results from mark-downs and additional markups taken by the department managers then not reported, thereby covering up poor buying."

In order to clearly explain what he was talking about the controller developed a hypothetical illustration. The illustration involved the three examples (A, B, and C) presented below. Only the "retail side" of the retail inventory computation was shown because the conversion to cost currently was not a problem. (The controller also illustrated *units* so that the effects could be traced easily. Obviously in an actual situation, units do not enter into retail inventory calculations.)

Example A: Assumptions—Data as given below are correct, including the shortage of $200 (20 units).

	Units		At Retail
Beginning inventory	1,000		$10,000
Add: Purchases	2,200		22,000
Net add'l markups			1,000
Goods available for sale	3,200		33,000
Deduct: Sales	2,080	$19,800(a)	
Markdowns		2,000	21,800
Book inventory at retail	1,120		11,200
Physical inventory at retail	1,100		11,000(b)
Shortage	20		$ 200

(a) 1,000 @ $ 8 = $ 8,000 (All units in Beg. inv. marked down and sold.)

1,080 @ $10 = 10,800 } (All units marked up were sold.)
Markup   = 1,000
                ———————
              $19,800

(b) 1,100 @ $10 = $11,000

In this case the departmental manager correctly reported all markdowns and all additional markups, consequently the computation shows the correct shortage which is assumed to be due to theft and which is slightly over the 1 per cent allowance.

This example indicates the method employed to determine the amount of theft—a comparison of the departmental retail inventory (book) results with the departmental physical inventory. Obviously, if there are no errors in either inventory, the shortage due to theft is correct as computed. In situations such as this one (where the shortage is over 1 per cent) a typical reply by the department manager involved was "the sales people were hired to sell and not to be store detectives— it's up to the store detectives to catch the shop lifters."

Example B: Assumptions—Exactly the same as Example A except that it is assumed that the department manager actually took *markdowns* of $3,000, but reported only $2,000. There were two reasons why he might fail to report the $1,000, viz., (a) the 10 per cent limitation on markdowns, and (b) as a result of "poor buys" the merchandise could not be sold at the established markup. Therefore, he had to take a markdown to sell the goods. The markdown was not reported because it would reveal the poor buying which was an important factor used by management in evaluating department managers.*

* The controller has been "pressed" by the general manager to control thefts, whereas the department managers are "pressed" to buy better.

	Units	As Reported		Correct	
Beginning inventory	1,000		$10,000		$10,000
Add: Purchases	2,200		22,000		22,000
Net add'l markups			1,000		1,000
Goods available for sale	3,200		33,000		33,000
Deduct: Sales	2,080	$18,800(a)		$18,800	
Markdowns		2,000	20,800	3,000	21,800
Book inventory at retail	1,120		12,200		11,200
Physical inventory at retail	1,100		11,000		11,000
Shortage	20		$ 1,200(b)		$ 200

(a) 1,000 @ $ 7 = $ 7,000   (All units in Beg. Inv. marked down and sold.)
$\quad$ 1,080 @ $10 = 10,800⎫
$\quad$ Markup $\quad$ = $\quad$ 1,000⎭ (All units marked up were sold.)
$\qquad\qquad\qquad$ $18,800

(b) The shortage overstated, by $1,000, the amount of the unreported markdown.

$\quad$ This example clearly illustrates what the controller meant by "inventory manipulation through unreported markdowns to cover poor buying." The computed shortage is over 6 per cent of sales.

Example C: Assumptions—Exactly the same as Examples A and B except that the department manager, in addition to taking markdowns of $3,000 ($1,000 of which was not reported), actually took *additional markups* (on newly received merchandise) of $3,000, but reported only $1,000. He failed to report the $2,000 in markups for two reasons, viz.: (a) he was "hiding" the unreported markdowns to prevent the result demonstrated in Example B (overstatement of shortages), and (b) the large markups, if reported, might indicate he was not competitive.

	Units	As Reported		Correct	
Beginning inventory	1,000		$10,000		$10,000
Add: Purchases	2,200		22,000		22,000
Net add'l markups			1,000		3,000
Goods available for sale	3,200		33,000		35,000
Deduct: Sales	2,080	$18,800(a)		$18,800	
Markdowns		2,000	20,800	3,000	21,800
Book inventory at retail	1,120		12,200		13,200
Physical inventory at retail	1,100		13,000(b)		13,000
Shortage	20		$ 800 (overage)		$ 200

(a) 1,000 @ $ 7 = $ 7,000 (All units in Beg. Inv. marked down and sold.)
$\quad$ 1,080 @ $\quad$ 10 = 10,800
$\quad$ Markup $\quad$ = $\quad$ 1,000 (Items marked up this amount sold.)
$\qquad\qquad\qquad$ $18,800
(b) 1,100 @ $10 = $11,000
$\quad$ Markup not
$\quad$ reported $\quad$ − $\quad$ 2,000 (New items marked up this amount not sold.)
$\qquad\qquad\qquad$ $13,000

In this example the department manager "overcompensated" resulting in a "computed" *overage* of $800 which is incorrect by $1,000, the net effect of the two unreported items.

After getting a clear picture of both the theft and manipulation possibilities as explained by the controller, the general manager stated: "We must determine what our theft losses are and also stop these manipulations—something must be done immediately!"

What are your recommendations?

Chapter 17

17-1. THE Z PUBLISHING COMPANY. The management of the Z Publishing Company developed an annual profit plan and presented it to the board of directors for approval. Approximately three weeks prior to the beginning of the current year, the board of directors approved the plan for the ensuing year. The plan was developed in some detail and included expense estimates for each item of cost in each department. The expenses in the profit plan approximated $80,000.

On February 16 of the budget year, the general manager requested that the board of directors approve the following expenditures as additions to the budget, for the reasons quoted below:

1. An additional $3,000 for circulation salaries—a 20 per cent increase in circulation during January has created more work than the present staff can handle efficiently.
2. An additional $9,000 for newsprint—this amount is needed to pay for additional newsprint made necessary by increased circulation.
3. An additional $2,000 for editorial expense—this amount is necessary for travel and coverage out-of-town events.
4. An additional $3,000 for printing expenses—this amount is necessary to cover unanticipated repairs to the presses.
5. An additional $2,000 for circulation expense—this item is to cover increased postage and other costs arising from increased circulation.
6. An additional $5,000 for promotion—this expenditure is needed to increase circulation and advertising commensurate with that anticipated in view of January results.
7. An additional $500 for insurance—this is necessary to increase the personal and public liability insurance on employees when they are acting as agents of the company.

These proposals for expenditures above the original budget gave rise to discussions by the board concerning the specific expense items, and budget policies and procedures generally.

Required:

Analyze the principal problems that should be considered by the board and present your recommendations with supporting reasons.

17-2. BIGFOOT PIPELINE COMPANY was organized soon after World War II to pipe natural gas to several metropolitan markets. The company, from beginning to present, has been engaged in the construction of new facilities and other expansion. The total assets of the company have increased approximately $5\frac{1}{2}$ times during the last 10 years. The large volume of construction required many blueprints and copies of various documents. To meet the demand for emergency prints and reproductions, the engineering department, under the supervision of the chief engineer and vice president, Stanley Meyers, initiated the operation of a "reproduction room" with three or four employees and some simple equipment. Mr. Meyers boasted that he ran the department, making it clear that he wanted no help. Initially, the work of the reproduction room was limited to emergency needs of the engineering department.

Ed Luther was placed in supervision of the reproduction room work and reported directly to Mr. Meyers. Mr. Ed, as he was known to employees and friends, was a charter employee of the company. He was a very friendly fellow, about fifty years old, and commanded the respect of all his associates. His warm smile and silvery-gray hair were well known throughout the company. In addition to his company activities, both he and his wife were active in civic and church affairs. The Luthers, their children married, appeared to prosper on his salary of $700 per month.

During the following three or four years the activities of the reproduction room increased. More and better equipment was acquired and its employees were increased to a dozen. It finally was made a section. Although a section in the engineering department, it became known as the "reproduction department." By this time it was doing considerable work for the entire company, including routine printing jobs. The 400 employees of the general office enjoyed a great deal of liberty in calling on the department for printing forms, reports, maps, etc.; to some extent, printing was done for nonbusiness organizations such as the Boy Scouts and professional societies. Due to the manner in which the department originated and expanded, few formal procedures or policies were established; policies resulted from practice and necessity. To meet his own needs, Mr. Ed printed "requisition on reproduction room" forms, which provided for the name of the department requesting work, a description of the work desired, and the operating or capital account to be charged with the cost.

The estimated cost at commercial rates of the items requisitioned was added by the reproduction room. No approval was required on the form. At the end of each month, the actual expenses of the department were accumulated. Based on the ratio of estimated commercial rates (total of all requisitions for the month) to actual expenses, a proportionate allocation was made to each requisition. In this manner, the actual expenses were exactly apportioned to the various requisitions for the month. "Actual" expenses of the department included only direct cost (labor, material, and supplies) with no charges for utilities, building rent, or equipment depreciation.

Paper and supplies were purchased in large quantities in order to receive more favorable discounts. Orders for supplies were usually placed directly with local vendors by Mr. Ed. Upon delivery, all purchases were charged to "reproduction-clearing," an inventory account. No perpetual inventory records were maintained, although inventories sometimes exceeded $20,000. A physical inventory was made of all stock on the last day of each month. The amount charged to expense each month was merely beginning inventory plus purchases less ending inventory.

Inasmuch as the reproduction department was doing considerable work for the entire company, all such work was routed to Mr. Ed; when a job could not be done by his men, it was "farmed out" to one of the several local commercial reproduction firms. Mr. Ed explained that this was necessary because of the rush nature of many large jobs; the capacity of the equipment in the department limited the output of work in any short period of time. Also, considerable overtime hours were being worked by the employees in the department. Mr. Ed stated that the pay scale for his department was too low to keep competent employees without allowing some overtime to increase their earnings.

Since the creation of the reproduction room, the internal audit staff had followed the growth and procedures of the section. Now that the volume of work had reached such a high level, the auditors were concerned about the apparent laxity of procedures, policies, and operations. As a matter of routine reporting, certain suggestions were made by the internal auditors for improving control of expenses in the department, including the following:

1. Establish perpetual inventory records,
2. Require the approval of the head of the department to originate a requisition,
3. Review pay scales and make adjustments, if necessary, to maintain a forty-hour work week,
4. Review budgetary procedures and reports.

These same recommendations were submitted annually from 1958 to 1962. Departmental lines in the company were difficult to cross, a fact which was well known by all; consequently, Mr. Meyers was never pressed to take action. When questioned by the auditors concerning their suggestions, Mr. Ed generally gave these answers: "Perpetual inventory records would require someone in the stockroom at all times, and we don't have that much business; I've got to keep the cost of this department down, you know. As for approvals on requisitions, that is OK if you can get them, but I don't think we need them. Most of the 'personal' work we do is for executives (implying such work would continue, regardless of approvals). If the last set of pay raises I requested for my boys is approved, they won't have to work any more overtime." In the opinion of the internal audit staff these statements somewhat exaggerated facts, but because of departmental barriers, no one made an issue of the matter.

Each October Mr. Ed was required to submit his "budget estimate" for the ensuing year. His latest estimate compared with January "actual" was:

REPRODUCTION DEPARTMENT REPORT

	Budgeted (Month Average)	January Actual	Variations *Unfavorable
Direct costs:			
Payroll	$ 6,000	$ 6,000	—
Supplies and expenses $7,000 to $10,000	8,500	9,500	$1,000*
Farm out work	5,000	4,200	800
Total	$19,500	$19,700	$ 200
Inventory of supplies	$20,000	$20,900	$ 900*

Comments: No action required.

Early in 1963, the situation took on a new light. A private detective called on the president of the company and gave this account: His client, a drilling contractor, had reasons to believe that his "electric logs" were getting into the hands of a competitor. He had been retained by the driller to determine the validity of this conclusion. The detective explained that the driller's logs were sent to a commercial reproduction firm to be developed and printed. He had found that the logs were being conveyed to the "Bigfoot" building. Subsequent investigation revealed that the commercial reproduction firm "farmed out" the log jobs to Bill Drake, who was an employee in the reproduction department of Bigfoot. Instead of reproducing only the number ordered by the client, Drake printed an extra copy of all logs, which he retained. Later the extra copies were sold to the competitor for a generous fee.

At this point, the president of Bigfoot also retained the detective to further his investigation within the company and "find out everything that is going on in the department." Among his findings were:

1. Bill Drake was processing the driller's logs with company equipment and supplies while working overtime on weekends.
2. Another employee of the reproduction department, Herbert King, was receiving 10 per cent of Drake's spoils as hush money because King was aware of the situation.
3. Mr. Ed was receiving a 20 per cent rebate on all "farm out" work sent to the same commercial production firm.

Drake, about twenty-seven years old, was married and the father of two children. After attending college for two years, he served three years in the navy before coming to Bigfoot. He was cooperative with all employees and always willing to accommodate those in need of rush work. In addition to his work, he was well known for his sidewalk conversations in front of the general office building during lunch hours.

Herbert King began working for a commercial photo lab soon after graduating from high school. Except for military service, he had worked for the same firm for ten years before coming to the company in 1957. Owning an expensive set of photographic equipment, he engaged in photography both as a hobby and a side-line trade. King catered to making photos for parties, weddings, and various other social functions. He enjoyed a great deal of favorable publicity from employees of the company.

The three employees, Ed Luther, Bill Drake, and Herbert King, were dismissed from the company immediately. Mr. Ed maintained his innocence on the grounds that any amounts received by him were commissions that otherwise would have been allowed to the salesmen of the reproduction firm, and therefore had not cost the company anything extra. Drake and King offered no explanations.

The president immediately sent for the files of the internal auditing department relating to the activities of the reproduction department. The auditors were asked to assist the new head of the department in establishing adequate internal control procedures; the budget director was requested to "review the budget procedures for the reproduction room."

Be prepared to discuss all aspects of this case, including suggested actions that should be taken.

17-3. THE HALE MANUFACTURING COMPANY

THE HALE MANUFACTURING COMPANY
1111 Travis Street
City, State

December 15, 19—

Mr. A. B. Smith
102 Pierce Avenue
(State)

Dear Mr. Smith:

I was fortunate to have been seated next to you during the Chapter meeting in (city) last week. Our conversation concerning *cost control* has since resulted in considerable thought on my part. I am writing this letter to convey some of my thoughts on this subject. I hope that you have time to draft a reply that may clarify my thinking. It is my hope that these preliminary discussions will interest you to the extent that we may obtain your services on a consulting basis.

You will recall that in our discussion I outlined briefly what we have done concerning organization structure and delegation of responsibilities. If I understood correctly, you thought our efforts were in the right direction. Our production planning function is performed very efficiently, although frequently it is necessary to change production schedules due to unexpected conditions such as a large unanticipated order. Our policy has been to keep finished inventories to an absolute minimum.

As I told you, our budgeting is kept to a minimum; we do what is required by the lending agency—that is, a cash forecast is prepared by the chief accountant. There has been no effort to use budget procedures for cost control purposes as you suggested.

According to the chief accountant, our accounting system follows traditional financial accounting procedures with some cost-accounting adaptations, particularly concerning burden application rates which are based on direct labor hours. I believe the accounting system is adequate for a small firm such as ours because product costs appear to be fairly accurate.

Frankly, the problem of cost control is one of my pet peeves. After perusing the monthly accounting statements, I always have the feeling that many costs are too high. As a matter of fact, every few months I call a meeting of the top supervisors and remind them in very strong terms that our costs are way out of line. In fact, we had such a meeting yesterday, at which time I told the group that the chief accountant had been directed to take definite steps to reduce costs and keep them in line. Subsequent to the meeting I talked to the accountant briefly; he seemed disturbed and uncertain. I hope our company has not outgrown his abilities.

I would appreciate a reply at an early date including any immediate suggestions you may have concerning the problem, with a view toward your consulting with us at an early date. The chief accountant is anxious to have your help in this matter.

Sincerely,

A. P. Bannister, President

Required:

Draft a reply to the above letter for Mr. Smith, who is a specialist in budgeting and cost accounting. Assume Mr. Smith is interested in the engagement.

17-4. THE BRAND BUTANE GAS & APPLIANCE COMPANY is an incorporated business located in a city of about 15,000. The company has been in existence about four years. Operations involve the sale of butane gas, installations of storage tanks, pipes, fittings, etc. for new users, and appliances such as stoves and heaters, which are adapted to the use of butane gas. In addition, the company handles large contract installations of air conditioning equipment. Sales of butane gas and related appliances are not confined to the city. A large rural area reaching into five counties is served.

Ownership of the business is vested primarily in two people, one of whom is the general manager; the other, for whom the company is named, is interested mainly as an investor as he is active in another noncompetitive business in the same city. In addition to the general manager, the company employs a bookkeeper-typist, three route men to deliver butane gas, a crew of five men for installations and repairs, and part-time help when needed.

There is another firm in the same line of business in the city. It is older, but not much larger than Brand. The ownership is vested in individuals who live about 250 miles south; the business in the northern part of the state is generally considered as a branch. One of the factors related to the competitive status of the two concerns is that the name of Brand has been well established in the city for over thirty years and carries considerable goodwill.

The management of Brand became seriously concerned with costs and related controls as the result of a loss of $16,427 last year. Their concern was particularly appropriate in view of the following additional information relating to last year:

(1) Capital invested in the business amounted to only $62,500.
(2) Debt exceeded the owner's equity in the business.
(3) The ratio of current assets to current debt was barely one to one.
(4) The volume of business was as follows: 38 per cent from the sale of appliances, 12 per cent from the sale of tanks, fittings, and pipe, 30 per cent from the sale of gas, and 20 per cent from contract installations. Materials, including goods for resale, accounted for approximately 60 per cent of all costs, labor 13 per cent, and selling and general administrative expenses 27 per cent.

The unfavorable results of Brand's operations last year resulted in a study by an outside consultant to locate the difficulties and make recommendations for corrective action. The following notations are from the files of the consultant:

(a) The first area analyzed concerned the materials used in Brand's operations. Because these materials, (which consist, in addition to appliances of pipes, copper tubing, joint connectors, etc.) account for such a large percentage of costs, it is logical that their handling should be investigated. Material handling involves several aspects: materials are kept in the sales room and warehouse in the main, except for the butane gas, which is stored in large storage tanks about a mile from the warehouse and sales room. Materials are taken from the warehouse and loaded on trucks for delivery to installations or repair jobs. Some materials are kept in the service trucks at all times. In most cases more materials, pipes, fittings, etc., are taken to installations than are required for the job, but this is done for convenience; the excess pipe, fittings, etc., are brought back to the warehouse, transferred to another job or left on the service truck. All pipe, fittings, etc., have a high resale value if stolen or lost. All materials are of such a nature as to make it easy to carry a perpetual inventory.

(b) The survey of materials procedures shows the following:

(1) Perpetual inventories are not kept on materials.

(2) No single person is charged with the responsibility of accounting for materials, either their receipt, their issuance, or their maintenance in the warehouse. When materials are needed for a job, some member of the installation crew simply goes into the warehouse and gets what he wants without question.

(3) There is no responsibily for materials put on the service trucks. Truck inventory sheets are not maintained.

(4) Requisitions are not issued for materials to be used on jobs; for example, if 150 feet of pipe are taken out, and only 100 feet used on the job, no one checks to see that the 50 feet are returned to the warehouse, or charged to the truck inventory if the pipe is kept on the service truck.

(5) A physical inventory is taken once a year. Spot inventories of various classes of materials during the year are thought to be impractical because of the lack of perpetual inventory records with which to make comparisons.

(6) No records are kept of butane gas taken from the storage tanks. Delivery tickets are turned in for the purpose of billing customers for gas put in their tanks, but no record of total receipts and deliveries—that is, purchases and sales of gas—is available to compare with any inventory in order to check evaporation or theft.

(7) The warehouse is freely accessible to all employees. There are no protective restrictions.

(8) Because no material records are kept, it is not possible to determine whether or not excessive stocks are carried on some items of material; furthermore, it is not possible to determine the most economical quantity to carry on each class of material in order to make the best use of working capital.

(c) The investigation of labor revealed the following:

(1) No record is kept of how time is spent—that is, as to jobs or classes of work—hence there is no accounting for:
a. cost of labor by jobs.
b. cost of labor by functions, such as delivery expense, installation costs, service costs, idle time, and so on.

(2) Time cards, or similar records to account for over-all hours worked, are not kept. An employee is presumed to have worked his full week, unless he reports "off" for a day for personal reasons, for sickness, etc.

(3) Labor standards have never been considered.

(d) The company contracts for large installations, such as institutional users of gas; it also handles large installations of air conditioning. The contracts for such installations usually vary from $8,000 to $10,000 and are often obtained as the result of competitive bidding. The procedure with respect to contracts was inadequate in that:

(1) No records are kept for the cost of materials and labor related to each contract, and

(2) Comparisons are not made of the actual cost of completing a contract with the bid price—either in total or by elements of cost, for the purpose of determining whether more or less material or labor is used than was contemplated in the bid or contract price.

(e) Because no cost records are kept for materials or labor, it is no surprise to find a coı..plete lack of control of overhead. There are no periodic control reports to show:

(1) Whether or not fixed overhead costs are being absorbed by the volume of business done, and
(2) Whether or not variable overhead costs are kept in line, particularly in view of the seasonal nature of the business.

(f) The company officials have no idea of the minimum volume necessary to absorb fixed overhead costs, though this is important due to the seasonal nature of the business. As a result, sales efforts are not particularly planned. Some incentives are used with respect to sales of butane gas, but there are no incentives with respect to the sales of the appliances which would increase the use of gas.

(g) The company bookkeeper-typist is unable to prepare monthly statements, cost reports, and the like, due to the absence of essential records and data as indicated above.

A resume of the report of the consultant follows:

Point (a)

What should be done about the easy access to the materials warehouse? Two points of entry may be necessary—one from the office and one from which trucks are to be loaded.

First, keep the points of entry locked at all times when not in use. All trucks load out early in the morning; therefore, one of the truckmen should be given the responsibility for checking outgoing materials against requisitions and truck reports, and seeing that the requisitions are turned into the office for accounting purposes. He should have one of the three keys to the loading entry, and one of the three keys to the entry from the salesroom-office area. The general manager should keep a key for each entry and a similar set should be kept in the office. If it becomes necessary for a truck to return to the warehouse during the day, either the general manager or the bookkeeper-typist should unlock the doors and see to it that requisitions are obtained for materials taken out. When materials come in on purchase, either the general manager or the bookkeeper-typist should open the doors for the receipt of the materials, and later the truckman referred to above should check the materials in on a receiving report, which he turns in to the office.

Next, warehouse procedures should be explained to all personnel, and their co-operation requested. Employees should understand that spot inventories will be taken frequently, and that the materials called for by the perpetual inventory records should be on hand. Employees should understand that it is extremely important that all receiving reports, requisitions, and truck loading reports be accurate and complete.

At the present time it is too expensive for the company to employ a supervisor to attend to the warehouse.

Point (b)

What kind of perpetual inventory records should be installed—should they be kept manually, or by a bookkeeping machine which could also be used for other accounting procedures? The determination of the proper kind of perpetual inventory records also should cover the related materials, receiving reports, and requisitions for material taken out.

A simple perpetual inventory card should be maintained manually, in the office. Because the bookkeeper will be required to keep it, the inventory record should be simple and not involve too much detail work. Thus, the record should be kept manually; and it should refer to quantities, but not values, on the theory that if quantities are correct, correct values will be reflected. Later on, as the business grows, the card details can be expanded to provide for values and a tie-in with the general ledger control—especially if a bookkeeping machine is used.

What is the best way to account for materials on trucks? Should weekly in-and-out and stock reports be used for each truck?

A study was made to determine a typical stock for each truck— that is, the kinds of fittings, pipe, etc., most likely to be used and, hence, carried on the truck. This standard list should be mimeographed down the left side of an 8 × 14 sheet. To the right, spaces should be provided for "in" and "out" for 6 days and, finally, on the right side, space should be provided for the quantity on hand at the end of the week. The set-up should be along the following lines:

Materials	Unit	Begin Bal	Mon		Tue		Wed		Thu		Fri		Sat		End Bal	
			In	Out	In	Out	In	Out	In	Out	In	Out	In	Out		
1" Pipe																
1/2" Pipe																
etc.																

Space should be left at the bottom for atypical items required during the week. At the end of each week, the quantity on hand is computed and transferred to the beginning of the report for next week. Completed reports are to be turned in to the office at the end of each week for checking and accounting procedures. Each truckman should be told to check his reports frequently against the actual materials on his truck, and that all trucks are subject to spot checks.

Point (c)

A small time clock should be installed.

How should labor be accounted for by jobs?

All workers for whom a distribution of time is essential for cost purposes should be given a weekly *time distribution report*, on which to report the number of hours spent on various jobs (or kinds of work), on off time, awaiting orders, etc. The total should agree with the total shown by the time clock. The reports are to be turned in to the office at the end of the week for inspection by the general manager and for accounting purposes.

Point (d)

Methods by which jobs may be *costed* should be developed. The cost of materials, labor, and overhead should be accumulated for each job so that:

(1) a comparison may be made with estimated costs used in determining contract prices, and

(2) the profit or loss on each job may be determined.

This can be accomplished by carrying a *job in process account* for each job until it is completed. The account should be charged with all materials used on the job as shown by requisitions, all labor as shown by the *time distribution reports*, and an overhead factor. When a job is completed, the total cost will be the debit balance in the account, and a comparison with the contract or bid price will tell the profit or loss story. The account will be cleared by transferring the balance to cost of sales. The sales income credit will be created when the customer is charged for the job.

Point (e)

A study was made to determine the minimum volume of business necessary to cover the fixed overhead.

This study embraced three basic steps:

(1) Determination of the *dollar* amounts of fixed charges, such as insurance, depreciation, salaries, ad valorem taxes, and other expenses that would remain more or less fixed in dollars regardless of volume of sales.

(2) Determination of the percentage relationship over the past four years of variable expenses to sales volume.

(3) Determination of the rate of gross margin to be expected on sales.

After the above factors were determined, a few test calculations were made to determine the minimum volume required to take care of fixed overhead. Variable expenses were estimated for various levels of sales. It is possible to establish estimated amounts for each variable expense, so that comparisons can be made with actual expenses.

A similar analysis was made with respect to selling and administrative expenses. Overhead, and selling and administrative expenses, should be controlled by budget.

Point (f)

Are sales incentives related to the wrong base in view of the fact that it is difficult to increase the use of gas without increasing the mediums through which it is used—that is, the number and kinds of appliances?

Sales incentives should be expanded to include appliance sales as well as gas sales.

Point (g)

Accounting procedures should be installed to obtain a monthly balance sheet and a profit and loss statement, as well as a report on expenses. The report on expenses should show (a) the amount of overhead not absorbed because of insufficient volume, and (b) whether or not variable expenses are in line relative to the volume of business done.

After providing ways and means of getting costs and, therefore, costs of sales, it will not be difficult to prepare a monthly balance sheet, profit and loss statements, reports on overhead expenses, and reports of the profit or loss on various jobs.

Required:

(a) Evaluate (1) the problems facing the Brand Butane Company, and (2) the recommendations of the consultant.

(b) Would you recommend a profit planning and control program? Explain.

Index